WIRE AND WORSE

RAF Prisoners of War in Laufen, Biberach, Lübeck and Warburg, 1940–42

WIRE AND WORSE

RAF Prisoners of War in Laufen, Biberach, Lübeck and Warburg, 1940–42

CHARLES ROLLINGS

Illustrated
With maps by Robert M Buckham and Paul Mathias

Ian Allan PUBLISHING

Author's Note

Every effort has been made by the author and publisher to trace the owners
of copyright material.

The author bears no responsibility for any embarrassment or inconvenience
caused to individuals mentioned in this text or to their relations or friends.

Dedication

Dedicated to all whose story this is.

First published 2004

ISBN 0 7110 3050 2

Published by Ian Allan Publishing

an imprint of Ian Allan Publishing Ltd, Hersham, Surrey KT12 4RG.
Printed by Ian Allan Printing Ltd, Hersham, Surrey KT12 4RG.

Code: 0409/A2

Contents

List of Photographs

Prisoners relaxing at Oflag VIIC, Laufen, summer 1941. *(Author's collection)*

James Heber Ward. *(J H Ward)*

Jack Best. *(Author's collection)*

Anthony Trumble. *(A J Trumble)*

Colin Dilly. *(Martin Dilly)*

Eric Sydney-Smith *(left)* and his Blenheim crew in Malta, prior to his returning to England in 1941. *(Author's collection)*

Jaroslav Zafouk. *(Author's collection)*

Wallace Cunningham: POW Photograph. *(W Cunningham)*

Peter Harding: POW Photograph. *(P Harding)*

William "Dutch" Bakker: POW Photograph. *(W Bakker)*

Peter Stevens. *(Marc Stevens)*

Gilbert Walenn. *(via Norman Canton)*

Lionel Casson. *(Author's collection)*

Douglas Bader being shown around the German fighter airfield at St Omer. Adolf Galland is second from left. *(via P B Lucas)*

Wing Commander Douglas Bader is allowed to sit in the cockpit of an Me109 at St Omer shortly after his capture. A German officer holds a pistol at the ready in case of any "funny stuff". *(via P B Lucas)*

Blenheim crews pose for the camera with a box containing a new pair of artificial legs to be dropped for Douglas Bader during a daylight raid over France. *(via P B Lucas)*

A cheerful Peter Tomlinson prior to take-off. *(P Tomlinson)*

Peter Tomlinson looking down in the mouth after being captured. *(P Tomlinson)*

A POW mess at Oflag XC, Lübeck, drawn by Bill Bakker. *(W Bakker)*

POW registration card filled in by Roger Bushell at Lübeck.

Aerial view of Oflag VIB, Warburg-Dössel. *(Author's collection)*

POW barracks at Warburg. *(Author's collection)*

Oflag VIB, Warburg, after the war with the barbed-wire fences and sentry towers demolished. *(Author's collection)*

The *Sportplatz* at Warburg. *(Author's collection)*

Dominic Bruce. *(D Bruce)*

Acting Squadron Leader Peter Mason, drawn by a fellow-POW, Major The Hon. G D Milne, RA, at Warburg. *(Author's collection)*

Pilot Officer Waclaw Krupowicz, drawn by Colin Dilly at Warburg. *(Martin Dilly)*

Sydney Dowse. *(Author's collection)*

The scaling ladders on the wire at Warburg, the morning after "Operation Olympia". *(Author's collection)*

The wire at Warburg, the morning after "Operation Olympia". *(Author's collection)*

List of Maps and Line Drawings

Preface

This book is both a companion volume and a sequel to my first book, *Wire and Walls: RAF Prisoners of War in Itzehoe, Spangenberg and Thorn 1939–42*, published last year by Ian Allan — a companion volume because the first half of the story treats of those Allied aircrew officer prisoners who, in 1940 and 1941, were sent not to those camps covered in *Wire and Walls* but, sometimes inadvertently, to Oflag VIIC (Laufen), Oflag VB (Biberach) and Oflag XC (Lübeck); a sequel because it follows the fortunes of the former Spangenberg prisoners from where *Wire and Walls* left off with them being transferred to Oflag VIB (Warburg), where they joined those prisoners who had been previously collected at Oflag XC.

As was the case with the previous volume, the subtitle of this book is something of a misnomer, for it concerns not only Royal Air Force prisoners of war during the period covered, but also Royal Australian Air Force, Royal Canadian Air Force, Royal New Zealand Air Force, South African Air Force, and Royal Navy Fleet Air Arm prisoners, along with one officer of the French *Armée de l'Air* captured during the invasion of France who remained with the RAF when his compatriots were purged from Spangenberg in the summer of 1940.

Although the prisoner of war camps in which they were incarcerated have featured in several diaries, memoirs, biographies, histories and anthologies of escape stories published since 1945 — the relevant ones of which are listed in the Sources and Bibliography — nobody, as far as I know, has yet attempted to reconstruct a coherent history of aircrew prisoners of war in camps administered by the German Army between June 1940 and September 1942. Even in Aidan Crawley's excellent *Escape from Germany*, the official history of RAF escapes during the Second World War, the coverage is brief (indeed, several escape attempts are completely overlooked), and most other accounts have regarded these camps as a somewhat intrusive and tedious prelude to the main event: the saga of Stalag Luft III and Stalag Luft VI, where the bulk of Allied aircrew prisoners were assembled under Luftwaffe authority as from 1942 and 1943 respectively.

In this respect, I can speak for myself as well. My intention, when I decided in 1989 to seriously study the subject of RAF POWs, rather than to continue passively consuming the kind of literature that I had been reading since 1970, was to write the complete history of Stalag Luft III to the exclusion of all other camps. But this proved unrealistic, for two reasons. Firstly, no history of Stalag Luft III could be attempted without reference, in some detail, to the experiences the prisoners had undergone in the earlier camps, most of which had been run by the German Army. Secondly, as my appeals for information bore fruit, an abundance of material on these early camps came my way — and so fascinating was this material that it became clear to me that to waste it would be nothing short of criminal. What finally tipped the balance, however, was the plain and simple fact that there was an enormous gap in the history of aircrew POWs, which would remain long after those involved had passed away — perhaps for ever — unless someone with the knowledge of and a passion for the subject did something about it.

Finally, the camps described in *Wire and Worse* — Oflag VB, Biberach; Oflag VIIC, Laufen; Oflag XC, Lübeck; and Oflag VIB, Warburg-Dössel — were only four of the many Army camps in which aircrew prisoners were held. Aircrew were also accommodated for a time in Oflag IIA, Prenzlau; Stalag IIIE, Kirchhain; Stalag IXC, the vast POW camp at Bad Sulza from which the Army POW hospital at Obermassfeld was administered; Stalag XXIB, Schubin; and Stalag XIIA, Limburg. Four of these camps, the Stalags, were for NCOs and "other ranks". These camps, along with the first all-aircrew camps, Stalag Luft I at Barth, will be covered in my third volume, *Hell Camp, Hell's Kitchen and Sandy Corner*.

Some aspects of this narrative might need some explaining, particularly in regard to spelling the names and indicating the ranks of prisoners. The spelling of surnames conforms to the RAF List and and to AIR 20/2336, the alphabetical list of Air Force prisoners in Germany, held at the National Archive. Ranks are a thornier issue. By the time AIR 20/2336 was compiled, almost every officer captured as a Pilot Officer or a Flying Officer during the period 1939–42 had received time-promotion to Flight Lieutenant. However, to avoid confusion, I have maintained the ranks they held at the time of capture.

I have also endeavoured to describe how each of the prisoners mentioned in these pages found himself behind the wire — at least to the extent of giving his squadron number and the type of aircraft flown, and some details of the operation, especially the date. However, some shot-down stories have eluded me, and should any reader be able to throw any light on these omissions I would be grateful. I have deliberately omitted the capture stories of those prisoners who were originally in Stalag Luft I and then transferred to Lübeck. Their accounts properly belong to the history of Stalag Luft I, and will be included in the third book in this series. The capture stories of the Spangenberg prisoners who were purged to Warburg are, of course, related in *Wire and Walls* (except, that is, for former Stalag Luft I inhabitants).

In order to provide some continuity between this book and my first, and to put the aircrew POW experience in its historical context, I have in my Introduction used some material from the first and last quarters of Chapter One of *Wire and Walls*; however, mindful of the fact that this is intended to be a stand-alone work, and that repetition can be boring, I have carried the information from the second and third quarters over as Appendices II and III.

Some readers, particularly the ever-diminishing band of ex-POWs still living, might take issue with my rendering of some of the events of that period. However, I would point out that the keynote of this book is accuracy. I have read almost every book on the subject; interviewed and corresponded with survivors and their relatives; pored over diaries, Wartime Logs and POW letter-forms; and consulted official records in England and Germany. I have tried to cross-check every anecdote, apocryphal or otherwise, and have discarded anything that could not be verified or which seemed spurious or beyond the realms of probability. As the years have passed memories have grown hazier, and some recollections have become muddled, while there were a few — *very* few — among my interviewees whose individual claims, particularly concerning escape attempts, I found to have been exaggerated. Anyone who attempts a work of this nature would like to believe he is writing a "definitive" history — indeed, should set out to do so — but my aim in this book has been to lay out the material to facilitate future studies and provide a starting point for aviation, social and family historians who for either academic or personal reasons might seek information on one or a number of POWs and camps. In that respect I am more of a compiler than an author, and I hope this book will be taken in that spirit.

At the same time, despite my best efforts, minor errors, if not major ones, are bound to creep into an ambitious project dealing with the minutiae of the day-to-day existence over two years of hundreds of men. It was particularly difficult to unravel the tangled and contradictory accounts that emerged from Warburg, but ultimately, the responsibility for any mistakes is mine. Corrections and suggestions will be gratefully received — but brickbats and lawsuits will not.

There are some major omissions, too: in respect of photographs. To the best of my knowledge, no photographs were ever taken of Oflag XC during its brief existence as a camp for British prisoners. As for Oflag VIB, the *Wehrmacht* did hire a local photographer to take group snapshots of prisoners, but as the Allies approached in 1945 he destroyed his entire collection, and only a few official photos of poor quality have survived.

Acknowledgements

This book would not have been possible without the help, co-operation and enthusiasm of those whose story it relates. They and their relatives answered detailed questions on their experiences, in both interviews and correspondence, loaned me diaries, Wartime Logs, POW letters, drawings and photographs, and egged me on when at times the mass of material confronting me made my head swim. My one regret is that during the fourteen years it has taken for the first two books in this series to emerge, many of the ex-kriegies have died, and to list their names would make depressing reading. They are listed in the Sources and Bibliography, and I would like to thank them collectively for all that they have contributed.

I would also like to thank the members of the Royal Air Force Officers' Ex-POW Association Dining Club for inviting me to their wonderful annual dinners on two occasions, and especially Captain H H Bracken CBE, RN (Retd.), who in addition to having a rich fund of anecdotes provided me with virtually the entire proceeds of his researches in the Public Record Office on prisoner-of-war conditions in Germany and in particular on the issue of POW pay.

Thanks are also due to: the Public Record Office (the National Archive) for providing camp histories, escape reports, and the files of MI9; the Imperial War Museum, Lambeth; the *Bundesarchiv* in Freiburg im Breisgau, which holds on file almost every issue of *The Camp*; and the *Stadtarchiv* Warburg.

I would also like to extend my gratitude to W R Chorley, whose excellent series *Royal Air Force Bomber Command Losses of the Second World War* rarely left my side during my researches, and to my wife, Isabel, who has gamely put up with my chaotic filing system and checked the German in my manuscript.

Glossary of Foreign Terms, Service Slang and POW Argot

AA ack-ack (qv)

AASF Advanced Air Striking Force, part of the **BEF** (qv) in France, 1939–40

Abort (Ger.) latrines

Abteilung (Ger.) section or department

Abwehr (Ger.) Military Intelligence Organization

ack-ack AA, anti-aircraft fire (see also: **fireworks, flak**)

AC1 (RAF abbr.) Aircraftman 1st Class

Amt (Ger.) office or service (plural, *Ämter*)

Anträge (Ger.) written complaints

Appell (Ger.) roll-call (plural, *Appelle*)

Arbeitskarte (Ger.) worker's identity card

Armée de l'Air French Air Force

Ausweis (Ger.) card (normally an identity card)

bag (RAF slang) to seize, score or capture. One can "bag" an enemy aircraft; the Germans can "bag" — ie, capture — one (one is thus "bagged"); one can be "in the bag" — ie, a prisoner; and one can "bag" — ie, find or steal — something

bale out (RAF slang) to take to one's parachute

bash (service slang) feast

beat up (RAF slang) strafe (qv)

"Beehive" (RAF slang) A tight formation of bombers (the hive) with an escort of fighters (the bees surrounding the hive)

BEF British Expeditionary Force

belly-landing (RAF slang) a landing with wheels up (also: **wheels-up**)

blitz (POW slang) an escape effected very quickly, from the German word for "lightning" and the (subsequent) Service slang for the clean-up that takes place when a "big noise" is due to visit a Station

Blitzkrieg (Ger.) lightning war

bomber boy (RAF slang) any member of a bomber crew

borrow (RAF slang) steal

brass (Service slang) collective for high-ranking officers (see also: **brass-hats, top-brass**)

brass-hats (Service slang) see: **brass, top-brass**

brew (Service slang) tea; (POW slang) illicit liquor

brolly (RAF slang) parachute

brown job (RAF slang) soldier

Bürgermeister (Ger.) Mayor

buttoned-up (RAF slang) sorted out (also: **sewn-up**)

'chute (colloquial) parachute

"Circus" (RAF terminology) daylight raid by small force of bombers with heavy fighter escort, usually over German occupied-territories, with the intention of drawing up German fighters and chipping away at German air superiority

CO (Service abbr.) Commanding Officer

cooler (POW slang) solitary confinement cell, from the Service slang for detention cells, where hot-heads can "cool off"

dicey (RAF slang) risky

Dienst (Ger.) duty, service

dienst (POW slang) task, escape operation — from the German *Dienst*

ditch (RAF slang) come down in the sea while still in one's aircraft

Dolmetscher (Ger.) interpreter

drill (Service slang) correct way of doing something

drink, the (RAF slang) the sea

duff (colloquial) incorrect, unfit, useless

duff gen (RAF slang) wrong information (see also: **gen**)

Dulag (Ger. abbr.) *Durchgangslager* — literally, "through-camp", or transit camp

Dulag Luft (Ger. abbr.) *Durchgangslager der Luftwaffe* — transit camp of the Air Force

Ersatz (Ger.) substitute

FAA (Royal Navy abbr.) Fleet Air Arm

Feldwebel (Ger.) Senior Sergeant

ferret (POW slang) *Abwehr* snoop who looks for signs of POW escaping activities

fireworks (RAF slang) flak (qv)

flak (RAF slang) anti-aircraft gunfire, from the German *Flieger-(or Flugzeugs)-abwehrkanone* (air-defence cannon) (see also: **AA, ack-ack, fireworks**)

flanker (RAF slang) trick

flap (Service slang) disturbance, excitement, panic

Flieger (Ger.) airman

Flight (RAF terminology) one-third or one-fourth of a squadron's strength — ie, four to six aircraft — led by a Flight Commander in Fighter Command, and a Squadron Leader in Bomber Command; also slang for Flight Sergeant

"Gardening" (RAF slang) mine-laying

Gefreiter (Ger.) lance-corporal

Geheime Staatspolizei (Ger.) Gestapo, Secret State Police

gen (RAF slang) information, usually genuine unless preceded by a qualification (eg, **duff gen, Elsan gen**)

gen man (RAF slang) one who gives gen (also: **gen wallah**)

gen up (RAF slang) swot up on a subject (see: **gen**)

Generalleutnant (Ger.) Lieutenant-General

genned up (RAF slang) well-informed (see: **gen**)

George (RAF slang) automatic pilot

Geschwader (Ger.) Wing formation (Luftwaffe)

Gestapo (Ger. abbr.) *Geheime Staatspolizei* (qv)

gong (Service slang) medal

goon (Service slang) stupid person, but also any German

goon-box (POW slang) sentry tower

goonery (POW slang) squad of goons or a collective (generally unfair) act by goons

goon-lamp (POW slang) improvised lamp usually made from "borrowed" materials; used as night-lights and for illuminating tunnels

goon-skin (POW slang) fake German uniform

Grand Blessé severely wounded, sick for repatriation, etc

Hauptmann (Ger.) Captain

Hauptlager (Ger.) main camp
Hauptmann (Ger.) Captain
das Heer (Ger.) The Army
Hitlerjugend (Ger.) Hitler Youth
hole (POW slang) tunnel
Hundmeister (Ger.) dog-handler

i/c (Service abbr.) in charge (eg, officer i/c escaping)
intercom (RAF abbr.) inter-communication telephonic system of an aircraft

Jagdgeschwader (Ger.) fighter wing (Luftwaffe)
JG (Ger. abbr.) *Jagdgeschwader* (qv)

Keintrinkwasser (Ger.) Metal water jug from which, however, water cannot be drunk
kite (RAF slang) aircraft
Klippfisch (Ger.) frozen cod, sun-dried, issued to early POWs as part of their staple diet
Kommandantur (Ger.) administrative quarters
krank (Ger.) sick
krank im Zimmer (Ger.) sick and confined to one's room
kriegie (POW slang) prisoner of war, from the German *Kriegsgefangener* (qv)
kriegiedom (POW slang) prisoner of war life
Kriegsgefangener (Ger.) prisoner of war
Kriegsgefangenschaft (Ger.) prisoner of war life
Kriegsmarine (Ger.) Navy
Kühler German for "cooler"

Lagergeld (Ger.) camp currency
Lazarett (Ger.) hospital
Leutnant (Ger.) Second- or Sub-Lieutenant
look-see (RAF slang), reconnaissance (see also: **recce, recco**)
loose off (RAF slang) fire a machine-gun
Luftgau (Ger.) Air Defence District
Luftwaffe (Ger.) Air Force

Machinenpistole (Ger.) machine-pistol; later known as a Tommy-gun
Mae West (official) Self-inflating life-jacket worn by aircrew, so called because it bulges in the
    right places
Met (RAF slang) Collective for Meteorological Officers
MI9 Military Intelligence 9; War Office department set up to foster escape and evasion
MO (Service abbr.) Medical Officer

Nachtjagdgeschwader (Ger.) night-fighter wing
NCO (Service abbr.) Non-commissioned officer (also: **non-com**)
NJG (Ger. abbr.) *Nachtjagdgeschwader* (qv)
non-com (Service slang) NCO (qv)

Obergefreiter (Ger.) corporal
Oberkommando der Wehrmacht (Ger.) *OKW*, High Command of the Armed Forces
Oberkommando des Heeres (Ger.) *OKH*, High Command of the Army
Oberleutnant (Ger.) Full or Senior Lieutenant
Oberst (Ger.) Colonel
Oberstleutnant (Ger.) Lieutenant-Colonel
Oberzahlmeister (Ger) Senior Paymaster

OC (Service abbr.) Officer Commanding
Offizierslager (Ger.) officers' camp
Oflag (Ger. abbr.) See: *Offizierslager*
OKH (Ger. abbr.) *Oberkommando des Heeres* (qv)
OKW (Ger. abbr.) *Oberkommando der Wehrmacht* (qv)
Old Man (Service slang) Commanding Officer
Op(s) (RAF slang) operation(s)
OR (Service abbr.) other ranks (ie, not officers or NCOs)
organise (RAF slang) wangle or steal something
Ostfront (Ger.) Eastern (Russian) Front
other rank (Service jargon) rank and file below most junior NCO
OTU (RAF) Operational Training Unit

Panzer (Ger.) tank
Posten (Ger.) guard or sentry
prang (RAF) crash-land; bombing raid
pukka gen (RAF slang) absolutely trustworthy information (see: **gen**)

recce (abbr.) reconnaissance
recco See: **recce**
Reich (Ger.) State
Reichsbahn (Ger.) State Railway
Reichswehr (Ger.) Defence Force
Reichssicherheitshauptamt (Ger.) *RSHA*, State Security apparatus
"Rhubarb" (RAF slang) fighter patrol, by a small number of aircraft, seeking targets of opportunity over enemy-occupied territory, usually when bad weather prohibits normal operations
Rittmeister (Ger.) Cavalry Captain
RM (Ger.) *Reichsmark*, coinage
RSHA (Ger. abbr.) *Reichssicherheitshauptamt* (qv)

SBO (POW officialese) Senior British Officer
Schütze (Ger.) infantry soldier (originally, bowman or marksman)
Schutz-Staffel (Ger.) *SS*, Defence Echelon
Schweinerei (Ger.) mess; dirty trick
SD (Ger. abr.) *Sicherheitsdienst* (qv)
second dicky (RAF slang) Reserve Pilot on an aircraft
Sicherheitsdienst (Ger.) *SD*, Nazi Party Intelligence Organization
skipper (colloquial) captain of an aircraft
SOE (abbr.) Specal Operations Executive (qv)
Sonderführer (Ger.) Nominal rank, equivalent to Warrant Officer given to civilian attached to the Armed Forces for special duties
Sonderlager (Ger.) Special Camp, for hostages, persistent escapers and general nuisances
Special Operations Executive SOE, British clandestine organization set up to create disruption in German-occupied territories
Speisefett (Ger.) literally, food (eating) fat — sometimes real margarine, sometimes substitute
Speisesaal (Ger.) dining-hall
Sportplatz (Ger.) sports ground
SS (Ger. abbr.) *Schutzstaffeln* (qv)
Staffel (Ger.) squad (Army), squadron (Luftwaffe)
Stalag (Ger. abbr.) see: *Stammlager*
Stammlager (Ger. abbr.) *Mannschaftsstammlager*. Literally, team camp — a camp for NCOs and other ranks

stooge (RAF slang) go on patrol; (POW slang) assistant, informer, POW lookout, keep watch

Strafe (Ger.) punishment

strafe (RAF slang) (to) rake with gunfire

Strafgefangenen (Ger.) prisoners undergoing punishment

Straflager (Ger.) Punishment or Reprisal Camp

streng verboten (Ger.) strictly forbidden

top-brass (Service slang) high-ranking officers (See also: **brass, brass-hats**)

type (RAF slang) chap, fellow; usually prefaced with "good" or "dim"

Unteroffizier (Ger.) Sergeant

verboten (Ger.) forbidden. See also: *streng verboten*

Vertrauensmann (Ger.) literally, "man who can be trusted"—Trusty or Man of Confidence

Vorlager (Ger.) front compound, ie, a coumpound in front of the main prisoners' compound wherein such buildings as library, coal bunker, woodshed, cooler, showers, etc, are located

Wehrkreis (Ger.) (Army) Defence District

Wehrmacht (Ger.) Armed Forces

Wimpey (RAF slang) Wellington bomber — after the cartoon character J Wellington Wimpey, partner of Popeye the Sailor

Wingco, the (RAF slang) Wing Commander (see also: **Wings**)

Wings (RAF slang) Wing Commander

WO (Service abbr.) Warrant Officer

WOP (RAF abbr.) pronounced as a word, the wireless operator of an aircraft

WOP/AG (RAF abbr.) Wireless Operator/Air Gunner

write off (RAF slang) kill, damage beyond repair

Wurst (Ger.) sausage

Zerstörer (Ger.) destroyer — ie, fighter aircraft

Zimmer (Ger.) room

Introduction

Colonel von Lindeiner — the second, longest-serving and most humane of Stalag Luft III's four commandants — was inordinately proud of the Allied aircrew prisoners in his charge. He was later to remark in his unpublished memoirs that a burgeoning diplomat would have received ideal training in his camp because it afforded the opportunity of studying the mentality of men from almost every country in the world. For Stalag Luft III was indeed a community of nations, with aircrew from the United Kingdom, Canada, South Africa, Australia, New Zealand, America, the Netherlands, France, Belgium, Greece, Denmark, Poland, Czechoslovakia, India and China — there were even Maoris and a Lithuanian.

The venerable commandant was no less intrigued by the variety of their skills and backgrounds. In addition to career officers and non-commissioned-officers, he claims to have found among them millionaires, Indian princes, lords, lawyers, policemen, private detectives, school-teachers, newspaper reporters, firemen, tram-conductors, bus- and taxi-drivers, chauffeurs, missionaries, bacteriologists, veterinary surgeons, coal-, diamond- and gold-miners, horse trainers, jockeys, racing drivers, professional hockey and football players, ski-ing instructors, singers, pianists, band-leaders, dancers, theatre organists, artists, photographers, actors, cinema projectionists, commercial travellers, plantation owners, hotel managers, waiters, porters, cowboys and even professional gamblers.

It is, perhaps, just as well that his memoirs — though translated into English — remain unpublished, as most ex-prisoners would doubtless be scornful of his remarks. One of them, former naval captain Hugo Bracken, points out that after leaving the aircrew transit camp, Dulag Luft, he only once exchanged more than ten words with a German officer — and that was in an earlier camp, Oflag XC, at Lübeck, in 1941. He is sure the same goes for the vast majority of those who were in Stalag Luft III. "Talk of studying my, or most of the other prisoners', mentality is pretentious nonsense," insists Bracken. "What he might have been able to study was the collective mentality of quite a large group of prisoners." The tenor of life in Stalag Luft III had largely been set by the early Royal Air Force prisoners, he says; those who arrived later merely fell in with what they found to be the accepted code of conduct.

Hugo Bracken is quite astute in his assessment. For von Lindeiner's somewhat select list was in fact culled from a more comprehensive one compiled by a prisoner, Flight Lieutenant Peter Gardner, not only at Stalag Luft III, but also at two previous camps: Oflag XC, and Oflag VIB, at Warburg-Dössel. Lübeck and Warburg had held officers from British Army and other land forces of the Empire as well as from the British and Dominion Air Forces and the Fleet Air Arm, and Gardner's list therefore embraced the peace-time occupations of men from all three services. Thus the cross-section of society remarked, at second-hand, by von Lindeiner was by no means unique to aircrew prisoner-of-war camps.

For most of the war it was, however, the British and Dominion Air Forces alone who carried the offensive into Germany and German-occupied territories — supported from 1942 onwards by the United States Army Air Force. RAF Bomber Command, with its strategic bombing campaign, was the most aggressive arm in prosecuting the air war. It also paid a heavy cost, with 55,573 aircrew killed and 9,784 taken prisoner. But neither did Fighter Command's air supremacy come cheap. When, in November 1940, Air Marshal Sir Sholto Douglas, who had taken over from Air Chief Marshal Sir Hugh Dowding as C-in-C Fighter Command, began his policy of "leaning towards" German-occupied France, he found it was costing him more fighter pilots than his predecessor had lost during the Battle of Britain. By the time Germany surrendered, the number of British and Dominion Air Force POWs was 13,022 (4,480 officers, 8,542 Warrant Officers and NCOs) — not counting those who had died in captivity, had been repatriated on medical grounds, or had successfully escaped. They were among the finest and most highly trained material in the British Empire. It cost £10,000 to train a bomber pilot, and £15,000 for a fighter pilot — enough to send ten or fifteen men to study at Oxford or Cambridge for three years. The total number of USAAF aircrew POWs in Germany was 24,000. Its officer aircrew were equally well-educated and highly-trained: only university graduates were commissioned, and the "washout" rate for pilots was high, with the failures re-mustering as navigators, and so on down the line.

Both air forces altered in character as the war progressed and losses increased. (This was more noticeable in the RAF, which had initially been much more socially stratified than its Dominion and American counterparts.) It made for a potentially volatile combination when confined behind barbed wire.

The POWs could be divided into three broad categories:

(1) Those shot down early in the war and who were Regular officers, NCOs and aicraftmen, officers who had joined the 1930s Short Service Commission programme, Volunteer Reservists and Auxiliary Air Force "weekend flyers". Many of these were former public school pupils and adapted to camp life fairly quickly, being used to spending time away from home. (Most public schools were pretty spartan in those days.) These officers felt badly about the fact that their "war" life had been so short and that they would never get another chance. They formed the backbone of the escape committees and the actual escape operations. After two or three years some of these became discouraged after so many failed escapes and took up other occupations — theatre, language courses, painting, music, writing, and so on.

(2) As the war went on the type of POW changed — no longer the Regular type, but "hostilities only" volunteers who literally came from all walks of life. To begin with, they threw themselves into escape activities with gusto, but as the war dragged on and bomber losses became greater, aircrew were having a pretty rough time and were only too happy that they were alive and out of it — and comparatively safe.

(3) The exception to all that was the attitude of the Poles and the Czechs — and the Free French to a degree. To a man the Poles and Czechs were determined to escape, and with their knowledge of the language return to their own countries or England. Having had their countries raped and destroyed by the Germans their hatred of the enemy was immensely greater than that of the average Briton.

Regulars with leadership qualities who resented being shot down and captured early in the war; volunteers from all walks of life with a variety of skills, all of which could be turned to the escaper's advantage; citizens of German-occupied countries eaten away with hatred for their enemy and able to speak a variety of languages: these men, whose backgrounds so intrigued von Lindeiner, would eventually coalesce into an escape organisation that would break him and shake the German High Command. The result would be at once a triumph and a tragedy.

When Stalag Luft III opened in March 1942 the Germans held almost 2,000 aircrew POWs (including British and Dominion Air Forces, Fleet Air Arm and Special Air Service). Most were already case-hardened prisoners who had at one time or another been dispersed among some of the grimmest camps in the Greater Reich. These were mainly camps for Army prisoners: Oflag XA, Itzehoe; Oflag IIA, Prenzlau; Oflag VB, Biberach; Oflag VIB, Warburg-Dössel; Oflag VIIC, Laufen; Oflag IXA/H, Spangenberg bei Kassel; Oflag XC, Lübeck; Fort VIII, Posen; Fort XV, Thorn; Stalag IIIE, Kirchhain; Stalag VIA, Hemer bei Iserlohn; Stalag VIJ, Krefeld; Stalag VIIIB, Lamsdorf; Stalag IXA, Zeigenhain; Stalag IXC, Bad Sulza; Stalag XIIA, Limburg an der Lahn, and Stalag XXIB (later Oflag XXIB), at Schubin in Poland.

Only two of the camps in which aircrew were accommodated had been specially built or adapted for aircrew: *Durchgangslager der Luftwaffe* (or *Dulag Luft*), at Oberursel, near Frankfurt am Main; and Stalag Luft I, at Barth-Vogelsang in Upper Pomerania. Both were run by the German Air Force, the Luftwaffe. The former was a transit camp and interrogation centre, the latter a "permanent" camp which, however, became full within less than a year, was expanded, and filled up again — with the result that, from then onwards, until Stalag Luft III opened at

Sagan, aircrew prisoners were sent in large numbers from Dulag Luft to Army camps. Conditions in these camps varied only from the cramped and spartan to the cramped and appalling. But aircrew were not exceptional in having to endure such privations, for the German Army treated almost all of it prisoners badly (along with its own soldiery).

This situation came about for a variety of reasons. Firstly, the German organisation for prisoners of war — under *Das Oberkommando der Wehrmacht* (*OKW*, High Command of the Armed Forces) — grew in a piecemeal fashion and was chaotic. Secondly, rivalry existed between the various branches, and departments, of the OKW responsible for prisoners. Thirdly, POWs presented a logistical nightmare of huge proportions, as the OKW consistently underestimated the number of prisoners it would take as the war progressed; its resources were constantly overstretched, with overcrowding and underfeeding as the inevitable concomitants. Fourthly — and perhaps mainly — no matter how pious the intentions of those bodies in charge of POW affairs, the fact remained that Germany was not only a military state but also a Nazi state. So over-arching was the ideology of Nazism that few members of the OKW, and few POW camp commandants, had the will to try to overcome the logistical problems they encountered — and those who did have lived in constant fear of being hauled up in front of a military tribunal charged with being "Anglophiles".

The OKW had begun formulating the policy it would take towards POWs long before the war, and evidence suggests that it intended to abide by international laws relating to POWs and to segregate them by service. Germany was one of the first of the thirty-eight powers represented in Geneva on 27 July 1929 to sign the Prisoner of War Code and the Red Cross Convention.

Fig 1. Camps holding Allied aircrew POWs, September 1939–April 1942

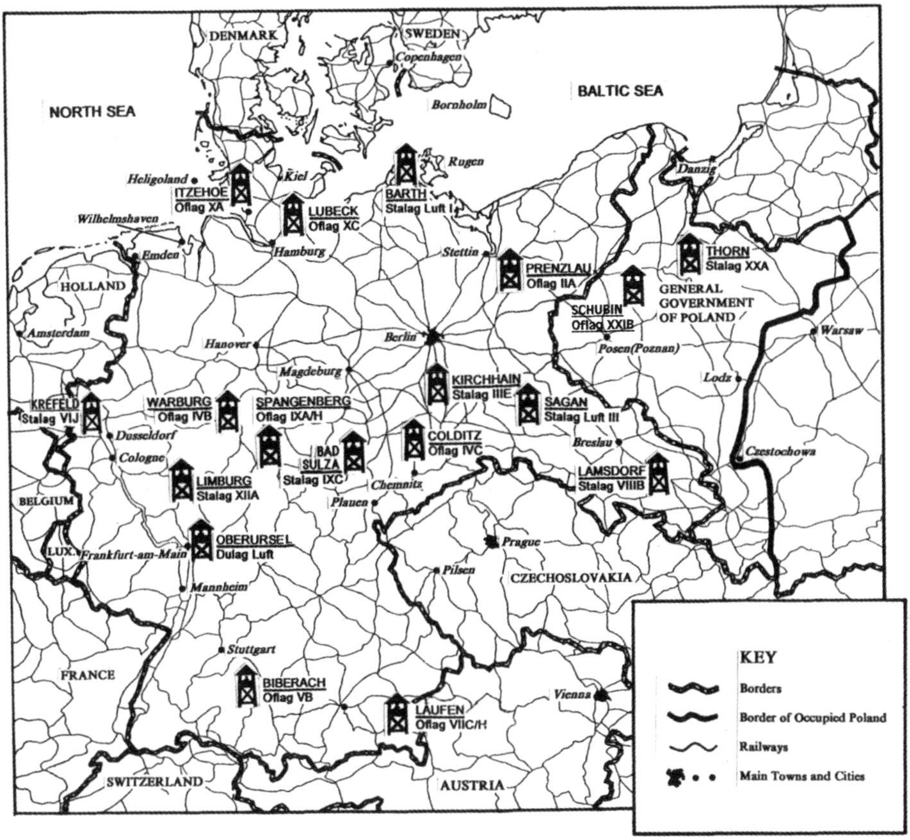

19

But the provision of a Prisoner of War Code was one thing; the question of whether it would be observed and could be enforced was another. It was hardly to be supposed that Nazi Germany — a regime which had torn up the Treaty of Versailles, made a mockery of the Munich Agreement, herded thousands of Jews, Jehovah Witnesses, Communists, clerics, dissidents, intellectuals, etc, into concentration camps, and would go on to attack Poland without any declaration of war, violate the neutrality of Holland and Belgium and break the Molotov-Ribbentrop pact — would give a *Pfennig* for the Geneva Convention, particularly as it was signed by the Weimar Republic, which the Nazis did not recognise. It comes as no surprise to the historian to learn that thousands of prisoners who passed through the Greater Reich between 1939 and 1945 never even saw a copy of the POW Code; nor that numerous POW camp commandants, particularly in the early stages of the war when Germany was winning, made it plain that they had no intention whatsoever of observing it; nor that, although in theory the OKW was accountable for anything that befell a prisoner once his "capture card" had been sent to the protecting power or the Red Cross, the Germans were largely indifferent to the fate of their prisoners; nor that there were no means with which to enforce the provisions of the Code.

Yet, for all that, it was possible for prisoners of war to appeal to German notions of fair play and thus ameliorate conditions in some camps. But the major factor in ensuring the Germans' compliance with the POW Code was the fear that their own men imprisoned in Great Britain and Canada might be ill-treated as a reprisal against their own unfair treatment of Allied POWs. As early as 1938 the OKW had foreseen that certain violations of International Law would undoubtedly occur among all sides involved in the impending war and — on the basis of "do unto others before they do unto you" — had drawn up a tat-before-tit list of those it would violate in advance. The OKW considered forcing prisoners to do "war work" quite justifiable, for example, and thus urged that discretion be used in reproaching enemies for this practice.

Throughout the war, POW affairs remained technically under the OKW, although in fact Hitler had the final say in POW matters. His immediate subordinate in this area was General (later *Feldmarschall*) Wilhelm Keitel, Chief of the OKW, who later testified at the War Crimes Trials at Nuremberg to the existence of a basic manual, *KGB-38* (Prisoner of War Directive No38), otherwise known as *The Prison Commandant's Handbook*, which contained all clauses in existing international agreements relative to POWs. These clauses applied equally to the Army (*das Heer*), the Navy (*die Kriegsmarine*) and the Air Force (*die Luftwaffe*). If Keitel is to be believed, every department down to the smallest unit had this handbook and every soldier received some instruction on its contents and on how to apply its directives. Special training courses were held in Vienna for those charged with the care of POWs. Finally, every soldier had instructions in his *Soldbuch* (pay-book) on the proper conduct towards POWs. On the other hand, German Regulation No9, Paragraph 462, advised POW camp guards that upon seeing an escape in progress, they should shoot prematurely rather than hesitate, while Regulation No32, Paragraph 504, added that no warning shots were to be fired and that should a guard ever need to fire weapons, "they must be fired with the intent to hit".

Directly below Keitel was *General* Hermann Reinecke, who oversaw the activities of the *Allgemeines Wehrmachtsamt* (*AWA*, Armed Forces General Office), a division within the OKW generally concerned with personnel, training and equipment, which also had some influence over POWs insofar as it provided camp staff and matériel. Within the AWA was an office with sole responsibility over POWs, the *Abteilung Kriegsgefangenenwesen im OKW*, or the POW Office within the OKW. For most of the war the staff officer in charge of POW Office was *Generalmajor* von Graevenitz.

At the beginning of the war the POW system was run entirely by Army personnel, with the camps being staffed by *Wehrkreiskommandos* (military district work groups) and guarded by *Ersatzheeren* (Army reservists), and prisoners from the British Army, Navy and Air Force being held in the same camps. But as the war progressed each service assumed control of its enemy counterparts, so that the POW Office found itself delegating authority to the Army, Navy and Air Force. These branches of the armed forces also had responsibility for communicating with the Protecting Powers — the United States of America until it joined the war in December 1941, and

Switzerland thereafter — through the Foreign Office, the Red Cross, and any other agencies concerned with the treatment of POWs. Representatives of the Red Cross, the protecting power and the various relief agencies had to get clearance from the OKW before visiting prison camps. Their activities were co-ordinated in the German Foreign Office by one of its under-secretaries, Baron Gustav von Steengracht, who from 1936 to 1938 had served under Joachim von Ribbentrop, then German ambassador to the United Kingdom.

Greater Germany itself was divided into twenty-two *Wehrkreise*, or defence districts. Occupied territories were similarly divided. The number of each prison camp was determined by that of the defence district in which it was located, with the first camp in that district being awarded the suffix "A", the second "B", and so on. There were three main types of camp: the *Durchgangslager* (*Dulag*, or transit camp), the *Offizierslager* (*Oflag*, for officers) and the *Mannschaftsstammlager* (*Stalag*, for NCOs and other ranks). Transit camps were mainly located on or near the front line and were either designated a *Feldposten* (field-post) or a *Frontstalag*. Attached to some main camps was a fourth type, the *Zweiglager*, or branch camp. This was usually designated by the letter *"Z"* following the Roman numerals. The combatant troops delivered their prisoners to *Dulagen*, and they in turn moved the POWs to the *Oflagen, Stammlagern and Zweiglagern* located in Germany, Austria and Poland. Orders concerning POWs reached camp commandants through a long and tortuous route, starting with the OKW and filtering down through the *Oberkommando des Heeres* (*OKH*, Army High Command), the commander of the reserve Army, and the Army district commander before finally arriving on the commandant's desk.

Up to 1942 there was also an *Inspekteur des Kriegsgefangenenwesen im OKW* (Inspector of POW Affairs). Usually an Army general, he examined standards at all levels of the POW organisation, from the command structure down to the camps themselves, and reported back to the *AWA*. He was also to ensure that all OKW directives concerning prisoners were carried out. However, the function of this office changed frequently, and its power and influence rose and fell accordingly. Most of its incumbents were ineffectual — or the *AWA* was simply indifferent — as conditions in the camps continued to be poor throughout its existence. In early 1942 a new post was created, the *Chef der Kriegsgefangenen im OKW* and another layer of administration was added, with the formation of the *Organisationsabteilung Kriegsgefangenenwesen im OKW*.

The effect of these changes on aircrew prisoners diminished during the latter half of the war, as Air Force camps came under the control of the *Luftgau* (Air District) commander. Ever since Britain's declaration of war, *Feldmarschall* (later *Reichsmarschall*) Hermann Goering, Commander in Chief of the Luftwaffe, had been determined to fight according to the chivalric code of the Great War and to keep aircrew prisoners under Luftwaffe jurisdiction. In September 1939 he had told his units: "During the Great War, in which I participated as an active pilot, there reigned between the rival air forces a spirit of chivalry which lasted even after tempers got hotter...I wish and hope that the newly formed German Air Force makes this chivalry, in the fighting which is about to start, their guiding principle also." Goering was further motivated by a desire to ensure that Luftwaffe personnel held by the British were also well treated. During the first nine months of the war in the West, most prisoners taken by the British were from the Luftwaffe. Their lot in captivity would be influenced mainly by the treatment given to British and Dominion Air Force personnel in German hands. It was therefore understandable that Goering should be interested in bringing the department holding Allied aircrew under his command. Thus, Luftwaffe camps were by and large free from Army and OKW interference, a factor that would benefit aircrew POWs. The Navy was accorded the same privilege.

But all prison camps, Luftwaffe or not, fell within the orbit of the German *Abwehr* — or Intelligence and Clandestine Warfare Service of the OKW — under the command of Admiral Wilhelm Canaris. Each camp was assigned one or more *Abwehroffiziere*. They were drawn from *Abt.III, Gruppe III-KGF. Abt.III*, under *Generalmajor* von Bentivegni, was responsible for counter-sabotage, counter-espionage and security. Its work frequently overlapped with that of the Gestapo, particularly where matters of national security were concerned. As for *Gruppe III-KGF* itself, this had been set up at the beginning of the war to prevent espionage and sabotage in POW camps. The personnel from *III-KGF* attached to each camp commandant's staff were primarily interested in security, searches and escapes, but they also reported to their superiors in the *Abwehr* chain of command.

The relationship of the *SS* (*Schutzstaffel*, or Defence Echelon) and the *Gestapo* (*Geheime Staatspolizei*, or Secret State Police) with the administration of the POW camps is also worth elaborating upon, as these two organisations were mainly responsible for affairs outside, rather than inside, the camps but would increasingly involve themselves in POW affairs as the war progressed. In this sphere of operations the Gestapo worked with the *Kriminalpolizei* (Criminal Police, or *Kripo*) in an organisation called the *Reichssicherheitshauptamt* (General Security Office of the Reich, or *RSHA*), established, commanded and built into a ruthless terror-weapon by Hitler's favourite, Reinhard Heydrich. From its creation at the beginning of the war the RSHA was divided into seven *Ämter* (offices or services), none of which had a direct interest in the affairs of genuine prisoners of war whose governments had signed the Geneva and Hague accords. However, *Amt IV*, which was the Gestapo proper, had six *Gruppen* responsible for seeking out and repressing opponents of the Nazi regime. *Gruppe A* comprised as many as six sub-groups, charged with, among other duties, counter-sabotage and general security measures. *Gruppe C* had the powers of preventive detention, protective custody, and the compiling of dossiers and card indexes; *Gruppe E* dealt with espionage, and *Gruppe F*, the Frontier Police or *Grenzpolizei*, was responsible for issuing passports and identity cards, detecting fakes, and patrolling the borders of the Greater Reich. The leader of *Amt IV* throughout the entire war was *Gruppenführer* Heinrich Müller.

Amt V was the Kripo. Led by *General* Artur Nebe, it had four groups and was strictly speaking responsible only for the prevention and detection of civil offences. Its executive groups were: A — Criminal Police and preventive measures; B — Repressive criminal police, and crimes and misdemeanours; and C — Identification and searches. It was, however, inevitable that in the normal pursuance of its duties it would encounter, and therefore arrest, errant prisoners of war.

These two *Ämter* had their headquarters in the same building at 8 Prinz-Albrecht-Strasse in Berlin, but their respective leaders loathed each other. Indeed, it is now a matter of record that Nebe, despite having been in the *Einsatzgruppen*, disliked carrying out Gestapo orders concerning POWs and later became involved in the plots to kill Hitler.

The RSHA had representatives in POW camps, often holding honorary Army or Luftwaffe ranks, from as early as summer 1940, and kept duplicates of RAF prisoner-of-war records in their Prinz-Albrecht-Strasse HQ. Aircrew prisoners were considered important by the Reich owing to their expensive training and, therefore, their value to the Allied war effort. It followed from this that they were most likely to make escape attempts, and their records were marked with a red flag and the word *"Deutschfeindlich"* — Enemy of Germany. In 1941 the Gestapo started to interfere systematically in POW affairs, following a meeting that July between Müller, Reinecke, General Breuer of the POW branch of the OKW, and Erwin Lahousen, a section leader from the *Abwehr*. Ostensibly, this conference was called in order to discuss measures against Russian prisoners, whose leaders had not signed the Geneva accords. However, its results, promulgated on 8 September 1941, were soon applied to other POWs:

> Insubordination, active or passive resistance, must be immediately broken by force of arms (bayonets, rifle butts, and firearms). Anyone carrying out this order without using his arms, or with insufficient energy, is liable to punishment. Prisoners who try to escape must be shot immediately, without being challenged. Warning shots are strictly forbidden...The use of weapons against prisoners of war is legal as a general rule.

In fact, this document was anticipated on 17 July 1941 by an order Müller issued to his agents in POW camps. He urged them to detect "all political, criminal or undesirable elements of whatever nature" in order to have them liquidated or subjected to "special treatment", and to seek out "all persons who could be employed in the reconstruction of the occupied territories". Any prisoners who "seemed trustworthy" should be used as spies to identify any fellow-captives who needed to be suppressed.

To carry out these orders the Gestapo set up a special department, *Gruppe IVa*, under

Hauptsturmführer Franz Koenighaus. It was hardly necessary. With agents already in all Oflags and Stalags, and Russian prisoners pouring in to them after July 1941, the RSHA already had a pretext on which to visit the camps. It was but a short walk, and a mere matter of another gate or two, for these functionaries to cross from the Russian to the British compounds.

However, from 1942 to1944 Goering was largely successful in his efforts to keep aircrew prisoners under his control — although the extent to which they were treated in accordance with his purported code of chivalry is open to question. For the first month of the war there was no camp in Germany for captured British personnel. But some 700,000 Poles had been taken captive and the first RAF officer prisoners, Squadron Leader S S Murray and Pilot Officers L H Edwards and A B Thompson, were held in one of the Polish camps, Oflag XA, at Itzehoe. On 2 October 1939 the Army opened Oflag IXA/H, at Spangenberg bei Kassel, for British and French aircrew. From December 1939 to July 1940 the only Luftwaffe camp for aircrew POWs was Dulag Luft, but this was only a transit and interrogation centre. From there prisoners were sent to Army camps. Officers (Army, Navy and Air Force) went to Spangenberg, which would accommodate the RAF at various times between 1939 and 1942. In June and July 1940 RAF officers were also sent briefly to Stalag XIIA at Limburg an der Lahn and Oflag IIA, another Polish camp, at Prenzlau. A small number were also held temporarily in Stalag VIA at Hemer, which was being used as a transit camp, and at Oflag VIIC, Laufen.

NCOs and "other ranks" went to Stalag VIA; Stalag VIJ, Krefeld; Stalag VIIIB, Lamsdorf; Stalag IXA, Zeigenhain; Stalag IXC, Bad Sulza; Stalag XIIA; and Stalag XXIB, Schubin.

These camps were rightly considered "undesirable" by the Luftwaffe, and on 5 July 1940 the first permanent aircrew camp run by the Luftwaffe was opened at Barth-Vogelsang, on the Baltic coast. As NCOs and other ranks would be in the majority, it was designated *Kriegsgefangenlager Nr.I der Luftwaffe* (or Stalag Luft I), and all subsequent aircrew camps were called Stalag Lufts even when officers were in the majority. But the High Command of Luftwaffe, like the OKW, had underestimated the number of prisoners that would fall into its hands. Some, but not all, of the RAF at Spangenberg were transferred there, and by the end of 1941 Stalag Luft I held, in one compound, 128 RAF officers, about 140 officers of the Dominion Air Forces and the Royal Navy Fleet Air Arm, a sprinkling of Royal Marine, Army, Commando and Special Air Service officers, and their thirty orderlies (a mixture of Army and Air Force NCOs and other ranks); and, in another compound, some 750 NCO aircrew, about six of them naval airmen. For a brief period, aircrew were also sent to the grim Polish forts of Posen and Thorn (Torun), administered from the nearby Stalag XXA, as a reprisal against alleged ill-treatment of German prisoners in Canada. Subsequently the RAF officers were returned to Oflag IXA/H, whilst new prisoners were sent to Oflag XC at Lübeck. Some were also held, by mistake, at Oflag VB, an Army camp at Biberach, and again at Oflag VIIC, Laufen.

In October 1941 Goering had ordered the construction of a new camp at Sagan, which was intended to be a model camp in which all Allied aircrew prisoners would be accommodated. In the meantime, the "old lags" from Oflag IXA/H would again be transferred, this time to Oflag VIB (Warburg-Dössel), where they would be joined by recently-captured officers from Oflag XC. New NCO prisoners would go to Stalag VIIIB and Stalag IXC, and another Stalag, IIIE, at Kirchhain. Even so, long after Stalag Luft III opened, some officer aircrew remained at Warburg, being sent to yet another Army camp, Oflag XXIB at Schubin (formerly a Stalag), in September.

Such, then, was the German state of preparedness for aircrew POWs between June 1940 and September 1942 — the limit of this narrative. During this period, as we shall see, Germany routinely breached almost every article of the Prisoner of War Code of the Geneva Convention, if not always in letter, then certainly in spirit. In some cases, newly captured prisoners were forced to march far longer distances than those stipulated and denied food, water and medical treatment. Under interrogation almost all were asked questions that went far beyond those required for the purposes of identification. In both transit and permanent camps many were held in substandard accommodation and denied fresh-air exercise; most were denied adequate food. They were collectively fined and punished for escape attempts and in some camps their food was tampered with and even stolen.

All RAF combatants, particularly officers, had been given to understand that in the event of being captured they should not merely sit out the war and await liberation by their own armed forces. It was their duty, by all possible and reasonable means, to escape.

Within the camps they were encouraged to escape by their senior officers and, indeed, from June 1941 all air force camps in which Wing Commander H M A Day AM, RAF, was Senior British Officer were declared "operational". Other SBOs, such as Squadron Leader B Paddon and Wing Commander J R Kayll DSO, DFC, of the Auxiliary Air Force, while less explicit, also fostered this spirit in Spangenberg and Warburg. If anything, far more aircrew officers tried to escape from Oflag VIB in 1941/42 than from Stalag Luft III from 1942 to 1945: almost the entire aircrew contingent were involved in tunnelling activities, for example, and even those who did not wish to make escape attempts were prepared to do escape work, such as forging documents, altering clothing, creating diversions and keeping an eye out for the Germans while others excavated tunnels, walked through the gate, crawled under the wire or leaped over the fence.

The extent to which the War Office considered escape a duty is indicated by the fact that as early as November 1938, two staff officers in separate branches of the War Office proposed creating an organisation to train servicemen in escaping if captured and to send intelligence back from POW camps. They were Captain (later Major) A R Rawlinson and Major J C F Holland DFC. Rawlinson had been in the sub-branch of the War Office responsible in 1917/18 for interrogating ex-POWs and promoting escape and evasion. Holland would go on to create the Commandos and Special Operations Executive (SOE). In autumn and winter 1939 the War Office held consultations with Holland and escapers from the Great War to decide how help could best be given to prisoners taken in the fresh outbreak of hostilities. Their proposals were passed on to the inter-services' Joint Intelligence Committee and on 23 December 1939, MI9 (Military Intelligence No9) was formed, under Major (later Brigadier) Norman R Crockatt DSO, MC, of the Royal Scots Fusiliers, to study the problems of escape and evasion in the light of their advice. Its office was in room 424 of the Metropole Hotel in Northumberland Avenue, a couple of furlongs away from the main War Office buildings.

Initially, MI9's brief was to interrogate enemy prisoners, to organise the escape of British prisoners and debrief them, and to help maintain escape routes set up in France, Belgium and Holland by patriotic civilians. But its scope soon increased, and its objectives were later defined retrospectively as follows: (i) to supply money and radio communications to escape lines; (ii) to drop supplies; (iii) to arrange pickups by aircraft and naval evacuations from the coast of France; (iv) to train new agents and establish new routes; (v) to train servicemen in evasion and escaping; (vi) to provide them with escape kits; (vii) to send escape equipment to POW camps in Germany, Poland and Italy; (viii) to gather and distribute intelligence from the camps and from interrogating escapers and enemy POWs; (ix) to deny information to the enemy; and (x) to maintain POW morale. In December 1941 the side dealing with enemy prisoners became MI19, while MI9 was divided into five sub-sections — b for liaison with other branches of the services and interrogation of returned evaders and escapers; d for training; x for the planning and organisation of escapes; y for codes; and z for tools.

Documentary evidence shows that MI9 was highly successful in aiding evasion. But even the late Airey Neave, who joined it in May 1942 and wrote the first full-length account of its exploits, found the records (now held in the Public Record Office at Kew) difficult to interpret. They contain little of relevance to any of the prison camps in which the Royal and Dominion Air Forces were held, but it is worth going into the history of MI9 at some length in order to establish how far the War Office went to foster escape activities amongst aircrew POWs.

After the Metropole suffered bomb damage in September 1940, Crockatt moved his HQ to Wilton Park, a country house on the eastern edge of Beaconsfield, in the Chilterns. Sections b and d at Beaconsfield — known as Camp 20 — collected Intelligence about Allied POWs from the interrogation of escapers and other sources, and built up a system of briefing the three services on how to avoid capture. The centre of operations for escape lines in North-West Europe was Room 900 of the War Office, with MI9b staff at an Interrogation Centre in the London Transit Camp — formerly the Great Central Hotel — in Marylebone.

Room 900 also provided information for evasion briefings, sent by agents in occupied territory. This included advice on what to do when shot down, and details of German controls in frontier and coastal zones and their methods of checking passengers on trains.

Travelling MI9 lecturers started briefing operational units of the Army, Navy and Air Force at least as early as January 1940. But it was in the middle period of the war that the number of lectures reached its peak. From 1 January 1942 to 25 August 1944 — that is, from three months prior to the opening of Stalag Luft III until five months after the mass escape therefrom in March 1944 — MI9 gave 1,450 lectures to RAF personnel, of whom 290,000 attended. Many memoirs by wartime airmen, and histories of fighter and bomber operations, have included accounts of these lectures. They were often given by successful escapers from the Great War — such as Squadron Leader A J Evans MC and Flight Lieutenant H G Durnford MC — and by returned escapers and evaders from Hitler's war. However, the talks tended to concentrate on how to evade capture, rather than escape from prison camps, since in North-West Europe the main objective of MI9 was to secure the return of trained men by the underground. Thus, the principal instruction passed on to airmen was that when they found themselves in enemy-occupied territory they should at all costs avoid capture. They were to endeavour to bury their parachutes and take cover until they were sure that search parties were no longer looking for them, or to take off across country as soon as possible. They should look for a suitable house or farm, but not enter until they had made sure the owner was alone and that no German troops were in sight. Schoolteachers, doctors and priests were invariably helpful and often spoke English. Priests could safely be approached at the confessional.

Once evaders had made contact, been given civilian clothes and had their wounds, if any, treated, they were to wait patiently in hiding. It might take several days, or even weeks, for those who sheltered them to contact an escape organisation and then pass them from contact to contact, and from one safe house to another, until they reached neutral territory. (Men thus passed down the escape lines were called "parcels".) On no account were they to attempt, through boredom and frustration, to make their own way to safety. Lacking authentic papers and, in all probability, unable to speak any language other than English, they would surely be arrested, in which case they should escape as soon as possible. Should they have to travel alone and unaided, they should move by day and observe the curfew by night. They were advised not to steal bicycles, as this might lead to detection, although more than one successful evader — as well as at least one successful escaper — had travelled vast distances on bicycles without incident. If they did secure bicycles, they had to keep to the right-hand side of the road, as failure to do so had more than once led to arrest by the local police.

Aircrew were also warned against opening friendly and unnecessary conversation and carrying cigarettes — especially such British brands as Players and Gold Flake — as these were rare on the Continent. Nicotine stains on the fingers could also lead to detection and arrest. Nor should they eat chocolate — again unknown in most places during wartime — in public, or carry a walking-stick or cane, as this was a British custom. Rope-soled shoes and a beret, if they could be acquired, were often the most effective means of disguise.

The recommendations for travel in Germany itself were the opposite of those for occupied territories, as there was no prospect of help from the population. Walking in Germany by day was extremely dangerous, so it was best to move by night, avoiding military installations with sentries and the streets of large towns. But POW-escapers, armed with passes and suitably disguised, could cover large distances by train.

Not only did these lectures provide information and advice which gave the men confidence in their ability to avoid arrest, but they also placed great emphasis on the security of MI9's agents and helpers. Hitler and Goering knew of the existence of escape lines and understood the impact on the Allied war effort of hundreds of airmen slipping through their hands. They gave orders that the lines were to be crushed. The *Feldgendarmerie* (Field Police) and Secret Field Police of the *Abwehr* repeatedly invaded the homes of helpers in the dead of night and carried them off for interrogation. In Brussels and Paris, Goering's Secret Police of the Luftwaffe collaborated with their political enemies in the *Gestapo* and *Sicherheitsdienst* (*SD*, or Security Service) in subjecting helpers and Allied airmen to brutality otherwise alien to the Luftwaffe. (After the German occupation of Vichy France they were also helped by collaborationist Frenchmen in the *Milice*, the French equivalent of the *Gestapo* directed by Joseph Darnand. Both the *Gestapo* and the *Milice* tortured captives by beating, ice-cold bath treatment and electric shock.) Thus, MI9 warned airmen that on no account were they to put in writing the names and addresses of those who hid them. Any airman captured by the *Gestapo* while in the hands of escape organisations was to give only his name, rank and service number, as he was obliged to do if captured in combat.

For the same reasons, MI9 lecturers withheld concrete information regarding the locations and members of escape lines. By the end of 1942 there were four principal lines in operation employing at the very least 12,000 helpers. The evader could only hope that once he had made contact with a patriot he would be handed on to one of these lines. The first — set up in July 1940 with the help of an MI6 agent, Donald Darling, then based in Lisbon — eventually ran from Paris, through Vichy France to Barcelona, as well as having collection points for evaders at Normandy, Rouen, the Pas de Calais, Marseilles and Toulouse; this later became known as the PAO (Pat O'Leary) Line. As many as two hundred and fifty people worked for it as couriers, forgers and suppliers of clothing. The guides were recruited in Perpignan and were paid £40 for each officer, and £20 for each "other rank", they led across the Pyrenees. As frontier controls tightened, the prices increased. The cost of sheltering and feeding evaders in one year alone was at least six million French francs, all of which the Treasury credited to accounts in England. Once in Spain, successful evaders were taken by train to the consulate in Barcelona. After a brief interrogation at the British Embassy in Madrid they went by coach to Gibraltar, usually as a party of "students". There, they were interrogated by Donald Darling, who had been transferred from Lisbon in January 1942 and who arranged their passage home. The PAO Line also evacuated evaders by sea from the coast of southern France to Gibraltar. By the end of the war it would rescue more than six hundred Allied airmen and soldiers.

Even more startling successes were achieved by the Comet Line, which in 1941 had started passing soldiers and airmen through a chain of "safe houses" in Brussels and Paris and down to San Sebastiàn and Bilbao. It cost 6,000 Belgian francs to pass an airman down to St-Jean-de-Luz and 1,400 pesetas for a guide across the Pyrenees. But between July and October 1942 alone this line escorted fifty-four men to Spain. In its three years of life it would return more than eight hundred soldiers and airmen.

A third line, though less successful, was run by an MI9-trained agent, Mary Lindell, Comtesse de Milleville, who passed evaders from Paris and Bordeaux to Perpignan and across the Pyrenees. The fourth, known as "Shelburne", was established to house and feed airmen in Paris and pass them on to Brittany for naval evacuation to Dartmouth or for passage down to Spain. It would not, however, achieve its first success until January 1944. By July 1944 Shelburne would rescue three hundred and sixty-five airmen.

MI9 provided money, radio links and trained agents for all these lines throughout the war. The officer in charge of maintaining these escape lines was Lieutenant Colonel J M Langley MC, MBE, of the Coldstream Guards, who despite the loss of an arm at Dunkirk had escaped to England via Spain in the spring of 1941. He was based in Room 900.

There was a fifth line, however, with which MI9 had no connection: the Dutch-Paris Underground, established in 1941 by John Henry Weidner, a Seventh-Day Adventist from the Netherlands. Stretching from Holland, through Belgium and France and down to the Swiss and Spanish frontiers, Dutch-Paris would eventually employ more than three hundred helpers and save more than a thousand Jews and a hundred and twelve Allied airmen.

Running parallel to the escape and evasion briefings given by MI9*d* lecturers was Intelligence School No9 (IS9) at Caen Wood Towers in Highgate, North London, where Intelligence Officers of all three services were briefed on evasion and escape so they could lecture their own units. IS9 had its origins in September 1941, when the RAF started a series of Intelligence Courses at Station "Z", Harrow, which eventually became known as the "A" Courses of the RAF Intelligence School. The Air Ministry approached MI9 with a view to starting an MI9 course at the school, intended to train RAF Intelligence Officers as instructors in escape and evasion. All IOs on

Operational Training Units and operational stations would undergo the course, and at least one officer on each station would be made responsible for instructing aircrew in MI9 subjects. MI9 lecturers would continue to brief aircrew directly, and successful escapers and evaders would go on lecture tours. The first MI9 course, known as the Special Intelligence Course No1 and later called "B" Course, opened at Station "Z" on 5 January 1942 and was attended by ten Senior Intelligence Officers from No6 Group, Bomber Command. A J Evans, Senior RAF Officer attached to MI9, was appointed Chief Instructor and was responsible for drawing up the original syllabus. He was assisted in lecturing by visiting lecturers from MI9 and other departments, while the administration was handled by the Intelligence School under Squadron Leader H M Parsons.

The first "B" Course covered evasion, early escape, prison camp conditions and organisation, POW security, codes, International Law, and conditions in Occupied Europe and Germany, took in a visit to MI9 Headquarters, and concluded with a short practice lecture in one of fourteen subjects by each pupil; a report was made on each pupil, assessing his suitability as a lecturer and instructor. It lasted five days. From then on B Courses ran almost continually, week by week, up to November 1944, and during this time expanded considerably in both size and scope, eventually becoming inter-service and embracing Intelligence Officers of the American Forces. Successful escapers and evaders detailed for lecture tours also attended. By September 1942 twenty-six of these Special Intelligence Courses had been run at Harrow.

Some aircrew fell asleep or made wisecracks during MI9 lectures — out of either cynicism or a blithe faith that they would never be shot down. There were others who, while on operations, never gave POWs a thought. But as losses — particularly on "Rhubarbs", "Circuses", "Beehives" and deep penetration raids to the Ruhr, Berlin and Nuremberg — continued to mount, so the prospect of "getting the chop" or becoming a POW preyed more heavily on the minds of aircrew. Thus, most airmen followed MI9 instructions, and some took them sufficiently seriously to learn languages and study the countries over which they were due to fly on operations.

In any event, to make audiences more receptive, MI9 lecturers told true stories of the adventures of other evaders and tried to lace them with humour. They also briefed airmen on what to expect if their efforts to evade broke down and they were interrogated at Dulag Luft and then passed on to a permanent camp.

Somewhat fancifully (did they think the Germans did not read?) MI9 also asked the British Museum to comb libraries and second-hand bookshops in Bloomsbury for copies of escape classics of the Great War. In all they collected fifty — among them H G Durnford's *The Tunnellers of Holzminden*, A J Evans' *The Escaping Club*, E H Jones' *The Road to En-Dor*, Duncan Grinnell-Milne's *An Escaper's Log* and M C C Harrison and H A Cartwright's *Within Four Walls*. They had the books summarised by the sixth form of Crockatt's old school, Rugby, into guidelines for a new generation of escapers. *Within Four Walls* was published in a Penguin paperback in 1940 and issued to aircrew.

The escape kits provided by MI9 and issued before each operation also served to underline the seriousness of evasion. Crammed into flat transparent acetate boxes, they contained a variety of escape aids: silk maps, £12 in foreign currency, a small compass, a hacksaw, nourishing food for forty-eight hours (such as Horlicks malted milk tablets, boiled sweets, liver toffee, chewing gum and chocolate made with 45% fat), a pint-sized water bottle, water purifying tablets (halazone), benzedrine, and such helpful items as soap, shaving tackle, a needle and thread, and a fishing line and hook. By 1942 they also contained a toothpaste tube full of concentrated milk manufactured by Nestlé. They were designed at MI9 headquarters in Beaconsfield under Christopher Clayton Hutton, a wayward genius who, with Charles Fraser-Smith — a civilian working ostensibly for the Ministry of Supply, but secretly under the direction of MI6 and MI9 — produced an astonishing variety of other ingenious devices. Known as "Q" gadgets, they included maps printed on rustle-free paper and hidden inside pipes, shaving-brushes, hair-brushes, playing-cards, dominoes and chess-sets; and tiny compasses hidden in tooth fillings, fountain pens, collar studs, the backs of cap badges and service buttons and, again, in pipes, shaving tackle and hair-brushes. Hutton and Fraser-Smith arranged for pencils and razor blades to be magnetised, for surgical hacksaws ("Giglis") to be hidden in bootlaces and small shaving mirrors and invented the "escape boot" — a pair of flying boots with removable leggings which could be converted into walking shoes and a waistcoat. Another one of their inventions was the escape blanket—a blanket which could be sent to a prisoner by a fictitious relative and which, when washed, revealed a pattern for a civilian suit. Their masterpiece, however, was the escape knife: as well as a strong knife-blade it had three saws, a lock breaker, a screwdriver and a small wire-cutter.

In April 1942, when Stalag Luft III opened, 2,338 purses of foreign currency, 3,857 escape kits and 3,220 compasses were issued to RAF personnel in Europe. During the same month, 208 "loaded" parcels were sent to POW camps in Germany in the guise of private parcels or gifts of some three-dozen organisations invented by MI9 to sponsor their traffic — such as the Licensed Victuallers' Sport Association, the Prisoners' Leisure House Fund, and the Welsh Provident Society. They contained two-hundred and nine maps, ninety compasses, 5,210 *Reichsmark*, 175 *Guilder*, one dye, forty-four patterned blankets, thirty-eight hacksaws, four sets of Me110 starting instructions, two sets of Ju88 starting instructions, one set of plans for aerodromes in Holland and Belgium, and six passports. Of twenty-two RAF personnel questioned by MI9 in May 1942 after returning from Germany or German-occupied territory, ten had been briefed by MI9 and nineteen had been issued with an escape kit.

From as early as 1940 MI9*y* had been trying to work out a satisfactory code by which prisoners could send home information, or request escape aid, in apparently innocuous letters. Many married prisoners had already made private arrangements with their wives, known as "dotty codes", since the portion of the letter in code was bracketed by a series of dots. With the help of C W R Hooker, a Foreign Office expert, the staff of MI9*y*, led by two of Crockatt's earliest subordinates, Major Leslie Winterbottom and A J Evans, developed a code known as "HK". The first code used by the RAF was called "Amy", which was based on a pocket English dictionary with pages measuring no more than 2 x 4 inches. By late summer 1942, Winterbottom had developed six codes, plus Hooker's; three more were in reserve by autumn. HK was a simple code, which was unusually hard to detect. The user indicated by the manner in which he wrote the date (in Roman numerals) whether the letter contained a message, showed by his opening words which part of the code he was using, and then went on to write an apparently normal, chatty letter, from which the inner meaning could be unravelled by MI9's decoders. The incoming messages, once decoded, were sent to Norman Crockatt, who then distributed them accordingly. Potential code-users were chosen by MI9 from amongst the more sober and level-headed members of lecture audiences — those who would be least surprised, once in a permanent POW camp, at receiving a letter from a fictitious relation or school-chum invented by MI9*y*. Code-users amounted to about one per cent of the Army and Navy, most fighter pilots and six per cent of other aircrew. Teaching the code and instructing the user in security took less than an hour. The first code-carrier to be shot down and made prisoner, on 20/21 July 1940, was a flight sergeant, N J Prendergast, from No61 Squadron, Hemswell. But at the end of August 1940, when the number of British prisoners in Germany stood at about 34,000, only four officers were equipped with an MI9 code — three from the RAF and one from the Royal Navy. They were Wing Commander Day, Squadron Leader W H N Turner DFC, Flying Officer J A Gillies (of the Auxiliary Air Force) and Lieutenant Commander J Casson RN. Several POWs were, however, communicating with London through coded letters by November 1940.

Unfortunately, MI9 was not without its own problems. For a long time it failed to gain the co-operation of senior officers. This owed itself in part to the distrust in which Regular officers held what they chose to call "cloak and dagger" work. To them, clandestine operations seemed essentially civilian in character (hence their opposition, also, to SOE), and neither were they disposed to encourage their men to ponder on the possibilities of capture. Although they softened in their attitude after the fall of France, when many soldiers — and some aircrew — reached home through Spain, even as late as 1944 there were many whose backgrounds made them reluctant to accept the need for training in escape and evasion. The Air Ministry was especially culpable, since aircrew were much more likely than the Army or the Navy to find themselves alone and unarmed in enemy territory. For much of the war it fell to a handful of staff officers in Bomber Command and the Directorate of Operations & Intelligence to pressurise the Air Ministry into issuing instructions and escape kits to operational aircrew. Although aircrew had been receiving lectures and escape equipment since January 1940, it was not until September 1941 that the Air Ministry initiated evasion and escape briefings at the RAF Intelligence School; and it showed little enthusiasm for the provision of aircraft for clandestine escape operations or for the parachuting of Room 900 agents, despite the fact that it succumbed to persistent pressure from SOE and other secret intelligence organisations. Military Intelligence itself considered returned POWs to be of little value to the war effort, and two years were to elapse before it would take the work of MI9 seriously. The Foreign Office suffered many attacks of "cold feet" when MI9 planned sea-borne evacuations in vessels painted in neutral colours, even though on one occasion thirty-five airmen, including the distinguished Squadron Leader Whitney Straight, were rescued in this way.

Not only were MI9's relations with other departments strained, but its own y and z sections were subject to the limitations imposed by the global war economy. POW post was slow and unreliable, and months could pass between y section asking for information and receiving a reply from a camp in Germany; seven weeks was considered fast. The alternative — for prisoners to build a radio transmitter and receiver — was accomplished in most camps, although in no case was a transmitter ever used; possession of either was, in fact, punishable by death, and MI9 gave strict instructions that prisoners should never use the transmitters except in dire emergency.

As it was, much of this activity occurred too late to be of benefit to the aircrew POWs who reached Sagan from Barth, Spangenberg and Warburg in 1942. Most had been shot down with no escape aids and few had heard MI9 lectures. In any case, by the end of 1941 the three services had expanded so much that visiting MI9 lecturers could not keep up. The RAF was in the worst position. With the large number of new formations, including operational squadrons, Operational Training Units (OTUs) and Heavy Conversion Units (HCUs) spreading all over the country, and the demands on manpower made by the campaigns in France and Norway, the Battle of Britain and the stepping up of the Bomber Offensive, it was becoming increasingly difficult, if not impossible, for the small number of MI9 instructors to cover all these units at regular intervals. Even when instructors did visit, the prior claims of operations and flying training, leave, sickness and other causes prevented adequate attendance by aircrew. Thus in 1940 and 1941 many aircrew were operating over enemy territory with little or no knowledge of a subject which the War Office looked upon as of vital importance.

Even assuming that most had been issued with escape kits, there are several recorded instances of evaders discovering that the money was in the wrong currency or that the rubber water-bag had rotted or that the chocolate had gone sour. The escape boots were totally inadequate — they failed to keep legs warm at high altitudes and, once cut down to make shoes, proved as uncomfortable and impractical as ordinary flying boots. In the end, MI9z abandoned them.

Some of the aircrew shot down in autumn and winter 1941 were captured because the escape lines, too unwieldy for proper security to be effective, were either afraid to handle them or were infiltrated by informers and broken up. Once in POW camps, aircrew found that the lessons they had learned from reading accounts by successful escapers of the Great War were outmoded, for all *Abwehr* personnel had read the books, which had been passed on from spies in America, Cuba, Mexico and Argentina and were stocked in their escape museums. In addition, the experience that POW camp staff acquired from thwarting escapes was passed on to the *Abwehr*, who each week produced a publication called *Das Abwehrblatt* (Security News), consolidating all the information regarding escape methods employed in the past seven days and circulating it to every POW camp commandant.

Assuming the initial achievement of escaping from a POW camp in Germany, prisoners then had to avoid the inevitable manhunt (or *Fahndung*, as the Germans called it). The moment an escape was discovered (usually early in the morning), the commandant alerted the local foresters, the local railway stations, and all police stations within five kilometres (approximately three miles). They raised parties of local inhabitants on foot and bike, who scanned the open country, beat forests and watched bridges, rivers and canals. The camp security officer sent off a posse of soldiers with sniffer dogs to track down the escapers within a radius of fifteen kilometres (9½ miles) of the camp. If, by midday, that had produced no results the dragnet would be extended to a radius of twenty-five miles. Once an identity parade, or snap *Appell* (roll-call), had ascertained exactly who was missing, the commandant phoned the area HQ of the *Kriminalpolizei*. Area HQ had duplicate records and photographs of all the POWs in the district, and could produce a profile of the escapees for publication in a *Sonderausgabe* (Special Issue) of the *Kriminalpolizeiblatt* (*Criminal Police Gazette*). Back at the camp, the *Abwehr* officers would have instituted a *Grossrazzia*, a class-one search, to discover the means of egress. It paid for the commandant and his security officers to recapture the escapees quickly and to find out their method of escape, for the *Abwehr* and OKW in Berlin would soon be on the line, asking: "How did they get out?" "When did they escape?" "What clothes are they wearing?" "Who is to blame?" "Has he been punished?" "What are you doing to stop similar escapes in the future?" And so on.

The *Kripo* and the *Gestapo* were no fools. They were well aware of the routes taken by fleeing aircrew: north to the Baltic and across to Sweden; south to Switzerland; west to Belgium and France where they might contact the Comet Line or Dutch-Paris, or east and south-east to Poland or Czechoslovakia, where once again they could hope to link up with Partisans. Switzerland was, however, unpopular with aircrew escapers. Once there they ran the risk of either being interned for the duration of the war, or of having to sneak out of the country and through France to Spain along the PAO Line, with all the attendant hazards of being captured yet again and, like their Resistance helpers, facing torture followed by death or incarceration in a concentration camp.

Of the RAF officer POWs who attempted to escape between 1939 and 1942, only two made home runs, both from Stalag Luft I and both via Sweden. MI9's contribution to these escapes was negligible. Its official historians — M R D Foot and J M Langley — themselves estimate that only about two-thirds of its loaded parcels actually reached prison camps in Germany, and their use is difficult to evaluate. MI9 records claim that dyes, maps, money, patterned blankets, and so on, were continually being smuggled in to the camps. But many of Clayton Hutton's tricks for hiding escape material — such as inside gramophone records and book-bindings — were discovered early in the war, and the convertible blankets were of too good a quality to pass for civilian suits, which were often of inferior cloth. (Incidentally, there is some rivalry and one-upmanship between former members of MI9, with several memoirists trying to take credit for what were, quite frankly, negligible achievements with pinprick value to the war effort.)

The grim reality was that, despite MI9's best efforts to foster escape from prison camps, the prisoners themselves — especially those captured in the first two years of the war — still had to rely mainly on bribery, theft, culling the German newspapers, improvised tools, papers and disguises, and the accumulation of knowledge borne of years of bitter experience in previous camps. The escape attempts by RAF prisoners from Warburg between September 1941 and September 1942 owed little, if anything, to MI9. In the official history of MI9 by M R D Foot and J M Langley, published in 1979, Oflag VIB receives one mention, and that concerns a mass escape to which MI9 appears to have made no contribution. The official history also fails to mention that, of the RAF contingent at Warburg, only two officers received loaded parcels, Squadron Leader Turner and Pilot Officer J E A Foster RAFVR. In general its references to escapes from POW camps are based on previously published accounts, most of them unreliable. Clearly, the history of MI9 suffers from "the bullfrog" effect, and the stark truth is that Royal and Dominion Air Force personnel captured between the outbreak of hostilities in September 1939 and the opening of Stalag Luft III in April 1942 received scant help from official sources.

However, perhaps the *Abwehr* should have the last word. After the USA joined the air war over Europe, Luftwaffe counter-escape intelligence compiled a report on MI9 gadgets found on captured aircrew. Despite the efforts of MI9 to disguise their maps, compasses, hacksaws and foreign currency, the enemy had discovered nearly every single device employed and ensured that information on new discoveries was passed to all units "charged to watch and arrest enemy Air Force prisoners…in order to enable them to take efficient counter-measures". After listing all the items "routinely" found on aircrew, the report concluded: "It must be conceded that the enemy works hard to provide constantly so many new additions to escape material."

Chapter One

Accidental Arrivals, Sudden Departures

Oflag VIIC/H, Laufen, June–September 1940 and July–August 1941; Oflag VB, Biberach, June–September 1941

T he charming Mediæval village of Laufen lies about eighteen kilometres north-east of Salzburg, on the banks of the Salzach River at a point where it separates Bavaria from Austria. It is dominated by an enormous, biscuit-coloured, block-like building, five storeys high and constructed of stone and brick with red tiled roofs. This is the palace of Laufen, once the summer home of the Archbishop of Salzburg, and later the place where Mozart composed and played some of his most famous works. Architecturally, it is remarkable only for its multitude of windows — in one wall alone more than sixty. In 1939 it became remarkable in quite another way, as it was one of three permanent structures in *Wehrkreis VII* requisitioned by the *Oberkommando der Wehrmacht* and converted by district headquarters in Munich into prisoner of war camps for captives from the *Blitzkrieg* on Poland.

Designated Oflag VIIC, it was opened, according to official reports, on 3 December 1939. On 9 July 1940 it became a *Hauptlager*, or main camp, and was redesignated Oflag VIIC/H. However, on 3 January 1941 it reverted to its original suffix. Almost a year later, on 28 January 1942, it was closed to prisoners of war and became Ilag VII, a camp for civilian internees. When Germany launched its *Blitzkrieg* in the West in May 1940 more than half the British army officers captured, along with four aircrew POWs, were sent to Oflag VIIC. It turned out to be a grim place, of which they would for years afterwards hold unpleasant memories. "Despite the attractive countryside around it, the lovely river Salzach which flowed by it and the breathtaking view of the Alps which it provided," wrote one Army officer, Lieutenant E G B Davies-Scourfield of the King's Royal Rifle Corps, "Laufen was in fact a vile place."

The first Army officers to reach Laufen arrived on Wednesday, 5 June. They numbered nearly three hundred. A further two hundred-odd arrived on Wednesday, 12 June. Included in this party were two pilots and an air gunner: Pilot Officers A H Deacon and L P R Hockey RAFVR, and a Fleet Air Arm lieutenant, A D Neely. More prisoners arrived on Friday, 14 June — some two hundred Army officers who had been temporarily held in Doullens castle and Oflag XIIB, a former military barracks in Mainz. Yet more arrived on Tuesday, 25 June, and still more on Saturday, 29 June, the night of Sunday, 30 June, and on Sunday, 7 July (three hundred alone in one evening). Among the 30 June intake was Pilot Officer J B Smiley.

The walrus-moustached, forthright Leonard Phillip Redcliff ("Len") Hockey had been a businessman in Bristol when he joined the RAF Volunteer Reserve before the war. Posted to No75 (New Zealand) Squadron, based at Feltwell, Norfolk, he had been promoted to Acting Flight Lieutenant and appointed gunnery officer. He then had the unenviable distinction of being its first officer to enter captivity — in the first of one hundred and ninety-three aircraft lost by the squadron, which was to suffer the second highest losses in Bomber Command. On the night of 21/22 May 1940, the squadron put up eight Vickers Wellingtons as part of the RAF's effort to disrupt communications in Germany, France and the Low Countries. Their target was the bridge at Dinant, Belgium, across which the Germans were pouring troops. Hockey, who wanted to find out what "ops" were like, flew as rear-gunner in a Wimpey piloted by Flying Officer J N Collins of the RNZAF. (This operation would also lead to the capture of Flying Officer D F Laslett, Pilot Officer G T Dodgshun and Pilot Officer J Whilton, all from No115 Squadron and all three of whom would be sent to Oflag IXA/H, Spangenberg.) Also in John Collins' crew were Pilot Officer F A G F J de Labouchere-Sparling, the second pilot, who was on his first operation; Sergeant G Thorpe (observer); and Aircraftman 1st Class J S Brooks (wireless operator/air-gunner).

John Collins took off from Feltwell at 2120 hours. The flight out was uneventful, and over Froyennes, east of Tournai, he prepared to lose height ready for the bombing run. But at about 3,000 feet the Wimpey was hit by flak and the starboard engine burst into flames. Pilot Officer de Labouchere-Sparling tried to douse the fire with extinguishers. Seeing they were having little or no effect, Collins banked to port, hoping the blast from the wind would put out the flames. But soon the entire wing was alight, engine included, so he ordered the crew to bale out. He told the second pilot to open the bulkhead door, make sure Sergeant Thorpe baled out and then follow him. By this time the fire had spread to the fuselage and the starboard side of the Wimpey was a mass of blazing fabric — only the geodetic airframe was still intact. Len Hockey was third man out of the aircraft. The last to jump was AC1 Stan Brooks. He had vacated his wireless position on crossing the coast to man the front gun-turret in case of fighters. Now only Collins was left, having courageously stayed with the burning aircraft to make sure the crew escaped safely. He was killed when it exploded in the air over Hainaut, four kilometres north-north-west of Tournai. Collins' second pilot, de Labouchere-Sparling, was also killed — hit by ground-fire as he descended by parachute. He had spent his early years in Belgium and, had he survived, would have stood a good chance of going to ground and returning to England.

Hockey, Brooks and Thorpe landed several miles apart but all three were captured straight away. Their captors gathered them at a farm and then took them another twenty miles to a beautiful château where they were handed over to the Luftwaffe. One by one the prisoners were escorted up a wide staircase to a vast room where each was interrogated for half an hour by a *Flak* major and two young Luftwaffe pilots. One of the pilots had a bandaged leg and the other an arm in a sling; obviously they were convalescing from combat wounds. Apart from saying "Good morning" in English, they asked no questions, leaving this to the major.

Len Hockey was alarmed by the procedure that followed. It began with softening up, the major bidding him to take a seat and proffering a packet of fifty Players'. After asking Hockey his name, rank and service number the major went on to ask questions about his squadron, aircraft and operations — which, of course, Hockey refused to answer. This went on for about twenty minutes, with the major becoming more and more annoyed. Suddenly, the enraged major opened a desk drawer, pulled out a revolver, pointed it at Hockey's chest and shouted: "If I don't get answers to my questions, I will shoot!" Despite their wounds, the two Luftwaffe pilots lunged at him, wrested the revolver from his grip, returned it to the drawer, and admonished him. It would have seemed melodramatic, even comical, in a film, but to Hockey it seemed all too real and frightening.

After that, the major calmed down. He ended the interview on what he clearly thought was a note of triumph, claiming to know that Hockey had been shot down in a Bristol Blenheim and the location of his airfield. As the Wimpey had exploded in mid-air, and only three men had survived, the German observers had wrongly assumed they were a Blenheim crew; but it was not for Hockey to straighten them out! When he was led back downstairs Thorpe was taken up, and Hockey whispered to Brooks that when his turn came he should give only his name, rank and number. Comparing notes afterwards, the three discovered that each interrogation had followed the same pattern, and that the business with the revolver had been a bluff.

Arthur Henry Deacon, from Invermay, Saskatchewan, had been a bandleader before joining the RAF. He was posted to No242 (Canadian) Squadron, equipped with the Hurricane MkI, on

6 November 1939, along with Flying Officer L E Chambers and Pilot Officer Smiley, both of whom he would soon join in captivity. On 16 May 1940 "Art" Deacon went to France with "A" Flight to join No85 Squadron at Lille-Seclin on attachment. The pace was hectic, with the squadron going up on patrol and interceptions three times a day. On 19 May Deacon flew four sorties; by the third he had been so exhausted that he had fallen asleep three times in the cockpit while over enemy territory. At last, on 27 May, the squadron heard it would be evacuating France in stages and gathering at Manston, Kent, where Art Deacon returned to his former unit.

The end came for Deacon the next day, Tuesday, 28 May, when ten of No242's Hurricanes took off in two sections from Manston for a lunchtime patrol over Ostend, on the Belgian coast. Deacon was flying in a section led by Flight Lieutenant D R Miller. The cloud over Ostend was dense, and the two sections lost each other. Flight Lieutenant Miller spotted a Ju88, led his section in pursuit, but lost the quarry in thick cloud. Then he and his fellow-pilots saw twelve Me109s flying below in loose formation. Miller led them down, going for the leading enemy aircraft. But the Hurricanes in turn were bounced by another sixty Me109s, which had been lurking above.

Deacon had seen them coming and broken formation, intending to enter their defensive circle, shoot quickly, then "get the hell out". He got in a quick burst but was hit from behind. Shells struck one of his legs and punctured the oil line, and the oil spurted over his cockpit canopy. He shut off the engine, slid back the canopy — with oil streaming into his face — then threw off the escape hatch and undid his harness. Meanwhile, he pointed his Hurricane towards the coast, in a shallow dive, hoping to crash-land on the beach or bale out if the aircraft caught fire. He just made it to the coast and, pulling back the stick, went almost straight in. Losing consciousness on impact, he came to in the garden of a hospital, where his face, which had been cut open on crash-landing, was stitched up.

In hospital he learned that Belgium had surrendered at 11am that day. There was no time to lose if he wanted to return to the Allied lines. He acquired some civilian duds and made his way to Antwerp, where he tried to get help at the American Legation. The staff agreed to take his home address and write to his father. (Deacon found out later that they welched on this promise). In the meantime, he was admitted to hospital to have the stitches in his face removed and his leg-wound cleaned up. A few days later the hospital was overrun by the Germans and, because he was in civilian clothes, Deacon was at first held in a camp for civilians. He was then transferred to Laufen.

Born in Mussoorie, India, Alexander Desmond Neely had gone to England with his mother at the age of five after the death of his father in 1922. The young widow and her son settled in Bedford and, in 1935, following a public school education, Neely joined the Royal Navy as an Executive Cadet (Public School Entrant). After undergoing the usual Executive Officer training, he decided in late 1939 to specialise in aviation. On 25 May 1940 he was posted to No825 (Fleet Air) Squadron, which was temporarily attached to Coastal Command and based in Kent at RAF Detling. Until recently, No825 had shared the aircraft carrier HMS *Glorious* with Nos 823 and 812 Squadrons — all three flying Fairey Swordfish — and No802 Squadron, equipped with Sea Gladiators. The *Glorious* had arrived in the Clyde from the Mediterranean on 18 April. Three days later, Nos 812 and 825 flew to Prestwick, while the *Glorious* took on RAF Gladiators urgently needed in Norway. On 18 May the squadron was seconded to Coastal Command and moved to Detling. It would shortly welcome a new commanding officer, Lieutenant-Commander J B ("Jimmy") Buckley DSC, RN.

Buckley was a Dartmouth-trained regular and had served on the *Glorious* as Senior Pilot of No802 Squadron during the Abyssinian crisis. In the first week of May 1940 he had formed No806 (Fighter/Dive-Bomber) Squadron, equipped with the Blackburn Skua, at Worthy Down, Sussex. At the end of the month, sporting the DSC ribbon, he took command of No825 Squadron. This would be both his and Neely's first experience of flying the Swordfish on operations.

The Swordfish was intended for torpedoing enemy shipping, "spotting" the fall of gunfire and carrying out reconnaissance for the fleet; hence it was known initially as a "Torpedo-Spotter-Reconnaissance" aircraft, or TSR. But bombing gradually assumed more importance than spotting, so that the aircraft was sometimes called a TSBR, or merely a TBR. Even more of an anachronism than the Skua, it was an open-cockpit, three-seater biplane with a fixed undercarriage, a conception which owed much to Great War influences. Indeed, the Swordfish was already being superseded by developments in the monoplane when it was on the drawing board in 1933. Fully bombed-up, it could just about clock up 139mph at service ceiling and was poorly armed, with only one forward-firing Vickers gun operated by the pilot and one Lewis gun mounted in the rear cockpit. However, it was incredibly versatile, carrying bombs, torpedoes and, later in the war, rockets. (Because it could carry almost anything, and was a maze of wires and struts, Swordfish crews called it the "Stringbag".) It was also very manoeuvrable in a dogfight, could take a lot of punishment, and had a staunchly reliable Bristol Pegasus engine. To give the Swordfish attached to Coastal Command sufficient range to carry out operations off the French, Belgian and Dutch coasts, each had been fitted with an auxiliary fuel tank between the pilot's and observer's positions. This had mixed results, many aircraft and crews being lost through fuel failure.

Unfortunately, neither Buckley nor Neely was to have time to appreciate the finer points of the Swordfish. They were shot down after only three or four days on No825 Squadron.

On Wednesday, 29 May, at 1200 hours, No825 was ordered to Hawkinge, another Kent station, to await further instructions. Buckley was about to lead his aircraft off the ground when he was told to wait for details of a German gun battery near Dunkirk that needed silencing. Finally, at 1700 hours, they took off. On arriving at Hawkinge they were told that from an area some seven or eight miles inland and to the south-west of Bergues a big gun was shelling the mole at Dunkirk. They were to attack without an escort, as RAF fighters were continually patrolling the coast.

Buckley led eleven of his squadron across the Channel without mishap. As they hit the French coast, they confronted a heavy flak barrage, but passed through safely and at 1855 hours reached the target area. However, they could not see the guns. After a fruitless ten minutes' circling, Buckley ordered two aircraft to stay on, in case the battery opened up again, and the rest dispersed, most flying further inland to look for other targets. Three of the aircraft bombed flak positions that were firing on them, but five others, including Buckley and Neely, were shot down.

"Sailor" Neely was attacked by an Me109, which his Telegraphist/Air-Gunner, Naval Airman F G Rumsey, disabled with Lewis Gun fire. After force-landing near the Belgian village of Dixmude, Neely and Rumsey were picked up by German soldiers and later marched past the Me109, which had crashed in a field. They spent the night in a church with some twenty Army prisoners who had been rounded up on their way to the beaches. Next morning the entire party joined a long column of prisoners and began marching to the German border-town of Bocholt. There, the officers were separated from the other ranks and put on a train to Laufen. It was the last time Neely was to see Rumsey. But he would later encounter Jimmy Buckley at Dulag Luft before being transferred to Stalag Luft I, where Buckley himself would eventually fetch up. They would remain together, both there and at Stalag Luft III, until Buckley was transferred to Oflag XXIB in the winter in 1942/43 — a camp from which he would not return — and Neely crossed to Stalag Luft III's newly opened North Compound, where he was destined to take part in the tragic mass escape of March 1944.

***

When Deacon, Hockey and Neely arrived on Wednesday, 12 June, disembarking from cattle-trucks with some two hundred Army officers, all of them tired, dishevelled, hungry, grumbling and in pain, they were at first surprised at how pretty a place Laufen was. Villagers lined the cobbled road and watched in silence as they all marched by. But the enormous slab-like palace dominating the skyline dispelled the fairy-tale image: it looked like a huge mental asylum.

When the column entered the main gates, three hundred starving Army officers were already hanging about in the courtyard and peering through the windows. They had arrived exactly a week previously, and now the camp authorities had the business of receiving new prisoners running to a smooth routine. Firstly, they paraded the newcomers while the Commandant, *Oberst* Frey, made an appearance, surrounded by his fawning retinue. *Oberst* Frey was of the old Prussian school, tall, smart and upright in spite of his white hair and seventy years. But any respect the prisoners might have accorded him dissipated when he delivered a long harangue, which he ended with a warning against escape attempts. "It is useless to try to escape," he shouted. "Look around you at the impregnable barriers, the formidable array of machine-guns and rifles. To escape is impossible. Anyone attempting it will be shot." He spoke English well and he spat out the word "shot" with staccato malice. "These are my strict orders to the guards, who will carry out the command to the letter."

When *Oberst* Frey dismissed the parade, the guards subjected each prisoner to an embarrassingly thorough search. Thirdly, they completely shaved his head. The fourth step was an issue of small aluminium discs, each stamped with "OFLAG VIIC" and a number. Len Hockey became *Kriegsgefangenennummer* 410, Desmond Neely 420, and Art Deacon 465. Finally they had their photos taken, were issued with a spoon, a fork and a bowl each, and were at last allowed into a small compound as officially recognised prisoners of war.

The grounds at Laufen were small, the buildings consisting mainly of two blocks, each with an inner paved courtyard, connected by another low, narrow building. Each of the main blocks — a small one to the south and a much larger one to the north — could accommodate more than two hundred officers in dormitories, and at times the number would be as high as five hundred, while the connecting building was used chiefly for German store-rooms, and contained accommodation for a few doctors and padres. For *Appelle*, and exercise during wet weather, there were two cobbled courtyards, one about fifty yards by thirty, and the other fifty yards by fifteen. Beyond some low stables, which were separated from the main block by an alley, stretched a wired-in compound for recreation in fair weather, known as "The Park". This was about seventy yards square and covered with sparsely growing grass, with one large tree in the middle. A small path ran round the perimeter. The buildings and the field were surrounded by a barbed-wire fence, three metres (ten feet) high and double-banked, which was floodlit at night; at every corner there was a raised sentry tower equipped with a machine-gun and a searchlight. All the courtyards and the walls of all the buildings were floodlit, too, and sentries were posted on most of the roofs.

The main Laufen-Salzburg road ran along the western side, but was cut off from view by a ten-foot-high wooden fence beyond the wire. The southern stretch of the barbed-wire was bounded by an orchard belonging to the convent nearby, and by a stretch of the rapid-flowing River Salzach.

Several of the newcomers, including Neely, were allotted to room No66. The dormitory was about fifteen yards long by twelve yards wide by twelve feet high, with a floor of bare wooden boards, grey and splintering with age. In this space there were nineteen wooden three-tier bunks, half a dozen pine tables, a small tiled heating stove, and ten small upright lockers. The bunk-beds were crowded so close together that it was barely possible to stand between them. They were of spartan design, with the bottom tier only one foot six inches off the floor and the top tier about six feet up. If you drew the top one, you were in constant danger of banging your head on the ceiling. Each tier consisted of a simple wooden frame spanned with an average of ten wooden bed-slats. Across this you laid your palliasse and pillow, both filled with wood shavings, your one sheet, your one blanket (thin and small) and your blanket cover (a large linen bag into which you put the blanket, so making a top sheet and counterpane). The blanket cover and pillowcase were exchanged for clean ones every month, but your blanket was never cleaned.

Despite the presence of a stove in each room, no coal was issued during the summer. As Laufen, like Munich and the rest of the southern Bavarian plateau, lay about fourteen hundred feet above sea level the nights were apt to be a bit chilly, even in July and August, and before long your precious bed-boards were being consumed in the stove.

Rumour had it that when the camp was full it would hold fifteen hundred officers — and before the month was out there would be nearly sixty men crowded into this one room.

The daily round was dominated by food. Breakfast was issued at 0700 hours, and consisted of one mug of acorn coffee, unsweetened and without milk, or tea made from the leaves of lime trees. Before long each dormitory established a roster for duty officers, who attended to the daily distribution of coffee, soup and potatoes and the weekly rations. The duty officer usually woke up ahead of everybody else in the dorm and at 0645 hours went down to the kitchen to draw his jug of acorn coffee. At 0700 you would roll, yawning, off your bunk, although you were so tired and listless you could easily have dozed on for another hour. Washing arrangements were barely adequate, the whole prisoner complement washing in two rooms, each containing sixty or seventy basins. Usually you had to wait five minutes before a basin was free. Soap was very limited, one small tablet (guaranteed not to lather) per man per month. There was no toothpaste, razor blades were scarce, and three or four people shared a single mirror. For a towel you were given a strip of flannel-like cloth two feet long by six inches wide. It had to last the week. Once washing was over, you drank your black coffee or leaf tea.

Appell, or roll-call, took place twice a day in the main cobbled courtyard, where prisoners drew up in different companies, arranged on a basis of rank, and stood three lines deep while the guards walked along the front counting *"Drei…sechs…neun…zwölf…"*, etc. (RAF prisoners would later claim that only Lufwaffe guards counted in threes, and that Army "goons" were dimmer and could count only in fives. Although it was true that the latter did indeed find counting difficult, it did not deter those in Laufen from trying to count in threes. But the guards at Oflag XXIB, in winter 1942/43, counted in fives.) Because of their poor diet, most of your fellow-prisoners were too weak to stand properly, and slouched listlessly, often leaning against each other for support. Many an officer keeled over. One minute he would be standing to attention next to you and then, the next second, without warning, he would hit the ground, making no effort to arrest his fall. Morning *Appell* was at 0930 hours, although as more prisoners arrived it would be moved forward to 0845. It was a rather tedious affair, and often took as much as an hour because the simple-minded guards often miscounted and stood in a huddle scratching their heads as they argued over each other's sums. The German officers always spruced themselves up, and arrived immaculately attired, even down to pressed riding breeches. This provoked much ridicule among the British, who were by contrast a motley and bedraggled-looking lot, many wearing torn battledress and remnants of Polish and French uniforms. The tiny RAF contingent looked the worst of all, their tunics and slacks unable to take as much punishment as British Army battledress.

Lunch was at 1100 — if, indeed, you could call one third of a bowl of soup and three boiled potatoes "lunch". In any case, the soup was ninety-five percent plain water with a very slight amount of flavouring from sawdust-like soup powders and a bit of thickening, such as sago, pearl barley, oatmeal, noodles or potatoes — never more than just a hint, mind. On days when the soup actually *was* potato soup the kitchen goons did not issue the three boiled potatoes separately, and you were left feeling hungrier than ever.

You ate your lunch in your dorm in almost complete silence and, half-starved, quickly dispensed with table manners. As you had not been issued with a plate, you ate everything out of a bowl, gobbling it up with unseemly haste. You then retired to your bed for a post-prandial snooze and to dream of real food. The canteen was shut in the afternoons, there was no other public room, and it was too hot in the courtyards and in "The Park". There was, simply, nothing to do…

At 1700 hours there was supper — again, a third of a bowl of soup, but this time issued without potatoes, and again eaten silently and quickly. Every five days you were issued with a loaf of black bread in a tin, which you had to eke out daily. The bread was the lowest quality *Wehrmacht* issue, often mouldy and the potatoes became progressively more and more rotten. Only a small part of each potato was edible — the rest was just blight, green mould, worms and stinking black slime. (Before long you were suffering from violent tummy troubles, variously called "colitis" or "enteritis", but really a mild form of dysentery. So you joined the long queues forming at the lavatories, of which there were few, sometimes being unable to hold out until your turn.) For some reason, the senior British officers refused to complain about the bad potatoes or to demand an investigation into the state of the potato-cellars, despite the fact that it was obvious that there was either gross negligence or peculation on the part of the German officers in charge.

That was your total food supply. But if you stretched your culinary abilities to the utmost it was possible to introduce a slight variation. You could, for instance, put one and a half potatoes in your soup to thicken it — and keep one and a half for later. Your meals then consisted of:

Breakfast: *ersatz* coffee, half a slice of bread spread with sliced cold potato
Lunch: soup with one and a half potatoes and half a slice of bread
Tea: soup with a thin slice of bread
Supper: one slice of bread spread with sliced potato

On "potato soup" days, because there was no separate issue of potatoes, you had to have dry bread for breakfast and supper. But very occasionally you were given a small pat of *Speisefett* or, if you were lucky, proper margarine, sufficient to spread on two days' bread ration. On Sundays the Germans distributed benison in some form of *Wurst* for lunch and a small Limburg cheese, two ounces in weight, for tea, along with a spoonful of turnip jam. But then you used up more of the day's bread ration than you could really spare — and the Germans cancelled the soup! Sometimes the bread was not issued on the day it was due, and then you nearly starved until it arrived, either the next day or the day after that. The cookhouse goons did not make up for these breadless days, but counted each five-day cycle from the time your loaf was actually issued. You were also permanently threatened with having your rations stopped if anyone upset the Germans. This threat was very real, as, despite the fact that the war was going well for "the Hun", he was very touchy and incredibly easy to offend.

"Speisefett" literally meant "food-fat", and was a form of lard or dripping. You dubbed it "man-fat", as it was rumoured that during the Great War the Huns had boiled down their corpses to extract the fat. To you it was inedible, so you used it as fuel for "goon-lamps" — night-lights made from cigarette tins with strips of pyjama cord for wicks.

For most of the summer of 1940 you saw no meat or sugar. The meat went straight into the soup, or so the British kitchen orderlies maintained, and the sugar was already added to your coffee and tea. But it was still undetectable. (Later, it was discovered that at nights the German kitchen officials had been taking the sugar away in sacks to sell on the black market.) You didn't see milk, fish, butter, oatmeal or eggs either, come to that.

Cigarettes were issued at the rate of eight per man every four days. Smokers endured agonies of indecision, trying to make up their minds whether it was best to smoke all eight at once, or two a day, or none until the fourth day and then smoke them all — and so on…

The Germans at Laufen were as fickle as could be, and would cut your pay, your food, your cigarette ration or your letter-form entitlement at the drop of a peaked cap. They would then tell you that this was because German prisoners in England were not allowed them. You determined to find out after the war whether German officer prisoners were treated as badly as you were. You could bet your boots they weren't.

Sometimes, the cookhouse arbitrarily cut off your ration of potatoes, or your occasional pats of *Speisefett*, or the milk you usually had in your morning coffee. They told you the potatoes were "in the soup". Then, when you did see potatoes in the soup you noticed that the amount used had been cut by three-quarters, and you were not issued with the balance of the ration.

The Germans did allow you to buy half a litre of skimmed milk a day, for the sum of 10 *Pfennige*. Unfortunately, it was usually sour and lumpy — and better made into something akin to cottage cheese, quite easy to do if you tied it up in an old sock and then suspended it from the side of your bunk.

On this diet you were permanently hungry. You never had any meat or anything you could sink your teeth into; it was always slops. You were getting weaker every day. Twice round "The Park" was about all the exercise you could manage in one day, and climbing the stairs back to your "dorm" afterwards was quite a problem. You had to sit down for a rest two or three times on the way, like an old man suffering from lack of breath. The camp Medical Officers gave the weaker ones only three months to live.

In officer camps there was usually a ratio of one private or NCO orderly to every five officers, but at Laufen the ratio was one to every thirty-two. They were supposed to clean the dorms twice daily and help carry food from the kitchens, but often you had to do it yourself because the Germans tried to sow discord between British officers and other ranks, encouraging the latter to be lazy and insolent.

After tea, time passed less slowly and a little more pleasantly. The temperature outside dropped, and you went to "The Park" and joined the knots of men sitting on the grass, chatting, yawning, day-dreaming…

Evening *Appell* took place at varying times, and then you made your supper from bread and any morsels you had managed to save. At night the blackout curtains had to be pulled to until "lights out" at 2230 hours, when the German Orderly Officer made his rounds; then you could switch off the lights and re-open the curtains. It was up to the duty officer for the day to ensure that you complied with the blackout rules.

Despite the association of Laufen with Mozart, Neely thought not of music but of escape. He was not alone. Before long he fell in with an arrival from the previous week, Kenneth Lockwood, a captain in the Queen's Royal Regiment, who also confided an ardent desire in trying to get out of Laufen.

On the face of it, however, Oflag VIIC looked impossible to crack. Firstly, as the camp had already held Polish officers, the German security staff was one jump ahead of the British prisoners. Security was in the hands of an English-speaking *Hauptmann* from the *Abwehr* who was assisted by several NCOs, also speaking English (or American English). "This officer was responsible for the whole system of defence against would-be escapers," wrote Lieutenant T C F Prittie of the Rifle Brigade,

and this system was the direct fruit of his labours and information service. The lay-out of sentry boxes, sentries' beats and the exact placing of barbed wire were the most obvious external signs of his activity, but at the same time he instituted his own system of checks and counter-checks on the gate or gates, making these as exact and as carefully defined as possible.

The front gate, for instance, was virtually impassable. Anyone entering or leaving had to sign his name in a book kept in the guard-room. On the way out his signature was matched with that given on his way in.

The *Hauptmann* and his NCOs were always alert to visible and audible signs of tunnels or other illicit POW activity — "loose panels or floor-boards, the noise of hammering and thumping underground, the presence of obvious look-outs at doors and windows, the most likely dumping-grounds for stones and earth evacuated, and even the unwary conversation of officers walking down passages and round exercise-grounds". According to Terence Prittie, he knew his job well.

But for the one tunnel brought to a successful conclusion, he remained master of the situation during the whole existence of Laufen as a British camp. He was a very much cleverer man than most of his counterparts in later days and at other camps, some of whom descended to a level of pure fatuity. The honours of the first round in the annals of escape might be said to have rested entirely with the Germans.

A second factor was the poor diet, as a result of which most prisoners were mentally incapable of planning an escape and physically unable to carry it out. Those who resided in the second- or third-floor dorms were seldom able to climb all the way upstairs without blacking out and having to rest for several minutes. In addition to sometimes fainting on parade, most had periods of giddiness and headaches. All had lost weight and dysentery was common. Soon all available hospital space would be occupied.

Thirdly, escape intelligence in summer 1940 was practically non-existent. There were few maps available, and they were inaccurate. Prospective escapers knew nothing about the various frontiers or how to cross them. Switzerland was a hundred and eighty miles away, Hungary more than two hundred and Yugoslavia little under a hundred and fifty. In 1940, still flushed with their victory in the West, none of the Germans was likely to impart information on identity papers or help kit out escapers with disguises.

There was also a psychological deterrent. Men who thought that the war was "as good as over" were unlikely to think seriously about escape. Not surprisingly, only eight British officers would escape from Laufen during the camp's sixteen months' existence. It took a peculiar kind of willpower in the summer of 1940 to even consider an escape, let alone to carry it out.

Nevertheless, besides Neely and Lockwood there were several other determined individuals, whose names have become legendary in the annals of escaping.

Two other residents of room No66 who had arrived on the same day as Lockwood were Captain R R F T Barry, of the Oxford and Bucks Light Infantry, and Lieutenant P R Reid, of the Royal Army Service Corps. Neely and Lockwood noticed that this pair devoted much of their time to reconnoitering the camp and entering into conspiratorial huddles. Indeed, Patrick Reid and Rupert Barry spent hours at a stretch examining the barbed-wire entanglements in the compounds and watching the traffic entering and leaving by the gates. When the searchlights were switched on at night, they sat by the windows, judging the depths and positions of shadows, timing sentries on their beats, sometimes staying up almost the entire night peering cautiously out to see if the guards became lazy or changed their habits in the small hours, giving them a possible opening. Finally, without trying to appear over-curious, Lockwood and Neely approached Reid and Barry, evinced an interest in their activities, and added that they, too, were bent on escaping.

A day or two later Reid invited them to an escape meeting. Reid himself opened the proceedings. He explained that he and Barry had concluded their escape reconnaissance and had narrowed the possibilities down to one particular corner of a tall building where there appeared to be a chink in the enemy's defences. Rupert Barry had suggested excavating a tunnel from the building, which meant tedious work for months on end, while Reid had proposed a long climb along the roofs and a descent by bed-sheet rope to a narrow alley or cul-de-sac outside the prison-camp precincts. A sentry marched up and down the street running parallel to this building and past the alley. After making a careful study of his routine, Reid had established that during each turn of his beat there was an interval of about three minutes when he could not see the alley. Reid hoped to make use of this, provided there was enough shadow in the alley to conceal their movements.

Reid's plan was for a "blitz" effort which, if all went well, would be over in a few hours. But he needed to conduct a survey of the alley and of its precincts at the dead of night in order to determine whether the climb was feasible, whether they could move at speed without making too much noise, and whether the shadows would provide sufficient cover. Captain Barry had agreed that it was worth experimenting with Reid's idea before finally deciding which plan to adopt. They wanted Lockwood and Neely to act as observers while Reid carried out a trial run across the roofs.

"For the trial run we need a night with no moon," said Reid. "The darker the night the better."

"Yes, but you don't want rain," said Neely. "You'll career off the roof like a toboggan." He suggested Reid wear plimsoles.

"A wind wouldn't matter," added Lockwood. "In fact, it should help."

"We need all these conditions if possible," said Reid. He explained that, between the window from which he intended to sortie and the sloping roof he needed to reach, there was a flat inter-connecting roof. Barry, as the strongest of the four, would lower him on to the flat roof by a rope made of bed-sheets.

"We'll need at least two sheets," said Lockwood; "better have three for the twelve-foot drop."

"I'll drop, and then carry on to the main roof," Reid replied, adding: "You will have to watch my whole journey and check for visibility, shadows, and noise." Turning to Neely, he went on: "You had better keep your eye on each sentry in turn as I come into his line of vision and area of responsibility, and watch for reactions."

The idea, explained Barry, who had been quiet and thoughtful during the meeting, was for Reid to sneak across the long roof to the far end and see if it was possible to make a sheet-descent outside the prison. There was a sentry in the road round the corner, but none of them knew how much he could see. That was another thing for Reid to check on. But the success of his look-see depended on the depth of shadow in the area.

The moon would be barely visible on 30 June, observed Reid. The 30th was a Sunday, and the guards might well be more drunk and sleepy than usual. Reid suggested he carry out his recce on that date provided the weather was reasonable.

The other three nodded their assent, and went on to discuss the details of the climb. Reid suddenly had an idea: "Wouldn't it be a cakewalk if I could fuse all the lights? I think I can do it."

"Oh! How?" asked Neely.

Reid had noticed that the wires ran round the walls of the buildings on insulators, and were only about eighteen inches apart. It was just a matter of shorting them.

"And how do you think you can do that?"

He thought for a moment, then exclaimed: "I know! One of the windows in room No44 is only about four feet above the wires and is in pretty good shadow. If we can collect about forty razor blades, I'll attach them to a piece of wood, using drawing pins. It will form a conductor and a sharp knife at the same time. I can screw the piece of wood on to a broom-handle and there we are!"

"Good idea!" said Barry. "But if June 30th is our zero date, then the sooner the fusing is done the better."

"I meant to fuse them on the 30th," Reid replied.

"I don't think that's wise. It might create an uproar, and they might get the lights working again just when you're hanging in mid-air somewhere. It would be better to make the fusing a try-out too. Then we can see how long it takes them to repair the fuse."

"All right," Reid agreed, somewhat reluctantly. "I'll do the job — and while I'm fusing, you three had better take up positions around the buildings to note if any sections of the lighting do not go out with the rest."

Pat Reid went ahead with the shorting a few nights later. His razor-edged device worked perfectly. With a gentle sawing motion he cut through the heavy insulation in only a minute, while his confederates stood at strategic points to monitor the German reaction. A brilliant flash, a noise like silk tearing, and all the searchlights within view went out. Some shouting and running from the vicinity of the guard-house. So far, so good. But after only three minutes the lights were on again, leaving too little time to carry out an escape — even a "blitz" along the lines that Reid had envisaged.

＊＊

Whilst Barry, Lockwood, Neely and Reid were absorbed in their escape plans, yet more prisoners were arriving. Two hundred were herded into the palace on Friday, 14 June. The "dorms" were so overcrowded it was getting to the point where you couldn't go anywhere and be alone, even for a minute.

From the upper rooms of the castle you had a superb view. First, looking straight ahead, you could see in the far distance the spires and steeples of Salzburg. Then, looking southward, to your right, you could see the Austrian and Bavarian Alps, snow-covered and magnificent. Tucked way among them somewhere was Berchtesgaden, the holiday home of Adolf himself. However, only the Führer, it seemed, was permitted the luxury of such a glorious view. During morning *Appell* on Wednesday, 19 June, the Germans issued a new and ominous notice. "British officers," they warned, "are not allowed to lean out of windows as it is dangerous for them; if they do so the sentries have orders to shoot." Their paranoia about prisoners leaning out of windows dated back to the recent occupation of the camp by Poles, who thoroughly disliked the Commandant. The guards let it be known that one of these Poles had tried to leap on *Oberst* Frey from a second-storey window. Unfortunately he missed, landing instead on the cobblestones and killing himself. Ten of his fellow-prisoners were taken out and shot against the wall. The British were even shown a bullet-marked wall, proving the veracity of this rumour and obviously meant as a warning. Another school of thought claimed that the Polish officers had made a habit of emptying dirty water and refuse on the heads of the German sentries and that, although the Commandant did not seriously believe that British officers would do likewise, he intended to remind them continually that they were prisoners and therefore of an inferior status. (All the same, one afternoon not long afterwards a young British Army officer, Lieutenant Deeds of the 6th Battalion of the Durham Light Infantry, was standing some yards inside a window sketching the mountains round Salzburg when a guard outside raised his rifle and put a bullet through his head. This unreasonable behaviour was typical in Army officer POW camps in the Greater Reich during the early part of the war. The guards, mostly drawn from the local *Ersatzheeren*, or Army reservists, were brutish and unimaginative to say the least, perhaps still harbouring some resentment over losing the 1914–18 War. They were easily insulted and would shoot a prisoner for the most minor infraction of the rules.)

You were, however, promised an issue of margarine with your evening meal. But nothing even resembling it arrived. It transpired that the POW Quartermaster had accused the German kitchen orderly of stealing prisoners' rations. The orderly complained to the Commandant, who severely reprimanded the Quartermaster and threatened him with solitary confinement for "Unbecoming conduct towards a member of the German armed forces". So now you had lost your "marg" ration.

Often you envied other ranks, such as the Quartermaster, because, although their lot was in many ways harder, they could at least get outside the barbed-wire and go out to work on the farms, in the quarries and elsewhere. But officers were forbidden to work and even parole walks were seldom allowed; you had no opportunity at all of seeing the world outside except through a screen of tangled barbed-wire six feet thick. Throughout the entire summer of 1940 you had no books, no magazines, no newspapers, and nothing to look forward to or to plan towards. Lucky indeed were the few who possessed a pack of playing cards.

According to the Prisoner-of-War Code of the Geneva Convention, an officer POW was entitled to write three letters and four postcards home per month. But the authorities at Laufen allowed you only two letters, each of twenty-two lines, and two cards per month. They also refused to issue camp pay until Friday, 21 June. Even then, they cut your pay by half because German pay was only half that of the British, and decided to issue it every ten days instead of once a week. Still, the *Lagergeld* made a slight difference to your feeling of well-being. You could now purchase a pint of beer and some tobacco or cigarettes from the canteen — even though the beer was watery and the tobacco of dubious origin.

As soon as *Appell* was dismissed you made a mad dash for the canteen, where beer was available from 0930 hours. The room was comfortably furnished with benches and tables. But unfortunately it was meant to hold only eighty to a hundred men, and often four or five hundred officers would be packed in, making the atmosphere fetid. Also, because you were effectively receiving less than half-pay, you could drink very little beer — perhaps a pint on "pay-day" and then half a pint a day for the rest of the week. Even so, sitting round a table with your friends and a mug of beer in your right hand, you felt a bit more like an ordinary human being.

The prices of the goods stocked in the canteen were out of all proportion to their value, as the exchange rate was the equivalent of only 9RM to the pound sterling. Thus, one biscuit cost sixpence, a small barrel of Bismark herrings £25 and a bag of walnuts £15. All your *Lagergeld* were gone by the second day, leaving you eight lean days in every ten. You were so hungry that you would pay almost anything for something remotely resembling food. You were allowed two cigarettes per day, for which you paid 5 *Pfennige* each, saving the butts either for smoking in a pipe or for barter. Cigarettes fetched high prices in the barter market. So did bread. A whole loaf was very rarely to be had, but you might occasionally be offered a slice in exchange for two cigarettes.

Although your view of the surrounding countryside from the upstairs windows had been curtailed by order of the Commandant, "The Park" lay on the southern side of the camp and opened before you a glorious vista of the Bavarian Alps. To the east, on your left, the Salzach River flowed rapidly towards what, before the *Anschluss*, had been Austria. The river was only forty yards wide at this point, and on the opposite bank you could see a quaint old red-roofed village. Occasionally a canoe, carrying a young man or a girl, swept downriver, going under the bridge that had once held the customs barriers of the Austro-German frontier. Beyond the river and the village the countryside was part-wooded, part-agricultural, with to the south hills gradually mounting in height and culminating in the Gaisberg, which towered 3,500 feet above its surroundings and 5,000 feet above sea level.

To the east of the Gaisberg lay the town of Salzburg, fourteen miles away. You could barely see it from Laufen, but sometimes the castle of Hohensalzburg was just visible through a thin blue haze. "High above Salzburg to the right, or west," wrote Terence Prittie,

> was the massif of the Untersberg, culminating in the tottering peak of the Salzburger Hoch Tron. The Untersberg is a beautiful sight in summer and winter alike, rising sheer from the plains, pale blue and purple through the flickering heat-waves, and dazzling white under a winter sun. Over its shoulder a series of graceful peaks stretched away to the horizon, where, on a clear day, were visible the 12,000-foot giants of the Gross Glockner, the highest mountains in the German Alps.
>
> The nearer mountains to the west were not as impressive as the Untersberg and its immediate neighbours. Some of the peaks overlooking Berchtesgaden and the dismally lovely König See peeped through from behind…West again, a slight ridge blocked out any view beyond an immediate vista of tree and field-covered slopes, with the occasional low red and brown clusters of farm buildings.

You could enjoy this landscape for long hours at a stretch, "particularly in the silence of the evening, with the river rippling in the foreground, grey-green willows and darker pine-trees beyond, and then golden and green and dark brown fields stretching a dozen miles across the plain to the line of great mountains that filled the whole southerly horizon". But there was "a certain irony" in the beauty of your surroundings, for you would always associate them with the worst days of your life.

***

On Tuesday, 25 June it was announced that on the 22nd the French had surrendered. The morale at Laufen was already low, mostly because of constant, nagging hunger but also because you felt useless now that you were out of the war and unable to lift a finger to help. There was also little to do but walk round and round the exercise yard in endless identical circles like a snail with some kind of nervous tick. Some of the older, more experienced, Army officers were now arranging a course of lectures on various subjects, and inviting anyone who knew anything about them to give the lectures. (An excellent and, as it turned out, prophetic lecture was given by Captain the Reverend Richard G Heard of the Royal Army Chaplain's Department, who was also a Cambridge don and erstwhile Dean of Peterhouse. He told his audience to expect the war to last another three-and-a-half years. He had carefully prepared his argument, backed by figures provided by Len Hockey showing how long it would take Britain to design and build the ships and aircraft necessary to blockade Germany so that it would run out of oil. The RAF would then bomb Germany into submission and it would be unable to retaliate.) You could also subscribe 2RM towards a library of Tauchnitz books, though when they would arrive was anyone's guess. Newspapers or a radio or a gramophone would have done much to ease your tedium, but such luxuries were *verboten*.

On Saturday, 29 June, the prisoners were given an interesting insight into the German mentality. The Archbishop of Canterbury had recently made a speech about Nazi Germany, and Josef Goebbels' propaganda machine had condemned it as "disgraceful". British chaplains were now barred from sitting on any committee in the camp. All bible classes and lectures on mechanics, wireless engineering and elementary German were also temporarily suspended.

Yet more newcomers turned up that day, all of them Army officers.

***

Sunday, 30 June dawned fair, heralding a fine day. And there was jam for breakfast! Granted, it was only small dollop of that *ersatz* stuff, but it was sweet and made a change. The Germans also promised you a slap-up lunch of meat- and potato-stew but, after looking forward to it all morning, you got exactly the same as usual with not a vestige of anything resembling meat, although there was one small cube of fat floating on the top.

Sunday afternoons were usually a chore to get through. On weekdays you could spend the afternoon and evening attending lectures, but on Sunday there was nothing.

Evening approached with no change in the weather and that night stars twinkled in a cloudless sky. Not a breath of wind stirred the trees. The night was almost perfect for Pat Reid's trial run. At 10.30pm Lockwood and Neely watched from their bunks as Reid, accompanied by Rupert Barry, crept out of room No66 and into the corridor that led to the room from which Reid would descend on to the flat roof. A few minutes later Barry returned alone and told Neely and Lockwood that after looking and listening carefully through the window Reid had decided that although the night was too bright, the dark shadows cast by the strong moonlight would provide adequate cover. He intended to go ahead.

Reid estimated the trip would take about an hour and said he would not return earlier than that. At 11.30pm — "zero hour" — he slipped a pair of socks over his feet (no plimsoles were available), old socks cut out as mittens on to his hands, and a borrowed balaclava helmet over his head to conceal his face. Neely and Lockwood took up their positions at key windows.

The window that Reid intended to use was in full view of a sentry about fifty yards away, who could play a searchlight at will on any desired spot. When the sentry's receding footsteps indicated that his back was turned, Reid dropped quietly and quickly to the flat roof and was soon hidden from view — but from where Neely stood he seemed to be making a lot of noise. A few minutes later a disturbance began in one of the courtyards, with officers bellowing orders and guards running back and forth with flashing torches. The hubbub increased, but did not approach the area where the four would-be escapers were operating. At about midnight they heard the sound of murmuring voices from the most distant of the four courtyards: another batch of prisoners had arrived.

Not long afterwards Neely heard a long rumble and the crash of slate against the guttering. He thought Reid had fallen off the roof, but couldn't see him because he was on the far side of the sloping eaves. Three and a half hours passed before Reid returned, unharmed but exhausted. Rupert Barry hauled him in. It made a hell of a racket, but surprisingly none of the sentries was alerted. At 3am the little league of pioneer escapers crept back to their bunks.

The next day they held another meeting, at which Reid conceded that the proposed point of descent was unsatisfactory.

Reid continued: "The nearest anchor for a rope will mean carting along with us about twenty-five sheets or blankets. We would also have rucksacks and boots. The alley is a cul-de-sac, but I'm afraid the shadows are not helpful. The rope would be clearly visible in any position."

"I heard you distinctly on several occasions," commented Lockwood.

Neely added that Reid had made such a racket that he thought he had fallen off the roof.

"I think we may as well call it off," opined Barry. "If one man without luggage makes all that din, what are four going to do?" Turning to Reid, he added: "Frankly, I think you were saved by the noise of the new arrivals — and, to clinch it, if the rope has got to dangle in the limelight, we shall never get away with it!"

Finally, they agreed that they would never be able to sortie, and cover their tracks, in the three minutes at their disposal. They would further examine Rupert Barry's tunnel idea.

As for the previous night's arrivals, they turned out to be some four hundred army officers, many of them from Scottish line regiments and the Rifle Brigade, which had been amalgamated into the 51st Highland Division under the leadership of Major-General Victor M Fortune and had been captured in the valiant rearguard action at St-Valery-en-Caux on 12 June. Amongst them was a lone youngster in RAF blue, Pilot Officer Smiley. A close pal of Art Deacon, his fellow-Canadian on No242 Squadron, Joseph Beverly Smiley was a former hard-rock gold miner from Wolseley, Saskatchewan. He had joined the RAF on 13 May 1939 and was posted to No242 on the same day as Deacon.

Smiley's final "op" took place on Thursday, 23 May, when he was slated to help escort a Bristol Blenheim on a recce over northern France. The escort would comprise one Hurricane flight from Smiley's outfit, and another from No32 Squadron. They took off from Biggin Hill at 0730 hours, refuelled at Manston and proceeded across the Channel and over the Continent. Over Ypres the Canadians were attacked by some eighteen Me109s, while a dozen more Jerries took on No32's Hurricanes from the rear. Four Hurricanes were lost, all from No242. Two of the pilots were killed outright, and another was wounded but managed to bale out and make it to Dunkirk. Smiley received shell fragments to his head, baled out, lost consciousness, and awoke in hospital to find Lorne Chambers in the next bed. Chambers had been shot down five days previously. However, the two pilots left the hospital separately, Chambers to go direct to Dulag Luft (thence to Stalag Luft I) and Smiley to join the hundreds of Army prisoners being entrained for Laufen.

Smiley would be the last RAF officer to be sent to Laufen until the summer of 1941 and was allotted *Kriegsgefangenennummer* 947. This meant crowding more men into the dormitories, and No66 finished up with fifty-seven occupants. They all lived, ate and slept in this one room, for at that time there was no common- or day-room.

Major-General Fortune now became the Senior British Officer, a burden he would carry in several POW camps for the next five years, including spells in Oflag VIB and Oflag IXA/H, both of which at that time held a large RAF contingent. For now, however, he had his work cut out trying to establish some kind of POW organisation in a camp jam-packed with starving, demoralised men. It would be an uphill task taking several months, for he was not even given a copy of the POW Code, an omission that was itself a breach of the Geneva Convention. "It would be wrong and thoroughly misleading to conceal or minimise the inexcusably bad treatment we suffered at German hands during the early part of the war," wrote Gris Davies-Scourfield.

They were winning and did not give a rap for anybody else. Later on, especially as the fortunes of war began to shift, our treatment improved, but meanwhile we had to grin and bear it. At this time, for example, it was no use quoting the Geneva Convention — the international agreement on the handling of prisoners-of-war — because the Germans announced they did not recognise it: the Weimar Government had in fact signed, but the Nazis did not recognise Weimar either! Later, when lots of Germans had been taken prisoner, they decided that they recognised the Convention after all.

Victor Fortune simply made it a principle to protest about everything, constantly deluging *Oberst* Frey and the Protecting Power with *Anträge*, or written complaints.

Monday, 1 July was, much to your surprise, bitterly cold and wet. The food situation had also deteriorated, although you wouldn't have though that possible. You had been promised a new loaf of bread at 0900 hours but, as usual, it did not arrive. You began to wonder whether it was all a plot to do you out of your bread ration. Lunch was entirely tasteless: pearl barley soup with three very old potatoes — mostly rotten and nearly raw. But that evening the bread ration was at last doled out, so you had dry bread and water for supper.

During the day several rumours did the rounds. Libya had been overrun and 45,000 Italians captured. The Russians had invaded Poland and captured Warsaw. The invasion of England would take place within the next ten days...You were better off out of it, lying on your bunk and dreaming about food.

The following day was the complete opposite. The weather was glorious, and the soup at lunch and tea much thicker. Letter-cards were issued, so you could now write home, and there was a new rumour: Italy was suing for peace.

Three hundred more officers arrived on the night of 8/9 July, but the Germans issued no extra food for them. The result was that throughout Tuesday the 9th the entire officer POW complement was on half rations. Breakfast was half a mug of coffee. Lunch consisted of three potatoes and some hot water. Tea was more coffee and three potatoes — mostly bad.

On Wednesday, 10 July a shot was fired at POWs exercising in "The Park". Two British officers, walking down the path along the wire, were laughing over a private joke. They passed a sentry who, perhaps because of an inferiority complex, imagined that they were laughing at him. He screamed at them and opened fire from a range of five yards, missing both but very nearly hitting another German sentry stationed on the roof of the garage. This sentry fell down his ladder and sprained his ankle, giving prisoners the opportunity to genuinely laugh at a German.

There were now 1,463 officers packed into Oflag VIIC, all of them Army except for three RAF and one Fleet Air Arm, and every one of them hungry, weak and anxious to hear news from home. During morning *Appell* on Thursday, 11 July they were informed that there was no longer any line of communication with England. No letters or parcels addressed to them would be arriving at Laufen and none of their letters were being sent. They were assured, however, that people at home knew that they were prisoners. The Germans also issued a warning, viz the incident that had occurred the previous day: the guards were liable to shoot if they thought they were being laughed at. As a result of this warning, the German sentries became very free with their firearms. "Another order issued to sentries gave them the unlimited right to fire on any officer who, in their opinion, was interfering with them in the execution of their duties," wrote Terence Prittie.

Officers were frequently fired at and missed by varying margins. One, who was shutting a window at the time, was hit in the arm…Sentries would fire without warning at any window insufficiently blacked out. As black-out materials were provided by the Germans themselves, there was very little that occupants of the room could do, beyond turning out the lights and readjusting the black-out boards at imminent risk of being shot in the process.

So hungry were the POWs now that they had taken to licking out containers, even if the meagre contents were poisonous. The struggle to make a loaf of bread last five days was becoming harder. Although the quality of the soup had improved slightly, the quantity had diminished. The potato ration had also deteriorated. Instead of three potatoes each, the prisoners now received two only, and often these were bad. All the potatoes stockpiled in the cellars were rotting, and the entire building stank of them.

The prisoners were also still very weak. They spent most of their time lying in their bunks, playing patience or bridge and, when the weather was warm enough, sun-bathing. This display of near-nudity prompted a lecture by the Germans on intercourse with their womenfolk, which was punishable with ten years' imprisonment or the death sentence. If any Laufen prisoner could get anywhere near a woman, German or otherwise, it would be a miracle. So terrified were the guards of escape attempts that they were continually taking extra precautions. They would not even allow parole walks. They expected German officer POWs to break parole and escape if they had the chance, and imagined the British would do the same.

They also subjected the prisoners to a propaganda war, telling them that the invasion of England was imminent, and that they intended to smash London to bits and send "the British plutocracy" to work in the salt-mines. The German news made dismal reading. First, the complete collapse of the French Army; then Italy's entry into the war; then the French capitulation in the Forest of Compiègne; then the signing of the Molotov-Ribbentrop Pact; then the British evacuation of Narvik; then the U-boat blockade; and then, worst of all, the Luftwaffe's air offensive on Britain. The prisoners reckoned that the official German daily communiqués divided their own losses by three and multiplied those of the RAF by four. (Back home, the British were likewise exaggerating enemy losses, with the RAF doubling and tripling the claims made by fighter pilots.)

There were some pretty unpleasant individuals on *Oberst* Frey's staff. The senior sergeant major, Herman, was a fat, beer-swilling Municher with a red face who enjoyed showing off his authority. Without any apparent provocation, he would scream hysterically at the prisoners, and often jostle them and threaten them with his revolver — behaviour that was acceptable in the German, Polish and Czechoslovakian armies, but illegal in the British armed forces. "He was a bully of the most obvious type," concluded Terence Prittie, "but there was another unpleasant side to his character. After several months it was discovered by the German authorities that he had been stealing food on a large scale, and he was removed from Laufen in disgrace."

Another was the NCO in charge of the kitchens, known as "Cook-house Joe". He was a rat-faced little specimen who had spent some time in America. "There was no hint of physical violence about him, and his line was cheap jibes at officers, made sometimes to his comrades, sometimes to British orderlies. He took an especial pleasure in announcing that London was in ruins and that the Luftwaffe would shortly blow up the Houses of Parliament and Buckingham Palace."

As for Frey himself, he "was a man of ungovernable temper bordering on hysteria, and in his wild moods as vicious and dangerous as any mad dog".

Frey's adjutant, *Major* Kreuznacher, was a different matter. A local shopkeeper, he was "harmless and ineffectual, pompous and paunched, but often genuinely concerned with bettering our conditions of life. There was no malice whatever in him."

To assist him in his duties he had an interpreter, "a ridiculous little black-haired Italianate person, who panicked badly on parade if there was the least murmur of dissatisfaction from the rear ranks. He was a complete cypher, far too nervous to be either a nuisance or to do anything constructive that might be required of him."

* * *

While Pat Reid had been concentrating on his abortive roof scheme, Rupert Barry had lighted on a small locked room in the corner of the building that backed against the cul-de-sac Reid had examined from the rooftops. The room was a semi-basement. One day, while Kenneth Lockwood kept watch for the Germans, Barry, Neely, and Reid removed the lock from the door and went in. They found a small flight of stone steps leading down to the floor, which was about five feet below ground level. "The room contained lumber," recalled Pat Reid in *The Colditz Story*, "including a large variety of rifle-range targets. There were painted French soldiers and English Tommies — lying, kneeling, and charging, as well as the usual bull's-eye type." Barry proposed piercing the wall at floor-level, digging a tunnel across the street, and through or under the foundations of an old stone building at the other side. But Neely had noticed a small lean-to shed against a private house on the other side of the cul-de-sac. The shed was made of vertical wooden slats with gaps in between. Through these gaps he had seen piles of wooden logs. He considered this wood-shed good camouflage for an exit hole and suggested they project the tunnel in that direction. Another advantage was that they would not have to circumvent any heavy foundations at the far end of their tunnel. Neely's suggestion was adopted without further ado.

They kept their plans secret from all but one officer, Major J S Poole of the 60th King's Royal Rifle Corps. Jack Poole had been a prisoner before, in the Great War, and his advice on all POW matters, clandestine or otherwise, was always keenly sought. He suggested that the tunnellers work during afternoons only. Fewer Germans roamed the camp after lunch, but there was a lot of civilian coming and going in the streets outside, the noise of which would help cover up the sound of tunnelling. This regimen would give enough time for two shifts of two hours each per day.

It was just as well that Barry, Lockwood, Neely and Reid had something with which to occupy themselves. A deep depression had now descended over the whole camp. "Absolutely nothing to do and everyone's tempers getting a bit short," recorded one Army officer, Captain Michael Duncan of The Glosters, in his POW diary. Saturday, 13 July was a

perfectly bloody day. Very cold. Coffee, short ration and nearly cold. Lunch half an hour late. Swindled out of half a day's bread ration. Potatoes worse than ever and nearly uneatable. Beer gets a shorter issue every day. It costs 45 pf. and mugs are less than two thirds full. This is a swindle worked by the men behind the bar who thus get a free beer for themselves in every four they issue. A complaint about the short measure was made, but a charge was cooked up against the complainant by the German orderly and he got five days' "holiday" for his pains. Even the lowest German private has got us by the short hairs as the Commandant always takes their word before ours in any dispute. The position is made worse by two of our British orderlies serving in the bar, who, for their own advantage, take the side of the Germans against us and are becoming very like them in manner. God help them when we get back to England.

Barry and Reid started to break through the wall on Sunday, 14 July. (Reid thought it "a propitious day — the anniversary of the storming of the Bastille!") They made the entrance to their tunnel in the farthest corner of the room where an old table stood. It would thus be shrouded in darkness. The digging routine thereafter was simple: one man hacked away at the wall; another man sat on a box inside the room with his eye on the keyhole of the door and looked along the passage; a third man sat on the stone steps a few yards along the passage at the only entrance to the building, reading a book or engaging in some other innocent-looking activity, and a fourth man lounged, or exercised, in the far courtyard. After two hours or so the two men outside and the two men inside changed places. Warning of approaching Germans was passed along the line by noncommittal signals, which varied according to the direction from which they appeared. The man at the tunnel face stopped work immediately on receipt of the signal.

Before the first shift of the day Reid opened the door, as he had on 14 July, by removing the screws holding the latch of the padlock. Once two men were inside, Reid screwed up the latch so that during each shift both the man at the wall and his stooge worked behind a locked door. Should a German enter the room, they would have to hide amongst the lumber or in a small triangular space beneath the stone steps.

The wall was made of stone and brick. They had only the most primitive of tools with which to attack it: three six-inch nails and a roughly shaped stone.

In the meantime there was no improvement in camp conditions. Indeed, things were going from bad to worse. The morning after the tunnelling syndicate started work the breakfast coffee ration was halved. Lunch was also a short ration, with the soup not much more than coloured water. For tea each man had only potatoes, as the cookhouse had run out of soup-mix. "The whole camp smells like a drain from the rotting potatoes," wrote Michael Duncan, "and twenty or thirty men are going down with dysentery every day. Most of us are also out of soap. The small tablet that was given us as a month's issue was finished a week ago. We were supposed to have a new tablet issued two days ago but, like most of these things, it just failed to turn up."

Personal items were also starting to disappear from lockers, "a potato here, elsewhere a mug or a razor strop. Little things, but when one is otherwise entirely destitute one sets enormous store on little things." It was the same with bread. "It is regrettable to record," wrote Davies-Scourfield, "that bread-stealing was by no means unknown, and literally 'to lose one's loaf' on the first or second day of issue could be a near-tragedy, and it therefore had to be carefully safe-guarded: it was not even safe in one's bed at night unless tied to one's arm or leg."

Rumour had it that a German doctor had condemned the kitchen as insanitary and inadequate. The local German who collected the rubbish considered the potatoes discarded by the cookhouse not only unfit for pigs but also useless as manure. He refused to take them and they were returned to the kitchen and issued to the prisoners. But there were a few encouraging rumours: the Germans had tried to land in England but had given up after being bombed by the RAF; the Canadians had landed at Calais and the enemy opposition had again been bombed by the RAF; there had been an uprising in Holland; all strategic points in Abyssinia and Lybia were being held by the British; and the USA had sent over three thousand aircraft, nine hundred of them bombers. None of the Army prisoners knew where these rumours came from, but in all likelihood they originated with the tiny RAF contingent; at any rate, they wanted to believe them and it helped cheer them up.

On Wednesday, 17 July, General Fortune saw *Oberst* Frey and complained, amongst other things, that prisoners were not being treated in accordance with the Geneva Convention. Frey's reply was that they had no intention of keeping to the Geneva Convention, which was drawn up by a lot of old women and not by soldiers. His bible was *The Prison Commandant's Handbook*, published four years prior to the outbreak of war.

After a few days the tunnelling syndicate received additional help in the shape of a small hammer. This was "won" from the Germans by Lieutenants W L B ("Scarlett") O'Hara and "Crash" Keeworth, both of the Royal Tank Regiment, when a lorry entered one of the courtyards to deliver goods to the canteen. A stolid-looking sentry guarded the lorry, and while Keeworth distracted his attention by pretending to steal something from the back, O'Hara rummaged in the tool-kit under the driver's seat, lifting the hammer and a very good road-map of Germany. Inevitably, the loss did not go undiscovered, and within the hour a snap-*Appell* was called. It gave the tunnelling syndicate some anxious moments. Neely was at the wall and Lockwood at the keyhole keeping a lookout, and Reid had to evacuate them from the lumber-room in frenzied haste.

"The Commandant appeared at the parade foaming at the mouth," recalled Reid. "All his subordinates duly followed suit and shouted themselves into paroxysms of rage, ...encouraged by derisive laughter from the British ranks." After another of his long harangues, both in English and German, the prisoners "were given to understand that all privileges would be withdrawn until the hammer and map were returned. The parade then broke up with catcalls, hoots, and jeers. Scarlet had pulled off his job superbly, and we found a muffled hammer a much better tool than a roughly shaped stone!"

Once they had pierced the wall they found loose earth on the other side. This was a tremendous relief, as they would now make much faster progress. But it was also obvious that they would have to shore the tunnel to keep the roof from falling in. They found some handy lengths of three-inch by two-inch timber in the lumber-room itself, and these, together with bed-boards removed from their wooden bunks, would carry them the whole length of the tunnel. A typical bed-board was about three-quarters of an inch thick and two feet six inches long. Bed-boards would become the escaper's most important raw material, as they could be used for shoring tunnels and carved into such items as dummy pistols and even rifles (as would happen in Oflag VIB in 1942 and Stalag Luft III in 1943). Prisoners engaged in illicit activities soon learned by experience how to spirit bed-boards from one room to another, and eventually Neely and his confederates were confident enough to pass a German officer with a couple of them tucked inside a loosely worn overcoat.

At first, the tunnel progressed at the rate of a foot a week, with the digger at the face working by the light of a "goon lamp". When each shift ended they tipped the soil and rubble into their trouser pockets, which they had adapted to knee-length, moseyed along into the exercise yard, and emptied their pockets surreptitiously as they lay on the grass. But now the tunnel was moving forward at a cracking pace. It was becoming impossible to dispose of the soil quickly enough, and Barry and Reid called a council-of-war. They reckoned that at the current rate of dispersal the tunnel would take at least six months to complete, and that the longer it dragged on the more certain it was that Jerry would cotton on. They concluded that they should make a "blitz" effort, and during the next week, working flat out and hiding the soil in the lumber-room, they progressed nine feet.

Another sidelight on German mentality, *circa* Sunday, 4 August 1940. The Army officers at Laufen had spent a huge amount of their precious *Lagergeld* hiring a piano and had arranged for Captain A H S Coombe-Tennant, a talented pianist in the Welsh Guards, to give a small recital on Sunday evenings at 9pm. But the Germans had decreed that entertainment on Sundays was *verboten*, so the recital was banned. On the other hand, Captain Coombe-Tennant was allowed to practise on the piano at this hour, and there was no objection to fellow-officers listening to him. But, as it was only a practice and not a recital, they were not to applaud.

From then on things started to improve — slightly. First, some books arrived, and each man now had about two books a week to read. Then prisoners were allowed to buy additional vegetables with which to thicken the soup. Better still, the rotten potatoes were at last condemned. The senior British medical officer, Colonel Morris, had finally forced the Commandant to allow him to inspect the potato-cellars. He found the cellars "in a truly disgusting state, most of their floors being literally awash with liquid manure" recalled Terence Prittie. The POWs were asked to make up working parties to remove the potatoes — "a filthy job, but at least it got rid of the permanent stench" wrote Michael Duncan. They were allowed to take what raw potatoes they could, but after cooking and eating them were doubled-up with the gripes. The British medical staff could do nothing, for they had no medicines — not even Germany's famous Bayern aspirin.

New potatoes arrived, and they were a great improvement, although they, too, were often diseased. Communal Red Cross parcels were also distributed. Mostly they contained cigarettes, jam, soup powder, condensed milk and chocolate powder. None of this was particularly filling, and it did not last long, but it did provide some much needed nourishment.

Major-General Fortune had put Captain A T Cameron, who had been captured with him, in charge of the cookhouse. As if by magic, the sugar ration started to appear and there was a good deal more meat in the soup.

This improvement went on until about 20 August, when there was a reversion to former conditions. Margarine, which had made a temporary reappearance, ran out — never to appear again — and the cookhouse returned to issuing that old German stand-by, *Speisefett*. Bread was also running short and from then onwards one loaf had to last for seven days; at one stage there was no bread at all, and prisoners were issued instead with *Knäckebrot*, a crisp-bread imported from Sweden. To cap it all, vegetable prices were highly inflated, and soon the prisoners ran out of money and so could buy nothing — not even the weak and ultimately unsatisfying German war-beer.

The handling of Red Cross parcels by the Army goons at Laufen in 1940 contrasted sharply with how the Luftwaffe would behave later on in such camps as Stalag Lufts I and III. Despite assurances by the Red Cross that no escape equipment would be hidden in any of their parcels, *Oberst* Frey soon insisted that every parcel be opened and every tin emptied. Soap, powdered milk, egg powder, chocolate, jam, meat loaf, M&V, and so on, were all mixed together in soup bowls and drinking mugs — which the Germans seemed to find frightfully funny.

In the middle of August, Desmond Neely had received the crushing news that he would soon be moved to a camp for aircrew. It was touch and go whether they would complete the tunnel in time, and his transfer would leave the syndicate short of manpower. As it was, with the tunnel lengthening, they already needed more workers. Reid, after seeking Major Poole's advice, recruited three more officers: 2nd Lieutenant A M ("Peter") Allan, of the Cameron Highlanders, and Captains R H ("Dick") Howe MC and H B ("Barry") O'Sullivan, both of the Royal Tank Regiment.

With the syndicate now seven-men strong the tunnel was under the lean-to woodshed at the other side of cul-de-sac by the end of August. After nearly seven weeks' digging, the tunnel was at last nearing completion. But it was too late for Neely. On Sunday, 1 September, the Germans carried out their promise and transferred Neely to Dulag Luft, along with Art Deacon, Len Hockey and Joe Smiley. Reid promised that, should the escape be successful, he would write to Neely's parents to let them know how he was faring. A few days later, on 4 September, six officers, including Reid, Lockwood and Barry, escaped through the tunnel, but all were recaptured and sent to Colditz. In the meantime, Deacon, Hockey, Neely and Smiley joined a purge of RAF prisoners to Stalag Luft I, at that time the only Luftwaffe camp for aircrew prisoners.

(2)

August 1940 was the last time Laufen held any Air Force prisoners until July of the following year. By then the Germans had captured so many RAF that the cage at Barth was again overcrowded. Spangenberg, too, was beginning to resemble the Black Hole of Calcutta, and Dulag Luft had a huge backlog of transients awaiting a move to permanent camps. Perhaps as a result of a recent spate of escape attempts, or merely by an administrative oversight — which ex-kriegies consider more likely — the Germans sent no more new RAF prisoners to Spangenberg between August 1941 and February 1942. Instead, in October 1941 Goering ordered the construction of another special camp for aircrew, at Sagan, in *Luftgau III*. However, the OKW had beaten him to it, converting a former artillery barracks at Lübeck, which lay on the Baltic coast in *Wehrkreis X*. Even so, the camp at Lübeck would not be habitable until the end of July 1941, and in the meantime, another group of officer aircrew prisoners found themselves incarcerated in the dreadful Oflag VIIC.

On this occasion, the Air Force contingent destined for Laufen numbered eighteen: Squadron Leader H J C Tudge; Flight Lieutenants C H MacFie DFC, AuxAF, and E A Masters; Flying Officers P Langmead, H A R Prowse and J Palka (Pole); and Pilot Officers J D Agrell,

B D Campbell RCAF, J G Crampton, D A Elliott RCAF, R C A Hunter RCAF, M Kozinski (Pole), P R I Pine RCAF, H J Sellers, J E Simmonds, W H Skinner DFM, J H Ward and P Ward-Smith.

Of this purge, twelve were from Bomber Command, three of whom came from Canada, and six were fighter pilots, one of whom was an American in the RCAF.

Taking the bomber crews first, Harry Sellers had been second pilot to a New Zealander, Pilot Officer R G Eccles, in a Vickers Wellington MkIC from No103 Squadron, based at Newton in Nottinghamshire. Their Squadron operated almost continuously throughout the war, carrying out more operations and suffering more losses than any other unit in No1 Group. Sellers was bagged on 15/16 May 1941 when 101 aircraft, mostly from Nos 40, 103 and 144 Squadrons, set out to bomb Hanover. On the way out, Eccles' port engine packed up; on the way back, over Emden, the Wimpey was hit by flak. Two of the crew — Eccles himself and the rear-gunner — perished. The aircraft crashed at Oude Pekela, some nine kilometres north-east of Veendam, in Holland.

Eccles' observer, Pilot Officer A W Sulston, was still in Dulag Luft, and Sellers would meet him again in Oflag XC in August. Another Bomber Command officer who would meet a fellow crewman at a later camp was Pilot Officer "Eski" Campbell, a native of Point Claire, Quebec. Campbell had flown as second pilot to Pilot Officer R A Walker on No106 Squadron, based at Coningsby, Lincolnshire (No5 Group). On Wednesday, 2 July thirty-nine Handley Page Hampdens set out to bomb Duisberg, Bob Walker taking off at 2310 hours. No fewer than twenty-one aircraft failed to find the target, and two crews from No106 Squadron were shot down. Walker's machine was attacked by *Leutnant* Reinhold Knacke of *II/NJG1*, killing the WOP/AG, Sergeant J Diggory. The Hampden crashed in Belgium with the crew on board. The survivors were separated at Dulag Luft, and Walker went to Spangenberg; he was destined to be reunited with Campbell at Warburg.

"Joe" Palka was an observer on a Wellington MkIC from No301 (Pomeranian) Squadron, based at another Nottinghamshire station, Syerston. No301 had been formed in July 1940 and became operational in No1 Group that September, the second Polish squadron to come into being in Bomber Command in one year. With almost a year on ops and training behind him, the fanatical and experienced Palka was due to go on leave after taking part in a raid by twenty-nine Wimpeys and thirty-nine Hampdens on Bremen on 3/4 July. The results of the raid were reckoned to be good, and only three aircraft were lost. Joe Palka's pilot, Flying Officer Butkiewicz, was carrying a supernumerary, Group Captain B Stachon from Station Headquarters at Swinderby in Lincolnshire, who had decided to go on the op for a "look-see". He got more than he bargained for, as would other Group Captains who thought going on ops was a joyride. Over Holland the Wimpey was bounced by *Oberleutnant* Helmut Lent of *4/NJG1* and at 0034 hours crashed at Eerste Exloërmond, some eighteen kilometres north-north-east of Emmen. "Groupie" Stachon was killed, but with the exception of the pilot, whose fate is unknown, the regular crew survived.

Pilot Officer "Junior" Simmonds was from No77 Squadron (No4 Group), flying that old warhorse the Armstrong Whitworth Whitley MkV. He took off from Topcliffe, Yorkshire, at 2240 hours on 6/7 July to take part in a raid with forty-five other aircraft on Dortmund. Haze obscured the target but the observer, Sergeant E H Alderton, saw some fires below and aimed his bombs at them. However, flak struck the Whitley and Alderton was hit in the chest by shrapnel. The damaged aircraft crashed eight kilometres south-east of Eindhoven. Alderton's wounds turned out to be only slight, and after treatment in the Hohemark clinic, attached to Dulag Luft, he was sent to Lamsdorf. The WOP/AGs, Sergeants D Bradley and S A Evans, were unharmed and sent to Stalag IXC.

Eric Masters, Johnny Agrell and the Canadian Donald Elliott were three survivors of a Wellington MkIC crew from No99 (Madras Presidency) Squadron, stationed at Waterbeach in Cambridgeshire (No3 Group). They were shot down in a raid over Cologne on 7/8 July. Bomber Command put up a hundred and fourteen Wimpeys that night, and three were lost. Masters had only recently been promoted and was looking forward to completing the thirtieth and last sortie of his tour as a pilot. He took off at 2323 hours, and the outward leg went smoothly until he reached the Rhine, where he tried to get a fix on his position from the river, which was reflecting the moonlight to the south. Flying between two flak batteries with his navigator, Elliott, peering over his right shoulder, he discovered they were to the south of Cologne — to get a good bomb-run to the city they would have to approach it from the north. Once the Rhine was behind him Masters turned north and flew along the eastern outskirts of Cologne, watching the activity over the target, then began his approach. Elliott now lay in the prone bombing position, just below and in front of him, giving course corrections.

By then all was peaceful over the target, and one of the gunners remarked: "Everyone seems to have gone home, skipper." Suddenly they were caught and held by the blue master-searchlight. They had flown straight and level, at the same speed, for too long. Six more searchlights coned them, and they came under a terrific flak barrage. Masters increased speed, holding the aircraft in a dive and still heading for the target, with flak following and tossing the old crate all over the sky. Suddenly the control column juddered and Agrell, the second pilot, who was in the astrodome, announced that they had been hit. Masters felt the fore and aft controls go rigid and struggled in vain to bring the nose up. Still the flak was after them. He told Agrell to jettison the bombs, hoping this would give the aircraft some "lift". It failed. They were out of control and losing height rapidly. At 10,000 feet Masters gave the order to abandon the aircraft. Once Agrell, Elliott and the rest had gone, he grabbed his chest parachute and followed them out. All the crew survived.

Flying Officer Peter Langmead's aircraft was shot down in a very convenient place from the German point of view: Frankfurt am Main. He was a pilot with No35 (Madras Presidency) Squadron at Linton-on-Ouse, Yorkshire, which had recently re-equipped with the four-engine Handley Page Halifax MkI, the first unit in No5 Group to do so. On 7/8 July —the same night Agrell, Elliott and Masters were "getting theirs" over Cologne — fourteen Halifaxes and three Short Stirlings set out for Frankfurt, Langmead taking off at 2300 hours. His was the only aircraft lost on that night's minor operations (the big raids were on Cologne and Osnabrück), falling victim to flak. The six sergeants in his crew went with him into the bag.

Squadron Leader Herbert John Charles Tudge was a veteran of No21 Squadron, which had been with No2 Group at the outbreak of the war but had thrice been detached to Coastal Command, flying Blenheim MkIVs from Bodney, in Norfolk, and Watton, Suffolk. On Thursday, 10 July twenty-four Blenheims escorted by fighters from No11 Group took part in "Circus No42", which involved coastal sweeps against ships and ports from Le Havre to Cherbourg. No21 Squadron was slated for Cherbourg docks, Charles Tudge leading his flight off from Watton at 1040 hours. His was the only Blenheim shot down. All his crew survived unharmed.

That night an entire Wellington MkIC crew from No300 (Masovian) Squadron were bagged: Pilot Officers J Kuflik, J Janicki and M Kozinski and Sergeants M Sztul, J Artymuik and A Suczynski, all of whom were original members of this first all-Polish squadron, founded in July 1940. They were on another maximum effort against Cologne, this one involving 130 aircraft. Jan Kuflik took off from Swinderby at 2249 hours. Bad weather dogged the raid, and it is not known why Kuflik's aircraft crashed, although it was probably down to flak. In any event, all the crew survived, albeit with injuries. Kozinski, the observer, was sent to Laufen. Janicki, the second pilot, spent nearly nineteen weeks at Hohemark and Dulag Luft before being sent to Oflag XC. Jan Kuflik, their pilot, was more seriously injured and was transferred from Hohemark to *Lazarett* IXC, and from there to Spangenberg.

Four days later it was the turn of "Crammy" Crampton to tread the path to Laufen. He was from No214 (Federated Malay States) Squadron, stationed at Stradishall in Suffolk (No3 Group) On 14/15 July, in yet another raid on Bremen, ninety-seven aircraft were sent to three different aiming points — the shipyards, the goods station and the *Altstadt* (Old Town), which had the reputation of making quite a nice fire. Crews reported afterwards that "the whole town was ablaze". But on the return trip four Wellingtons were lost. Crampton's kite fell to a night-fighter while still over Germany, crashing near Quakenbrück. The observer was killed.

The following night No3 Group put up thirty-eight Wellingtons from Nos 57, 75, 115 and 218 Squadrons to bomb Duisburg (again). Thick cloud, heavy flak and ubiquitous night-fighters made bombing difficult and led to the loss of four aircraft — and to one of those incidents which is quite funny, but only in a droll sort of way. Although he was from Toronto, Ontario, and early in the war had joined the RCAF, training as an observer, Robin Hunter was susequently posted to a New

Zealand bomber squadron, No75, which was still based at Feltwell. He was crewed up with Pilot Officer W J Rees, second pilot Sergeant D C Joyce, wireless operator Sergeant J W Lewis, nose-gunner Sergeant D H Conibear and rear-gunner Sergeant Gwyn-Williams. Over Duisburg they were caught in the searchlights, then hit by flak and then attacked by a night-fighter from *I/NJG1*. Cannon-shells exploded in the cockpit and blew open the escape hatch midway along the fuselage. Sergeants Joyce, Conibear and Gwyn-Williams were all wounded, while Lewis, sitting at his radio, was dazed and deafened. Only the pilot, Rees, and the observer, Hunter, were unscathed. With Rees wrestling to steady the bucking aircraft, Hunter left his position to go aft and help Gwyn-Williams. Unaware that the hatch had been blown open, he literally fell through it. Luckily, he had strapped on his parachute, and once he had sufficiently recovered from the initial shock of finding himself hurtling through enemy sky, he pulled the D-ring, and the 'chute — much to his relief, undamaged — opened with a reassuring crackle.

While Hunter floated down to face German hospitality, further aloft Rees had steadied the Wimpey and Lewis had recovered and was helping the wounded. Lewis also managed to repair his radio, collect Hunter's maps together and help Rees work out a course for home. The aircraft made it, but Conibear had to be rushed to hospital where he died of his wounds on 30 July. Rees was awarded a DFC, and Lewis a DFM. Robin Hunter was awarded a trip to Dulag Luft. His stay was only brief, however; the cells were overcrowded and, truth to tell, the interrogators felt a wee bit sorry for him and let him into the compound within twenty-four hours. As for Hunter himself, he was to spend the next four years wishing he had never left his home in Toronto.

Of the six fighter pilots, Colin Hamilton MacFie, Harry Arthur Robin Prowse and Wilfred ("Bill") Skinner had all fought in the Battle of Britain, and subsequently each was shot down within a day of the other. Harry Prowse, captured on Friday, 4 July 1941, had initially been in No266 Squadron, Wittering, Northamptonshire. He was then posted to No603 (City of Edinburgh) Squadron, an Auxiliary Air Force outfit that in May 1941 became part of No11 Group's Hornchurch Wing — and which, after the capture of Wing Commander J R Kayll DSO, DFC, in June, came under the tactical leadership of Wing Commander F S Stapleton DSO, DFC. In Prowse's last engagement with the enemy his squadron had provided top cover for "Circus No32" to Choques power station. Prowse bagged two Me109s but was then hit by flak. He pancaked in a field and set his Spitfire MkVA alight with his Verey pistol before being captured. (This operation also led DFC holder Flying Officer Keith Ogilvie into the bag; he was now at Spangenberg, awaiting repatriation, on medical grounds, that would never take place.)

Colin MacFie, of the Auxiliary Air Force, had flown first with No611 (West Lancashire) Squadron and then with No616 (South Yorkshire) Squadron, Westhampnett, Sussex, where he commanded "B" Flight. In February 1941, equipped with Spitfire MkIIBs "borrowed" from No65 Squadron, No616 became part of No11 Group's Tangmere Wing, led by the legless ace, Wing Commander D R S Bader DSO*, DFC*, and known as "Bader's Bus Company". On Saturday, 5 July 1941 aircraft from Nos 54, 74, 145, 308, 312, 485, 610, 611 and 616 Squadrons took part in "Circus No33", escorting three Stirling bombers to Lille and a single bomber to Abbeville. The Luftwaffe came up to play, but ignored the bombers. Three Spitfires were shot down. One ended up in the Channel, its pilot being picked up by Air-Sea Rescue; another crashed, killing the pilot, and MacFie baled out over France and was captured.

Bill Skinner, shot down the next day, 6 July, was the longest-serving member of No74 ("Tiger") Squadron, which he had joined as an NCO on 10 June 1939. Originally based at Hornchurch, Essex, No74 Squadron was operating from Gravesend, Kent, and being re-equipped with the Spitfire MkVB when Skinner flew his last sortie, yet another job providing top cover for a "Circus", this time No35. There were two "Circuses" that day: No34 escorting six Stirlings to Yainville, and No35 providing cover for another three heading for Lille. Again, no bombers were lost but several fighters were. Bill Skinner was shot down over the French mainland, one of three RAF fighter pilots captured that day (the other two were NCOs).

Another fighter pilot in the purge to Laufen was Peter Pine, a Californian who had gone to Canada to join the RCAF in 1940. After training he was posted to No145 Squadron, also part of the Tangmere Wing, also stationed in Sussex (at Merston) and also equipped with the Spitfire MkVB. During the afternoon of Tuesday, 8 July 1941 his squadron provided high-altitude escort for "Circus No40" to Lille. Some savage dog fighting ensued between the Spitfires and the Me109s from St Omer, resulting in Pine being shot down.

Peter Ward-Smith, of No610 (County of Chester) Squadron — another Auxiliary Air Force unit in Bader's Wing and based, like No616, at Westhampnett — had fought as a Sergeant Pilot during the Battle of Britain and had been commissioned in June 1941. He was shot down two days after Peter Pine on "Circus No42", when Spitfires of No11 Group escorted Blenheims on the raid that led to Charles Tudge's capture. His aircraft damaged by an Me109, he baled out and was captured soon afterwards.

James Heber Ward, of the Middle East Air Force, was captured in North Africa. A relatively inexperienced pilot, he had joined No73 Squadron, based at Sidi Haneish, from the Middle East Pool at the end of April. On Saturday 14 June 1941, flying a Hurricane MkI at low level, he was shot down by an Me109. After crash-landing he started to walk towards British lines, and was free for three days before being caught by an Italian patrol, who handed him over to the Germans. (Shortly afterwards Acting Squadron Leader A M Crawley joined No73 Squadron. Captured a month later, he was to encounter Ward at Schubin in September 1942. Another No73 Squadron alumnus, Flying Officer P O V Green, was soon to meet Ward at Oflag XC.)

***

The RAF prisoners at Laufen, by dint of the administrative oversight that had led them there in the first place, received no personal Red Cross parcels during their brief stay, and had to subsist on German rations and the generosity of the Army prisoners. However, conditions had been steadily improving since September 1940. To begin with, communal Red Cross parcels were arriving with some regularity and the letter-form and letter-card traffic was running smoothly, with the caveat that officers' rights on this head were still seriously curtailed — a routine contravention of the Geneva Convention that *Oberst* Frey so despised.

Secondly, the German rations were slightly better — or, at least, not as bad. The potatoes, now free of blight and worms, were just about edible. Now that the despised "Cookhouse Joe" had been booted out of the camp, there was meat in the soup, albeit leaving a greasy patina. The black market racket in sugar had also been uncovered, so now sugar appeared in the acorn coffee and lime-leaf tea. Prisoners could actually attend *Appell*, exercise in "The Park" and walk up and down the stairs without keeling over.

Thirdly, the camp was less crowded. In the second week of March 1941 five hundred officers, mainly of junior rank, had been sent to the *Straflager* at Fort VIII, at Posen. (However, Major-General Victor Fortune had gone with them, leaving Laufen with a less than inspiring British camp staff.) Once the *Strafe* was lifted in June, the Laufen contingent did not return; they were sent instead to Oflag VB at Biberach.

Fourthly, there was now reading fodder, mainly badly written American crime novels and Tauchnitz books. The latter were in their own way as unappealing as the crime fiction: cheap copyright editions of British novels published in Leipzig from the late 19th Century onwards for British expatriates, printed in uneven type on yellowing, porous paper and without any pretence at proper binding. But there was also a series of lectures, music concerts and plays, laid on by the Army using instruments, costumes and props paid for with their precious *Lagergeld*.

However, they RAF contingent were mere spectators to most of this activity, receiving no parcels, no letters and no camp pay, and having no chance to settle in. Between 4 and 7 August, having spent only two weeks at Laufen, they were transferred to Oflag XC, Lübeck, which, they were told, was a brand-new camp with flushing lavatories. They were not to know that the commandant there would be as big a bastard as *Oberst* Frey and that the food situation would deteriorate. Not for these prisoners the old proverb, "abundance of things ingendereth disdainfulness".

(3)

As a result of yet further administrative bungling by the Jerries, several RAF officer POWs were sent in 1941 to Oflag VB, the camp at Biberach to which the Army *Strafgefangenen* had been sent after their stint at Posen. Biberach was a small German town in the middle of the triangle formed by Ulm, Memmingen and the River Danube. On the outskirts of the village was an army barracks comprising a large parade ground bounded on one side by six long, low brick huts and on the opposite side by another two. After the fall of France the local *Wehrkreis*, whose HQ was in Stuttgart, began converting it into a POW camp, adding two more brick barrack blocks, a canteen, a bath house and a hospital. At one end was an open space for exercise purposes and the whole was surrounded by the usual double fence of heavy barbed-wire, three metres high and two metres apart, overlooked from every angle by the usual raised wooden sentry-towers. Running close to the ground one metre from inside the fence was a trip wire, delineating a no-man's-land between it and the fence into which it was forbidden to step on pain of being shot. The camp was opened to POWs on 28 August 1940, and initially held French officers. No British inhabited the camp until June 1941, and even then its life as a British camp would be brief, as the new occupants would be transferred in September of the same year.

In mid-June four RAF officers reached Oflag VB via Greece. They were Acting Flight Lieutenant H W Lamond and Pilot Officers J W Best, R Edge and L J E Goldfinch.

Richard ("Dickie") Edge was an air observer with No11 Squadron, of Middle East Command.

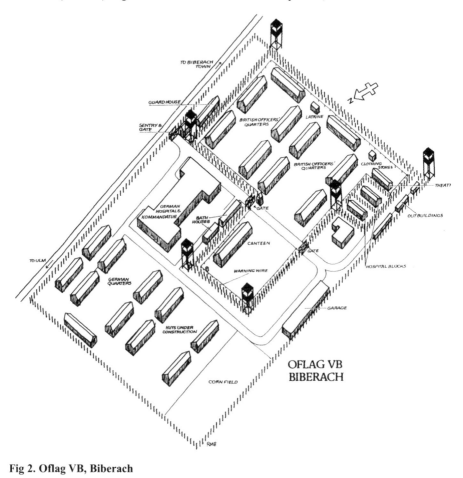

Fig 2. Oflag VB, Biberach

54

The bulk of his squadron had in fact been stationed in Singapore until the Italians entered the war, and was then hastily recalled to Aden. Constantly short of manpower and aircraft, their shiny new Blenheim MkIs either being given to the Balkan states as diplomatic sweeteners or being shot down through enemy action, No11 and its sister squadrons were moved to Egypt and then to the Greek mainland — based firstly in the south at Elevsís (Eleusis), then in the north-east at Almirós and later even further north at Lárisa — to help stem the German invasion of Yugoslavia and Greece. In time No11 Squadron received replacement aircraft, mainly Blenheim MkIVs, and in March 1941 became part of the newly formed E (for "Eastern") Wing. But the relentless German advance and the strafing of Lárisa airfield on 15 April forced No11 Squadron to retire south on 16 April to Menidi — an airfield east-north-east of Elevsís and thus pretty well back where the squadron had made landfall three months earlier. Although five Blenheim squadrons were gathered at Menidi, half their strength was transferred to Crete and one squadron had been completely wiped out. When the remnants of these units were consolidated under the leadership of No11 Squadron, the ground crews reported that they had only fourteen serviceable Blenheims.

Dickie Edge's brief but eventful operational career came to an end on Friday, 18 April 1941. Earlier during the day Blenheims had temporarily delayed the German advance by blowing up a bridge near Kozáni, up towards the Macedonian border, and Pilot Officer Patrick Montague-Bates was ordered to bomb and strafe the troop column. Taking Sergeant H Murphy as WOP/AG and Dickie Edge as observer, he carried out his task successfully, killing eight soldiers and wounding a further fifteen. But as he turned for home his Blenheim was bounced by an Me109E of 9//JG77, flown by *Oberleutnant* Armin Schmidt. The Messerschmitt raked the Blenheim from end to end, killing the pilot and Murphy, who had put up a valiant fight despite guns that kept jamming. Dickie Edge alone walked away from the crash and was captured almost immediately by soldiers from the column he and Montague-Bates had bombed. He was not at all popular. However, he was reported next day as safe and a POW, and shortly afterwards was flown to Salonika by a Ju52 transport aircraft. He fetched up at Dulag 185, where he would eventually meet with Henry Lamond, Bill Goldfinch and Jack Best.

Henry William Lamond, nicknamed "Piglet" because of his small stature, had been born in Auckland, New Zealand, on 26 August 1915. In common with most boys at that time he grew up with a tremendous enthusiasm for flying. But his father, a poorly paid school-teacher, had little money to spare, so flying lessons were out of the question. Instead, young Henry

joined the Auckland Gliding Club and learned to fly the hard way — in basic gliders. We did all the work ourselves, of course, including the servicing of old, heavy motorcars which we used as a makeshift winch by jacking up one rear wheel, chocking the other, and putting on a wheel without a tyre on which we wound a steel cable to get a launch. Eventually we built a stream-lined cockpit around the seat of an American WACO basic glider and in that I held, or rather set-up, a NZ gliding record of a whole 15 minutes or so in the air.

In 1937 Lamond won a flying scholarship, a small number of which were provided by the New Zealand government, and learned to fly powered aircraft at government expense on de Havilland Gipsy Moths at the Mangere aerodrome in Auckland. The Gipsy Moth was a very basic aircraft with few instruments — an altimeter, a compass, an oil-pressure gauge and an air-speed indicator that was no more than a flap on one of the struts. "Real seat-of-the-pants flying and the most wonderful fun in the world," recalls Lamond today.

His final "A" Licence flying test was conducted by an RAF Flight Lieutenant on secondment to the RNZAF, and through him Lamond joined the RAF, although he still did his RAF flying training in New Zealand. On completing the course in June1938, his intake was supposed to go to England, but the Munich Crisis intervened and the batch was kept in New Zealand until early 1939. That March, Lamond was posted to a General Reconnaissance (GR) course on RAF Thorney Island, Sussex. From there he went on a flying boat conversion course at Calshot, Hampshire, and finally, a few days after the war started, joined No210 Squadron, a No15 (GR) Group unit, flying Short Sunderland flying boats out of RAF Pembroke Docks.

Lamond's flying experience on Sunderlands was haphazard, as from March 1940 he was "detached" and sent on GR instructional duties to various Blenheim squadrons at Bircham Newton, West Raynham and Hatston, and then to No2 School of GR, Blackpool. He rejoined his old squadron, No210, in October, by which time it had moved to Oban. Then, in December 1940, he led a crew delivering a new Sunderland to No228 Squadron (also from No15 Group), which had been the RAF's third Sunderland unit and had moved to Kalafrana, Malta, on 10 June 1940. But instead of being allowed to return to Britain, as they had expected, Lamond and the ferry crew were kept in Malta. Italy had begun its invasion of Greece in October 1940, and the brass-hats were predicting that by spring 1941 the Germans would be advancing through Greece and threatening Crete. Every Sunderland crew would be needed to keep British supply-lines open. Lamond, then a Flying Officer, was promoted to Acting Flight Lieutenant and given his own crew, one of whom was Bill Goldfinch. On Lamond's first operational flight as a skipper of a Sunderland, on 27 January 1941, his observer spotted an enemy convoy of four ships and the wireless operator sent a message to base. Lamond shadowed the convoy and watched it being attacked with torpedoes by naval Swordfish from Malta. It was the first time a combined operation of this sort had been carried out in the Mediterranean.

As No228 Squadron had so few flying boats, Lamond got to be skipper only occasionally. In mid-March the squadron was bombed out of Malta and was more or less broken up. The CO and the senior staff returned to London, while the two remaining flying boats went to Alexandria. Some of the ground crew stayed behind in Malta to service visiting flying boats; others went to Alexandria by ship.

On Thursday, 24 April, Lamond was made skipper of another Sunderland, T9084, and sent to Suda Bay in Crete. The next day, Friday, 25 April, was a day of operations with hardly a respite and which ended with Lamond and Bill Goldfinch being captured. First, they were ordered to reconnoitre the Greek coast around a place called Githeon to see if they could find and pick up any members of the RAF trying to evade capture by the German invaders. They found a party, picked up as many as they could and flew them back to Suda Bay. Almost at once Lamond was ordered to fly out to Kalámai (Kalamáta), where he saw signals being flashed from a hand-held mirror. On landing he saw what looked like the entire British garrison assembling — they were in fact 101 officers and men of No112 Squadron. By now Lamond's Sunderland was low on fuel, but he still managed to pick up seventy-four of them. With a ten-man crew that made a complement of eighty-four — the record number carried in an aircraft up to that time.

Later that same evening he was woken up and ordered to fly back to Kalámai with an urgent message that the Navy would endeavour to lift off as many troops as possible by ship. The operation meant Lamond would have to take off from Suda Bay at night with no flare-path — and there were several obstructions, such as sunken ships, in the harbour — and a night landing at Kalámai, again with no flare-path. "I should have refused to go, I guess," he recalls now, "but in those days one didn't. I managed the take-off but it was a lousy night with very poor visibility, much sea-mist and no wind, so I knew that I could not use the landing lights to help with the landing — and to cut a long story short I never made it, and in the attempt crashed the aircraft."

Lamond's Sunderland had hit an obstruction in the water — though what it was he never did find out. Only four of the crew survived the crash, three with injuries — Lamond, Bill Goldfinch and an NCO, Danny Davies — and the other, Pilot Officer Briscoe, unhurt. They clung to one of the wings, which was floating upside down with one of the floats in the air, and after several hours adrift were rescued by a Greek search party in a small boat. It had taken them ages because of the mist. When the Greeks took the survivors ashore, Briscoe made off. (He managed to get back to Suda Bay by boat.) On Monday the 28th the Germans overran the area and took the wounded to a hospital in Kalámai, where they encountered Jack Best.

John William ("Jack") Best, born on 6 August 1912 at Llangollen, North Wales, had attended prep school in the village of Rottingdean, outside Brighton, before going to Stowe School. From 1931 until the war he managed various farms in Kenya and in April 1940 bought his own. Best had got his "A" Licence in 1937 with an eye to joining an Air Force Reserve should one ever be formed. None was, so he joined the RAF in 1940, spending three months on No3 War Course in

Kenya training on de Havilland Tiger Moths. The day after he bought his farm he was posted to Habbanyia in Iraq for six months on Airspeed Oxfords. After a conversion course on Blenheims at Ismailia in Egypt he was posted to No39 Squadron at Cairo. No39 was a reconnaissance squadron that saw action mainly in North Africa and the Mediterranean with a rag-bag of aircraft that included Blenheims, Beauforts, Beaufighters, Marauders, Mosquitos and Martin Marylands, although in the early summer of 1941 only half of the crews were equipped with aircraft. In May and June of 1941 the squadron was carrying out almost daily recces and nuisance raids from a forward base at Maaten Bagush. These were exhausting and uncomfortable operations, flown at 20,000 feet and often lasting for more than six hours, and attracting enemy fighters. The Maryland was not cut out for air combat: the crew positions were isolated and the only means of communication was by intercom. The combination of cold, fatigue and Me109s led to increasing losses. One flight was posted to Fuka Satellite to do photo-reconnaissance, and the other joined soon afterwards to temporarily replace Sunderlands on sea reconnaissance. The Sunderlands had flown round the clock during the evacuation of Greece and had now been grounded.

Early on Monday, 5 May 1941, Best took off in a Maryland with Sergeants Martin (Observer) and Kerry Cobb (WOP/AG) and another air-gunner, Sergeant J A Quitzow, whose first trip with Best this was. They flew first to the most easterly point of Greece, south of the Gulf of Corinth, and then on to Malta. They were due to arrive in time for lunch; another crew would fly the Maryland to Greece and back. This was many more miles than the Sunderlands flew, but roughly the same of amount time spent over the sea. As Best was approaching Malta his Maryland hit cloud and Cobb asked base for a bearing. There was no answer. So Best decided to go north to Sicily, get a position once there, and then use a square search to find Malta. He hit bumpy weather over Sicily and the next time he tried to use the intercom it was dead. In a Maryland the observer was below and well in front of the pilot, and the other two crew were completely isolated by the bomb bay, which was loaded with an extra fuel-tank. It was impossible to navigate accurately in these conditions, so Best made another decision: return to Crete, which had not yet been invaded by the Germans. Unfortunately, the fuel ran out over the southern Peloponnese. After flying for nine-and-a-half hours with no second pilot or "George", Best was exhausted. He flopped the Maryland into the sea near Cape Akritas, and the crew tried to scramble aboard their dinghy. It blew bubbles and sank. They swam ashore in their Mae Wests, which was tough on two of the crew, who were poor swimmers. Once ashore they received a tremendous welcome from the local inhabitants, who dried their clothes and gave them food. Two different parties vied to help them obtain a boat to Crete. Mentally flipping a coin, Best chose one and they went off together, marching all night and finally reaching a road and a little building where they were to wait for news of a boat. Dog-tired, Best and his crew fell asleep. But instead of waking up later in the day to friendly helpers, they saw a squad of Germans in uniform. That night they were taken to Kalámai, where they met Lamond and Goldfinch.

The following morning Best and his crew were taken in a captured Ford V8 to Corinth, and it was some time before he again met Lamond and Goldfinch. At Corinth, they were each put into a tiny bell-tent with one sentry for each by day and two by night. They were with a Luftwaffe squadron and had the same food. But on the second or third night a bunch of army thugs appeared, toting machine-guns and demanding to take custody of the prisoners. The Luftwaffe CO was reluctant to let the airmen go, but the matter was out of his hands. The soldiers shoved the captives, who were wondering what was going to happen next, into the back of a lorry, where the guards were uncommunicative. Eventually they reached the port of Corinth, where again each was put into a plundered British bell-tent on the gravel beach and spent a very uncomfortable night. They were there two days and were fed only once. Across the road was a restaurant full of German soldiers that the Italians were afraid to enter. That, at least, boosted Best's morale.

On the third morning, suddenly and without warning, they were put in the back of a lorry and taken to Athens, where they were at last allowed to talk to each other and were interrogated. None of them had ever had any instruction on what to say — let alone what not to say — upon becoming a POW, but had agreed early on to claim that they had been flying a Blenheim, as the Maryland was new to the Middle East. "I only hope that between us we did not give any valuable information away," Best remarked fifty years later. They spent the night with an Army unit who stuffed them with food and British chocolate and biscuits, telling them to fill their pockets as they would see no such luxuries in a POW camp. After about a week in a Greek army barracks, they boarded a boat with some Army prisoners and a wireless operator from the Merchant Navy. They were at sea for twenty-four hours without being fed.

Eventually they reached Salonika, where they were herded into Dulag 185, a temporary POW camp that had until recently been a Greek Artillery barracks. Dickie Edge was already there, but weeks were to elapse before the arrival of Goldfinch and Lamond. After Best had left them in Kalámai, Goldfinch, the most badly injured of the Sunderland survivors, had been taken to a hospital on a hillside at Kokinia, between Piraeus and Athens. A modern building of white concrete, which had once been a borstal, it consisted of four blocks, each four storeys high. Before its capture by the Germans, it had been the 5th Australian General Hospital run by Major E Moore, RAMC, aided by a staff of Australian doctors, male medical orderlies and female nurses. When Greece was evacuated, all the nurses and many of the doctors had gone with them to Egypt, but Major Moore and several others volunteered to stay behind to look after the wounded from the beaches. They were assisted by staff from the 26th British General Hospital. Now, surrounded by barbed-wire and guarded by the SS, it was used as a hospital for POWs under the command of a German doctor. The medical treatment was good, but the diet was inadequate, consisting of a wedge of bread issued each morning and intended to last the entire day.

In the meantime, Henry Lamond, who had only slight head injuries, joined about 20,000 Army prisoners destined for Dulag 185. He was the only RAF officer amongst them until Goldfinch returned to the fold. "The Germans were quite phlegmatic about the whole thing," recalls Lamond:

> They said they would starve us until we were weak enough not to cause them any trouble as they carted us back to Germany. (Sensible when one comes to think about it...) Anyway, we starved. I don't remember getting anything much, other than what was supposed to be a "stew" in the middle of each day but which turned out to be simply greasy water. Unfortunately, in the heat and dust and miserable sanitary conditions many of the men got awful dysentery and some died in great pain as there were no medicines.
>
> It was weeks before we were carted off by train in filthy cattle trucks. Railway bridges and tunnels had been blown up...so we had to walk occasionally. The worst walk was over Mount Olympus, which was long and difficult. Without proper footwear and socks for Bill Goldfinch and I, our feet turned into raw meat. However, even when starved it is surprising what strength remains and bloody-minded men did cause a lot of trouble by trying to escape, sitting down and refusing to go on and the like. Unfortunately some were so sick that they couldn't make it, and the German answer was simply to dump them into a horse and cart — those on the bottom just suffocated as more and more bodies were piled on top.

Salonika was a bad camp in every respect. Comprising seven long, low barrack blocks, it had been built by the Turks during the years of the Turkish occupation, and the sanitary arrangements were primitive in the extreme, with hardly any drainage. When the Greeks, and then the Germans, took it over, they had had allowed it to deteriorate badly. The only addition made by the Germans were five raised sentry towers, twenty feet high, and a wire tangle ten feet high and ten feet wide surrounding the buildings. They had then opened the gates to more than 24,000 prisoners, and left them to fend for themselves with hardly any food or facilities. The rooms stank abominably, and many of the doors, tables, benches and bunks had been used to fuel the small stove in each room. Now there was only enough wood for one stove to be lit in each building. Few of the windows were intact and all the rooms were thick with dirt and dust. There were still some iron bedsteads, but the frames and mattresses — as well as what timber was left in the barracks — were infested with bugs. "It was unbelievable how many bugs there were in those timbers, so we tried to sleep out in the open," says Lamond. The cookhouse was in a distant shed near the wire fence and was poorly equipped. Flies by the million swarmed around the cookhouse and the latrines, and formed

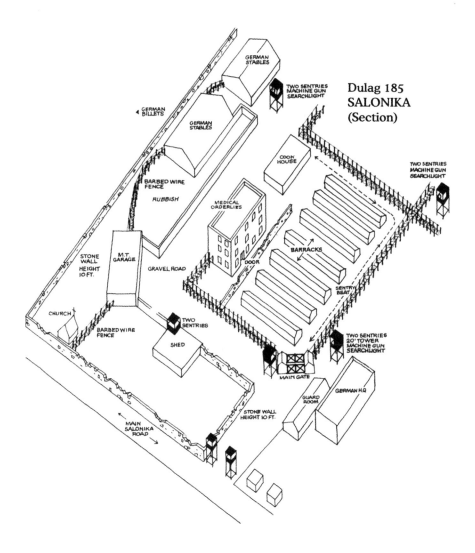

Fig 3. Dulag 185, Salonika

ugly black heaps where refuse was dropped. Scores of mangy cats slunk among the barrack rooms, and during cool weather the rats from the sewers would boldly roam the compound.

The Commandant, *Hauptmann* Severin, was a middle-aged farmer from Westphalia, who evinced concern at conditions in the camp but did nothing to improve them. Every morning, accompanied by two British Army warrant officers who spoke good German, he would carry out an inspection of the camp, during which the prisoners had to parade by their beds. His inspection was thorough and his solicitousness disarming, but given the chance he would sooner engage in a dialogue on his favourite subject — farming — and then conveniently forget to make the promised representations to higher authority regarding living conditions and diet. He was to some extent hampered from behind the scenes by an SS *Gefreiter* (lance-corporal), who commanded the guard, and by constant observation by the Gestapo.

Twice a day the prisoners were called out on *Appell*. Able-bodied men had to form up outside in two ranks, while the sick and wounded sat on their beds or in their hospital wards while the Germans went round and checked their names against a list. The rest of the day they paced up and down inside the wire and thought and talked about food. Only the British warrant officers, who occupied an office in the administrative block outside the wire, had plenty to do. They interpreted for the Germans, provided fatigue parties, ran the cookhouse, and were allowed to take parole walks into town. Consequently, they were despised by their fellow-prisoners, especially as most had to live on nothing but thin stew — made from water, beans and tiny fragments of meat — and were forced to endure the utmost squalor. Life was also made difficult by the SS corporal, whose main preoccupation seemed to be thinking up new rules and regulations by which to restrict the prisoners' freedom of action.

Many shocking atrocities were committed by the guards, most of whom seemed to be former *Hitlerjugend*. One of them threw a grenade into a latrine packed with dysentery cases; the carnage was frightful. The only explanation given was that the men had been whispering in a suspicious manner. Three men caught trying to escape were shot out of hand and their bodies left for days in the hot sun. Other escapers were bound with barbed-wire and whipped as a warning to all. Drunken guards would walk into the compound and beat unarmed prisoners, and rumour had it that the SS corporal would ask daily of his guard how many *englische Schweinehunde* they had killed and congratulate the murderers effusively.

Best fell in with two officers of the 4th Hussars. They decided to make an escape before the Germans finished putting up the barbed-wire round the Army quarters, ready for the arrival of the rest of the captured Hussars. But Best was suffering from dysentery and had to pull out. The other two tried it and the first to go was shot and killed.

At last they were put into ever more cattle trucks for the journey to Germany. Best again mucked in with the 4th Hussars, although this time none tried to escape. At stops throughout Yugoslavia the local population would turn out and give them yoghurt — "which was nectar". Finally, on Monday, 16 June, they were shoved into Oflag VB.

Biberach was a vast improvement on Salonika — it was well run, relatively comfortable and received Red Cross parcels: a good camp as prison camps go. The barrack blocks were clean, spacious and well appointed by previous standards. The entrance to each barrack block was halfway along one of the two longer sides, and directly opposite was a washroom, its walls lined with deep metal troughs and taps providing permanent cold water (alas! "H&C in all rooms" was not a feature of German POW hospitality). Running from either side of the lobby was a long passage illuminated by skylights and electric lighting running flush with the ceiling. Flanking the passage were the POW living rooms, furnished with stools, tables, lockers and a tiled stove. The one drawback was that, instead of sleeping in bunk-beds, the prisoners had to sleep four men to a large wooden shelf secured to the wall. However, in the middle of July the shelves were replaced with proper bunk-beds.

The small RAF contingent had no opportunity to escape as, despite the dubious comforts of Biberach, the Army officers were constructing two major tunnels and had imposed a moratorium on individual attempts. Eventually, six of them would make a home run from Oflag VB, a record equalled by very few camps.

***

Between Thursday, 17 July and Thursday, 31 July 1941 a further five RAF aircrew officers arrived at Biberach. They were Acting Squadron Leader W R Williams and Pilot Officers I P B Denton, K C Edwards, AuxAF, W J ("Red") Hunter RAFVR and J G Ireton.

During the Battle of Britain Kenneth Charles Edwards had been an air-gunner on Blenheims in No600 (City of London) Squadron, an Auxiliary Air Force unit in No11 Group, Fighter Command. But in January 1941 he was transferred to bombers, joining the Wellington-equipped No150 Squadron (No1 Group), based at Snaith in Yorkshire. He was on his fifteenth operation with this squadron as an air-gunner, a raid by 107 aircraft on Hamburg on 16/17 July, when his aircraft was hit by flak, exploding at a height of 14,000 feet.

Fortunately for me, the explosion blew me out of the aircraft and I found myself in pitch darkness, floating down on my parachute. Imagine my horror when, as I came nearer to the ground, I discovered that I was immediately over the River Elbe — dead centre — into which I sank complete with high-flying gear and a water-logged parachute, to hamper survival drill. Here I was, swimming, gurgling, and sinking, until finally around dawn I was fished out by a German patrol boat.

Though Edwards was safe and uninjured, all his crew had perished. Their bodies were recovered by the Luftwaffe and buried in Hamburg. A few hours after being rescued Edwards was taken by lorry and train to Oflag VB. (His one consolation was that three weeks later, on Friday, 8 August, he received time-promotion to Flying Officer.)

Acting Squadron Leader, Walter Rice Williams was a Flight Commander in the Halifax-equipped No76 Squadron (No4 Group), based at Stanton Harcourt in Oxfordshire. A total of 278 members of this squadron would become prisoners of war, and "Taffy" Williams, his second pilot, Jim Ireton, and the rest of his crew were among the first. On Thursday, 24 July fifteen Halifaxes from Nos 35 and 76 Squadrons set out to in broad daylight at 1030 hours to attack the German battle-cruiser *Scharnhorst* lying in harbour at la Pallice. Originally the plan had been for a hundred or more aircraft, a mixed force of Halifaxes, Hampdens and Wimpeys, to mount a dawn attack on Brest, where not only the *Scharnhorst* but also the *Gneisenau* and *Prinz Eugen* were harboured. The plan was called "Operation Sunrise". At the last minute, however, the three battle-crusiers moved down the coast to la Pallice and the plan was modified, with the force dividing in two to attack both harbours. The Hampdens and Wellingtons, with a heavy fighter escort, were to hit Brest. The two Halifax squadrons drew la Pallice, and were to go in unescorted, although a series of diversionary raids by Blenheims, Hurricanes and Spitfires would be laid on over Cherbourg to draw enemy fighters eastward.

In the event, the Halifaxes scored five direct hits on the *Scharnhorst*, although she was only slightly damaged. The cost to Bomber Command was high: five aircraft lost and the rest badly mauled. The flak barrage was intense and Me109s from *I./JG2* and a combat-ready operational training unit, the *Ergänzungsgruppe* of *JG53*, both based at la Rochelle, had been lying in wait for the unescorted heavies. Taffy's aircraft was hit by flak over the target and finished off by an Me109. He ditched in the North Sea off la Rochelle. All the crew survived, and were picked up by a French fishing boat. The Frenchmen were unable to help Williams and his crew to evade capture because the rescue had been seen by a German naval vessel, whose captain became somewhat covetous and ordered that Williams and his crew be transferred aboard. Once they were ashore the officers and NCOs were separated, the five Sergeants destined for the recently opened Stalag IIIE at Kirchhain, while Taffy Williams and Jim Ireton were sent to an army barracks outside Brest, where another officer POW who had also been involved in attempting to attack the *Scharnhorst* was now being held.

Pilot Officer William James Hunter, a navigator in Coastal Command, was generally known as "Red" because of his wavy ginger locks. A lean six-footer, he was Scottish on his father's side although he had been born in Wales, in 1920, where his father was a surface worker in the coal-mines. The family later moved to Coulsdon, near Croydon in Surrey, and Hunter won a scholar-ship to Caterham School, a public school whose fees stretched the family's finances. After leaving Caterham he became a bond bearer in the City of London and later a junior clerk in Barclay's Bank. When war seemed imminent he mounted his push-bike and presented himself at the local RAF recruiting station. The Recruiting Sergeant took his name and address and said: "Now, you run along home, sonny." But Hunter went back every Saturday for the next few weeks, until, one day, the Recruiting Sergeant finally took him seriously. He was given a medical examination, measured for a uniform and told to await orders. Several weeks later a letter dropped on the doormat ordering him to report for training.

Hunter was determined to become an officer and a pilot. However, there were too few aircraft for pilot training, so he trained as an Observer; the navigation exercises were done in Tiger Moths and the bombing practice in Fairey Battles. He was then posted to the OCU (Operational

Conversion Unit) at Chivenor, near Barnstaple, where he crewed up with Sergeants A J ("Pip") Appleby and E Taylor, who had trained as WOP/AGs. Shortly afterwards Hunter was commissioned. But they were still without a pilot. The first skipper they were supposed to team up with was posted to another squadron to join a crew there. The next one was taken off flying for medical reasons. They were beginning to wonder if they were jinxed when in April 1941 all three were posted to No217 Squadron, a No15 (GR) Group unit in Coastal Command. Stationed at Warmwell, in Dorset, at the outbreak of the war, the squadron had moved to St Eval, in Cornwall, a month later, its docile old Avro Ansons being replaced in May 1940 with the Bristol Beaufort MkI. Although the Beaufort was a torpedo aircraft as well as a bomber, few crews were fully trained in torpedo attacks, so No217 Squadron mainly carried out daylight bombing raids, mine-laying (otherwise known as "gardening") and anti-submarine patrols.

A few days before they arrived at St Eval the CO, Group Captain Guy Bolland, had been relieved of command for complaining that using Beauforts on daylight raids was suicidal. Bolland declared all his squadron's aircraft unserviceable and was called to Coastal Command HQ at Plymouth, where he told the RAF and RN top-brass that "sending young men to their deaths on useless missions is not on". Bolland was replaced by Wing Commander Leslie ("Dickie") Bower.

Now, at last, Hunter and his two WOP/AGs had a skipper, Acting Squadron Leader L E ("Digger") Collings, RAAF. Les Collings, a flight commander, had previously flown Lockheed Hudsons, and had already been at St Eval for some time before Hunter, Appleby and Taylor arrived. Leslie Collings was unusually quiet and well spoken for an Australian, his accent more like that of a southern Englishman. He wore a trim handlebar moustache, the ends of which he would twirl when deep in thought. When he was angry, however, his moustache would bristle and the air would become blue with the choicest Australian adjectives.

"Digger" Collings and his crew took part in sixteen ops, including a night bombing raid, along with thirty Armstrong Whitworth Whitleys from Bomber Command, on 23/24 July against the pocket-battleship *Scharnhorst*, which was harboured at la Pallice. The following day it was reported that the *Scharnhorst* had sneaked out of la Pallice overnight and would soon be in the Bay of Biscay, escorted by six destroyers as she made a dash northwards for Brest. As the most heavily defended port in the world, Brest was a much more desirable refuge for *Kapitän zur See* Kurt Hoffmann, the commander of the *Scharnhorst*, than the anchorage at la Pallice, and even though the damaged vessel could only make about 20 knots and would be exposed to attack from the air.

That afternoon six crews and a reserve crew from No217 Squadron were briefed to rendezvous at dawn on Friday, 25 July, with Beauforts from No22 Squadron and find and attack the *Scharnhorst*. The main attack was to be carried out by No22, who would go in with torpedoes, whilst No217, carrying semi-armour-piercing bombs (SAPs), made a diversionary attack on the destroyer escort from a height of 5,000 feet. In the event of the force becoming scattered or the torpedo-bombers failing to make the rendezvous, Collings' aircraft should attack the main target.

At the final briefing the next morning, the Station Intelligence Officer announced that instead of semi-armour-piercing bombs, Collings' Beaufort would be carrying land mines (known as magnums). The mines would make a much bigger bang than a few 250lb SAPs, but it meant that the diversionary attack would now have to take place from about 1,000 feet, as the MkIX bomb-sight could not achieve accuracy above that height. Another snag was that the mine was too big to fit properly into the bomb bay of a Beaufort, so the bomb doors had to be left slightly ajar, increasing drag and reducing airspeed. Hunter therefore had to revise his flight plans.

"Digger" Collings led No217's Beauforts off at 0530 hours. Once aloft, Hunter scanned the horizon with some anxiety. The gunmetal grey of dawn had given way to a yellowish sky, heralding a fine day. They needed good cloud cover for the task ahead, say 5/8th at around 3,000 feet. As they flew east the weather obligingly deteriorated, thick cloud and patchy mist hiding them from enemy aircraft. Unfortunately, the cloud also hid the Beauforts from each other; the force became scattered and there was no sign of the aircraft from No22 Squadron. Soon, visibility was down to a mile and thick banks of fog were rolling in from the north. Collings warned the crew to keep a close lookout. Seven minutes from ETA, and flying at about 500 feet, they kept plunging into patches of thick fog.

Only Collings found the target. Two minutes from ETA, Ted Taylor noticed some "large ripples" on the port side. Climbing a little and banking to port, Collings saw between the patches of fog a large, ominous wake, and ahead of it a huge dark form. It had to be the *Scharnhorst*. Collings decided to fly along the wake and take their quarry by surprise. So thick was the cloud that they didn't see the *Scharnhorst* until they were directly over it. There was no time to drop the mine, so Collings, without saying another word, went round again. As he was making the second run the Beaufort ran out of cloud cover and immediately encountered a storm of flak. The aircraft, receiving its first hit, shuddered. Smoke began to appear from the port engine and from behind the pilot's seat. Jim Hunter, lying in the nose, was still trying to give Collings bomb-aiming directions. But soon the Beaufort started to dive and veer too far to starboard, and the intercom went for a Burton. The port engine was over-revving and pouring forth billows of white smoke. Realising that he now had no chance of reaching the target, Collings, struggling with the control column, jettisoned the mine; perhaps then the Beaufort would regain height. It leapt a few feet into the air but just as quickly went back into its dive. It was now being hit repeatedly — by the 20mm and 105mm guns of the *Scharnhorst*, by 37mm flak, and by the light armament of the escort destroyer *Erich Steinbrink*.

There was a fire somewhere aft of the main spar, so Hunter grabbed a fire extinguisher and went to investigate. The W/OP's cabin had been badly hit and "Pip" Appleby was dead. There was nothing Hunter could do for him. Leaning over Appleby's corpse, he tried to send a signal to base, although the cabin was such a shambles that he very much doubted whether the radio was still working. Through the side window he could see the undercarriage wheel hanging down uselessly beneath the starboard engine. Although the engine was on fire, it still seemed to be working at full throttle.

Meanwhile, Collings, who was peppered with shrapnel, was still pulling back on the control column. The crippled aircraft was not far off the sea, although its descent was now very gentle. Part of the nose had been shot away and wind was howling through the fuselage. Hunter sat with his feet against the instrument panel and Ted Taylor was operating his gun-turret manually so that he could jump into the sea at the moment of ditching. Shortly before it hit the water, the aircraft was fired at again, this time by tracer from a Heinkel He115. Collings executed a textbook ditching, and in the eerie silence that followed made his way out through the hatch above the cockpit, with Hunter not far behind. Within seconds of them entering the sea Sergeant Taylor appeared from his turret, having apparently suffered no real harm. They had to leave Appleby in the aircraft. With its back broken it sank in no time, leaving not a trace. The three survivors trod water, inflated their Mae Wests and waited to be rescued.

In the distance they could see the battleship and some other craft; the *Scharnhorst* had her gangway down. The Heinkel He115 that had attacked them with tracer was circling overhead. After a while a largish ship started towards them. With a few deft movements and with the aid of a sailor wielding a boat-hook in the stern, they were towed some distance and then hauled aboard, very subdued and full of water. Once aboard they were stood beside what appeared to be a hot boiler and it was not until then that they realised just how cold they were. They were then stripped naked and their uniforms were taken away. In due course their uniforms were returned, a little scorched but dry.

Collings made the most senior looking of the Germans an offer. Would he be so kind as to take them across the Channel to England? If so, he would be handsomely rewarded by the British government. This suggestion elicited a stern rebuke, ending with: "For you the war is over."

When the war definitely was over, Jim Hunter discovered that the detachment from No22 Squadron had not even set out, and that in all probability there had been a recall signal, which Appleby had missed.

Collings was seriously wounded in both legs and Hunter was concussed by the impact of the ditching — one eye was knocked askew with the result that for some time it did not point in the same direction as the other. Following their transfer from ship to shore the three survivors were ushered into a lorry. Their destination was a large barracks, somewhere near Brest. Upon their arrival at the barracks Collings and Hunter were put in a large but gloomy room with a few iron bedsteads and barred windows. Taylor was taken away to join a couple of other NCOs — bomber types captured during a daylight raid on Brest two days earlier. Soon afterwards Collings was taken to Brest hospital to have the shrapnel removed from his legs.

Hunter lay back on the straw palliasse and looked at the ceiling, while the armed sentry outside the door paced up and down. For lunch he was given dry, sawdust-like bread and a bowl of tasteless soup; for tea, some hot liquid made from mint leaves and a slice of hard bread with a dollop of sweet red *ersatz* jam; for breakfast, more bread, and coffee made from acorns.

After a couple of days Hunter was joined by Acting Squadron Leader Williams and Pilot Officer Ireton, and they were transferred by lorry, train and lorry again to Biberach.

***

Paddy Denton, who before the war had served an apprenticeship with a company manufacturing marine and industrial diesel engines, had been in the Army Reserve before transferring to the RAF in 1940 and training as an observer, bomb-aimer and pilot. After a posting to Abingdon as second pilot he joined No102 (Ceylon) Squadron, based at Topcliffe and equipped with Whitleys. He was crewed up with Sergeants H G Benfield (pilot), W R Gibson (WOP/AG) and R V Harnett (rear-gunner). Denton doubled as second pilot and observer. On 25 July 1941, their usual Whitley was taken out of commission and they were given a replacement, which had come up from a Maintenance Repair Unit. The crew took her out on a forty-minute test flight, marvelling at her new bomb-sight but less happy about her sluggish performance and temperamental radio. Reporting afterwards to the Flight Commander, Denton and Benfield complained that the new aircraft was hardly airworthy, let alone operational, as nothing had been run in. The news appeared to depress him, but what he had to say in reply gave them a severe jolt. "I have news for you," he said. "One of the reasons she is not like the others is that she is much-modified, and you lucky little lot have been chosen to take her out tonight. The mods are simple: a bloody great bomb bay and the biggest bomb we have yet taken to Germany. So you can stuff your belly-aching and get on with it. See you at briefing."

The briefing and everything else that followed turned out to be routine — a raid by thirty Hampdens and twenty-five Whitleys on Hanover, with good cloud cover on the way in — except that for this trip they were given a new, inexperienced observer, Sergeant K S Carter. On the way to dispersal, and boarding their new aircraft, the crew felt distinctly uneasy. "It was strange, this sense which seemed to intrude upon us," Denton recalled years later, "not fear exactly, but a pervasive feeling of something not right." Indeed, nothing *was* right, as the gremlins played up from the start. As the first aircraft took off into the evening sky, Benfield awaiting his turn, Gibson, the radio-operator, reported that his set was duff. They called the ground staff and a radio mechanic boarded to carry out repairs. Two squadrons were airborne by the time the set was fixed. Finally Benfield was able to take off, but the rest of the Whitleys were well ahead and Benfield's crew were to all intents and purposes alone as they flew over Yorkshire, out across Flamborough Head and over the North Sea. Testing the rear guns, Harnett found they had jammed, and they passed the next few minutes in anxiety until he announced they had cleared and fired off a few bursts. When they reached altitude they hit another snag: on autopilot the Whitley see-sawed and they had to switch to manual, "which meant a lot of flying by the pilots".

Over Holland they hit the flak belt, but droned on, appearing to have escaped it. Then, without any apparent feel or shock of a hit, the Whitley shuddered and the cockpit filled up with smoke and acrid, white fumes. The instrument panel was obscured. Denton's eyes streamed and every breath became a choke. Benfield opened a sliding hatch and the cockpit cleared a little, though not enough. But at least they were able to see what the problem was. Flak had hit the port engine, the heater vent had come off the manifold, and glycol coolant was running down to form a gaseous mix in the heater intake. Benfield sent Gibson into the root of the wing to stop up the fumes with flying jackets and gash gear. Slowly the cockpit cleared, and they could see the instrument panel again. Flak was still coming up at them, but mercifully it missed.

Sergeant Benfield decided they should jettison their bomb load, and Denton went down into the front turret, switched on the bomb-sight and fused the bombs. As the bombs dropped, the aircraft surged upwards. Harnett got quite excited when the big one went off. It put out the blue searchlight and the other lights tailed away and left the Whitley in peace. Turning her to starboard and on a course for home, Benfield complained that she was flying heavily. Then she started to drop sharply. The port engine had locked solid in coarse pitch. Normally a Whitley could fly straight and level at about 4,000 feet on one engine, provided the dead one was free to windmill; however, with the dead port engine locked in coarse pitch this was impossible. After a quick discussion he and Denton decided they would rather try to reach England than bale out. At worst they could ditch in the North Sea and take to their dinghy. But at this point the gremlins played another joke. Gibson, the WOP/AG, tapped Denton on the shoulder and reported: "Radio gone." That meant no intercom. So any messages had to be passed verbally, involving a long crawl down the fuselage to Harnett in the aft turret.

With the drag on the port side and the starboard engine flogging its guts out the Whitley was flying like a crab and losing height relentlessly. After what seemed an age, Carter piped up suddenly: "We should be over the coast, captain." There was a thin layer of cloud below, so they couldn't see, but the sense of relief was quite something.

It didn't last long. As they broke cloud at about four hundred feet they saw not sea but land, and that, worse still, they were approaching a night-fighter aerodrome. (It was outside Maurik, inland from Amsterdam.) The Germans must have thought they were a friendly aircraft coming in to land, for suddenly the runway lights and floodlights came on, and the Whitley flew over with its starboard engine screaming in fine pitch. It had nearly cleared the aerodrome when the Germans realised their mistake and threw up a heavy barrage. The Whitley was flying too low for the heavy stuff to be effective, but the light fireworks seemed pretty dense. Not that it made much difference, as the aircraft was barely under control. Denton was by then lying on the steps to the front turret holding Benfield's feet on the rudder pedal. As they hit the ground Denton saw before them — just for an instant — a grove of trees. "Luckily for us, as we found out later, they turned out to be young poplar saplings which acted like a shock absorber and to a great extent minimised the impetus of the crash. Otherwise we would have been in for a deep fry or a quick death." Then all went black.

Denton awoke to find himself in the front turret, unable to see out of one eye, which was covered in blood. His mind was not at its best and he thought being in the turret was "a bit rum", so he went back to the pilot's seat. This did not offer much in the way of solace, as the aircraft was gently burning. He decided to get out, but found that the front and emergency hatches were jammed. Sitting alone in the burning aircraft he tried to apply some detailed logic to the situation. *If I am here, where are the others, and how did they get out? Through the main hatchway and down the fuselage.* To get there he had to go straight into the fire, which was glowing well in the tunnel through which he had to crawl. It was a question of staying and frying, or frying as he tried to escape, and the latter course was the least unpromising. He started to crawl backwards through the tunnel. However, he was still wearing his helmet with its intercom lead dangling and, in the middle of the tunnel and the flames, he found he was caught by his head. To discover what was wrong, he had to inch forward with his legs still in the tunnel, which was warming up nicely. The Whitley had slatted panels to stiffen the floor and the lead had neatly jammed itself between the slats. He let the strap in his helmet go and resumed his backwards crawl. As he did so he became acutely aware that the top of the tunnel was the bridging fuel tank between the wing-tanks.

One-hundred-octane fuel was pretty combustible and this was no place to dilly-dally. His movements toward the main hatch were as rapid as possible in the circumstances, but once there he found to his disappointment that this hatch, too, was jammed. Logic again: *They must have got out somehow.* He went further aft until, flaming a little, he fell out of the fuselage, into a ditch and onto some of the crew.

Whereupon the Whitley's tanks exploded, the woods caught fire, and the ammunition belts for the rear turret, which stretched down the fuselage, ignited, screeched over the men skulking in the ditch and nearly blew their heads off. When the drama had subsided, Benfield turned to

Denton and remarked: "My God, you weren't meant to die in an aeroplane. What the hell were you doing?" As Denton tried to explain, it dawned on them that Harnett was missing, and that their Whitley was without its tail-plane and rear turret. By now the woods were fairly crackling with flames and they could feel the glow of the fire on their faces. The thought struck them that Harnett might still be in there. They went round the woods and, at the far end, found him hanging upside down in his straps in the turret. They asked him why he didn't get out and he replied that if he released his straps he would fall and break his bloody neck — did they take him for a fool?

We got him out but he did not appear overly grateful, in fact complained that we had been rather a long time coming...Actually, to see his rather solemn and lugubrious face hanging suspended in his straps, illuminated by flames, was one and perhaps the first of many funny moments of what turned out to be an interesting war.

However, levity must end, and as by this time we were clearly visible for some distance against the burning aircraft and wood, it seemed discreet to make a move. Across the field was a shadowy hedge so we got there — somewhat gradually as by this time I was feeling a little below par...my head and nose were bleeding quite a lot and in the shunt I had lost my left boot. Most of my left-side trouser-leg and socks had apparently been burnt away. A small sense of singeing was becoming noticeable...

We found the hedge and had a short period of detente. Overhead we could hear but not see the early boys going homewards. It gave an intense feeling of isolation. We moved on for some way and came across a farmhouse. The crash had obviously caused some alarm and despondency because, as we came close, a door opened and an extraordinarily pretty girl came out to us. She gave us some milk to drink, which was the finest thing I have ever tasted.

The farm was isolated and she pointed us to a village where there were more people who, she said, could between them hide us and help us.

So once again we trudged off. After about three-quarters of a mile, to our surprise and discomfort, two Germans emerged in the dawning light from behind a wall where they had been keeping quietly out of trouble. Then the old rigmarole of revolver or whatever: *"Hände hoch"*, and so on. So, disconsolately, we were marched into the village and to the Mayor's Parlour, which was also German HQ for the village. Everyone was frightfully embarrassed and formal until the Mayor arrived. He was a jovial soul and most hospitable, offering us slices of cheese, and he produced a box of cigars, which he formally offered to us. Then, turning his back on us and facing the Germans, [he] selected one for himself and deliberately slapped the lid of the box shut.

At this point there was a great kerfuffle of vehicles outside and three Luftwaffe characters burst in. The top brass was a *Hauptmann* and clearly overcome with adrenalin excitement. He kept claiming that his lot had shot us down and that he had been to the scene of the wreckage to assure himself of the fact. It was, I think, at this point, that I decided I would not speak German again until the war was over. This proved to be a useful decision.

He kept shouting at us and of course we stayed with the system of name, rank and number. Shortly after, a Dutch interpreter was brought in. He was clearly on our side, so there was no difficulty in explaining that our obligation was to give name, rank and number and nothing else. This did little to please the *Hauptmann* who promptly adopted the German drill of shouting louder and spitting a little. I found this to be a characteristic of the Germans. It seemed to give them a sense of satisfaction although, so far as I could judge, never contributed very much to the solution of any problem.

He then played his trump card. Quite quietly, through the interpreter, we were told that he had found a circular object with the words, as he pronounced them, ETLEEN GLEEKOL. This, he seemed to think, was a new secret weapon: chemical warfare perhaps?

As I was the only officer in the aircrew the Germans naturally thought that I was the Captain of the aircraft, which was not the case... Therefore all the questions were addressed to me.

In response to the query about our Merlin coolant I said that as far as I was aware it was a liquid much used in Southern Ireland as a wood preservative and couldn't understand why he should have found it as our aircraft was made of metal. This reply seemed to baffle the chap a bit as he kept shaking his head and saying "Etleen Gleekol" quietly to himself, while looking rather strangely at me and the others.

This charade went on for a short while and then another truck drew up outside and within minutes we were lobbed somewhat unceremoniously aboard before the sympathetic eyes of the assembled villagers. The canvas tilts came down and off we set accompanied by four Luftwaffe guards. They behaved extremely well and gave us cigarettes from time to time, although they were discourteous enough to keep pointing guns in a very hostile fashion, which left us little doubt as to their intentions in the event of our making any provocative step. Eventually this became rather dull so we mostly had a bit of a kip. There was the most fearful row at some toll bridge or other which we had to cross and no one was prepared to shell out for the vehicle or passengers which included us. The toll keeper, needless to say, was Dutch and thoroughly enjoyed exercising his authority, which was indisputable. Eventually the matter was settled and we rumbled on.

After an hour or more it was evident that we were in a town. Horns and general traffic noises, stop, start, stop and on again.

We turned, reversed and finally stopped. The back flaps were opened and all we could see were some iron gates, heavily wrought. Through them we went, turned left and clang, clang into individual cells. There seemed little to be done so I lay down on the rather unsavoury bunk and decided that a snooze would be a good thing.

How long this lasted I can't tell because I was woken by a banging of doors and keys and removed sharply left and then right down a corridor to a largish room with one barred window high up on the top left and a bunk, a chair, whitewashed walls and nothing else. All a bit queer. I decided, when left almost immediately alone, to continue my kip.

Then the most interesting part started as a very well-turned-out bloke in the uniform of the International Red Cross came in and started talking in accented but perfectly fluent English. Very sympathetic. "Head OK? Not too badly burnt? What bad luck, old chap. I'm here, of course, to help you and your family. Where are you from, so that I can tell them? What squadron, so that I can get a message? By the way, where were you going to, what aircraft?" Smooth as a piece of silk. But a fearful blunder. My mother always smoked Gold Flake and he produced a packet. They were a very good resemblance but somehow the mere gesture and the memory of them triggered something off. So I did the old routine: name, rank and number. I thought he was going to burst into tears.

Didn't I trust him? He was only there to help. "Come on old chap." I said I was rather tired and could we talk again later. This pantomime went on for a few days at intervals of hours, sometimes minutes, during any period of twenty-four hours. He seemed to get a bit fractious towards the end and actually confessed that he knew my blasted name, rank and number and don't blame him if my whereabouts didn't reach my nearest and dearest and the Squadron.

I felt rather sorry for this forlorn figure so pretended to break down on the promise that he would help me. To this, of course, he agreed. I told him that the aircraft was a Hartford, powered by the new Wright Whitworth Cyclone engines and that our destination was Cologne. Quite fascinating to see this basically nice chap solemnly writing all this bull down in his little book with a look of childish satisfaction on his face.

Shortly after this we were again loaded into a truck with Luftwaffe guards and set off. This time, instead of leaving by the wrought-iron gates, we were taken out on the other side of the building where a narrow causeway ran alongside the canal. We turned left over a bridge and then along a road of pavé. After a few miles, as the back flap was open, we were most encouraged to see a very pretty girl on a bicycle wearing a pink polka dot frock. It was quite evident that her legs stretched up to her shoulders. Very good for morale.

The Goons behaved impeccably, giving us the odd cigarette and almost creating a feeling of camaraderie.

After some miles the lorry stopped at a minor railway station and they alighted from the lorry and were escorted to a third-class railway carriage. This was the beginning of a journey that would eventually take Denton to Biberach and Oflag VB. He was surprised and disappointed, on the way there, to see how little damage Bomber Command had done at this stage of the war, despite fairly strenuous efforts. His guards pointed out Cologne Cathedral in all its grandeur.

> There was a great temptation to tell them that in our book this did not constitute an industrial target. I decided not to.
>
> At the odd station where we stopped, the populace indicated quite forcibly that we did not rate too highly in their popularity ratings. *Terrorflieger, Bomber, Kindermörder*, and other such phrases came to their lips and our ears. We maintained a dignified silence and merely contracted British phlegm and a look of utter contempt. I don't think that this attitude endeared us to them particularly.

Some time later, at a railway siding, Denton was separated from his crew and put aboard a carriage with wooden seats. After a long, hot journey southward he arrived, next day, at Oflag VB.

He had not been expected and was taken to the guards' quarters and locked in for several hours. An English private was, for some odd reason, sent to see if he was okay and give him some *ersatz* coffee. Denton knew that a friend of his from pre-war days had been bagged at Dunkirk, and asked the soldier if anyone of his name was in the camp. The answer was "yes". Some hours later, when he was allowed into the camp proper, he "was met by one mate and some remembered names".

> The first question startled me. "Are we mad?" To this I could honestly answer that the one I knew was no nuttier than when I had known him previously. Then there was: "When were you last in England?" "What's going on?" "What happened to you?" "What happened to your clothes?" All great fun and an enormous relief and relaxation for us all.

The weather in southern Germany was sunny that July, warm enough for them to lie down in the recreation ground and contemplate the sky. From Biberach you could even see the Swiss Alps, their snow-covered peaks glinting in the sun.

Such respite could, however, be only short-lived. The Germans soon realised that the aircrew officers had been sent to Biberach in error. Denton had been there only two days when on 31 July he, Williams, Edwards, Hunter and Ireton were told to pack their belongings immediately, as they were being moved out forthwith. None of the prisoners knew their destination, and the guards wouldn't tell them. Denton considered this "gross incompetence and most aggravating", Packing was easy: they had nothing. Within minutes they were boarding a tired-looking lorry, which conveyed them to a train in a goods siding. The trio were now *en route* to Dulag Luft, to which they should have been sent in the first place, and would arrive there on Friday, 1 August. On Sunday, 3 August, they would be purged to Oflag XC, reaching that camp on Monday, 4 August.

On arrival at Dulag Luft they were immediately stripped of their uniforms and given a shower. Their uniforms were then returned and they were marched to the cell block for interrogation. Paddy Denton was again offered a Gold Flake. When the interrogator departed, he left the packet "as a gesture of goodwill". After about eighteen hours Denton was escorted to the transit camp.

> It was here that I first came into contact with German service soap. The scented stuff almost turned my stomach, it was so sweet and yet somehow quite corruptly evil. I don't know why. Like an old tart trying to disguise her BO with scent. Repulsive. Never forget how it permeated everything.
>
> The transit camp was an almost frightening experience as it was filled with recently shot down Royal Air Force personnel. The cross-questioning that went on put any German interrogation into the pale. Luckily I found one friend there who had been with me in England and Canada, so eventually I was accepted as genuine.

In the main compound they were fed reasonably well from Red Cross parcels, which went into a communal pool and were distributed as meals from the "canteen". The *Abwehr*-appointed commandant, Major Theo Rumpel let it be known that they would be well treated if they behaved themselves. The war, he said, would soon be over anyway so there was absolutely no point in trying to escape. Furthermore, they might well have the chance to ski in the winter — and after the war was over the British and the Germans would all be playing football and cricket together!

***

Meanwhile, the authorities had overlooked Jack Best, Dickie Edge, Bill Goldfinch and Henry Lamond, who would remain at Biberach for another two months.

During that time, the Army officers finished converting one of the huts into a theatre and put on some quite spectacular productions, including Arnold Ridley's classic *The Ghost Train*, for which they built a machine out of wood and canvas so as to re-create the noise of wind and rain, and a lavish musical in which some of the Maori prisoners dressed up — very convincingly — as Polynesian women.

By the end of August two Army officers had already made a home run from Oflag VB. On Saturday, 13 September another twenty-six broke out, four of them making it to Switzerland. Twelve days later all the Navy and RAF officers were removed, the former going to Marlag und Milag Nord, at Westertimke near Tarmstedt, and the latter arriving at Dulag Luft on Saturday, 27 September. From there the four RAF officers were sent to Barth.

Chapter Two

The "*Ex-Kreta*" of Lübeck

Oflag XC, Lübeck, July–August 1941

According to German records, the prisoner of war camp at Lübeck, Oflag XC, had been opened on 1 June 1942, although evidence suggests that it did not in fact open until Tuesday, 29 July. It was staffed — once again — by the Army. Lübeck, in the province of Schleswig-Holstein and about thirty kilometres from the Baltic coast, was an old German Hanse town, of relatively minor industrial importance, known chiefly for the Mediæval houses that hugged each other in the town centre. It was only lightly defended by the Germans, but because it was near the coast and, according to "Bomber" Harris, built "more like a fire-lighter than a human habitation", from February 1942 it would be on Bomber Command's list of targets which aircrew could find easily and utterly destroy, although in the event it was bombed less often than Harris would have wished and than legend has had it. Oflag XC itself had recently been an artillery barracks, whose former inhabitants were now at the Russian front. It was spacious, with twelve white-painted brick huts in which there were — unusually at that stage of the war — flushing lavatories. Washing troughs, with running water, stood in the open. Otherwise its layout was typical — the usual double barbed-wire fence, sentry towers and warning rail — and as bare as a billiard-table. But where it differed most from previous POW camps was in the way it was run. With the exception of Oflag XXIBand Oflag XXIB (the latter opened in September 1942), it was the worst camp in which Allied aircrew officers were contained up to the time aircrew camps were evacuated to escape the Russian advance in January 1945. It was also one of the most crowded. Although it held British POWs for only nine weeks, the Germans crammed in a record number of purges, not only RAF and Fleet Air Arm, but also — and mainly — Army.

The aircrew officers at Lübeck fell into four main groups: officers captured in Crete and sent to Lübeck from Dulag 185 at Salonika; the eighteen from Oflag VIIC; a party of thirty from Stalag Luft I who arrived on Friday, 8 August, 1941; and new prisoners collected at Dulag Luft in 1941 who were being sent to Lübeck right up to its closure that October. The Dulag Luft purges arrived on 4, 11 and 25 August; on 8, 12 and 21 September; and on 5 October. Occasionally, sick and wounded officers arrived from Obermassfeld, although most were kept at *Lazarett* IXC until the camp at Warburg was opened to British and Commonwealth POWs in September.

The first arrivals, a party of thirteen RAF officers from Salonika, reached Oflag XC the day it was opened. They were Acting Wing Commander A J Trumble; Squadron Leader C H Deakin (Southern Rhodesian); Acting Squadron Leader P Mason; Flight Lieutenants D R S Bevan-John, C H Fry DFC, R Garside, C R C Howlett and E H Lewis-Dale; Flying Officers T F C Churcher, C N Dilly RAFVR and P J Valachos DFC; and Pilot Officers F P N Dyer and R D May. All had been captured on Crete.

Anthony John Trumble, who in June 1939 had become the envy of other RAF boys by marrying a beautiful model, had flown the ill-fated Boulton & Paul Defiants in the Battle of Britain, and after a series of postings was in March 1941 appointed to HQ Middle East (Air Staff Plans), known as "Z" Wing. The Germans had mined the Suez Canal and Churchill wanted it cleared "at all costs". Based in Crete, "Z" Wing was to amplify the Middle East Air Force (MEAF) in preparation for the capture of the island of Skarpanton. From there the RAF was to attack the Italian base on Rhodes.

Tony Trumble was put in charge of planning and set-up operations at RAF Heraklion, the only modern aerodrome on Crete. However, when the Germans invaded the Balkans and Greece, Air Chief Marshal Sir Arthur Longmore, C-in-C MEAF, called off the Rhodes operation. British personnel from Greece were to be evacuated through Crete, and Trumble was given the job, as Acting Wing Commander (unpaid), of re-organising landing grounds for Hurricanes. He also became effectively station officer at Heraklion.

On the face of it, the RAF and Royal Navy Fleet Air Arm presence on Crete was impressive. HQ Creforce, at Canea, had twenty-three Naval personnel and ninety-five RAF, including signals officers. Based at Heraklion were No220 Air Ministry Experimental Station (AMES), with fifty-one personnel, and No112 Squadron, with 141 men. At RAF Maleme there were No252 AMES, with fifty-six men; Nos 30 and 33 Squadrons, with 229 men; and No805 Fleet Air Arm Squadron, with fifty-five men. At Suda Bay there were a further thirty-six RAF officers and other ranks. In all, 686 men of the Air Ministry, the Admiralty, the RAF and the RN were based on Crete, and before long it would be overrun with even more from Greece.

The Air Force contingent at Heraklion included Flight Lieutenants Charles Horace Fry and Ronald Garside, Flying Officers R J Bennett and T Hutton, and Pilot Officer L L Bartley, all fighter pilots on No112 Squadron, originally formed during the Great War, disbanded in 1919, and re-formed again on 16 May 1939 for service in the Middle East; and on Trumble's staff, Peter John Valachos, and two Air Ministry works branch civil engineers, "Deak" Deakin and Peter Mason, put in uniform for the war. Deakin and Mason had been sent to Crete for airfield work, and had vast amounts of money with which to employ local labour.

Charles Fry, an Australian, had led a flight of four No112 Squadron Gladiators from Egypt in December 1940 to join No80 Squadron in Greece. As more Gladiator reinforcements arrived in January, Fry took command of "B" Flight and, later, the seven aircraft of "C" Flight. When Greece was evacuated, the No112 Squadron detachment was ordered to fly to an airfield being prepared at Pediada Kastelli, west of Maleme. But the airfield was not ready. Instead, the squadron established itself at Heraklion. By now only six of its fourteen Gladiators were serviceable, and the pilots eagerly awaited re-equipment with new Hurricanes. In the meantime, HQ ordered one flight back to Egypt. The Flight Commanders decided the issue on the flick of the coin. "A" Flight won, and the eight pilots took off, leaving ten pilots at Heraklion under Charles Fry. Their numbers were reinforced some days later by the arrival of six new pilots from No1430 Flight, recently transferred from North Africa. Among them were Flight Lieutenant Ron Garside and Flying Officer Thomas Hutton.

Eventually two new Hurricanes arrived, but only three pilots had flown the type before and of them only Fry had any real experience. On Friday, 16 May thirty Me110s of II/ZG26 approached Heraklion, lining up for a strafing attack, and the two Hurricanes and three Gladiators were ordered up to intercept. Fry aimed for a flight of eight Messerschmitts flying at 6,000 feet and managed to bounce one of them, piloted by *Unteroffizier* Erhard Witzke of *Nr4 Staffel*. However, as Fry broke away, Witzke's gunner, *Feldwebel* Karl Reinhardt, got in an accurate burst which hit the Hurricane's engine. It started streaming glycol, and Fry had to bale out. As he did so, he collided with the tail-plane, which knocked him senseless. Luckily his parachute deployed, and when he came to he found he had landed three miles from the airfield with a badly bruised chest. Fry, who had become one of the highest-scoring pilots in the campaigns in Greece and Crete, was taken off ops and attached to the ground staff. So, as aircraft losses mounted, were Garside, Hutton and other aircrew from No112 Squadron.

Of Trumble's permanent staff, Deakin was a Southern Rhodesian and Peter Valachos a Canadian of Greek descent who had learned to fly at the local aero club near his native Brantford, Ontario, and joined the RAF in 1938. The war, however, caught him by surprise. Writing to his parents from England in August 1938 he asserted that there would be no war in Europe "for ten years". He had even arranged to return to Canada in 1942 to become a commercial pilot. Surprised or not, he went on to complete thirty ops on Wellingtons with No99 Squadron (No3 Group), then based at Newmarket in Suffolk, and to earn a Mention in Dispatches and a DFC in 1940. He then went to Malta and flew another ten ops with No148 Squadron, another Wellington outfit. It always struck him as ironic that after all that he should be captured on the ground. He was in Crete largely through his own impatience. "Tour-expired", he had been assigned a desk job at MEAF HQ Cairo, but requested a posting to HQ Athens, which he preferred because of his Greek extraction. Meanwhile, he was rested for three months. Towards the end he became bored and asked for something to do until his next assignment came up. So he was sent to Crete to plan air defences at RAF Heraklion. Together, the Army and the RAF did a good job on the ground defences — the airfield was protected by well-placed Bofors guns and by the 14th Brigade of the Black Watch, which, with reinforcements, had a strength of more than 8,000 — and many of the "aircraft" were, in fact, dummies.

Another of those at Heraklion was Colin Noel Dilly. He had flown RE8s and DH9s with the Royal Naval Air Service in the Great War and had afterwards been a commercial artist, well known for his evocative travel posters depicting the delights of ocean liners and steam trains. In 1939 he was commissioned in the RAFVR and served as codes and cyphers officer in Egypt and Greece before being posted, at the age of forty-one, to Crete. He was based in the HQ cave near the Heraklion airfield perimeter, along with another cyphers officer, Charles Robert Compton Howlett.

On Monday, 19 May, Tony Trumble received a confidential message from HQ Middle East asking him to "establish with all speed" a landing strip for Hurricanes on the most southern part of Crete possible, and have it stocked with aviation fuel and ammunition. Deakin and Mason were building an airfield south-east of Heraklion, in the middle of the island, but this was too far north for Hurricanes operating from Egypt and needing to refuel and re-arm.

On the night of 19/20 May, Stukas dive-bombed Crete heavily. Heraklion aerodrome was subjected to a three-hour assault, with every bomb finding its target: the Bofors guns and the Black Watch surrounding the airfield perimeter. Trumble, Dilly and Howlett took shelter in the HQ cave, with Steele, another cyphers officer, also sleeping there for safety. Leaving the cave at 0805 hours, they were joined near Heraklion by an off-duty pilot, Flying Officer R J Bennett of No112 Squadron. Despite the previous night's bombing and warnings that an attack might occur, they had no reason to suspect, recorded Dilly, that an invasion was imminent — although later on at Warburg he learned from some men of the Black Watch, who had been based in another HQ cave fifty yards from his, that they knew an attack was expected on Tuesday, 20 May, as did another RAF officer, Flight Lieutenant F H Babcock, based at Maleme. Yet Creforce headquarters at Canea, which had a direct line to Cairo, had not informed the RAF codes and cyphers officers.

Construction work on the airfield at Heraklion was now abandoned, and Trumble set off by car to look at a site at Messaras Plain that had been found by either Deakin or Mason. He took Colin Dilly with him, along with his cypher gear. A radio operator and other equipment would follow later. They established a temporary RAF HQ in an old church in an olive grove near the camp of the Argyll and Sutherland Highlanders, not far from Ay Dehka, north of the Messaras site. The Argylls, noted Dilly, were "in evident state of readiness and anticipation". Yet that afternoon, "other ranks" from the aerodrome at Heraklion were allowed into town, provided they were armed; "so it appears," recorded Dilly, "no one there expecting anything, and evidently no messages received up to say 2pm. F/Lt Cooper assumed duties as station c/o in Trumble's absence."

Then the airborne invasion commenced, wave after wave of gliders and Ju52s swarming over the island and disgorging their cargoes of assault troops. Deakin, on his way to Canea, hadn't even reached Retimo when he was stopped and told the place was in the hands of the Jerries. He returned to Heraklion to find it under fire.

The first objective of the German parachutists, XI Air Corps, had been to take serviceable airfields — Maleme, Retimo and Heraklion. The capture of Heraklion was entrusted to *Oberst* Bruno Bräuer, commanding No1 Parachute Regiment, reinforced by a battalion from No2 Parachute Regiment and a further two companies — a total of 2,600 men. Of these, II Battalion was to attack the airfield from both sides, while another would storm the harbour from the west.

However, it was to be a costly victory for the Germans. The drop took more than three hours, many of the parachutists falling into a murderous barrage from the defenders. Within an hour II Battalion was nearly wiped out — twelve officers and three hundred men killed, and another eight officers and one hundred men wounded. By nightfall more than half the Germans who had invaded Crete were dead. Nevertheless, the attack continued at dawn, but by the following dawn, Thursday the 22nd, the parachutists had been ordered simply to prevent the Allies from using the airfield.

On Monday, 26 May, the airfield at Messaras Plain, equipped with fuel and re-arming facilities, was declared open — although, recorded Dilly, "on arrival of Deakin and Mason, Trumble refused to show them [the] selected site, giving one the impression that they had already been given particulars of its situation". After lunch they went on for another four or five miles without looking at any sites, and at about 1430 hours started back towards Heraklion. They had not gone far before they found themselves under attack from enemy aircraft flying at about eight hundred feet. Abandoning the car, they took cover beneath the trees and waited for the aircraft to finish making their pass. Proceeding on their way, they were attacked again in the hills to the north-east of Ay Dehka and again had to take cover. Attacked a third time a mile or two further on, they were hurriedly pulling in to take cover when their car hit a swampy patch. It took them an hour to push the car back on to firm ground, during which time they once again came under aerial attack. Eventually they crossed over a hilly ridge and, at about 1630 hours, within sight of Heraklion,

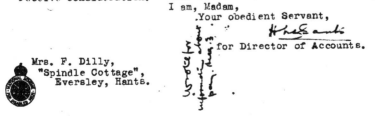

Madam,

I am directed to refer to this department's letter of 25th June 1941, and to the further report of which you have been advised, that your husband is a prisoner of war, and to state that in consequence temporary allowance cannot continue in issue to you.

While your husband is a prisoner of war, issue of his Royal Air Force pay will be made to his bank account monthly in arrear by the Royal Air Force Agents as from the date of previous suspension, subject to deduction of the amounts paid to you in respect of temporary allowance to 31st July 1941, and to regular deductions at the rate of £5.8.0d. a month, which are being made from the pay of prisoners of war of the rank of Flying Officer in German hands, in respect of sums understood to be in issue by the German Government. In addition married allowance at the appropriate rate will be issued to his banking account monthly in arrear by the Senior Accountant Officer, Station Accounts Section, No. 1 Royal Air Force Depot, Uxbridge, Middlesex.

I am to explain that it is the responsibility of an officer to arrange either through his bankers or otherwise for the supply of funds to his family during his absence on service, and if such arrangements were made by your husband you should have no difficulty in obtaining funds. If, however, you should experience difficulty in this connection it is requested that you will communicate with this department as soon as possible in order that the matter may receive consideration. Your son's birth certificate is enclosed.

I am, Madam,

Your obedient Servant,

for Director of Accounts.

Mrs. F. Dilly,
"Spindle Cottage",
Eversley, Hants.

Fig 4. Letter from Air Ministry sent to Flying Officer Colin Dilly's wife after he had been captured, explaining the pay procedure for the families of POWs

stopped by the roadside for an hour to brew up. As they sat there they saw an RAF lorry carrying aviation fuel coming towards them, towing another lorry. The driver leaned out and told them he had been bombed just outside Heraklion, that German parachutists had landed and that all avenues of retreat had been cut off. So back to Ay Dehka they went, holing up in their temporary HQ in the church ruins.

Tony Trumble could recall only one Hurricane landing at Messaras before Crete was overrun by the enemy. "We had a primitive radio link from here to HQ Middle East and had told them of the location of the strip and the facilities available."

The stalemate at Heraklion continued until Tuesday, 27 May when, following the fall of Suda and Canea to the Germans, General Bernard Freyburg, C-in-C Crete, ordered his troops to evacuate the island. Only sixty-four of the RAF personnel at Heraklion were evacuated. Those left defending Heraklion had no choice but to surrender. Trumble and his party took refuge high in the mountains at Ay Galene, but eventually ran out of food. They were surrounded by German parachutists and captured on Friday, 6 June. Also bagged with Trumble's party were the three No112 Squadron pilots (Fry, Garside and Hutton), and Pilot Officer A J C Hamilton of No274 Squadron, who had force-landed at Heraklion on 25 May. (Bartley and Bennett reached the south coast and were evacuated.) Peter Valachos remembers the moment of capture well. "A German officer walked up to me and said: 'May I have your pistol, please?' " The following day they were driven away in their own vehicles, brand-new Ford trucks, which the Germans had captured. For two days they were held in the Helvitia Hotel in Heraklion, and on Monday, 9 June, were force-marched to Canea — a distance of some eighty miles — to the agricultural prison at Ay Canea. This was "a sort of American jail," recalls Trumble, "and quite new". They arrived there on Friday, 13 June, "tired and hungry — our guards had been relieved every few hours and went by truck until the next bout of escort duty was due, while we staggered on".

Trumble's party was now minus Flying Officer Hutton and Pilot Officer Hamilton. Tom Hutton would arrive in Germany later and meet Trumble again at Warburg, whilst Hamilton would wind up temporarily at Spangenberg before reaching Oflag VIB. But in addition there were Flight Lieutenants David Richard Spencer Bevan-John and E H Lewis-Dale, an assistant civil engineer with the Air Ministry Works Staff, who had been captured at Maleme on 25 May; Pilot Officer F P N Dyer, also rounded up on 6 June; and finally Flying Officer Churcher and Pilot Officer May.

Thomas Frederick Collie Churcher and Roderic Douglas May had been pilot and observer in No45 Squadron, another Great War unit that had been disbanded in 1919 only to be re-formed later. However, unlike No112 Squadron, No45 had been re-formed as early as 1 April 1921 at Helwan in Egypt as a heavy-bomber squadron, eventually flying Bristol Blenheims from Fuka. On Monday, 26 May 1941, six Blenheims, drawn equally from Nos 45 and 55 Squadrons, had been briefed to make a dusk attack on Maleme. Take-off was scheduled for 1700 hours. In the meantime, however, two Hurricanes from No274 Squadron, Gerawla, had been sent out to strafe the airfield. They had returned safely, but when the Blenheims reached the target they found the defences alerted, and the No45 Squadron Blenheims, led by Tom Churcher, were intercepted by patrolling Me109s of 6/JG77. The *Staffel* leader, *Oberleutnant* Walter Höckner, hit one Blenheim, which caught fire, killing all the crew. He then turned his attention to Churcher's aircraft, causing severe damage. Churcher and his crew baled out, and he and his observer, Rod May, were captured by German parachute troops as soon as they hit the ground. (The gunner, Sergeant H G Langrish, evaded capture, eventually reaching the south coast where he was picked up by a British destroyer. The third Blenheim from No45, flown by Pilot Officer J Robinson, got out to sea without a scratch, only to run out of fuel over the desert.)

On Sunday, 15 June Trumble's party was taken by lorry to Maleme airfield and at 1300 hours put aboard a Ju52 (number IZ-AS). During the flight, Howlett, Dilly and Trumble were forced to sit over the hatch while a burly Luftwaffe NCO sat opposite with his hand on the lever. He had orders to open the hatch if they moved. One hour and thirty-five minutes later they landed at Megara airport, outside Athens, where they were interrogated. When Lewis-Dale was questioned, he was shown the cyphers and documents that the Germans had captured. Again the dead hand of

HQ Canea was revealed: none of the cyphers had shown any inkling that Crete was about to be invaded.

From Athens they were escorted to the old Greek barracks in the suburb of Guidi, where they were visited by representatives of the Greek Red Cross — but they could only offer sympathy. Trumble's party remained at Guidi until Sunday, 22 June when they were put on a train of cattle-trucks, which eventually began to clank and rattle slowly in a northerly direction. It was a long journey. On the night of Monday, 23 June, the train stopped at Lárisa, and on Tuesday, 24 June (Tony Trumble's second wedding anniversary), they arrived at Dulag 185, Salonika — the same ghastly hole to which Jack Best, Dickie Edge, Bill Goldfinch and Henry Lamond had been taken. At night Trumble's party slept with hundreds of other prisoners on the road running through the camp, Trumble sharing his greatcoat with Acting Squadron Leader Aidan Crawley, who had been captured in North Africa. It was a bad time for Trumble, who on Saturday, 19 July suffered a bout of malaria. On Tuesday, 22 July his party were put on board a cattle-truck, and endured a long journey through Yugoslavia, Hungary, Austria and Germany. On the way, Trumble contracted dysentery. Finally, on Tuesday, 29 July, they arrived at Lübeck, without having gone first to Dulag Luft. "As the officers with me in Crete were captured on the ground wearing khaki tropical shirts and shorts with only rank stripes," suggests Trumble, "I think the Germans thought we were Army, and for that reason we were sent directly to Oflag XC without being interrogated at Dulag Luft."

At Lübeck, the German Medical Officer took Trumble to the sick quarters, gave him some tablets for his dysentery, and subjected him to several jabs in the backside for his malaria. The latter brought tears of pain to his eyes, but while he was occasionally to get dysentery again, the malaria recurred only once.

For two days, they were the only prisoners in the camp. Although there were twelve blocks, each containing eight rooms on either side of a central corridor, the prisoners were squeezed into one room in Barrack No4. The rooms measured sixteen feet by twelve by ten feet high and were furnished with six — and sometimes ten — two-tiered wooden bunks, with palliasses and pillowcases resting on wooden slats. In each room was an iron or tiled stove burning coal briquettes. The only other furniture consisted of a wooden table and six stools, which meant that if six officers sat at the table the other six had to sit or lie on their bunks.

On the night of Thursday, 31 July, a gaunt- and desperate-looking mass of 600 Army officers arrived from Crete, having travelled in cattle-trucks by way of Salonika, Scopia, Agram (Zagreb), Marburg and Leipzig. After being deloused, finger-printed and issued with their POW identity discs, they were paraded in front of the commandant. This was the first time the RAF contingent had seen him.

Oberstleutnant Freiherr von Wachtmeister was a cadaverous, cropped Army reservist aged seventy-four, whose son, it was claimed had been killed on the Western Front in the Great War. He thus had an abiding hatred for the British, and openly told them that as far as he was concerned the Geneva Convention had been "drawn up by a load of old women" and that he had no intention of observing it. Inspecting the faces of the new arrivals, he asked if any of them were Jews. Afterwards he ordered them to be numbered off and led to their huts. They were packed in to as few huts as possible, leaving most of them vacant.

Three nights later, on 4 August the twenty-two aircrew officers arrived from Dulag Luft, bringing the aircrew contingent up to thirty-five. The twenty-two included the five officers who had inadvertently been sent to Biberach: Acting Squadron Leader Walter ("Taffy") Williams and Pilot Officers Paddy Denton, Kenneth Edwards, William Hunter and Jim Ireton. The other seventeen were: Acting Squadron Leaders F L Campbell-Rogers, T W Piper and E Sydney-Smith DFC; Flight Lieutenants G M Fuller and P J S Shaughnessy DFC; Acting Flight Lieutenant M C G Sherwood; Flying Officers D Graham-Hogg, N W McLeod and J Zafouk (Czech); Pilot Officers L B Barry RAFVR, O Cerny (Czech), P L Dixon RAAF, P A Leuw, S Maciejewski (Pole), A W MacKay and R G M Morgan; and Lieutenant (A) A T Easton RN.

Most batches of new POWs sent on to other camps from Dulag Luft consisted predominantly of Bomber Command aircrew, and this party was no exception, although it did also include a few officers from Fighter Command, Coastal Command and the Fleet Air Arm.

The first of the bomber types to enter the bag was Patrick John Shaw Shaughnessy, an experienced pilot from No44 (Rhodesia) Squadron, based at Waddington in Lincolnshire. No44 Squadron was part of No5 Group, and one of only two RAF operational units to see continuous service with Bomber Command throughout the war. On 12/13 June ninety-one Hampdens were sent to Soest to hit the railway marshalling yards, Paddy Shaughnessy leading his section off at 2300 hours. Visibility was poor over the target and fewer than half of the crews bombed the primary target. Two Hampdens were lost to flak. Shaughnessy ditched his crippled aircraft in the sea. His observer was killed, and the body never recovered, but the WOP/AGs, Sergeants C W Townsend and J E Hughff, survived.

Pilot Officer Ronald Morgan found himself a prisoner a month later, when on 14/15 July No405 (Vancouver) Squadron, set off from Pocklington, Yorkshire, to join in a raid on Hanover involving eighty-five aircraft from No4 Group. Their aiming points were the city centre and the rubber factory on the outskirts. No405 Squadron, flying Wellingtons, had been formed on 23 April and was the first nominally Canadian squadron in Bomber Command, although only a few of its aircrew were Canadian. Morgan was second pilot to a twenty-one-year-old Sergeant, D B Thrower, who took off at 2230 hours. The outward leg was uneventful but on the run-in to the target the starboard engine blew up. Even so, the observer, Sergeant V R J Slaughter, still managed to release the bombs, stoking the many fires he could see below. Derek Thrower then turned for home. Although his aircraft was constantly losing height, he made it to Holland. But there the Wimpey was picked out by searchlights, pummelled again by flak and chased by night-fighters. The already crippled aircraft could not withstand such heavy punishment. Thrower knew that all was lost, and ordered the crew to bale out. Ronny Morgan stayed behind to make sure they had all gone, then shook hands with Thrower before hitting the silk himself.

All but two of the crew were rounded up within a few hours. By dawn Thrower, Morgan, "Todd" Slaughter and one of the WOP/AGs, Sergeant J N Kirk of the RCAF, were under lock and key in an upstairs room in the town hall at Zwolle. They talked quietly about the way each had been captured, but when one of the crew mentioned their squadron Thrower cautioned him to be quiet, for it was obvious that the guard on the door was listening attentively and probably knew some English. To find out for sure, one of them asked the guard, in English, how much longer they were to be kept in this small room, and he answered in English before he could check himself. The guard was most put out and a minute later was removed. Another soldier then appeared in the doorway, camera in hand. He quickly took photographs of them, while they grinned at him and pulled faces. None of this worried him and he disappeared without any fuss. They concluded that he had taken the photographs for his own benefit.

Although there were now no guards in the room, they began to feel anxious. They had been there too long, and wondered whether the room had been wired for sound. So they discussed *fortississimo* the personal habits of the Germans and in particular of *Herr* Hitler himself, and sure enough, the door soon burst open and an irate officer strode in, followed by his subordinates. Red in the face, he waved his clenched fists and bellowed loudly. The four prisoners were hustled downstairs and out on to the front steps of the town hall to await the transport that was to take them to their next destination. Standing next to the still-raging officer was the guard who had taken their photographs. Sergeant Thrower interrupted the voluble officer and explained to him about the guard and the camera. The officer shouted for a *Dolmetscher* (interpreter), and turning on the visibly paling offender demanded the camera from him and gave it to Thrower. Thrower returned it, replying that it was not his and that he did not want it. When the interpreter translated, the officer lost his temper and booted Thrower down the steps.

They were driven to Amsterdam and soon found themselves locked in separate cells in a proper gaol, where they stayed for seven days, from time to time being interrogated by a relay of German officers from the Carlton Hotel, the Luftwaffe's HQ and a satellite of Dulag Luft. Morgan's first visitor offered him a cigarette and lit it for him, then handed him a Red Cross form, which, he insisted, had to be completed in full. This would then be sent to the Red Cross authorities in Switzerland, who in turn would pass the information to England, where his parents would learn that he was alive and well and a prisoner of war. The form looked genuine enough, thought

Morgan, so he filled in his name, rank and number; but when he came to questions which asked for the number of his squadron, where it was located, what kind of aircraft it used, and so on, he drew a line through the form and handed it back. The German affably repeated that the questions must be answered before the form could be sent off, and reminded Morgan of his family's anxiety about whether he was alive or dead.

Morgan's next visitor was more aggressive. On entering the cell he waved a gun at him, all the while stamping and shouting and threatening to shoot him if he did not complete the form. Morgan refused, and the German left, still ranting. The next day a fine, handsome German officer appeared. He was gentle and refined and spoke excellent, well-accented English. Introducing himself, he offered Morgan a cigarette and threw a large packet of them on the bed, saying that he could keep them. He went on to talk about England, remarking upon what a pleasant country it was and how he had spent many years studying in London. He had had a girlfriend when he was there and asked if Morgan had one, and where they went on their dates. He was a clever man and seemed so perfectly innocuous that if Morgan had not been on his guard he could easily have given something away. Eventually Morgan simply stopped answering him. His interrogator did not appear annoyed, but he took back the cigarettes, Morgan noticed.

Then the first visitor reappeared, and again presented him with a Red Cross form — this one complete with all the information the Germans had wanted from him in the first place. Morgan was shocked, but sat still and said nothing. The interrogator told him that there was now no reason why he should not fill in his own form. They had all the information they needed, so it was now only a matter of formality. Morgan remained still and silent until the German left the cell, taking the forms with him; with his departure the interrogators went out of his life for the time being.

From Amsterdam, Morgan and his three crewmen were escorted to Dulag Luft. The first part of the journey was by covered lorry to Utrecht. From there they were to travel by train to Frankfurt. They were given a strong escort of armed soldiers for the journey. They found out why outside the station at Utrecht. When the local civilians recognized them as RAF prisoners, they gathered round, giving the V-sign and throwing cigarettes and chocolate to them, until the guards, fearful at being swamped by such numbers, threatened to start shooting if they did not move away.

Derek Thrower, who had been identified as a troublemaker, was separated from the group and thrust into an empty carriage on his own, while the guards took Morgan, Slaughter and Kirk to other carriages. The crowds had made their way on to the platform and were peering through the windows. It felt good to receive such encouragement. The train steamed out of the station, the three prisoners in Morgan's compartment sitting on one side of the compartment, the guards sitting opposite, their rifles at their sides. They reached Dulag Luft at nightfall, and again Morgan found himself alone in a cell. Once again he had his quota of visitors, pleading, beguiling, threatening — "Just fill in the form and all will be well. If not — well, we are in no hurry." Morgan's uniform and underwear were taken away — for "de-lousing", he was told. After three days the clothes were returned and he was escorted to the main camp. There he found Thrower, Slaughter and Kirk, along with the two gunners, Sergeants E Jones and W J Dossetter, who had managed to evade capture for a little longer. All the NCOs were eventually sent to Bad Sulza.

Morgan also met Pilot Officer Les Dixon of the RAAF. From No149 (East India) Squadron, based at Mildenhall in Suffolk, he had taken off at 2305 hours, destined for the same Bremen raid that had led "Crammy" Crampton into the bag. Dixon's Wellington was brought down by flak and his crew of Sergeants also survived to join him behind barbed-wire.

Eric Sydney-Smith, a pre-war journalist who wrote under the name of "Sydney Smith", had recently been posted to No139 (Jamaica) Squadron at Oulton, Norfolk, after returning from a tour of duty in Malta, where he had earned a DFC for attacks on enemy shipping. No139 Squadron had the distinction of carrying out Bomber Command's first sortie of the war on the first day of the war, saw continuous service in one theatre or another throughout the war, and carried out the most bombing raids in No2 Group. Sydney-Smith himself was about to go on a spot of well-deserved leave when his flight was put down for a large-scale operation against the harbour at Rotterdam.

This port was of great strategic importance to the Germans. Not only was it used for shipping raw materials such as Swedish iron ore, which was transported in huge barges down the Rhine directly to the steel mills in the Ruhr Valley, but it was also an important ship-building and maintenance depot. Despite the fact that the Germans had set up a very strong defensive ring of flak batteries, searchlights and fighter squadrons, along with the crack *Vorpostenboot* flak-ship flotilla No13, the city was a tempting target for the Royal Air Force. During 1940 and the first half of 1941, Rotterdam had been raided dozens of times, mainly by heavy night bombers.

In accordance with Churchill's Maritime Directive, a daring daylight bombing raid against the harbour had been planned for Wednesday, 16 July 1941. Photographic reconnaissance and Dutch Resistance reports had revealed that the 17,000-ton vessel *Strassburg* was moored at the quay. The *Strassburg* was the former Dutch liner *Baloeran*, which had been confiscated by the Germans and was now in service as a hospital ship. There were also several merchant vessels and warships that the Blenheim crews of No2 Group had to put out of action. The attack was to be carried out in two waves — the first, comprising eighteen Blenheims from Nos 21 and 266 Squadrons, based at Watton, and led by Wing Commander Tom Webster, No21's commanding officer; and the second of another eighteen aircraft from Nos 18 and 105 Squadrons at Horsham St Faith, Norfolk, and from No139 Squadron at Oulton. They would be led by Wing Commander Tim Partridge DFC, the CO of No18 (Burma) Squadron.

The Blenheim crews practised hard on low-level formation flying, and at last the great day arrived. Eric Sydney-Smith was given a "scratch" crew, as his usual observer and WOP/AG were in hospital. They were recovering from wounds received on 27 March when Sydney-Smith had dive-bombed a German destroyer, then gone round again using machine-guns. This effort was held up by the Wingco i/c flying as an example for all to follow, but the badly shot-up crew thought it suicidal. As for his replacement crew, neither the observer, Pilot Officer R A White, nor the WOP/AG, Flight Sergeant E G Caban DFM, had flown together before. Adrian White's usual pilot was not available, and Ted Caban had been posted to No139 Squadron in a non-flying capacity as a gunnery leader/instructor after completing a tour of operations. (He had been awarded the DFM for shooting down an enemy fighter.)

At 1535 hours on a bright, sunny afternoon, the first wave of bombers from Watton took off, until there were eighteen formatting above. The number was reduced to seventeen when Acting Squadron Leader F L Campbell-Rogers of No226 Squadron dropped out owing to hydraulic problems. Horsham St Faith's Blenheims had taken off some twenty minutes earlier. Those from Oulton took off at 1600 hours. Crossing the North Sea at wave-top height on a dogleg to the south-west of Rotterdam, they reached the target area at 1700 hours. Wing Commander Webster's formation approached the harbour with Partridge's wave a few minutes behind. As the latter formation went in, Sydney-Smith could see Dutch civilians waving and cheering at them from the streets. He also noticed an Me109 on a satellite airfield taxi-ing for take-off — not a comforting sight. Each crew selected a suitable target and made hay over a wide area, bombing and strafing ships, installations, storage buildings and railway lines. Among other buildings, a dock used by Wilton-Feyenoord shipbuilders was set ablaze, and according to a report by the Dutch Resistance twenty-two ships were damaged.

It was a miracle that none of the Blenheims collided, as the sky over Rotterdam was a hornet's nest of bombers. But throughout the entire raid the Germans put up fierce flak barrage and four Blenheims were destroyed, which was considered a small loss for such a daring raid in broad daylight. Three complete crews were killed, but Eric Sydney-Smith and his crew survived a successfully belly-landing in the middle of the city. As Sydney-Smith flew across the docks, looking for his own target, he ran more or less broadside on to a cargo ship — quite a good sized one, and fully laden at that. It looked as if it was being towed across the docks. A very slight course adjustment took Sydney-Smith right over it, almost amidships. After letting his bombs go at low level, he lifted the Blenheim's nose and flew over it. On the other side he put the nose down — and then saw that he was flying straight into the guns of a flak-ship, moored about five hundred yards away on the far side of the dock. He could see the ship sparking from end to end with gunfire and hear and feel some of it striking the Blenheim. Within a few seconds Ted Caban was on the intercom warning that the port engine was on fire and that he had been hit. Sydney-Smith took a sideways glance at the engine and saw that thick black smoke was pouring out from the top of the cowlings. He busied himself at once, opening the cowlings and pulling switches in order to put out the fire.

All this had taken only a few seconds and he realized later that he had probably switched the engine off by accident, although the propeller continued to turn. When he looked up again, out of the cockpit, he saw a church tower looming towards him. It seemed to rise well above his aircraft, and it was so close that his first thought was that they would crash into it and be stranded there. However, in the few seconds necessary for his subconscious to analyse this idea, it rejected it and, without any calculated intention, he heaved full back on the controls. The Blenheim went straight up and over. (Had there been a weathervane on top, it would not be there now!) They came down on the other side, but with only one engine working, and that close to stalling. Sydney-Smith carried on over the rooftops, flying tail-down and nose-up with a nasty, sinking feeling in the pit of his stomach. He was still heading north-east — the wrong way for home. But he was flying too low and too slow to attempt turning north-west, and he felt the safest place to do a wheels-up crash-landing was the countryside on the other side of the city. It would have to be soon, before they blew up or crashed among the rooftops.

Suddenly there was an almost empty space ahead of them. It was about the size of a football pitch and strewn with rubble, as if a block of buildings had been bombed and the area partially cleared. Sydney-Smith cut the engine. He could not remember afterwards whether he put the flaps down, but had he done so they would not have worked. He turned slightly to port, and then side-slipped to starboard, until the Blenheim was straight and level. It did not seem to hit the ground very hard and it bounced along for a short distance before coming to a stop, upright and with the fuselage still more or less intact. Both wings, with their engines, had been cleanly torn from the fuselage and left behind, and the fire had gone out.

Sydney-Smith was unhurt except for a very slight bump on the forehead. He unclipped his harness and the aircraft rescue axe, and climbed out of the cockpit and down onto the port wing-root to help Ted Caban out of his gun-turret. Almost as soon as he stepped to the ground, crowds from the surrounding streets began rushing towards the stricken Blenheim. Within seconds — before he had any time to do anything — the first man reached him, snatched the axe from his hand and started attacking the turret, trying to rescue Caban. Another few seconds, and the crowd was so thick that Sydney-Smith could get nowhere near the wreckage. He went round towards the nose and, standing on tiptoe, saw a knot of anxious Dutch civilians attending to Adrian White. He was smiling reassuringly, although he appeared to have a broken leg. But in any event, he was being looked after, and Sydney-Smith was being pushed further and further away by the crowd. Nobody was paying him any attention. He decided to clear off. As he was not wearing his jacket, nor his collar and tie, he might pass muster as a civilian. He walked quickly to the nearest stretch of street, crossed it and walked along the pavement away from the crash-site. After a while a man fell in beside him and started talking in a low voice. He said, in English: "Are you from that plane?" Sydney-Smith replied: "Yes," and told him that he would like to find the American Consulate. The Dutchman told him that he was a merchant seaman. The US Consulate, he continued, was back in the dock area from which Sydney-Smith had been fleeing.

Guided by the directions of the Dutch seaman, who also gave him a handful of small change, he made for the docks. When he arrived at the US Consulate he did not like the look of it. German soldiers patrolled the pavement on each side of the main doorway. It was almost on the very edge of the docks. He realised that he had taken a route almost identical to the one in which had flown — so much so that a moment later he saw the flak-ship that had shot him down tied up along the quayside and, out in the middle of the dock beyond it, the ship he had hit, sitting on the bottom. The crew, all talking and shouting like mad, were busy cleaning the guns and putting things in order. Sydney-Smith stood for a minute or so on the quayside, watching and listening. Looking at the flak-ship, bristling with multiple pom-poms and other armament, he found it hard to imagine how his Blenheim had not been blown to bits, and felt that if he had ever seen a flak-ship at close quarters before it would have had a horrible effect on his "moral fibre".

He then decided to move out of the docks and into the country. However, the Germans were already combing the area and he had no chance of getting anywhere. Late that evening, he was taken prisoner. The manifest Dutch sympathy for the Blenheim raid and the help that the people of Rotterdam had given to Sydney-Smith and his crew immediately led to German reprisals. The *Wehrmacht* Commander in the Netherlands announced that in future any Dutch expression of sympathy towards shot-down RAF aircrew would lead to armed force.

The two Czechs, Jaroslav Zafouk and Otaker Cerny, were shot down after the same raid on Hamburg, on 16 July 1941, as Kenneth Edwards. They were an observer and a WOP/AG in a Wellington MkIC of No311 (Czechoslovak) Squadron, formed in 1940 from aircrew who had fled their country in 1938, fought in Poland in 1939 and served in France in 1940. Their pilot, Sergeant Jaroslav Nyc, took off from East Wretham, Norfolk, at 2307 hours. Four hours later, on the return journey, his aircraft was attacked by a night-fighter from *4/NJG1*, flown by *Oberfeldwebel* Paul Gildner. The tail-gunner was killed. With the exception of Sergeant Nyc, who stayed with the aircraft and ditched in the IJsselmeer, the rest of the crew baled out. All but Cerny were rounded up within a few hours, and taken to Amsterdam for interrogation and thence to Dulag Luft. Cerny was on the run until 19 July, and re-joined his crew a few days later.

Flying Officer Dennis Graham-Hogg, of No21 Squadron, had taken part in the Rotterdam raid that had led to Eric Sydney-Smith's capture. He was up again on Friday, 18 July, by which time the squadron was operating from a forward base at Manston, the former Battle of Britain aerodrome, for "Channel Stop" operations. His flight of Blenheim MkIVs took off at 1115 hours to attack shipping off Gravelines, but all were shot down by a combination of marine flak and Me109s from Wissant and Calais-Marck. Graham-Hogg's WOP/AG, Flight Sergeant D W Wyatt, was killed, leaving his aircraft defenceless. He ditched off Cap Gris-Nez and along with his observer, Sergeant J Marsden, was picked up be a German patrol boat.

Squadron Leader Thomas William Piper was one of those unfortunates who, as a Flight Commander on No15 Squadron, Wyton (No3 Group), had flown Short Stirlings, which, owing to their lack of height, were rapidly gaining a lousy reputation. On Saturday, 19 July, his flight was slated to take part in "Circus No51" to bomb Lille power station or, as a secondary target, Dunkirk. No fewer than eight fighter squadrons, from the Biggin Hill, Hornchurch and Tangmere Wings, flew as escort, drawing up every Me109 and Me110 for miles around. Three enemy aircraft were definitely destroyed, seven probably destroyed, and two damaged, for the loss of two Spitfires. The three Stirlings, however, failed to reach Lille, and bombed Dunkirk instead. Tom Piper's aircraft was hit by flak over the target and the tail unit caught fire. Wisely, the air-gunner abandoned his position and took to his parachute. The fire then spread to fuselage.

As the blazing Stirling went into a vertical dive, two Me109s attacked, their gunfire setting the port wing alight. All elevator control had gone, and Piper decided it was time he, too, was gone. Struggling out of the escape hatch, he hit against something, probably the aerial mast, and the parachute harness became partly detached. When he pulled the rip-cord he turned "arse over tit" and hung from the parachute by his feet, the pack casing banging into the back of his calves. Then another Me109 approached, but luckily for Piper the pilot had only come to see what was going on. Having made up his mind that he did not fancy falling out of the harness and plummeting to his death, Piper began to think about how to make a landing without breaking any bones. As terra firma rushed towards him he rolled himself tightly into a ball. He landed on his back in a cornfield, which knocked the wind out of him, and five minutes later the Jerries arrived. His Stirling had dived into the ground at Killem. The only other survivor was the air-gunner who had baled out. (Tom Piper was in worse shape than he thought. The previous year, on 17 April, he had been injured during a stint as a Flight Lieutenant instructor at No15 OTU at Harwell in Oxfordshire. He had taken a pupil up for night-time instrument training in a Wellington when, over Berkshire, the engine lost power and he had to force-land in a field sixteen miles north-east of Reading. The Wellington then caught fire, and both Piper and his pupil suffered serious injuries to their arms, backs and shoulders. Piper made a good enough recovery to resume ops in 1941, but his parachute descent in 19 July exacerbated his old injuries, and he would eventually be admitted to *Lazarett* IXC at Obermassfeld and repatriated in 1944.)

That night's operations also saw Pilot Officer "Fiji" MacKay, a Whitley second pilot, and his observer, Peter ("Rudy") Leuw, enter the bag. Except for occasional detachments to Coastal Command, their squadron, No51, had been in No4 Group since pre-war days, and had flown the first sorties over Germany on the first night of the war. No51 would go on to fly more ops in Whitleys than any other RAF squadron. On this particular night the squadron was down for a raid on Hanover. A total of forty-nine aircraft were to aim for the main railway station. The captain of MacKay and Leuw's Whitley, Pilot Officer A R Thomas, took off from Dishforth, Yorkshire, at 2114 hours. There was little German fighter activity that night, and Thomas's aircraft was probably shot down by flak. Thomas himself was killed.

Exactly one week after aborting from the Rotterdam raid, Acting Squadron Leader Frank Landseer Campbell-Rogers, who had now been transferred to No21 Squadron, followed Eric Sydney-Smith into Dulag Luft. On the afternoon of Wednesday, 23 July, seventeen Blenheims from Nos 18 and 21 Squadrons flew on a "Roadstead" anti-shipping operation along the Dutch and Belgian coasts, escorted by Hurricanes and Spitfires from the Tangmere Wing. The Luftwaffe was also up in force, and six Blenheims were lost. Campbell-Rogers, whose flight had taken off from Manston at 1400 hours, was shot down off Ostend and ditched in the North Sea. His observer was killed, sinking with the aircraft.

Flying Officer McLeod, a Halifax tail-gunner, was from the same squadron, No76, as Acting Squadron Leader Williams and Pilot Officer Ireton; he was also bagged as a result of the same 24 July daylight raid on la Pallice. His skipper, Flight Lieutenant A E Lewin, took off from Stanton Harcourt slightly ahead of Williams, at 1034 hours. Lewin and three other members of the crew were killed when the aircraft crashed south-west of Luçon after being chased inland by Me109s. The two surviving NCOs were sent to Stalag IIIE.

Another crew bagged on the same night as Paddy Denton's, 25/26 July, was that of Acting Flight Lieutenant Michael Colin Gordon Sherwood. He was a pilot on No7 Squadron (No3 Group), stationed at Oakington in Camridgeshire, which on 10/11 February 1941 had been the first squadron to use the Short Stirling on operations. On 25 July, in addition to ordering aircraft to Hanover, Bomber Command also sent seven Stirlings and two Halifaxes to Berlin, Sherwood taking off at 2250 hours. His was one of two Stirlings lost, falling victim to the flak belt on the Dutch/German border. He crash-landed at Oudorp in northern Holland. All his crew survived, and his navigator, Flight Lieutenant Fuller, remained with him on the journey to Oberursel. The NCOs, like those in Denton, Shaughnessy and Williams' crews, were sent to Stalag IIIE.

The one fighter pilot — and only Pole — amongst this crop was Stefan Maciejewski, from No308 Squadron, a Spitfire MkIIA unit in No9 Group and based at Baginton in Warwickshire. On Thursday, 17 July a planned "Circus" (No50) was aborted, so the eight fighter squadrons down for escort duties carried out "Rhubarbs" instead. No308 Squadron went out that evening to draw up some Me109s. Three "kills" and two "probables" were reported, but three Spitfire MkIIs were lost. Two of the pilots were killed and Maciejewski baled out and was taken prisoner.

Thirty-two-year-old Pilot Officer Louis Brull Barry was an air-gunner from Coastal Command, who had served on the same squadron as William ("Red") Hunter but was posted missing two months before his arrival. He had grown up in Hungary, where his father, the noted rower W A Barry, taught him to scull and to horse-ride on the estate on which he was employed. After the Great War Lou himself became a professional sculler, winning the Doggett's Coat and Badge in 1927, and gaining the championship of England in 1936, beating Ted Phelps — only to lose the championship later that year when Ted's younger brother Eric beat him. Barry was also working as a professional rowing coach, first in Ireland and then in Italy, where in 1936 he coached the Italian Olympic team and was, much to his amusement, given a medal by Mussolini. He took a great deal of ribbing over this, and used to joke that he just happened to be at the end of the welcoming line when Mussolini made a visit and, since everyone was getting a medal, there was no way of avoiding it. When war broke out again in 1939 he joined the RAFVR and qualified as a navigator, wireless operator and air gunner.

Barry was posted to No217 Squadron, part of No15 (GR) Group, which in 1939 had been based at Warmwell, from where it flew Avro Ansons. But in 1940 it moved to St Eval to convert to Bristol Beauforts. Barry was crewed up with the experienced Flight Lieutenant A V Hunter (pilot), and Sergeants P H Clarke (navigator) and G D Holiday (WOP/AG). On Wednesday, 12 February 1941, Arthur Hunter took off from St Eval at 1215 hours on a routine "Rover" patrol over the Bay of Biscay, taking with him a supernumerary, Flying Officer J H Wybrant, a pilot instructor from Group HQ who was present to observe proceedings. As was often the case with passengers, he brought bad luck to the crew and, fatally, to himself. Sergeant Holiday, at the radio, got a fix on an enemy aircraft fifty miles west of the Isle of Ushant, just off the Brest coastline. They set off in pursuit, but were shot down by coastal batteries, crash-landing on the Brittany peninsula. Wybrant was injured and taken to the naval hospital at Brest, where he later died, but Hunter, Barry and the rest of the Beaufort crew survived. After fetching up at Dulag Luft, they all were distributed to a variety of camps: Hunter and one NCO going to Stalag Luft I, Barry to Oflag XB and the remaining sergeant to Stalag IIIE.

The one Fleet Air Arm officer, Lieutenant Easton, was a telegraphist/air-gunner in a two-seater Fairey Fulmar MkII from No809 Squadron. He had taken part in a disastrous daylight raid on Petsamo, in the northernmost tip of Norway, on Friday, 25 July. His pilot, Sub-Lieutenant (A) T E Blacklock RNVR, was still at Dulag Luft, along with eighteen other Fleet Air Arm officers captured on raids on 25 and 30 July, several of whom had been badly wounded.

***

After a journey from Dulag Luft lasting almost two days, they reached the railway station at Lübeck at 10pm on 4 August. "The station looked as inviting as a small version of Manchester Central on a wet Sunday night," recalled Paddy Denton. It was barren of people except some Luftwaffe characters and a singularly unpleasant-looking officer.

We stumbled out and the officer then indulged himself in a typical fit of German hysteria. *"Schwein Mörder, Flieger Mörder, Kindermörder,"* and so on. It was bad-mannered and quite unnecessary.

We were then marched off from the station, with rather a heavy guard, to what was to be the climax of the evening for the good citizens of Lübeck and their teenagers and children since, on the command of the officer, they started to throw brick ends, stones and epithets at us. They were pretty inaccurate so we only suffered a small sense of resentment at this undignified behaviour.

We walked on, for about three miles, to a typical barracks camp which is common to all nations world-wide.

We were taken into a bare building and to the great hilarity of the Goons had to strip naked and parade. I had a silver watch which was a 21st birthday present from an uncle...That went. I also had a birthstone signet ring from a great grandparent. That went. All this while standing naked and cold tended to make one feel irritable if not actively hostile, but there was not much one could do.

Eventually, [they] having had their fun, we clambered back into our bits and pieces and entered the compound of Oflag XC.

Each man was issued with two blankets, straw to stuff into his palliasse and pillowcase, and, for messing, a mug, bowl, knife, fork and spoon. (There were no plates, so instead they used the small bread-boards acquired from the canteen). They were then taken to Trumble's barrack block. Much fitter and better fed than the contingent from Crete, the ex-Dulag Luft boys referred to them as "ex-*Kreta*" — a pun on the German word for Crete and the effects of dysentery.

A few days afterwards the Laufen party arrived; the aircrew contingent at Oflag XC now numbered fifty-three. However, on Thursday, 7 August Trumble, Deakin, Mason, May, Churcher, Dilly, Garside, Howlett and Valachos were removed from the camp, de-loused, searched and walked two miles to a *Panzer* division headquarters, where they were locked in one of the barracks for the night. The following morning they were put on a passenger train for Dulag Luft, which they reached on Saturday the 9th. After a night in the cooler and interrogation the next morning, they were released into the compound. The interrogators had treated them to their familiar "brothers in arms act" which, recalls Trumble, "went down with us like a lead balloon. We were tough and angry nuts to try cracking at interrogation. The Luftwaffe decided we were bad news." From Dulag Luft, on 10 August, Trumble wrote his first POW letter to his family.

***

Back at Lübeck, the tiny Air Force contingent from Biberach had made a football out of pieces ripped from a palliasse cover, which they kicked around on a fair-sized patch of sand near the trip-wire. The Army officers from Crete, watching from the sidelines, envied them their strength and stamina, and on one occasion three of them stood behind one of the improvised goals and tried to kick any stray shots back on to the field of play. But their efforts were derisory. They had no control over their feet, and simply collapsed in a heap and blacked out, to hoots of laughter from the Air Force boys. One day the ball trickled over the trip-wire. Another prisoner, a senior Merchant Navy officer from the freighter *Huntsman*, was standing nearby. After making his intention plain to the guard in the goon-box, he stepped across to retrieve the ball. The guard shot three rounds at him. Fortunately, only one bullet hit, nicking him on the thigh. A German officer ascended the goon-box and shook the guard by the hand, then a squad of guards appeared and took the wounded officer away to Lübeck hospital. Although the wound was not serious, the RAF prisoners were furious. They thought it, Paddy Denton records, "a totally unnecessary and unfair piece of Goonery":

It was a useful lesson again since the sound of the shots brought everyone off their bunks and out of the huts and we surrounded the Goon-box of the offensive little man. We expressed ourselves and our opinions of his forebears in perfectly explicit, grammatical English language, the purpose of which seemed to make some impression. Within minutes however we were involved in a mêlée of Germans with Stens or some form of chatter-gun in a high state of excitement and were reluctantly returned to our two blocks and locked in, the normal drill in this camp, for some hours and then released.

Not long afterwards the Germans supplied them with a large white flag and a cap to wear whenever they wished to retrieve the football from the no-man's-land. But the prisoners did not trust the trigger-happy guards, and there was no more football after that.

Chapter Three

"A Very Bad Camp..."

Oflag XC, Lübeck, August–October 1941

O n the night of Friday, 8 August, while Trumble & Co were still at Dulag Luft, the purge of thirty from Stalag Luft I reached Lübeck. Among them were Wing Commander N C ("Hetty") Hyde; Squadron Leaders R J Bushell, AuxAF, K C Doran DFC*, F J B Keast RAFO, E H Lynch-Blosse and W H N Turner DFC; Acting Squadron Leader F A Willan; Flight Lieutenants R J ("Liffey") McConnell and J W Stephens DFC*; Flying Officers C Y Buckley, J C W Bushell, M N McF ("Bush") Kennedy, C D ("Snowy") Milne, M I Murdoch, S H ("Percy") Palmer RAFVR and M H ("Maggie") Roth; Pilot Officers R F Beauclair, J R Denny, H E L Falkus, J H Green, T G Hynes, K Jones, D F M Mackarness, J F McPhie, E R Mullins, R E W Pumphrey, AuxAF, J P ("Paddy") Quirke and J L Scott; and Lieutenant C H ("Fairey") Filmer DSC, RN.

There was no apparent logic behind purging these kriegies from Stalag Luft I. Some of them — such as William Turner, John Stephens, Michael Murdoch, Robert Pumphrey, Michael Roth and Ernest Mullins — had originally been sent from Dulag Luft to Spangenberg in May 1940 and then transferred to Barth. One, Hugh Falkus, had begun *Gefangenschaft* proper in June 1940 at Stalag XIIA, Limburg, before being transferred to Oflag IIA at Prenzlau and thence to Luft I. The rest were Barth "originals", most having been shot down in the summer of 1940 and sent there direct from Dulag Luft. The Luftwaffe goons claimed they were being purged because they were known to have taken part in escape activities. This was certainly true of Noel ("Hetty") Hyde, Roger Bushell, Kenneth Doran, Melville Kennedy, Hugh Lynch-Blosse, Frank Willan, Robert McConnell, Cecil Milne, Stanley Palmer, Robert Beauclair and Cecil Filmer. Indeed, Doran and Kennedy had been amongst the foremost of the early escapers at Barth. As for Hyde and Bushell, they had taken part in the mass escape from Dulag Luft under Wing Commander H M A Day's leadership in June 1941, and upon recapture had been banished with him to Stalag Luft I. At least two of the officers, Willie Turner and Francis Keast, had been trained in secret letter-codes. However, some of them had no connection at all with escape or any other clandestine activity. All Michael Roth wanted was to be left alone to practise his conjuring tricks. (His nickname, "Maggie", was short not for "Margaret" but for "magician".)

They therefore believed that their hasty departure had been impelled less by their reluctance to embrace Stalag Luft I's hospitality than by a wind of change that was now blowing through the camp following the arrival of "Wings" Day. When Day had been head of the British Permanent Staff at Dulag Luft, many of the prisoners who passed through on their way to Barth felt Harry Day and his cohort were living the life of Reilly and that their relationship with the German authorities was a little too cosy. They had made potentially libellous references to the British Permanent Staff in their letters home and, indeed, had gone so far as to involve the Air Ministry, write a letter to the commandant of Dulag Luft and hold a court of inquiry into Day's activities. This was rank insubordination and a clear breach of service etiquette. Not only that, but Day's own junior officers had humiliated him in front of the enemy. When he was sent to Barth he was seething with suppressed fury, and was well aware of the rancour that some officers still felt towards him. It was no coincidence that, apart from Roger Bushell, there were no fewer than six squadron leaders on this purge, most of whom had been in Stalag Luft I at the same time as two successive Senior British Officers, Squadron Leaders Brian Paddon (from 12 July 1940 to 20 February 1941) and Geoffrey Stephenson (June–July 1940 and 20 February–7 June 1941). Paddon was now in Colditz *Sonderlager* and Stephenson would join him there on 1 September).

Harry Day was also intent on streamlining the escape committee, and there is good reason to believe that he connived to have those who resisted his measures removed from the camp. At any rate, for the rest of the war the loyalty of Royal Air Force kriegies would be split — between "Wings" Day and his entourage, who believed in maintaining superficially good relations with the Germans while organising large-scale escapes and carrying out intelligence work, and the younger and more spirited nay-sayers who preferred things a little less streamlined and who felt that the short-term satisfaction to be gained from "goon baiting" and generally raising Cain was as least as useful to the war effort as escaping, as despite the disruption it caused and the reprisals that resulted it showed "the Hun" that they would not be pushed around. The two camps would become known as "the sheep" and "the goats". The former were, by and large, ex-Dulag Luft and ex-Barth; the latter ex-Spangenberg, ex-Laufen, ex-Lübeck, ex-Warburg and ex-Schubin.

By train Lübeck was seventy miles west of Barth. The prisoners from Stalag Luft I arrived late in the evening. Every light was blacked out against air raids. Inside the station they "were met by a company of green-coated Goons — those unimaginative dolts — the behind-the-lines barrack troops, dregs of the *Wehrmacht*," recalled Michael Roth:

> We groaned, knowing from experience what was in store: true to form, they began shouting orders; these cretins could never do anything without excessive verbal babbling. A horse-drawn cart was laid on for our heavy luggage. Then, at walking-race pace they marched us uphill towards the camp shouting hurry, hurry, hurry, every three steps. It was very dark. No moon. No stars peeped through the heavy overcast. Part way, an old man on a bicycle going in the opposite direction plowed [*sic*] full tilt into the leading Goons. The language! Served them right. It was their own fault for being on the wrong side of the road. They were knocked, bruised, and tossed in a heap. The old man picked himself up and started arguing. They weren't interested. They clubbed the poor sod with their rifle butts and pitched him semi-conscious into the ditch. For good measure they threw his bent bike on top of him. On we went, sorry for the old man, but glad of the brief rest. If this was the way they treated a civilian, what would they do to us?

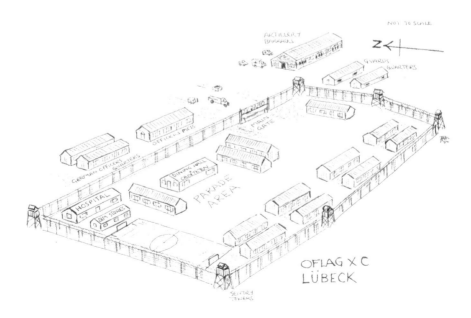

Fig 5. Oflag XC, Lübeck *(Paul Mathias)*

Absolutely pooped, we reached the camp and found ourselves herded into a large empty garage without bedding for the night. We decided then that the letter C after the camp's number could only stand for Concentration camp, or *Straflager...*

First thing next morning was an inspection for lice by a Yankee-born interpreter, *Obergefreiter* Edwards. "Sorry fellas. Ain't nuthin' I can do about it." That was his lingo. Where the hell did they think we'd come from to have lice? We refused point-blank to be deloused. We challenged Edwards to find any lice on any of us. He looked behind everyone's collar and found none. This apparently was a 100% foolproof test. We were lice-free. So the garage doors were folded back and several tables carried in. Two creepy Goons waited behind each table. Then some German officers appeared and gave the order for the search to begin. Some search! It was nothing more than a pretext for stealing anything of value. They took everything, even underwear. When my turn came and I carried my gramophone and suitcases to a table, I could see anticipation of plum goodies on the faces of the two weasels eager to start their pilfering. First they took the gramophone; *verboten* at this camp. It would of course bring a high price on the local Black Market. When the two thugs started pitching the contents of my suitcases into a sack, I protested this was in violation of the Geneva Convention.

They sneered and grinned at each other. *"Hier haben wir keine Genfer Konvention."*

Useless even trying to reason — what can one expect from a pig but a grunt? I turned my back, and despite their yells of *"Komm zurück,"* I marched up to and saluted a tall German captain, one of a group viewing the larceny.

"Bitte sehr, Herr Hauptmann. Ihre Soldaten haben meine Dinge genommen. Können die deutschen Soldaten Kanteen mir meine Dinge zurückgeben?" The captain appeared to be interested. So with all the emphasis I could, I explained that the confiscated articles included magical apparatus, allowed me on the express personal permission of *General* Wolffe when he inspected our camp at Barth, and that therefore these two soldiers were now by their actions countermanding the orders of a general. Would the captain please see that the general's orders were respected?

The captain was convinced. He strode over to my table and gave the two thieving bastards hell. They stood stiff as sticks muttering *"Jawohl, Herr Hauptmann."* The captain ordered the immediate return of my property. It seemed one could always appeal to a German officer on grounds of fair play — if he was a member of the Old School.

Inside the compound we were greeted by a very dispirited bunch of plump rose-cheeked RAF kriegies who'd been in the bag barely three weeks. They were lost, cheerless sheep without a shepherd or a leader — their morale seemed at a very low ebb already. The RAF senior officer was a wing commander, a slovenly, sloppy type both in appearance and personality, the very last person one would have chosen as a liaison officer, simply because the Germans respected smartness and nobility of bearing and speech. He had neither. If only we'd had Paddon!

The Wing Commander to whom Roth referred was in fact the SBO of his own group from Barth, Noel Challis ("Hetty") Hyde. Opinions as to the efficacy of Hyde as an SBO vary widely, although most ex-kriegies consider him to have been "a gentleman", even if a bibulous one. He and Roger Bushell had still not done their time in the cooler as a result of their involvement in the Dulag Luft breakout in June. On recapture, all had been sent to Stalag Luft I, where the cells were fully booked. Thus, when they arrived at Lübeck they were promptly escorted to the cooler — the first RAF officers at Lübeck to be conferred with this dubious honour.

(2)

By now, more than enough prisoners had been gathered at Dulag Luft to make up another purge, which left for Lübeck on Monday, 11 August. It included Trumble's party, yet more officers captured in the Mediterranean, and the largest number so far of Fleet Air Arm officers to fall into German hands in any one raid. Bomber crews were in the minority. The officers with Trumble and his "ex-*Kreta*" were: Flight Lieutenants G G F Draper, T R Kipp RCAF, F L Litchfield, T H B Tayler, R F Terry RAAF, and F Thompson RAAF; Flying Officers J H L Blount, J F Clayton DFM, A P Culverwell AFC, RAFVR, and M Marcola (Pole); Pilot Officers G A Eperon, F T Clayton, C A S Greenhill DFC, E Hewson, I A Kayes, A W Sulston, and K F Thornton; Lieutenant I M Coetzee SAAF; Lieutenant H H Bracken RN; Lieutenant (A) P J Greenslade RNVR; Supply Lieutenant H F Bond RN; Sub-Lieutenants (A) T E Blacklock, C V Howard, A P Keep RN, R S Miller RNVR, J F Olsen RN, and G L Turner RNVR; and Probationary Temporary Sub-Lieutenant (A) W W Parsons RNVR.

Amongst the Bomber Command kriegies in this catch, Archibald William Sulston was by now an "old lag". An observer in a Wellington from No103 Squadron, he had been in the same crew as Harry Sellers on the night of 15/16 May when the squadron had bombed Hanover. Sellers had been sent to Laufen.

The next to enter the bag was that of Flying Officer Marcola, a Wellington observer from No305 (Ziemia Wielkopolska) Squadron, one of two bomber units formed in August 1940 from Poles who had fled their homeland in September 1939, joined the *Armée de l'Air* (the French Air Force) and then escaped again when France fell. No305 became operational in April 1941 when it moved to Syerston, in Nottinghamshire, joining No1 Group. On 9/10 July, fifty-seven Wellingtons from Nos 1 and 3 Groups set out to bomb Osnabrück. Marcola's pilot, Sergeant J Mikszo, took off from Syerston at 2312 hours. It appears from subsequent reports that the crews missed their target and dropped their bombs on two nearby villages by mistake. Of the bomber force, two were lost, most of the men going into captivity. One of Mikszo's crew, Flying Officer B P Okonski, who was also his squadron's senior gunnery instructor, was killed; but Mikszo, Marcola and the rest baled out and all were rounded up by dawn.

John Clayton and "Ep" Eperon were bagged two weeks later on Thursday, 24 July, during "Operation Sunrise" — in which "Taffy" Williams and Jim Ireton, from No76 Squadron, had also been involved. Eperon was an observer in a Halifax of No35 Squadron, which was operating from Stanton Harcourt and, like No76, was slated for la Pallice. His pilot, Flight Sergeant C A Godwin, took off at 1040 hours. Their bomber was attacked over Angles by two Me109s from *I/JG2*. Godwin was killed, along with the second pilot, the two flight engineers and two air-gunners. Only Eperon and one WOP/AG survived.

Clayton was from the same squadron as Patrick Shaughnessy, No44, which had moved to Coningsby for its part in "Operation Sunrise" — the daylight attack on Brest harbour. Clayton took off in his Hampden at 1100 hours, and along with the rest of the squadron rendezvoused with more Hampdens from Nos 77 and 144 Squadrons and the Wellingtons from Nos 12, 40, 75, 101, 103, 104, 218 and 405 Squadrons. They tucked themselves in under heavy fighter escort provided by Hurricanes from No316 Squadron and Spitfires from Nos 66, 118, 152, 234, 317 and 501 Squadrons. However, the Luftwaffe had put up aircraft in overwhelming numbers and were waiting for them. The result was a slaughter. Two Hampdens and no fewer than ten Wellingtons were lost. Several fighters attacked Clayton's aircraft, which hit the sea off Brest. The wounded navigator was unable to leave the aircraft and went down with it.

Flight Lieutenants Frank Thompson and Thomas Henry Bryan Tayler, from No15 Squadron, were bagged on 25/26 July, taking part in the same Berlin operation that had led Fuller and Michael Sherwood into kriegiedom. Along with No7 Squadron, No 15 had put up seven Stirlings to bomb Berlin, accompanied by two Halifaxes from No35 Squadron.

Bryan Tayler's RAF service had been somewhat erratic and his operational experience virtually non-existent. He had joined up on a Short Service Commission at the age of twenty-two. Posted to Hatfield, Hertfordshire, as a pupil pilot, he carried out his first flight in a Tiger Moth on 24 May 1937. After clocking up some sixty-eight hours' flying, he was posted to the RAF Depot at Uxbridge, Middlesex, where he was commissioned, kitted out and drilled. Two weeks later, scheduled for heavy bombers, he was sent to No10 Flying Training School at Tern Hill, Salop, for advanced flying training in Hawker Harts and Avro Ansons. On 26 March 1938 he was posted to No148 Squadron, at RAF Stradishall, to fly Vickers Wellesleys. The squadron retained its Wellesleys until August, when the aircraft were sent to the Middle East, and was then re-equipped with the Handley Page Heyford MkIII, some of which had come from No99 Squadron. Throughout March and April 1939, the squadron re-equipped again, this time with Wellingtons. On 4 September, the day after war was declared, it moved to RAF Harwell in Berkshire, where it became a training squadron within No6 Group, Bomber Command. Exactly seven months later, on 4 April 1940, the squadron merged with No75 to form No15 OTU. At the end of the month, the squadron was re-formed in its own right as a bomber squadron, only to be disbanded on 23 May 1940. Whilst the future of No148 was in some doubt, Tayler made plans for his own future; on 12 October 1940 he married his fiancée. He stayed with No15 OTU for some sixteen months, as an instructor, giving dual instruction to a large number of pilots that came through the unit, both on Wellingtons and later on Stirlings. But having never been on ops himself he eventually decided it was time to practise what he was preaching, and asked for a posting to an operational squadron. On 22 July 1941, he joined No15 Squadron, which flew Stirlings from Wyton, a No3 Group Station.

As one of his closest friends, Squadron Leader Tom Piper, was already based at Wyton with No15, Bryan Tayler was happy with the posting and looked forward to seeing his friend again. However, his feelings turned to sorrow when on arriving at Wyton he was informed that Squadron Leader Piper had been shot down during a daylight raid over France three days earlier and was listed as "missing". Tayler found the set-up before him most depressing, especially as the squadron commander, Wing Commander Patrick Ogilvie, informed him he was to take over Tom Piper's flight.

The following day Tayler's name appeared on the battle order. He was detailed to fly as second dickey to Pilot Officer Needham on a daylight operation against the German battle-cruiser *Scharnhorst* at la Pallice. Three crews from No15 were detailed to join three crews from No7 Squadron for the attack. Unfortunately, the raid was a failure. One crew bombed a ship at Fromontine, instead of la Pallice. Flying Officer Campbell RAAF was forced to ditch some fifty miles off Milford Haven on the return leg and the entire crew perished. Pilot Officer Needham, unable to raise the undercarriage of his aircraft, was forced to dump his bombs and fuel and return to base.

After a dual conversion flight on 24 July, Tayler was passed fit to fly solo. But he was still required to fly another operation as a second pilot to an experienced crew. The next opportunity arose the following night when seven Stirlings and two Halifaxes were detailed to make a diversionary raid on Berlin whilst main force aircraft attacked Hanover and Hamburg. Two of the Stirlings came from No7 Squadron and the other five were from No15.

A raid on Berlin was bad enough for an experienced crew, let alone a novice. But Tayler was not unduly worried, as he had been assigned to fly with Frank Thompson, an experienced bomber captain. The rest of the crew were Sergeant J T Day, flight engineer; Sergeant B Beecroft, navigator; Sergeant F Smith, wireless operator; Sergeant L C Titterton, front-gunner; and Sergeant H N Guymer RNZAF, rear-gunner. Sergeant Guymer had flown thirty trips.

Frank Thompson took off in Stirling N6029, "K for King", with five 1,000lb and seven 500lb bombs. The crews had been briefed to bomb the city at ten-minute intervals. This was asking for a lot of attention from the flak, which they duly received. Nevertheless, the Stirlings damaged some military establishments, two railway stations and an armaments factory, which was still burning the following day. Searchlights swept the sky and a barrage of hot steel exploded around the bombers. But Thompson's Stirling escaped unscathed. Sergeant Smith sent the "Operation Completed" signal, and Sergeant Beecroft set course for home.

However, something went awry with the navigation. As dawn broke, and the features of the earth below began to take shape, the crew looked out anxiously from their Stirling. To their consternation and disappointment they saw beneath them not the North Sea, but dry land. The question now was: *Where the — are we?* A check of the compass and charts revealed that their bomber was way off course. Thompson quickly asked Beecroft for a course correction, then turned onto a southwesterly heading.

They began to feel vulnerable now that it was dawn. The night-fighters had all gone to bed, but the flak gunners were wide awake and could see the Stirling's silhouette against the pale yellow sky. As the aircraft left the Dutch coast behind it, Thompson dropped to 7,000 feet, and the rear-gunner, Sergeant Guymer, saw the waves breaking on the beach. Whilst watching the sky for fighters he felt sure must soon appear, he occasionally glanced down, until the distant waves became an unbroken line of white surf as the bomber flew out over the sea. The flight engineer, Sergeant Day, had been watching the fuel gauges closely. He was worried, as the needles were fast flickering towards the zero reading. Day kept Thompson posted, and at 0540 hours Thompson told Sergeant Smith to radio Wyton that the aircraft was short of fuel. Then one of the engines packed up. Thompson warned the rest of the crew and after a brief discussion they decided to press on rather than bale out. But some forty kilometres out to sea the remaining three engines, starved of fuel, stopped dead. Thompson would have to ditch. The Stirling began to sink towards the vast expanse of water below, flying only on the vapour left in the tanks.

As the sea grew nearer, Thompson ordered the crew to their ditching positions. Air whistled eerily through the aicraft, and the crew could hear unusual knocking and clinking sounds as bits of equipment rolled about. Thompson made a good job of ditching, and each man was able to scramble through the escape hatches and climb safely aboard the dinghy. After making sure no one was injured, they sat quietly in the gently bobbing dinghy, sometimes watching their aircraft — which floated for three hours — and sometimes looking at each other, feeling cold, wet and miserable. They wondered how long it would be before they were rescued — and by whom.

When Thompson's Stirling failed to return, a search was ordered on the last reported line of bearing. Wing Commander Ogilvie immediately took off in a Lysander, and two Hawker Hurricanes departed from the No11 Group station at Martlesham Heath in Suffolk. Squadron Leader A R Oakeshott, flying a Beam Approach Training Flight Wellington, searched for two hours together with three other Wellingtons from No40 Squadron. Although there were a few local rainstorms, the sea was calm and visibility was good; but there was no sign of the dinghy.

At 1300 hours the men in the dinghy heard the sound of aircraft engines, and their hopes rose. Scanning the sky they spotted three aircraft flying in a wide "vic" formation about half a mile away. To their dismay they turned out to be Dornier Do17s, but they fired off a rocket flare, to which there was no response. Later on they tried to paddle towards a buoy, but the dinghy continued resolutely to drift on the current and soon they were "all in" and had to give up. The sea was turning rough and during the night it rained heavily, soaking them to the skin.

Not long after dawn they heard aircraft engines again, but low cloud prevented them from sighting any aircraft. The weather stayed lousy all day, and continued into the night and all the following day. Luckily, the dinghy rode the waves very well, and shipped in only small quantities of water. During their ordeal, which was to last for five days, the Stirling crew survived on rations consisting of one biscuit, two Horlicks tablets and a piece of chewing gum per person per day. They drank no water until the fourth day, when each man swallowed only one mouthful, although they did take a tot or two of rum.

At about 1900 hours on the evening of Tuesday, 29 July, their morale was given a boost when they saw two ships with a fighter escort about three miles away. The remaining flares were useless because soaking wet, so they tried waving — although this was by no means easy, as too much activity would capsize the dinghy. The fighter escort flew to within half a mile of them, and just carried on, protecting the ships. Thompson and his crew sank back into their state of cold, wet misery.

Finally, a little before 0730 hours on Wednesday, 30 July, the crew saw a thin dark strip on the horizon and realised it was land. They were drifting in towards it, so didn't bother to paddle. An hour later they were two miles away from the shoreline, but began to drift out to sea again, so they started paddling to keep land in sight. But the current was so strong that again the dinghy drifted away. They paddled flat out until 1600 hours, when they arrived safely at Haamstede on the island of Schouwen, off the Dutch coast. A party of German troops had seen them and awaited their arrival. The seven men were wet through, cold and weak around the knees, but otherwise none the worse for their five-day ordeal.

On landing they were given sweets, cigarettes, coffee and bread. They were then taken to a Luftwaffe aerodrome and given a change of clothing and some more food and coffee. After spending the night in the Luftwaffe barracks, they were sent by lorry to Amsterdam gaol, where they spent four days in solitary confinement.

In an effort to extract information from their new prisoners, the Luftwaffe pulled their usual trick of sending bogus Red Cross officials into the cells to ply the men with cigarettes, give them fake forms to fill in, and assure them that their names would then be quickly passed on to their respective families and the competent authorities. But such questions such as CO's name, time of take-off and place of take-off were all too obvious to catch them out. They may have got wet when they ditched — but they were not wet behind the ears

At 0830 hours on Saturday, 2 August, they were moved out, and by way of Utrecht arrived the next day at Dulag Luft, where they were interrogated again. When he was released into the compound after his period in the cells, Tayler heard that Tom Piper had in fact survived being shot down, and had only recently left Dulag Luft, bound for Oflag XC.

Tom Kipp, a doughty Canadian Wellington pilot from Winnipeg, Manitoba, and his Australian second pilot Ron Terry, were shot down on the night of 2/3 August, when three Wellington squadrons mustered forty aircraft to support eight Halifaxes and five Stirlings in a raid on Berlin. Kipp, from No405 (Vancouver) Squadron, took off from Pocklington at 2210 hours. The weather was hazy over the target, but the flak gunners were pin-point accurate and crippled three Wellingtons and one Stirling. None of the Wimpeys made it home. One plummeted into the North Sea; another crew ditched. There were no survivors from either aircraft. Kipp and his crew were lucky: all six baled out, to face four years behind the wire.

Pilot Officer Ian Kayes was an observer in a Whitley from No77 Squadron, Topcliffe (No4 Group). He was captured on the night of 5/6 August. Two of the crew, Pilot Officer D G Baber, the captain of the aircraft, and Sergeant A Day RCAF, the second dickey, had evaded the searching Germans. Day made it home, but Douglas Baber was eventually captured and would reach Lübeck on a subsequent purge.

Bomber Command mounted three major raids that night, on Mannheim, Karlsruhe and Frankfurt am Main. Forty-six Whitleys and twenty-two Wellingtons set out for Frankfurt, but heavy cloud and poor visibility resulted in some crews bombing Mainz, twenty miles away from the intended target, while others bombed the alternative target, Koblenz. Duggie Baber, who had taken off at 2207 hours, was one of those who bombed the alternative. But on the return leg, whilst climbing through thick cumulus cloud-banks, his aircraft was hit by flak over Ghent at about 15,000 feet. The rear-gunner, Sergeant M B C Delaney RCAF, put up a fight with his four Brownings, but searing lines of red-hot tracer raked the port wing and the side of the cabin, ripping open the instrument panel as if it was paper. Then Baber saw the first lick of flame over the port engine cowling, and Albert Day pointed a gloved hand towards the wingtip, which was starting to buckle. The Whitley became heavy in Baber's hands and was near stalling. Over Meulebeke, in Belgium, he set off the magnesium flares, warning the crew to abandon the blazing aircraft. All baled out safely, Baber remaining in his seat and crash-landing.

Flight Lieutenant Frederick Lorne Litchfield, a Wellington pilot on No115 Squadron (No3 Group), based at Marham in Norfolk, was captured the same night as Kayes, when sixty-five Wimpeys and thirty-three Hampdens targeted Mannheim. Fred Litchfield took off at 2247 hours. The raid was considered very successful, but three aircraft were lost, two complete crews being killed. The only injuries to Litchfield's crew were sustained when they abandoned the aircraft, Sergeant D A Boutle (observer) fracturing his skull, and Sergeant J G S Walker (rear-gunner) breaking his leg on landing.

An observer in a Whitley MkV of No51 Squadron, and the only officer in his crew, Francis Clayton was captured on the night of 6/7 August when forty-six Whitleys and twenty-two Wellingtons set out to bomb Frankfurt am Main. Clayton's pilot, Sergeant R J Allen, took off from Dishforth at 2200 hours but over Holland, on the return leg, was attacked by a night-fighter from *I/NJG1* flown by *Oberfeldwebel* Reinhard Kollak. One of the air-gunners, Sergeant G Haines, was injured in the exchange of fire, and the damaged aircraft crashed at twenty past two in the morning on Ginder Farm, eight kilometres south-east of Eindhoven. All five crew survived the crash, but in hospital a few hours later Haines died from his wounds.

Pilot Officer Hewson was a Blenheim MkIV pilot on No53 Squadron, a former Fighter Command unit that had been transferred to No 16 (GR) Group, Coastal Command on 3 July 1940, and then to No19 Group on 20 March 1941, being based at St Eval. Hewson had already survived one dicey operation, a "Bust" (anti-shipping) patrol on Friday, 6 June when his Blenheim was hit by flak and had limped home to a forced-landing at St Eval. The crew escaped injury (they were back on ops the next day) and the aircraft was patched up, although, unusually in these circumstances, no gongs were handed out. On Monday, 23 June, Hewson took off at 1800 hours in a replacement Blenheim on another shipping sweep, and came under fire again, but this time his aircraft did not return. His crew, Sergeants R A Dawson (observer) and W G McCorkell (a WOP/AG from Southern Rhodesia) went into captivity with him, though all three ended up in different camps and did not see each other again for the duration.

Another Coastal Command type was Arthur Philip Culverwell, a pre-war reservist who after call-up was posted to No22 Squadron, a No16 (GR) Group unit that on the outbreak of war had been based at Thorney Island and equipped with the Vickers Vildebeest Mks I, III and IV. It had since re-equipped with the Blenheim MkI and the Beaufort MkI, as well as a few Martin Marylands. It had been shunted around a lot, too, from Thorney Island, to North Coates, Lincolnshire, and back to Thorney Island again. At the end of July 1941 a detachment was flown to Manston and from there carried out "Rover" Patrols in the North Sea and the English Channel. On Saturday, 2 August, Arthur Culverwell took off at 1358 hours in company with several other aircraft to patrol the Belgian and Dutch coasts. But over Ostend, as they flew north towards Zeebrugge, they hit low cloud and fog and lost sight of each other. Culverwell's Beaufort was atacked by patrolling Me109s, fatally wounding his air-gunner, Flight Sergeant W H Dulwich. At 1525 hours the Beaufort ditched seven miles off Vlissingen (Flushing). Two of Culverwell's crew, Sergeants H C Friend (observer) and R Tanfield (wireless operator), survived the ditching with him. But Flight Sergeant Dulwich was unable to escape and his body was never recovered.

Twenty-year-old Gilbert Graham Farley Draper was one of a number of Battle of Britain veterans falling victim to German fighters in daylight sweeps on the Continent. He was with No610 Squadron at Acklington from 3 September 1940, and then on 29 September was posted to No41 Squadron, Hornchurch, equipped with the Spitfire MkVB. In the early afternoon of Thursday, 7 August 1941, his squadron comprised part of an escort for Blenheims on "Circus No67" to Lille power station. This was an unpopular target for fighter boys as it brought them within easy range of the Me109s at St Omer, but a diversionary attack had been laid on to prevent the German aircraft leaving the ground. However, the Luftwaffe still managed to put up some opposition and Gilbert Draper was set on by Me109s over Fruge, and had to abandon his aircraft.

Flying Officer John Hubert Lemprière Blount was a photo-recce Sptifire pilot from No3 PRU at Oakington, Cambridgeshire. On Wednesday, 9 April he took off in X4712 to photograph enemy shipping movements off the Dutch island of Texel, but on the way back at 1325 hours was intercepted over Holland by an Me109E flown by *Feldwebel* Mickel of the Katwijk-based *1/JG1*. His aircraft ablaze, Blount baled out.

Ian ("Tiger") Coetzee of the South African Air Force was a Martin Maryland pilot in the RAF's No39 Squadron, the recce unit in which Jack Best had also flown before failing to return on 5 May. Coetzee's crew was one of the last of No39's to be lost during an exhausting period of round-the-clock operations, carrying out a high-level recce over Crete on Friday, 13 June.

The naval officers had been among nineteen captured during two daylight raids inspired by a report compiled by Lieutenant Hugo Bracken in 1940 and eventually carried out on Friday 25 and Wednesday 30 July 1941. During the Norwegian campaign, "Bungie" Bracken, a regular officer, had commanded No701 Squadron, equipped with six Walrus amphibious aircraft that had been shore-based at Harstad in northern Norway. He had flown up to Bøkfjord, in the extreme north near the Finnish border, to investigate a reported sighting (erroneous) of German parachutists at Kirkenes harbour. When writing his report on his return to England, he had suggested that if the Germans started to use the large deepwater port at Kirkenes to export iron ore from the big mine situated near the town, this might be a suitable target for a carrier-based torpedo attack. He then forgot all about it. A year later, while "flying a desk" in the Ministry of Aircraft Production (MAP) in Thames House, London, where he was in charge of cockpit design for single-seater aircraft for the RAF and FAA, the Germans invaded Russia. Bracken was surprised in early July to receive a telephone call ordering him to report to the Admiralty, where the Vice-Chief of the Naval Staff wanted to see him. *Good God*, he thought, *what have I done wrong?* Feeling a bit apprehensive, he hopped into a taxi and, arriving at the Admiralty, was taken in to see the top-brass, who told him: "Winston Churchill says we have got to do something to assist the Russians. Other than bombing Germany with the RAF there's nothing we can do. The only plan that exists is your plan to attack Kirkenes, which the Germans are now using as their main base in North Norway for attacking towards Murmansk. We're going to send two carriers up there to attack shipping at Kirkenes and Petsamo, and, under cover of that operation, send vital supplies to the Russians in a fast mine-layer."

Bracken was flown up to Scapa Flow and embarked on HMS *Victorious,* where he joined No827 (Albacore) Squadron, in which he had served as Senior Observer immediately prior to his posting to the MAP. *Victorious* had another Albacore squadron, No828, and a squadron of two-seater Fairey Fulmar II fighters, No809. The other carrier was HMS *Furious*, with one squadron of Swordfish (No812), one of Albacores (No817), one of Fulmars (No800) and another of Sea Hurricanes. It would be the first time Sea Hurricanes were embarked in a carrier.

Towards the end of July, under the flag of Rear-Admiral W F Wake-Walker in a cruiser, *Furious* and *Victorious* set out from Scapa Flow with a destroyer screen. On the way to Norway the force put in at Iceland so the destroyers could refuel. "One of the escorting destroyers ran into one of our own minefields," recalls Bracken, "and had her bows blown off, which was hardly a good start." When they finally set out they encountered bad weather, which, had it persisted, would have favoured the impending operation, which would deploy slow but manoeuvrable biplane torpedo bombers.

The plan was for Swordfish and Albacores from HMS *Furious* to attack the ships in Petsamo on 25 July, and for Albacores from *Victorious* to bomb those in Kirkenes on 30 July, with Fulmars from both carriers providing a fighter escort. Both bombers and fighters were to approach the target at low level, but on making landfall the fighters were to climb not only to protect the bombers but also to attack the Luftwaffe airfield at Petsamo. Only light opposition was expected, as the airfield was supposed to be equipped with training aircraft. This piece of news was received with some dubiety, as they were in the proximity of the Russian-German Front.

Among the Albacore crews on HMS *Victorious* serving in No827 Squadron were Sub-Lieutenant (A) P J Greenslade RNVR, pilot, Sub-Lieutenant (A) W W Parsons RNVR, observer, and Leading Airman H Pickup, telegraphist/air-gunner; Sub-Lieutenant (A) D Myles RNVR, pilot, Sub-Lieutenant (A) A P Keep RN, observer, and Leading Airman H C G Griffin, T/AG; Sub-Lieutenant (A) J S Olsen RN, pilot, Sub-Lieutenant (A) A J Bulford RNVR, observer, and Leading Airman H J Wade, T/AG; and Lieutenant (A) A Turnbull RNVR, pilot, Lieutenant H K ("Betsy") Serjeant RN, observer, and Leading Airman J D James, T/AG. Crewed up with Bracken were Supply Lieutenant H F Bond RN, and Leading Airman E Lancaster, T/AG.

In No828 Squadron, also on the *Victorious*, were Sub-Lieutenant (A) C V Howard RN, pilot, Sub-Lieutenant (A) G L Turner RNVR, observer, and Leading Airman D E Polmeer, T/AG; Lieutenant (A) R Ross-Taylor RNVR, pilot, Sub-Lieutenant (A) S Clayton RNVR, and Leading Airman L W Miles, T/AG. Also in No828 were Sub-Lieutenant (A) L E R Bellairs RN and his observer Sub-Lieutenant (A) D M Lubbock RNVR. David Lubbock, a big, wavy-haired Scot, was a nephew of Lord Boyd-Orr, and had carried out nutrition research under him at the Rowett Institute, Aberdeen. They had co-written a book on the subject, *Feeding the Nation*, which had become the basis of the government's food rationing scheme. However, in 1940, feeling he could do more to help Britain in its hour of need, Lubbock joined the RNVR and underwent training as an observer. He was eventually posted to No828 Squadron, where he joined the crew of Lionel ("Skid") Bellairs, whose telegraphist/air-gunner was Leading Airman Jan Beer.

Among the Fulmar crews from No809 Squadron on HMS *Victorious* were Lieutenants (A) T E Blacklock RN, pilot, and T E Easton RN, the telegraphist/air-gunner; and Sub-Lieutenant (A) R S Miller, pilot, and Leading Airman Barrow, the T/AG. Tom Blacklock had joined the carrier as a pilot only in early July, when No809 Squadron was formed. He and Stan Miller were among those down to provide fighter cover for the attack on Petsamo on the 25th.

As it turned out, there was nothing to bomb at Petsamo. Any shipping there had been was long gone. So the Swordfish and Albacores lobbed their torpedoes at the empty wharves. Nevertheless, the Germans had expected the attack, and Me109s and Me110s from Petsamo were in position, resulting in the loss of three British aircraft. Tom Blacklock was forced to ditch, but both he and Easton survived. "Picked up by German patrol boat," records Blacklock laconically. "Three days at Kirkenes. Transported by coach to Rovaniemi [in Finland]. Two days there, then by air to Helsinki, Berlin and Frankfurt. Spent a few days at Frankfurt where we were interrogated…"

At Dulag Luft, Blacklock and Easton had become temporarily separated, as Easton was sent to Oflag XC in an earlier clear-out. Stan Miller was also attack by Me109s. His T/AG, Barrow, was killed by gunfire.

Despite the fiasco at Petsamo, the operation against Kirkenes took place on the 30th as planned, and again in broad daylight; it was an unmitigated disaster. *Victorious* lost thirteen aircraft, with forty-four men lost and the rest taken prisoner. Despite the weather, which gave only about two miles' visibility, all went well until the aircrews went on deck ready to climb into their aircraft. Then there was a slight change of temperature, as sometimes happens in the Arctic, and suddenly they could see a hundred miles. The commander of No827 Squadron, an observer, had also introduced a gremlin of his own. Although Bracken had been sent by the Admiralty to join the force attacking Kirkenes because he knew the area and could guide it to the right fjord, the CO of No827 Squadron insisted that he should fly in the leading aircraft himself and direct them to the target. After a furious row, Bracken was relegated to flying as Observer to Supply Lieutenant Bond in the third sub-flight of No827.

Forming up after take-off they noticed that one of the destroyers was firing on a German reconnaissance aircraft; the Germans had spotted them. Despite this the carrier-borne aircraft still flew in at low level. As the Kirkenes formation approached the target the commander of No827 Squadron led them up Kjøfjord — the wrong fjord. Roaring: "We're going to the wrong place, for Christ's sake!" Bracken forced his pilot to break off. So his sub-flight, one or two others from No827 and all of No828 went up Bøkfjord, which was the right fjord. The others soon realised their mistake and flew across to join the main formation, but by then they had lost much precious time. As they flew into Kirkenes harbour they saw directly ahead a German gunnery training ship, the *Bremser*. Bracken's pilot selected this as his target, went down and dropped his torpedo. It passed right under the *Bremser* without exploding. The torpedoes were armed with Duplex heads, which were set to detonate on coming into contact with a ship's magnetic field. However, with Kirkenes being so rich with veins of iron ore, there was obviously a risk that the Duplex heads might not function normally. This Bracken had pointed out. He had suggested fitting contact heads instead, but once again he was overruled —"We don't need lieutenants from the Admiralty to plan this operation."

As each Albacore dropped its torpedo it headed back out of Bøkfjord and set a return course for the *Victorious*. It was then that the Messerschmitts from Petsamo airfield went into the attack. One of them got on Bracken's tail, making six passes as the Albacore kept turning inside him. "But we weren't going anywhere," recalls Bracken.

[We were] making very little distance. When we were being attacked, I didn't feel very frightened at all. There was so much going on, and I was trying to talk to the pilot, telling him when to turn, and looking around…Then finally a cannon-shell hit the rudder and we crashed into the sea from a height of about 200 feet. I was flung out of the rear cockpit and went through the air for about a hundred yards or so, and landed in the sea. When I surfaced, I looked back and I saw the pilot and the air-gunner had been able to get out. After about twenty minutes a German mine-sweeper came and picked us up.

We were taken back into the harbour, alongside this ship, the *Bremser*. We were stark naked with blankets round us, and the German captain came down in his white suit and with his dirk, gave us a big salute and said: "Bad luck, gentlemen. Your torpedo went under my ship without exploding." We were then taken ashore and we had a very brief interrogation. Then we were taken down by bus to a place called Rovaniemi, in Finland, where we were kept for a couple of days before being flown down in a Ju52, first of all to Helsinki, then to Königsberg, and then to Stettin. Then we were taken to Berlin, and to Dulag Luft.

I had no complaints about the way we were treated. I think most people's experience was that front line troops, unless you were caught in the heat of combat, normally treated prisoners better than second-line or third-line troops. It's quite a shaking experience being shot down and taken prisoner and we were very, very depressed. It was quite obvious as we were taken past the harbour in the mine-sweeper that none of the ships had been hit — none of the torpedoes went off, not one of them, except when they hit the shore. We lost eleven aircraft out of twenty, and the fighters lost four out of twelve. So, having achieved absolutely nothing, I must be honest about it, my morale was pretty damn low, and I think everybody else's was, too.

With the gift of hindsight, we should have made an attempt to hijack the Ju52; but our morale was very low and the Germans had obviously envisaged such an attempt, since we could see through the cabin door that both pilots had pistols on the dashboard in front of them. An attack by a prisoner on a guard with a weapon was a court martial offence resulting, at best, in a lengthy prison sentence with hard labour. The chances of success had to be very good to take such a risk.

At that stage in the war the Germans were terribly cocky. They were really winning in Russia and they thought they'd got it all sewn up. They were rather saying to us, Why are you fighting against us with those ghastly Russians? When we were taken to Berlin there was practically no damage at all there. The Germans...tried to adopt the V-sign as their sign.

At Dulag Luft, I was interrogated by the Commandant, *Oberst* Rumpel, but to be honest I don't think they were very interested in us Naval people. They knew perfectly well which aircraft-carriers we came from...They knew the type of aircraft we were flying. His interrogation of me was really very cursory. But he was very nice and chatty and all the rest of it; there was no question of any sort of pressure being applied at all.

At least four more aircraft from No827 Squadron were shot down attacking ships in Bøkfjord. Sub-Lieutenant Keep's Albacore was hit while he was lobbing his torpedo at a ship at anchor; he made it across Finnmark only to crash east of the island of Reinøy. All his crew survived, but Myles was injured and would remain at Dulag Luft and Hohemark clinic for several months before going to Stalag Luft III in April 1942. (The tail of Keep's Albacore was salvaged in 1984 and presented to the Fleet Air Arm Museum.) John Olsen's Albacore was crippled in the same attack. He and Bulford were taken prisoner, but Leading Airman Wade was killed. Bulford, like Myles, would later be sent to Stalag Luft III. Greenslade and Parsons were shot down while similarly engaged; they and their T/AG also survived. Angus Turnbull and "Betsy" Serjeant were attacked by an Me110 and crashed in the sea off Vardø, north of Kirkenes and on the easternmost tip of the Varangerhalvøya peninsula. All three of the crew were wounded. Turnbull was another who would be sent to Stalag Luft III after several months at Hohemark.

Of those from No828 Squadron, Howard and Turner were shot down over the target. All three of the crew survived. Robin Ross-Taylor and his crew also came out of their wrecked Albacore alive, Clayton eventually being sent to Stalag Luft III.

Lionel Bellairs, also of No828 Squadron, came under fire from Me110s on the return leg. The T/AG, Jan Beer, returned fire and probably downed the Messerschmitt, but one of the Albacore's wings was badly holed and Beer was killed in the exchange. David Lubbock received metal splinters in one eye and was temporarily blinded. As they did not have enough wing surface left to land on the carrier, Bellairs decided to turn east and cross the German lines into the USSR. He was amazed that the Albacore could still fly on three wings. They then had a dogfight with an

Me109, which finally peeled off after running out of ammunition. By then the Albacore was riddled with holes, and Bellairs had to put her down in the tundra, which he did with consummate skill. He and Lubbock started walking towards the USSR but had to walk through Finland and the German lines. They were captured on Saturday, 9 August, at Grense Jacobselv.

The metal splinters David Lubbock had received soon began giving him eye trouble. "Those sticking out of the eyeball were very carefully and well removed by a young German doctor in the front line," he later recalled, "but one or more within caused a weakness in my vision such that I could only read the first couple of lines of a book before it all became blurred."

There is an interesting postscript to the Bellairs and Lubbock story. Bellairs was a friend of George Miles, chief designer and technical director of Miles Aircraft, Reading, and his wife Corinne. A few nights before Bellairs was shot down George dreamt that he was Lionel and that he was in the cockpit of a severely disabled Swordfish. His vision became obscured, apparently owing to a blowback of hot oil from the engine. He then awoke sweating and told Corinne about the nightmare. In early August they read an announcement in *The Times* that Lionel was missing. Once they had established that he was a POW, Corinne wrote telling him about George's nightmare. By the time he received it he was in Oflag VIB, Warburg, and he wrote back: "I was very interested in George's dream. I think there must be something in it."

Fifty years later a group of Norwegians found and recovered Bellairs' Albacore. Inside was the skeleton of Beer, minus the skull. The Norwegians reconstructed the rest of the skeleton, packed it into a suitcase and handed it to the Naval Attaché in Oslo.

By the time Lubbock and "Skid" Bellairs reached Dulag Luft most of the other officers shot down at Kirkenes and Petsamo were either in Hohemark clinic or had already left for Lübeck. Only Ross-Taylor and Serjeant remained in the transit camp. They and Bellairs would be transferred to Lübeck on 25 August, but Lubbock was asked to stay on. Acting Wing Commander D R S Bader DSO*, DFC*, who had lost his legs in a flying accident in 1930 and yet gone on to become a legendary Battle of Britain fighter "ace", had recently arrived at Dulag Luft, and Lubbock, who was the only prisoner with any medical experience, was asked to look after Bader's stumps and artificial legs. He did not reach Lübeck until 5 October.

Prior to leaving Dulag Luft Tony Trumble's much-increased party was issued with Red Cross parcels, not only for themselves but also for the rest of the Air Force contingent at Lübeck. They travelled in third class railway carriages. On arrival at the camp, in the late afternoon, each was issued with a white towel and two blankets; they were then crowded in barrack No4. Bryan Tayler was given a warm welcome from his chum Tom Piper, with whom he was able to share a room. On Monday, 18 August, the Germans took away the blankets — they were destined for the *Ostfront* — and gave each prisoner a poorer one in return.

Every Friday they had to take their towels on morning parade for inspection by the *Lageroffizier* (compound officer), *Hauptmann* Schultz, to see whether they were soiled enough for exchange. They were being treated like schoolboys, and found it tiresome and irritating.

The prisoners were counted twice daily, parading in ranks determined by block numbers, each called a "company". Morning *Appell* was at 8.30. As the companies paraded, a German non-com called out the prisoners' names, in very bad English. On hearing his name, each officer stepped forward and said: "Here!" If for some reason a particular officer wasn't present, a confederate would answer to his name and the Germans were none the wiser. Meanwhile, soldiers went round each company, counting. This gave the prisoners the opportunity to have a bit of fun, moving around during the count and greeting the figure reached by the Germans with cries of "Rubbish!" The entire farce had then to be repeated. "I don't think they ever knew who or how many were there," recalled Paddy Denton, "but they followed their drill and we had our chuckle."

After *Appell* the men returned to their messes for thin mint tea, very slightly sweetened. It was issued in large metal jugs from the cookhouse and was usually lukewarm by the time it reached the messes. Most men treated themselves to a small slice of their meagre bread supply, with perhaps a scraping of *Speisefett* saved from the previous days' rations. These were issued each morning and consisted of a loaf of black bread per man weighing between 200 and 300 grams, plus a piece of fat the size of two walnuts which might be margarine or some form of cooking fat, a tablespoonful of potted meat or tinned horseflesh, and the same amount of *ersatz* jam or whey cheese. Each prisoner divided his rations in such a way that they would last him for three or four meals.

Morning tea was followed by ablutions and washing up the crockery. As the Germans issued each man with only one cake of soap per fortnight, the crockery was cleaned with sand. Many of the prisoners grew beards to avoid the unpleasantness of shaving with cold water, little soap and blunt razors. Once these chores had been performed, there was nothing for prisoners to do except lounge about until lunchtime. The library of English books was small, and the only other reading fodder was the stock of German language textbooks obtainable through the canteen. Thus, many prisoners turned to learning the language. German speakers were the most fortunate, as they were employed on the British camp staff; those not on official camp duties were much in demand as tutors.

The midday meal — issued, like the mint tea, from the cookhouse — consisted of a bowl of watery cabbage soup per man along with three or four medium-sized potatoes boiled in their skins. Some men ate the skins, some removed them. Those who preferred to peel the potatoes let their companions draw lots as to who should eat the skins. But after a time, hunger became so acute that there were no peelings left over. In the afternoon, there was more time to kill until a further issue of mint tea at 6pm, followed by another hour on *Appell*. Now and then they were issued with *Blutwurst* (black pudding).

Red Cross parcels would arrive only intermittently, and the prisoners shed pounds in weight. This was particularly hard on the "ex-*Kreta*", the majority of whom were sick with dysentery and malaria when they arrived. The diet and conditions did nothing to hasten their recovery and some of them went down to seven stones in weight.

After his spell in the cooler, Wing Commander Hyde assumed the mantle of Senior RAF Officer and appointed Bushell as Adjutant. Bushell was aghast at the appalling German rations and made strenuous, but unavailing, attempts to remedy the situation. He was also surprised that the Army officers had received no Red Cross parcels: they should be issued at the rate of one per man per week. He also informed them that they were entitled to receive three private clothing parcels a year with up to one pound in weight of chocolate. To the discredit of the RAF contingent, some of the younger, more ebullient types who had passed through Dulag Luft and Stalag Luft I regaled them with mouth-watering descriptions of the contents of food parcels, which for the starving Army officers was pure torture. For their part the "ex-*Kreta*" made clear their objection to being so called, and so to the former Barth contingent they became the "Cretan Freaks".

Camp money was issued weekly, but the canteen was so poorly stocked that it was worthless to the prisoners. All they could buy were useless items such pepper, pepper-pots, various synthetic sauces (mainly a weak equivalent to chop sauce), vases, plates, bowls, cutlery, brushes and combs, safety razors and blades, matches, cigarette-making machines, cigarette papers and Balkan tobacco. They were, however, issued with twenty *Caporals* per man per week. By saving the butts and rolling them into second-runs with the Balkan tobacco, the issue could just about last the week, though the cigarettes got thinner day by day. The *Unteroffizier* in charge of the canteen kept meticulous records of the pay and expenditure. Unfortunately, because Germans issued the scrip according to their own pay scale, the credit balance remaining once British and Commonwealth officers had made their purchases was low.

The "brown jobs" were more organised than the RAF, and before long they set up an exchange and mart, with a currency based on cigarettes; they also put out a camp newspaper and discovered ingenious ways of making the German issue rations palatable. Michael Roth copied one of the newspaper articles, along with a recipe, into his diary:

Extracts from a camp handwritten newspaper run by enterprising Army officers:

Exchange and Mart — Lübeck

Oflag XC's market has been one of the world's most unstable. The Financial Reporter has produced a list of exchange rates using cigarettes as common currency. Freak deals have been included. For example:

One mess tin (British Army issue) for a promised pair of artificial silk vests and pants-underwear.

Ten Marks for one cheese ration.

Five Marks for one English cigarette.

Bread has been the highest basis of exchange, camp money the lowest, and cigarettes the most usual. Types of cigarettes on the barter market include:

English, Belgian, Yugoslavian, American, Greek, Portuguese, Dutch and Canadian.

Current rates of exchange using cigarettes as the unit of currency. (This was before any bulk issue of cigarettes arrived from the Red Cross):

Item	Maximum	Minimum
Bread ration (1/5 loaf)	40 cigarettes	10
Fig-biscuit ration	3 for 2	1
Potatoes	2 for large one	1 for small
Large billy-can	60	40
Hag-cola-*ersatz*	2	
Margarine ration	6	
Sausage ration	4	
Fat ration	4	
Can pea soup	15	
Jam ration	10	5
Cheese	10	5
5 fig biscuits	15	5

Cooking Recipes

Jam Pudding, Lübeck:

Take three parts of breadcrumbs, a quarter of them roasted, to one part of mashed potatoes. Mix in one packet of powdered hag-cola, half a week's jam ration, moisten the lot to a dough. Steam the mixture in a tightly covered bowl for half an hour, and the result will have the consistency and taste (?) of Plum Pudding.

NB. The editor it not responsible for statements made by correspondents, but will accept cooked samples.

To make steak and kidney pudding Lübeck, substitute a ration of liver sausage for the sweetening above, and cook in the same way. Says the cook: "Close your eyes when eating and it really is steak and kidney pudding!"

(3)

On Monday, 25 August, another purge arrived from Oberursel. Under the leadership of Squadron Leader A F H Mills of the RCAF, they were: Squadron Leader S G Long RAFO; Acting Squadron Leaders H Budden DFC and L E Collings RAAF; Flight Lieutenants C C Cheshire, R McD Durham and A D Gosman; Flying Officers L H Casson DFC, AuxAF, M G Geoghegan and J A Little; Acting Flying Officer W A Staniland; Pilot Officers W C Chadwick, J R Gibbon, G H Hill and J H O'Byrne RAAF; Lieutenant H K Serjeant RN; Lieutenants (A) L E Bellairs RN and R Ross-Taylor RNVR; and Sub-Lieutenant (A) R A Burroughs RNVR.

Squadron Leader Mills, Acting Flying Officer Arthur ("Hank") Staniland and Pilot Officers Hill and Chadwick were all from No18 Squadron, and all were captured on the same day, Tuesday, 12 August, when No2 Group mounted "Circus No77". This was part of Bomber Command's campaign to help the Russians by harassing the Germans into drawing fighters from the East. The plan called for a daylight attack on the electricity power stations at Knapsack and Quadrath-

Fortuna, near Cologne, with thirty-six Blenheims setting out for Knapsack and eighteen for Quadrath. Force I, the smaller formation, would comprise three boxes of six aircraft from Nos 21 and 82 Squadrons, led by Wing Commander J O C Kercher, the former squadron's CO; Force II, six boxes of six aircraft from Nos 18, 107, 114 and 139 Squadrons, would be led in by Wing Commander J L Nichol. They would rendezvous with their fighter escort over Martlesham Hearth, leave the English coast at Orfordness at 1000 hours and then fly to the Schelde estuary at low level with a heavy fighter escort, including the Westland Whirlwinds of No263 Squadron. However, as the Belgian coast was the limit of the Whirlwinds' endurance, other fighter boys would be making elaborate diversionary raids on St-Omer and Gosnay along with a force of Hampdens. There would also be a series of supporting raids by Flying Fortresses.

Despite these elaborate diversions and spoof raids, the operation seemed suicidal to the Blenheim pilots, who would have to hedge-hop 150 miles across enemy-held territory, unescorted and in broad daylight, to attack important, heavily defended targets in mainland Germany, and afterwards (assuming the initial achievement of actually reaching and bombing the target) make their way back with the formation widely dispersed and vulnerable to attack by enemy fighters, which by then would have been alerted and awaiting the moment to pounce.

Pilot Officer Hill took off from Horsham St Faith at 0920 hours, and Mills five minutes later. Mills had left Calgary, Alberta, to join the RCAF long before the war, and his observer, "Hank" Staniland, had joined No18 Squadron at Oulton, in Norfolk, in June 1941 and had survived twelve low-level operations. Each carrying two 500lb bombs, the Blenheims picked up their fighter escort as planned and flew tight box formations the entire way at fifty feet. Mills was leading the last box of six. This meant he would be last over the target, and as the two leading sections would be bombing at fifty feet using twelve-second delayed action fuses, he would have to attack from 800 feet to escape the blast. The formation crossed Holland without incident and, although the Whirlwinds reached the limit of their endurance well short of Cologne, most bomber crews reached Germany. They soon knew they were over Germany: the farm labourers in the fields below stopped waving and, instead, looked for cover or fell flat on their faces.

The Me109s were soon upon them, and two Blenheim crews were shot down without even seeing the target; another hit a power cable and spun in, and a fourth turned for home. As Mills approached Cologne and started to climb, Sergeant L C ("Mitch") Mitchell, the WOP/AG, reported an Me109 on their tail, so he dived back to fifty feet to throw him off. Mills succeeded, but ahead of him loomed Knapsack with its intense flask barrage. Eventually the Blenheim reached bombing height, but as Staniland was releasing his bombs, flak hit the port engine. Mills turned for home, but with the propeller juddering violently, the Blenheim was losing air-speed and lagging behind. Mitch then reported a large hole near the starboard engine and bullet-holes in the wing. So Mills alerted the rest of the box and advised them to rejoin the main formation and carry on home. Then, to cap it all, the port propeller flew off and another Me109 came in to attack, leaving a jagged hole eight inches long just below Mills's seat.

Flying at fifty feet on one engine, they eventually neared the Dutch coast. Just when they thought they had a good chance of crossing the North Sea and lobbing the Blenheim down on the nearest airfield, they were hit by flak from one of the batteries based along the northern stretch of River Schelde. It was then attacked by an Me109, flown by *Oberleutnant* Baron *Freiherr* Hubertus von Holtey of *JG26*, based at Wevelgem. Mills made it to the coast, but had to ditch in the Westerschelde. The aircraft came to rest in shallow water 800 metres from the flak post, the tail unit still visible from the coast. Mills had sustained a minor head injury and was feeling groggy. Staniland and Mitch inflated the dinghy and they drifted on the tide until they were picked up a few minutes later by a small *Kriegsmarine* vessel. They were put ashore at Flushing and taken to the local airfield, where they were interrogated by a Luftwaffe officer. On Thursday, 14 August, after a spell in hospital, they were entrained for Dulag Luft.

For the rest of the Blenheims, it was a similar story. Another aircraft was hit by flak over the target, and although the Luftwaffe had risen to the bait put out by the diversions, they were not fooled for long. On the return leg the Blenheims were savagely mauled by fighters, and another five were destroyed. Pilot Officer Hill's aircraft crashed at Diest, in Belgium. Chadwick, his observer, badly injured his leg and the crew stayed with him to ensure he received medical help. Another two Blenheims, detailed to act as navigation leaders for the fighter support, also failed to return. Thus the total number of Blenheims lost that day was twelve — twenty-two per cent of the aircraft that set out, or 18.50 per cent of the force that actually attacked. Every aircraft in No107 Squadron was damaged, and six Spitfires were also lost in the diversionary "Circuses". However, No2 Group felt it had been let off lightly, as most crews had reported accurate bombing. Even so, Group was in no hurry to mount another such daylight deep-penetration raid.

That night saw the capture of Harry Budden, Christopher Cheshire, "Mac" Durham, Michael Gerald Geoghegan, Ray Gibbon, Alexander Douglas Gosman and James Alexander Little, who were among seventy crews — manning Wellingtons, Halifaxes, Stirlings and Avro Manchesters — briefed to bomb the *Reichsluftfahrtministerium* (Air Ministry) buildings in Berlin's Wilhelmstrasse. Christopher Cheshire was a Halifax pilot in No76 Squadron (No4 Group), which had been formed at Middleton St George, in County Durham, in June 1941. Tall and blond, with a youthful, sparkling laugh, he was, at twenty-one, two years younger than his brother Leonard, who would go on to win the VC and lead No617 ("Dam Buster") Squadron. He had been in the middle of his second year studying law at Oxford when the war started and had immediately thrown it up to join the RAF, initially being posted to a Whitley squadron in Yorkshire. He was now due to go on a staff posting at Bomber Command HQ, but insisted on returning to ops.

Both Christopher and Leonard were slated to take part in the 12/13 August sortie. Earlier in the day Leonard had been told by his Flight Commander: "You're going missing tonight." "Who told you that story?" asked Leonard. "Just a premonition, but my premonitions are always right." As it turned out, he was only half-right, for it was Christopher, in Halifax "L-London", who went missing. He was flying above 15,000 feet over a murderous flak barrage near Bremen when his Halifax was caught and held by a group of searchlights. Try as he might to escape them, he could not, and a shell burst on the tail-wheel, killing the rear-gunner and putting the aircraft out of control. It went into a dive and Christopher gave the order to bale out. The wireless operator, observer and second pilot all jumped in turn. Christopher was next at the escape hatch, with his flight engineer close behind. By this time the Halifax was diving steeply and Christopher stepped over the escape hatch and let the engineer go first. Then Christopher followed. All those who had abandoned the aircraft landed safely, but the front-gunner had no time to escape and was killed when the aircraft crashed.

Jim Little and Mick Geoghegan were pilot and second dickey in a Manchester from No97 (Straits Settlements) Squadron, based at Waddington (No5 Group). The Berlin raid was only their third operation. Their Manchester hit by flak, they ordered the crew to bale out over Münster. All the NCOs in the crew survived, although one of them, Sergeant G L Scott of the RNZAF, broke his leg and was admitted to hospital.

Harry Budden was on No104 Squadron (No4 Group). He had previously been on No51 Squadron, which he joined before the war, and had completed his first tour of operations by July 1940. Budden led his flight off from Driffield at 2125 hours. His aircraft, too, was hit by flak, and Budden ordered the crew to abandon. Again only one of the crew was injured, when Sergeant L G Smalley, the wireless operator, landed heavily and broke an ankle.

Alex Gosman, Ray Gibbon and "Mac" Durham were pilot, second pilot and observer on the same Wellington from No142 Squadron (No1 Group). They took off from Binbrook, Lincolnshire, at 2046 hours. Although it was a lovely, clear, moonlit night, there were 60mph gusts, and when Durham reported that they had reached their target Ray Gibbon was sceptical, as they were seventeen minutes ahead of their estimated time of arrival. They dropped a flare, and within seconds flak came up at them from everywhere. It was "The Big City", all right! However, they had by now overshot the target, so went round again on a reciprocal course — and missed it. So, naturally, they went round again. Gosman made a steady bomb-run, and they dropped their load. By this time they had been more than five minutes over their target, and the flak had found them, hitting the port wing and putting the engine out of action. Gosman and Gibbon struggled to maintain height on one engine, but the Wimpey continued to sink, and the only options they had were to abandon the aircraft or risk buying it when the crippled crate crashed. They baled out.

Lionel Harwood ("Buck") Casson and Justin O'Byrne were both Spitfire pilots with the Tangmere Wing and both were shot down on the same day. Casson had fought throughout most of the Battle of Britain with No616 Squadron, Leconfield, Yorkshire, and O'Byrne was from No452 (RAAF) Squadron at Kirton-in-Lindsey, Lincolnshire.

In early March Wing Commander Douglas Bader had arrived as the new Wing Leader. The following month No616 Squadron started bomber escort and offensive patrols over Northern France. A few weeks later they moved from Tangmere, Sussex, to the nearby satellite airfield at Westhampnett. Thereafter, the Tangmere Wing was continually in action escorting "Circuses" to France. Usually Bader led with No616 Squadron, providing the middle airspace cover, while No145, from Merston, another Sussex airfield, gave top cover. The Tangmere Wing's "kill" rate mounted, but so did the losses. In July No616 Squadron, which hitherto had flown Hurricanes, re-equipped with the Spitfire MkVB, armed with cannon in the wings. Sweeps over Abbeville, St Omer and Gravelines brought further success. However, Colin MacFie, the commander of "B" Flight, was lost and Casson was promoted to take over. During July the Squadron was credited with fourteen kills and many probables and damaged, almost all the victims being Me109s.

On Saturday, 9 August, following some poor weather, the Wing was ordered to escort six Blenheims to Gosnay power station on "Circus No68", but the sortie went badly from the beginning. Bader's radio was faulty and the top cover squadron, flying its first operation since relieving the experienced No145 Squadron, failed to make the rendezvous. Crossing the coast, they spotted some Me109s climbing towards them in formation; led by Bader, No616 dived to attack, while No610 Squadron remained to give limited top cover. Casson was behind Bader and to starboard with three other aircraft from "B" Flight. More Me109s of *JG26*, led by *Oberstleutnant* Adolf Galland, pounced on the Spitfire squadrons and in the ensuing mêlée all formation cohesion was lost. It was every pilot for himself as the Spitfires tried to disengage and return home. Lionel Casson, Douglas Bader and Justin O'Byrne were all shot down to spend the rest of the war as prisoners.

Casson noticed that the other aircraft in "B" Flight were lagging behind and throttled back as Bader peeled off to port. He had a quick squirt at two Me109s, flying together, from the rear, and then saw another enemy aircraft on its own and turned on him. He used up nearly all his cannon ammunition, destroying its tail unit, and the pilot baled out at 6,000 feet. Casson then spotted four Spitfires, three of them from "A" Flight, circling at 13,000 feet with numerous Me109s around, and climbed to join the formation. A running combat took place, but about fifteen miles from the coast he saw a lone Spitfire, well below and about half a mile to starboard. The Spitfire was moving very slowly and seemed to be in trouble. Casson failed to attract the pilot's attention with his radio calls, so left the formation to assist, telling the other Spitfires to follow. They did not. Instead, they dived into a layer of cloud to the south-west and disappeared.

Hauptmann Gerhard Schopfel, the *Gruppenkommandeur* of *III/JG26*, spotted Casson's Spitfire, and he and his wingman closed for an attack. As Casson drew up alongside the lone Spitfire he heard shells thudding into his fuselage and wing, saw the two Me109s in his mirror and realised that the other Spitfires had not followed him. He broke for some cloud at 5,000 feet, but found it was too thin to provide cover. The Me109s were still in hot pursuit. He dived to treetop height, hoping to cross the Channel at low level. Some damage had been caused to his engine, which was overheating and running rough. By now two more Me109s had joined the party, and they soon gained on him and began firing again. They were flying from port to starboard and delivering quick bursts. Shells pounded into his aircraft from behind, hitting his armour plating, instruments and fuel tank. One passed between his right leg and the joystick, taking off part of the rudder and lodging in the fuel tank. With the cockpit filling with fuel, oil pressure dropping, and glycol overheating, he tried one more desperate attempt to shake off the enemy fighters, but his engine seized. He sent a message to Bader, having no idea where he was, then blew up the wireless and made a hasty forced-landing in a field on the edge of a wood near

St Omer. The German fighters circled overhead, giving his position to a cavalry unit in the corner of the field. Casson set his aircraft on fire, and a posse of shrieking Germans rushed towards him. He was marched off to captivity as Schopfel returned to base to record his thirty-third victory.

Casson was taken before a Luftwaffe *General*, and spent the night in a room with two German guards. The next day he was escorted to Dulag Luft. He spent only one day in the cooler before being released into the compound. On Thursday, 21 August he and O'Byrne were surprised, but delighted, to see Douglas Bader stump through the gate. Within a few days they were split up and Casson and O'Byrne left for Lübeck.

Of the two Coastal Command officers, Squadron Leader Samuel Godfrey Long, of the Reserve of Air Force Officers, was, like Henry Lamond, that rare thing in a German prison camp — a Short Sunderland pilot. On Tuesday, 17 June, at about 2200 hours, he had taken off from the River Itchen at Winchester to deliver the flying boat from No119 Squadron, Pembroke Docks, to "Gib". The Sunderland was a converted civil aviation model, formerly known as *The Golden Fleece*. Among the fourteen crew and passengers on board were Brigadier R L Taverner, of the King's Shropshire Light Infantry, bound for a posting in the Middle East, and Corporal L G Corcoran, an RAAF air-gunner, who on 21 April had been one of five survivors out of an eleven-man crew of a Sunderland that, owing to bad weather, had become lost on patrol and ditched in the North Sea. Today, the weather was very calm. But as Squadron Leader Long flew south they began to encounter a warm front and almost tropical winds. The oil temperature rose and, even with the coolant on maximum, it was far too high. By 0300 hours the temperature outside had started to drop, but by then the oil system for the port outer engine had developed a fault. Deeming it best to return to England, Long turned back. But fifteen minutes later the same problem occurred with the port inner engine. So he turned again, towards Spain and Portugal. It soon became clear, however, that he would have to put her down. As he did so, the Sunderland broke up and Taverner, Long, Les Corcoran, Sergeant J E Hill and AC1 J Anderson scrambled into the dinghy. The other nine men disappeared into the deep with the wreckage of the Sunderland, their bodies never to be recovered. The survivors sat mournfully in their dinghy and waited for dawn to break.

They drifted for three days. Twice a day an He115 floatplane patrolled the area, and they did nothing to attract its attention. But they did holler and wave frantically at a coastal steamer and a fishing fleet — to no avail. Finally, on the fourth morning, confronted with another bright and windless day, they had no alternative but to attract the attention of the patrolling He115. The pilot waited for another floatplane to arrive, and while it circled overhead, dropped down and picked up Long and the rest. They were taken to a *Kriegsmarine* base near St-Nazaire, where they spent forty-eight hours in the naval hospital. The Germans and the hospital staff treated them well, providing them with the best red and white French wines. There were worse ways to enter captivity. *En route* to Dulag Luft they bade farewell to Brigadier Taverner, who was being sent to an Army camp and would eventually become Senior British Officer at Oflag IXA/H.

Acting Squadron Leader Les Collings, the other Coastal Command type, had been skipper of the Beaufort from No217 Squadron in which Pilot Officer William Hunter had been observer on 25 July. Both of Collings's legs had been peppered with shrapnel, some of which had been plucked out by doctors at Brest hospital. His treatment continued at the Hohemark clinic and he could now walk again, albeit with the aid of sticks.

Of the four Fleet Air Arm officers, three of them — Lionel Bellairs, Robin Ross-Taylor and "Betsy" Serjeant — almost completed the quota of Albacore crews captured during the disastrous daylight raids on Kirkenes on 30 July and destined for Oflag XC. (David Lubbock was still at Dulag Luft.)

The remaining naval aircrew officer, Sub-Lieutenant Ronald ("Box") Burroughs, was another Fulmar observer from No809 Squadron. He had the good fortune to escape the massacre over Petsamo and Kirkenes, but Lady Luck stopped smiling on him on Monday, 4 August, when the aircraft from *Victorious* attacked shipping at Tromsø, on the north-west coast of Norway. His pilot is also reported to have been taken prisoner, although efforts to trace him have proved fruitless.

* * *

At Oflag XC Casson was reunited with his former Flight Commander, Colin MacFie, who had recently been awarded the Distinguished Flying Cross in his absence. A few days later Casson learnt that he, too, had been awarded the DFC. The citation highlighted his service from Dunkirk throughout the Battle of Britain and the "large number of offensive patrols over Northern France. His efficiency, leadership, and courage have set an excellent example…"

There was another, cooler, reunion when Alex Gosman recognised Michael Roth. Gosman had been acting adjutant on his squadron in 1940, and although their friendship had only ever been lukewarm, he invited Roth to mess in his room, where there were a few vacant bunks. Also in Gosman's mess were Ross-Taylor and Lionel Bellairs, whom Roth thought somewhat embittered at the way in which the daylight operation on which they had been shot down was conducted. "Taylor and Bellairs were already preparing some choice remarks for the Admiral after the war," Roth recalled.

Lionel Casson kept a laconic record of his experiences in Lübeck. His recollections for September make for gloomy reading: "Much of POW Reich ration was sold off in Lübeck. Cold at night with only one blanket. Walked round compound. Lost a lot of weight. Inoculated TAB." Michael Roth also kept a record, some pages of which escaped the *Abwehr* searches. His entry for Sunday, 7 September reads: "Fire in camp — caused by cooking in one of the huts. Germans furious. Shots. One chap wounded."

Nights were enlivened only by the passage of British aircraft overhead on their way to Berlin and other targets. The flak at Lübeck always opened up and it was the only time when the prisoners did not mind having their sleep disturbed. One exception was Michael Roth, who regarded the raids as a "peril…The Goons had batteries all round the camp, and after they'd pumped away half the night we were a pretty shaken lot. We spent a lot of time on the floor either under the table or under our bunks. It was frightening."

On the night of 7/8 September a bomber passing over the camp started circling. The German gun batteries opened up, and the bomber jettisoned a stick of incendiaries. Most of them landed in the German compound, hitting the *Lazarett* and the German Officers' mess, completely gutting it, but some hit one of the barrack blocks and went through the roof. The prisoners cheered the hits and fires in the German compound — until the garrison threatened to shoot them. Later, they discovered that one of the HEs had landed on the bed of an Army Major, Anthony Holden of the Nottinghamshire Yeomanry. He was injured so badly that one of his legs had to be amputated.

(4)

On Monday, 8 September another party of RAF arrived, the fourth direct purge from Dulag Luft. On it were: Squadron Leaders M M Kane MBE and B G Morris; Flight Lieutenants J A Cant, W Cunningham and D N Sampson; Flying Officer E A Rance RAFVR; and Pilot Officers W W Chciuk (Pole), G W Cole, D Cowley, R R Henderson RCAF, F M V Johnstone, H G Keartland SAAF, W L MacDonald, J P McKechnie, E C Maskell, C D Roberts, H B Robertshaw, T M Robinson, F W Shorrock RCAF and M G Williams.

Of the bomber crews, Flight Lieutenant "Sammy" Sampson and Pilot Officer Cole had both fallen victim to night-fighters on 14/15 August, when 152 aircraft had set out to plaster Hanover, with railway stations as aiming points. Both were from No102 Squadron at Topcliffe, the Whitley squadron on which Paddy Denton had flown. Sampson took off at 2202 hours. Cole was a second dickey to Sergeant A W Hawkes, who took off at 2210 hours. Both aircraft were shot down on the outward leg. Sampson's Whitley was attacked by *Oberleutnant* Ludwig Becker of *4/NJG1* and crashed in Holland at about a quarter past one on the morning of the 15th. All his crew survived. Sergeant Hawkes's aircraft crashed half an hour later near Jögel in Germany. The rear-gunner was killed, but Hawkes, Cole and the rest, along with Sampson, became hyperboles — "not dead, but prisoners".

John Arthur Cant, Hugh Keartland and Robinson had been captured on 16/17 August. That night Bomber Command put up seventy-two aircraft for yet another raid on Cologne, this time to bomb the railway marshalling yards. The squadrons slated for the op were Nos 10, 12, 58, 78 and

104. There was also a raid on Düsseldorf, again on railway targets, involving fifty-two aircraft from Nos 44, 97, 106 and 207 Squadrons. John Cant, of No78 Squadron, took off from Middleton St George in his Whitley MkV at 2305 hours, destined for Cologne. The target was obscured by haze and smoke and the results of the raid were uncertain. Seven aircraft were lost. Cant's Whitley crashed in Holland at 0315 hours on the return leg. Two of his crew were killed.

Keartland and Robinson, pilots in No207 Squadron, Waddington, and No106 Squadron, Coningsby, were on the Düsseldorf op. Both were shot down by night-fighters. Keartland's Manchester was attacked by *Hauptmann* Werner Streib of *I/NJG1*. Shell splinters from his gunfire entered the back of the rear-gunner, Sergeant W Hart, who was seriously wounded but not fatally. The aircraft crashed at Oberkrütchen. All the crew survived. Robinson, flying a Hampden, was shot down by *Oberleutnant* Wolfgang Thimmig, also of *I/NJG1*, and crashed at Meijel, north-east of Weert in Holland. His crew, too, came out alive.

Pilot Officer Maskell, of No50 Squadron (No5 Group), fell victim to the next night's operations, when fifty-nine aircraft were sent to bomb the Focke-Wulf factory at Bremen. He took off from Swinderby at 2255 hours, reached the target safely, but on the way back was attacked by a night-fighter flown by *Oberleutnant* Ludwig Becker of *4/NJG1,* who two nights earlier had shot down Flight Lieutenant Sampson. Maskell's Hampden crashed at 0144 hours at Paterswolde in Holland. He was the only survivor.

The night of 18/19 August was an early Christmas for the Luftwaffe, with no fewer than twenty-two aircrew being shot down and captured. Those who turned up at Lübeck on the 8 September purge were Squadron Leader Morris Michael ("Flush") Kane MBE, whose younger brother Terence was also a POW in Spangenberg; and Pilot Officers Henderson, Derek Roberts, Robertshaw and Shorrock. Three of the four were bagged as a result of yet another raid on Cologne, when sixty-two crews from Nos 10, 51, 106 and 218 Squadrons were briefed to take the *Westbahnhof* (West Station) as their aiming point. Mike Kane, of No10, led his flight off from Leeming, Yorkshire, at 2214 hours. Sergeant J A B Jamieson, of No51, took off from Dishforth at 2134 hours with Frederick Shorrock as second dickey. Another No51 Squadron pilot, Sergeant W B James, took off at 2144 hours, with Derek Roberts as his observer. Pilot Officer Robertshaw, of the same squadron, took off at 2125 hours. The raid was not a success and the bomber force suffered ten per cent casualties. Mike Kane's Whitley crashed at Lanaye, on the Dutch-Belgian border, and three of his crew perished. Sergeant James's Whitley, with Pilot Officer Roberts on board, was hit by flak fifteen minutes after he had left the target. He ordered the crew to bale out, but one of the WOP/AGs said his parachute had been ripped to shreds by shrapnel, so James gave him his own "brolly" and stayed with the aircraft. He crash-landed near Maastricht. Pilot Officer Robertshaw was attacked by a night-fighter, mortally wounding one of the WOP/AGs. His aircraft crashed south-east of Hasselt in Belgium. His second dickey, Pilot Officer H G ("Rocky") Trites RCAF, also went into the bag, and by yet another administrative oversight by the Germans was sent to an NCOs' camp, Stalag IIIE, at Kirchhain. Sergeant Jamieson's Whitley was also attacked by a night-fighter (with which it might have collided), and he and two other members of his crew were killed. The aircraft crashed at 0200 hours near Malden in Gelderland, five kilometres south of Nijmegen. Only Fred Shorrock and a WOP/AG survived.

Pilot Officer Henderson, the other aircrew officer captured that night, had been a Wellington observer on Les Dixon's old outfit, No149 Squadron, Mildenhall. His was one of forty-one Wimpeys sent out to bomb railway yards at Duisburg, an operation also involving Nos 218 and 300 Squadrons. Henderson's pilot took off at 2329 hours and all went smoothly until the return leg when a night-fighter homed in on them. The rear-gunner, Pilot Officer M I A Mendoza, was hit during the exchange of gunfire, and the captain of the aircraft, Pilot Officer J C Lynn, stayed at the controls after the rest of the crew had baled out, not knowing whether Mendoza was dead or alive. Lynn was killed when the aircraft crashed at Haelen in Holland.

No fewer than six members of this purge were Spitfire pilots, the first of whom to enter captivity was Wladyslav ("Chucky") Chciuk, from No308 Squadron at Baginton. His squadron had been among the top cover for the raids on la Pallice and Brest on 24 July that had sent John Clayton,

Eperon, Ireton, McLeod and "Taffy" Williams into the bag. Another Pole who had fled his country in 1939 and then flown in France, Chciuk had fought the last of his three brief campaigns.

Pilot Officer Mark Williams was from No41 Squadron at Hornchurch. On Monday, 18 August, four squadrons of Spitfires escorted Blenheims on "Circus No78" to Lille and Marquise, where they attacked trawlers. The Luftwaffe had been quiet for most of the day, but on this occasion they reacted, and one Blenheim and three Spitfires, including Williams' were shot down. The other two pilots perished.

Another fighter pilot was captured the next day: Pilot Officer Jock McKechnie, an Australian who had been posted to No242 (Canadian) Squadron, at North Weald, Essex, from No56 OTU on 18 February 1941. On 19 July the squadron was moved to Manston to take part in "Operation Channel Stop", an attempt to hamper enemy shipping movements from Holland to the River Seine by air power, with Hurricanes and Spitfires acting as escort to marauding Blenheims. McKechnie scored one "probable" before being shot down on Tuesday, 19 August, when twenty-two Hurricanes from Nos 1, 3 and 242 Squadrons attacked shipping in Ostend harbour. The operation was muddled, with pilots shooting up many barges and drifters, but making no concerted attack, and with Hurricanes coming at each other from all directions. McKechnie was hit by flak early in the attack and baled out, coming down in the sea.

Squadron Leader Brenus Gwynne Morris was the CO of No403 (RCAF) Squadron, which had originally been formed at Baginton on 1 March for Army co-operation and equipped with Curtiss Tomahawks. In May it transferred to Fighter Command and started to convert to Spitfires at Tern Hill, a No9 Group station. In August the squadron moved to Hornchurch to join No11 Group. Bren Morris was captured on Thursday, 21 August, when in the early afternoon "Circus No84" was flown to bomb the chemical factory at Choques. It was the second attempt to raid on Choques that day. This time the RAF brought the Messerschmitts up in strength, and the bombers did not even reach their target. Although no Blenheims were lost, Bren Morris and a Sergeant Pilot from No403 Squadron were shot down.

Denis Cowley and Wallace Cunningham, a dour Glaswegian who had fought in the Battle of Britain, were from No19 Squadron, led by Squadron Leader Walter Lawson DFC. In common with many fighter pilots, Cunningham and Lawson each had a dog — Cunningham a mongrel and the CO an Alsatian. On 27 June 1941, when the squadron had been based at West Malling, the mongrel had got into a fight with Lawson's Alsatian. Trying to separate them, another pilot, Flying Officer Harold Oxlin RAFVR, who was down for a late evening patrol of the area along Hardelot–St-Omer–Gravelines, had his thumb bitten. His place was taken by Pilot Officer Denis Cowley, a pre-war barrister, who was due to go on leave. That evening ten Spitfires took off and carried out their patrol at 20,000 feet with aircraft from Nos 65 and 266 Squadrons. At 2140 hours they ran into heavy and accurate flak, which attracted the attention of five or six Me109s who attacked in line astern. Cowley failed to return.

On 21 August the squadron was re-equipped with the long-range Spitfire MkIIs, which they took over from No234. A week later, on Thursday, 28 August, No19 Squadron was ordered to take off from Matlaske, Norfolk, at about 1500 hours and rendezvous with eighteen Blenheims from No2 Group over Coltishall. The fighter pilots were to provide escort, along with Nos 41 and 152 Squadrons, for the Blenheims on a low-level daylight raid on shipping in Rotterdam harbour. But take-off was delayed because the Wing Commander leading the Blenheims crashed on take-off and was killed. It wasn't until 1800 hours that the Spitfires left the ground and started forming up. Led by Lawson, with Cunningham commanding "B" Flight, they made their rendezvous with the seventeen remaining Blenheims and flew across the North Sea at sea level to go under the enemy radar. Then they climbed to approach Rotterdam from 2,000 feet. The Blenheims turned towards the harbour in line abreast while, to draw the enemy fire, Cunningham took his flight round and past Rotterdam and down the estuary. However, the flak coming up from both ships and coastal batteries was heavy and mainly for the bombers, seven of which were shot down.

Of the Spitfire pilots, Lawson and Cunningham were lost turning westward for home. Although no one witnessed Lawson receive any flak hits or engage in combat with enemy aircraft, he peeled off and was never seen again. Cunningham's Spitfire was hit by pom-poms from one of the enemy vessels. Glycol streamed from the engine, and Cunningham climbed, hoping either that the engine would settle and enable him to make a steady descent towards the English coast, or that if it cut he would gain height and bale out. He had reached 1,000 feet when the engine went dead and the aircraft stalled and turned over. Cunningham made a controlled dive towards the beach south of the harbour, where he crash-landed. He had banged his knee on impact, but was otherwise unhurt. Scrambling out of the aircraft, he attempted to set it on fire, but was thwarted by a machine-gun post opening up on him. Bullets whined over his head, then a posse of German soldiery turned up and led him to an artillery Officers' Mess. They tried to claim him as their "victory", but Cunningham pointed out that it was a ship that had shot him down, not a shore-based battery. Although none too happy about having their claim disputed, they treated him pleasantly and gave him tomato sandwiches and champagne, accompanied by the favourite German phrase, "For you the war is over."

Afterwards he was escorted to Amsterdam, and locked up in the civilian gaol. Three Blenheim boys were also being held there: Pilot Officers W Beckingham, F M V Johnstone and W L MacDonald. Logie MacDonald, from No21 Squadron, had taken off from Watton at 1445 hours, with William Beckingham as his WOP/AG. Johnstone, from No226 Squadron, had taken off from Wattisham, another Suffolk airfield, five minutes later. The Blenheim formation was bounced by Me109s from *6/JG53* and the flak was fierce. Although two large freighters were hit and there was some damage to the docks, seven Blenheims were lost. MacDonald's observer was killed and Bill Beckingham badly injured. The aircraft crashed near the target. Johnstone's

Fig 6. Wallace Cunningham's impression of his interrogation in Amsterdam

Blenheim crashed nearby at Maashaven. The two NCOs in his crew survived, but were being held elsewhere.

After two nights in the cells they and Cunningham were taken by train to Frankfurt. It was a pleasant trip, the train meandering past the beautiful Rhine castles, and Cunningham thought it a great pity that he had to be introduced to such a lovely view under POW circumstances. At Dulag Luft, Beckingham was sent to Hohemark and thence to *Lazarett* IXC. He would turn up at Lübeck later. Cunningham, Johnstone and MacDonald were kept in the cells for about three days. "We were too dumb, I'm sure, to provide the Germans with any great amount of useful knowledge," recalls Cunningham, although he was surprised that one interrogator knew that the strike had been delayed owing to the Blenheim leader crashing on take-off.

On being let into the compound at Dulag Luft, the first familiar face he saw was that of Denis Cowley. The first words Cowley uttered were: "You and your —ing dog!" Cowley quite naturally blamed Cunningham's mongrel for his incarceration.

The one Coastal Command officer on this purge was Edward Arthur ("Flip") Rance of the Volunteer Reserve. Like Leslie Collings, Lou Barry and William Hunter, he was from No217 Squadron at St Eval. At 1205 hours on Monday, 11 August he had taken off in company with other Beauforts to conduct a shipping search. Some time after 1344 hours his aircraft was brought down into the sea by ground fire from St-Nazaire. His observer, Sergeant A G Wilson, and his air-gunner, Sergeant S J Austin, went with him into captivity, but the wireless operator, Sergeant A Chiplin, was killed. Chiplin's body was never recovered.

***

When this purge arrived at Oflag XC, ten British soldiers from a nearby working camp were clearing the rubble left from the bombing raid the previous night. Wallace Cunningham was amongst the officers watching: "It was the British workman at his best — picking up a brick and passing it round and back onto the pile again. The pile never got any smaller."

Paddy Denton:

> I shall never forget the sight of the British Army personnel.... Those who had been given the job of cleaning up the rubble smiled at us paralytically pissed. They had found booze at the officers' end [of the German mess]... They threw bottles over to us but their aim was somewhat impaired. Most of them fell back laughing at their failure but some of those who were in the legless, two-eyes stage kept on trying. One actually knocked himself out with a nasty blow from his own hand-held bottle which caught him unawares on the back of the neck.
>
> The Germans, for some reason, didn't see any humour in the episode but we all found it most comical...

In the aftermath of the raid, the Commandant, on the assumption that prisoners had been signalling to the bombers, ordered the guards to shoot in the direction of any lights still on after hours and posted sentries inside the camp with fixed bayonets. Twice when prisoners struck matches on the way to the lavatory the guards popped off at them. But no one was hit.

Happily for the kriegies, a German inspecting general came to report on the damage, saw the guards inside the compound, and immediately threw them out. Michael Roth recalled that the general:

> then gave *Oberst* von Wachtmeister a terrific raspberry. Wachtmeister was a senile, hateful old basket — he had to stand to attention at the salute for twenty minutes while the general gave him his "cigar" (the German expression for a severe reprimand) right in front of the kriegies. Served him right. He was the most hated man around. He always shuffled about in his First Great War uniform trailing a nickel-plated sword scabbard. On one day entering the compound, he caught the flukes of his scabbard in the barbed wire, wrested it free, then got it between his own legs and tripped and fell to the ground. He was livid, since he was seen by dozens of

Fig 7. Wallace Cunningham in solitary confinement in Amsterdam gaol

Amsterdam is a Lovely City.

grinning kriegies. Morale rose a point — a long malicious laugh enjoyed by all. One of life's highlights at the time.

The two No19 Squadron pilots, Denis Cowley and Wally Cunningham, had moved into a room with Gosman and Roth. Although they were pals and "mucked in" together they seldom spoke, much to the bemusement of Roth — but then he did not know about Cunningham's mongrel.

(5)

In their determination to crowd as many officers as possible into one camp, the Germans shipped another batch from Dulag Luft to Oflag XC on Friday, 12 September. This party included Flight Lieutenants E C Cathels RCAF, T Griffith-Jones, V Kilian (Czech), B Mickiewicz (Pole), Z Prochazka (Czech), E R Templer, and K Trojacek (Czech); Flying Officers P Harding RAFVR and H Skalski (Pole); and Pilot Officers M T H Adams, J E T Asselin RCAF, D G Baber, M H Gifford RCAF, A E Hayward, H Heaton, F G Horner, D E Kennedy RAFVR, J W McCarthy RCAF, W R Oldfield, D B Organ, H W Pickstone and I G St G Pringle.

The three Czechs — Václav Kilian, Zdenek Prochazka and Karel Trojacek — had been prisoners since 23/24 September 1940. They were from No311 Squadron, East Wretham, the only Czech squadron serving in the RAF, and were shot down in the same Berlin raid that had claimed Squadron Leader Anthony Bridgman, who had been sent to Spangenberg. Bomber Command had put up 129 aircraft, a mixed force of Hampdens, Wellingtons and Whitleys, and dispersed them to eighteen different targets in Berlin. Surprisingly, only three aircraft were lost: one each from Nos 77, 83 and 311 Squadrons.

No311, like the Polish bomber squadrons, was equipped with Wellingtons. Karel Trojacek, a pilot, became a section leader, Prochazka his observer, and Kilian his rear-gunner. Also in Trojacek's crew were Sergeants A Zabrs (second pilot), K Kunka (WOP/AG) and F Knotek (WOP/AG). Shot down by flak over southern Holland, they crash-landed at 0435 hours near Leidschendamall, a village ten kilometres south-west of Leiden. All six escaped safely from the wrecked Wellington. However, they were the first Czechs to crash-land in Germany and were anxious about their reception. The Germans might accuse them of being traitors, and torture and kill them. Karel Kunka shot himself with a Very pistol to avoid capture. But all were found, locked in police cells and withheld from the protection of the Luftwaffe, Sergeant Kunka dying the next day. Their Wellington was towed to Rechlin, the Luftwaffe equivalent to Britain's Royal Aeronautical Establishment at Farnborough, where it was put through the hoops by test pilots.

The commandant of Dulag Luft, Major Theo Rumpel, heard of their dilemma and sought the opinion of the Senior British Officer, "Wings" Day, who told him that all foreign nationals in the British armed forces were legally British citizens and had the same rights. Rumpel pulled strings to get them released, but they remained in solitary confinement at Dulag Luft for eleven months. Thin and pale, they stood out amongst the rest of the purge. Within minutes of arriving at Lübeck, they were slapped in the cooler again. (The two surviving Sergeants, Zabrs and Knotek, had been sent to Lamsdorf.)

Another one who had been a kriegie for some time was Pilot Officer Henry Heaton. A Yorkshireman from Leeds who had been in the clothing trade before the war, he was a Wellington second dickey in No40 Squadron, a former No2 Group unit and now part of No3 Group and based at Alconbury in Cambridgeshire. Heaton's pilot was Cranwell-trained Hugh Lynch-Blosse, the commander of "A" Flight, who had joined the squadron at Wyton in September 1940 when it was still a Blenheim outfit. The rest of the crew were Flying Officer S H ("Percy") Palmer (rear-gunner), a brush manufacturer from Portsmouth; and Sergeants D R Clay (navigator), A ("Wally") Hammond (wireless operator), and H Caldicott (front-gunner). Heaton and Palmer, both approaching their thirties, were the "old men" of the crew, while Lynch-Blosse was twenty-four, and the NCOs barely nudging twenty. Heaton was a married man and Palmer had a girlfriend on the station.

Hugh Lynch-Blosse's twenty-third operation, on 12/13 March 1941, was one he had long awaited: a trip to Berlin — "The Big City". Bomber Command would put up two hundred and forty-six aircraft that night — eighty-eight against Hamburg, eighty-six against Bremen, and seventy-two to Berlin. No40 Squadron took off at 2100 hours. It was a beautiful, bright moonlit night — ideal if you wanted to get "the chop" from night-fighters. But they flew across Europe with no sign of the enemy at all.

A warm reception awaited them over Berlin, however. Flak was coming up thick and fast and Lynch-Blosse counted more than forty searchlights. He could have sworn they were all coning him. He told Heaton to stand in the fuselage between the engines, which was the safest place, in case he (Lynch-Blosse) was hit and Heaton had to take over. After weaving and jinking in an effort to avoid being hit he found himself flying at only 7,000 feet. He had just shouted: "Bombs gone!" when the Wimpey was hit by flak, peppering it with holes. A shell entered the front gun-turret, fabric came off the fuselage in big strips, the port engine was hit, a gaping hole appeared near Palmer's rear gun-turret, and Heaton was struck in the leg by shrapnel. He made the announcement in a crisp, matter-of-fact voice. Then Caldicott, with similar equanimity, informed the crew that ammunition in the front gun-turret had exploded. Otherwise, apart from the wind howling through the framework, all was quiet within the aircraft.

Berlin was not far behind them when the damaged engine gave out a loud bang and started surging violently. Then the starboard engine started to play up. About twenty minutes later the port engine packed up completely. L-B struggled to maintain height on one engine, but by the time they had gone fifty miles on the homeward leg the Wimpey was down to 2,000 and still losing altitude. Then the starboard engine seized. L-B had to toss up now between crash-landing and ordering the crew to bale out, and opted for the latter because it would give everyone a better chance of survival. He promptly gave the order, urging them to land as near as possible to Heaton to make him as comfortable as they could. Once they were clear, he took to his own parachute.

Heaton broke his injured leg on landing. The rest of the crew — apart from Lynch-Blosse, who came down further away and tried to leg it — landed nearby. When the goons rounded them up they made sure Heaton was taken to hospital. He was there for seventeen weeks before being transferred to Dulag Luft and thence to Lübeck, where he would meet Lynch-Blosse and "Percy" Palmer, both of whom had been purged from Barth,

Yet another interesting case was Pilot Officer Douglas Baber, of No77 Squadron, who had been shot down as long ago as 5/6 August. He was the pilot who had stayed with his Whitley and ordered his observer, Pilot Officer Kayes, and the rest of the crew to bale out over Belgium after the aircraft was damaged by a night-fighter. Once they had gone, Baber crawled to the escape hatch, his heart bursting with fear, the aircraft heaving and rocking, nose up, out of control. As he poised himself to jump, the slipstream caught his dangling legs and knocked him against the escape hatch, cutting open his forehead. When finally he did jump, he pulled the rip-cord too early, and realised with horror that he was within feet of the Whitley's blazing tail-plane and could very well be burned alive. But the moment soon passed, and he was floating through the night, sick with relief. Wounded in the head and the left foot, he made a heavy landing in a field. It was about 0030 hours, and he decided that as first light could only be four or five hours away he should get clear of the area as soon as possible. Determined to bury his parachute, he clutched it tightly and moved slowly forward on his hands and knees, dragging his injured foot. However, a strong wind tore the parachute from his grasp and sent it trailing across the field. Hauling himself painfully across the field, he heard it flapping against a hedge, found it, rolled it into a bundle and stuffed it deep into the thicket. From there he worked his way along the edge of the field, through a half-open gate and across a sloping meadow to a canal-bank.

Some way ahead of him he saw a light flash briefly and made towards it, coming across some outbuildings of a farm tucked alongside the canal. His ears strained for the sound of movement. From a shed on his right he heard snuffling, then the clink of a bucket: an animal searching for food with its snout. Then in front of him he saw a slender bar of light from beneath a closed door. Climbing to his feet he crossed a yard, limping painfully, and pulled himself along the side of the house with his hands. At the door he reached down for the heavy Service automatic tucked into his flying boot, cocked it and heard the snick of a cartridge slip into the firing position, pushed open the door and stood blinking dazedly in the light.

The farmhouse in which he stood, five kilometres from where his Whitley crashed, was owned by the Rigaux family — a farmer, his wife and their daughter and two sons. When they first set eyes on Baber, covered in mud and blood and pointing his revolver, they were both aghast and afraid. But once they had established his identity — his crippled Whitley had apparently staggered on over their farmhouse — they sat him down, removed his flying boots and set about bathing and bandaging his foot, which had suffered nothing more than a sprain. One of the sons went out and unearthed Baber's parachute, which he brought back, tore up and burnt, along with his Irvine sheepskin flying jacket and the silk maps from his escape kit. Anything incriminating that could not be burned they threw into the canal.

Duggie Baber's first impulse, after a good night's rest, was to strike off towards France and contact the Underground, but the Rigaux family decided he should stay until his foot was healed, as the going would be mainly across country and through thick woodland. The nearest village was two kilometres along the canal, with one or two outlying farms on the low ground and the main road well on the other side of the village. After about four days his foot had improved sufficiently for him to take evening walks alongside the canal, wearing a suit provided by the family. But the next night a car full of SS pulled up outside the house, followed by lorries bristling with armed troops. Baber and the Rigaux family had been given away by an informer. The SS put Baber in the car, forbidding him to either talk or smoke, piled the Rigaux family into one of the lorries, and took them to the Gestapo prison in Brussels. There, Baber was ordered to strip and made to stand naked on the stone floor of a reception room while two corporals examined every inch of his clothes. Removing his possessions, they tossed him his clothes back. After taking his name, a soldier escorted him through long gloomy corridors, lined with cells, and locked him up.

A dim blue lamp shone from the ceiling, and in its light he saw a bed made of wooden slats with a straw palliasse and two blankets, a chair, and in one corner a bucket heavily encrusted with excreta. He could walk the length of the cell in four paces, its width in two. The door was made of oak, reinforced with iron strips, with a Judas-hole at eye level. On the opposite wall was a tiny barred window. Baber went to the bed and lay down. He covered himself with the blankets, but the stench they gave off sickened him so much he threw them off.

When he awoke next morning a grey light was filtering through the window and from the corridor came the sound of metallic clanging. Eventually the noise reached his own cell and the door was thrown open. A soldier handed him a chipped enamel mug, filled with *ersatz* coffee, and two slices of black bread. Baber sat on his bed and tasted the coffee. It was bitter, but he was cold and thirsty and drank it to the last drop. The bread he tossed into the bucket.

Later in the morning two soldiers took him down the long corridor, and on the way he counted the number of cells they passed: more than sixty. They came to a small office, where a man was sitting behind a table. He rose to his feet as Baber entered and the guards closed the door and stood one against each wall, flanking him. The man opposite was dressed in drab civilian garb and was clearly Gestapo. He invited Baber to sit down and offered him a cigarette. Baber sat, but curtly refused the cigarette. "You don't smoke, Mr Baber?" "Not yours." Then the interrogation began. It started innocuously, with a request for name, rank and number, then moved on to: "When were you shot down?" "How long were you with the family Rigaux?" "Where did you get your civilian clothes?" "What sort of aircraft were you flying?" Baber said he couldn't remember when he was shot down, that he had not been staying with the Rigaux family, that he had been caught crossing the road with a stranger he had encountered, that he had stolen the clothes from the farmhouse and that he had been flying a Tiger Moth. The interrogator's eyes narrowed at this reply, and he advised Baber not to make jokes. "You are in a most unenviable position, do you realise that? Caught in civilian clothes in the night. To us you might be a spy...an agent...we're entitled to shoot you for that." Baber invoked the Geneva Convention. His interrogator had an answer to that: "In this prison there is no Geneva Convention. No Convention exists for spies." Then he turned on the charm, telling Baber that there was no need for any unpleasantness. All he had to do was answer a few simple questions and he would join his comrades in a POW camp. "We have nice camps you know. Plenty of good food, games, books, concert parties...they have a fine time. Your Douglas Bader is there, did you know? Yes, we have him, and hundreds of others, so you won't be lonely. Now, how long were you with the family Rigaux?" Again Baber refused to answer his questions, and finally the interrogator revealed that he already knew what aircraft Baber was flying and the names of his crew. Telling Baber they were going to have to hold him a long time, he motioned the guards to bustle him back to his cell.

They didn't bother him again that day. During the morning a trusty brought him a tin of swede soup and more black bread. Baber asked if the Rigaux family was still in the prison and the trusty, hearing footsteps coming along the corridor, nodded briefly and slammed the door. Baber ate the soup, thin watery stuff with one piece of hard swede floating in it, and managed this time to eat the bread as well. Later on he went to the outer wall, jumped up at the bars and gripped them so as to see out of the tiny window. Down in the prison yard, prisoners with shaven heads were exercising. Round and round the yard they went, all staring at the ground. Baber dropped back to the floor and began a study of the walls. Messages had been scratched into the plaster — a prayer or two, an obscene drawing of a German soldier, crude calendars with dates crossed off, but mostly farewell salutations. On the wall above his bed was a great brown stain like a map, with more stains spattered beneath it. He didn't try to imagine what it was...

In the afternoon he lay on his bed and tried to sleep, and it was then that he discovered the palliasse was infested with bed-bugs. He caught several and squashed them between finger and thumb. They exploded in a bubble of blood and gave off a musty smell. The blood was his, and his body was itching all over.

During the next two days he was interrogated twice more. He felt humiliated before his interrogators. He had been refused permission to wash and shave, his clothes stank and he was covered from head to foot in weeping bed-bug sores. When he wished to relieve himself he was forced to use the bucket, and the stench seemed to cling to his body. The nights were like a bad dream. A hot-water pipe ran through the cells, and late each night the prisoners would tap out messages on it, the news travelling in hollow metallic clangs and bangs around the prison.

On the fourth day they again shoved him along the corridor, through locked doors and into the little office. His original Gestapo interrogator was there, accompanied this time by a much larger man, again obviously Gestapo. Baber was warned this was his last chance. He remained tight-lipped, and this time they confronted him with the informer, a local woman who had been going with one of the Rigaux boys. She identified him as the pilot who had been given shelter by the Rigaux family. Then he was manhandled back to his cell and dumped on the bug-infested palliasse.

The following morning he was startled by a Luftwaffe *Major* hurrying into his cell. He looked dapper and clean in his smart blue uniform, and behind him were three other Luftwaffe men, all fresh-faced and cheerful in contrast to the lugubrious, sickly-looking prison guards Baber had been used to seeing for the past week. "Baber?" the Major asked, glancing around the cell and wrinkling his nose in disgust. Baber sat up. "Come," said the Major. "We're taking you with us."

"Where?"

The Major looked surprised. "Where? Why, to a Luftwaffe prison camp in Germany. Where else?" Although Baber didn't yet know it, the *Major* was none other than Theo Rumpel himself, come from Dulag Luft to rescue him.

The Rigaux family was deported to Dachau, remaining there until liberated by the Allies in 1945. Baber's crew also survived, all but Albert Day preceding him into captivity. Day made contact with the Comète escape line and escaped to England via Spain.

Of the other bomber aircrew, Eric Roy Templer was an observer from No51 Squadron, which had already lost "Fiji" MacKay, "Rudy" Leuw, Frank Clayton, Freddy Shorrock, Derek Roberts and Bob Robertshaw to captivity. On 24/25 August forty-four aircraft set out to bomb Düsseldorf. Templer's pilot, Sgt J C W King, took off from Dishforth at 2059 hours, but neither Templer nor any other observers were able to locate the target because of cloud. They bombed on an estimated position. On the way back King's Whitley was attacked by a night-fighter from *I/NJG1* flown by *Leutnant* Hans-Dieter Frank and crashed in Holland. All the crew survived.

Antony Hayward and "Pring" Pringle were from No144 Squadron, based in North Luffenham, Rutland (No5 Group). On 25/26 August forty-five aircraft bombed Mannheim with poor results for the loss of three Hampdens to flak and night-fighters. One crew was killed outright, and Hayward, an observer, was the only survivor from his crew. As his pilot, Sergeant Donald Whiting, turned for home, flak hit the aircraft, setting the fuselage ablaze. Hayward baled out over Brussels. The Hampden crashed at 2300 hours near the castle of Puttenburg, at Beert, with the rest of the crew still on board. Two Belgians found the injured Hayward, carried him to a house and fetched a doctor, but at dawn the Germans started a house-to-house search and they were obliged to give him up. He was taken to a hospital in Brussels. One of the nurses took his details and smuggled out a note in her apron; his parents received it before the Red Cross notified them that he was a prisoner of war.

Pringle's crew were more fortunate. He force-landed his damaged Hampden on Ypenberg airfield, Holland. Though none of his crew was hurt, running for it was out of the question.

"Barney" Oldfield, another bomber pilot, was not shot down at all. He was from No103 Squadron, a Wellington unit in No1 Group and based in Elsham Wolds, Lincolnshire. On 29/30 August ninety-four Wellington's took off to bomb Mannheim and encountered bad weather. Oldfield's aircraft was struck by lightning and crashed near Flushing. All but Oldfield and the tail-gunner were killed.

The weather was still bad on 31 August, when a hundred and three aircraft set out to bomb the railway yards at Cologne. The losses that night, however, were put down mainly to flak and night-fighters. Douglas Bruce Organ — born to be nicknamed "Sex" — was the observer for Flight

Lieutenant E P Willcox, a DFC holder in No83 Squadron, Scampton, another Lincolnshire aerodrome in No5 Group. Their Hampden was attacked by *Unteroffizier* Pahler of *I/NJG1* and crashed twenty minutes after midnight at Meijel. Willcox was killed in the crash.

Michael Thomas Henry Adams, like Hayward and Pringle, was from No144 Squadron. His aircraft was the only one shot down on the night of 1/2 September when twenty Hampdens and thirty-four Wellingtons bombed Cologne. It crashed near the target area with all the crew on board, and only Mike Adams came out alive.

Joe McCarthy, a Canadian from Hamilton, Ontario, was the first of forty-two officers and NCOs to enter Dulag Luft after a raid on Berlin on 7/8 September, when Bomber Command sent a mixed force of 197 aircraft to three different aiming points in the city. Aircraft were also sent to bomb Kiel and Boulogne, and losses from all three operations were heavy — at nearly six per cent, the highest so far in a single night. Taking part in the Berlin raids were Squadron Nos 7, 9, 12, 15, 51, 58, 104, 106, 115, 144, 149, 207, 214, 218 and 405, drawn from Nos 1, 3, 4 and 5 Groups. Joe McCarthy was an observer in a Wellington MkII from No 12 Squadron, Binbrook. His pilot, Squadron Leader P F Edinger, led his flight off at 2150 hours, and of Edinger's crew, McCarthy alone survived.

Yet more Spitfire boys were on this purge to join Cowley and Cunningham — Flight Lieutenants Cathels and Mickiewicz, Flying Officer Skalski, and Pilot Officers Asselin, Horner and Pickstone. All had served on No11 Group squadrons, providing escort at high-altitude for "Circus" and "Roadstead" operations, often as part of Douglas Bader's "Big Wing". From No610 Squadron, Westhampnett, there was "Jackie" Horner, who had been in the bag since 8 July, when he was shot down during the same operation, "Circus No40", as Peter Pine. Then there was "Pick" Pickstone, from No130 Squadron, which had been formed at Portreath, Cornwall, as recently as 20 June. The squadron was still a week short of becoming fully operational when Pickstone was shot down. On the morning of Thursday, 21 August — the same day that Squadron Leader Bren Morris was captured — No130 Squadron flew a "Roadstead" to IJmuiden. Their Spitfires were bounced by Me109s from the *Ergänzungsgruppe* of *JG53* and lost two pilots, one of whom was killed.

Flight Lieutenant Cathels and Flying Officer Skalski were shot down on the same day. Edmund Charles Cathels was from No403 Squadron, which until 21 August had been commanded by Bren Morris and was now in the hands of Squadron Leader R A L Knight DFC. The Polish Henryk Skalski had been with no fewer than five fighter squadrons since arriving in Britain in 1940, including Nos 46, 249, 242 and 306, flying both Hurricanes and Spitfires, sometimes into high-tension cables, sometimes into other aicraft. Since 3 March 1941 he had been in No72 Squadron, first at Acklington, then at Gravesend. On the morning of Wednesday, 27 August No72 Squadron was supposed to provide top cover for "Circus No85", but the operation was aborted because the Blenheims failed to make the rendezvous. The escorts segued into fighter sweeps. Meanwhile, No403 Squadron was acting as top cover for "Circus No86" to Lille. As usual they succeeded in drawing up the Luftwaffe, and eight Spitfires were shot down. Only Cathels and Skalski survived to become prisoners.

Bronislaw Mickiewicz had begun his RAF career in No307 Squadron in 1940 and after a spell at No5 OTU had been on Nos 303, 43 and 316 Squadrons before being posted to No315 Squadron in April 1941, three months after it had been formed at Acklington. No315 consisted mainly of Polish pilots who had been trained at the Deblin Air Force Academy, seventy miles south of Warsaw, in the 1930s, when as many as 6,000 hopefuls would compete for only ninety places and who, like Mickiewicz, had fought in France after the collapse of Poland and defied orders by the French authorities that they should surrender to the Germans, instead making a mass exodus to England. Mickiewicz was shot down on the morning of Friday, 29 August, when the Deblin squadron — as No315 was called — provided high-altitude escort for six Blenheims on "Circus No88" to Hazebrouck. There were several dogfights and five Spits were knocked out of the sky. One of the pilots baled out over the sea and was rescued, but Mickiewicz's combat took him over dry land, where he was chopped down and captured.

Six days later Eddie Asselin, a Canadian from Westmount, Quebec, entered the bag. He was on No92 Squadron, based at Biggin Hill (No11 Group), and failed to return from sweep on the afternoon of Thursday, 4 September, a day when no fewer than eight Spitfires were shot down.

From Coastal Command there were Derrick Evan Kennedy and Peter Harding, both of them Volunteer Reservists. Kennedy was a Blenheim MkIV pilot from No59 Squadron, No16 (GR) Group, based at Detling. Despite staggering losses (36 per cent in two months alone) Coastal Command was still carrying out strikes and offensive recces, albeit with fighter escort. On Monday, 16 June, No59 Squadron contributed several aircraft to "Circus No13", when twenty-five Blenheims went on a coastal sweep off Holland and Germany. Kennedy took off at 1559 hours and in company with other aircraft met an escort of six fighter squadrons over Canterbury. But some of the bombers were late to the rendezvous and the fighters used up a fair bit of fuel waiting for them. They also met with heavy opposition across the Channel, where *JG26* pounced on them. In the ensuing mêlée, Kennedy was wounded and forced to ditch. His observer, Pilot Officer P S E Briggs RAFVR, and his WOP/AG, Sgt C H Edgar, survived uninjured. Air-Sea Rescue launches escorted by Nos 1 and 91 Squadrons failed to find them; they were picked by the *Seenotdienst* instead. Briggs was sent to Spangenberg but Kennedy was treated at Hohemark and remained in Dulag Luft for nearly three months.

Flying Officer Peter Harding, a pre-war metallurgist who had joined the RAFVR in June 1939, was another photo-reconnaissance pilot, like John Blount, from No3 PRU at Oakington. On 15 August 1941, however, No3 PRU was disbanded and absorbed into No1 PRU at Benson. Harding was on his twenty-third trip when on Wednesday, 27 August, 1941, his Spitfire MkV (PR) let him down. His was yet another case of an officer being captured as a result of volunteering for an operation on which he was not scheduled to fly. He had reported for briefing, only to be told there would be no flight that day. However, another pilot, Flight Lieutenant Roy Elliot, who was down for ops, had a cold and decided he would rather not go up.

I asked where he was going and he told me Kiel. I liked Kiel so I volunteered to take his flight. I took off about 1100 hours, dropped into Horsham St Faith to top right up with fuel, and set out across the North Sea, along the north coast of Germany. I saw Denmark coming up in front of me, but as I passed over Wilhelmshaven my engine packed up. Thinking my two 30-gallon wing-tanks were empty, I switched to main tanks, behind my seat, and waited the three or four seconds for the engine to pick up. It did not. Flying at 30,000 feet, I had plenty of time so I checked the wing-tanks — the port tank was empty, and the right tank full. I stood the Spitfire on its left wing and tried gravity-feed from the right wing-tank. Nothing. I turned all the tanks on, smashed the stick into the dashboard, hauled it into my stomach, wiggled it, shook it and called it all the bad words I knew.

I then tore up my maps and things in my pockets and scattered them from a great height. I looked for my Very Pistol, could not find it, and had no matches or even a penknife. All I had was the automatic gun in the side of the fuselage. The only way to destroy the Spit was to bale out. Always I had said I would never bale out if the aircraft was flyable. Had another go at starting the engine — the prop was still windmilling — and found that it would fire on the Ki-gas pump. Clouds of black smoke, a lot of bangs, but that was all. Rolls-Royce engineers have told me since that almost certainly my carburettor had iced up and that there was nothing I could do. At 10,000 feet I decided I had to get out. I trimmed the Spit very tail-heavy, tried the Ki-gas again, opened the cockpit cover, undid my straps, had a final check round and at 8,000 feet rolled the Spitfire onto its back and pushed the stick forward. I did not see it go, and felt only a shot of pain as my knee banged against the windshield as I went. I felt for the rip-cord but it was not there. I looked down and saw to my surprise that it was in the middle and not round the side, where I thought it should have been. I pulled it, saw the drogue 'chute pull out the main — and, bang! I was hanging, one ball trapped under the harness, which I had not adjusted since it was repacked the day before. I suffered agonies before I hit the ground, at least a mile below.

I saw the Spit spinning below me, wind screaming in the open cockpit. It went into a cloud and I heard it hit the ground with an almighty bang. There was about a 30mph ground-speed wind blowing, so I drifted rapidly away from the site of the crash. I saw a pond coming up, and in my effort to avoid it, turned round and landed on my back just beside it. I lay there for a while relieved to be out of my agony. I put my parachute under a hay cock and dived into a ditch, luckily dry. I made off along the ditch towards distant woods. I was in a square of roads and wherever I went there were Germans hiding behind trees. A large elderly policeman came over towards me, pistol holster still buttoned up, and spoke to me. There was no way out and he searched me for arms. *"Kommen Sie mit,"* he said, and took me to a cottage, putting me on the settee in the lounge, whilst the *Hausfrau* gave me a cup of coffee and a biscuit. They were very kind to me.

A while later a Mercedes pulled up outside and three German officers arrived. I was asked where my crew were. Five parachutes had been seen coming down. Was I flying a Blenheim? "Peter Harding. RAFVR 73046. Flying Officer," was all they got from me. I was taken to Jever and interrogated by the Station Commander. Same questions and same reply. He took me into the hangar and showed me his latest Me109F. I told him it was a bit slow, and was locked up.

Half an hour later I was called back.

"You were flying a Spitfire."

"Was I?"

"Here is a plate from it, saying Spitfire 1937." (It had just been upgraded to a Mark V.)

So I said: "Still faster than yours."

He told me the engine was ten feet down and that I had really wrecked it. He then said I was the first officer prisoner they had had and I was to be guest of honour at dinner that evening.

I was offered every drink under the sun and had to be very careful, though I would have liked to have got legless. The following night, after being entertained by the junior officers, I was taken by train to Dulag Luft, arriving on 29 August.

***

Trevor Griffith-Jones had been an observer in a Blenheim from No110 (Hyderabad) Squadron. On 29 June the squadron had left Wattisham, bound for Malta, to relieve No82 Squadron, which had been carrying out anti-shipping operations from the island since April. At 0430 hours on Wednesday, 9 July 1941, seven Blenheims from No110 took off on their maiden operation against enemy ships harboured at Tripoli. Although they damaged four large merchant vessels, an equal number of Blenheims were shot down over the target by flak and fighters. Griffith-Jones was wounded and his WOP/AG, Sergeant D Wythe, killed. The pilot, Flight Lieutenant M Potier, crash-landed nearby and he, too, was killed. Despite his wounds, Griffith-Jones escaped from the stricken aircraft, to be captured soon after. He was taken by ambulance to Bu-Setta hospital, where he underwent treatment for ten days. On the 29th he was taken to a German prison camp where, he later noted in his Wartime Log, "the prisoners were weak and ill". However, he was there only until the morning of 31 July, when he was taken by car to Castel Benito aerodrome. He was flown to Tripoli and from there by Ju52 to Catania, Sicily. After spending the night in a barracks he was taken by first class railway carriage to Messina, then by train ferry to Reggio in Italy. From there he travelled second class to Naples, spending the night in the train, and eventually reaching Rome on the morning of 2 August. There, as his Wartime Log again cryptically records, he was "taken to Nazi HQ". The next day, again travelling second class, he was taken to Munich, going via Florence, Bologna, Brenner and Innsbruck, where again he spent a night on the train. On the morning of 3 August: "Am taken to Nazi HQ for interrogation in Munich." The interrogation over, he was taken from Munich to Frankfurt am Main by third class, from there to Oberursel by second class, and finally to Dulag Luft by car. "Spend all night in cell and undergo further interrogation. Am then admitted to camp."

The newcomers arrived at Oflag XC on 13 September and were thoroughly searched and fingerprinted before being allowed into the main camp. Henry Heaton was surprised — and delighted — to see his former pilot, Hugh Lynch-Blosse, and his rear-gunner, "Percy" Palmer, at Lübeck, as they had originally been sent to Barth. Heaton moved in to their room. Bruce Organ moved in with Gosman, Roth, Cunningham and Cowley. Before the war, Organ, an Irishman, had been actor-manager of a Shakespearian touring company, "and as such had developed stomach ulcers," recalled Michael Roth:

> He was a hilarious mimic and impersonator, and entertained us with parodies of bosomy ageing operatic females he'd met in his travels. One of his best was from *Sampson and Delilah*, in which the actress playing the young and seductive Delilah was actually a sixty-year-old bird who sang with hands under the chin: "I am young, am I not?" Ludicrous. Organ had a vast, fascinating store of managerial anecdotes, most of which had to do with eluding the duns (bailiffs), or getting across the border in or out of Scotland without paying his company's bills. Organ filled our days with laughter, bless him.

* * *

On Wednesday, 17 September, the Germans held a "bed-board parade" to determine whether any prisoners had been using their bed-boards for firewood. "Everyone had!" noted Michael Roth. The following day the former Barth kriegies were given blank prisoner-of-war registration cards to fill in and send to their next of kin. These cards were essentially the same as those they had completed shortly after interrogation at Dulag Luft, but in this instance the purpose was to inform the folks back home that they had been transferred to another camp. Even so, the German administrative staff had been somewhat dilatory, as by then the Barth contingent had been in Oflag XC for more than six weeks. The Senior RAF Officer, "Hetty" Hyde (who had been a prisoner since 9 April), wrote a proper letter to his wife on the 18th; it appears to have been the only one he sent from that camp.

MY DARLING KAT
HOW ARE THINGS? SORRY I HAVE NOT WRITTEN BEFORE THIS MONTH. I AM AFRAID THAT I HAVE BEEN WICKED AGAIN & HAVE BEEN MOVED TO THIS CAMP AND HAVE JUST COME INTO CIRCULATION AGAIN. I RECEIVED YOUR LETTERS DATED 17/6, 14/7 & 20/7 JUST BEFORE I CAME HERE, THAT WAS GRAND. THERE WERE TWO PARCELS ARRIVED FOR ME, ONE FROM EGYPT (M.P. PRESUMABLY) & ONE FROM SWITZERLAND, BUT I DIDN'T GET THEM. THEY SHOULD BE SENT ON HERE SOON. THE TOBBACCO [sic] & PERSONAL PARCELS HAVEN'T ARRIVED YET, BUT SHOULD ROLL UP ANY DAY NOW. MARGARET BROWN'S HUSBAND IS HERE [...], HE WAS TAKEN PRISONER IN CRETE. HE SENDS YOU HIS SALAAMS. WE HAVE NOT GOT ANY RED CROSS PARCELS HERE YET, BUT HAVE WRITTEN TO GENEVA, SO ARE HOPING THAT THEY WILL TURN UP SOON. [...] WE ARE ONLY ALLOWED 2 LETTERS & 4 POSTCARDS A MONTH HERE SO INSTEAD OF 3 LETTERS I WILL SEND YOU 2 LETTERS & 1 P.C. IN FUTURE.

In his diary for that day, Micheal Roth recorded: "Margarine replaced fat ration. Previously marg. was pinched by Goon in cookhouse. Big day. Jam and Limburger cheese ration."

(6)

Two days later, on the night of Sunday, 21 September, another group of officer aircrew arrived from Dulag Luft. They were Squadron Leaders J H Barrett, H D H Cooper and S S Fielden; Acting Squadron Leader D M Strong; Flight Lieutenants W Bakker (Dutch), H T Beare RCAF, P O V Green, W J Lewis DFC, W J Peat RCAF, and G W Walenn; Flying Officers R T R Cowper, J O Hedley RAFVR, G S Williams and H C Winter-Taylor; Pilot Officers J I Davies RCAF,

R O H Down, A J Hibell, J B Leetham, W K Mackey RCAF, P Stevens, T L Walker RCAF, R A White, R T C O White and F R Wilbraham; and Lt A S Ruffel SAAF.

Squadron Leader Herbert Douglas Haig Cooper — named after the Great War Field Marshal — was nearing completion of his second tour in bombers when he was shot down as a Flight Commander in July. His first tour had been with No110 Squadron, flying Blenheim MkIVs from Wattisham. He then joined No21 Squadron, stationed at Watton. This, too, was equipped with Blenheims. On the evening of Tuesday, 1 July, twelve Blenheims took off to block the Kiel Canal under cover of cloud. "Unfortunately," recalls Cooper,

> the latter was very thin at about 1,000 feet and the German AA very accurate, shooting away the controls and killing the air gunner. When the observer and I baled out he got caught up in the tailplane so I was the only survivor — almost landing in the arms of the German gun crew.

Pilot Officer Robert Adrian White had been Eric Sydney-Smith's observer in the 16 July raid on Rotterdam. When Sydney-Smith's Blenheim pranged, White was sitting in the nose, and as it hit the deck he was catapulted through the Perspex. He landed some way ahead of the aircraft, and lay stunned and breathless until some Dutch civilians rushed up to him and cut off his collar and tie so he could regain his breath. The Dutch crowded round him, all very attentive, but then some German soldiery arrived and bundled him into an open car. On the way to the military hospital, the pavements were crowded with civilians, jeering at the Germans. One of the guards stood up and threatened them with his gun, while another sat in the back with White, sticking a pistol to his ribs. Flight Sergeant Ted Caban, the WOP/AG, was also in the hospital. A cannon-shell had exploded under his feet, and he was having shrapnel removed. Adrian White was only slightly injured and after a few days was removed from hospital and transferred to Dulag Luft.

Pilot Officer Leetham, from No83 Squadron, was shot down by flak on the night of 6/7 September when twenty-four Hampdens went on a "Gardening" op to Oslo. His observer and rear-gunner were killed and the aircraft crashed near Sandvika, Norway.

Peter Stevens was a London-born Jew whose German-Jewish family had returned to Germany during his childhood but had fled the Continent again in 1929. Stevens interrupted his studies at the London School of Economics to join the RAFVR in September 1939, and on 1 April 1941 was posted as a pilot to No144 Squadron, which flew Hampdens from Hemswell, and later from North Luffenham. He flew his last sortie on 7/8 September, taking part in the same Berlin raid that had led to Joe McCarthy's capture. Stevens had dropped his bombs and was turning for home when his Hampden was hit by flak and badly damaged. He ordered the crew to bale out (the tail-gunner was killed when his parachute failed to deploy), but the observer, Sergeant A W Payne, stayed with the aircraft. With most of the crew gone, the Hampden became marginally flyable and Stevens asked for a course home. He flew on gamely as far as the Dutch coast, but by that time had neither the height nor the fuel to attempt a crossing of the North Sea — and he didn't fancy his chances of surviving a ditching since, as he put it later, he "was no swimmer". Instead, he turned back inland to Amsterdam, deciding to crash-land on the outskirts. He made a belly-landing in a farmer's field some eight kilometres north-east of the city, setting fire to the aircraft and destroying all the documents. Then he and Payne started walking towards Amsterdam, hoping to contact the Underground. They met a farmer, who took them to his house, gave them food and promised to put them in touch with "the organisation". In the meantime, he suggested they hide up locally. They walked across country and after an hour came across a football field where there was a little hut in which goalposts and nets were stored. They decided to hide there. However, later in the day they were discovered by German *Feldgendarmerie* and taken to a military prison in Amsterdam, where they were locked up for two days.

Another victim of the 7/8 September raid was Wilfred John ("Mike") Lewis, a Canadian from Port Hope, Ontario. He had joined No44 (Rhodesia) Squadron, flying Hampdens from Waddington, in August 1939 and completed a tour as a pilot before being posted to the Manchester-equipped No207 Squadron, also at Waddington. There he finished a second tour. Returning to base after some well-earned leave, he discovered he had been posted back to No44

Squadron to help convert it to the Avro Lancaster, a four-engined variant of the under-performing Manchester. However, he was asked by the CO to do one more operation, as it was a "maximum effort" on "The Big City". With the exception of the observer, Sergeant Ron Macleod RCAF, and the wireless-operator, Flight Sergeant Doug Kingston, who had completed forty-four operations with Lewis, he would be flying with an untried crew. The mid-upper gunner was Sergeant Charles Hall, and the rear-gunner Flight Sergeant E S ("Dusty") Miller RCAF.

On the way out they were attacked by a night-fighter, which pounced on them from below, took out the port engine and peppered the fuel tank with holes. Lewis coaxed the crippled aircraft as far as Ameland, one of the Dutch Frisian Islands, but at about 0100 hours was forced to crash-land on the beach. The only one of the crew to sustain injury was Miller, who broke a bone in one of his hands. Once out of the wreckage they chopped up the aircraft and started to cross the island, hoping to find friendly inhabitants. They reached the other side of the island and started looking for a boat, but without success, and at about 0900 hours were picked up by a Wehrmacht search party who had found the remains of their Manchester. They remained on the island until noon when they were taken by ferry to the mainland, thence to Amsterdam, where they were put with half a dozen other shot-down aircrew and taken in stages to Dulag Luft.

Another Canadian, Jeff Peat, from Port Arthur, Ontario, also turned up at Dulag Luft around that time, along with Squadron Leader Samuel Spencer Fielden — yet more victims of the 7/8 September Berlin raid. All three were from No12 Squadron at Binbrook. Fielden, a former Captain in the Royal Artillery, took off at 2150 hours. Jeff Peat, his observer, and all the other members of the crew, went with him into captivity. McCarthy, another observer, was the only survivor from his crew. Two more captives from the Berlin fiasco were Pilot Officers Kenneth Mackey, a Canadian observer from No405 Squadron, Pocklington, and Frank Wilbraham, a second pilot in a Whitley from No58 Squadron, Linton-on-Ouse. Ken Mackey was also the only officer in his aircraft, a Wellington. All his crew survived. Frank Wilbraham's pilot was killed.

David Malcolm ("Dim") Strong, a Flight Commander in No104 Squadron, and his Canadian navigator, Pilot Officer "Hal" Beare, from Calgary, Alberta, had become prisoners owing to navigation error. On 10/11 September 1941, seventy-six aircraft were sent to bomb the Fiat factory in Turin. Strong had taken a crew whose captain and navigator were on leave. The second pilot was a six-foot three New Zealander, Sergeant G T Woodroofe. Sergeants J A Chubb, N S Fisher and R Ritson (rear-gunner) made up the rest of the crew. Strong's own navigator was sick, and to fill the slot he had sought the advice of the Squadron Navigation Officer, who strongly recommended Beare. He had only been on one operation, to Berlin, but had acquitted himself well, and if he could navigate a Wellington to Turin and back he would prove himself a sound navigator early in his operational career. Having received these assurances from the SNO that Beare was up to the task, Strong selected him as navigator.

Normally based in Driffield, Yorkshire, the squadron had to operate from a forward base at Stradishall, in Suffolk, as the Wimpey could not carry enough fuel to get them from Yorkshire to Turin and back with a safe margin. The flight out was uneventful; navigation was by dead reckoning, and although they were above cloud, Mont Blanc showing clearly to port indicated that they were on course for Turin. After bombing the target from 16,000 feet they turned for home but found the weather had deteriorated, and were soon flying through thunder-clouds. At one stage the aircraft was struck by lightning, which badly affected R/T reception. Nearing the Channel coast, Strong dropped to 2,000 feet, but they were either in or above cloud the whole time. Nevertheless, from that height Strong could catch intermittent glimpses of seawater. Judging that they were over the North Sea, he lost height to get below cloud and found that they were 300 feet above sea level and it was belting down with rain. Estimating that the wind was from the west, Strong turned on to a course of 300 degrees, but Beare, who had had a difficult return flight with no positive sightings to go on, insisted they were over the Channel and should steer NNE. Strong remained sceptical but told Beare to obtained two loop aerial bearings to confirm their position. In the meantime Strong continued to fly west while urging Beare to get a move on as the fuel was running low. Five minutes later Beare piped up that Strong had been wrong after all—they were over the Channel and he should steer 035 degrees. But it was too late. They were out of fuel and Strong told the crew to prepare for ditching. Gordon Woodroofe fired off Very lights, to attract the attention of friendly shipping in the vicinity, and they took up crash positions.

It was a good ditching, as ditchings go, the only member of the crew to sustain an injury being Ritson, who had been hit in the eye by a parachute flare. They took to their dinghy and for half an hour sat there with a gale blowing. Two of them were sick. Then a Danish fishing boat hove to, part of a fleet that had been forced to fish with Germans. Strong asked if the captain would take them to Scotland, but the captain said it was impossible. They hadn't the fuel and, besides, the Germans held their families as hostages. He had to take them to Esbjerg and hand them over. While Ritson was taken to hospital to have his injured eye treated, Strong, Beare and the rest were taken to a nearby fighter base.

The Adjutant, *Hauptmann* Hans-Kurt Graf von Sponek, of the *Richthofen Staffel*, met them at Esbjerg with two cars. Von Sponek saluted Strong and invited him to share his car, while the others followed in the second car. They were driven in style to the base where, recalls Strong, they "had one hell of a party". In the Officers' Mess, Strong was introduced to the Squadron Commander, a Major, who told him he had ditched in the Channel during the Battle of Britain and had been picked up by one of his own floatplanes. He gathered all the aircrew together, and they consumed large quantities of food, and Danish beer, brandy and fifty tins of Players, all liberated from Dunkirk, to the reedy sounds of Flanagan and Allen's "We're Going to Hang Out Our Washing on the Siegfried Line", playing on the gramophone. The party went on all night, and when it finally broke up, Strong's crew slept under guard in the Mess. Before falling into sweet oblivion, Strong was told: "We are front-line chaps. You won't be treated like this in the rear."

When daylight came Woodroofe showed the Luftwaffe what he thought of their hospitality by trying to escape. He was caught at the gate and on the train to Frankfurt was kept handcuffed in a separate compartment.

After their customary few days in the cells, Strong and his crew met another officer who had experienced similar problems on the Turin op, Flying Officer Gerald Standish Williams, a Halifax pilot in No35 Squadron at Stradishall. Gerry Williams' observer also had navigation difficulties on the way back, mistaking the Cherbourg peninsula for the English coast. The W/T operator radioed for a plot, but the fuel ran out and Williams had to make a forced-landing in France.

Pilot Officer Robert White was another Whitley second pilot from No58 Squadron to join Wilbraham. He was the only officer in his crew. On 11/12 September thirty-three Whitleys had been put up to bomb the docks at Warnemünde, but most bombed the town by mistake. His aircraft was brought down by the *Marinenflakabteilung*, the pilot ditching in the North Sea. All members of the crew survived.

Squadron Leader John Henry ("Birdie") Barrett, and Pilot Officers Anthony Hibell and James Davies found themselves prisoners on 15/16 September, when Bomber Command sent 169 aircraft to bomb Hamburg, using railway stations and shipyards as aiming points. A Flight Commander in No15 Squadron, John Barrett was flying as flight engineer to Pilot Officer H J Brown, who took off from Linton-on-Ouse in his Stirling at 1955 hours. Davies, from Bangor, Saskatchewan, was a Whitley observer on No51 Squadron. His pilot, Sergeant J C Gowland, took off from Dishforth at 1905 hours. Finally, Tony Hibell of No455 Squadron, Swinderby, was in the air in his Hampden at 1924 hours. Conditions over the target were clear, but the intense glare from the multitudinous searchlights prevented them recognizing their targets. It did help flak and night-fighters, though, and eight aircraft were lost. Brown's aircraft was hit by flak over the target. Although Barrett and the rest of the crew hit the silk, Brown was unable to abandon the aircraft in time and it crashed with him still inside. Gowland's Whitley was attacked in the target area by a night-fighter and both his WOP/AGs were killed. Gowland, Davies and the second pilot, Sergeant J H Davis, survived. Tony Hibell was also shot down by a night-fighter, flown by *Oberleutnant* Walter Barte of *I/NJG1*. The observer and one WOP/AG were killed, but Hibell and the other air-gunner survived. The Hampden crashed at 2354 hours near Winkelhof, twelve kilometres south-south-west of Zeven.

Gilbert William Walenn and his Australian companion, Thomas Walker, shouldn't have been over enemy territory at all — indeed, should not even have wandered beyond the shores of Blighty. For both were instructors on an Operational Training Unit. Walenn, always known as "Tim", was a smooth-faced bank clerk from Golders Green with a huge handlebar moustache, and had joined the RAFVR in December 1937. The following March he was released from his bank to do six months' training with No166 Squadron at Leconfield, where, at that time, "Dim" Strong was also serving. With the outbreak of war, Walenn became a flying instructor at No10 Elementary Flying Training School (EFTS). In August 1941 he was posted to No25 OTU at Finningley, in South Yorkshire. On the night of 10/11 September Tim Walenn and Flight Lieutenant Tom Walker of the RAAF took three crews of senior NCOs on a practice bomb-run over the firing ranges near Misson, a few miles to the south-east across the county line of Nottinghamshire. They were to fly a circuitous route there and back, as a night-navigation exercise. Walenn led them off in his Wellington MkIC at 1955 hours, with Tom Walker and three warrant officers on board his aircraft. They dropped two bombs, letting the last of them go at 2043 hours. But, turning for home, they flew off course and at a little before 2200 hours called Finningley for directions. Finningley responded, but the Wimpey ended up over Rotterdam where it was hit by flak. According to subsequent accounts, this occurred some *seven hours* after the exchange by radio. With no prospect of getting the aircraft back to England, Walenn ordered Walker and three warrant officers, P A Edwards, S C Stevens, and W A Platt, to bale out; he was the last to leave, and the Wellington crashed further north in the IJsselhaven.

Flight Lieutenant William ("Dutch") Bakker, Flying Officers Roderick Thomas Redpath Cowper and Hylton Clement Winter-Taylor, and Pilot Officer "Dickie" Down were all four from Coastal Command. Bakker had originally been in the Royal Netherlands Army, graduating from the Dutch Military Academy as a regular officer in 1933. He then opted for flying duties and earned his "wings" in 1935, being posted to the only fighter squadron in the Royal Netherlands Army Air Force, which operated from a corner of Schiphol airport. "There were no runways then," he recalled; "only grass." In 1937 he transferred to Soesterberg as a flying instructor. He escaped from Holland in May 1940, joined the RAF as an instructor on Blackburn Bothas, and then transferred to the Royal Netherlands Naval Air Service at Porthcawl in Wales.

> As I wanted to stay in England (and not go to the Dutch East Indies or the USA), in summer 1940 I had to join the naval unit at Porthcawl. I became a naval officer, but — for what reason I don't know — with two others like me, we were posted to the OTU at Silloth. We were very much on our own, and only the naval uniform was a link with the unit we belonged to.

In June 1940 the Dutch Navy's flying unit had become No320 Squadron, joining No15 Group, Coastal Command, and swapping its Fokker T-VIIIWs for Avro Ansons. It was part of No18 Group from October to January 1940, when it re-equipped with the Lockheed Hudson MkI. In January 1941 it absorbed another No15 Group squadron, No321, and in March was returned to No18 Group and stationed at Leuchars, in Fife, Scotland. For much of this period Bakker was the chief flying instructor, converting newcomers — most, like himself, from the Royal Netherlands Naval Air Service — to twin-engined aircraft, usually Avro Ansons, while in the meantime trying to familiarise himself with the Lockheed Hudson. He was also officer i/c instrument flying and did ferry jobs to the Shetland Isles.

On Saturday, 30 August he flew his seventh and final operation. Four Hudsons were ordered to carry out a strike on a German convoy that had been reported moving southwards along the coast of Norway off Egersund. It was a clear day — good for spotting a convoy, but also good for marauding enemy aircraft adding to their tally of kills. The Hudsons took off at 1135 hours and, flying to the limit of their range, found only one ship, dropped their bombs, then turned back. Ten minutes later, they were bounced by two Me109s and three of them were shot down. Bakker's rear-gunner, Sergeant H J Heeren of the RNNAS, was killed in the first burst and his Hudson set on fire. There was nothing for Bakker to do but ditch. When the aircraft smacked into the sea he was thrown out through the hatch in the cockpit roof. Three of his crew were still alive: Sergeant C E van Huijstee (co-pilot) of the RNNAS, and Lieutenant K Deen (navigator) and Sergeant E H Chateau (wireless operator), both of the Royal Netherlands Navy. Although the wireless-operator and the co-pilot were badly wounded, all managed to escape through the doorway, the door having automatically ejected on contact with salt-water. The Hudson sank straight away, a peculiarity of that aircraft.

On hitting the water, Bakker submerged, but his Mae West brought him back to the surface, where he found his crew bobbing on the surface. Only Lieutenant Deen was in good shape. Bakker himself, although not wounded, was a bit "bashed about; but at first I had so many other things on my mind that I took no notice of that. There was quite a swell, and when on top of a wave I could see the coastline, far away." Bakker, van Huijstee and Chateau clung to the navigator, and Bakker took off his shoes so their weight wouldn't drag him under. "I have always been a good swimmer," Bakker recalled,

and as a boy, born and bred in Den Helder — with sea on three sides — I had done a lot of risky swimming in the sea. But this was of course quite different. I also lost blood and, although I started to swim in the direction of the coast, I don't think I made more than half a mile. We got separated very soon, just drifted apart, and gradually one got desperate. Tired, cold, seasick. The thought of drowning becomes very real, and several times I was on the verge of giving up. The Mae West keeps floating alright, but you have to keep your head out of the water, and with the waves rolling over you that becomes very difficult eventually...

After a long time — one hour, two hours, I don't know — a twin-engined aircraft came searching over the area. Was I surprised and relieved to see that! He started to circle, and fired a flare, almost overhead. That was encouraging, too. But he went away and nothing happened for a long time. Then an aircraft on floats appeared...a Heinkel He59...started to circle, moved away, landed half a mile away from me, and stayed at the same place for quite some time. But then he opened up and slowly approached. He pushed me under with one of his floats, but then stopped ten yards away and they started to try to get me out of the water. I couldn't move an inch...it took a long time to get hold of me with a boat-hook. Once aboard I realised what they had done before they came to me. They had picked up my co-pilot. He was screaming his head off and obviously badly wounded. When I said there were two other crew members, they said: "No, we have seen nobody else. We are going back to base." It will forever be a mystery what happened to them. Were they drowned? When you drown, do you sink? The W/O was badly wounded, but my navigator—I had given him more chance than myself.

We two survivors were flown back to Stavanger and taken to hospital. The second day in hospital, two officers came to visit me, one Army, one Air Force; also one civilian. Not to be sociable but for information, of course. They told me they had also found the floating door. They had gone through all the items found on me and, as a joke, asked me what I had planned to do with the Norwegian money, the maps and the escape rations, etc. I said that I obviously was not in a good position to plan anything at all and that being alive was all that mattered. They agreed.

I spent one week there. I was then considered fit enough to be transported to Oslo for interrogation. There the Germans told me that they had shot down two more aircraft, no survivors. I did not believe them, but much later I heard it was true.

Also, years later, I heard what happened to my co-pilot. Apparently, he stayed in hospital a long time. Then he also ended up in a POW camp...he was soon repatriated. Did he never recover properly? I have never seen him again.

When I moved on from Oslo to Stettin, and then to Berlin, all I had with me was a *Feldwebel*, and not even a keen guard at that. He was terribly airsick in the Ju52. At Templehof he did not know how to get me to the railway station. So we stood there at the gate, trying to get a lift...You must picture me as a tramp, dressed in Polish Army trousers, a bashed about sweater (my own) and an Army overcoat (also Polish), with a black eye, a swollen face and an unhealthy complexion, and by my side a *Feldwebel*, thumbing a lift. We just stood there until

— thank God — a mighty fine car came to the gate, and the driver and my guard knew each other. The driver stopped and, looking at me, said: "What is that?" In a whisper the *Feldwebel* told him.

The driver was delighted to be of service, and with the two Germans in front and me, the vagabond, in the back seat, we went on our way. They knew I spoke German, but were not secretive at all. We did not go to the railway station. No, they were going to show me the sights of Berlin and, they said, show me that there was not all that bomb-damage the BBC claimed there was. We stopped somewhere for coffee and food, and then I asked what had happened to *General* Ernst Udet (a famous pre-war pilot and a very big wheel in the Luftwaffe), now presumed to be wounded or killed. The driver said: "No, no, he is very well. In fact you are being driven around in his car!" That was not a joke, it was true! At the end of the trip the driver gave me his name and address, and said he would like me to contact him after the war. I kept the note for a while, but soon realised that the name and address of *General* Udet's personal driver in the pocket of a POW, when discovered during a search, could spell a lot of trouble for him.

In the train from Berlin to Frankfurt am Main my guard even left me alone. He found a girl in one of the other compartments! Of course, when you are sitting there, all alone, it comes to your mind that — normally — you think of escaping. But in fact nothing was normal about it. It was physically and mentally not possible to get off an inter-city train, guard or no guard. He knew it, I knew it. When he finally delivered me at Frankfurt am Main, he said goodbye and added: "I am very, very sorry about all this."

It was Sunday, 7 September when Bakker reached Dulag Luft. As the first and, for a long time, the only Dutchman there he stayed a week longer than was usual. "I think they did not know what to do with me. The camp commandant [Major Theo Rumpel] was a nice chap. He was married to a Dutch woman and spoke Dutch fluently." On being released into the compound after the customary spell of "solitary" on Thursday, 11 September, Bakker shared a room with Eddy Asselin, and "Barny" Oldfield. They were purged to Lübeck the next day, and Bakker was joined by Acting Flight Lieutenant Frank Welburn, who would subsequently be sent to Stalag Luft I. On Saturday, 13 September, seventy-three NCOs were purged to Lamsdorf. Acting Flight Lieutenant Frank Welburn did Bakker's washing, because his badly wounded hands were taking time to heal. Bakker had his first hot meal in the Mess that day, sitting next to a young Flying Officer, "Tint" Winter-Taylor, who was a 13 September arrival. They engaged in conversation, and Bakker discovered that "Tint" was a survivor from a Whitley he and five other Hudson crews had been searching for the day before he was shot down.

"Tint" Winter-Taylor was from No612 Squadron, which had been in No18 Group since the beginning of the war, when it was stationed at Dyce in Aberdeenshire. The squadron had then flown Hectors and Ansons, but in March 1940 converted to Hudsons. Eight months later it re-equipped with the Whitley MkV and at the end of March 1941 relocated to Wick, in Caithness.

On Tuesday, 26 August "Tint" took off at 0815 hours to investigate a reported U-boat sighting. He carried out a series of square searches between Wick and Iceland but five hours after take-off was attacked by enemy fighters and had to ditch. His wireless operator had sent Wick an SOS, but the signal was faint and the aircraft hit the sea before he could complete his message. The Whitley remained afloat for a while and the crew clambered aboard the wreckage. Then the U-boat surfaced and took them aboard. Two of the crew, including the rear-gunner, Flying Officer John Grocott RAFVR, were badly wounded and given medical treatment.

The SOS received at Wick galvanised search parties into action, and Coastal Command and Air-Sea Rescue combed the sea for three days. On 29 August panic broke out on board the U-boat carrying "Tint" and his crew. British aircraft were approaching — probably Bakker's six Hudsons. The U-boat crash-dived and proceeded on its way to Le Havre unmolested. From there Winter-Taylor was taken by train to Dulag Luft. As "Tint" related his story to Bakker, it struck them that if the aircraft had been Bakker's Hudsons, and if the U-boat captain had not crash-dived, he might

— just might — have been killed at Bakker's hands. The coincidence forged a bond between them, and they became close friends.

Down and Cowper were pilot and navigator in a Hudson MkV from No233 Squadron, which since the start of the war had been shunted between Nos 15, 16 and 18 Groups before finding its final resting place at St Eval with No19 Group on 16 August 1941. Less than a month later, however, on Saturday, 13 September, Down was ordered up to search for a U-boat, taking off at 1220 hours and finishing in the North Sea. Only he and Cowper are recorded to have survived.

Two members of this purge were from the North African Theatre: Anthony Stanford Ruffel and Percy Oliver Valentine Green. Tony Ruffel, a huge South African with a personality to match (one officer prisoner described him as "Quite a lion of a man"), had been born and raised in Bloemfontein. Before the war he had worked for Cooper, MacDougall & Robinson, the leading manufacturers of animal health products — famous amongst sheep-farmers for "Cooper's Dip". In 1940 Ruffel had left the firm to join the SAAF in Pretoria and about the middle of May 1941 was posted with five other new pilots to No1 Squadron SAAF at Fuka. No1 SAAF, under the leadership of Major T Ross-Theron, was a Hurricane unit in No343 Wing that had racked up an impressive rate of "kills" against the Italians in East Africa but would a take beating in the Western Desert and suffer crippling losses when matched against the Me109Es of *I/JG27*. Ruffel was on the squadron for two weeks only before he was captured. Nine Hurricanes had been sent out at sunset to escort destroyers to Tobruk, which the British still held. They were jumped by a *Staffel* of Me109s and three were shot down. Cannon-shells ripped through Ruffel's Hurricane, holing the glycol tank and passing through his right knee. The aircraft caught fire and he baled out, coming down in the Mediterranean. A tough character, he started swimming towards the coast, and made landfall twenty-four hours later.

Unfortunately, he ran into an Afrika Korps unit. It was only then that his right knee started to give him trouble, and they took him to a field hospital at Derna where the knee was treated and bandaged. Then began the long and tortuous journey to Dulag Luft — by sea to Crete and Italy, and by rail to Vienna and Frankfurt am Main, where he was sent to the hospital at Hohemark.

Flying Officer Oliver Green — usually addressed as "Ollie" — had been with No112 Squadron flying Gloster Gladiators before being posted in May 1941 to No73 Squadron, a former Great War fighter squadron like many others subsequently disbanded, re-formed (with Gloster Gladiators), all but wiped out, and re-formed again (with the Hurricane MkI). In November 1940 it was transferred to North Africa, and since April had been based at Sidi Haneish, Egypt, not far from the Italian-held frontier near Bardia. "Ollie" was in charge of "B" Flight, and two weeks later "A" Flight was put under the command of Acting Squadron Leader A M Crawley, who had been told he would play an active part in leading the squadron, a position he viewed with misgivings. Having recently returned from an Intelligence posing in Sofia, he had limited flying experience, had never commanded a Flight and had not yet fired a shot in anger. The squadron itself consisted of only two flights and most of its pilots were only eighteen or nineteen years old, and their flying was limited to patrols over the sea. The only exceptions were Oliver Green and two Frenchmen who had fought in France in 1940.

At the end of May, No73 Squadron was given the job of protecting British barges delivering supplies to the beleaguered garrison at Tobruk, but early in July Middle East Command decided to take the offensive by putting up fighter sweeps over enemy-occupied territory. The object of these sweeps was to destroy columns and aircraft on the ground. Crawley and Green were horrified. There would be no cloud cover, and from any ridge or escarpment they occupied the Germans would see for at least twenty miles. They would thus have ample warning of the approach of marauding British aircraft and make sure their forward bases were evacuated while those in the rear would be able to scramble to a convenient height from which to intercept the strike. Crawley visited the AOC, Western Desert — Air Commodore R Collishaw, a Canadian "ace" of the Great War — to lodge his objections and suggest alternative tactics. Collishaw was unimpressed. No73 was to lead the first sweep of eight squadrons in strafing operations against the enemy airfield at Great Gambut, about eighty miles west of the frontier. They would assemble over Sidi Haneish, the top squadron flying at twenty thousand feet and the rest in steps downwards.

At 1710 hours on Monday, 7 July, six squadrons duly gathered above Sidi Haneish, where No73 Squadron joined them. The eighth squadron, which was supposed to provide top cover, failed to show. Crawley decided to press on nevertheless. A member of his flight dropped out straight away, claiming his engine had seized up.

No73, as leading squadron, flew at a height of 8,000 feet while the others stepped up behind. They crossed the frontier south of Sollum, and as they flew across eastern Cyrenaica saw more than one airfield where Gambut was supposed to be. Green, who had been across the frontier before, broke radio silence to tell Crawley which strip was the right target. As they descended, Crawley could see that there were few aircraft on the field. But they went down to about twenty feet and swept it with gunfire. Crawley noticed that two of the "aircraft" he hit were in fact dummies. Green followed Crawley down to strafe Gambut, but when he saw that the aircraft on the ground were either dummies or wrecks, he turned back to the south-east with his flight to try to get across the frontier south of Sollum and reach Sidi Haneish. One or two of Crawley's flight joined him, but Crawley's Hurricane was nowhere to be seen. Green kept low, but his flight was bounced by an Italian squadron, which had been waiting for them further west. Three Hurricanes were shot down, then Green himself was attacked from above. His engine caught fire and as he had just enough height to take to his parachute, he baled out. He was captured immediately and was flown by transport aircraft to Salonika, where he was thrust into Dulag 185. Two days later, Crawley turned up. Dulag 185 was a bad camp (the appalling conditions and many atrocities committed by the Germans against non-British prisoners have already been described in Chapters One and Two), and Crawley and Green were relieved when they were summoned to the guardroom after three weeks and informed that they would be leaving for Germany by train that afternoon.

Though the journey to Germany sealed their fate as prisoners, it was surprisingly exciting. Soon after the train pulled out of Salonika the engine slowed to a crawl as they passed a line of railway oil tankers, derailed and lying on their sides. Altogether they passed fourteen derailed trains — mainly oil tankers — before reaching the Austrian frontier.

At Belgrade their guards bought some German newspapers and magazines, which they passed to Crawley and Green when they had finished reading them. As the train wound its way through the valley of the River Sava, where the railway occasionally ran along the riverbank, Green, sitting opposite Crawley, leaned forward and handed him a copy of the *Berliner Illustrierte Zeitung*, saying: "I think you might be interested in this." To Crawley's surprise the frontispiece was a picture of him, described as a great explosives expert of the former British Embassy in Sofia and a dangerous member of the British Secret Service. A long article alleged that Squadron Leader Crawley had misused diplomatic bags to import bombs, which he had distributed to the Underground before being smuggled out of Sofia. Though the article substituted him for Cavan Elliott, the real bomb-smuggler, there was some truth in the story, and Crawley supposed a member of the Embassy staff had been interrogated by the Germans and substituted him either deliberately or through ignorance. He was thankful for his dishevelled appearance — he had several days' stubble and was still wearing the dirty khaki shirt and shorts in which he had been shot down — and dropped the magazine out of the window as soon as he could.

At Dulag Luft Oliver Green lost contact with Crawley, who remained there until he was sent to Spangenberg in February 1942. They would meet again in September 1942, when several hundred RAF officer POWs were temporarily accommodated in Oflag XXIB. From then on they would remain together until the evacuation from Stalag Luft III in January 1945. In the meantime, Green was transferred to Hohemark, where he met Tony Ruffel.

Regardless of his gammy leg, the leonine Ruffel hatched a plot to escape with him. One night, still in their pyjamas, they picked the lock of their ward door, sidled past the guards, hobbled downstairs and out through the main door. They had a few nasty moments avoiding a machine-gun post, but got clean away. Their aim was to cross the Rhine and make for France, where they hoped to link up with the Resistance. All they had to eat was some hoarded Red Cross food and they knew the chances of success were slim — but they were on the run for two or three days. They got away with a lot they shouldn't have, stealing clothes from a gamekeeper's hut and scrumping apples, which caused a lot of unwelcome bowel movements. Again, however, they succumbed to the mental exhaustion and lack of judgement that overtook all hard-arsers who had embarked on such an escape endeavour ill-equipped, and made the mistake of walking straight through a village, where they were baled up by a German farmer. So it was back to Dulag Luft and a spell in the cooler.

On Friday, 19 September, whilst Bakker was having a conversation with Frank Wilbraham and Lieutenant G A Haller of the South African Air Force, word came through that most of the transient officers were to be purged the next day. This was confirmed at evening *Appell*, when the SBO, Squadron Leader E D Elliott, read out the names of those being purged. They were to be packed and ready to leave by morning roll-call.

Also on the list were Flight Lieutenants R P Wallace-Terry and C M Hall RAAF, but they escaped in transit. Clive Hall, an Australian second pilot from No7 Squadron, Oakington, was another victim of the Berlin raid of 7/8 September that had accounted for Fielden, Lewis, McCarthy, Mackey, Peat, Stevens and Wilbraham. Hall's pilot, Sergeant A Yardley, had taken off in his Stirling at 2100 hours. They were shot down over Germany by a night-fighter and crashed at Recklinghausen. The entire crew, all of whom but Hall were NCOs, entered kriegiedom.

A highly experience RAF regular, Richard Patrick Wallace-Terry had suffered appalling head injuries when his Stirling had been hit by flak during a special operation over Berlin. He was a skilful pilot whose cool demonstration, in the Middle East, of how a Bristol Bombay Freighter reacted to an uneven distribution of passengers, had led to the invention of the "load sheet" — a compulsory document completed by every transport pilot, civil and military, prior to take-off to ensure proper distribution of load. He had been in No216 Squadron at Heliopolis before being posted to "Oxford's Own", No15 Squadron, at Wyton in Huntingdonshire, in 1941. No15, whose motto was "Aim Sure", was the second squadron to be equipped with the new Short Stirling twin-engined bomber.

In early September, Terry was selected for a special exploratory raid on Hermann Goering's secret radar and predictor control HQ for anti-aircraft and searchlight defences. Goering had taken these over in 1935, when he won control of the Luftwaffe from the Army. After the first Allied bombing of Berlin he initiated new defence measures for the German capital, embracing the latest technological developments. The nerve-centre was near one of his own homes, in a small triangle of woodland on the north-western reaches of Berlin. British Intelligence had been monitoring its progress for a year, and by mid-1941 had decided to mount an operation against it. Terry was to have a good look at the target, bomb if possible, and return with reliable photographs as a prelude to large-scale attacks.

Following a main bombing force to Berlin, Terry was to veer off as he neared the HQ and decide his run-up. It would rest with him and his navigator, Warrant Officer R B ("Pin-Point") Pape, how best to use their bombs. Night-fighter and flak opposition was expected to be intense. So the bomber fleet would fan out ahead over the capital, activate flak and searchlight batteries and, as far as possible, divert attention from Terry's operation. He and Richard Pape studied in secret everything relevant to the target. Patiently they pored over maps and photographs until they could see the target in the mind's eye. They marked the environs into categories for possible bombing runs from every point of the compass. Then, on the night of Tuesday, 2 September, with little warning, they set off for the 1,200-mile round-trip. "Met" predicted excellent conditions: bright moonlight.

Flying south of Wittenberge, and skirting Berlin to make for its north-western belt of forest, they met only moderate opposition. The main wave of bombers was drawing most of the searchlights and flak as Terry and Pape sought their target. Glorious moonlight made locating the triangular forest amazingly easy — and the Stirling easy prey to searchlight batteries, flak and night-fighters. But Terry made two dummy-runs to test wind speed and direction, and — impossible to believe — not a searchlight beam nor a single shot was aimed at him. Either British

Intelligence had been misled, or the Germans were deliberately being low-key to keep the forest's secret. After a final run-up from the north-east, they straddled the centre of the forest with bombs and then — as if by a flick of a switch — every searchlight and flak battery over Berlin went dead. Seven minutes later, as Terry was cruising over the thickly populated southern Berlin, all switched on again and caught his Stirling in coning searchlights and a vicious box-barrage. The accuracy was frightening. But, weaving madly, he got the aircraft clear, though not before Pape's course and speed calculator had been dashed from his hand by shrapnel. Pape had to navigate the aircraft back to Wyton by dead reckoning.

The brass-hats were jubilant when the photographs were processed, and rewarded Terry and his crew with thirty-six hours' leave. Getting nicely plastered in Cambridge, Terry and Pape made up their minds to quit ops after their current tour and apply for an instructor's course. Both intended to marry, and neither could bear any longer watching his "intended" checking her tears every time he went on a raid. But on the afternoon of Sunday the 7th they learnt that another raid on Berlin had been scheduled for that night, with 197 bombers from several squadrons taking part. Their squadron would put up ten Stirlings. Terry and his crew were to carry out another lone sortie over the same triangular forest, but slightly north-west of the former position. It would be a provocative attack to bring up fire and further evidence. They were warned to expect real opposition this time.

Most of the route would be above blankets of cloud with little view of the ground, which meant navigation by dead reckoning at its very best. There should be reasonable moonlight with scattered cloud over Berlin. Wallace-Terry wanted to use the same Stirling as he had flown on the previous operation. But she was unserviceable. One of her wing spars had almost been severed by flak and a deep line had been scored across the fuel tank. Next, he asked for more fuel and fewer bombs, as cloudy conditions could mean more time looking for the target. His request was denied. He was to carry eleven 500lb armour-piercing bombs, a new type of incendiary, photoflashes — and less fuel than before.

The operation seemed doomed from the start. As the Stirlings at Wyton were warming up, German bombers attacked the airfield with incendiaries and the squadron was ordered to do a quick-succession take-off.

After leaving the English coast, Terry's Stirling entered unbroken cumulus cloud, which stretched to the outer reaches of Berlin. There, as "Met" had predicted, gaps opened up and a watery moon allowed Pape to discern ground features and get a fix. Zigzagging towards the north of the forest, they were welcomed by searchlights and flak far more intense than anything they had experienced five nights previously. Again, Pape pin-pointed their target with little difficulty, and Terry stood off to judge his approach. Then, with infinite care, Terry lined up his aircraft's nose and began his bombing run. The flak suddenly let up, but just as Pape released his bombs and photoflashes, the Germans sent up a stream of shells. "Funny," said Terry, "Jerry taking pot-shots at us now." At 0052 hours the radio operator — Sergeant C S Aynsley, a former reporter on *The Daily Express* — sent the message: "Task completed", and Terry veered westward over the outskirts of Berlin.

But this time the searchlights and anti-aircraft fire over Berlin did not fail. Intense, blue searchlights stabbed the aircraft. "I'm diving," yelled Terry. "Hold on!" But before he could push the control column forward, the flak found its mark. A thunderous explosion, a mighty green flash, and Terry felt a blow to his forehead. Blood trickled from beneath his helmet and down his face. But he had no time to contemplate his wounds. The Stirling was bucking and shuddering in his hands. The starboard outer engine had been smashed and the fuel pipelines severed. Blazing petrol gushed from the 300-gallon tank, and flames danced along the wing. For the second time, Terry plunged his machine into a steep dive, shipping back the flames to the trailing edge of the wing. The fire went out and he pulled up, but the port wing was listing alarmingly.

The aircraft shuddered. Its starboard inner engine, out of alignment and synchronization, was over-revving and in danger of wrenching itself from its mountings. But at least the port motors were functioning evenly. Still Terry continued doggedly westward, flogging the port engines to the limit. Finally, the starboard inner petered out, and they began to lose height in the teeth of an unpredicted 50mph headwind. At 0128 hours Cyril Aynsley sent his last, laconic, radio message:

"Hit by flak". Any further radio contact would alert enemy night-fighters. In any case Terry knew the game was almost up. The aircraft was flying wing-down on two port engines, with little fuel and a damaged tail-plane. Wind howled through the gaps in the fuselage. Height was slipping away. To keep the aircraft aloft, he ordered the three air-gunners to unlock their guns and jettison them, the ammunition and anything else removable and expendable. He wanted to get as far as possible across Germany — perhaps even Holland — before making a crash-landing. His second pilot, Sergeant R Harper, and the flight engineer, Sergeant W C ("Jock") Moir, continued to nurse the engines and manipulate the petrol cocks, trying to squeeze as much juice out of the tanks as they could, even though the gauges registered "zero".

Terry jerked the aircraft along, rebuffed by 70mph headwinds. He ordered his crew to check their parachutes and open the escape hatch by the bombing well. Then the port engines spluttered, gulped and died. As the bomber started to fall, Terry, ashen-faced, with blood trickling from underneath his flying helmet, yelled over the faltering intercom: "Jump! Bale out!" The tail-gunner, Sergeant J E Dodd, and the front-gunner, Sergeant R D Hooley vanished through the bombing well, followed by Aynsley and Harper. Richard Pape, William Moir and the mid-upper-gunner, Sergeant H J Dunnett, stayed. The flak had torn a hole in the fuselage and ripped Pape's parachute. While Terry struggled to get the Stirling into gliding position, Moir was frantically shutting off all petrol flow, a vital task with a crash-landing inevitable. Sergeant Dunnett was concussed, lurching beside Pape's navigation table. Pape came forward and, heaving on the control column, helped his ailing skipper level out the Stirling. But a few minutes later the nose fell and a church steeple loomed out of the darkness. Uncannily, a sudden, upward draught lifted the Stirling lazily over the roof.

But the ground was terrifyingly close. Turning to avoid a small village, then again to miss a farmhouse, they braced themselves for impact. Then thirty tons of bomber hit the ground at more than 150mph. It bounced upwards, then down, then up again, and ploughed deeply across a small field. One of the wings struck a stout oak tree standing splendidly alone at the edge of the field. The Stirling spun, and lurched to a standstill. A blinding flash, a hideous grinding of metal...then...silence. They had crashed some twenty kilometres inside Holland, on Boer Enzerink's farm between the villages of Hengelo and Steenderen.

William Moir was the first to come to. A bit knocked about, but otherwise none the worse for wear, he found Pape unconscious, with a wicked contusion on his head and three fingers badly gashed at the palm of his right hand. He grabbed the first-aid box and was bandaging his fingers when Pape came to. Terry and Dunnett were still out. It took all the strength Moir and Pape had to drag them down the long, broken fuselage and into the open. Rain was falling heavily and a pale dawn cast a coppery glow across the flat landscape. Pape was appalled when he saw Terry's face for the first time. An ugly wound on his forehead had exposed a white mound of bone. The gash was pouring blood. There was coagulated blood around a smaller wound, which had probably been inflicted by shrapnel. At first Pape thought Terry was dead, and was relieved when he heard him give out low moans. "Jerry bastards mustn't get a clue," he was muttering. "Destroy everything, burn everything, mustn't get a clue, mustn't get a clue." The young gunner, Dunnett, had roused, but was in a state of shock.

After ministering what aid they could, Pape and Moir set about smashing up all the instruments in the aircraft and burning everything inflammable. The glow inside acted as a beacon: two red rockets flared into the sky some distance away, followed quickly by the crackle of rifle-fire. Terry came round, sitting up, retching violently and bowing his head up and down. Moir and Pape decided to make good their escape. Their skipper looked up, paused in his vomiting, and waved his hand in a vague effort at salutation. The same thought hammered at his muddled brain: *walk and walk until you drop...escape, escape, escape*. But the surrounding fields were flat, and the shallow ditches provided scant cover from the Germans, who were searching methodically. Motorbike patrols scoured the countryside, and men on foot crossed the fields, firing green flares and shooting at random to warn Dutch civilians to stay indoors. Fine rain, falling fast and cold, chilled Terry to the marrow. In dire pain from his head injuries, and half-blinded by blood, he had no choice but to give himself up and seek medical treatment.

Wallace-Terry received the best medical attention the Germans could give and, serious though his head injuries were, he had retained his memory and his wits. He was to need them, for while he was undergoing treatment, Moir and Pape, who had contacted the Dutch Underground, were betrayed. Captured in civilian clothes, with no RAF identification, and in possession of incriminating evidence, they were not far from death by firing squad when Moir buckled and gave them details of their crew, aircraft and mission. Luftwaffe Intelligence was notified and set about locating other members of their crew.

Terry was questioned in Luftwaffe headquarters at 46-47 Knesebekstrasse in Berlin, where the chief interrogator was *Oberstleutnant* Lindermann, a courteous Cambridge graduate who spoke English fluently. Terry knew something was afoot when his interrogators claimed to know he had been on an independent bombing mission, that twice in five days a four-engined bomber had attacked a forest north-west of Berlin, and that they did not believe that his crew had pin-pointed the target without the aid of some secret target-finding device. He gauged from their questions and inferences that if he talked freely, the Luftwaffe would do everything in its power to persuade the Gestapo to release Moir and Pape into the custody of Dulag Luft. Delving into the recesses of his mind, he concocted a story that Pape had been testing a secret radar device, which presumably he had switched on when nearing Berlin. He knew a lot less about it than did Pape, he said, but apparently it operated with the co-operation of people on the ground near the target; they sent signals on a special frequency which provided Pape with a cross-beam for a perfect fix on the target. When the interrogators told Terry that his Stirling had been dismantled and expert examination had revealed no secret apparatus, he told them that the device was so valuable that after testing it Pape had jettisoned it. A time-bomb had destroyed it in mid-air. The interrogators were dumbfounded: a secret, deadly accurate navigational aid, and treachery on the ground!

Soon Moir and Pape were in the cooler at Dulag Luft, where the Luftwaffe tried to pump them for more information. But by the time they found out that Terry's navigational aid was sheer fantasy, it was too late. Terry was at Lübeck, and Moir and Pape had wangled themselves a quick transfer to Stalag VIIIB, where Pape exchanged identities with a New Zealand soldier.

***

With Squadron Leader Barrett in charge, the purge left Dulag Luft at 7.40am on 20 Setpember, travelling by *Strassenbahn*, or street-car, to Oberursel, where they boarded a local train, which took them to the cavernous old *Hauptbahnhof* at Frankfurt am Main. There they boarded a train of second class coaches plundered from the French railway network. In one of the compartments there were "Dim" Strong, John ("Birdie") Barrett, Clive Hall, "Jock" Fielden, Tony Ruffel, "Ollie" Green, Gerry Williams and Richard Wallace-Terry. Despite his head-wounds and the incessant rain, Wallace-Terry was determined to escape. He went into a huddle with Tony Ruffel, who created a diversion by elaborately folding a blanket and thus obscuring the vision of the guard in the corridor. This allowed Wallace-Terry and Clive Hall to jump out of the window. Both were caught. Wallace-Terry, after landing heavily, stumbled and hit his head on the railway line. As a result he had to spend several weeks in hospital. Clive Hall made good progress, but was beaten by wet weather and had to give himself up. He reached Oflag XC a few days later, while Wallace-Terry would join the RAF kriegies at Warburg.

The rest arrived at Lübeck on Sunday, 21 September. "March to the camp. Search. POW nos. Fingerprints. Locked up in cold cell for the night. Ruffel keeps up the spirit," recorded Bakker laconically. Clive Hall and Wallace-Terry missed out on this process (they grieved not) and did not receive their POW numbers and identity tags until they arrived at Stalag Luft III.

(7)

A few days later more Army officers turned up from the campaigns in North Africa and Crete. Among them were some RAF and Free French Air Force personnel attached to the RAF: Flying

Officer A R Butcher; Pilot Officer W E Myhill; and Captain (Flight Lieutenant) P J F Jacquier, Lieutenant (Acting Flight Lieutenant) A D Péronne, and Lieutenant P Courcot, all from the Free French Air Force.

Arthur Richard Butcher and Pilot Officer Myhill were captured in Crete on Thursday, 22 May, after the German paracutists had finally got their hands on the airfield at Maleme. The Germans began gathering in the sick and wounded and any stragglers in the area. Dick Butcher had been a Gladiator pilot in No112 Squadron, and was then posted to No33 Squadron, equipped with Hurricanes, in Greece. He had been evacuated to Egypt after the fall of Greece, while the squadron had been re-formed and sent to Crete. On 12 May he was flown in a Sunderland to Suda Bay with Wing Commander Edward Howell, No33's new CO, along with a number of other pilots to replace those who were going on leave. He didn't even get a chance to fly on ops. Myhill had been an administrative officer on Maleme airfield .

Pierre Courcot, Paul Jacquier and Antoinne Péronne had been serving in Syria with the *Armée de l'Air* when France fell, and on 27 July 1940 had flown their aircraft to Egypt, where they volunteered for the RAF. Courcot, an observer, was attached to No24 (SAAF) Squadron, flying Martin Marylands, while Péronne and other French evaders were formed under Jacquier's leadership into No2 Free French Flight and operated from El Amrya, flying the various aircraft in which they had fled Syria — Morane Ms406s and Potez 63.11s. Eventually they were re-equipped with long-range Hurricanes and attached to No274 Squadron at Gerawla, where Jacquier was appointed a Flight Commander. A few weeks before the invasion of Crete he was married in Cairo.

On Monday, 26 May 1941 six Hurricane pilots were briefed to attack German transport aircraft flying into Maleme. The first three would set out at fifteen-minute intervals starting at 1310 hours, followed by the other three at 1415 hours. Jacquier was in the second section. On nearing Crete the three pilots separated and hunted for the transports individually. Jacquier was flying about twenty kilometres north of Maleme at 10,000 feet when he saw a Ju52 heading for Crete at a height of between a hundred and two hundred metres. He attacked from behind, got in a quick burst, and banked upwards to starboard. The Ju52 disappeared into the sea. A few minutes later Jacquier saw another lone Ju52 flying at about the same height, and repeated the performance. In each case the enemy gunner had managed to return the fire at the last minute. With two kills under his belt, Jacquier climbed and continued to Maleme to strafe aircraft on the ground. While he was attacking, five Me109s and two Me110s were circling slowly at about three thousand feet. Their undercarriages were down — no doubt to identify themselves to the airfield's defences as friendly aircraft. Jacquier shoved his engine through the gate and dived, heading east with the sun behind. Attacking another Ju52, which blew up, he levelled out a few metres from the ground. As he approached the airfield's eastern perimeter his engine cut; it had been hit by flak. Petrol flooded the cockpit. Using his speed he glided along the beach between Maleme and Canea, and did a wheels-up landing amongst the German forward positions. He was slightly injured in the crash, and was pulled out of the wreckage by Austrian mountain troops, who handled him roughly.

They took him to Maleme, where he was interrogated. At first, he deemed it safest to claim he was a French-Canadian, but later, when he was taken to the nearby POW cage, he met up with three other Frenchmen — Courcot, *Sergent* Roger Lefevre and *Adjudant-Chef* Albert Marteau — all of whom had proudly proclaimed their French identity, and decided he would share their fate. From the same Maryland crew, the three had been captured the same day as Jacquier, when two aircraft from No24 SAAF, under the leadership of Captain K S P Jones (SAAF), had taken off to drop medical supplies and ammunition to the defenders of Retimo. Following Jones's lead, Courcot's pilot, *Commandant* Georges Goumin, skimmed the waves on approaching the island, climbed to 2,000 feet when ten miles out, then dived down to drop his load. Having accomplished this, Goumin then decided to strafe Maleme. Goumin sprayed the airfield with his machine-guns, and Marteau, the WOP/AG, joined in with his two machine-guns. On the way out, they were intercepted by a swarm of Me109s from *III/JG77*, one of which, piloted by *Leutnant* Emil Omert, raked the Maryland from all sides. As the aircraft banked, the other gunner, Lefevre, fell from his turret and inadvertently pulled out his intercom wire. Marteau tried to rescue him, but became entangled with his parachute, which was billowing out of its pack. In total silence, they tried to extricate themselves. While this grim farce was unfolding, Goumin, who had been hit in the chest, was slumped dead over his controls. Courcot tried to take over, but too late; the Maryland crashed into a ditch, and slid along on its belly until its progress was brought to a jarring halt by a dirt bank. He and Marteau were injured in the crash, and the engines were now ablaze. As they were struggling out of the aircraft a patrol of Austrian mountain troops appeared and took them into captivity.

In due course Jacquier and the survivors from the Maryland were flown to Athens, and at the interrogation there Jacquier admitted that he, too, was French. He was then taken to the prison hospital at Kokinia. The hospital was surrounded by barbed-wire and nominally commanded by an SS corporal, who took his orders from the German *Arzt* in charge of the unit. The doctor took little part in treating the prisoners, leaving arrangements to Major Moore, and the staff who had volunteered to stay behind and look after the wounded when Greece was evacuated. As it happened, the casualties from Greece had been light, but wounded were pouring in from Crete. Although the building could easily accommodate five hundred beds, the number of needy cases was too great, and the beds were crowded together in wards with little space between them; patients were even lying in the corridors. The kitchen was inadequate, the supply of food short, and the orderlies overstretched. Jacquier volunteered to help, accompanying the orderlies, supplying the patients with water, encouraging them to eat, swatting the flies off their dressings, and washing and shaving them. Every morning Jacquier would visit the priest, and together they would kneel and pray for the prisoners.

After about three weeks he was told he was to be flown to Germany. A rumour circulated that he was to be handed over to Vichy and shot as a traitor to discourage other Free Frenchmen from fighting, as he was one of the first to have been captured. He took it phlegmatically, his only concern being that someone should tend for one of the most badly wounded prisoners, Wing Commander Edward Howell, and that Howell should get a message to his wife in Cairo. When his escort came to take him away, he walked out with his head high, smiling and waving at the other patients. He set a fine example, and it came as a relief to those at Kokinia when they discovered that he was destined for a POW camp in Germany.

Antoinne Péronne was shot down on Monday, 16 June, when at 1655 hours No274 Squadron sent out ten Hurricanes to ground-strafe the Acroma-Capuzzo road, where there was a concentration of enemy motor transport. The operation went smoothly until, on their way back, the Hurricanes were attacked by Me109s and four of them were shot down. Péronne force-landed behind enemy lines and was captured immediately.

(8)

On Wednesday, 1 October, Michael Roth recorded: "Winter coal issue — 8 blocks per day per room." Two nights later there was a minor sensation in the camp when the legendary legless Battle of Britain "ace", Acting Wing Commander Douglas Robert Steuart Bader DSO*, DFC*, was seen being escorted into the administrative barracks outside the camp.

Probably the most famous fighter-pilot of the Battle of Britain, "Tin-Legs" Bader was in March 1941 appointed leader of the Tangmere Wing, comprising Nos 145, 610 (County of Chester) and 616 (South Yorkshire) Squadrons. In fighter sweeps and "Circuses", Bader led No616 Squadron, with Ken Holden's No610 providing top cover, and No145, led by Stan Turner, on a flank between them. By August 1941 Bader was fifth on the list of the RAF's top-scoring pilots, with more than twenty confirmed victories and a personal tally of nearly thirty. He had done more sweeps than anyone else in Fighter Command and still insisted on leading the Tangmere Wing on every raid, pushing himself to the limit and driving others to keep pace. In one week alone in July 1941 he did ten sweeps — enough to knock out the strongest of men, still more one who had to get around on artificial legs. He was the last of the original wing leaders still operating — the rest were dead or, like Joe Kayll, prisoners of war; or, like Tuck and Malan, screened for a rest. He was noticeably on the verge of exhaustion, the skin around his deep-set eyes dark with fatigue. His wife, Thelma, his relations, his friends, and above all the AOC No11 Group, Air Chief Marshal Sir Trafford

Leigh-Mallory, were repeatedly urging him to take a rest. Bader refused. He lived for the Tangmere Wing, and battle was an intoxicant that answered his search for purpose and fulfilment. Leigh-Mallory, however, resolved to rest him in September.

The end came before that — on Saturday, 9 August 1941, when he led the Tangmere Wing to escort five Blenheims on a "Circus" operation to Gosnay power station. (It was the same op on which "Buck" Casson was shot down.) Their job that day was to go for German fighters where they found them. By this time No145 Squadron was being rested and the replacement squadron, No41, led by the Canadian Lionel Gaunce, was still relatively un-blooded. From the start things went wrong. Bader's No2, Flight Lieutenant Allan Smith, was suffering from a heavy cold and running a temperature. He was replaced by a New Zealander, Flight Lieutenant Jeff West. His No3 and No4 were Pilot Officer J E ("Johnny") Johnson (who would be promoted to Flying Officer the following day) and Flying Officer H S L ("Cocky") Dundas, leader of No616's "A" Flight.

Take-off was off from Westhampnett at 1040 hours. They met up with No610 over Chichester, and were now supposed to rendezvous with No41 Squadron over Beachy Head, but the formation had somehow gone astray. Climbing over the Channel, they could still see no sign of No41, but Bader refused to call it as that would mean breaking radio silence. Then, halfway across, his air-speed indicator broke, the needle slipping back to zero. This would mean trouble timing his rendezvous with the "Beehive" over Lille, and afterwards a difficult landing at Tangmere, not knowing during the critical approach how near the aircraft was to stalling. Trying to hand the lead over to Hugh Dundas, he found that his R/T was not functioning properly. He ought to have turned back. But he signalled Dundas to take over and for now he pushed the problem to the back of his mind. It was a good day for a fight, with patches of layer cloud at about 4,000 feet but a clear vaulting sky above and a high sun. Dundas climbed the squadrons to 28/30,000 feet so that they, not the Germans, would have the advantage of height and sun.

As they crossed the French coast south of Le Touquet, Ken Holden, top cover leader, spotted the German fighters. A mile ahead and about 2,000 feet below, a dozen Me109s from Adolf Galland's JG26, based at Wissant (a satellite of St-Omer), were climbing to attack, spread in "finger fours" abreast, the formation which Bader had done so much to promote in RAF Fighter Command. Then Bader saw them, flying in the same direction as his No616 Squadron, none of them looking behind; they were sitting ducks.

Bader warned Holden's squadron to remain as top cover, and ordered the rest down. With Hugh Dundas, James Johnson and Jeff West beside him and the others close behind, he plunged down at the leading four. The Germans were still climbing placidly ahead. It was the classic "bounce". Bader picked out an Me109 to port and closed in swiftly, but the Me109 seemed to slam slantwise at him. Trying to lift the nose and get a squirt at him, Bader misjudged. The two aircraft were about to collide. At the last minute Bader jerked hard on the stick and rudder, and his Spitfire sheered off, dropping nearly 4,000 feet. Angrily, he flattened out again at about 24,000 feet and found himself alone, thirty miles inside France. It was deadly to be alone in this dangerous sky. He must rejoin his men.

As he started climbing he was startled to see six more Me109s ahead, spread out in three parallel pairs, line astern, noses pointed away from him. More sitting ducks! He knew he should pull up and leave them: he had repeatedly drummed it into his own pilots never to attack on their own. But the temptation was too good to resist, and for the second time that day he pushed discretion aside. It was indicative of how much mental exhaustion was now clouding his judgement. He glanced behind, saw it was all clear, and sneaked up behind the middle pair. None of them noticed. From a hundred yards he fired at the nearest one and saw a thin blade of flame lick out behind it. The flames spread all over the aircraft, which dropped on one wing and plummeted downwards. Still the others flew blindly on. Bader aimed at the leader, 150 yards in front, and gave him a three-second burst. Again his shells found their mark. Pieces flew off the aircraft, white smoke gushed from beneath the engine cowling and the nose dropped. The two fighters to port were turning towards him. Crazily elated, as though he had just pulled off a big robbery, Bader wheeled violently to starboard to break off, but saw that the two Me109s on that side were still flying doggedly ahead — he could pass between them. In sheer bravado, he held course. Then something hit him. He felt the impact but his mind was numb and he could not account for it. There was no noise, but something seemed to be holding his Spitfire by the tail, pulling it out of his hands and slewing it round. It lurched suddenly and plummeted straight down, the cockpit filling with dust that had floated up from the floor. Bader pulled back on the stick but it fell inertly into his stomach like the neck of a sleeping swan. His Spitfire was spiralling earthwards and he looked round, bewildered, to see if anything was following.

Then he got the shock of his life. The whole of the Spitfire from behind the cockpit — fuselage, tail, fin — had gone. Only the little radio mast stuck up just behind his head. In his dazed frame of mind he could only conclude that the second Me109 had hit him and sheered off the back of the Spitfire with its propeller. (This has been bitterly disputed by Galland and by German records. According to them, Bader was in fact shot down by cannon-fire by *Oberfeldwebel* Max Meyer of *Nr.6 Staffel, JG26* — Meyer's eleventh victory. Bader had mistaken the impact of the cannon-shells for a collision.) He knew his aircraft was finished but hoped desperately that he was wrong. Seeing his altimeter unwinding fast from 24,000 feet, he thought how foolish it was to have to abandon his aircraft when the closed cockpit was so nice and warm. Then the survival instinct re-asserted itself. In a moment of panic a jumble of confused instructions fought for supremacy in his addled brain: *Christ! Get out! Wait! No oxygen up here! Get out! Get out!* He was already descending at 400mph and had no time to lose. Tearing off his helmet and mask, he yanked the little rubber ball overhead and the cockpit canopy flew off, leaving him battered by a screaming slipstream. He removed the pin from his harness and took a grip on the cockpit rim to lever himself up, wondering if he could get out without thrust from his helpless legs.

Pushing himself upwards, he felt as if he was being torn in two directions. The wind was sucking him out, but something else was holding on to his artificial right foot. It had snagged under the rudder bar. The broken Spitfire was now spinning down at 500mph, dragging him by the leg, while the wind buffeted him and clawed at his face. The nightmare seemed to drag on and on into an eternity of confusion. Only by hanging on to the D-ring of his parachute would he have the slightest hope of getting out alive. Suddenly, at about 4,000 feet, the leather harness of his artificial legs snapped and he was dragged out, minus his right leg. The noise and buffeting had stopped. He was floating upwards in peace. *It is so quiet, I must have a rest,* he thought. *I would like to go to sleep.* In a flash his brain cleared and he knew he was free. He pulled the D-ring, and the parachute cracked open.

As he floated earthwards — thankful, for once, to have lost his legs and had detachable ones — he heard the noise of an aircraft engine. Turning in his harness, he saw a lone Me109 heading towards him. Surely, after all he had been through, he was not going to be shot at now? But the pilot turned and roared past fifty yards away.

Bader was captured immediately upon landing by three German soldiers, who bent over him and removed his harness and Mae West. They carried him to a car and drove him to the hospital at St-Omer, where orderlies laid him out on a passed casualty table. A thin *Arzt*, wearing rimless spectacles, looked down at him and frowned at his empty trouser-leg. Pulling the torn cloth aside, he stared in amazement, then looked at Bader's face and at the wings and medal-ribbons on his battledress jacket. Puzzled, he said: "You have lost your leg." Bader spoke for the first time since his aircraft had been hit. "Yes," he said. "It came off as I was getting out of my aeroplane." The doctor examined the stump again, and realised it was an old injury. "You have lost both your legs — your real one and your artificial one!" He seemed to find it mildly funny, and Bader thought: *God, you haven't seen anything yet*, and was looking forward to the real joke. He had to wait a little longer for this, however, as the doctor suddenly noticed he had a cut on his throat. Bader poked around his neck and was surprised to feel a large gash under his chin. It was sticky with blood, but did not hurt. The doctor peered at it, then stuck his fingers between Bader's teeth and felt around the floor of the mouth, checking to see whether the cut went right through. Bader felt a chill of horror, but apparently it was all right, though the doctor was anxious to sew it up. After putting in the stitches he started to examine Bader's other leg. *This is going to be good*, thought Bader, and raised his rump so the doctor could ease his trousers over the hips. The doctor froze, staring transfixed at the leather and metal that encased the stump of the left leg. After a pregnant silence, the doctor sucked noisily and declared: "*Ach!* We have heard about you."

Once he had satisfied himself that Bader was otherwise unhurt, he had two grey-uniformed orderlies carry Bader upstairs to a narrow room, where they dumped him on a white hospital bed. They removed his clothes and his left "tin-pin", wrapped him in a white nightshirt, pulled the bedclothes over him and, standing the left leg against the wall, left the room. He lay motionless, aching all over. Every time he shifted in his bed, pain stabbed at his ribs. His head was singing like a whistling kettle. Suddenly he felt utterly exhausted, too tired even to think. After being fed soup by a nurse, he watched dusk gather in the room and then dozed fitfully. Some time later he woke in darkness, wondering where he was, and when he remembered he fell into a deep gloom, wishing he could turn back the clock. But time moved resolutely forward to his first dawn in captivity. It was only then that he began to think clearly, resolving to get his artificial legs back and somehow let Thelma, his wife, know that he was safe.

That morning, Sunday, 10 August, two young Luftwaffe pilots from Wissant paid him a visit. They were both friendly and curious, asking what it was like to fly without legs. As they spoke an elderly administrative officer came in and said: "Of course, it would never be allowed in Germany." After agreeing that both the RAF and the Luftwaffe flew good fighter aircraft, the pilots left. Next came a bald-headed Luftwaffe engineering officer, who asked more questions about Bader's legs. Bader cut him short, asking if they could radio England and arrange for a new leg to be flown over, and suggesting they search the wreckage of his Spitfire in case the other leg could be found. The German said he would see what he could do.

Later on, while trying to have a strip-wash, he noticed a big, dark lump at the top of his right thigh. He touched it gingerly with his fingertips. It was terribly sore. The doctor from the day before had a look at it and said: "We will have to cut this." Bader was horrified at the thought of some amateur taking the knife to his stump and refused to allow it. The doctor grudgingly agreed to leave it for a while.

At lunchtime a dark, plump girl came in and gave him a bowl of potato-water soup, two thin slices of black bread smeared with margarine and a cup of lukewarm *ersatz* coffee. Up to the moment he put the food in his mouth he thought he was hungry, but the bitter taste took away his appetite.

Then it was the doctor again, this time with two orderlies. They were going to put Bader in another room with "friends". The orderlies carried the mystified Bader along a corridor into a larger room with five beds. Three of them were already occupied. In the far bed was Pilot Officer Tommy Harrison, a WOP/AG in a Blenheim from No107 Squadron who had been shot through the mouth on Monday, 23 June, when "Circus No20" had attacked Mardyck airfield and Me109s had pounced over Dunkirk. His pilot, Flying Officer E T Fairbank, had been sent to Spangenberg. Next to Harrison was a Pole, Sergeant Pawel Kowala, a Spitfire pilot from No308 Squadron. His face and hands had been badly burnt when his aircraft had been shot down on "Circus No29" on Wednesday, 2 July. Nearest Bader was an American, Pilot Officer W I Hall. A former bush pilot in Alaska and at Val d'Or, Quebec, William Hall had been one of the original members of the first Eagle Squadron, No71, based at North Weald in Essex. He had the less colourful distinction of being the first Eagle to become a POW, shot down on the same "Circus" as Kowala. At 1150 hours twelve Hurricanes from the squadron took off to escort twelve Blenheims to Lille power station. Hall, sleeping on and off at dispersal, was awoken from a nightmarish dream by the dispersal gong. He had been imagining that he was being shot and that his right side was paralysed. So vivid was the dream that he awoke in a cold sweat and mentioned it to the station IO on the way to his Hurricane.

The Hurricanes rendezvoused with the Blenheims 12,000 feet above the east coast, formating above and slightly to the rear and heading across the Channel. As they crossed the French coast the Germans hurled flak at them. The shells burst well above and behind the aircraft, but as they progressed south towards the target the flak batteries tracked them and they came under fire all the way. When they reached the target, flying at 10,000 feet, the ack-ack was intense. Flak struck Hall's right wing, partly destroying it. He started to lose altitude, and spun out. At about 1,500 feet the Hurricane straightened out and Hall began to follow the formation at low altitude. Then, as the

Blenheims released their bombs, about thirty Me109s swooped down on them. Hall soon had a Messerschmitt on his tail, pouring cannon-shells and machine-gunfire into him. The shells slammed into his tail and the armour plating behind his seat, then started coming up through the cockpit and into his reserve fuel tank, dumping fuel into his lap and setting the aircraft on fire.

One of the shells hit him in the thigh and paralysed his right side. His nightmare was now a reality. He rolled his Hurricane upside down, opened the canopy and dropped out. In his haste, he had forgotten to disconnect his helmet from its radio cord and oxygen line, and as he fell out he got wrapped around the tail fin. Trying to open his parachute with his right hand, he couldn't, so he had to use the thumb of his left hand to assist his right hand in pulling the rip-cord. By the time his parachute opened he was dangerously near the treetops. He swung once in one direction, then in the other, then landed behind a hedge in a daze.

Nearby were some French peasants hoeing. They were shouting and gesticulating at him to run, but he couldn't get up. Almost immediately German soldiers were upon him, charging through the hedge with fixed bayonets. Two of them went away to fetch a stretcher, then carried him to a German Officers' mess hall some fifty yards away on the other side of the hedge. He lay in the hallway of the Mess, on the stretcher, for seven hours until at last, at 9pm, an ambulance arrived. In the meantime, he was an object of curiosity to the soldiers, who gaped at him and spoke to him in German and English. After pouring liberal quantities of brandy into him they investigated his wounds: his right kneecap had been shot off and he had shrapnel down his right side.

After a three-hour ride, in which the ambulance kept stopping to pick up German wounded, he reached the hospital at St Omer. The doctors operated on him that night. Before putting him under ether, the surgeon, with a couple of nurses looking on, pulled up his hospital gown, rapped his testicles with a scalpel, and said: "You won't be needing these any more, will you?" "No," replied Hall, "not for a while." The doctor laughed. When Hall awoke next morning the first thing he did was check to make sure they were still there.

Altogether Hall underwent nine operations on his leg, and after each was put in a body-cast. One busy morning, while he was waiting to enter the operating theatre, a German pilot was brought in. He had baled out of a blazing Me109. His face was badly burned and the skin was hanging off the ends of his fingers, like melting toffee. When the orderlies arrived to take Hall into the operating room, he urged them to take the German pilot first. Some time later, in the middle of August, the pilot's mother brought her son some wine and a birthday cake, and together they went upstairs to Hall's ward and shared them with him. Before the disfigured pilot left he dropped in to say goodbye.

At night the door to the ward was left open and guarded. For the first three or four days the guards outside played records. It was always the same two: "Roll Out the Barrel" and "We're Going to Hang Out Our Washing on the Siegfried Line". At first Hall thought they did it to amuse him, but before long realised they did it to annoy.

Despite their condition, Harrison and Hall plotted to escape. With the help of Sergeant Kowala, who had fought with the *Armée de l'Air* in 1940 and spoke fluent French, they persuaded a French ward-maid called Lucille de Becker to smuggle in a small surgical saw, and with this Hall slit his body-cast all the way down and, at night, practised walking. The next step was to get back their clothes, as these had been taken away, leaving the pair only in nightshirts. As the window offered the only means of escape they would also need a rope, which would have to be smuggled in. Another snag was the ten o'clock curfew in St Omer. Then Hall's knee turned gangrenous and the German doctor decided he needed another operation.

Hall was now back in a body-cast, and in traction; for him, escape was impossible. To fight the gangrene the doctor had opened the cast at the knee. So many wars had been fought in France that the earth was full of gangrene bacteria. All day Hall lay near the window, in the sunlight, so that bacteria-carrying flies would land on the gangrenous knee and lay their eggs. The maggots then ate the dead flesh away. Eventually the leg was cured.

Occasionally the German nurse, Sister Erica, would slip him a lemon, or a couple of cigarettes or some sweets — little acts of kindness that Hall would forever appreciate.

Bill Hall had been in hospital six weeks when Bader arrived. Almost the first thing Bader asked was whether, assuming he could persuade the doctor to return his uniform, there was any means of escape. Harrison and Hall told him the French girls working at the hospital might smuggle in a rope, but he would have to escape at night before the curfew. Bader slept on it.

When he awoke the next morning, Monday, 11 August, his stump felt less sore: a good sign. Then the plump girl came in with black bread and acorn coffee. She was accompanied by another local French girl, whom Bill Hall introduced as Lucille. Bader tried to joke with her in his schoolboy French, but although she smiled and coloured slightly, she said nothing — a German guard was standing within earshot at the doorway.

During breakfast the doctor came in to look at Bader's stump. The swelling had gone down, much to Bader's relief. While he had the doctor's ear, Bader waved a slice of black bread in his face and told him the food was "bloody awful". They had a shouting match and the doctor stormed out. There was no improvement for lunch: more potato-water and black bread. Afterwards a tall, smart Luftwaffe officer dropped in; he was aged about forty and wearing the red tabs of the flak regiment. Saluting and clicking his heels, he announced that they had found Bader's leg in the wreckage of his Spitfire. A jackbooted soldier marched proudly through the door, jerked to attention beside the bed, and held out one arm to its fullest extent. Hanging from it was the artificial, yellow-painted, duralumin leg, covered in mud; the harness was torn, the shin was dented and the foot was smashed. Bader took the leg and, removing the sock, found that the instep had been stove in. He asked if the engineers at St-Omer airfield could repair it. After pondering a while, the officer said he would take it and see. After a mutual exchange of compliments, the officer again clicked his heels and saluted, then turned smartly about and left.

Dinner was delivered by a new girl, with fair hair and spectacles, called Hélène Lefèvre. She set the tray down on Bader's bed and he looked goggle-eyed at its contents: real tea and a slice of greyish-white bread. So the shouting match had been worth it. Later on, the doctor returned to examine Hall's leg. Bader, who had done so well on his artificial legs, advised the doctor to amputate. But to Hall's relief *der Arzt* was dead against it.

By the following morning, Tuesday, 12 August, the swelling on Bader's stump had cleared completely — just in time, as after breakfast the flak officer returned with his jackbooted stooge and proudly presented Bader with his repaired leg. The engineers at St-Omer had done a magnificent job, supplying a completely new harness of good-quality leather, hammering out the dent in the shin, putting the foot back in position and correctly setting the rubbers in the ankle so that the foot would be strong and resilient. They had cleaned and polished the leg, and apart from a patch bare of paint on the shin it looked normal. Bader was impressed and very touched. "It's really magnificent," he said. "It is very good of you to have done this. Will you please thank the men who did it very much indeed?"

Bader strapped on his duralumin legs and eased himself off the bed. For a moment he felt a little unsteady, but was soon propelling himself round the room, feeling ludicrous in his long nightshirt with shoe-clad metal legs underneath. His right stump-sock had been lost in the parachute descent, and the leg felt strange, clanking loudly as he swung it. Tommy Harrison, Pawel Kowala and Bill Hall looked on, fascinated. The Germans beamed with pleasure. When they left, Bader crossed to window and looked thoughtfully out at the grass courtyard, three storeys and forty feet below. To the left were the gates — open and unguarded.

Later on, a Luftwaffe *Feldwebel* entered and told Harrison and Kowala to prepare to leave for Germany after lunch. He would bring their clothes later. Bader began to worry whether it would be his turn next. Once in Germany and behind barbed-wire his chances of escape would be slim; he had to escape while still in France, and contrive to delay as long as possible any move to Germany. When Lucille brought lunch, Bader whispered to Kowala: "Ask her if she can help me get out or put me in touch with friends outside." In a low voice the Pole started talking to Lucille in fluent French. She stole a look at Bader and whispered an answer to Kowala. Keeping their eyes on the door, they went on talking in fast, urgent whispers. Bader listened eagerly, but their flow of words was too fast. Then they heard the heavy footfalls of a guard in the corridor, and Lucille left, giving Bader a quick, nervous smile. Kowala went over to Bader's bed and told him the girl was willing to help. She could not get him a rope, or arrange the return of his clothes, but she had heard there were British agents in a village nearby and would go there and contact them on Sunday, her day off. That was four days away. In the meantime he must prevent the move to Germany. From now on he would pretend to be too weak to travel.

The Germans came for Kowala and Harrison that afternoon; Bader would now have to converse with Lucille in his schoolboy French. On the morning of Sunday, 17 August, when she handed him his breakfast — the usual bread and acorn coffee — she slipped a note into his hand. Written in French in a clear, child-like hand, it read:

My son will be waiting outside the hospital gates every night from midnight until 2am. He will be smoking a cigarette. We wish to help a friend of France.
J Hiècque

Tingling with excitement, Bader tucked the note inside his nightshirt and stuffed a handkerchief on top. He knew he must destroy the note. If it were discovered, Hiècque, and probably Lucille, too, would be put to death. He must also get his clothes and think of a way of escaping from the hospital. But first the note. Strapping on his legs and lurching to the lavatory at the end of the corridor, he struck a match, burnt the note, and flushed the embers down the pan. As he walked back up the corridor, the sentry gaped at him, and this gave Bader an idea. He would explain to the doctor how self-conscious he felt at being an object of curiosity and use that as a pretext to get his uniform back. When the doctor came to inspect the right stump again, Bader told him about the sentry, and added that in bed the nightshirt got tangled up in his stumps. Half an hour later a German nurse came in with his uniform and, smiling briefly, put it in a neat pile on his bed. It was that easy. Sister Erica had even sewn a new button on his damaged battledress jacket.

Back in bed, Bader racked his brains for a foolproof way out of the hospital. He had no rope, and walking out was impossible, as guards were on duty in the corridor all night from midnight. He crossed to the window, and again looked down wistfully at the grass courtyard. He was still there when the two Luftwaffe pilots from St Omer returned. They told him they had brought him two bottles of champagne and invited him for drinks in the doctor's room downstairs. During the party — a cheerful affair in which they chatted amiably about tactics and aeroplanes — the pilots told Bader that Goering had given permission for the Luftwaffe to radio England and allow the RAF free passage to drop Bader a new artificial leg. Bader chuckled inwardly. If he knew Leigh-Mallory and Sholto Douglas, they would arrange for it to be dropped during a "Circus". They also told him that commander of their airfield at Wissant was *Oberstleutnant* Adolf Galland, one of Germany's greatest fighter aces with ninety-five victories. Galland had invited Bader to tea at the Officers' Mess that evening. Having heard of Galland by reputation, Bader was intrigued and said he would be delighted to meet him. It would add a note of chivalry to a war that was now modern and impersonal. Neither could the value of visiting an enemy aerodrome be underestimated. It was a chance to spy out the country and compare a German fighter station with those back home. He might even steal an Me109 and fly back!

That evening a car came for him and he sat in the back with the bald-headed engineering officer. It was a fifteen-mile journey to Wissant, the sun was out, and Bader soaked up the experience of being driven through the open countryside after four days in hospital. They pulled up in front of an attractive country house of red brick. German officers stood outside. It was the Officers' Mess. As Bader climbed out of the car, a dark-haired man about his own age stepped forward. He had burn marks round the eyes and a little moustache. Round his neck hung the Knight's Cross with Oak Leaves and Swords.

Extending his hand, he said: "Galland."

Shaking hands, Bader introduced himself, the engineering officer interpreting.

Then one by one the other officers introduced themselves, clicking their heels and bowing slightly.

Followed by his entourage, Galland led Bader down a garden path lined with shrubs. As they walked, they compared their experiences of baling out. Then they went through a long, low arbour filled with an elaborate model railway on a raised platform. Galland pressed a button, and the little trains started rolling past little stations, rattling over points, past signals and through tunnels and cuttings. Smiling wistfully and his eyes sparkling, Galland suddenly looked boyish and fun-loving. The interpreter said that outside flying this was Galland's favourite hobby. The layout was a scale replica of Goering's railway.

Afterwards came the moment for which Bader had been waiting. Galland, tiring of his model railway, led him and his pilots several hundred yards along hedge-lined paths and through a copse of trees to the aircraft dispersal. There, tucked inside one of the three-sided blast walls, stood an Me109. Bader looked at it with fascination, and Galland motioned him to climb in. Hauling himself up on the wing-root, while the Germans looked at him with surprise, he grabbed his right "tin-pin" and swung it into the cockpit, into which he climbed unaided. As Galland leaned over and explained the cockpit layout, Bader was seized by a mad impulse to start her up and take off. (It wasn't until after the war, when Galland sent a snapshot of the scene, that Bader discovered that a German officer had been standing next to the cockpit with pistol drawn. He wouldn't have stood a chance.) Bader asked the interpreter if Galland would allow him to take a spin in the aircraft. Galland chuckled and answered. "He says that if you do," the interpreter told Bader, "he'll be taking off right after you."

As Bader stepped out of the cockpit, he looked across country and saw the Strait of Dover. He fancied he could see the White Cliffs far beyond, and for a moment felt sick. If only they would leave him alone for a moment, he could steal the Me109 and be back home for tea.

But for Bader tea was in the German Officers' Mess, where waiters in white coats served sandwiches and real English tea (probably captured). Like many RAF captives before and after him, Bader was struck by the similarities to his Mess back home; only the different uniforms and the German language spoiled the picture. The atmosphere was a little strained, too — everyone was formal, and the conversation stilted. Perhaps in Galland's presence the junior officers were less boisterous. No one tried to pump him for information. The interpreter told him that on the day he was shot down the Luftwaffe had destroyed twenty-six Spitfires without loss — such arrant nonsense that it bucked Bader no end. It confirmed the RAF's scepticism of German claims. Bader himself had destroyed two that day. After the war he found out that his wing had destroyed eight Me109s for only two losses from No616 Squadron — himself and "Buck" Casson. (What he did not know, however, was that another eight Spitfires from other squadrons had been shot down.)

That night they showed him some camera-gun footage, including an odd film of an Me109 strafing a British ship. The last few frames purported to show the ship half-submerged, but it was obvious to Bader that it was a different ship. The other films, one showing the demise of a Spitfire, were authentic. Afterwards Galland gave Bader a tin of tobacco. When it was time to leave, he told Bader that things would be different in a prison camp, but if Bader ever needed anything he would do his best to help. With that, he smiled warmly, shook hands, clicked his heels and bowed. The other assembled officers, standing at a discreet distance behind, likewise bowed and clicked heels. Bader slid into the car with the engineer and they drove back to hospital. The engineer escorted him to his ward, shook hands, clicked his heels and bowed himself out.

More black bread stood by Bader's bed. Lucille had been in with "dinner". After his tea with Galland, he had no stomach for it.

In the meantime another Spitfire pilot had joined him and Bill Hall. Sergeant Pilot G B Russell, from No485 (RNZAF) Squadron, had been shot down on 12 August and had just had an arm amputated. Russell lay comatose in the bed by the window, stinking of ether. He was still under the influence of the anaesthetic.

The door opened and a German soldier came in. He was wearing a coal-scuttle helmet, the first Bader had seen. The soldier, who must have been awaiting his return, saluted and told him in heavily accented English that he should be ready to leave for Germany the next morning at eight o'clock. The news hit Bader in the pit of his stomach. When the soldier left, Bader slumped on the bed and swore.

"Tough luck, sir," said Hall. "Looks like you've had it."

But Bader was not finished yet. "Well, I've got to get out tonight, that's all," he said crisply.

Crossing to the window, he pushed it open and peered out. It seemed a long way down, and directly below, bordering the lawn, were flagstones. With his duralumin legs, he could hardly jump — he would split himself in two. He turned round and surveyed the room, with its bare floorboards and five neat beds. *Beds...bed-sheets. My God! Sheets! Knotted sheets!* Each bed had a single under-sheet and a double, envelope-type top-sheet, stuffed in the continental style. He stripped his bed and the two empty beds, ripping the top-sheets down the seams to make two out of each one. The tearing was bound to alert the Germans, and Bader told Hall to make a noise. In a loud American voice, Hall launched himself on a long monologue, talking nonsense, saying anything that entered his head and laughing mirthlessly. They heard jackboots scuffling across the floor outside and Bader looked up like a hunted animal. Then the wicker-chair outside the door creaked as the guard sat down.

Bader went back to work, tying the sheets together without skill in huge granny-knots. When he had finished, the knots took up so much linen that the sheet-rope was too short. Hall offered his sheets, but still the rope was too short. There was no help for it — Bader would have to take the sheets from the comatose Russell. Gently easing the sheet from under him, he turned round and told Hall: "This is frightful, but I've just got to do it." Hall said he would explain to the Sergeant Pilot when he came to.

Soon Bader had fifteen sheets knotted together, strewn across the floor, and he prayed no one would come in. He pushed Russell's bed towards the window — it screeched terribly — and knotted one end of the rope round the leg. The rest he stuffed under the bed, but it still looked obvious. Then he straightened the white blankets on all the beds and climbed into his own. He lay there sweating, his heart thumping. *Pray God that darkness comes before the guard.* Time dragged like a ball and chain as he waited for nightfall. He and Hall tried to talk in low voices, but Bader couldn't concentrate on the words. At about nine o'clock, just before darkness fell, a German soldier craned his neck round the door and looked in. Bader lay there with bated breath. The guard muttered *"Gute Nacht"*, withdrew his head, and closed the door behind him.

In three hours' time, provided the nurse did not come to check on Sergeant Pilot Russell, Bader would be away.

It seemed that time had stood still when at last a clock tower somewhere in St-Omer chimed midnight. Bader eased himself to the edge of his bed, trying to stop it creaking and conscious of the silence surrounding him. He strapped on his legs, donned his uniform and, hoping the guard outside was asleep, took a step towards the window. He winced as the right leg squeaked and thumped on the creaking floorboards. Hall started coughing to cover it up, and Bader, unable to tiptoe, swung himself painfully and unsteadily across the floor. He didn't know which of them was more likely to wake the guard — Hall or himself. Finally making the window, he pushed it open and leaned out. But it was pitch dark and he could not see the ground. Trusting that his improvised rope would be long enough, he grabbed the knotted sheets and lowered them out. Suddenly Russell started groaning; Bader or Hall must have inadvertently awoken him. All Bader needed now was for a nurse to hear the Sergeant Pilot's cries of agony and come running.

Holding the sheet-rope, Bader leaned his chest on the windowsill and tried to swing his legs out sideways. They seemed more clumsy and unmanageable than ever. He took one hand off the rope to lift the right ankle up to his rump and bend the knee. He clambered through and, with both hands holding the rope, dangled from the windowsill. A pain shot through his ribs, making him gasp. "Good luck," whispered Hall; it sounded loud enough to wake the dead and Bader hissed at him to "Shut up". Then: "Thanks," he said, and started lowering himself, hand over hand. This part was easy — for, although his legs dangled uselessly and scraped against the wall, his arms were strong and took his weight without difficulty. Luckily, his granny-knots were holding. In a few seconds he came to a window; it was open and he recognised it as the room in which he had drunk champagne earlier in the day. He hoped the doctor was asleep. Sitting on the windowsill for a breather, he looked down again but could still not see the ground or tell whether the rope reached it. Anyway, it was too late to go back now. He eased himself off the ledge and pressed on.

At last his feet touched the flagstones. He let go the rope, and noticed, without paying much attention, that there were yards of sheet lying in the courtyard. Piece of cake, he thought, and started to make for the gates, cursing his noisy legs. When he reached the gates, he found to his horror that they were closed. In a feeble hope that they might be unlocked, he slid his fingers through the crack between and to his relief one of them opened about a foot. He slid through and on to the cobbled road and straight away saw the glowing cigarette end, directly opposite. The mysterious Frenchman was there. Bader crossed the road diagonally and the cigarette end moved towards him. It came to his side and the shadowy figure behind it hissed "Douglas!" in a heavy French accent. *"Oui,"* said Bader, and the figure grabbed his right arm and guided him along the road, the darkness and silence resounding with the clattering of his legs on the cobblestones. The Frenchman applied pressure on his arm and they turned right. After a while the Frenchman started muttering superlatives, and Bader, beginning to find the situation faintly amusing, broke into giggles. The Frenchman said: "Ssh! Ssh!" But that only made Bader giggle all the more; the harder he tried to stop, the worse his fit of giggles became. Then the Frenchman joined in and, absurdly, the pair were soon laughing loudly. Slowly, as their pent-up emotions were released, the laughter subsided into sniggers and at last they regained their composure.

The trek through St-Omer seemed to last for ever, and before long Bader's right stump, without the protection of the stump-sock, began to chafe. After about half an hour it became sore and painful. Ten minutes later Bader started limping. The Frenchman made soothing noises, as if to say, "Not far now." But on and on they went, the duralumin rubbing the skin off Bader's right groin at every agonising step. On the point of exhaustion, Bader stumbled and clung with both arms to the Frenchman's shoulders. In the end the Frenchman had to pull Bader's arms round his neck, pick him up, and carry him on his back like a sack of potatoes. After a hundred yards of this the Frenchman, worn out, put him down. Bader leaned against a stone wall, and saw to his relief the Frenchman pushing open a gate beside him.

With the Frenchman leading the way, Bader stumbled up a garden path, through a doorway and into a small, low-ceilinged room. In the dim light of an oil-lamp on the table, he saw flowered wallpaper and an old man and woman in a black shawl rising from their chairs. The woman, Madame Hiècque, embraced and kissed him. She was more than sixty, plump and with a lined, patient face. Monsieur Hiècque, her husband, was thin and stooping with a grey moustache, which he brushed against Bader's cheek. Bader caught only a fleeting glimpse of his guide, a young man wearing a cap with a shiny peak drawn over his face. With a faint smile, he shook Bader's hand and left.

Madame Hiècque asked: *"Vous êtes fatigué?"*

"Oui," Bader replied, leaning on the table.

Holding a lighted candle, she led him up some stairs into a room filled with a double bed. He flopped on it. Madame Hiècque put the candle on the table, smiled and left the room. With a wave of relief, Bader unstrapped his legs, stripped to his underclothes and slid under the sheets into a soft feather bed. *That's foxed the bloody Huns*, he thought. *I'll be seeing Thelma in a couple of days.* Then he fell asleep.

At about 7am he was awoken by a hand on his shoulder. Monsieur Hiècque was smiling down at him, revealing tobacco-stained teeth. He left Bader a razor, hot water and a towel. After a wash and shave Bader examined his right stump. It was raw and bloodstained and terribly sore, but he would just have to grin and bear it. He strapped his legs on and after an agonising walk down the stairs found coffee and bread and jam ready on the table. Madame Hiècque put on an old straw hat and went out, leaving Bader in a plush, red chair trying to talk with the old man. Their conversation was friendly but stilted, and time passed slowly. At last, after about two hours, Madame returned, smiling gleefully. *"Les Boches,"* she said, *"sont très stupides."* She explained that she had taken a walk to the hospital and stood watching while hordes of Germans ran around frenziedly searching the area. In his schoolboy French Bader tried to make her understand that they were taking a grave risk in harbouring him. If found, he would only be sent to a prison camp, but they would be shot. He ought to leave and find somewhere to hide up. But Madame would have none of it; the Germans would never find him here. That evening, her son-in-law, who spoke English, would come, and they would discuss a way of getting him to the Underground.

She examined his right stump and improvised a stump-sock. Taking a pair of long woollen underpants, she cut off one of the legs and stitched up the end. Then she powdered the stump and carefully put the stump-sock over it. The leg felt much better.

After giving Bader cold pork for lunch Madame Hiècque made another trip to the hospital. Her pleasure when she returned far surpassed that which she had displayed earlier. Convinced that Bader could not walk far, the Germans had cordoned off an area round the hospital and were searching every house within it. They had not come anywhere near this part of the town.

Madame went out again later in the afternoon. She was enjoying herself! But for Bader time dragged, and he sat in the red chair, twiddling his thumbs and wishing the English-speaking Frenchman would hurry up. At half-past five there came an urgent rapping on the front door and Bader's blood ran cold. The old man nearly jumped out of his skin. He peered furtively through the curtains, turned and whispered: *"Les Boches!"*

Grabbing Bader's arm, he led him towards the back door, giving Bader just enough time to grab his battledress jacket. They stumbled into the garden, Bader moving as fast as his artificial legs would carry him. Three yards from the back door an old galvanised-iron shed stood on posts against a wall. Inside were baskets, garden tools and straw. Monsieur Hiècque pulled the baskets and straw away, and Bader, using his hands as a pillow, lay on his stomach against a corner of the wall while the old man piled the straw and baskets on top. The old man hurried back inside.

Within a minute Bader heard loud voices and then scurrying jackboots by the back door. Through the straw he could see nothing. The boots echoed down the path towards the shed. Baskets were being kicked about, and the straw over him was moving and rustling. He thought the game was up, but then the footsteps retreated and died away. He couldn't believe his luck. Then suddenly the boots were coming back up the path. Confound it! They were back in the shed! Standing no more than a yard away, the Germans were tossing the baskets aside as they searched. Seconds later he heard a definite, metallic clang; a movement in the straw just above him, and another clang. A bayonet passed within an inch of his nose, pierced the wrist of his battledress jacket and hit the stone floor. The next stroke would surely go into his neck or back. Instantly, he jerked up on his hands, straw tumbling off his back. A young soldier, poised to make another jab with his bayonet, leapt back in shock and stared at him goggle-eyed. He started yelling hoarsely to his comrades. Three more soldiers, all armed, ran towards the shed and stood round Bader in a semicircle. They raised their bayonets, the tips poised about four feet away from him. Slowly he put up his hands.

They were joined by a small *Stabsfeldwebel* with a dark, thin moustache, who covered Bader with a pistol. He looked pleased with himself. "Ah, Wing Commander," he said in unaccented English. "So we have caught you again."

Bader asked if he could order his men to lower their rifles; after all, he was unarmed. The *Stabsfeldwebel* obliged, and the soldiers lowered their rifles. Then a surreal conversation ensued.

"You speak English very well," said Bader, still with his hands raised.

"Thank you, Wing Commander," replied the staff sergeant. "I lived at Streatham for eleven years."

"Did you really? I used to live near Croydon myself."

"Ah, I know Croydon well. Did you ever go to the Davis Cinema?"

"Yes. And I used to go to the 'Locarno' at Streatham."

"Did you? Many Saturday evenings I have danced there."

It was a peculiar way for Bader's escape bid to end — making polite party-conversation with the enemy who had captured him. Just another of the incongruities of war, like his drinking champagne with the Luftwaffe pilots from Wissant and his meeting with Adolf Galland. What a damn silly business war was! It confirmed his belief that it was the politicians, not the ordinary people, who started wars, and that the world would be well rid of them. He felt no animosity towards the Germans who had found him and, as far as he could see, they felt none towards him. It made Hitler and Mussolini look pretty bloody stupid...

But when he reached the house grim reality re-asserted itself. The Hiècques were standing in the backroom, under guard. They looked pale. Bader walked stiffly past, showing no sign of recognition. Outside, he told the *Stabsfeldwebel* that the couple did not know he was in their garden. He had entered it the night before through a gate in the wall.

"Yes," replied the German, quite pleasantly, "I understand that."

As they approached the waiting car the back door opened and Hélène got out. So it was she who had betrayed him. He said "Hallo", but she walked past him with her eyes down.

There had been ructions in the hospital when Bader's escape was discovered. Hall was rushed to the operating room, where his body-cast was replaced with a travelling cast, and the next day he was transferred to a German hospital, staffed by British doctors, at Holmark on the Belgian-German border.

During Monday the 18th, Bomber Command Blenheims had carried out "Circus No80", another raid on Lille and Marquise. While they were over France a Blenheim from No18 Squadron, Manston, detached itself from the formation and dropped a three-ply wooden box by parachute. It was marked with red crosses and addressed:

WING COMMANDER BADER, RAF
KRIEGSGEFANGENER
BITTE AN FOLGENDE ADRESSE LIEFERN
FLIEGERHORSTKOMMODORE, DEUTSCHE LUFTWAFFE
FLIEGERHORST ST OMER (LONGUENESSE)

Bader was taken to the Luftwaffe headquarters in St Omer and questioned, unavailingly, by a German officer before being escorted to another room where he saw the box that had been dropped that afternoon. Inside, to his surprise and delight, was his new right leg. Thelma and his batman, Stokoe, had stuffed it with spare stump-socks, talcum powder, pipe tobacco and chocolate. The Germans took a photograph of Bader standing by the box — good for propaganda — then, to his annoyance, refused to let him have it, instead ushering him to a room upstairs. There, for the first time since his captivity, they really infuriated him: they took away his artificial legs. In response to his protests, the officer said he was acting on orders from above, and left Bader on the bed, helpless and humiliated, with two guards standing over him with loaded rifles.

There he remained the whole night. It was stiflingly hot in the ward, but the officer would not allow a window open, again on "orders from above". His captors were obviously taking no more chances. Bader did not sleep at all that night, with the guards talking and coughing, and with the possibility nagging him that the Germans knew about the Hiècques helping him and probably about Lucille, too. Although he knew Hélène had betrayed them, he felt no resentment towards her; she had probably been threatened.

The next morning, Tuesday, 19 August, two guards carried Bader downstairs to a waiting ambulance, while another followed with his artificial legs wrapped in a blanket. The ambulance bounced over the rutted roads, jostling Bader against his taciturn guards. Through the windows he could see angry, low clouds and pouring rain. It was one of the most depressing journeys he had ever known. He worried about Lucille and the Hiècques and wondered why the Germans looked so square-headed and stupid — the first stirring of the anti-German sentiments he would harbour throughout his four years as a POW.

At last they arrived at Brussels. Led by a strutting officer, the two guards again carried Bader while a third minced behind with the legs. As he was borne, with mounting fury, across the square to the railway station, people turned and stared. He was carried aboard a second class railway carriage with — thank God! — upholstered seats, and the officer put his legs on the luggage rack above. Then, with a series of jolts, the train got under way. The officer tried to make conversation once or twice, but Bader maintained a tight-lipped silence, staring out of the window at the rain-swept landscape. They passed Liège, then crossed into Germany. Bader decided to pay his respects to the Fatherland by going to the lavatory. He asked for his legs. The officer refused. A guard carried him down the corridor and sat him on the lavatory seat, then held the doorway open and covered him with a pistol. "You stupid clot!" growled Bader. "How the hell d'you think I can get out of here?" The guard, who understood no English, drew the correct inference and simply said: *"Befehl ist Befehl!"* From that moment on Bader loathed the Germans implacably.

It was midnight when they reached Frankfurt am Main. Once again the two guards carried the helpless Bader, this time to a car that, half an hour later, drew up outside Dulag Luft at Oberursel. Two Luftwaffe men now took over the job of carrying Bader. Dumping him on a wooden bunk in one of the cells, they stripped him down to his underclothes and locked him in. This time, dog-tired, he slept well.

His first visitor in the morning — it was now Wednesday, 20 August — was *Sonderführer* Heinrich Eberhardt, the camp liaison officer, who handed him the usual bogus Red Cross form. Bader filled in his name, rank and service number and handed it back. Eberhardt then charmingly suggested he fill in the rest — "It will help the Red Cross inform your relatives and forward your letters. Just a formality, you know" — and Bader went over to the offensive. "That's all you're getting," he said. "I'm not half-witted. Now if you don't mind, I'd like a bath, a shave and my legs. Then I'd like some breakfast."

Eberhardt said he would call the Commandant. A few minutes after he left, Major Rumpel entered. Rumpel assured Bader that they would try to make him as comfortable as they could, and that because he had been a pilot in the last war he wanted to keep alive the tradition of chivalry between pilots.

Bader was unimpressed. "We're enemies," he said, "and that can't be overlooked."

Despite Bader's truculence, Rumpel pressed on, asking probing questions about his squadron and trying to wheedle out information on technical matters. But Bader simply responded: "If you know, why the hell ask me?" Then Rumpel turned to politics — never a favourite subject of Bader's — and ended by saying what a shame it was that Britain and Germany should be enemies. "Of course, we know you call us Jerries, but — "

"No we don't," Bader interrupted. "We call you Huns!"

That did it. Rumpel's face turned to stone and he stood up and walked out. As the door closed behind him, Bader yelled: "Send my legs and some tea, damn you!"

Much to his surprise, a Luftwaffe orderly came along a few minutes later bearing Bader's legs (including the new one), some soap and a towel. Bader strapped on his legs and the guard escorted him to the bathroom. A tray of English tea, with milk and sugar, and some bread, butter and jam, were waiting in his cell when he returned. An hour after breakfast he was taken from his cell and released into the compound.

In his biography of Bader, Paul Brickhill asserts that at Lübeck and Warburg Bader knew none of the other aircrew prisoners. This is completely untrue and an unaccountable oversight on the part of both biographer and subject. From the Tangmere Wing there was "Buck" Casson, who was at Dulag Luft when Bader arrived in the compound on the 21st and left for Lübeck on the 25th; from 1940, when Bader had been on Nos19 and 222 Squadrons, there were Wally Cunningham and Hugh Falkus, whom he would meet also again at Lübeck. Meanwhile, he fell in with David Lubbock and another new prisoner, Acting Flight Lieutenant P M Gardner DFC.

David Lubbock, it turned out, had been captured the same day that Bader had been shot down. "Since I had a degree in natural sciences and was likely to be the nearest to a medical doctor that he would come across," recalled Lubbock, "Bader asked me to stay with him to help him look after his legs. Actually, the only doctor I came across as a POW was a gynaecologist!"

Peter Melville Gardner, a dark twenty-three-year-old fighter pilot from Grimsby, had distinguished himself during the fall of France and the Battle of Britain. He had been posted to No54 Squadron at Hornchurch as Flight Commander in June 1941. On Friday, 11 July — four days before he was due to be married — his Spitfire MkVB was shot down on "Circus No45", escorting Blenheims over Lille. He later made light of the affair by saying he was fast asleep and suffering from "finger trouble", and should therefore have been awarded "The Order of the Irremovable Digit".

Bader, Lubbock and Gardner shared a room in Middle Block with Flight Lieutenant V G L D ("Paddy") Byrne, who had been on "Wings" Day's British Permanent Staff. After swapping stories Bader asked if Vincent Byrne if he knew the whereabouts of Day, whom Bader had served under in the 1920s. Byrne told him that Day had been purged to a permanent camp in June after leading a mass escape by tunnel. For Bader, the word "escape" was like a red rag to a bull. He asked Byrne to describe the tunnel, and afterwards suggested to Lubbock and Gardner that they also give it a whirl. They agreed. A day or two later they started work in an end room of Middle Block, cutting a trap in the floorboards under one of the bunks. The idea was to come up in a wooded area near the apiary on the other side of the road running north of the compound. Without legs, Bader was unable to cut holes or turn sods, so he acted as stooge, watching for Germans at the window while Gardner and Lubbock took turns hacking at the tunnel face and dragging the soil to the surface in a basin. They spread the soil in between the floorboards under the bunk.

For Bader, brimming over with impatience, the days passed slowly. He could think of little else but escape, although his plans were hazy. He refused to regard his legs as a barrier. Make for Switzerland...steal a car...or stow away on a train or a barge... What fools the Huns would look if a legless man escaped and reached home!

But, for Bader, the scheme was coming to a sticky end. One day, Heinrich Eberhardt strutted into the compound, sought out Bader, and told him that next morning he would be taken to Brussels to attend a court martial. His mind in turmoil, Bader asked what the hell for. "I do not know," said Eberhardt, "but you must go."

Bader, seething at the thought of missing the tunnel as well as at the prospect of facing a court martial, told Byrne, Gardner and Lubbock. The canny Byrne said it was a wonderful chance to crack off, and gave him a slip of paper bearing a name and a Brussels address. "If you can duck the guards and contact these people, they'll try to pass you on to the escape chain."

Bader simmered down. But next day the resentment boiled over again. Although he was allowed to keep his legs, he was closely watched throughout the train journey by a blond young *Sonderführer* and two helmeted soldiers, who never left his side. When the train pulled into Brussels that night he was escorted to a car, which took him to a civilian gaol. Bader, furious, tried to bluff them. "I'm not staying here," he declared.

The *Sonderführer*, clearly upset by Bader's fulminations, pleaded with him to behave. Bader demanded to see the general in charge of the district.

"I do not think he is at home," came the reply.

It was such a lame excuse that Bader was near to laughter. "Well, go and get the clot!" he demanded.

The *Sonderführer* turned and spoke to an Army *Feldwebel*, who appeared to be the gaol reception clerk. He turned back to Bader and said that perhaps if they accompanied Bader to his room he would be prepared to stay. Bader, of course, had no choice: sooner or later they would apply force, perhaps even take his legs away. The humiliation would be unbearable. So, deliberately taking his time, he let them lead him through a barred gate and down a passage flanked with cell-doors. Finally they stopped at one of the doors and opened it. Bader looked into a whitewashed cell so tiny he could touch both walls if he extended his arms. A narrow bed nearly filled one side, and near the ceiling was a small barred window. Bader tried his game of bluff again, demanding that the door be left open and that a table be brought with a cloth and tea. The *Feldwebel* went away and Bader waited by the door until he returned with an orderly carrying a table and stool. Satisfied, Bader entered the cell. Putting down the furniture, the Germans retreated, leaving the door open.

Alone at last, Bader quickly shoved the table under the window, put the stool on top, and climbed up until he was balanced precariously on the stool, clinging to the window-bars. Pulling himself up, he tried to look out, but the walls of the gaol were so thick he could not see the ground. He shook the bars in frustration. Then he heard a discreet cough from behind and, as he turned round, saw the little orderly, carrying a tray of tea and looking up at him completely po-faced. A glimmer of hope moved Bader to ask, in his schoolboy French, if he was Belgian. *"Nein,"* said the orderly. *"Ich bin Deutscher."* Feeling foolish, Bader started climbing down. The orderly helped him, removed the stool, put the tray on the table, nodded deferentially, and padded out on rubber-soled shoes. Stretching out on the bed after tea, Bader found it about as comfortable as lying on a table. Lifting the palliasse, he discovered that the bed beneath was solid wood. He spent a sleepless night, in which all his anxieties about being a captive, the court martial, the tunnel, the Wing and Thelma crowded in on him, giving rise to intense frustrations and resentment.

At about ten in the morning the *Sonderführer* returned with the two guards. They drove him to a large house and led him into a big room with a long table at one end. Sitting at the table were six German officers, three of them generals. At the other end were the doctor, staff and soldiers from St-Omer hospital, who eyed him sourly. A young Luftwaffe interpreter motioned Bader to a chair in front of the table and invited him to sit down. Bader refused. The six officers at the table, obviously judges, put their heads together and muttered amongst themselves, and the middle one, a bald, hatchet-faced general, spoke to the interpreter. Would Bader swear to tell the truth? "No," Bader answered. "Certainly not." The interpreter looked as if he had misheard. Bader repeated his answer, adding: "Go on. Tell the Court." Nervously, the interpreter spoke to the judges. The bald general raised his eyebrows. He wanted to know why Bader would not tell the truth. "Well," said Bader. "If you're going to ask me questions about the French I will obviously lie." The judges muttered some more, then via the interpreter informed him that the French had already been punished. Bader was horrified, and was wondering what punishment the Germans had meted out, when the interpreter asked him whether he thought the hospital staff at St-Omer had been careless. It suddenly occurred to Bader that it was not he who was being court-martialled. He asked who was in fact on trial. The interpreter, surprised, said: "Why, the hospital staff, of course."

Bader was relieved. His anger evaporated, and he told the Court that it was unreasonable to punish the staff. They had taken all the proper precautions in guarding him. How were they to know that he, a legless man, would climb out of the window? When he had finished, the *Sonderführer* led him out and the hospital staff beamed at him.

The next day he was back at Dulag Luft. No chance of escaping had presented itself as the guards had once again watched him closely. The first thing he asked on reaching the compound was: "How's the tunnel getting on?" Lubbock said it was plodding along quite nicely, and introduced him to a newcomer, Flight Lieutenant P Tomlinson RAFO, who had been allocated a bed in their room and had been co-opted onto the digging team.

Twenty-five-year-old Peter ("Tommy") Tomlinson was the great-grandson of a London property developer who had built a hundred and ninety houses in Hammersmith and Chiswick. Tommy's father was a London solicitor who in the Great War had left his practice to join up, had received a commission and served on the Western Front with the Royal Army Service Corps. His mother was a stepsister of Captain Albert Armitage, who had been second in command of Captain Scott's first Arctic expedition. His older brother, Michael, had joined his father's legal practice, while his younger brother, David, was an actor on stage and screen. (In 1950 he would play the Oliver Philpot role in the film *The Wooden Horse*, set in Stalag Luft III to which Peter was subsequently sent.) Peter himself had joined the Reserve of the RAF while working for P&O. When the war started he was appointed pilot and personal assistant to Air Vice-Marshal Arthur T Harris — then AOC, No5 Group. After two years with him at HQ Grantham he volunteered for operations and joined No3 Photographic Reconnaissance Unit, based at Oakington in Cambridgeshire. However, No3 PRU was disbanded on 21 August 1941 and absorbed by No1 PRU at Benson in Oxfordshire.

On Sunday, 21 September Tomlinson took off at 1100 hours on a photographic mission to Hamburg. But over Holland, on the return leg, his Spitfire's engine seized up. He made a gliding crash-land on Deelen airfield, where the port undercarriage leg collapsed and the aircraft swung round on its starboard wheel, the tail-wheel acting as a brake and sparks flying off the port wing-tip. By the time the Spitfire had skidded to a halt Tomlinson was surrounded by a lorry-load of German soldiers. The airfield at Deelen was the home of *Oberst* Wolfgang Falck's night-fighter wing, and Tomlinson was taken to the crew-room where he sat feeling depressed and dejected. Luftwaffe technicians examined the wreckage of Tomlinson's Spitfire and realised he was a PRU pilot. By rights, they should have handed him over to the Gestapo, but Falck took pity on him, instructing his technical officer to fly Tomlinson to Frankfurt in his Me110 and hand him over to the staff at Dulag Luft. Tomlinson was baffled by this gesture, but gratefully accepted it, along with a gift of cigarettes and chocolate. At Oberursel, Theo Rumpel allowed Tomlinson to telephone Deelen and thank Falck for his kindness and "a marvellous flight", which had enhanced his admiration for the Me110.

Back home, when "Bomber" Harris heard that Tomlinson had failed to return, he was understandably aggrieved. Peter Tomlinson was almost a member of the family. Subsequently two of his brothers, Michael and Paul, served a stint as Harris's personal assistant. The Germans did not know of Peter's association with "Bomber" Harris, and for the rest of the war he wrote to him via a "Mrs Harris" at a private address.

During digging operations for the next three days Bader resumed his stooging duties at the window. With three men now working in shifts, the tunnel forged ahead and reached the wire. A few more days and it would be finished. However, a fit of recalcitrance on the morning of 2 October put an end to Bader's involvement. He was lurking near the entrance of Middle Block, with hands in pockets and pipe in mouth, when one of the interrogation officers, *Hauptmann* Müller, walked pass. Bader did not salute him. Müller stopped, turned, and said: "Ving Commander Bader, you should salute me."

"Why?" Bader demanded.

"All prisoners of war should salute German officers."

Bader quoted the Geneva Convention, which held that a POW should only salute enemy officers of equal or superior rank. Müller was only a captain, whilst Bader was equivalent to a lieutenant-colonel.

"I am the Commandant's representative, and you should salute me," insisted Müller.

"I don't salute the Commandant either," pursued Bader. "He's only a major."

"Those are the Commandant's orders!" yelled Müller.

This only made Bader even more disagreeable. "I don't give a damn if they are!" he said shortly. "They're wrong and I'm damned if I'm going to salute you."

Half an hour later an orderly entered Bader's room and told him to be ready to leave for a permanent camp in twenty minutes. Beside himself with rage, Bader gathered his kit.

Glowering, he was driven to Frankfurt in an Opel staff car and put in a third class railway carriage with hard wooden seats. By then it had started raining — a monotonous drizzle which didn't let up for the entire two-day journey. On reaching Lübeck on the night of the 3rd he was helped into a farm wagon, which trundled across the bleak sandy flats to the camp, where he was searched and fingerprinted. The Germans removed his watch and signet ring, the last present he had received from his father.

(9)

Two days after Bader's arrival, on Sunday, 5 October, yet more RAF and Fleet Air Arm turned up. They were Squadron Leaders S Pietraszkiewicz (Pole) and S Scibior (Pole); Acting Squadron Leader D L Armitage DFC, RAFVR; Flight Lieutenant P Tomlinson RAFO; Acting Flight Lieutenant P M Gardner DFC; Flying Officers J Grocott RAFVR, K W Mackenzie DFC, AFC, RAFVR, and J A G Parker RAFVR (Southern Rhodesian); Pilot Officers A J Beales, C Daszuta (Pole), S A Graham RCAF, J Janicki (Pole), J F Knight RNZAF, G F Lowes, R Shuttleworth, W J S Smith RNZAF, and W B Towler; and Sub-Lieutenant (A) P M Lubbock RNVR.

Douglas Bader was surprised to see Pete Gardner, David Lubbock and Peter Tomlinson. When he had left them the tunnel was near completion and they should have been free by now. "What the hell happened to the tunnel?" he asked. Lubbock explained that almost as soon as Bader left, a posse of goons had entered the camp and gone straight to the trap-door of the tunnel. They even knew who the culprits were. "Hence our arrival," concluded Lubbock.

Of the bomber crews in this batch, Pilot Officer Janicki, from No300 Squadron, had been in the bag almost nineteen weeks. He was the second pilot in a Pilot Officer Jan Kuflik's Wellington, shot down during the raid by 130 bombers on Cologne on 10/11 July. Most of the six-man crew had been seriously wounded, Jan Kuflik the worst of all, and had been sent to the hospital at Obermassfeld, while Janicki had remained at Hohemark.

Pilot Officer Lowes, from No21 Squadron, Manston, was shot down by a flak ship off Ostend on the same 23 July daylight raid as Frank Campbell-Rogers. Lowes was the observer in his aircraft; the pilot and WOP/AG were killed. Squadron Leader Scibior was a Flight Commander in No305 Squadron, which in July had lost Flying Officer Marcola and which had since moved from Syerston to Lindholme in Yorkshire. On 5/6 August No305 took part in the same raid on Frankfurt that had led Duggie Baber, Ian Kayes and Fred Litchfield into the bag. All but two of Scibior's crew were killed; the survivors evaded capture.

Pilot Officer W J S Smith was a second pilot on a Wellington MkIII from the same squadron as Len Hockey and Robin Hunter, No75 (New Zealand), which was still stationed at Feltwell. Smith was bagged on 17/18 September when thirty-eight Wimpeys set off for Karlsruhe. No75 Squadron suffered the only loss. Set ablaze by flak, fire, Smith's aircraft crash-landed in Germany at Holsthum, on the River Prüm. The pilot, navigator and front-gunner were killed. Smith went into the bag with the rear-gunner, Sergeant A H Heard, and the wireless-operator, Sergeant J W Reid. Unfortunately, Reid, who was sent to Stalag VIIIB, Lamsdorf, would be killed trying to escape on 29 December.

Pilot Officer Towler, of No405 Squadron, was the second dickey — and the only officer — in one of only two Wellingtons lost on 19/20 September, when seventy-two aircraft aimed for Stettin. It was a long haul and twelve aircraft failed to reach the target. Towler's aircraft ran out of fuel and the crew baled out over Germany.

The most recent of the Bomber Command prisoners was Reg Shuttleworth. He was a rear-gunner from No115 Squadron, Marham. On 29/30 September ninety-three aircraft had set out to bomb Hamburg. Shuttleworth's pilot, Sergeant A R Hulls, took off at 1931 hours. Searchlight glare prevented accurate bombing, and on the way back the Wellington was shot down, crashing at Blijham, in Holland, at 2252 hours. A pilot from *4/NJG1*, *Oberleutnant* Ludwig Becker, took credit for the victory, although his claim is rather doubtful, as the rest of the crew were killed and it would have been highly unlikely for the rear-gunner to survive a night-fighter attack unless the Wellington was raked by gunfire from beneath.

Apart from Pete Gardner, there were several other fighter boys in this intake. "Good-time Charlie" Daszuta flew Spitfires on No306 Squadron, stationed at Northolt in Middlesex, in the No11 Group sector. In June the squadron had converted from the Hurricane Mks IIA and IIA to the Spitfire MkIIB, and in September was re-equipping with the MkVB. On the afternoon of Wednesday, 17 September, the MkVBs provided top cover for "Circus No95", when twenty-three Blenheims bombed Mazingarbe power station and chemical works. The Luftwaffe rose in great numbers to give battle, but no bombers were lost. However, nine Spitfires were brought down, including that flown by Daszuta.

Allen Beales was from No607 (County of Durham) Squadron, an Auxiliary Air Force unit formed in 1930. It had started life as a bomber squadron and in 1936 converted to a fighter role, flying Hawker Demons, Gloster Gladiators, Hurricane MkIs and, from July 1941, the Hurricane MkIIB. The current CO, Squadron Leader G D Craig, had been with the squadron since the early 1930s and had fought in the Battle of France, the Battle of Britain and in subsequent cross-Channel operations. Beales, a newcomer, felt safe in his hands. However, shortly after Beales arrived the squadron was selected to be the first Hurricane fighter-bomber unit of the RAF, and the pilots started training at Martlesham Heath with their aircraft fitted with either eight 40lb or two 250lb bombs. This training was interspersed with some on-the-job practice — escorting Blenheims and Hampdens on their daylight sweeps of the Continent. During the afternoon of Thursday, 18 September, No607 was one of three squadrons providing close escort for "Circus No99", when eleven Blenheims were dispatched to Rouen power station. The Luftwaffe came up in force to meet them, but although no Blenheims were lost, six fighters were shot down. Allen Beales ended up in the drink and was picked up by the *Kriegsmarine*.

Three days later Dennis Lockhart Armitage, CO of No129 Squadron, was one of two squadron commanders chopped down on "Circus" operations. "Bill" Armitage had fought in the Battle of Britain as a Pilot Officer with No266 Squadron, and on 20 June1941, by then a Flying Officer, he was given a war-substantive Squadron Leader rank and given command of No129 at Leconfield. On Sunday, 21 September, two "Circuses", No101 to Gosnay and No102 to Lille, took place at the same time, with thirteen Spitfire squadrons and one Hurricane squadron providing escort. Despite having to split their forces, the Luftwaffe shot down fifteen RAF fighters and damaging four others. An Me109 got under Armitage's tail, hitting his Spit and wounding him in one hand. At first Armitage thought the aircraft was still undamaged, but as he was about to turn in on the Jerry it burst into flames, engulfing the cockpit. Armitage's only thought was to "get the hell out of it", and he tried to undo his straps. He was in a bit of a panic and couldn't undo them, so tried to pull himself up, hoping they would snap. When this didn't work he tried to collects his wits together and had another go. This time they came undone. But then the Perspex hood wouldn't slide back — so he went straight through it. He left the aircraft at a height of about 2,000 feet, and was so worried that his brolly wouldn't open that he pulled the rip-cord directly and took an age to float down. As he was descending, an Me109 flew around him, and he remembered all the stories he had heard about other pilots who had baled out and landed looking like sieves. But the Jerry didn't try to plug him and he landed safely, with soldiers scurrying towards him to give him the usual greeting. They took him to a temporary hospital at Boulogne, and when he had recovered from his wound he was transferred to Dulag Luft.

The other squadron commander shot down that day was Stanislaw Pietraszkiewicz, another Pole from No315 (Deblin) Squadron to join Bronislaw Mickiewicz. This had been his fifth posting in less than a year. He had joined No303 Squadron on 21 August 1940. On 10 September he had been posted to No307 Squadron. Two weeks later he returned to No303, then two weeks after that he was transferred yet again, to No616. Pietraszkiewicz had taken command of No315 Squadron on 21 January 1941. His squadron was among those escorting twelve Blenheims to Gosnay. Attacked, like Armitage, by an Me109, he force-landed his Spitfire in France.

Another September captive was Kenneth William Mackenzie, a Belfast-born engineer who had learnt to fly at the North of Ireland Aero Club at Newtownards and had joined the RAFVR early in 1939. In one year of Hurricane combat with No501 Squadron, Kenley, and No247 Squadron, Predannack, he had dispatched ten enemy aircraft, damaged four and shared in the destruction of a further four. He found fame in the Battle of Britain by chopping bits off an Me109's tail-plane with his prop when he ran out of ammunition, and his exploits had been written up by David Masters in his embarrassingly jingoistic tribute to the RAF, *"So Few"* (published the month Mackenzie was shot down). His Battle of Britain kills earned him the DFC in October 1940, and in June 1941 he was posted to No247 Squadron, equipped with the matt-black night-fighter Hurricane MkIIC, as a Flight Commander.

On Monday, 29 September his luck ran out. Four pilots from the squadron were hurriedly briefed to follow up an attack on Lannion airfield in Brittany by Whirlwind fighters from No263 Squadron. They protested that the airfield did not present a worthwhile target, as their own reconnaissance had revealed that, apart from one Me109 (damaged), there were no aircraft based at Lannion. In any case, the element of surprise was already lost, owing to the initial attack by the Whirlwinds. But their complaints fell on deaf ears. Consequently, when they took off at 1850 hours, they were pretty bloody-minded. Mackenzie, for his part, was determined to give the airfield a good "going over".

Crossing the Channel, they dipped to about two hundred feet to sneak in under the German radar, spreading out into two flights of two aircraft each. Red 1, Flight Lieutenant D Smallwood, and Blue 1, Mackenzie, flew slightly ahead of their No2s, Pilot Officer S S Hordern and Sergeant Deutzer. Throttling back to a cruising speed of 230 knots, they set a course of 152°. The weather was hazy, with some high stratus cloud, and the sea was calm. Keeping radio silence, they skimmed over the water and after about twenty-five minutes made out the French coast. Further inland, low cloud was drifting towards the area of Lannion. West of Les Triège Islands, the four pilots selected full power, checked their instruments, switched the gyroscopic gun-sights and guns to "Fire", and pulled up to six hundred feet ready for a diving attack. Flying in line abreast, two hundred yards apart, they dived at the airfield from a hundred feet, Smallwood and Hordern taking the western perimeter, Mackenzie and Deuntzer the east.

The flak opened up immediately — an intense and accurate barrage coming from all sides of the airfield and from well beyond it. Even with their cockpit canopies open, the four Hurricane pilots could make out little in the fading light, which only made the flak look even more deadly. Mackenzie and Deuntzer weaved in and out of the buildings and dispersals, firing as they went, and Mackenzie silenced a gun-post about half a mile north of the aerodrome. The flak missed him by no more than a few feet, and as he weaved he could fire his guns only sporadically.

Smallwood and Hordern pulled away, but Mackenzie was determined to make a last, quick attack on his way out towards the coast. By now the sky was throbbing with flak, and Mackenzie, sweating profusely, was angry because the mission, which had in any case seemed pointless from the start, was yielding poor results. He silenced another gun position, and skirted south of the airfield at a height of about fifty feet to upset the enemy's aim. Suddenly, his Hurricane was caught in a cone of fire, and shells thudded into the engine and across the top of the windscreen, striking his flying helmet. He pulled straight up, nursing the engine, and tried to gain height in order to coax the Hurricane back to base. The flak was still following him, his engine was running rough and his head was sore, but he continued weaving to shake off the flak. The temperature gauges were rising to dangerous levels, and at a height of 1,800 feet he felt the engine slowing and could smell hot metal, a sure sign that the Hurricane was about to burst into flames.

He knew then that he would have to bale out or ditch, and tried to get as far away from the French coast as possible. Levelling off, he trimmed the Hurricane into a gentle glide at 120 knots and crossed the coast. He could make out below him the dim outline of the coast and pick out scattered lights. Ahead, the sea was hardly visible. Then, with a grinding clatter, the engine seized up and the propeller stopped turning. He re-trimmed to maintain gliding speed. He was now too low to bale out. Ditching it would have to be. As he glided down he ejected the hood, tightened his harness, checked the oxygen, selected full flap and switched on his landing lights so as to judge his height as the sea came up to meet him. He was about five miles from the coast. About six feet above the water, and gliding at about seventy knots, he stalled the Hurricane, which struck the surface immediately. It pitched forward violently, raising a wall of spray. The engine hissed and banged as it cooled. Then...silence.

Mackenzie undid his harness and eased himself out of the cockpit. The Hurricane was sinking by the nose; he would have to move quickly. That was the last thought he had until he came to some minutes later and found himself floating in his "K"-type dinghy, wet through, sitting in about three inches of ice-cold water, dazed and with a sore and bloody head. The Hurricane had already sunk. He realised he must have carried out his well-rehearsed dinghy drill automatically.

The next step was to work out his position and assess his chances of survival. He estimated that he was a hundred and twenty miles off the Cornish coast. His watch had stopped but he guessed it must be about 2100 hours. The French coast — a mile or so away — was visible in dark silhouette, with dim lights flickering here and there. Barely visible against the southern horizon were a few small islands. Mackenzie reckoned he must be somewhere in Lannion Bay, but beyond that he had no accurate idea of his position. Although eventual capture was inevitable, he decided that he should at least make an effort to get as far away from the enemy-held coast as possible. Luckily, the sea was calm, although there was a light wind from the west, and broken cloud scudded across the moon. He put on the paddles, which fitted on the hands like mittens, and after some experimenting discovered that the only way he could make any progress was by turning round and paddling backwards. That meant he could not see where he was going. He put the small sea anchor out astern so that the drag would keep him in a straight line, but it also meant rowing required more effort.

It soon became obvious that he was making little, if any, progress. He paused to clean the wound on his head with salt-water, and suddenly remembered that because of the abnormally low tide along the coast the French kept their fishing boats moored out to sea; perhaps he could steal one and sail home. Turning round, he started paddling in a southerly direction towards the coast, resting every twenty minutes or so and occasionally glancing over his shoulder to judge his progress. By about midnight it seemed to him that the coast was definitely nearer, and after another hour he could make out dim shapes between himself and the coast, which slowly resolved themselves into the outline of several boats. Reaching them at last, he found that the first was motor-driven, much too large and chained to its mooring; the second was smaller but still too big, and also motor-driven; but the third only about eighteen feet long, with mast, lug-sail and rudder in place — and no motor. This boat it would be. He got on board, tied the dinghy to the stern, cut the two mooring ropes with his knife and hoisted the sail without difficulty. Before long he was out to sea, and decided to let the wind drift him clear of the little knot of other boats before setting a course. But his dinghy was slowing the boat down, so he hauled it on deck.

Owing to the light westerly wind the boat was moving sluggishly, and it was obvious that, even if he reached one of the islands, he would still not be far enough away from the coast by dawn to avoid being seen. By about 0400 hours the sky began to lighten towards the east. Tacking close to the wind, he made for one of the larger islands, which was now only about half a mile away. He reached it just as dawn was breaking, hove to alongside a small cove and moored the boat. Taking the dinghy to use for shelter, he scrambled ashore. He found a spot where there was a gap between a low wall and a bush, tucked the dinghy between them, climbed underneath...and fell asleep.

Suddenly he was being prodded by a rifle. Shaking off the last vestiges of his slumber, he saw German sailors surrounding him. One of them, seeing he was still groggy, and cold and stiff, helped him to his feet. They took the dinghy and escorted him to a lighthouse. Below the lighthouse was a small harbour, with a jetty where a German patrol boat was moored. It turned out that no downed British flier had been reported, but the lighthouse keeper had seen the boat approaching and, thinking it might be laden with Frenchmen escaping to England, had summoned the crew of the patrol boat. They were surprised to find that their quarry was *"Ein englischer Flieger"*. After giving him some hot acorn coffee, they took him and the dinghy aboard the patrol boat and made for the mainland. There he was kept in a *Kriegsmarine* orderly room and given bread, sausage and milk. A plain-clothed official he took to be Gestapo made a desultory attempt at interrogation, in halting English, and Mackenzie wrote down his name, rank and number. Then a Frenchman arrived and started jabbering about the boat; as far as Mackenzie could make out, the Frenchman was telling him that he should have stayed hidden in the boat and the French would have helped him. Afterwards, a succession of people — military and civilian — came to gape at him. He gathered he was the first British pilot they had encountered.

Finally he was escorted to an office where he was mildly interrogated by a *Kriegsmarine* officer who spoke passable English. After taking down Mackenzie's name, rank and number (which he had already given to the plain-clothed official) the German asked if he was aware of the penalties for stealing a boat. The interview was interrupted by the arrival of the Luftwaffe, who took Mackenzie off at pistol-point and bundled him into the back of a waiting staff car. Eventually they arrived at Lannion airfield where, much to Mackenzie's surprise, he was greeted by an elderly Luftwaffe *Oberst* and taken to the Officers' Mess. He was then treated to a slap-up lunch, which included a delicious steak. Whilst Mackenzie was eating, the *Oberst* asked him if he minded the French Mess staff coming to look at him. Though he was in no mood to fraternise, he let the old man have his way and in they came, staring at him, shaking hands, commiserating...all very touching.

After lunch the *Oberst* took Mackenzie to his office, where once again his particulars were noted. The *Oberst* said the Red Cross would be informed of his POW status that day; and, as it happened, news that he was safe and a prisoner filtered through to No247 Squadron within a few days.

During the interrogation the *Oberst* expressed surprise that the RAF had bothered to attack Lannion again, although he gave out no details concerning the results of either raid. Then he took Mackenzie over to a wall-map of Russia, showed him how far the Germans had advanced and, much to Mackenzie's surprise, declared: "No matter who wins the war, they will have to fight Communism ever after. Britain and Germany should join forces now!"

Mackenzie spent his first night of captivity in a cold, bare cell in a guard-room on the airfield. It measured about ten feet by six, with concrete walls and a small window near the ceiling. Furniture consisted of a bed and a chair. In one corner stood a bucket. The bed was made of a hard wood and had no mattress; the pillow was filled with straw, and only one blanket was issued. Unable to sleep, Mackenzie paced up and down. But the cell was so small that he could take only a few paces. So he lay on the bed and cursed himself for putting himself out of the war just when Fighter Command was going over to the offensive. Continuing to chastise himself, he realised that he had allowed his anger to cloud his judgement, and that he should never have gone round a second time to make another attack. His attempt to evade capture had been hampered by lack of preparedness. Night-intruder pilots were flying across enemy-held territory without side-arms or escape and survival equipment and had never been briefed on evasion. It put their chances of getting home once shot down somewhere between slight and nil.

The following morning he was taken to Morlaix, where he and a middle-aged guard boarded a Paris-bound train. It was packed like a Bank Holiday special but the guard found room in a second class carriage. The presence of the British POW seemed to pass unnoticed. At Le Mans, where the train made a brief stop, the guard left Mackenzie alone and bought some peaches and grapes from a station vendor. The guard gave them to Mackenzie. When they reached Paris, the platform was crowded. Mackenzie instantly seized the opportunity to escape, although he had formed no coherent plan. While the guard went ahead, Mackenzie walked in the opposite direction, against the flood of passengers making for the ticket-barrier. Seeing what appeared to be a workers' store — it was full of picks and shovels — he ducked into it and, leaving the door slightly ajar, hid behind a wheelbarrow laden with tools. Cramped and uncomfortable, he waited to see what would develop. After about half an hour, in which no one had come near the store, he crept out. There were still a few people about, but nobody paid him any attention. He walked further down the platform and reached some steps leading down to a yard. As he walked through the yard he saw a platoon of Luftwaffe *Soldaten* approaching at the double. He turned and ran back up the steps, then heard a "Halt!" from behind. Looking round and down he saw a *Hauptmann* and some of the men waving guns at him. The *Hauptmann* beckoned him down and had him escorted to the station headquarters where he was handed over to the railway police. This time there could be no escape. He was flanked by two burly soldiers brandishing sub-machine-guns. Later, he was put into a small open lorry with four guards. They delivered him to the Gare du Nord, where he was handed over to another pair of guards who hustled him aboard a train for Frankfurt am Main. Worn out, despondent, and feeling a little foolish, he slept most of the way, occasionally waking up to eat some army rations.

At Frankfurt he was given over to the custody of the station police and then to a two-man Luftwaffe escort, who took him to Dulag Luft. He had been lectured about Dulag Luft whilst serving with No43 Squadron and knew the ropes. After a couple of days in the cells, and an interrogation by the glib-tongued Eberhardt, he was released into the compound, where he was questioned by the SBO, Squadron Leader Elliott, and the Adjutant, John Casson, and his bona fides established.

John Grocott was the lone Coastal Command officer among the 5 October arrivals. He had been the rear-gunner in "Tint" Winter-Taylor's Whitley, shot down on 26 August looking for a U-boat. Badly wounded, he had been in the Hohemark clinic ever since, and in 1944 would be repatriated.

(10)

The overcrowding at Lübeck was by now acute, particularly in the RAF block. In Room 6, for instance, there were no fewer than twenty men, representing four of the nations fighting alongside the Old Country against Hitler: Hal Beare (Canada), Bill Bakker (Holland), Roderick Cowper, Jim Davies (Canada), "Dickie" Down, Eperon (Canada), Oliver Hedley, Tony Hibell, John Leetham, Wilf Lewis, Ken Mackey (Canada), Jeff Peat (Canada), W J S Smith (New Zealand), Peter Stevens, Gilbert Walenn, T L Walker (Australia), Adrian White, Robert White, Frank Wilbraham and Winter-Taylor, who Peter Tomlinson nicknamed "Wagger-Tagger". Even officers of Squadron Leader rank and above, who normally occupied a single- or double-room, had to share with up to half a dozen others. "Dim" Strong initially messed with only "Birdie" Barrett and "Jock" Fielden, but later on Tony Ruffel and Oliver Green increased the number.

By now the prisoners were suffering from malnutrition. The whites of their eyes had become clear and bluish and their stomachs and thighs swollen. Trevor Griffith-Jones recorded: "No Red Cross food or cigarettes. Lose 2 stone. Pulse 40. 22 per room." Peter Harding recalls that he lost half a pound in weight a day. "To say that the food supply was poor would not be in any way an overstatement," wrote Paddy Denton later,

> consisting as it did of a cup of greasy water and a rotten potato with a slice of German bread cut so thin that I don't know how it was done. However, we staved off some of the pangs of hunger by drinking vast quantities of mint tea and saccharin, which we could get from the so-called canteen.
>
> In order to prepare this delicate brew we made electric kettles, which gave us a good laugh. These comprised glazed pots of about 6" internal diameter [which] we filled with salt-water solution or uric acid as an electrolyte. Then with the help of some borrowed electric cable from unused huts we were in business.

Once sufficient electrolyte had been tipped into the pot and the electric cable put in place, Denton — or whoever was taking his turn as kitchen "stooge" — filled a tin with water and carefully lowered it into the pot. He then connected the other end of the cables to the circuit, and pushed a hand or shoulder heavily against the spring-loaded fuses.

> Hey presto! Boiling water and an enormous overload in the entire electrical circuit. All jolly good, clean, decent fun.
>
> We, while perhaps experienced in war, were entirely innocent so far as the requirements of survival as prisoners demanded.
>
> The rations were totally inadequate to sustain life, let alone health, therefore we learnt pretty quickly how to contrive to surmount these obstacles. Grass picked from the perimeter track, round the huts or wherever it could be seen, could [be] and was made up in the kettles which have been described into a mush not quite like spinach but full of nutritious value, even if not satisfactorily filling an empty belly.

Because the prisoners were crowded into a few barracks and there was congestion at the stoves, some had to build fires in the communal *Abort*, using the straw stuffing from palliasses for fuel and cooking in jam tins. "Even though cooking in the huts was forbidden," recalled Michael Roth, "a few made small stick fires in the latrines (we actually had flush toilets at Lübeck), on which they tried to make their bread rations more palatable by frying them in fat. I recall seeing one poor sod drop his bread into the urinal by accident; he quickly retrieved it, shook it off, refried and then ate the soggy mass."

The Sunday Peter Tomlinson arrived has become a landmark in RAF POW folklore. It was the day a small number of their contingent had cat stew. As so often happens, the facts have become obscured as a result of reminiscences long after the event, in which the names of the protagonists have become confused and reflection has bathed it in an effulgence undoubtedly not experienced at the time. According to Hugh Falkus, Paddy Denton and Wally Cunningham, the Commandant's cat, well fed and plump, lurked outside the wire and had preyed on Falkus's mind for days. The hunting skills he had learnt from his father served him well as he and Wallace Cunningham lured the cat into the compound, stalked it, finally cornered it and put it to death. The stewed meat was divided amongst nine or ten men: Hugh Falkus, Wally Cunningham, Paddy Denton, Denis Cowley, Edwards, Greenslade, Robertshaw, Ruffel, "Hank" Staniland and Tomlinson. Cunningham thought it "very enjoyable", Denton considered it "extraordinarily good", and Ruffel

Fig 8. Stalking the Commandant's cat at Lübeck, as drawn by Wallace Cunningham

recalls it being "marvellous...great fun". The bones, once scrubbed, made good stock. Falkus used the cat's skin to make himself a pair of mittens.

However, Tomlinson's recall is at variance with this account. He is adamant that the cat wandered into their room and that Robin Beauclair delivered the fatal blow — which is how he earned the epithet "Basher". The stew that resulted was far from excellent, but "absolutely revolting", and the cat's fur was enough to make only one mitten. William Hunter also came up with an alternative account: he claimed that Tony Ruffel grabbed and killed the cat, an incident Hunter considered brutal, and that they did not even enjoy the resulting stew. However, it is perhaps for the best that recollections remain hazy — there can be few men who would want to take the credit for having killed a domestic pet, despite the extreme provocation brought on by hunger. Michael Roth took the view that the men responsible for killing the cat must have been "prompted by a streak of sadism as well as hunger...They battered it to death in the latrine with heavy stones and then tried to cook it — a cruel and horrible *débâcle*. It was a tough brute and defied all efforts to make it edible. Its executioners were not hungry enough to eat it raw."

The days that followed were mostly dull, their monotony relieved only by plotting escape. Bader picked the brains of the older kriegies from Barth, absorbing the lore they had gathered on the subject. But the determining factor of their existence was food, and all escape plans took on a fanciful quality in comparison to the needs of the human frame. Paddy Denton:

Hunger reveals aspects in men of which they are totally unaware. To see oneself literally eyeing the floor in case a friend has dropped a crumb from the unbelievably meagre rations and to observe in oneself an utterly primeval lust to assuage an appetite which has never before been subjected to such disciplines brings one up a bit sharpish. One really does have to take a hold on the animal instincts which lurk beneath the formally accepted civilised skin. The self-discipline, good manners and [self-]sacrifice were quite magnificent...

There were, of course, no [British] cigarettes, no booze, and to men used to these little amenities the loss and withdrawal symptoms imposed thereby added to the tension which was experienced, endured and triumphantly overcome. There was no aggression, no bitching, a great amount of co-operation and the overall determination that this part of our lives was not to be allowed to distort or dominate the traditions which we valued. It sounds trite stuff but was as strong as fine steel and kept us bound in our resolution.

Most former inmates of Lübeck have described the atmosphere there as "spiritless". This was perhaps more true for Army prisoners than for RAF, as they were in much poorer shape. Neither did the "brown jobs" have the RAF's enthusiasm for escape.

Unfortunately, this enthusiasm could rarely be translated into action, not only because of the poor diet but also because all schemes had, perforce, to be vetted by Army officers. For their part, the Army considered the Air Force unruly and were afraid their high spirits would lead to reprisals. In any event, hardly any ex-aircrew POWs have a good word to say about Oflag XC today. Wallace Cunningham:

It really brought the harsh realities of life home to us because Dulag Luft had been a very cushy business, with the Germans kidding us along, and we certainly quickly realised that when we got to Lübeck. It was a tough camp. We were hungry. The camp Commandant and his staff were pretty bloody-minded, so altogether we were unhappy there. The first spell in getting used to a big cut-down in food intake is waiting for your stomach to shrink. It's not so bad later on. After a year or two years, you become accustomed to just existing on 14-1500 calories per day, but when you suddenly get cut down to that swiftly the pangs of hunger occupy your mind a great deal. At Lübeck we weren't given much food. It was very watery soup made from *kohlrabi* or cattle-feed. Once we detected a rat in it. So altogether it was a miserable place.

Hugo Bracken:

This was a very bad camp. It was the worst camp I was in in Germany... The commandant was a real bastard. He was a real old Prussian, and he hated the British and was going to take it out of us as much as he could. And all German officers were superior to all British officers and all British officers had to salute them every time they met them, and that sort of thing. People went to endless lengths to avoid meeting the German officers, and so forth.

The Germans wouldn't let the Protecting Power — which at that time was America — come to the camp because, they said, there was an outbreak of typhoid — which was completely untrue. He [the Commandant] restricted the number of letters we were allowed to write, which was contrary to the Geneva Convention. The other people in the camp, with one exception, took their cue from him. Now, the one exception was the security officer — who was in charge of preventing escapes — a *Hauptmann* Leipold. Now he was a really decent man. He really was absolutely correct, I think, in his attitude to prisoners.

Bill Bakker had his wounds and his personal anxieties to contend with:

My English was not good enough to pick up all the conversations around me. The good things — very few. And the beefs — very many. It was only for a few months. My wounds still bothered me. I was worried about my family in Holland. I did not know many people. The ones I knew best were the people from Dulag, those on the train, in the cell, and my room-mates, some of them also in Dilly's drawing class. Contrary to how I really am, at Lübeck I was too self-centred to pay much attention to what was going on around me.

Michael Roth expanded at length in his unpublished post-war memoir:

By far the greater number of kriegies at Lübeck were British Army officers, some captured on Crete, others in Albania. Their train journey to Lübeck had taken days and days in overcrowded cattle trucks, with so little food or water that many had died. After the ordeal of that terrible journey, to them Lübeck was a paradise. To us, after Barth, it was hell.

Aside from the bloody-minded attitude of Wachtmeister and his Goons, the worst thing about Lübeck was the hunger trouble, made more intense by the lack of books. Wachtmeister had confiscated them as a personal reprisal for the RAF raid; what had angered him most was the total destruction of his wine cellar. Wachtmeister further refused to inform the Red Cross at Geneva of the existence of the camp, so we were denied this source of possible supplementary rations. The official German rations were about half what they should have been: the *Feldwebel* in charge of the cookhouse and our rations was a thief who, aided and abetted by the Administration, kept back half for his own trading operations on the Lübeck Black Market. The weekly sausage and margarine rations for five hundred kriegies — small though it was when divided — made a sizeable amount for barter when in one piece. We complained about this to the German officer in charge of our company (the RAF were quartered apart from the Army). He investigated our complaint, found it true, and said: *"Es ist eine Schweinerei,"* meaning literally it was the sort of conduct one would only expect from a pig. He at once protested on our behalf to the *Kommandant* and quoted German Army Regulations. Wachtmeister had to yield. From then on, our own kriegie representatives divided the rations and took over the operation of the cookhouse.

In some small way we benefited from Wachtmeister's corrupt administrative staff. It sold us — at fantastic prices — through the canteen items such as fig biscuits, gherkins, pickles, *ersatz* tomato and Worcestershire sauces, plus German mustard made by the Popp and Popp Chemical Company in Hamburg. Obviously our *Lagergeld* was still backed by genuine currency, and the middlemen were making a packet. Along with the meagre bread ration and daily spud, these condiments became part of the monotonous diet. Each kriegie had his own eating plan: I ate one very thin slice each of potato, with gherkin, mustard and ketchup; cutting each so-loaded slice into four, I would literally chew each mouthful thirty-two times — a health hint of Prime Minister Gladstone's. Some kriegies bashed their daily rations at one swoop, leaving nothing to look forward to for the next twenty-four hours. Others got so hungry they were not above pinching each other's grub — inevitable under conditions of extreme hunger. Some kriegies foolishly swapped their bread for cigarettes: their craving for smokes being greater than their hunger...

In spite of our intense hunger, there were several neurotic looney types who felt they had to keep in shape (physically fit). "In shape for what?" one asked. So they organised fierce deck-tennis tournaments and running races round the inside perimeter. Completely barmy. In a very short time they found themselves flaked out flat on their backs far less fit than those who had sensibly desisted from this idiocy. These fiends lost their stamina for months to come as a result. They had to learn the hard way.

Lübeck was not a safe camp in which to be a prisoner because the Goons were habitually firing their rifles into the compound during the night, pretending they'd seen someone lighting a match inside the huts. They used to shoot through the doors, and the bullets would whistle down the corridors and out the other end. Luckily no one was hit. Our complaints regarding this were ignored. The guards were definitely looking for any excuse to kill us.

Each week, in parties of thirty, we marched out of the compound to the shower building. Here the water was turned on for exactly one minute. In this time we were expected to get wet and lathered with *ersatz* soap. A second minute's supply supposedly sufficed to wash off the soap — quite impossible with four kriegies fighting for a place under one weak nozzle. But since the Goon in charge of the wash-house was selling the coal he saved out of the ration provided to heat the water, this was understandable. It was during one of these shower parties that I witnessed a sample of the kind of Hunnish bestiality prevalent in the concentration camps. Beside the path we took to the showers was a heap of coal clinkers. One of us picked up a piece that had rolled onto the path. At once came the order to halt. A guard seized the wretched kriegie, marched him a little distance away and made him stand against a white brick wall. The guard then retreated a few paces, cocked his rifle, and aimed it at the figure in front of the wall. Ages passed. The guard fired. Some of us were sick. For an instant the kriegie was showered in brick dust. The bullet had grazed his shoulder and ricocheted off the wall. When he didn't collapse in a heap the guard turned his moronic face in our direction and grinned. Vocal pandemonium. Had it not been for the other guards who threatened to shoot all of us, we'd have thrown caution to the winds and lynched the swine on the spot. Terribly shaken, the wounded kriegie was marched off to the cooler and charged with stealing.

On Wachtmeister's orders huge Tannoy outdoor loudspeakers were put up around the wire so that we had to hear the German war-news about the Eastern front. Every communiqué was preceded by the opening bars of Beethoven's Fifth Symphony, sounding like the International Morse Code signal "V for Victory" — German of course. *Obergefreiter* Edwards had lived several years in New York City; he spoke like a cloth cutter from the Bronx. We told him not to believe this German war-news, and that it was a pack of lies. We constantly assured him that Germany would never win the war and, what worried him most, that the war would go on for at least another five years, ending in his country's defeat.

"Aw, come off it fellas. You must be kiddin'." We weren't and he knew it. He paled at the thought of another five years of service. He hated his job, but so far as we were concerned, he was just another bloody-minded Goon, a nasty two-faced nonentity, doomed to die later from frostbite and starvation in Russia — at least that's what we kept telling him. We had little mercy for his ilk.

A few days before we left Lübeck, I received a personal food parcel from Denmark forwarded on from Barth. Since I was sharing a room with seven others I realised that decency demanded that I at least offer them part of it. It would be too embarrassing to sit down and guzzle away on my own, even though I needed the food far more than they did. So I handed over the kilo of Ryveta biscuits, the kilo of butter and the kilo of sausage for a general share-out. Gosman sat at the head of the table and measured off various segments of butter and sausage with a ruler. Then we drew cards to see who had first choice of the portions. I didn't think this equitable in my case, since after all the grub was mine. It was the last parcel I was to get from my friends in Denmark, too — they were not allowed to send any after this. Subsequently, at the next camp, we stayed together, but not one of these types ever made a gesture towards repaying my generosity — even though they began to receive more parcels than I did, and could well afford to have done so. It was convenient to forget.

Once, the Commandant tried to pull his sword on Eddie Asselin, who was walking past him with his hands in his pockets and failed to salute. But *Oberst* Wachtmeister was too old and stiff to draw the sword successfully, so he pushed it back into its scabbard and had Asselin sent to the cooler.

Despite the hunger and Wachtmeister's intolerable regime, some of the former Barth kriegies, under Roger Bushell's leadership, set up an escape syndicate. Amongst its members were Squadron Leaders Ken Doran and Hugh Lynch-Blosse, Flight Lieutenant Tom Kipp, Flying Officers Melville Kennedy and "Percy" Palmer, Pilot Officer Robin Beauclair, and Lieutenant Cecil Filmer. They decided to dig a tunnel from their barrack, and kept their "dienst" secret from the Army prisoners. As the tunnel had its entrance under one of the bunks in Tom Kipp's room, and Hugo Bracken was the senior officer of the Mess, they included Bracken in the team. It says much for their security that nobody outside the tunnelling syndicate and Bracken's Mess knew of the project. Bracken had been taught the "Amy" letter-code before he was shot down, and wrote home to "Control" asking for MI9 escape equipment. Unfortunately, Oflag XC was broken up before his communication could yield any results, but the tunnel made good progress, projecting some sixty or seventy feet before Lübeck was evacuated. It was a pretty primitive affair, and would not have fooled the ferrets at Barth for more than five days, if that; but then the Army Goons at Lübeck were considerably dimmer and less experienced in combating escapes than the Luftwaffe.

With the onset of the Baltic winter the days were generally fine, if chilly, but the nights were freezing. The Germans had confiscated much of the prisoners' decent clothing for their soldiers at the *Ostfront* and in turn given them old Polish trousers and other poor-quality items from their booty of Polish, Greek and French uniforms. This left the kriegies with no greatcoats or adequate winter clothing. The Germans had plenty of overcoats in their stock of "liberated" uniforms but refused to issue them. Finally, in response to repeated requests by the SBO, they agreed to sell the coats for *Lagergeld*.

The coats, when they were at last brought into the compound, were of poor quality, and in varying shades of khaki and sky-blue. It was a swindle, but the prisoners had no choice. To keep warm in their bunks they slept fully dressed and kept the windows closed; with the smell of eighteen to twenty-two men and the fumes from the coke stove the rooms became stuffy. Even then, the fire didn't last long: the coal issue was one and a half briquettes per room per two days.

For one Air Force prisoner, there was nothing to dispel the gloom. Pilot Officer G H Batchelor, a young Spitfire pilot who had been badly wounded when he was shot down, was suffering from septicaemia. Gordon Herbert Batchelor had joined No54 Squadron at Catterick in October 1940, when it was part of No13 Group. He was still with the squadron when it moved to Hornchurch as part of No11 Group. During the early afternoon of Wednesday, 9 July 1941, the Hornchurch and Tangmere Wings flew as top cover for "Circus No41", when three Stirlings were dispatched to Mazingarbe. As usual, the Spitfires got caught up with Me109s and cannon-shells thudded into Batchelor's aircraft from below, passing through the cockpit, severing the elevator and rudder cables and hitting him in the legs. The Spitfire went into a spin from which it could not recover. Batchelor had no choice but to bale out, but as he did so his R/T plug became entangled in the aircraft. When it jerked free it was with such force that he fell several thousand feet without a parachute before pulling his rip-cord. The parachute was badly torn, and Batchelor landed heavily in a cornfield, further injuring his legs, but also his hips and spine. He was unable to move.

Within about five minutes he was surrounded by Germans, who took him on horseback to an armoured car. After bandaging his legs and giving him something to drink, they took him to an Army headquarters at Vitry-en-Artois, where he was searched and questioned. He was then moved to a hospital in Arras. X-rays revealed two pieces of shrapnel deeply embedded in his left leg and one in the right, but as they were small the doctors decided not to remove them. All they did was pick out the pieces that lay under the surface of the skin. He spent the next ten days in Arras, with little to do but lie in bed and read a few English books that the doctors had brought him. They also gave him pen and paper so he could write home.

On Tuesday, 29 July they took him by ambulance to Brussels, where there was a bigger hospital. Again his legs were X-rayed and again the doctors decided not to operate. Neither Batchelor nor the doctors realised the severity of his injuries. From then on he went from hospital to hospital until finally arriving at Obermassfeld and being transferred to Oflag XC.

When he arrived at Lübeck he occupied a bunk at right-angles to Paddy Denton's. He lay there day and night groaning with pain. At first his fellow prisoners were disinclined to feel sympathetic: they thought he had a touch of the twitches. Then, one night a few weeks later, they heard one of his bones breaking softly as he turned over in his bunk. It was only then that they realised how ill he was. Two weeks later he was taken away and put in the so-called sick bay. By this time more Army officers had arrived from Crete. Among them were a number of chaplains and an MO, who volunteered to look after the incurably ill pilot.

Finally, in early October, the camp received a surprise visit from two officials from the American Embassy in Berlin. "Despite Wachtmeister's precautions," wrote Michael Roth, "we were able to sneak them a written statement of our complaints and the many violations of the Geneva Convention. We hoped they'd lay it on thick so that the next bunch of inmates would fare better than ourselves."

This produced immediate results, for on Monday, 6 October, there was, recorded Roth "Sauce of soya bean extract and potatoes for lunch. Food! Issue of tin of 50 Players cigarettes per person. Red Cross now know we are here. Bonanza day."

On Tuesday the 7th the Germans announced that two thousand Red Cross parcels had arrived. But an hour later they announced that the entire camp would be evacuated the next day, as it was needed for others. They would be going to a "reconciliation" camp at Warburg, near Kassel. The parcels would travel with them by train and be distributed at the new camp. This was a bit of a blow, and the senior officers from each of the four services — Army, Royal Navy, Merchant Navy and RAF — ganged up on von Wachtmeister and demanded that he at least issue some cigarettes. After much arguing, he finally relented, agreeing to a ration of ten cigarettes per man.

The news of a transfer came as a tremendous relief to the RAF contingent. Any camp would be better than Lübeck, and the journey itself would be a welcome break in the monotony, and offer opportunities to escape. The mere fact of being outside the wire would allow the mind to unwind. "Wachtmeister and his gang didn't let us go without a last 'squeeze', however," recalled Roth:

On 7 October they called a special *Appell* with orders that we were to bring all our blankets on parade with us. At pistol-point they then took two blankets away from all who had two — the fact is they'd only issued one blanket per man in the first place. They insisted that we'd been issued with two blankets: the ones they took belonging to us were clearly Red Cross issue from Geneva.

Our Wing Commander [Hyde] — not having himself an extra blanket — told us to give up our blankets without making a 'fuss'. Asinine creature. Squadron Leader Roger Bushell, a great Goon-hater and superb linguist, got into a terrific shouting match with Wachtmeister's loathsome adjutant, who yelled out that all Englishmen were liars and told seventy-thousand lies. Bushell replied we were not liars and demanded that the adjutant produce the papers we had signed on our arrival for the original issue of one blanket per man. The adjutant refused. I

Fig 9. Personal search on leaving Lübeck *(Wallace Cunningham)*

believe that some kriegies forestalled the adjutant's plan by tearing a single blanket in half, folding it, and then handing in two halves as two whole blankets. It was a very unpleasant *fracas*, and our hatred for everything German became written on our faces.

One of Bushell's tunnelling syndicate, Tom Kipp, suggested that he should stay behind, hidden in the tunnel. It was quite probable that when the camp was evacuated the guards would be taken off and after about twenty-four hours he could sneak out and cut his way through the wire. The next morning, 8 October, it was announced that the move would take place that day. So, stocked up with food and water, Kipp was battened down in the tunnel.

It did not take the Air Force contingent long to pack their meagre belongings. Apart from flying boots — good for keeping out the cold — Kenneth Mackenzie, for example, had only a kitbag, an Army forage cap with ear-muffs and a pair of Army boots (from a bulk issue of POW clothing), some paper, an exercise book and a pencil.

Pilot Officer Batchelor remained behind, along with the Army MO, and was subsequently moved to another hospital at Hamburg. He died there on 15 April 1942, at the age of twenty-three.

The final head-count before the prisoners left Lübeck was a tedious and long-drawn-out affair. Forming "companies" between the barrack blocks, the prisoners had their belongings searched, their blankets checked and their identities confirmed against their *Personalkarten* — buff-coloured A4-sized documents that followed them to every camp. Kipp's absence was covered up by cooking the list of prisoners in the infirmary. The hospital bed-count was carried out by a British orderly, under German supervision, and as he crossed the compound to the parade ground he altered the figures. After several checks and recounts by various German officers there was a half-hour wait while figures were compared. The count was found to be correct, but during the pause, Squadron Leaders Kane and Morris sneaked off parade into their hut via an open window. "How they managed this without being spotted was a miracle," recalled Michael Roth. "They were taking a hell of a chance. In turn, they waited until the guard watching the rear rank walked his beat in the opposite direction, during which interval, in broad daylight, they nipped across the space between the rear ranks and the hut. It was a shaky do. Once inside the hut they hid themselves under a trap door that they had constructed in the floor."

At first the ruse appeared to have worked. But the Germans knew something was amiss, because after issuing rations for the journey about a hundred guards marched the kriegies to the *Panzer* HQ, half a mile away, where Trumble's party had spent the night before going to Dulag Luft. Lining the prisoners up on one side of the parade ground, they set up a trestle table and held an identity check. As his name was called each prisoner trudged across the parade ground with his belongings and presented himself before *Hauptmann* Leipold. When Kipp's name was called, the man who had just been checked dropped his belongings, and the Germans were so busy yelling that they forgot all about Kipp. They also overlooked the absence of Kane and Morris. But at the end of the check they were still rubbing their chins dubiously.

Company by company, the prisoners slowly filed out of the HQ and down across a field to a train of cattle-trucks waiting on nearby tracks. As the last of them passed through the wicket gate, the goon checking the count realised he was short of prisoners, and the *Abwehr* embarked on a thorough search of the camp. The march to the railway station was like a funeral procession, as the pace was dictated by some of the less healthy among the "Cretan Freaks" who struggled under the weight of their cardboard boxes. A few of them passed out, and had to be carried to the rear of the column, which was brought up by a ration lorry.

Meanwhile, the rest of the prisoners down at the railway station were boarding the cattle-trucks. The train was well guarded by the standards of the German Army. *Posten* sat on the roofs, and at the end of the train was a "flat-top" with eight guards and a machine-gun. The goons were taking no chances. They ushered the prisoners into the trucks in an orderly fashion, according to the rooms they had occupied at the camp, counting them as they boarded. When the men from Bracken's mess were boarding, the guards noticed that Kipp was missing and hauled them back on to the railway siding. A few minutes earlier the count had checked correct. The guards were completely bamboozled. They bundled the prisoners into a lorry, took them back to the camp and locked them up in the cells. Fortunately, the train was geared to a timetable, so the Germans couldn't drag everybody back to camp for interrogation. This time the joke was on them, and Wachtmeister would receive another big "cigar". Leipold interrogated the prisoners who had been held back one by one, and throughout they maintained that Kipp had escaped four days previously by hanging underneath a lorry — a trick well known to the Germans. Leipold still didn't believe them, and they remained in the cells.

Finally, back at the railway sidings, two guards joined the prisoners in each truck and the doors were slid shut. This was the Barth contingent's first experience of travelling by cattle-truck. "It was not pleasant," Roth noted. But for those captured on Crete the trucks were an improvement on their previous mode of transport, as they had each been fitted out with three wooden benches. This was a blessing during the day, when prisoners could take turns sitting down. But at night it was a curse, because there was less room to lie flat on the floor when trying to kip down.

The journey to Warburg took more than thirty-six hours — a long time to be cooped up in cattle-trucks. But they had one advantage over the third class passenger carriages favoured by the more security-conscious Luftwaffe: they provided a better opportunity to escape. Before long the Air Force prisoners produced jagged knives — made into saws by serrating the edges on the concrete steps to the barracks at Lübeck — and began hacking at the floorboards and levering them up. The rattling of the train covered the noise of the sawing and splintering. In Bader's carriage, Hugh Keartland, Robinson and Cecil Filmer cut a hole in the floorboards and started

Fig 10. The move to Warburg. Impression by Wally Cunningham (Note incorrect date)

158

slipping out while the train was in motion. Keartland got out safely — to be caught soon afterwards — but Robinson mistimed his exit. He fell under the wheels of the train, had both his legs cut off and died immediately. That put a stop to escapes from Bader's truck. But in others, escapes went on. As the train slowed down between Hamburg and Hanover, four officers escaped from one truck alone. Whilst two ex-Barth kriegies, John Denny and Robin Beauclair, finished cutting a semicircular hole in the back of the truck under cover of a group playing cards, "Mike" Lewis and Peter Stevens climbed through the ventilator. Beauclair and Denny were then ready to follow. Beauclair slipped out first, Denny passing him the food and escape clothes. Unfortunately, as Beauclair clambered across the buffers to the next wagon, he accidentally broke the air-brake line, which alerted the Germans. All four took off under a hail of bullets and reached the woods, but Beauclair and Denny missed each other — it was a very dark night — and had to travel separately. Later, while the train halted briefly at a siding in Hanover, Roger Bushell and Jaroslav Zafouk escaped (bringing the number of aircrew officer "train-jumpers" at large in Germany to six). Their absence went unnoticed by the Germans. They reached cover and set off for Czechoslovakia, where Zafouk's brother lived. Seven months would elapse before they returned to the fold.

The two squadron leaders left behind at Lübeck — Kane and Morris — waited until dark, climbed the now-unguarded wire, made their way to the docks, boarded a Swedish freighter unseen, and then had the worst luck. Overcome by exhaustion, they fell asleep, and their snores echoed up from the coal-bunker and attracted the attention of a pro-German Swedish sailor. He called the dock police, and the game was up. "They turned up six weeks later at Warburg and gave us the details," recalled Michael Roth. "They had a merry old time with that bastard Wachtmeister, who would cheerfully have shot them for causing him so much grief with his superiors."

Back at Lübeck, the day after the move, "Bungie" Bracken was horrified to see Leipold enter his cell with his pistol drawn. *Christ,* thought Bracken, *what's going to happen now?* He was surprised when Leipold said, quite pleasantly, "Come along," and escorted him outside, where two guards were waiting, also with drawn pistols. They walked him down to the *Panzer* HQ, took him to a garage and ushered him into a car. Suddenly it backed into the wall and Bracken and his escort ended up in a pile on the floor; the driver had locked the car in reverse gear. Luckily, no pistols went off and nobody was hurt, and after the usual German shouting match they drove to the town hospital. Bracken was told to wait in the passage, where sinister-looking grey-uniformed *Sicherheitsdienst* men passed to and fro, shouting and yelling. Then Leipold returned and took him into a room furnished only with a bed. Lying in the bed was a man Bracken had never seen before in his life. He looked frightened. Sweat was pouring off him and his eyes were swivelling from one side to the other. Wondering if the man was a British agent, Bracken said: "Hallo, Kipp." But the man made no reply. While the Germans looked on, thunderstruck, Bracken made one or two banal remarks; then they led him out and took him back to his cell.

The next morning Leipold again entered Bracken's cell. This time he was grinning. "Kipp has escaped," he said. "Yes, I know," replied Bracken. "Five days ago, under a lorry." "No, from that tunnel in your room. Come on," said Leipold, and he led Bracken back into the compound and straight to his hut, where the tunnel entrance was lying open. Then Leipold took him to the wire and showed him the hole Kipp had cut. Leipold was very sporting about it. He said he recognised that it was their duty to escape, and while he would always do his duty and try his best to prevent it, he would also do his utmost to ensure that the prisoners were tolerably treated. Then he explained that the man in the hospital had been picked up in the docks at Lübeck wearing only his underclothes. He was in a peculiar mental state and was therefore admitted to hospital. At first they had mistaken him for Kipp, and had taken Bracken down to identify him. But when it became obvious that neither had ever set eyes on each other, they started making enquiries. It turned out that some time previously the RAF had raided Hamburg and had hit the gaol. Some of the prisoners had escaped and this man, who was due to be hanged for killing his girlfriend, was one of them.

"So, what will happen to him?" asked Bracken.

"He was hanged this morning."

Now the affair was cleared up, Bracken and the others undergoing cell-arrest were taken to Warburg in a third class railway carriage.

A last word on Oflag XC, provided by Mike Roth:

The two guards on duty inside Beauclair's cattle-truck were court-martialled and sent to the Eastern Front six months later in a penal battalion.

A fitting epilogue to our hateful sojourn at Lübeck was that three nights after we left, it received one of the heaviest raids of the war — a fitting retribution for the unjustified treatment we'd received there — though I hardly think there was any connection.

Roth's recollection is, unfortunately, clouded by wishful thinking. The RAF did not raid Lübeck until 28/29 March 1942, although it is true that the city took a terrific hammering. However, there were no further major raids on Lübeck, as the International Committee of the Red Cross (ICRC) negotiated an agreement with Britain that it would not be bombed again because the port was being used for the reception of Red Cross supplies. This was to the advantage of POWs and the annoyance of "Bomber" Harris, who continued to authorise small-scale operations against the city throughout the war. Mostly these were nuisance raids without much result.

Prisoners relaxing at Oflag VIIC, Laufen, summer 1941. *(Author's collection)*

l

Above: James Heber Ward. *(J H Ward)*

Above: Jack Best. *(Author's collection)*

Below: Anthony Trumble. *(A J Trumble)*

Below: Colin Dilly. *(Martin Dilly)*

Eric Sydney-Smith *(left)* and his Blenheim crew in Malta, prior to his returning to England in 1941. *(Author's collection)*

Above: Jaroslav Zafouk.
(Author's collection)

Below: Peter Harding: POW.
(P Harding)

Above: Wallace Cunningham: POW.
(W Cunningham)

Below: William "Dutch" Bakker: POW.
(W Bakker)

Peter Stevens. *(Marc Stevens)*

Above: **Gilbert Walenn.** *(via Norman Canton)*   *Above:* **Lionel Casson.** *(Author's collection)*

Below: **Douglas Bader being shown around the German fighter airfield at St Omer. Adolf Galland is second from left.** *(via P B Lucas)*

Above: Wing Commander Douglas Bader is allowed to sit in the cockpit of an Me 109 at St Omer shortly after his capture. A German officer holds a pistol at the ready in case of any "funny stuff". *(via P B Lucas)*

Below: Blenheim crews pose for the camera with a box containing a new pair of artificial legs to be dropped for Douglas Bader during a daylight raid over France. *(via P B Lucas)*

Left: A cheerful Peter Tomlinson prior to take-off. *(P Tomlinson)*

Above: Peter Tomlinson looking down in the mouth after being captured. *(P Tomlinson)*

Right: A POW mess at Oflag XC, Lübeck, drawn by Bill Bakker. *(W Bakker)*

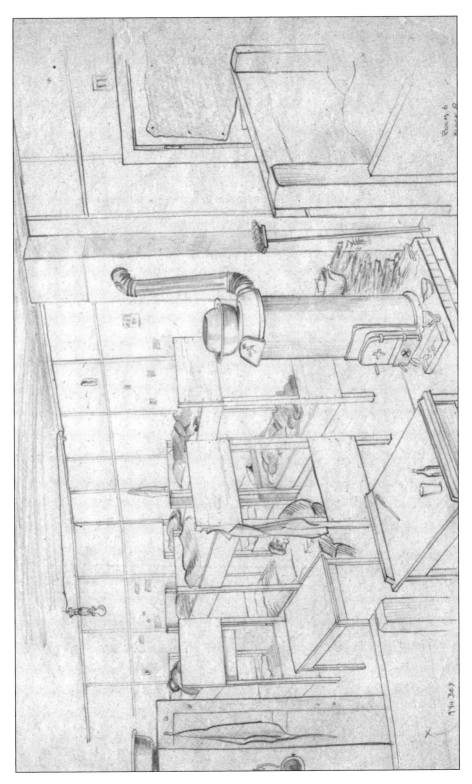

Kriegsgefangenenlager **Stalag X C** Gef. No. **621.**   Datum **18·9·41.**
Prisoner of War Camp   Date

Name **BUSHELL**   Vorname **ROGER**
Surname   Christian Name

Dienstgrad u. Truppenteil **R.A.F.**
Rank and Unit

Geburtsdatum **30·8·1910·**   Geburtsort **SPRINGS, SOUTH AFRICA**
Date of birth   Native-place

Lager Wohnort **STALAG LUFT I**
Last dwelling

Adresse meiner Angehörigen **R.D. BUSHELL, BROADMERSTON,**
Home Address

MOOOI RIVER, CAPE PROVINCE, SOUTH AFRICA

~~Unverwundet~~ — ~~leicht verwundet~~ — in deutsche Kriegsgefangenschaft geraten —
~~Unwounded~~ — ~~slightly wounded~~ — prisoner of war in Germany —

Befinde mich wohl.
I am well

(Nichtzutreffendes ist zu streichen)
(Passages not apposite to the point to be cancelled)

                        Signature

Left: POW registration card filled in by Roger Bushell at Lübeck.

Above: Aerial view of Oflag VIB, Warburg-Dössel. *(Author's collection)*

Below: POW barracks at Warburg. *(Author's collection)*

Above: **Oflag VIB, Warburg, after the war, with the barbed-wire fences and sentry towers demolished.** *(Author's collection)*

Below: **The** *Sportplatz* **at Warburg.** *(Author's collection)*

Right: Dominic Bruce. *(D Bruce)*

Below left: Acting Squadron Leader Peter
Mason, drawn by a fellow-POW, Major The
Hon. G D Milne, RA, at Warburg.
(Author's collection)

Below right: Pilot Officer Waclaw Krupowicz,
drawn by Colin Dilly at Warburg.
(Martin Dilly)

Sydney Dowse.
(Author's collection)

The scaling ladders on the wire at Warburg, the morning after Operation Olympia.
(Author's collection)

The wire at Warburg, the morning after Operation Olympia. (*Author's collection*)

Chapter Four

"A Very, Very Bad Camp..."

Oflag VIB, Warburg-Dössel,
September–December 1941

Oflag VIB was administered by *Wehrkreis VI*, with its headquarters in Münster, and lay on the flat windswept plains of Westphalia to the west of the village of Dössel bei Warburg. Originally, the site had been intended for use as an aerodrome, but by the time the war started only the accommodation huts for the airfield construction workers had been completed. It was then converted into a *Hitlerjugend* training compound. On 9 July 1940 it became a POW cage for Polish officers, who had recently been moved out.

The first British arrivals were Royal and Dominion Air Force and Fleet Air Arm officers from Oflag IXA/H at Spangenberg who, along with an RAF orderly, reached the camp on Tuesday, 16 September 1941. They were:

Acting Wing Commander J R Kayll DSO, DFC, Auxiliary Air Force;

Squadron Leaders A O Bridgman DFC, D B Gericke, S S Murray, M E Redgrave, E T Smith and F G L Smith DFC;

Acting Squadron Leader R N Wardell;

Flight Lieutenants J C Bowman RAFVR, J Bryks (Ricks) (Czech), L S Dunley RNZAF, F G Dutton, R H Edwards, R A G Ellen, M J Fisher RAFVR, E Hubicki (Pole), F W S Keighley, L Kozlowski (Pole), S Z Król (Pole), J N Leyden, R I C Macpherson, S G L Pepys, A A Rumsey RAFO, J R T Smalley DFC, N H Svendsen DFC (Dane), T E Syms, P F R Vaillant, M C Wells and G O M Wright;

Flying Officers T A Bax, D Blew, R J E Boulding, P E Bressey, D Bruce, R M Burns, E F Chapman RAFVR, C A R Crews DFC, W H Edwards DFC, E T Fairbank, J H Frampton, B W Hayward, D S Hoare, R H Jacoby, D F Laslett, W N Lepine, A C MacLachlan, R C D McKenzie, J C Milner, K H P Murphy, W M Nixon, S T Sedzik (Pole), J M Taylor, N M Thomas, J Tilsley, P D Tunstall, G E Walker and P G Whitby;

Acting Flying Officer W F Jackman RAFVR;

Pilot Officers M F Andrews, R S Ayton DFM, G M Baird, J Barker, H R Bewlay, R M M Biden RAFVR, H R Bjelke-Peterson RAFVR, A J Brewster, P S E Briggs RAFVR, P G Brodie, H F Burns, M G Butt RAFVR, S Carter RAFVR, W Cebrazynski (Pole), E J Clelland, P W Cook, R M Coste, R V Derbyshire RAFVR, G T Dodgshun, N M Dunn RAAF, L H Edwards, R F J Featherstone RCAF, J E A Foster RAFVR, W M W Fowler, G M Frame RAFVR, J T Glover, A H Gould, T H Hadley RAFVR, A J C Hamilton, W C Hartop RAFVR, D K Hayes, D G Heaton-Nichols, W Hetherington, K N Holland, W H Holland, J R Hoppe RAFVR, F Hugill, A M Imrie (Southern Rhodesian), K Jaklewicz (Pole), T F S Johnson, T M Kane, J McB Kerr RNZAF, I C Kirk, W Krupowicz (Pole), N Maranz (American), J D Margrie, A W Matthews, A F McSweyn RAAF, L Miller DFC, A W Mungovan, H M Murray, B T J Newland (Southern Rhodesian), D G O'Brien, T L W Officer RAAF, G Parker, D Paterson, J W P Perkins, I G G Potts, R G Poulter, S Reeves, R Roberts, C I Rolfe, W J Sandman RNZAF, H A T Skehill, W A Sojka (Pole), A J J Steel, H H Taylor, P A W Thomas, A B Thompson, K S Toft, R E Troward, P P Villa, R A Walker, R D Wawn, J Whilton, R A R White RZNAF, and I K Woodroffe;

Aircraftman 1st Class L J Slattery;

Captain K W Driver DFC, SAAF;

Lieutenant E C Newborn SAAF;

Lieutenant-Commander N R Quill RN;

Lieutenant (A) A O Atkins RN, (A) M A J J Hanrahan RN, J C Iliffe RN, (A) D T R Martin RN and A Taylor RN;

Sub-Lieutenants (A) R E Bartlett RN, (A) R L G Davies RN, (A) H Deterding RNVR, (A) H N C Hearn RN, (A) D A Poynter RN;

Lieutenant N M Hearle RM;

Capitaine Larmier, *Armée de l'Air*

The Spangenberg contingent fell into four main categories: (1) officers from the Advanced Air Striking Force (AASF), the Air Component, Bomber Command and the Fleet Air Arm captured during the "Phoney War" from September 1939 to April 1940, most of whom had been sent more or less directly to Oflag IXA/H without first going through Dulag Luft; (2) officers from Bomber Command, Fighter Command, Coastal Command, the AASF, the Air Component and the FAA, plus one officer from the *Armée de l'Air*, captured during the campaigns in Norway, the Low Countries and France from April to May 1940, including those who had taken part in raids against Germany itself, and some of whom were moved from Spangenberg to Stalag Luft I, Barth, in July 1940 and then returned in February 1941 for transfer to the *Straflager* at Fort XV in Thorn; (3) Barth originals, also a mixed party of Bomber Command, Fighter Command, Advanced Air Striking Force and Fleet Air Arm, who were transferred to Spangenberg and Thorn in the same purge; and (4) relatively new prisoners, including Photographic Reconnaissance Unit pilots and high-speed launch crews from Air-Sea Rescue, transferred from Dulag Luft to Spangenberg from June 1941 onwards.

Most were therefore seasoned prisoners, and some twenty-two of them— Mervyn Andrews, Joe Barker, Harry Bewlay, Dominic Bruce, Maurice Butt, Phil Cook, Robert Coste, Geoff Dodgshun, Robert Edwards, Ronald Ellen, Eric Foster, Ray Hoppe, William Lepine, Nat Maranz, John Milner, Allan McSweyn, Eustace Newborn, Warren Sandman, Neil Svendsen, John Tilsley, Eric Troward and Peter Tunstall — had endeavoured to escape from Spangenberg or other camps. Harry Bewley, the head of the RAF's escape committee, had alone notched up four attempts; Eric Foster, five.

When the train carrying them from Spangenberg finally ground to a halt in the afternoon of 16 September it was not at Warburg station but Menne, a town to the north of Warburg and to the west of the village of Dössel, near which their new camp was situated. They were met by guards from Oflag VIB, who augmented the escort from Spangenberg, and a torrential rainfall. As they marched eastwards to the camp they passed on old woman, who must have been at least eighty, weighed down with several lengths of heavy timber. One of the prisoners stepped out of the ranks to help her and, as the guards made no attempt to remonstrate, he carried her load for about a mile whilst two other prisoners shared his kit between them, as well as carrying their own packs. At the gates of Oflag VIB they had to stand in the rain for some time while the guards carried out a head-count and all the necessary paperwork was signed for the handing over of prisoners. They were cold, wet and miserable. Eric Foster noticed a guard standing next to him and asked what sort of a camp it was. The guard, looking straight ahead but speaking out of the side of his mouth like a screen villain, said: "It is a very, very bad camp. You should complain about the conditions. If you do, perhaps they will close it down. We are prisoners here almost as much as you are." He stopped speaking abruptly and stood a little more erect, as an *Unteroffizier* was passing.

Eventually they were led into the camp and marched directly to the search hut, Barrack No29, to the left of the gates. Their kit was thoroughly inspected and they were subjected to an embarrassing personal search. But owing to the hopeless inefficiency of the searchers, the old lags managed to smuggle through a good deal of escape equipment — including maps, compasses, cloth-caps and civilian jackets. Maurice Butt even managed to hang on to an Irvine jacket and a black leather jacket he had stolen whilst at Thorn *Straflager* the previous spring.

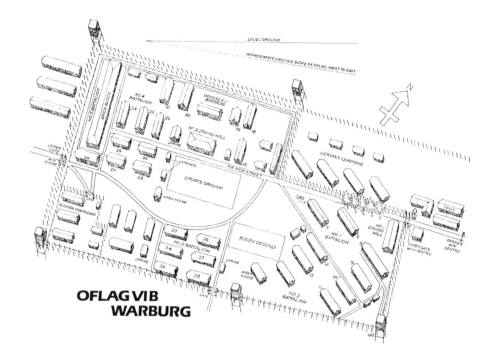

Fig 11. Oflag VIB, Warburg

Shortly after their arrival, Dominic Bruce and Peter Tunstall were sentenced to six weeks in the cells for an escape they had made from Spangenberg on 3 September. When they protested that they had already served a similar sentence there, they were told that had been for "insulting the Third Reich" after recapture. This sentence was for the escape itself. Grumbling, they were led off to the cell block on the eastern outskirts of the camp.

The cells at Warburg were damp, badly lit and very small — just wide enough for a bed, table and a stool, and just long enough to leave a little space beyond the bottom of the bed. But each was equipped with a stove. At Warburg there were two grades of cell-arrest, which the Germans politely called *"Stubenarrest"* — "room-arrest" — and *"Zellenarrest"*, even though both varieties involved spending time in the cooler. The only difference between the two was that in the latter case the prisoner under punishment was forbidden to smoke. Officers of the rank of Major (or Squadron Leader or naval Lieutenant-Commander) and above could not undergo *"stern*-arrest". Either grade of solitary entitled the prisoner to the normal German rations, plus one tin of Red Cross food per day, which could be heated on the stove, and half-an-hour's exercise a day on a small lawn. Writing materials and any number of books were also permitted. The door was locked from 9pm to 7am, but for the rest of the day was unlocked. In the passage was a tap for washing and drinking. The latrines were filthy, but the prisoners were allowed to use the guards' latrines. All in all, solitary was a bit of a rest cure, away from the dirty, crowded barracks, the bustle of human activity and the constant babble.

In the meantime, some of the former Spangenbergers started digging gardens, using makeshift spades. One of them was surprised when his spade hit a solid obstruction. Carefully digging round it, he finally unearthed a cannon-ball — a relic of the Napoleonic Battle of Warburg.

On Thursday, 9 October, the bulk of the Lübeck prisoners arrived. Unlike the Spangenberg contingent, they disembarked at a little halt the other side of Dössel but they, too, encountered a heavy shower. To some of them it seemed as if rain would accompany all moves from camp to

163

camp. When Wing Commander Douglas Bader had been transferred from France to Germany it had drizzled throughout the journey; it rained again when he was moved from Dulag Luft to Oflag XC; now once again the skies had opened.

As the guards prepared to march the kriegies to their new camp, some of the local children appeared, fell in as a choir, and sang "We're Going to Hang Out Our Washing on the Siegfried Line": a dispiriting experience for travel-weary, rain-soaked prisoners who had had nothing to eat for thirty-six hours. They got their own back, however, by singing it properly — and with gusto — on the march up to the camp. One who did not join in was Tony Trumble, who was hardly in condition for anything, let alone singing: he had suffered another outbreak of dysentery. In any case, as the column trudged westwards up the large slope, running with water and mud, all eventually lost their enthusiasm for singing. Eventually they saw several big barrack blocks, and, reaching the crest of a small hill, were once more confronted by the familiar barbed-wire entanglements and long, low wooden huts. "I had felt a bit put down before, over the last few months," Paddy Denton wrote later, "but going through the gate was really depressing. All dripping wet and vast and grey and black and bleak. In the long term it became one of the most entertaining places, as the Army boys were already there and some organisation was in hand."

Just as they had been searched on leaving Lübeck, so the prisoners were searched again at Warburg. They moaned and groaned at this, and protested to the *Abwehr* officer, a blond, Cheshire-cat-faced dwarf called *Hauptmann* Rademacher, who when provoked spat out his words and jumped up and down like an angry marmoset. "You think I not search because you have search before? You English — crazy ..."

However, the search was less grim than it might have been, thanks to Michael Roth, who mellowed Rademacher's attitude:

My suitcases lay open before him on the counter; his small, suede-gloved hands ferreted among their contents, but finding nothing *verboten*, began tossing things willy-nilly over his shoulder. His movements were jerky, erratic, like a dog kicking up dirt with its back legs. Once in a while he looked up and grinned with a "how do you like my little game?" look. This was a different situation to the one at Lübeck, and luckily I knew how to stop him.

"Bitte sehr, Herr Hauptmann..." is all I said. Then I quickly snatched a red wooden ball from a suitcase, threw it a couple of times in the air, popped it in my mouth, grimaced, and appeared to swallow it. I opened my mouth to show it had really gone. For a moment Rademacher couldn't twig what had happened. I had swallowed a red ball? Impossible—but he wasn't sure because he said what everyone says when they are mystified: "Again!"

I picked up another ball and swallowed it too, and then produced it from under my sweater. Rademacher beamed. He dug the *Unteroffizier* beside him in the ribs and told him to watch me do it again. He waved the rest of the search staff to gather round. Years before I had seen a busker outside Lyons Corner House in Piccadilly performing this ball trick. All he had done was to swallow the ball and reproduce it from his stomach, over and over and over again. He did nothing else, and still the passers-by threw coppers into the cap at his feet. Thanks to that old man, I knew I had something good — audience tested!

"Sie Sind ein Zauberkünstler, Ja?" ("You are a magician, yes?")

"Jawohl, Herr Hauptmann."

"More, *bitte*, more."

The search was held up while I did tricks with cards, handkerchiefs, cigarettes and small apparatus. I ended the impromptu show by pulling a string of spring sausages from the jacket of a *Gefreiter*. There were "huzzas" and "bravos". Rademacher was happy. Chortling to himself, he picked up the things he had thrown on the floor and tossed them back into my cases and nodded for me to go. Subsequently, whenever he saw me inside the compound he called out: *"Ach, der Zauberkünstler!"*

Once the search and final head-count were over and the prisoners were allowed into the compound, there were many reunions as former squadron pals recognised each other. But the warmest would be that between Terence Kane, a former Spangenberg kriegie, and his brother Michael Kane, who would reach Warburg once completing his cooler sentence for escaping from Lübeck. Terence, shot down in 1940, had not been aware that Michael, too, was now a prisoner.

The Army officers from Spangenberg arrived on the 10th. They managed to smuggle their wireless set ("The Canary") through the search. It had travelled from Spangenberg to Thorn and back again in a medicine ball. They were followed on Saturday, 11 October, by Hugo Bracken and the others from Lübeck destined for cell-arrest, and on 12 October by the Army officers from Biberach, which was being closed down. On Monday, 13 October yet more Army officers were brought in from Oflag VIIC, Laufen, and Oflag VIID, Tittmoning. Most of them had been in the bag since Dunkirk. There were also some thirty Indians who had been captured in North Africa.

About that time Tom Kipp, Wilf Lewis, Peter Stevens, Robin Beauclair and John Denny were seen being escorted to the cooler. Kipp had reached the Danish border, but developed frostbite. Unable to go on, he hid in a railway wagon and was found by a railwayman. Lewis and Stevens had jumped a goods train to Hanover, which they reached later that night. There they made contact with some of Stevens' pre-war acquaintances who gave them food, money and civilian clothing. After staying with them about an hour they struck out towards France, where they hoped to contact the Underground. Travelling on foot and by train they reached Frankfurt am Main. By then they were tired, cold, wet and hungry, and went into the station restaurant to order a coupon-free meal, where they were picked up during a routine check by the *Bahnhofspolizei*.

Robin Beauclair and John Denny had a bad time. When they broke out of their cattle-truck, Denny carried the maps and Beauclair the food and clothes. However, because they failed to meet up afterwards and had each to "go it alone", neither had adequate escape equipment. They were caught within a week. But Denny culled some humour out of his experience. One night he was so hungry that he began exploring a railway marshalling yard in Hamm, hoping to find a truck with some food inside. Suddenly a figure loomed out of the darkness and asked: "Is that you, Carruthers?" Denny was so startled, all he could say was "No", and before he had gathered sufficient wits to ask for some food the figure had vanished into the night.

After his escape from the train alerted the Germans, Beauclair had dived down the railway embankment and at the bottom had found a gap in the fence that he could wriggle through. He ran across the field and heard gunshots, which startled him so much that he tripped over. Picking himself up, he ran on, and a few yards further on fell into a stream. He picked himself up again, and ran on for about an hour, until he was exhausted. After stopping for a breather he resumed his journey at walking pace, and was out for two days and two nights before being caught by a railway worker. In the nearest village, he was handed over to the local garrison, which consisted of an Army NCO and six men. This was a big moment for the NCO, who clearly liked to lord it over his minions, and made a great deal out of subjecting Beauclair to a thorough search. As they felt his greatcoat they came across a suspicious lump in the seam. It was a concealed microphone, but they were not to know this, and when the NCO asked Beauclair what it was, he refused to answer.

At this point they produced a pair of scissors and proceeded to cut up his greatcoat. Beauclair then decided to have a bit of fun at their expense. He plucked the microphone out of the seams and laid it carefully on the table, saying: *"Eine kleine Bombe"*. This rattled the Germans, and the NCO carefully picked it up and poked one of the terminals. Beauclair ducked behind one of the soldiers and within seconds the Germans fled the room, leaving Beauclair standing alone, feeling a bit silly. After a while a hand came round the door, holding a gun, followed by an arm, a shoulder, and the flushed face of the NCO, whose voice made it quite clear that Beauclair needed to be taught a lesson. They searched him again, more thoroughly and personally this time, and then marched him to a cellar beneath the village school. The previous occupant had quite clearly not been allowed out for some months for any hygienic purposes. It was filthy and sickening. Beauclair was relieved when the next day an escort arrived to take him to Warburg.

These influxes of prisoners — one as strong as 1,500 — plus subsequent purges from Greece and Crete and from transit camps, eventually brought the camp strength, according to some memoirists, up to 3,700. However, this estimate is open to dispute, as official reports have it that the number of officers at Warburg never exceeded 2,600. Adding a further 300 NCOs and other ranks transferred to the camp as orderlies, one arrives at a figure of 2,900. But it is possible that during the year that Warburg was accommodating British POWs, up to 3,700 passed through the camp. "Certain that the war would be over by Christmas 1941," wrote Michael Roth

the German High Command wanted most of its allied officers prisoners in one camp before then. As a result, there were twenty-five nationalities among the POWs at Warburg: officers from many parts of the Empire — Indian officers (Viceroy's Commission) captured in France and North Africa, Arabs, Maoris, men from Australia, New Zealand, South Africa, Canada, and far Fiji. There were Polish, Czech, Dutch and French Air Force officers who had got to England before Dunkirk. There was a Greek general and his aide. And besides these and more, officers from the British Navy, Air Force, Fleet Air Arm, and Army officers from Laufen, Biberach, Tittmoning and Spangenberg. In all, three thousand, under the command of Major General Sir Victor Fortune KBE, CB, DSO.

Oflag VIB, as Denton had noted, was indeed a vast camp. The entire complex, taking in the prisoners' compound and the *Kommandantur* (administrative area), stretched for more than a quarter of a mile on an east-west axis and 350 yards from north to south. The prison compound itself was more than three-quarters of a mile in circumference. A main road twenty feet wide and known by the Germans as *Zum Lager* ran almost the entire length of the camp from Dössel in the east, and towards the rolling agricultural countryside to the west, with the compound, guards' quarters and *Kommandantur* strung out on either side.

Most of the compound — more than two-thirds — lay to the south of the road. In that area alone there were thirty-eight huts. They included a dining hall (referred to as No1 Dining Hall), two wash-houses and two latrines. No1 Dining Hall was later partially converted into a theatre, with a large stage and an auditorium for three hundred and fifty seats. There were also two clear areas which, covered with cinders, became sports grounds; the prisoners would use them twice a week for rugby and soccer. Halfway along *Zum Lager* — which the kriegies called the "High Street" — another road led off in a wide loop, leading south and turning west. In the smaller part of the camp, to the north of the "High Street", stood sixteen huts, some set aside for orderlies, and the No2 Dining Hall. All these huts were of wood. Running down the western fence, cutting across the end of the main road and almost reaching the gate, was a long barrack built of bricks. Surrounding it was a neat path. From above, the compound resembled two oblongs, the one to the north of the main road about half the width and half the length of that to the south. German guards' quarters lay outside the western and eastern fences of the smaller oblong and to the north-east of the larger oblong. The camp was built on a slope, with the southern and eastern fences stretching along the bottom and the northern and western fences meeting at the top, and the terrain was treacherous, criss-crossed with ditches, drains and low earth walls.

At the easternmost end of the High Street was the main gate — or "lower gate". This gate (in fact two gates, one set in each fence) was used only by guards and officers passing between the compound and the administrative barracks. It was manned by two sentries, one at a barrier and the other in a goon-box overlooking it. Twenty yards down the road was another sentry manning a movable pole barrier. To the left of the gate, strung out along the road, were the cells, clothing store, coal cellar and German dining hall, where off-duty guards lounged on the steps. Beyond them, over the brow of a hill, lay the rest of the *Kommandantur* buildings and a small, hutted compound. About two-thirds of the way down the western fence, at the far end of the looping subsidiary road, was a smaller double-gate — "the upper gate"—used by civilian workers. This, too, was manned by two sentries, one of them in a red-and-white striped box.

By contrast with Oflag XC, however, not all the huts within the compound were laid out neatly parallel to one another and the wire. Those to the east ran diagonally across the compound, with the exception of the No1 Dining Hall, which ran parallel to the eastern fence.

Some prisoners considered conditions at Warburg almost as bad as they had been at Thorn and Lübeck. To begin with, the camp was overcrowded, as the OKW had decided to concentrate as many officer POWs as possible in one huge *Offizierslager*. According to the latest propaganda, Warburg was a "reconciliation" camp, an atonement for prisoners having been held in Thorn. The official version, according to Red Cross and other reports on Oflag VIB, has it that "the Germans had assembled as many officers as possible in one camp because plans were under discussion for an exchange of prisoners with the British". It was equally true, however, that in a matter of only three months no fewer than six Army officers had made home runs from Oflag VB at Biberach, and to forestall further successes the OKW had turned the Polish camp at Dössel over to British POWs. It was three hundred and fifty miles from Switzerland, three hundred miles from the Baltic ports, and nearly two hundred miles from Holland. As for the aircrew prisoners, David Lubbock opined:

> I understood that our contingent, which came from Lübeck, was sent to Warburg in transit until the new "escape proof" camp of Stalag Luft III was made fully ready for us. I would not therefore refer to our move as a purge. We were all prisoners of the Luftwaffe.

At any rate, Hugo Bracken did not share the opinion that Warburg was as bad as the previous camps. "In pure physical terms, " recalls Hugo Bracken, "there may not have been much to choose between them, but there can be no doubt that morale was far higher at Warburg than it was at Lübeck." David Lubbock took a similar view: "Here to our joy we met practically all the British army officer POWs of that time, including, of course, many friends."

When the Spangenberg contingent arrived, only fifty or sixty men were allocated to each barrack block. But with the arrival, in October, of the parties from Biberach, Laufen, Lübeck and Tittmoning, as many as a hundred and thirty men were jammed into each hut. The barracks measured fifty feet by twenty-six, and were divided into rooms fifteen feet square, each for between eight and ten men. However, in some huts there were as many as twelve officers per room. As the rooms were supposed to accommodate no more than ten men, extra bunks had to be moved in. This left floor-space for a stove, a table, ten stools and one locker to every four officers. As it was, in some messes there was no table at all. There was also a shortage of fire-irons. Mattresses were damp and infested with bed-bugs, and the roofs leaked so much that when it rained — as it mostly did before the snows fell — everything became wet.

Orderlies (or batmen, as the Army still called them) were allotted at the rate of three to every two rooms. These orderlies were supposed to be at the disposal of the officers all day, but the Germans kept taking them away on working parties and communal duties, such as peeling spuds. Some the Germans employed as their own batmen. Consequently the British and Commonwealth officer POWs had to sweep and tidy their own rooms and do their own washing up. Many of these orderlies were Sergeants and Warrant Officers and had used the privilege of rank to wangle a transfer from other ranks' camps such as Lamsdorf, Moosburg (Stalag VIIA) and Mühlburg (Stalag IVB) in order to avoid working parties and find themselves "a better 'ole". The Sergeants attached to the camp hospital spent the day practising in their dance band. This was not at all satisfactory from the officers' point of view. Another vexing issue was the supply of eating utensils and crockery. In direct contravention of the Geneva Convention, the Germans refused to issue each prisoner with a knife, fork, spoon, bowl and cup, which meant that the only such items in Oflag VIB were those that prisoners had brought with them from their former camps. The Spangenberg contingent had to drink out of glass jam-jars bought there from the camp canteen.

Tea was brought round the camp by orderlies at 8am, and the first *Appell* of the day was at 9.30am. It was supposed to last about a quarter of an hour, the prisoners forming up around the recreation ground and facing inwards, but often lasted longer. Many prisoners rose early, sometimes at 7am or 7.30am, to get a quick wash in one of the four wash-houses. Each wash-house was divided into two rooms. One had a central trough with ten taps; near the entrance, and two feet above the concrete floor, were another two taps. There was always a queue of shivering men waiting their turn at the trough (in the entire camp there were only twenty-three taps for some 3,000 officers). In order to cut down the waiting time, it was forbidden to shave at the trough. With a great deal

Queuing for coal, clothing, parcels, abort — or just queuing.

Fig 12. Kriegies queuing for rations at Oflag VIB, Warburg
(*Wallace Cunningham*)

of contortion, the most determined types could just about take a cold shower under the taps near the floor; more often than not, however, the only visible result was a flooded floor. The nearest any POW could get to a bath was to take a strip-wash in a zinc basin, one of which was supplied to each mess. During wet weather, the prisoners visiting the wash-houses brought heaps of mud in their train, and it was not cleaned up until later on in the morning as the orderlies were kept on parade until 8.30. There was supposed to be a stove in each wash-house, but every time the Germans installed one prisoners stole it for use in the barracks. The other room, leading off the trough-room, was for washing up and dhobying. It was equipped with a large wooden table, at which each prisoner stood and did his washing-up and laundry in a bowl (if he had one). Usually, two such bowls were issued to each mess, and they had to be used for everything — mixing pies, washing feet, shaving, washing clothes, and so on. Some messes made a rule that the bowls were to be used only for cooking. The idea of mixing food in a bowl that someone had just used for washing his feet was too disgusting to contemplate. At any time during the day a prisoner could walk into the trough-room and see another prisoner washing himself, his teeth and his greasy feeding bowls in the same water.

It was much the same in the four latrines. These were adjacent to the wash-houses and of a standard pattern familiar to all old stagers who had been held in Army camps. Each latrine block was divided into two with a flimsy partition wall. One half contained rows of wooden benches, with holes sawn at intervals, over which prisoners sat and defecated onto a heaving cesspool beneath; the half other contained the urinals. The cesspool itself stretched beyond the latrines, and collected not only the issue from them but also the residue from the drains and ditches that criss-crossed the compound. At about two feet below ground level it had a cover with a permanently open trap. Through this trap the peasant who emptied the cesspool stuffed the pipe from his horse-drawn tank so as to suck up the waste, which was then spread across the fields beyond the camp as manure. Unfortunately, the cesspool was emptied at irregular intervals, and during the particularly bitter winter of 1941/42 its contents rose to ground level, threatening to flood the area between the latrines. As the "lats" were only about the length of a cricket pitch from the barrack blocks, the stench was overpowering. Many of the older kriegies considered Warburg a reversion to 1940 and Thorn conditions.

Breakfast, usually taken after *Appell*, consisted of *ersatz* bread (sometimes fried) with margarine and jam or sardines, washed down with *ersatz* coffee. The coffee was always cold, as it had to be carried — usually by officers — in open cans from the kitchens in No1 Dining Hall, which was a quarter of a mile away from some of the barracks. Orderlies — if available — would then clean the rooms, and this was the best time for officers to "bash the circuit". At about midday stooges would be posted at the windows and doors of each barrack block and the "gen-men" would appear to read the news taken down from the secret radio. This seldom went off without a hitch, as three *Abwehr* personnel — known as "ferrets" — prowled round the camp every day and there were always other Germans roaming the compound looking for suspicious activity. Consequently, the news bulletins suffered frequent interruptions. It became a rule never to discuss the news in the barrack blocks, lest a German with ears agape should overhear and twig that the prisoners were suspiciously well informed.

Lunch — usually a meagre ration of half a litre of soup per man — was held at 1pm in the No2 Dining Hall, on the northern side of the main road and run by an Army officer, Captain W Earle ("Bill") Edwards of the Royal West Kents, who had helped a number of RAF prisoners escape from Thorn back in May 1941. The food was brought to the dining halls in dixies by horse-drawn cart. Lining up along the High Street, officers stood in a queue hundreds of yards long to draw their ration. Some had spoons, but most did not. Those without spoons had to sup straight from bowls. Once inside the dining room they had to scramble for space at the wooden benches and tables, as there were not enough.

Evening *Appell* was at 5.30pm. At about 7pm — or any time after evening *Appell*, sometimes as early as 6.15 — the prisoners were locked into their huts and the windows secured and shuttered. Only twenty per cent of the huts had electric lighting. Those messes without electricity were each issued with two carbide lamps for illumination at night (theoretically one between every five officers). The carbide was issued every three days, but in such tiny amounts that the prisoners could usually afford to use only one lamp. They would light up as late as possible — at about 6.30pm — and extinguish it at about nine o'clock so that it ran down by ten o'clock without wasting any carbide. There was not enough room for more than half the prisoners to sit within its glow, which was not even sufficient to read by. Prisoners soon started making their own "goon lamps". Emptying a tin of S*peisefett*, they would wind wire in a circle in the bottom of the tin, leaving two prongs sticking up. Round the prongs they would wind pyjama cord as a wick. They would then replace the S*peisefett* and heat the tin, saturating the cord, which they would then light. Even this proved difficult, as there were never enough matches. Each room also had a stove, with coal briquettes being issued every three days. It wasn't even enough to boil water for tea. Sanitary facilities for each barrack consisted of a "thunderbox" in the passage. Visits to this evil-smelling night latrine were always unpleasant and, if possible, best avoided.

Prisoners were not allowed to write anything in their letters home concerning conditions in the camp. Some mentioned that the camp was hutted, that they messed fifty to a hut measuring only fifty feet by twenty-six, and that they were locked in at 6.15pm. These letters were returned to the authors by the camp censors.

Warburg, like all POW camps, also had a canteen, from which items were taken round the huts for officers to buy with their *Lagergeld*, which from 14 November onwards was issued monthly in accordance with the Geneva Convention. "However, the amount was small after the contribution to the Communal Fund had been deducted," recalls Hugo Bracken, " and probably averaged not more than RM65 (or £3.75)." In addition, as a result of a misunderstanding between the British and the Germans regarding naval ranks (which resulted in the latter mistaking an Acting Sub-Lieutenant, Commanding Officer, Warrant Rank, as an NCO instead of the equivalent to an Army Second-Lieutenant or an RAF Pilot Officer) there was a mix-up about rates of camp pay. Naval officers were paid at a rate one rank lower than their equivalents in the other two services. "At least the Naval types had the comfort," writes Hugo Bracken, "that less was deducted from their pay at home than would have been the case had they been paid according to their true rank."

Prisoners could afford to buy very little in the way of luxuries and had to write IOUs. Clothing was issued — very rarely — from the store in the *Kommandantur*. The Germans insisted that clothing (and personal parcels) be handed out to prisoners according to whatever camp they had been in previously; thus there would be an issue for, say, former Spangenberg inmates followed, days or weeks later, by an issue for those who had been at Lübeck. The prisoners would parade at the gates and march under escort to and from the clothing store. The same procedure was adopted for the issue of coal, carbide and so on, except that hut representatives were appointed to draw these rations collectively for an entire barrack or group of barracks.

The German garrison at Warburg was the typical mixture of the genuinely sympathetic, the weak and hypocritical, and the downright brutal. In the first category was the *Lageroffizier*, *Hauptmann* Kraus, the only German, apart from the *Rittmeister* (cavalry officers), who conducted *Appelle*, with whom the prisoners had daily contact. Known by the prisoners as "Gremlin George", Kraus was diminutive and well mannered. In the Great War he had been a prisoner and had escaped successfully. He therefore had little time for Nazism or the war, and had some sympathy for the men in his charge. Generally tolerant of their ebullient behaviour, he was considered by the prisoners to be "a good guy" and "a nice simple little egg". He was the only German in the camp who was never the victim of "goon-baiting". At the same time, he went about his job efficiently, regulating traffic in and out of the camp, issuing sentries' orders, and having an invariably good nose for sniffing out tunnels. He had an order posted on the notice-board which caused hoots of laughter: "POWs are forbidden to feed the German police dogs as the dogs have been ordered not to accept food from the prisoners."

There were three successive commandants at Warburg. The first was *Major* (later *Oberstleutnant*) Gall, who bore a faint resemblance to von Hindenburg. He fell into the weak and hypocritical category. Gall's posting to Warburg had been a bit of bad luck, as he had been appointed only two days before the first prisoners arrived. The camp was not yet ready to receive them, but he had been told to "get on with it". His task was not helped by the presence on his staff of a junior officer, a *Leutnant*, who was a Nazi Party member and could countermand any order issued by a non-Party member, even to the extent of overruling the Commandant. Consequently, Gall, although himself sympathetic, came in for a lot of flak from the executive Senior British Officer, Brigadier the Honourable N F R Somerset of the Glosters, who complained that Warburg had all the features of a *Straflager*. Gall argued that this was not so, but that the Army and Air Force officers had been assembled there as a result of repeated escape attempts from previous camps. The conditions in Warburg were thus a reprisal for their own recalcitrance.

By far the most loathsome individual on the German staff was *Hauptmann* Harger, a large, red-necked, ruddy-faced brute the prisoners dubbed "Horrible Harger the — of the Lager". Vying with him for unpopularity was the adjutant, *Hauptmann* Mählaw, a revolting, twenty-stone pig of a man whom the prisoners nicknamed "Bulk Issue", and whose personality was as disgusting as his appearance.

Another character cordially disliked by the prisoners was the Security Officer, *Hauptmann* Rademacher. He was capable of being a playboy and tyrant by turns. About fifty years old, with handsome features and grey hair, he bore a strong resemblance to Joachim von Ribbentrop. Rademacher laid it down that at night dogs should roam the compound without a leash. The security searches his staff made on barrack blocks were sudden, unannounced and often led to prisoners' property being stolen or vandalised. At first Rademacher would be courteous and charming to the prisoners, while concentrating his outbursts of anger on his subordinates. But as time passed and the search revealed nothing, he would order his men to hurl bedclothes, books, clothing and even crockery out of the window. Then he would draw his sword and spear walls, floors, palliasses and window blackout shutters. If prisoners protested, he drew his pistol and fired shots into the air. He insisted upon all prisoners saluting him; all those who failed to do so went to the cooler. Under Rademacher were "Gremlin George" and the three grey-overalled "ferrets", who poked about the camp every day.

The *Oberzahlmeister* — the goon in charge of the cookhouse — was another cause of friction. He often held back rations of potatoes, meat, sugar and margarine to which the prisoners were entitled and of which they were badly in need.

One advantage that Warburg had over Barth and Lübeck, from the topographical point of view, was that it had a lovely view beyond the wire of agricultural countryside very redolent of the North York Moors and in particular the Cleveland Hills. Often, in autumn, spring and summer, the prisoners could see labourers — men and women — working in the fields. Through the eastern gate they could catch a glimpse of Dössel village, with its attractive spired church. Evenings were blessed with some beautiful sunsets. These surroundings awoke the artistic instincts of many a prisoner, including Colin Dilly, who turned out a prodigious amount of pencil sketches and watercolours and also taught art classes, with Bill Bakker and William Hunter among his pupils. When Red Cross musical instruments arrived from the USA, the musically inclined got together and set up two dance bands and a sixty-piece camp symphony orchestra. "I am surprised," Joe Kayll claimed later,

how many people thought that Warburg was an unpleasant and dirty camp. My memory of it is that it was far the most interesting because of the presence of the Army with quite different experiences and views to the RAF detachment, and it was by far the best for escape attempts as there was a gate at each end and it had not been designed as a POW camp, so had many advantages for escape attempts.

On Tuesday, 14 October, a cold, bright day, Douglas Bader was paid a visit by some of the Army officers who come from Spangenberg. Bader was regarded with admiration and awe by the officers at Warburg — Army, Navy and (most, but not all) Air Force. Those who had dismissed the legend of "the legless ace" as mere propaganda now had to revise their views. From him the Army officers heard the first full account of the Battle of Britain, and his forceful personality, infectious grin and almost unwavering optimism provided a welcome tonic to the pessimism that prevailed amongst older kriegies.

Dinner that day was *Klippfisch* soup. With the number of prisoners from the various purges bringing the camp to near-capacity, there was, recorded one captive, a "Hell of a queue". At 3.15 the entire prisoner complement was paraded for a visit by the Commandant. But at 4.45 the prisoners got an extra meal out of it — barley stew. There was a mad rush for this, as it helped to keep out the cold.

The compound next day was a sea of mud and it was impossible to keep both barracks and oneself clean. A familiar face greeted Tony Trumble that afternoon — Commander G H Beale OBE, RN, who had been in command at Maleme, the Fleet Air Arm aerodrome on Crete. On 20 May, the day Maleme was bombed and then overwhelmed by German parachutists, the tall, lean George Beale had set out with Wing Commander Edward Howell, whose No30 (Hurricane) Squadron shared the airstrip, to check the forward defences. German glider troops, who had just landed in the riverbed, were forming up nearby. Trying to keep out of sight, Beale and Howell found a slit trench where they discovered two airmen with rifles. Taking the airmen with them, they pressed on, creeping quietly. But German paratroopers spotted them, and started firing. Beale was hit in the stomach and, coughing and grunting, pitched forward about five paces. Luckily the bullet had come out between his ribs without injuring any of his vital organs. As Howell was tending him he, too, was hit, machine-gun rounds striking his left shoulder and right arm and sending him spinning through the air. One of the airmen was hit in the ribs. The other airman and Beale, doubled-up in excruciating agony, crawled across to Howell and applied a tourniquet to his right arm. More bullets were whining overhead between them, and they helped Howell to his feet and ran towards the slit trench. They had to cross a hundred yards of terrain exposed to gunfire from two enemy positions. Five paces away from the slit trench, Howell collapsed and Beale and the airmen, despite the gunfire, crawled across to him and carried him to a dug-out in the hillside. The Germans then started lobbing grenades at them. Luckily the grenades fell short.

Beale, white and haggard and still doubled-up, was determined to find help and on his own set off towards the Allied Lines. He reached an aid post, and sent out a rescue party, which fought its way to Howell and found him unconscious in a pool of blood. Beale was captured when the aid post, where he was being tended to, was overrun. He was taken to the prison hospital at Kokinia, where he met up again with Howell. Paul Jacquier was there at the same time. Beale's wound healed up nicely, and he was one of the first POW patients to be shipped out to Germany.

The day Beale arrived at Warburg the water was turned off, without warning or explanation, preventing prisoners from brewing up, washing and shaving. At 10am there was a camp inspection by "Gremlin George". This was followed by a visit from the Protecting Power (at that time the USA) and Swiss representatives of the International Committee of the Red Cross. The American was shocked at conditions in the camp and declared it "not fit to live in, particularly [for] POWs and even more particularly Officers". He had already visited NCOs' and other ranks' camps in Poland where, he said, the prisoners were in good spirits and much better off than those at Warburg. He considered that 1,500 officers — or 1,000 at the very least — should be evacuated to another camp until Warburg was made ready to accept them. After inspecting the rooms, he said all should be equipped with electric light. He was also worried about the flow of food parcels; a million and a half parcels were stockpiled at Geneva.

Fifteen censor staff had arrived, to deal with letters and parcels for more than 2,600 officers and men. They had not yet even started censoring the letters. The Red Cross representative said that there should be at least a hundred censors for a camp the size of Warburg. The Air Force contingent were largely unaffected by this, as their outgoing mail was censored in Berlin and their incoming mail censored at Dulag Luft by *Hauptmann* von Massow and his security staff. They thus received more letters than the Army prisoners. The Commandant himself visited the camp hospital; it was said that he was so disgusted he had a heart attack. Later in the day the Germans promised to issue more sheets and towels. That night, unaccountably, the lights went out suddenly at 8.30 in the few barracks that had electricity. Groans from the kriegies. Once it was clear the lights would not come on again, they chatted in corners to the light of carbide lamps and *Speisefett* candles, or huddled round stoves. The huts were full of smoke.

Meanwhile, the prisoners were getting properly organised. As Warburg was predominantly an Army camp, internal administration fell to Army officers, mainly "the old and bold" — those of the rank of Major and above. Although strictly speaking Major-General Fortune was the SBO, he appointed Brigadier Nigel Somerset to this post, which he had also held at Spangenberg. Army officers were also responsible for administering parcels and post, and running the laundry, canteen, library, entertainments and the camp newspaper, "The Quill", which they had started back at Elbersdorf, where there had been a satellite of Oflag IXA/H. All services — meals, haircuts, shoe repairs and entertainment — were to be provided by roster, with each prisoner being issued with a ticket when his turn arrived.

Michael Roth had the greatest admiration for the "British Army types":

They were a courageous bunch with terrific morale. They had the knack of finding something positive in the grimmest situation. At first the RAF felt superior and poo-pooed their "let's get organised, chaps; let's improvise; let's put on a good show so the Goons see we don't give a damn for their bloody-mindedness". But eventually, even the cockiest RAF types had to admit this attitude paid off. For example, one could either moan about the mid-day soup ration, or one could look forward to drinking it in the main dining-hall to the music of the camp dance orchestra. Within ten days of their arrival, the Army put on a professional variety show. The General had bullied the Goons into giving us wood and lighting equipment for improving the skeletal stage that the French [*sic*; in fact, the Poles] had left behind. Soon after this, new shows were planned every two weeks. I recall the first full-length musical, *Behind the Scenes*, about the trials of a producer in rehearsal. It was a zinging success due to the extraordinary talent of one officer who when on stage virtually became a woman. Offstage, he was a visual nonentity, but on, he blossomed into a personable and totally believable female — a fine actor. Among the shows at Warburg were *George and Margaret, Coriolanus, Henry V, Rhapsody in Blue, The First Legion*, a Christmas pantomime and several revues, as well as symphony concerts.

The Army types organised everything to the *nth* degree. Apart from entertainments and lectures by competent teachers in more than fifty subjects, they bullied the Goons into letting us run our own chapel, barber's shop, tailoring and shoemaking establishments, hot shower hut, library, piano and music practice rooms, gymnasium, hospital, dental clinic, and carpenter's shop. One most valuable contribution was an organisation that called itself "Foodacco" — a barter market. Practically all our everyday needs (except food) could be taken care of from inside the camp. We were a self-supporting society.

The organisation of escape was also the province of the Army, and all plans had perforce to be vetted by its Escape Committee. There was some dispute amongst the Army officers as to who should sit on the committee, as the previous incumbents from Biberach, Laufen, Spangenberg and Tittmoning could all lay some claim to one post or another. In the end, the issue was decided according to seniority, which, as it turned out, left those from Biberach and Spangenberg in charge.

Despite the camp's unfavourable position in the heart of Germany, it was an escaper's paradise. The guard company was too small to maintain a secure watch on the camp perimeter, and the barracks had not been designed with security in mind. Although the double-floors were raised off the ground on piles eighteen inches high, the space beneath was skirted with bricks, while the topsoil was loose and turned easily. Tunnellers could therefore crawl through trap-doors and dig, unseen, from beneath their rooms, packing the earth round the inside of the brick skirting. Almost every hut therefore provided a favourable site for a trap. There was also plenty of scope for making hidey-holes: the hollow partition walls, the space between the double-floors, the attic roofs, windows, wainscoting, door-jambs and palliasses. A single palliasse could take two "ferrets" up to twenty minutes to search thoroughly, and as there were more than 2,600 in the camp the Germans usually gave up after about five minutes. Thus palliasses were ideal for storing small objects such as maps and compasses. During barrack searches some officers carried contraband on their persons and wore civilian clothes under their uniforms.

The OKW's intention to concentrate officers of all three services in one camp was itself a tactical error. Many of the Army officers were sappers and engineers, and thus ideally qualified for tunnelling operations. In addition, they already had a wealth of experience in map-making and forgery. For the RAF, Oflag VIB became an escape academy, with the Army genning them up on digging and shoring tunnels (known by Army engineers as "spiling"), surveying, mapping and forgery, all of which would prove invaluable in later camps. Returned Army escapers also passed on information regarding conditions outside the wire.

Unfortunately, perhaps because of lack of organisation at the outset, the prisoners had already missed the best escape opportunities. During the first week the camp was full of civilian workmen, erecting new huts, laying paths and cutting down trees. At lunchtime and in the evening they left the camp in droves. Security at the upper gate was lax, with no password, system of passes, or identity discs. The workers were required only to wear a white armband each. By the time the escape-minded prisoners cottoned on, it was too late. Notices were posted warning prisoners not to go within fifteen yards of the gates on pain of being shot without warning; civilians leaving the camp were stopped and relieved of their armbands; guard commanders made regular checks to ensure that sentries were alert and knew their orders, and telephones were installed in the watch-towers.

As it was, despite the establishment of an Escape Committee, the organisation continued to be a shambles. For the most part, escape was left to private enterprise with little back-up from the committee. Would-be escapers had to hoard their own escape rations, make their own maps, forge their own passes (or elicit help from camp artists), convert their own uniforms and rustle up their own stooges to keep watch while operations were in progress. Escape intelligence was not pooled, but simply passed on from one escaper to another. As a result, escapers were seldom well prepared for their journey beyond the wire. Although ninety-five men succeeded in escaping from Warburg between October 1941 and September 1942, when the camp was closed down, only six reached home — none of them RAF.

Neither was there any co-ordination in the siting of tunnels. In a camp as big as Warburg, where there were so many recalcitrant prisoners and so many potential tunnel sites, it was imperative that the committee provide a lead by giving advice and assistance in establishing a programme. Alas! this was not forthcoming, and as a result, escape attempts clashed and often went off at half-cock. Another result of this lack of control was that, despite all the ingenious hidey-holes the escapers had created, a great deal of escape equipment was discovered by Rademacher's three "ferrets". Descending on a particular hut, they would conduct a minute and exhaustive search of the floorboards, walls and roofs. They had constructed trap-doors in the brick skirting, and through these they crawled with torches, carefully investigating the soil for as long as two hours at a stretch in the hope of disturbing a tunnel entrance. They soon became experts at their job. Other Germans passing barracks on routine business were also dangerous. If they saw a face at a window, or an unusually large gathering in one room, they would pounce instantly, often discovering a mapping or tailoring factory. So much skill, ingenuity and hard work wasted, and so many opportunities lost! The only department in the camp that had an unblemished record was the security team for the forgers, who lost nothing.

(2)

On Thursday, 16 October those who had been at Lübeck were issued with a Red Cross food parcel each. So far they had each received a parcel and a half, while those from Spangenberg (and the Army officers from Laufen and Tittmoning) had received none. Two days later the weather turned really foul. It rained all day and blew a gale. But it turned out to be a blessing in disguise, for on the following day the prisoners woke to find the ground almost levelled. More parcels arrived that day, but the Germans refused to issue them. As usual in times of no parcels, rumours abounded. One rumour had it that Warburg was to be broken up, with all the prisoners returning to their former camps. Another had it that the Army administration intended to put all the RAF prisoners together in one barrack and that the Germans were trying to prevent it.

A further blow to prisoner morale came on Monday, 20 October, when the Germans forbade the use of *Speisefett* for night-lights. The next day another rumour circulated: *Major* Gall was dying. But for the prisoners the most pressing issue, apart from the poor diet, was the fact that none of them had had a hot shower for three weeks. That day, at last, the weather turned mild, which came as a relief to the prisoners who for nearly two weeks had had to squelch through mud to the wash-house, bringing mud and water in their wake. There was another improvement on 22 October when the Army parcels officer, Lieutenant-Colonel G W Kennedy of the East Surrey Regiment, persuaded the Germans to approve a new system of parcels distribution. One Red Cross parcel per man would be distributed throughout the entire camp the following day, and starting on Friday personal parcels would be issued daily until stocks were finished. However, the silver lining had a cloud. The Germans ordered that, to prevent prisoners hoarding food supplies for escape attempts, all cans were to be opened and their contents poured into containers. This meant that unless they bolted all the food at once, it would turn sour. Worse still, from the point of view of health, the parcels hut, made of wood, was infested with fleas, and the regular distribution of parcels caused a flea epidemic in the camp. "Regarding the opening of Red Cross parcels," Joe Kayll later recorded:

> The original reason for this was the security department realised that escaping equipment was being sent from the UK and getting into the camp — such as maps, money, compasses, etc. Their reasoning was as follows: The Red Cross had given their word that no contraband of any sort would be allowed in Red Cross parcels. The security thinking was that if the UK were sending stuff, they would put it in Red X food parcels.

So all the tins, etc, were opened and of course nothing of any kind was found. The small amount that was sent was in individual clothing parcels, about which no promises had been made, and in some rather infantile games sent by a phoney welfare organisation. Also new uniforms for Fleet Air Arm pilots, sent I think from Gieves', were very cleverly made so that the removal of buttons and some stitching made a very good business suit.

It was also on 22 October that Brigadier Somerset and his staff had decided to run the camp as a Brigade, divided into five Battalions with the requisite administrative officers. The Air Force and Fleet Air Arm contingents were to be segregated from the Army and allocated two barracks, Nos 6 and 7, running diagonally across the north-eastern part of the compound. Henceforth they would be known as No1 Battalion, whilst the Army officers were organised according to which camp they had been purged from: No2 Battalion, Laufen; No3 Battalion, Tittmoning; No4 Battalion, Spangenberg; and No5 Battalion, Biberach. The camp-wide reshuffle would begin immediately, starting with the RAF and FAA, and would not be finished until Thursday, 24 October. On the day the SBO made his announcement, the prisoners were issued with bed linen — the first they had been given — and winter greatcoats. They were also informed that laundry for each Battalion would be done once every two weeks. The contract to wash POW clothing had been given to an elderly civilian in Warburg called *Herr* Kamm, who ran his own laundry business. He liked to pretend he was sympathetic to the prisoners, and it was indeed true that he had little respect for the Nazis and could be persuaded to bring small *verboten* articles into the camp, including civilian duds. However, money or Red Cross rations, particularly cigarettes, chocolate and coffee, always had to change hands, and it became clear he was less an anti-Nazi than a money-grubbing old git. With few exceptions, the prisoners steered clear of him. This turned out to be a tactical error, because he did eventually help two Army officers to escape.

On the day of the move, there was more entertainment for the RAF — provided, unwittingly, by the Army. One of the Battalions had been ordered to parade after *Appell*, as some of them did not know how to drill. The parade was a fiasco, and as the RAF moved off they bleated at them like sheep. That night there was a Bomber Command raid on Frankfurt, and most of the aircraft got lost in bad weather and dropped their loads too far to the north. Hearing the noise, the men in the aircrew barracks threw open their shutters and started to cheer. They were met with shots fired from the sentry towers and the patrol outside the wire. Wisely, they withdrew, and no one was hurt.

The new dispensation meant that the RAF and FAA were near the No1 Dining Hall but also opposite the guards' quarters on the other side of the northern fence. All day the loudspeaker belted out the *"Horst Wessel Lied"*. Prisoners got pretty sick of it after a while; but so did the Germans who, unlike their charges, did not have the satisfaction of being able to sing, instead, "There'll Always be an England" or "Land of Hope and Glory".

The RAF barracks were also overcrowded, with as many as sixteen men to a room. One sixteen-man room was a League of Nations: "Dutch" Bakker, Courcot (French), Sydney ("Blackie") Graham (from London, Ontario), Alex Gould (Australia), J F Knight and Bill Smith (both from New Zealand), Kenneth Mackenzie (Northern Ireland), John Parker (Rhodesia), Acting Squadron Leader Walter Williams (Wales) and from England, Allen Beales, Hibell, G F Lowes, Peter Tomlinson, Frank Wilbraham and "Tint" Winter-Taylor. Later, on Tuesday, 4 November, Williams moved out and was replaced by Pilot Officer T R Gilderthorpe, a new arrival. Wally Cunningham messed with Mackey, Bryan Tayler, Mark Williams, Hugh Falkus, Christopher Cheshire, Paddy Shaughnessy, Paddy Denton, Derek Roberts, Harry Budden and Cecil ("Snowy") Milne. Some of the senior officers and several other special cases had smaller rooms to themselves or shared with one or two companions. "Dim" Strong occupied a room in Barrack No6 with, among others, Dennis Armitage, Lionel Casson and Douglas Cooper. Douglas Bader shared a small room — almost a cubicle — with David Lubbock and Peter Gardner. Curiously, the SBO and Major-General Fortune lived in Barrack No7, as did "Hetty" Hyde and, later, Squadron Leader Williams, who messed with Army officers of Field Rank.

The Air Force barracks were the untidiest in the camp, as despite being accommodated in rooms of up to sixteen men, they preferred to mess in small units of two or three. This meant that in any one room several messes were preparing breakfast, tea and supper in turn throughout the day. Consequently the floor was seldom swept and the table never cleared. There was no room at the table to read or for the carbide lamps, for all day long the table was strewn with tins of ingredients and dirty, greasy dishes. The dirt and grease inevitably found their way over the table itself, onto stools, books, writing materials and clothes, and eventually onto the beds. Modellers' tools would be all over the room, and their wood-shavings littering the floor. Artists covered the place with paint. Meanwhile, other inhabitants of the room, or visitors, would be coming in and out, bringing cakes of mud in their train. "A sort of 'social life' began at Warburg," recalls Alf Mungovan, "and it became the custom to visit friends in other rooms and huts for a 'brew-up'." The mud they let in would be hardened by the heat of the stove, eventually crushed underfoot and turned to dust. Everything in the room would then have its film of dust, which was unlikely ever to be removed. Reading on one's bunk was impossible, as the room was a constant hive of activity, with all its attendant noise.

On the walls along which the bunks were ranged were a plethora of coats, scarves and towels hung on home-made hooks, and shelves made of bed-boards or Red Cross boxes and suspended by a Heath-Robinson array of strings from the wall or ceiling. Some shelves were built up precariously from the frames of the bunks. Covering whatever space was left on the walls was a collage of snapshots pasted onto cardboard, cuttings from newspapers, pictures of women, and drawings of aircraft. Adding to the gloom were the double-glazed windows, which trapped the dirt and were never cleaned.

Once the initial disruption caused by the barrack shake-up was over, the Army's Escape Committee decided that for escape purposes the camp should be divided into operational territories also bound by Battalions, limiting each officer to seek opportunities only within range of his own quarters. This was of little use to those who wanted to try wire or gate schemes, and there was such an outcry that it was abandoned. After weeks of arguing, they made another stab at establishing some measure of order with the compilation of a register of those who were interested in making an escape bid. The result was a huge waiting list, which only led to frustration on the part of would-be escapers, who had to wait weeks or months before they were given the green light, and could not understand what reasons, if any, there were for such a long delay.

Several of the RAF from Spangenberg and Lübeck went along to the Escape Committee to put their names on the list of potential escapers. Few had schemes of their own, but hoped they could jockey themselves into favourable positions on one of the Army projects. Tough little Czech Joe Bryks was co-opted onto an Army tunnel, but was keen to start his own, and even had a site in mind. He intended to run the hole from one of the huts near the perimeter wire, which meant that the distance to be dug would be fairly short — a matter of some thirty feet. When Dennis Armitage put his name down, the committee told him about Bryks's scheme and asked him if he would like to run the show. Armitage jumped at the chance, but was less impressed when Bryks described how small he intended the dimensions of the tunnel to be. It needed to be small, though, as the chief difficulty would be in disposing of the earth that they dug out.

The tunnel was not much more than a rat-hole along which the diggers could just about crawl on their toes and elbows. Kneeling in it was impossible. It was horribly claustrophobic. To disperse the excavated soil they made long stockings out of any spare material they could find, filled them with dirt, suspended them inside their trousers and spread the soil round the compound, under the huts, and down the "lats". It was a very laborious task.

Hugh Falkus's first tunnelling effort was a "blitz" scheme similar to one he had tried earlier at Barth. Not far from the trip-wire was a potato clamp; he decided to start there, thus reducing the length to be dug. Burrowing into the clamp, he excavated a cave. It was dark inside and he worked completely by touch. Crawling out of the clamp one evening he bumped into a sentry, who demanded to know what he was doing. Rather than face another sentence in the cells, Falkus took to his heels, the sentry shouting after him. Falkus expected the sentry to discover the tunnel, but heard later that he hadn't, so went back to work. However, the Germans did find it a few days later. To prevent any further similar attempts, they constructed a wooden hut in which to store the spuds, oblivious to the fact that for POWs another hut meant another wooden floor in which to cut a trap-door and under which to hide spoil.

Eric Foster and Stanislaw Król joined one of the Army tunnel schemes. The tunnel had its entrance under an Army officer's bed and was projected towards a farm hut a hundred feet outside the wire. Two men at a time worked at the face, one hacking at the clay and the other filling a cardboard Red Cross food carton with the spoil and then, moving backwards, dragging it along the tunnel to the dispersal gang at the entrance. Progress was slow, and before long Król was helping out on Armitage's tunnel as well.

Within the Army organisation, the RAF now had its own, subordinate, administration, with Noel Hyde as Senior Air Force Officer, Anthony Trumble as Adjutant and Sydney Murray as official interpreter and *Vertrauensmann*, or "Man of Confidence". Commander George Beale became Adjutant in charge of Air Force and FFA parades. On *Appelle*, prisoners paraded in their respective Battalions.

Not long after his appointment Beale received a clothing parcel from home, among the contents of which was a brand-new uniform with a naval Commander's cap complete with "scrambled egg" on the peak. This he put on for the next *Appell*, and there was a certain amount of ribald banter from the RAF and FAA officers in his charge. The German officer taking the parade promptly arrested him for appearing on roll-call "in fancy dress". After a heated row, Beale was released and the Commandant apologised.

"Hetty" Hyde, as well as being Senior RAF Officer, was also the aircrew contingent's escape spokesman. The RAF and FAA also had its own, subordinate committee with "Nellie" Ellen as Officer i/c Escapes, and all prospective schemes had to be registered with him, then debated and passed on by Hyde to the main committee. Also on the aircrew committee were "Taffy" Williams, "Pop" Bewlay, Joe Kayll and Norman Quill. They normally met in a room in Barrack No6, with several stooges posted inside and out.

Most of the large-scale escapes from Warburg would be all-Army efforts, although the Air Force contingent became involved in several of them, as well as instigating a number of spectacular mass and individual attempts. The Air Force contingent embraced the idea of escape whole-heartedly. They set up their own Duty Pilot system — which had been in its infancy at Barth when "Hetty" Hyde and company had left for Lübeck. This involved keeping a permanent watch, from a discreet vantage point, on all Germans using the lower gate, and employing a network of "runners" to warn those involved in clandestine activities of their whereabouts. Thus tunnellers, forgers, carpenters and the like could close down activities at any sign of danger. Two pre-war artists, Gilbert Walenn and Colin Dilly, were taken under the wing of the camp forgers, whose factory was known, for security reasons, as "Thomas Cook's". Bill Bakker, Andrew Willan and Gordon Wright also learned the art of forgery. "Mike" Lewis was in charge of the RAF mapping section, which also included Johnny Clayton. "Percy" Palmer, Hugh Lynch-Blosse, Hugh Falkus and Willan (again) all joined "Burtons", the tailoring and make-up department. The tunnelling fraternity included "Dim" Strong, Dennis Armitage, Lou Barry, Christopher Cheshire, John Clelland, Douglas Cooper, Wally Cunningham, Paddy Denton, Falkus, Eric Foster, Dennis Graham-Hogg, Henry Heaton, Oliver Hedley, William Hunter, Joe Kayll, Melville Kennedy, David Lubbock, Lynch-Blosse, Kenneth Mackenzie, "Liffey" McConnell, Allan McSweyn, Alf Mungovan, Palmer, "Flip" Rance, Eric Sydney-Smith, Bryan Tayler, Peter Valachos and nearly all the Poles and Czechs — although all tended to be unlucky in their digging endeavours. In all, a hundred and ten tunnels were started at Warburg, mostly by Army officers, but the aviation contingent took part in two of these schemes and originated several of their own.

David Lubbock drew on his experience as a nutritionist to produce a concentrated ration that was easy to carry and would keep an escaper going for several days. "In escape attempts in the past," Lubbock recalled, "I found that people took as much fat as possible for their food, realising that it had more than twice the energy (calories) for weight than protein or carbohydrate. That diet would make them sick. I devised two balanced replacements, a dry powder to be taken with water and a slab, both made up from ingredients of Red Cross parcels."

The basic recipe for the "slab" consisted of two tins of rolled oats, and a heaped teaspoonful each of salt, powered milk and cocoa. This was mixed together, then supplemented with a tin of margarine (preferably American) and half a pound of sugar, which had to be melted together and then stirred into the dry mixture. The mess that resulted was then kneaded, with enough water to make it workable, and moulded into a block and slowly baked. The finished cake was good, solid, highly nutritional stuff, although it took some getting down. Although usually known as "Lubbock's Mixture", it attracted several uncomplimentary names, such as "Fudge", "Goo" and (later in the war) "Dog Food". Lubbock perfected the recipe over the next two years, but it always carried the warning: "Don't bash!" The dry version consisted of oats, sugar, cocoa and raisins, which could be carried in pouches and sewn into the lining of one's escape outfit.

It is perhaps worth pointing out that, in terms of escape activity, the RAF officers at Warburg were unusually persistent, perhaps because of the inspiration provided by the skilled and seasoned Army practitioners. Hugo Bracken's recollection is that: "Although attempts to escape went on for much of the time, they only involved a relatively small number of POWs, and deliberately so for security reasons. Most of the other POWs in the camps did not know what was going on until the very last moment. For this majority, life was one of boredom and frustration."

By now, the tunnel being run by Dennis Armitage and Joe Bryks was ready to break. Bryks, as the originator of the scheme, was first in line to escape, and the rest of the team drew lots to determine their places in the queue come the big night. Armitage drew number eight. The break was planned for the night of the 28th.

On Sunday, 26 October, Tony Trumble recived his first batch of mail — old letters redirected from the Middle East — and "Hetty" Hyde received two from his wife Kat. The day afterwards Hyde wrote his first letter home from Warburg:

...I AM THAT AFRAID MY LETTERS HAVE BEEN RATHER ERRATIC RECENTLY AS WE HAVE MOVED TO ANOTHER CAMP AND I HAVE NOT BEEN ABLE TO WRITE TILL NOW. THE LAST ONE I WROTE WAS ON THE FIRST OF THIS MONTH EXCEPT FOR A CHANGE OF ADRESS [sic] POSTCARD. SINCE THEN I HAVE RECEIVED YOUR LETTERS OF 31/7, 12/8, 18/8 + 7/9. TWO OF THEM YESTERDAY...WE ARE GETTING RED CROSS PARCELS HERE, WHICH IS GRAND. A LOT OF THE OLDER KRIEGIES (POWs) HAVE PLENTY OF TOBBACCO [sic], SO LIFE IS LOOKING UP. I AM SHARING A ROOM WITH 8 LT. COLONELS — GOOD CHAPS — AND SHARING PARCELS WITH ONE FELIX COLVIN [Lieutenant-Colonel F B Colvin, The Dorset Regiment]...WE ARE GETTING QUITE GOOD AT COOKING & HAD YORKSHIRE PUDDING FOR BREAKFAST THIS MORNING...YOU SHOULD HEAR FROM ME AGAIN SOON AS I AM ALLOWED 5 LETTERS AND 5 PCs A MONTH HERE!*

The parcels staff had another victory that day: the Germans agreed that only one can of food in twenty need be opened, thus giving prisoners a chance to plan their meals. Tuesday, 28 October, was a day both foul and fair. It started off without promise — cold and dark with incessant rain. But in the afternoon there was an issue of personal parcels. This was the usual long drawn-out affair, and it did nothing to improve POW tempers when they discovered that the cellophane wrapping had been removed from their cigarette packets and that the Germans had taken out the silver paper (thus preventing the escape-minded from melting it down to make the silver eagles on "goon-skins"). That night there was another air raid warning, and the guards ran round ordering prisoners to extinguish all lights.

Under cover of the raid the RAF escapers went down their tunnel in pairs. Bryks broke the last remaining crust of soil in the heathland outside the camp and poked his head out of the hole. The exit was only about fifteen feet beyond the wire, and two searchlights continuously swept around the area around it. A further problem was that guards with dogs regularly patrolled the perimeter. Bryks was forced to wait for the moment when neither searchlight was near him and when the

*This was the rule for Lieutenant-Colonels and above.

dog-handlers were out of sight. Finally, he squeezed himself out, as did his running-mate, Otaker Cerny. The next two, Koslowski and Król, then went down, and they were followed by Eddie Asselin and "Basher" Beauclair. Once they reached the end of the tunnel they had to wait for the right moment to make a run for it. Despite the evident hazards, all six managed to evade the sentries, only to be rounded up within a few days.

Just as Armitage was making his way down the tunnel the breakout was discovered. The man in front of him must have lost his nerve and gone too soon, because he was spotted and all hell broke loose: sirens blared, searchlights blazed, and goons were all over the place, shouting. Armitage had to back out of the tunnel with a great pack of food and all his escape equipment attached behind him. It was a hell of a job backing out, but he managed to reach his hut before the goons arrived. The escapers had arranged for the necessary number of people to sleep in their beds, and hung their escape paraphernalia amongst the others' innocent clothing.

On the morning of the 29th the first snow fell, and by lunchtime was quite thick; prisoners were warned to expect it to settle at a depth of four feet. It was going to be a tough time for those without winter clothing. That afternoon the Germans ordered an extra roll-call. It was very cold, and to most prisoners the extra *Appell* was just a bloody nuisance. Afterwards there was a bit of a set-to with the Germans in the parcels office. Despite the agreement reached on the 27th, the German *Leutnant* — the one who was a Party member — insisted on every food-tin being opened. Colonel Kennedy thereupon walked out, his entire staff following. A conference between the Commandant and the SBO was called for that evening. However, it resolved nothing. The Nazi Party member overruled the Commandant. The prisoners were due to have a Red Cross parcels issue the following day. Again the Party member spoiled the broth by insisting that every can be opened, and again Kennedy and his staff walked out. Another conference with the SBO followed and finally a halfway measure was reached: one can in ten would be opened, and parcels would be issued on Friday, 31 October. Meanwhile, on the 30th, a frost had set in and a number of prisoners got to work lagging the pipes in the wash-house with straw. But the endeavour was a complete failure. The wash-house became a quagmire of water, mud and straw, and the lagging failed to keep out the frost. Health was also deteriorating, with five cases of "the dip" being reported; but at least the flea epidemic was subsiding.

The snow was back again the next morning (31 October). It was very slushy underfoot and the wash-houses looked like pigsties. Some Battalions received the promised parcel issue but were warned by the Germans that as bulk stores of vegetables and other foodstuffs had arrived from Geneva the German ration issue would be cut. The SBO replied that if this happened he would order the British staff to leave the bulk food in the store. That day another three officers contracted "the dip" — bringing the number to eight in all.

New German Standing Orders were circulated on the same day. They were the usual mixture of punishment and reward. As a special concession, prisoners were allowed to open their windows at night. They were also permitted to play games in their leisure hours, but any form of gambling was forbidden, as was using the German form of greeting (that is, the Hitler salute, which prisoners used to bait the goons).

By November most of the camp had settled down into a fairly smooth routine. This was perhaps not so difficult for those who had been captured as early as 1939 or 1940, and who were also able to help smooth the transition from freedom to captivity for those rounded up at Crete. Only the new Air Force prisoners had trouble settling in. They had known home so recently that they found their new environment hard to bear. Nor were they entirely popular with the Army POWs. The Army took the view that, as most of the aircrew officers had been prisoners for only three to six months, they had no conception of the deprivation suffered by older prisoners, especially the Army. "They think they are undergoing severe treatment," wrote one Army officer rather tartly in his diary, "but they just don't know what lack of food and clothing means. They have walked straight into luxury." This reveals a peculiar blind spot on his part. Syd Murray, Alf Thompson, Laurence Edwards, Derek Heaton-Nichols, Colin MacLachlan, Harry Bewlay, Bob Coste and John Tilsley had been prisoners since 1939. Of those who had been purged from Barth to Lübeck, and thence to Warburg, several, like Hugh Falkus and Ken Toft, had been in the bag since May or June 1940. Still others, like Alf Mungovan and Percy Thomas, as well as several of those mentioned above and the likes of Rupert Davies and Alex Gould, had been at Thorn. They knew what it was like to go without. One can only assume, if one is to adopt a charitable stance towards this Army diarist, that conditions in Warburg at the time of this entry were giving rise to some bitterness, thus clouding his judgement.

Douglas Bader was by this time suffering a great deal not only with his stumps but also with back trouble. His stumps had shrunk as a result of the poor POW diet. They chafed more easily when he walked and, because the supply of talcum powder was limited and there was no Elastoplast to be had, they became sore and blotchy. In fact, he was in constant pain. Instead of using his stumps to propel himself forward, he took to using his back muscles, which ached day and night. Every morning either Peter Gardner or David Lubbock gave him a massage. They also did the daily chores. Walking in the compound was hazardous for Bader in any case, as it was at a slope and criss-crossed by ditches and other obstacles, round or over which he had to be manhandled by other POWs. Mostly he lay on his bunk and read (usually poetry). Unable to take part in camp sports or pound the circuit for any length of time, he had no conventional outlet for his natural vigour.

He found it, however, in "goon-baiting", and taunted all Germans with the exception of "Gremlin George". His favourite target was *Hauptmann* Harger, with whom he had several violent altercations. The situation came to a head one morning when Bader refused to attend *Appell* in the

Yus - I was flying Battles in France

Fig 13. Reality attack, Warburg
(Wallace Cunningham)

180

snow. Harger found him in his room and angrily ordered him out. Bader refused to budge and in the shouting match that followed Bader taunted: "My feet would get cold in the snow. If you want to count me, come to my room and do it." Drawing and levelling his pistol, Harger shouted: "You-will-go-on-*Appell*!" Bader could see Harger wasn't bluffing. He beamed at him. "Well, of course I'll go on *Appell* if you really want me to," he said, whereupon he picked up a stool, carried it out and planted it on the snow among his Battalion. Harger was seething.

On more than one occasion after that he goaded Germans into drawing their pistols. It was at that point that he would disarm them by submitting and turning on the charm, leaving the taste of moral defeat in the mouth of the enemy.

"Gremlin George" thought he was doing Bader a favour when he protested to the Commandant that Bader should not be expected to attend *Appell*. It was incorrect, he said, and humiliated Germany. The Commandant agreed, and let Bader stay in his room for *Appell*. It only provided Bader with another opportunity to provoke Harger. He went out and joined the others in the snow, where again Harger drew his pistol.

Maurice Butt has particularly vivid memories of Bader:

Bader was a natural goon-baiter — he provoked mischief and fun with the Germans at every opportunity. On *Appell*...he would stand on his pins swaying slightly to maintain stability, and then, when the German officer or NCO came within range, he would manage to fall all over him, much to everyone's glee, except the Germans'...All Germans steered clear of him to avoid a pull-down whenever they spotted him about the camp.

One morning some of the more boisterous RAF lads were playing snowballs and, despite his "tin-pins" and chaffing stumps, Bader joined in the fun. Suddenly, a young *Leutnant* rushed up to him waving a note from the *Kommandantur*. Bader took the note and handed his snowball to the German, saying: "Be a good chap and hold this for me, will you?" The callow German obligingly took the snowball and stood next to Bader, looking uncomfortable and not knowing quite what to do, while several hundred prisoners jeered, laughed and whistled at him.

Bader was not the only "goon-baiter". Douglas Cooper recalls another incident on *Appell* that aroused kriegie mirth:

Earlier on when Red Cross [musical] instruments started to arrive, a consignment came from the USA consisting of violins, saxophones, clarinets, etc, and included an American instrument known as a Sousaphone ("oompah! oompah!") — a huge thing which seemed to wrap around the body. Nobody wanted to play this, except one — no names no pack drill — so I will call him "Charlie". But where to play and practise this instrument? It was decided that the only place was the *Abort*, a hole in the ground in the far corner of the field with a shed over it. Here Charlie practised. Morning and night the Germans would have a parade for us to be counted, but bloody-minded German officers would hold a parade at any time just to annoy. It so happened that one such German came into the camp, blew the whistle, and shouted: "On *Appell*!" Having assembled us, they started to count — *"eins, zwei, drei, vier, fünf"*, and so on until the end of the line. One short! Pandemonium —panic — and we looked at each other wondering who was missing. Someone remembered Charlie over in the bog practising. "Charlie! Charlie! On *Appell*!" and Charlie came running across the field, still with his instrument slung over his shoulder, and stood on the end of the line.

But the methodical Germans had to count again, and when the guard arrived at Charlie, he blew him a RASPBERRY down the Sousaphone! Can you picture the situation? The German whipped out his pistol and would have shot the first one to move, and here we were standing stiffly at attention with tears of laughter streaming down our faces.

The RAF contingent had goon-baiting down to a fine art. They were nearly always unruly on parade, to the despair of Commander Beale and the ire of the Germans. When the Germans could not match the figures — and they seldom could on the first count — their scurrying to and fro would be accompanied by jeers and catcalls from all the British officers, but loudest of all from the RAF. As one, they would then begin chanting: *"Eins, zwei, drei, vier, fünf, sechs, sieben, acht, neun, zehn,"* and break into singing "Oh, why are we waiting?"

They had a complete disregard for German regulations. "Bulk Issue" had ordered that POWs were to stay in their ranks on *Appell* and were not allowed to smoke. But the RAF continued to stroll about, smoking. The guards, on seeing cigarette smoke curling into the air, had to walk amongst the ranks and flush out the offenders. But the RAF nicotine addicts did not even bother to conceal themselves. They walked to the middle of the square, reported to "Bulk Issue" or Harger, and returned to their ranks to finish their cigarettes. Any Germans they loathed they greeted with sallies like "Why aren't you at the *Ostfront?*" They particularly enjoyed baiting "Bulk Issue". Whenever they saw his ample figure waddling down the High Street, they would shout: "Room for 'Bulk Issue!' Make way there! Give the fellow space!" and back away, hanging onto each other, as though waiting for a large vehicle to pass down a narrow lane, while another, pretending to be a traffic policeman, would wave him on. "Every opportunity was taken to harass and annoy the Germans," recalls Alf Mungovan. "There were also some weird ideas from some to amuse themselves, such as piggy-back rides round the circuit, and when this was found to be too easy there were 'wheel-barrow' races with one person holding another by the legs who then moved forward on his hands."

One of the Army orderlies — Gunner C G King, a Territorial in the 92nd Field Regiment, Royal Artillery, who had arrived at Warburg with the Army officers from Laufen — recorded that the RAF officers "made a big difference" to the camp, though not to the good:

> Now these men had no regard whatsoever for German discipline, they did not wish to keep their uniforms in a tidy condition, were not willing to appear at regular times for roll call, and clashed on many occasions with the opinions of the higher ranking Army Officers. Quite frankly it was a very large, ugly camp and there was no unison of spirit amongst the men whatsoever.

To some extent, the RAF attitude was dictated by the fact that unlike Army officers, who often — though not always — entered captivity with their full kit, aircrew arrived on German soil in what uniform they stood up in, provided any of that was left by the time it had been torn by bullets and shrapnel, burnt, doused in petrol, immersed in seawater and spattered with phosphoros. If RAF prisoners were slovenly on *Appell*, it was largely because of the state of their uniforms. Their reaction to this misfortune, to be unruly on parade, matched their (lack of) kit and was, recalled Paddy Denton, "an inverse form of Service pride". When they did receive replacement uniforms in clothing parcels, they were grateful and spruced themselves up. Generally, however, they had to wait months for such parcels. Hank Staniland, whose tunic had been ruined when he ended his operational career in the North Sea, did not receive a replacement until he was in Warburg, after having already gone through Dulag Luft and Oflag XC. Even then, it was a battledress and not a tunic.

The least unruly prisoners were the Indians, who always turned out smartly on parade — to the amazement of the RAF — and were extremely polite and courteous. Most of them had medal ribbons from the Great War. They regularly observed their religious rights, and whenever the RAF went to tea with them would start by standing to attention and toasting the "King and Emperor".

The RAF kriegies also saw much in their own behaviour to keep them amused. John Parker, the Rhodesian who bunked below Peter Tomlinson, contracted acute appendicitis and had to be taken to hospital in Kassel. When he returned he regaled the Mess with colourful stories about the German nurses. They said, rather enviously, that he was damn' lucky to be have been sick. Shortly afterwards Bill Bakker remarked that Tomlinson's hair was getting thin on top. "So is yours," replied Tomlinson, adding: "Dutchy, never forget: there is no romance in a bald head."

Warburg was a great gambling camp and the prisoners there would bet on anything. It was nothing for a game of bridge, *chemin-de-fer* or poker to go on for seventy-two hours, and when cards were laid down for roll-calls or such like it was a point of honour that no one touched them. However, the level of winnings ran into tens of thousands of pounds. Debts were paid in

Lagergeld or promissory notes, some of them artistically drawn to resemble cheques. A friend of Percy Thomas's was at one point £1,600 ahead — a considerable sum of money in those days — and Thomas begged him to hang on to half of it. But within days he had lost the lot. "Betting and boredom were twin afflictions," recalled Michael Roth. "In one hut a room was turned over entirely to gambling; here, every day, vast sums changed hands at baccarat and *chemin-de-fer*. Payment of losses was made either in *Lagergeld* or by cheque written on an official POW letter-form — these the London banks honoured. In those days, officers did not pass dud cheques — it was a cashier offence." Roth compiled a list of some of the more outrageous bets:

10,000 *Reichsmark* were among the top clearing hands for *chemin-de-fer* at Warburg in 1941. 500 *Reichsmark* was the initial minimum. In those days there were around 12 Marks to the pound.

Three thousand pounds was lost in one game of backgammon.

Eleven thousand, five hundred pounds was lost by a bookee on a soccer book; the bookee later recovered an equal sum at *chemin-de-fer*.

32,000 Reichmarks was paid for one bank at *chemin-de-fer* in 1942.

Ken Toft bet 1000:1 against a pick-up football team beating the camp champions. He lost and couldn't cover his bet. So his major creditor told him he could erase the debt if he pushed a ping-pong ball with his nose the full 1,650 yards of the inside perimeter. Toft made himself mittens, kneepads, and a special cover for his nose. Six hours of crawling cleared him of debt, by which time he was being cheered by hundreds of spectators. The guards, watching from the sentry towers, were now convinced that the British were barmy.

Warburg even had official camp bookmakers. One, Edmund Cathels, gave odds on anything under the sun: when the next load of parcels would arrive, if a certain tunnel would break, when the war would end or which team would win a soccer match. His most unusual wager was a 5:1 offer against anyone eating the contents of a Canadian Red Cross parcel in twenty-four hours without being sick. Bets often ran to thousands of pounds, but Cathels never had to pay up because no one managed it. The closest anyone came was all but one biscuit; the bloated, gasping, stuffed-to-the-gills kriegie had half an hour left to choke it down, but he just couldn't make it. One two-ounce soda cracker was all that stood between him and a thousand pounds. He had swallowed 14 ounces of hard tack dry biscuits, 12 ounces of corned beef, 12 ounces of Spam, 8 ounces of salmon, 16 ounces of butter, 4 ounces of processed cheese, 8 ounces of sugar, 16 ounces of Klim full-cream milk powder, 5 ounces of milk chocolate, 12 ounces of jam, 4 ounces of powdered coffee, 3 ounces of sardines, 8 ounces of prunes and 7 ounces of raisins.

Eventually the gambling situation became so ridiculous that Brigadier Somerset instituted an inquiry. He set up a committee comprising senior officers of all three services, and over a period of several days all officers in the camp were called before them. Afterwards Brigadier Somerset issued an order cancelling all debts, prohibiting the sending of IOUs to England and banning all further gambling in sterling.

It is perhaps because of the shafts of light that kriegie humour cast on the otherwise dismal prospect at Warburg that former RAF POWs did not condemn the camp as roundly as they did Lübeck. "Oflag VIB was the liveliest of all the camps," recalled Alf Mungovan, "and one in which I found prison life to be the least disagreeable." Wally Cunningham thought the camp well administered by the British staff and that the opportunities for education, with classes and lectures by experts in all fields, were excellent, especially as some of the younger RAF types were already thinking in terms of post-war careers. Hugo Bracken, who often visited Major-General Fortune for tea, observes: "I've been reading the reports of the Protecting Power. They described it as a very, very bad camp. I didn't think it was all that bad. I mean, it was no bed of roses, God knows! But I didn't think it was all that bad." David Lubbock and Hugh Lynch-Blosse were quite delighted at being amongst so many Army prisoners, some of whom were close friends from pre-war days. One of them, an erstwhile colleague at the Rowett Institute, sought Lubbock out to congratulate him on being a father and to tell him that mother and daughter were doing well. "The best news I ever had, after an agonizing age of no news!" In a letter to Corinne Miles, Lionel Bellairs wrote:

THERE ARE A LOT OF US HERE SO IT'S NOT AS BAD AS IT MIGHT BE...THERE ARE A LOT OF SEERS AND PROPHETS HERE, AND SPIRITUALISTS, WETHER [sic] THEY ARE CORRECT IN THEIR PROPHESIES REMAINS TO BE SEEN. I AM AFRAID ONE IS VERY LIMITED BOTH IN SPACE AND MATERIAL IN LETTERS FROM HERE. YOU MENTIONED SOME BOOKS IN YOUR LETTERS. I'D SIMPLY LOVE SOME AND THEY WILL COME TO ME PERSONALLY, THEY ARE A GODSEND HERE.

Unfortunately, the books were a long time arriving. He wrote to George and Corinne some weeks later:

I HAVE NOT RECEIVED THE BOOKS YOU SO KINDLY SENT ME YET. BUT I EXPECT THEY ARE STILL BEING CENSORED, WHICH UNFORTUNATELY TAKES RATHER A LONG TIME. I AM GREATLY LOOKING FORWARD TO RECEIVING THEM.

As at Lübeck, most of the kriegies fell back on the old stand-by of learning languages. Lynch-Blosse studied Spanish for a couple of months, and also picked up some Urdu from the Indians in the camp.

Meanwhile, now they were installed in their own barracks, a considerable number of the RAF turned their attention to long-term tunnels. The enterprise on which Foster and Król were working was almost literally running into sand. As the length of the tunnel increased, lack of air became a major problem. There were now five men working in each shift and they soon consumed all the available oxygen. The goon-lamps also used up a fair amount of air, and flickered and died. The tunnellers tried to avoid boring an air-hole through the ceiling of the tunnel, as during cold weather (and there was now snow on the ground) hot air would rise from the tunnel and form little clouds of steam on the surface. They solved the problem to some extent by hacking out a chamber at the entrance. The chamber was two feet six inches square, while the tunnel itself was two feet high by one foot nine inches wide. There was little room to manoeuvre in the tunnel itself, but the chamber allowed sufficient elbow-room for the dispersal gang to turn around when coming to and fro with the spoil-filled Red Cross cartons, and their activities pushed some air along the tunnel.

Król was a dependable and indefatigable worker, and it came as a great blow to him when, owing to a lapse in security, the tunnel was discovered. By then the tunnel was outside the wire. "Veeks and veeks of work vasted!" fumed Król, who was inconsolable for days.

Foster, once he had got over his depression, registered two schemes with the Escape Committee. The first was a solo effort through the guards' compound from the clothing store outside the lower gate. This was based on the fact that the Germans occasionally allowed prisoners in to the store to receive their clothing parcels. Next to the room where the parcels were issued was another, empty, room which was always kept locked. Foster reckoned the lock could be picked and that he could sneak into this room under cover of a diversion and remain there until nightfall, provided the count was muddled when the bulk of the prisoners returned to the compound. Breaking out of the room at dusk, he could make his way down the "High Street" into Dössel. The second scheme was for a tunnel from the newly built potato store, which would probably take eight months to dig. Nat Maranz and Warren Sandman, two other former Spangenbergers, would also be in on the tunnel scheme.

Another tunnel scheme began under the leadership of "Bush" Kennedy. It was an ambitious effort, which deserved to succeed, but was dogged by one mishap after another. The trap was hidden under a bunk in Barrack No7. From there the tunnellers sunk a shaft, using a trowel made from the spout of a zinc jug with a wooden handle attached. While digging they wore long-johns, or sometimes combinations, which protected the stomach, elbows and arms from the abrasions caused by tunnelling in cramped conditions. When they had dug down about ten feet they widened the walls to make a huge chamber in which they stored bags full of earth from the tunnel. In elevation, it looked like a big, fat bottle. Then Robert McConnell had a brainwave, which was later taken up in several other camps. Halfway down the shaft they started a dummy tunnel, which went forward about forty-five feet. Then it stopped. A few feet before the face McConnell sank another shaft, which went down a further ten feet. At that level they hacked out another chamber, this time about five feet square. Once the second chamber was completed they used it as a "changing room" but also as the starting point of the main tunnel. This was to be driven uphill towards the southern fence, running under the Army barracks of No2 Battalion. Thus they would be digging at a constant depth of twenty feet — unheard of in 1941 — although near the wire they would start digging at a gradient until they were only twelve feet below the surface. The last thirty yards would rise to a level of six feet and would emerge — they hoped — into the field beyond. The tunnel was three feet high and about two feet wide. Ultimately it would be 140 yards long, and the longest tunnel ever dug from a POW camp.

While digging the shaft they ran into a dispersal problem. Whereas the topsoil was dark brown and loose, it turned to very clinging, light-grey clay a few feet down. It made for hard digging and, if dispersed in the compound, would give the game away. Some was stored in the big dispersal chamber, and some tipped down the communal toilets, where it mixed with the ordure and was pumped out periodically by the "honey-wagon". The rest was packed between the double floor and in the hut roofs (one of which subsequently collapsed).

The diggers worked in teams round the clock. At first, the teams were small. One man lay facing the face and hacked away at the clay with his trowel. The clay was wet and slimy and while the digger sweated above the waist, his nether regions and legs were always frigid with the cold and damp. His No2 dragged the excavated clay to the shaft where it was stored until it was time for dispersal operations to commence. At the end of the shift they crawled back to the "changing room" and handed over to the relief shift. Each man on the outgoing shift had to strip off his soaking wet long-johns or combinations and give them to an incoming digger to wear. Putting on trousers and battledress jackets, he climbed out of the shaft and, back in his room, tried to get as much dirt as possible off his face and hair. Then he went to the shower block to remove all traces of earth and mud under an ice-cold tap. Back on his bunk he shivered with cold and fatigue.

As they made headway they had to start shoring the tunnel. Because there was a shortage of suitable timber, and its absence from the camp would be conspicuous, they stripped the under-flooring from the huts. This was noisy and time-consuming, so the shoring was done piecemeal. To drag the clay from face to shaft they constructed a sledge about a foot long and two feet wide, pulled by rope. They spent hours laboriously weaving the string from Red Cross boxes into three-ply ropes about thirty inches long. For every two or three feet of tunnel dug they had to make more rope, take it down the tunnel and bind one end to the rope already on the sledge. At this stage the size of each shift was increased. No2 loaded the excavated clay onto the sledge, and when it was full tugged on the rope. At the hut end of the tunnel a third man pulled the sledge towards him, emptied it and tugged on the rope to let No2 know he could retrieve it. Every so often they dug blimps where they could change sledges or turn round. However, for the sake of speed and economy, they forsook this luxury after the halfway mark. To illuminate the tunnel they made "goon-lamps" using *Speisefett* as fuel.

Before long, sixty men were working shifts in the tunnel, no fewer than three of them squadron leaders (Douglas Cooper, David Strong and Eric Sydney-Smith), along with Melville Kennedy himself, Hugo Bracken, Paddy Denton, Hugh Falkus, Dennis Graham-Hogg, Kenneth Mackenzie and Peter Valachos. As they worked twenty-four hours a day this meant having to fix roll-calls and arrange for stand-ins in the bunks at night in case the Germans sprung a sudden night-count.

"This was probably the beginning of perhaps the most utterly physically demanding period of my prison life," Denton later wrote. "By hazard and not in any way design I became the best tunneller in the sense of digging more in my shift than anyone else. I also suffered from claustrophobia which, from where I was sitting or lying, did not add much to the gaiety of nations."

The tunnellers were nearing the wire when one day there was a torrential rainfall. Part of the tunnel was flooded and had collapsed, and Hugh Falkus, one of the shift leaders, asked Denton, who had a reputation as an engineer, to go down and assess the damage. None too enthusiastic owing to his claustrophobia, but unable to think up a suitable excuse, Denton went along with Falkus, donned some filthy, wet combinations and stuck his head in the tunnel. Falkus tied a rope to Denton's wrist and waited at the foot of the shaft, while Denton grabbed a goon-lamp and elbowed along the tunnel for about seventy yards. Some goon-lamps were still burning eerily in the little warren, and Denton could feel his pulse racing. Reaching the site of the fall, he was shocked to discover that not only the roof but also the walls had collapsed. The subsidence was big enough to bury a car, and had left only about six feet of soil between the roof and the surface. He was worried that if he attempted to climb over the fall he would displace more clay and be buried alive. His first impulse was to go into reverse, but his common sense was overcome by the fear of being thought a coward. He edged over the slippery slope and found that between the top of the mound and the roof there was a gap of about fifteen feet. After another moment's hesitation, he forged ahead and discovered that the rest of the tunnel was undisturbed. His inspection complete, he now had to crawl backwards to Falkus, using his toes and elbows and snaking gingerly backwards over the hump.

They decided to prop up the roof over the area of the fall, packing as much displaced clay as possible behind the shoring, and disperse the rest as best they could, before proceeding at a lightning pace to break earlier than planned. But some weeks after the completion of this Augean task, Rademacher and his men came along with probes and discovered the dummy shaft. So the tunnellers sunk another shaft from the nearest barrack, which accommodated Army officers from No2 Battalion, and linked up with the main tunnel. This was also discovered. But still the tunnellers would not give in. They dug yet another shaft from a third barrack. As this block was well forward of the entrance to the main tunnel, where the dispersal chamber and changing room were located, they dug down diagonally and towards the interior of the compound, so that together the linking shaft and the main tunnel formed a switchback. Then winter sent in and put a stop to operations.

***

On Sunday, 2 November the prisoners stood along the fence and watched lorries laden with parcels — probably communal food parcels — draw up outside the camp. As there was now a lack of storage space the prisoners felt that the Germans would be forced to distribute them. But the Nazi Party member was still hanging on to them.

The following day news arrived that sick and wounded prisoners who had left Spangenberg on 28 September to be traded with German prisoners in England were still at Rouen. Among them were kriegies who had been gathered from Barth, Lamsdorf, Thorn and Colditz, plus a number of former Spangenberg inmates, including Flight Lieutenant G Skelton, Flying Officer G E Grey-Smith, Pilot Officer P J Coleson and Sergeant G F Booth. The German prisoners in England had been embarked, but negotiations had broken down.

More parcels also arrived, but just as the German security officer, *Hauptmann* Rademacher, was giving his orders, news reached him that a number of prisoners had attempted to escape. Two had already been caught. A snap-*Appell* took place at 12.30. Many prisoners were having a "bath" (a strip-wash standing in a zinc basin), which made the count difficult, but for the rest it meant standing in three or four feet of snow, which had fallen between 6.30 and 7.30 that morning. The Germans also returned POW letter-forms that mentioned conditions in the camp. The SBO took this up with the censors, who replied that they were not concerned with the truth, but with what the authorities allowed to be written.

After the prisoners' failure at lagging the pipes in the wash-house, the Germans decided that in future, to prevent the pipes from freezing, the water would be turned off from the main stop-cock at 5pm. That meant no one could wash after about 6pm. Wooden seats also started to disappear from the lavatories; the wood went into the stoves.

On Tuesday, 4 November two more RAF officers who had been wounded when they were shot down arrived from Obermassfeld. They were Pilot Officers H J Bell-Walker and T R Gilderthorpe. Thomas Roberts Gilderthorpe, captain of a Manchester in No207 Squadron, Waddington (No5 Group) had been on the same Cologne raid on 31 August as Bruce Organ. Of the six Manchesters taking part, only Gilderthorpe's was lost. The aircraft was hit by flak as he approached the target and four of his crew were killed before it crashed near Oberkrütchen.

Pilot Officer Howard John Bell-Walker, another veteran of the Battle of Britain, in which he had flown Spitfires as a Sergeant with No72 Squadron, had been commissioned as a Pilot Officer on 7 August 1941. Posted to No602 (City of Glasgow) Squadron (No11 Group), he flew as No2 to the CO, Squadron Leader A C Deere DFC. On Tuesday, 12 August, No602 Squadron's Spitfire MkVBs provided close escort for "Circus No70", in which six Blenheims were to make a daylight attack on Gosnay. Flying as top cover were Nos 452 and 485 Squadrons. This operation was part of the elaborate diversion laid down to support "Circus No77", the ambitious raid on the power stations at Cologne that led to the capture of Squadron Leader Mills, Flying Officer "Hank" Staniland, and Pilot Officers Chadwick and Hill.

Towering banks of cumulus cloud, interspersed with layers of thin cirrus, covered the route to Gosnay — making escort difficult, though not enough to hamper the operation, and providing ideal conditions for the Me109s. Barely had the formation reached mid-Channel before R/T silence was broken by the Controller giving warning of heavy enemy activity over St-Omer. Owing to the dense cloud, the top cover squadrons had to reduce height to keep the Blenheims in view, and the scene was set for a classic bounce. Me109s dived through the clouds ahead. Wheeling to port, they lined up to attack. Al Deere was leading a section of four to the port of the bombers, with Bell-Walker hanging on to his tail. Two Me109s turned in behind to attack, and as soon as he was sure his section was the target Deere gave the order to break to port. The attack averted, Deere formated his section back into escort position ready for the next pass. Suddenly a voice screamed over the R/T: "Break, Toddy Red, Break!" The warning came too late for Bell-Walker, who was bounced before he could break away. Tracer hit him from behind, and his Spitfire caught fire and went into a dive. Badly burned, he baled out and was taken prisoner.

Tom Gilderthorpe moved into the "League of Nations" room with Bill Bakker, Peter Tomlinson and company. Despite the wounds he sustained on being shot down, he would prove an inveterate escaper. Gilderthorpe, says Bakker, "could not cope with kreigie life at all". (But then, who could?)

Two more late arrivals were Flying Officer T Hutton and Pilot Officer J A Timmis. Thomas Hutton had been captured with Tony Trumble's party on Crete. He moved into the same Mess as Peter Harding. Pilot Officer Timmis was a fighter type from No111 Squadron, flying the Spitfire MkIIA from North Weald, Essex, a No11 Group aerodrome. In February 1941 command of No111 was given to Squadron Leader J S McLean, who was to preside over its change of role from escort work to night-fighting. The squadron was in the midst of this transition when Timmis, a relative newcomer, was shot down. On 19 August, the same day as Pilot Officer McKechnie was bagged while escorting bombers on a shipping strike, No111 was gearing itself up for "Circus No82", an early evening raid by eighteen Blenheims on Hazebrouck, with Nos 71, 111, 222, 308, 315, 609, 611 and 616 Squadrons providing top cover. It would mean some of the pilots (such as those in Nos 308 and 609 Squadrons) flying two or three sorties in one day and by evening being totally flaked out. As it was, all the day's operations were heavily opposed by the Luftwaffe and almost every RAF fighter squadron involved suffered losses. No111 lost three aircraft, with one pilot killed and two, including Timmis, being taken prisoner.

More German Standing Orders on Wednesday, 5 November — prisoners were not allowed in their letters to write any more than eighteen syllables per line. Letters returned by the censors were not to be re-written. A list of *verboten* subjects had been compiled: the number of men in the camp; the hutted accommodation; lighting, feeding and washing arrangements; keeping cats (which implied there were mice); asking for Keatings' flea-powder (implying there were fleas) and comparison with previous camps. Altogether the list of forbidden subjects came to about thirty, which did not give the prisoners much to write home about. Shades of Thorn all over again!

The next day more parcels were issued, and prisoners who had been at Spangenberg received mail. On this — and other — occasions, the Air Force prisoners were the luckiest and received the most. On Friday the 7th there was a canteen issue: one thin notebook, one bottle of ink and three bed-boards per man, along with a supply of raisins. But there the Germans' goodwill ended. They were now trying to enforce a new rule about blankets. If a blanket arrived for an officer in a personal parcel, it would be issued only if the officer in question gave up his German blanket.

On Saturday, 8 November "Hetty" Hyde again wrote to his wife. Since his last letter he had received hers dated 4 and 28 August, and 2, 15 and 18 September, plus three others from friends and relations.

A LOT OF CHAPS HERE [he added] ARE GETTING U.S. PARCELS & THEY ARE VERY GOOD...I'M AFRAID THAT NONE OF YOUR PARCELS HAVE ARRIVED YET. THE TWO WHICH ARRIVED FROM EGYPT & SWITZERLAND AT STALAG LUFT IN AUGUST HAVE NOT GOT TO ME YET, ALTHOUGH I GOT ANOTHER BOOK PARCEL WITH NOVELS...

On Sunday, 9 November the Germans announced that henceforth prisoners would be able to visit other huts and the theatre after dark, as long as they returned to their own huts by 10pm. This was a welcome improvement not only in relations between captors and captives but also in conditions, as the prisoners, no longer confined to barracks from 6.15pm, would be able to use the communal *Abort* rather than the evil-smelling "thunderbox" in each barrack's corridor.

Three days later the first parcels showed up for Tony Trumble's party: five from Portugal. The day was also helped along by the introduction at lunchtime of a dance band playing in the No2 Dining Hall, a welcome innovation that made lunch bearable for the first time since the camp opened. Many prisoners stayed longer than usual, waiting for their favourite tune to come to an end.

The following day, Thursday the 13th, the three Czechs in the cooler, Flight Lieutenants K Trojacek, Z Prochazka and V Kilian, were at last let out. They had spent eighteen months in solitary detention in one camp after another and their sudden release could only be put down to the *Major* Gall's bewildering capriciousness. Their severely curtailed existence, with only an hour's fresh air exercise a day and a near-starvation diet, had left them pale and gaunt, and months would pass before they lost the harried look of men who lived under the constant threat of death. The same day they were released into the compound, the Commandant issued a statement expressing his wish to dissociate himself from Party orders regarding a number of restrictions imposed on POWs and parcel issues. This came as no surprise to the kriegies, as they had read in the German Press a report of Winston Churchill's statement that there would be no patched-up peace with the Nazi Party. The Commandant's statement was interpreted as clear evidence that some Germans were getting cold feet.

On Friday, 14 November the Germans discovered an Army tunnel started in one of the northernmost huts. It was followed by a tightening up of security, which made it difficult for the tailoring and mapping factories to work without interruption. Camp money was also issued for the first time, enabling officers to pay their canteen bills. The weather the next day was appalling — an easterly gale, and snow and sleet squalls — but the 16th, though cloudy, was one of the most glorious days since late summer and the sports grounds were in use all day for rugger, soccer and hockey. There were quite a number of professional sportsmen at Warburg: Laurence Edwards, the first officer POW of the war, had been an All Blacks trial; Derek Heaton-Nichols had played cricket and rugby for Natal; and Colin MacLachlan was a Midlands Counties rugby player and an association footballer of League standard. Together they were responsible for arousing interest in and increasing the standard of POW games. Along with some RAF enthusiasts and a few Army officers they had levelled out a football pitch, almost full-size, and formed a league of six clubs (five Army and one RAF) with second elevens. The matches were intensely competitive and the standard of playing high, especially that of the NCO orderlies.

It had to be. The players had a captive audience, most of them very excitable, highly critical and inclined to rank the games as equal in importance to a cup-tie back home. Douglas Bader, who had played rugger for the RAF before his flying accident in 1931, developed into an eager and boisterous spectator.

At Warburg the RAF prisoners, for the first time, received daily news bulletins, but not from "The Canary." The Army officers from Tittmoning had also brought a wireless set with them — indeed, there were now three or four sets in the camp — and gave the RAF kriegies the use of it. The radio was hidden under a seat in the *Abort* nearest the No3 Battalion barracks, which were occupied by the Tittmoning contingent. Very few people inside the compound knew its location, as POW security was very efficient. (Michael Roth only discovered it by accident after having been in camp several months — much to the umbrage of the "brown job" keeping a watch on it.) The daily BBC bulletins gave their morale a terrific boost. A copy of the latest "gen" was read out inside each hut once a day by Eric Sydney-Smith or Lou Barry, and then burnt. *Hauptmann* Rademacher knew they had a set, but his "goon squads" could never find it. "Had they examined the small and rarely used *Abort* by the south-east corner it's unlikely they would have found it even then," wrote Michael Roth:

From this source we learned about the Wehrmacht's mounting setbacks on the Eastern Front even before the local Goons. In the latter part of November 1941, the temperature west of Moscow dropped to 20 below; the weather was to save Moscow. First the dust, then early rain and mud, and finally the cold, paralysed the gargantuan effort to capture the city. Even behind the wire we knew of the desperate call throughout the Reich for warm clothing: civilians were told to give up their scarves, blankets, overcoats, furs, muffs, gloves, woollen underwear, boots and stockings for the soldiers in summer uniforms freezing to death in the East.

So we had news — "pukka gen" — from three sources: Russian, German, and our own. Sometimes the Goons put on movies in the dining hall featuring the weekly battlefront newsreel (*die Wochenschau*). These never showed Germans killed or wounded, only Russians by the thousands. We heard there were Russians without number: Siberian divisions from Manchuria, and unarmed divisions herded into battle by Commissars who marched behind them with sub-machine guns. The men had no weapons and were expected to scrounge them from what they could find on the battlefield from the dead of either side.

On Monday, 24 November, three hundred Russian prisoners arrived, some of them as young as sixteen. They were herded into three barracks in the south-west corner of the camp, where an area had been fenced off. The British and Commonwealth POWs threw cigarettes and Red Cross food over to them, and the next day the SBO announced that in future potato peelings would be reserved for the Russians, and that he was arranging a donation of Red Cross parcels. On Wednesday, 3 December the British were still showering the Russians with cigarettes, and the guard in his box leaned out and shouted to them: "Keep throwing them over. I shall shout loud at you, but don't take any notice." Later on the Commandant made an announcement over the loudspeaker. He forbade prisoners to throw any more cigarettes over the wire, but said he would welcome contributions given through the proper channels. Dickie Troward remembers that "we were asked not to give them soap, as they would eat it. I recall someone dropping a packet of biscuits, which resulted in a swarm of Russian POWs grovelling on the ground like a flock of vultures, picking up the broken remnants and even the crumbs."

It transpired that "only Russian prisoners who were fit enough to work got food," recalls Hugo Bracken. "The Germans agreed that we could give up part of our daily soup ration to feed them. I can still see the column of sick Russians coming down very slowly to the mess hall to get this soup. The Germans also agreed that British MOs could treat them."

There was an unfortunate incident when some of the Russian prisoners were brought into the main camp for a de-lousing shower. Joe Kayll:

> We knew the day before that our showers were to be made out of bounds for this purpose, and we also knew that the Russians were practically starving, so we all agreed that the kitchen should put two buckets full of stew in the shower-room for the Russians. The strongest got to the buckets first and ate so much that two of them got stomach cramps and died on the spot.
>   From the little contact we did have with the Russian POWs we found they had no conception of sharing; it was everyone for himself, and eventually we gave up trying to help them. Anything we gave was kept by the receiver, and we expected him to share but the idea seemed quite foreign.

As November faded into December, the Army officers who had been selected for repatriation under the POW exchange scheme began trickling into the camp, smarting at having been let down by the British and German foreign offices. At the eleventh hour the Germans had demanded, in contravention of the POW Code, that the exchange should be strictly on a one-for-one basis, and not simply sick, wounded and protected personnel as previously agreed, as more British prisoners than German were benefiting. The British, considering this a breach of trust, and worried that conceding to such a demand might set a precedent, dug their heels in — and sent all the German POWs back to their camps. Now the sick and wounded British prisoners were doomed to spend God alone knew how many more years behind barbed-wire for the sake of what seemed a pretty thin principle — and a principle being upheld by a government that did not segregate its German prisoners according to which service they belonged and that sent them across the Atlantic Ocean to Canada, and therefore itself breached the Geneva Convention.

Only one of the RAF turned up at Warburg, and that was Pilot Officer Dan Hallifax, who was in desperate need of plastic surgery; but he was soon sent back to Obermassfeld for further treatment. So anxious was he to reach home that he made persistent and strenuous attempts to escape, and was eventually sent to Colditz. The other RAF prisoners on the "repat" list were either returned direct to Obermassfeld or to their original camps at Barth and Lamsdorf.

On Monday, 1 December a party of thirteen officers from all three services had attempted to bluff their way through the upper gate. The scheme was based on the regular movement of French POW orderlies in and out of the camp on fatigue parties, escorted by an *Unteroffizier* and two guards armed with rifles. The British had decided to lay on a fatigue party of their own, with Peter Stevens, who spoke fluent German, disguised as the *Unteroffizier* and two others, one of them "Percy" Palmer, posing as the guards. Once outside, those suitably equipped and with a smattering of foreign languages would make for the railway station at the village of Nörde, five kilometres (a little more than three miles) to the north-west. Fake "goon-skins" were made by Dominic Bruce and Peter Tunstall, who had been involved in the now-famous "Swiss Commission" walk-out at Spangenberg and done two spells in the cooler for it. They were also taking part in this particular "dienst", disguised as French orderlies, along with the bulk of the party. Dummy rifles and a gate pass were also made, and food saved from Red Cross parcels. Thus equipped, Stevens proceeded to the gate, followed by two "guards" watching over the "orderlies" trudging along in two columns of ten. Unfortunately, the sentry at the gate was not satisfied with the pass. He let them get fifty yards away, then called them back. He told the *"Unteroffizier"* that the gate-pass had not been signed by the duty-officer of the day. Stevens had to march the party back in to the camp. As the guard had been unaware that the party was not genuine, the Escape Committee decided to obtain a replica of the duty-officer's signature and have another go in a few day's time.

According to an announcement, made a few weeks previously, the coal briquette ration was supposed to have been increased from one box per room every three days to one box a day as from 1 December. However, by 3 December, a bitterly cold day, the promised increase had not materialised. Indeed, the Commandant warned the prisoners that owing to transport difficulties they might have to stretch the current ration for four or five days. In some messes, rather than light the stove, men stayed in bed, fully dressed except for boots, or sat swaddled in blankets. At night they slept in pyjamas, thick underclothes, socks, pullovers, scarves and balaclava helmets, or piled their clothes on their bed with their boots on top to stop them falling off. By the following day the flow of parcels had halted, and the Germans were also refusing to issue Red Cross clothing. However, they relented the next day, and handed out greatcoats and underwear. As usual, they gave something in one hand and took something back with the other, cutting off the water supply at 8.30am. Not that it mattered: the entrance to the ablutions hut was blocked with six inches of mud. That evening a notice from Brigadier Somerset was circulated throughout the camp. It said that German Foreign Office officials had declared conditions in Oflag VIB impossible. They recommended the camp be cleared of prisoners and insisted on 1,000 leaving.

On Sunday, 7 December, the Germans took away ninety orderlies to make up a working party to unload coal and stockpile it in the stores. Lorry-loads of coal had been arriving for the past two days, and the Commandant was anxious to have it stored in the camp because he expected three or four feet of snow, which would block the roads and make further deliveries impossible. That night the prisoners heard of the Japanese attack on Pearl Harbor. "The local Goons were exultant," recalled Roth.

> They asked us what we thought about it. "Good news," we said. "The Americans will now fight openly on our side." And from that moment on, regardless of Japan, the Goons never again showed — to us at any rate — their former confidence in their country's ultimate victory.
>
> But life in the camp was as before. We waited — for the war to end. Forty-two months.

America was now in the war. For the men at Warburg the most immediate question was who would now be the Protecting Power. Two days later, on Tuesday, 9 December, an OKW representative, an *Oberst*, visited the camp with a member of the International Red Cross. The *Oberst* ordered a parcel issue but insisted that the Security Officer, Rademacher, open one tin in ten. However, he had reckoned without the Red Cross representative. He insisted that all food and clothing parcels should come under the direct control of the SBO. He also said that now America was no longer neutral, POWs would come under the protection of the Swiss government. Another result of his visit was that Rademacher's dogs were no longer allowed to run loose but had to remain on their leads.

On the morning of Saturday, 13 December Peter Stevens again tried to march his party of ten "orderlies" out of the camp. Again, Palmer was with him disguised as a German soldier, but on this occasion the escapers were one "guard" short. The sentry at the upper gate was immediately suspicious. A party of ten orderlies had to be escorted by at least two guards as well as an NCO. Detecting a slight wavering in the orderlies' ranks, he demanded the guard's *Soldbuch* (pay-book). The party quickly dispersed, running for their barrack blocks pursued by an NCO and another sentry (both genuine). The guard at the gate, who still hadn't twigged Stevens' real identity, shouted at him and Palmer to stop the orderlies from running away. When they failed to do so, he realised they were impostors and had them marched off to the cooler, where they were joined by Bruce, Tunstall, Cecil Filmer and "Bush" Kennedy. Meanwhile, a number of prisoners had gone into hiding within the compound as "ghosts", so that when the Germans put on a snap *Appell* they would be several prisoners short. As at Barth, the Warburg prisoners did this as a matter of routine.

The Germans now knew that prisoners were hiding fake German uniforms in their barracks. They were also worried about the "rifles" carried by the phoney guards, which they thought might be real. They announced that unless these were handed over by 2.45pm there would be an intensive search. By three o'clock it was obvious that no "goon-skins" or dummy rifles had been given up, and about two hundred troops marched into the compound. They ousted prisoners from their barracks with their rifle butts, sometimes even at bayonet-point, and at least two prisoners were injured, one having a couple of teeth knocked out and the other being stabbed in the face. Another officer was thrown down the steps, landing on his backside, and had to be taken to hospital. While the prisoners stood on *Appell*, Rademacher's men — some of them *Hitlerjugend*

— carried out their search which, Trumble noted in his secret diary, was "Very rough". The Commandant was sick, and Rademacher had been left in charge. He took full advantage of his position, ordering his men to sweep everything — food, books, photographs, the lot — out of cupboards and off shelves and onto the floor, where they sat in disordered heaps while the soldiers trampled on them. They grabbed suitcases, cut round the locks with bayonets and added their contents to the heaps. They prised open wooden boxes. In one hut a soldier opened a tin of jam and probed the contents with his dirty fingers. The RAF barracks came off worst. In one room, bedding, food, cigarettes, clothes and books were strewn across the floor and water poured over them. From some of the rooms the soldiers stole cigarettes and chocolate. Luckily for the prisoners, one of the *Rittmeister* intervened and countermanded Rademacher's orders. From then on he accompanied the soldiers to every hut to make sure they conducted the search in a civilised manner. Bill Bakker remembered the "bloody mess":

Of special interest to me is the story of the search by the *Hitlerjugend* types and the way they did it. When I got back to my block I too found all my things on the floor and trampled on. I made an entry in my diary to the effect that Germans are just all brutal criminals, a lower class of humans. And then to think that they treat my people in Holland in the same way…! When we were purged from Warburg I handed in my diary. That would speed up the procedure of evacuating the camp. I thought, it is all in Dutch and very small writing so they can't or won't read it through anyway. I did not think of the entry I had made. But the censor read it through alright. When I got my diary back I found a note attached to that page with a paper clip. It is still all as it was then, tho' the paper clip is very rusty. He apologised for their behaviour. The Germans were not all like these people, he said.

The search went on until dusk, and that night a rumour swept the camp that it would be resumed at 8am the next day. However, Sunday, 14 December came round and there was no search. Overnight, the dummy rifles had been piled conspicuously in the middle of the camp. The German panic subsided. On *Appell* the *Rittmeister* who had intervened the day before made a public apology for the chaos left in some of the huts. He said that a conference had taken place between the Battalion leaders the night before and that it was unanimously agreed that the whole affair was to be deprecated. A written report had been sent to higher authority. He added, angrily, that he was ashamed that German soldiers should have behaved in such a way. Later in the day prisoners received an assurance that the guilty soldiers, and the two officers supervising them, would be punished. However, this did not come to pass. Instead, *Major* Gall was removed (albeit temporarily), and replaced by the Party member, newly promoted to *Hauptmann*, with the result that again relations between the prisoners and their guards deteriorated.

The Germans' rough approach to barrack searches was perhaps understandable: "One of the factors behind the behaviour of the German troops during this — and many other — searches," says Hugo Bracken, "was that in order to muster enough men all leave had to be cancelled and men of the watches off-duty turned out; this the troops very much resented and took it out on the belongings of the prisoners. There were similar incidents in British POW camps for the same reason."

That Sunday, Noel Hyde wrote again to his wife, and again his letter concentrated on letters and food. After three weeks without any mail he had on Saturday, 13 December received her letter dated 11 October.

…I ALSO HEAR AN AMERICAN PARCEL HAS ARRIVED FOR ME! I HAVEN'T SEEN IT YET THOUGH…MY RAISIN WINE IS GOING STRONG — I TASTE IT EVERY DAY TO SEE HOW ITS [*sic*] GETTING ON — FELIX COLVIN DOES THE SAME AND SO DO ODD VISITORS — CONSEQUENTLY THE LEVEL IS RAPIDLY DROPPING! ITS [*sic*] RATHER GOOD — I WILL MAKE YOU SOME WHEN I GET BACK!…KAT II SOUNDS RATHER ATTRACTIVE — HOPE SHE HAS YOUR NOSE AND EARS! COULD YOU SEND ME SOME TOOTH PASTE OR POWDER AS IT IS RATHER DIFFICULT TO

OBTAIN, ALSO SOME THREAD AND MENDING WOOL — IF THE WAR LASTS ANOTHER FEW YEARS THEY MIGHT ARRIVE!

On Monday, 15 December John Blount and Louis Barry treated Tony Trumble to a birthday party, with a cake they had cooked especially. The camp had no beer, so they washed down the meal with fizzy lemonade, which seemed to be in good supply. The atmosphere in Bader's room, meanwhile, was less cordial. He was having a bath — the usual strip-wash in a zinc basin — when in walked Rademacher and an interpreter. They had come to search his room. (It was the only one searched that day.) The search was very thorough, and conducted without a word by the two Germans. Bader's remarks, and those of Gardner and Lubbock, were obscene and stinging, causing the interpreter to go red-faced with embarrassment.

Two days later fifty of the Russians were removed from their compound. There were now only two hundred and fifty. That night many prisoners experienced pangs of nostalgia when the camp choir stood between the barracks singing Christmas carols. The carol party raised 7,000 *Reichsmark*, some of which would go to the POW Benevolent Fund and the balance of which would be donated to people made homeless by the war. Afterwards, their thoughts turned to the

Fig 14. Cooking Red Cross food at Warburg *(Wallace Cunningham)*

parcel situation. Would there be more food and tobacco in time for Christmas? A good deal of their tobacco, and something like 33,000 cigarettes, had been donated to the Russian prisoners.

Although Red Cross and personal parcels were trickling in, the RAF kriegies sill lacked adequate food and clothing. "I tried to eat a raw turnip, I was so hungry," recalls Peter Harding, "but it made me sick. An Army man gave us a 2 oz packet of raisins and some tea. We had to share this in the room." One morning, as they were getting up for *Appell*, Tom Hutton told Harding: "My socks are so bad they hurt if I put them on the wrong foot."

(4)

Winter was the "off-season" for escape, but David Lubbock and Peter Gardner started plotting with a Commando captain, C J A Smith, to make a bid from the clothing store. Gardner, who had been taught how to pick locks by one of the Army prisoners, believed he could open the door of the adjacent room. He proposed that on a normal clothing parade they lock themselves in this spare room, hide until nightfall, then climb out of the window, walk down the High Street, past some German huts, and into Dössel. They would catch a train from there to Occupied France, where they hoped to contact the Underground.

When they put their proposal to "Hetty" Hyde and "Nellie" Ellen, they encountered two obstacles. Ellen said they were mad to try escaping in winter, and in any case the clothing store was already earmarked for Eric Foster. Otherwise they viewed the plan favourably, telling them that as long as Foster was willing to give up his reservation, the Escape Committee would provide the escapers with several hundred *Reichsmark* (smuggled into the camp), forged passes, maps and a compass. They also recollected that Foster had a useful photograph of the cockpit layout of a Ju52, which the camp censors had failed to rip out of a book he had received from Berlin University...

Having made their plans and received the approval of the Escape Committee, Lubbock and Gardner approached Douglas Bader. "We've got an idea for escape. Would you like to come with us?" "What, in winter?" replied Bader. "Yes," said Lubbock, who on being shot down over Norway had tried to evade capture by walking across the tundra. "Why not?" Bader needed no more persuading. "I'm in," he said.

✗ For food, Lubbock had baked some blocks of his patent mixture, adding Ovaltine, glucose, condensed milk, raisins and ground biscuits to the recipe. When the ingredients were mixed and beaten, the result looked like old glue, but once baked had the consistency of margarine. The cake was then packed into flat cocoa tins. One four-ounce tin had enough calories to last a man two days and also obviated the need to carry bulky and perishable food like bread and potatoes.

But there still remained the question of what to do about Eric Foster and his photograph of the Ju52 instrument panel. Bader volunteered to approach Foster and twice invited him to tea. On the first occasion, Bader asked if he could have the Ju52 cockpit photograph. Foster said he would like to keep it, but would be happy to trace it for him. In the event, Gardner did the tracing. On the second occasion, Bader steered the conversation towards the subject of the clothing store and asked him if he was ready to go, as the execution of Lubbock's scheme only awaited a suitable opportunity. Foster said he was not yet ready and that it would be unreasonable of him to hang on to his reservation under the circumstances. He agreed to drop his scheme in favour of Bader and his team.

Now all the foursome had to do was wait for a bona fide clothing parade. They hoped it would be sooner, rather than later, as Rademacher and his security staff were very much on the alert, despite the snow and the run-up to Christmas.

On Friday, 19 December, Rademacher conducted another camp search and discovered two more dummy rifles. The following evening the choir held a carol service in the church in the No2 Dining Hall. It was the first of a six-night run. The Germans, too, must have been infected with the Christmas spirit, as on Sunday, 21 December they announced that Red Cross parcels would be issued on the Monday and Tuesday, and that there were enough parcels stockpiled for a further three issues. On Tuesday and Wednesday personal parcels would also be handed out. The camp had also received 3,000 Christmas puddings and 3,000 cans of beer, sent via Portugal by Mrs Campbell, wife of Captain Ian Campbell, later Duke of Argyll. With luck, the beer would be issued in time for New Year's Day.

About fifteen of the aircrew officers — including Alex Gould, Ray Hoppe and Peter Tunstall — formed a syndicate to produce a Christmas dinner highlighted with a German bread pudding and a suitable cognac. They unscrewed twenty glass light fittings and filled the bowls "with water, potato peels, yeast and odds and ends," recalled Gould. "All fizzed well enough, but tasted vile...what to do?" Using copper piping they distilled the hooch. The result "was tasteless and colourless but combustion tests were satisfactory. Our ration was less than half a glass each." They stored the liquor down one of the tunnels, and waited for Christmas Day.

Peter Tomlinson chose Tuesday, 23 December as the day to start a diary, and that afternoon made his first entry:

I have decided to keep a daily diary from now on, though day follows day with the utmost regularity. A PofW's life is of necessity dull and one's chief bugbear is boredom, so that if this does no more than while away a short part of the day it will have served its purpose. One writes so little here — three letters and four postcards a month — so that I feel the urge to get things down on paper. Two days to Christmas. It seems strange, as it can be no more than a name this year. Here one only remembers the days of the week by the events which mark them. On Saturdays and Sundays we get ½ a loaf of bread each, instead of the daily 5th. The only other day of note in our week in Thursday, when — if we are lucky — we draw our weekly Red X parcel. In my last I found a small tin of coffee. Great rejoicing. I made a percolator...out of a round 50 Gold Flake tin and lavatory paper and drank Bert [Harris]'s and Jill's health. Result awful and lukewarm. Have felt out of sorts today but hope to get a letter. John Parker had his first from Rhodesia yesterday but it has only made him moody and depressed to hear of the good times everyone is having at home. I know the feeling well!

The day before Christmas the Commandant received an order from the OKW to the effect that all cooler sentences were to take effect within twenty-four to forty-eight hours and that the backlog of sentences was to be cleared. It meant the cooler would be fully booked until September 1942. Peter Tomlinson wrote in his diary:

It still rains having rained all night. Outside a morass of mud and my one and only pair of shoes (present from Ian [Lieutenant I B Macaskie, Royal West Kents]) leak, so I am spending today in bed. The light has not been turned on by the goons for two nights and the evenings have been screamingly tedious. We make lamps out of margarine (if we can spare it) and pyjama cord which gives us enough light for John and I to prepare some sort of supper. Afterwards a long talk on sex with I—, who tells me he didn't have intercourse with his wife for a year after they were married. Then bed — very hard and cold. Everyone kept awake by fleas. Luckily they prefer Dutch Bakker to anyone else in the room. We get hell. He gets very hell. Ian has painted a picture of my corner of the room which I share with 15 others. It looks brighter and cleaner than it really is.

There was, inevitably, a definite lack of festive spirit on Christmas Day. It had blown a hurricane and rained all night, and Christmas morning was cold and dark, with the compound presenting a marsh-like picture of mud and water. About five hundred prisoners rose early to attend a Communion service held at 8.30, which had to be cut short for *Appell*. The roll-call itself was chaotic and dragged on longer than usual because many prisoners failed to turn up. A long *Appell* in the cold, with mud underfoot, was bound to cause tempers to fray, and even the most jovial Germans became surly. Three prisoners were taken to the cooler. Afterwards many of the five hundred dashed back to the church to finish off the Communion service, which developed into a shambles, while the rest attempted to wash. In the wash-houses it was pitch dark, with officers and orderlies tripping over one another. The concrete floor was a sea of mud and squelched underfoot.

Breakfast, for most, was perfunctory. Despite their promise four days previously, the Germans had failed to make a camp-wide issue of Red Cross parcels. Only those who had been at Laufen received a plentiful supply. The only extra the Germans issued was *Sauerkraut*. And no beer. A Christmas without liquor was a sorry affair indeed. It soon became apparent that wishing anybody "A Merry Christmas" would cause blows to be swapped; the only permissible greeting seemed to be: "A happy Christmas — next year". After breakfast there was a morning service, with carols accompanied by a bad pianist on a creaky piano and a sermon on the advisability of not over-indulging in beer at Christmas. Oh, for the chance!

After *Appell* Peter Tomlinson was invited to tea by Ian Macaskie.

Thank God — we have very little food and this hunger is a bit grim. We sat on my bed and talked. His room have made Xmas cake, which makes one's mouth water as we talk. At one o'clock he has to go to lunch with Mike W——. Lucky chap. They have almost enough food to eat with their supply of private parcels. We haven't! Ian goes. Meanwhile everyone in the room has been preparing a Christmas dinner of sorts and we all sit down to our individual efforts. John Parker has made some custard from our Red X parcel and we have saved a tin of raspberries and a tin of figs which we eat with great relish. The custard alas is like billposters bucket — John is no cook — but it blows us out in the true Xmas fashion. My stomach has shrunk enormously and I feel podged out after a few mouthfuls which is all to the good. The German soup we get at midday is a good example, but it has disadvantages. One good belch and you've had your lunch. After lunch lay down on my bunk but not for long because John Mertens [Lieutenant J C Mertens, Black Watch] drops in to ask me to Christmas dinner at 8. What luck — bless him. I know I shall get plenty to eat. My room-mates are very envious — poor sods. I wish I could help them but they don't seem to know anyone in the army and my friends do more than they can afford for me. Clean my tunic for the first time and having lost a button sew on a Polish one John P has given me. Magnificent time with Ian, Mike Trevor [Lieutenant C M Trevor, Royal Armoured Corps], Mickey Farr [Lieutenant M Farr, Durham Light Infantry] and Michael Lindley [Lieutenant M L Lindley, Royal Armoured Corps]. Great fun and the cake excellent. Made with Reich bread, raisins, dates and covered with nuts in true Dundee style. Several people have made a form of wine (!) out of raisins to mark the occasion and some — more ambitious than others — have brewed large quantities and separated the alcohol which they drank through the day so that by evening they were "tight" or imagined they were. The greater part of the distilled drinkers succeeded in time in making themselves really ill and the abort was filled with people heaving in the most soul searing way. Obviously powered by fusel oil and looking and feeling like death. The raisin wine which I tasted was most pleasant and having a very small alcohol content had no effect. Parade for once quite amusing. Several officers being supported in a standing position. Directly after *Appell* went up to John Mertens' room and was the guest of honour at a party which would have done John credit at home. 14 of us. The room consisting of 14 [*sic*] army officers — mostly Australians. I the only flyer. Sat next to Major [G C] Coull RA who I found knew Cecil [Rhodes] well having spent most of his life on the Gold Coast. Known as Armitigger to the natives and apparently to the P of Wales as "the gentleman who swallowed a football". The dinner amazingly good. Cooked by John. The table was decorated and each member had a menu card with suitable picture on front…Started with salmon cooked up in a delicious way under Bun's eagle eye. Next hot tongue (I couldn't believe it), peas and potatoes. Then a home made Xmas pudding (nearly the real thing) and custard. The main ingredient I learnt was the crusts saved from many Reich loaves, mixed nut, figs, raisins, dates. (We get these occasionally from Turkey.) I was pretty blown out by this time but there was more to come. The Xmas cake was then cut. This being the same as the last only covered with melted chocolate and iced with proper icing sugar sent from Holland with "Happy Xmas" on top. All this the result of 6 months' hard saving. My nose suddenly started to bleed but after lying down for 5 minutes on John's bunk I was able to rejoin the table to toast the King in raisin wine. I was then called on to make a speech and although completely unprepared acquitted myself fairly well. One Australian affectionately telling me that I'd sure kissed the blankety-blank blarney stone. All this food, after being empty so long, made me very flatulent so I craftily (I thought) eased myself. After about the 4th — everyone having denied claim to it — true Australian investigations were carried out and I was nailed (purple in the face with embarrassment) as the culprit. The investigation consisted of Bun going to each individual in turn[,] parting the neck collar from the neck and putting his nose inside!! Songs — jokes — speeches but I wouldn't shoot a line or talk shop which made them a bit sore, but there are so many pilots here who do and I hate it. Got back to my room by 9.50 just in time to be locked in. Damned enjoyable evening.

Tomlinson had been lucky to be "invited out" for Christmas. But for most of the RAF and Fleet Air Arm contingent the day passed in a joyless fashion. Gould and his syndicate washed down their dinner with their illegal brew. "Christmas Day someone made up an *ersatz* orange to top each glass. A couple of senior guests offered toasts," recalled Gould: "Our cognac was good... good enough to forget the mud and *Gefangenschaft*. . . it generated warmth and peace. I went to sleep."

There was a heavy snowfall during the night, and by morning four or five inches of snow lay on the ground, with thick drifts alongside some of the huts and in the ditches. Inevitably, on the way to the wash-houses, the younger and more ebullient spirits skulked in the ditches and surprised passers-by with snowballs. But on the whole it was a day to be spent in bed, for although there were some bright spells, it was intensely cold. The wind was strong and later increased to gale force, carrying with it the drift-snow and making visibility nearly impossible. The snow did, however, bring one benefit. It sealed up the cracks and crevices in the huts and made them feel cosy for the first time.

But for some of the prisoners the shortage of food was still acute. Those from Spangenberg had so far received no personal parcels; but half a Red Cross food parcel was due per man, and an issue of Geneva bulk stores had been promised for the end of next week.

"My God it's cold," wrote Peter Tomlinson in his diary on Boxing Day.

Shutz [?] came for me at 2.30 and we watched the football match. Officers v orderlies. Back to Shutz's room for tea. 3 pieces of "scientific" toast, jam and hot tea. Most welcome — I was frozen. Had a row with John [Parker] in the evening. Quite heated. From sheer *ennui* he decided to amuse himself by sticking needles into my leg as we sat on my bunk. After the 3rd I hit him hard in the face. This very effective but in spite of apologies on my part he can't see my point at all. Very un-English these Rhodesians etc! Tempers often frayed particularly in a room where 16 people live, eat, wash, scratch, cook, shout, sleep and make solo love. The shouting and noise nearly send me mad at times. Still it's a wonder we get on as well as we do. Very few fights. Snowing like hell when we climbed into our bunks at 11 o'clock. I got to bed with all my clothes on + a balaclava. Bugger the fleas!

In Peter Tunstall's room, Alex Gould was the butt of all jokes:

Boxing Day evening...with some motivation and encouragement, I walked out to *Appell*. Some subdued goon baiting with some of the syndicate missing...apparently in the cooler. Patiently waiting to be counted, Pete Tunstall kept calling me a zombie. After some remonstrance he advised that he and Hoppy [Ray Hoppe] had taken me out to evening *Appell* on Christmas Day and further advised that he had failed to awaken me after blowing a cornet full blast in my ear.

No more snow fell during the night, but on the 27th the weather was "Bitterly cold", recorded Tomlinson, with "Thick snow" and 28°F (-2.22°C) of frost. The night of 27th/28th was even colder. "Too cold to sleep," wrote Tomlinson. "Water jugs in rooms froze up solid."

On Sunday, 28 December the frost hardened the snow underfoot. Skating enthusiasts flooded the area beyond one of the wash-houses to make a skating rink. They did this by dint of turning on all the taps in the wash-house and letting the water flow out from the drain. But the most memorable part of the day was the view. In the morning there had been a magnificent sunrise; the compound was bathed all day in brilliant — almost dazzling — sunlight, and that evening the sunset was magnificent, turning the snow purple and incandescent. The Germans issued each prisoner "with a Red X blanket in addition to our German apology".

That night, too, was bitterly cold, and the following morning not only were the taps in the wash-houses frozen but so was everything in the barracks: the water in the carbide lamps, water in the *Keintrinkwasser* jugs, and the lemonade. In one room, water in a bucket behind a stove, which had been on all night, was frozen over. The only place where one could draw water was the cookhouse, but by 5pm all taps were off. On *Appell* most prisoners wore balaclava helmets.

At a meeting with the SBO — his third since he had taken over — the new Commandant complained that prisoners lacked discipline on *Appell*. Brigadier Somerset replied that this was mainly festive spirit and the Commandant then accused the prisoners of being drunk. The SBO said this was impossible, as the camp had no beer. (This was true, but they had made brews from raisins.) Then the Commandant complained that the prisoners were failing to salute German officers and to return their salutes. Brigadier Somerset pointed out that under the Geneva Convention prisoners had only to salute captors of equal or superior rank, and that in any case the Germans themselves were not so punctilious about return salutes. He suggested that German officers be compelled to read the Convention. The next item on the Commandant's agenda was escape. He said he could not forbid escape attempts, but could prevent them, and had accordingly ordered the Guard Company to shoot to kill. There was supposed to be an issue of Red Cross parcels that day, but he had decided to postpone their distribution.

That night (Monday, 29 December) there was a pantomime called *Citronella* performed by the army officers in No1 Dining Hall, which Peter Tomlinson attended.

1st Class entertainment. It's amazing what one can do with such a little equipment. The dining room holds about 300 so it takes about two weeks to send the whole camp. One sees a new show every 3 weeks with luck but the Germans clamp down on entertainment as soon as we are "uncultured" and we always are!

The Red Cross parcels issue, postponed from the previous day, finally took place on 30 December. But this again caused friction between the SBO and the Commandant. In breach of the OKW order of 9 December, the Commandant had ordered that all tins were to be opened, rather than just one in ten. It took so long to open every tin that it meant parcels would be issued at a rate of only one per man every eighteen days, and no one would receive personal parcels. The issue for Peter Tomlinson's mess was disappointing: "Today issued with ? Red X parcel plus bulk issue of 3 tins of sardines amongst 10 men!" Neither was there any joy to be gained from German rations. The Reich bread was stale. No fresh bread had been baked since 11 December, and the *Oberzahlmeister* in charge of the cookhouse held back rations of potatoes, meat, sugar and margarine, which the prisoners badly needed.

The last day of 1941 was perfectly bloody. It had thawed during the night and the snow turned to slush. In the evening water poured off the roofs. A new order went round that no one would be allowed out of the huts to visit the latrines after 10.45pm, so it was back to the delights of the "thunderbox". The only good news, which the prisoners received with mixed feelings, was that the old Commandant, *Major* Gall, was back. Gall postponed the 10.45 lock-up order and permitted traffic between blocks up to one o'clock in the morning.

Peter Tomlinson made his last diary entry for 1941:

Ian and the 3 Mikes [Farr, Lindley and Trevor] went to the panto so I cooked a New Year's Eve dinner in their room, 12 feet by 6 feet! On their return I dished up soup made by Dutch cubes given by [?] Shutz. Mashed meat roll, peas and broccoli stolen by me under a sentry's nose. All mixed together and served up piping hot. Great success. Finished with crushed pineapple and orange jelly. Saw New Year in with great man Gates (stone deaf, very broad Australian but brilliant with his hands-point!!). John [Parker] was to have been with us but threw temperament last minute. Most enjoyable party.

As the New Year dawned, a somewhat less than sober Senior RAF Officer, "Hetty" Hyde, wrote his last letter of 1941 to his wife Kat:

A HAPPY NEW YEAR TO YOU! I HOPE I WONT HAVE TO WISH YOU THE SAME NEXT YEAR BY *KRIEGSGEFANGENEN* POST, BUT WILL BE ABLE TO DO SO IN PERSON! SO DONT SEND MY LONG SERVICE & GOOD CONDUCT MEDAL, MY MONKEY GLANDS AND BATH CHAIR, OUT IN MY NEXT UNIFORM PARCEL! I WISH I COULD HAVE GONE TO SEE "TARGET FOR TONIGHT" WITH YOU. I HOPE IT WAS BETTER THAN "THE LION HAS WINGS". MOST OF THE PAST SERVICE FILMS HAVE BEEN RATHER TRIPEISH. IT WOULD BE A HELL OF A THRILL TO GO TO THE FLICKS WITH YOU AGAIN. EXCEPT FOR A BRACE OF HISTORICAL GERMAN FILMS & SOME NEWS REELS AT STALAG LUFT, I HAVEN'T SEEN A FLICK SINCE I TOOK SILK! INCIDENTALLY, MY CABBAGE, IF YOU HAVEN'T ALREADY DONE SO — WOULD YOU INCLUDE A G.S. CAP, FIELD SERVICE, OFFICERS FOR THE USE OF — ONE, IN MY NEXT CLOTHING PARCEL (THE TYPE ONE CAN SIT ON — THE CAP, NOT THE PARCEL — NOT THAT I WANT THE CAP FOR SITTING ON.)
  SORRY THAT THIS LETTER IS FULL OF SUCH TRIPE — THERE ARE SO MANY THINGS THAT I WANT TO SAY TO YOU, BUT NOT TO THE CENSORS, NOT THAT THEY KNOW EITHER OF US FROM ADAM (OR EVE?). BUT YOU KNOW HOW I FEEL, MY DARLING. GOD BLESS & KEEP YOU. THIS SEPARATION WILL ONLY BE LIKE A SHORT & UNPLEASANT DREAM IN A FEW YEARS TIME.

So ended 1941 in Oflag VIB, Warburg. The past year had been one that most prisoners would prefer to forget. But 1942 would not exactly be all beer and skittles, either.

Chapter Five

Sorrow Behind Sorrow

Oflag VIB, Warburg-Dössel, January–May 1942

When the prisoners at Warburg awoke on Thursday, 1 January 1942, it was to a compound oozing mud and spattered with puddles. Owing to the visits exchanged the night before going on until one o'clock in the morning, many rose late, but Peter Tomlinson was among the few early risers: "Collected my utensils from room 21 in morning. Thawing hard. Place a mass of mud. Michael Lindley very kindly lent me a pair of boots. Enormous but serviceable. Sleeping better since receipt of extra blanket." The following day, Tomlinson

> Managed to get a loaf of bread on the Mart at 75 [points]. Great rejoicing. This bread is the best thing if you're really hungry. It fills one up admirably. When I first had it I couldn't touch it owing to its horrible smell, and also it seemed to be covered in fine sawdust. Since when necessity has forced me to eat and enjoy it. It is the German black bread. Not really black but dark brown and very sour tasting and smelling. Made of rye. It seems to keep fairly well, though inclined to mildew. Very satisfying when it is really hard because it takes so long to chew that it makes a meal quite a lengthy affair. The loaves are stamped with the date on top but we get them months old. 1/5 of a loaf a day. I wish it was three times as much!

On Saturday, 3 January the mud was worse than ever, but the Army still held a "Fun Fair" in the afternoon. In an interview with Brigadier Somerset the Commandant said he was tired of the endless flood of complaints from him, and that prisoners of war were there to receive orders, not to complain about them. The SBO replied that if the Germans adhered to the Geneva Convention he would have less to moan about. Peter Tomlinson recorded that day that "The SBO complained to the Swiss Commission that we were being given horse [meat] but it seems to be considered a delicacy in Switzerland. We were told we were very lucky!"

So bad was the food situation at this point that it had become an obsession, as Tomlinson felt moved to list the daily rations.

> My average daily meals: Breakfast 1/10 loaf of black bread. Margarine. Jam (if any). Tea or coffee. The Germans make tea from mint and coffee from acorns. Both filthy. 12.00. Plate of Reich soup (one good belch and you've lost it). Main meat ingredient horse. But not enough to impress it on you. Very stringy…Supper varies thank God. Depending on what we get from our ½ Red X parcel. Stew or bully or bacon, potatoes followed by prunes or raisins. Luckily I sometimes get asked out to tea by friends who receive private parcels. One eats all one can get trying hard to be polite and not too obviously famished. Ian MacKaskie [*sic*, Macaskie] is wonderful. From the moment I arrived he took me under his wing. He gave me a towel, tooth paste, tooth brush, cigarettes, tobacco and even a blanket. He is short himself I know. One becomes very selfish here — but not Ian or the 3 Mikes. I am always (it seems) feeding with them and when I am really starving they find out and feed me. Such kindness is golden. No letter since Xmas Eve. 7 in all [arrived for 16 men]. One has never looked forward to anything in one's life as one does to letter time. In most cases one draws a blank and hides one's

disappointment somehow. Supper tonight 1½ boiled potatoes, ½ tin apricots, ½ tin creamed rice, 3 slices of bread and jam. The place is still a mass of mud. How one longs for snow again and dryish feet. But most of all for the feel of grass underfoot and the sight and smell of flowers.

On Sunday the 4th conditions outside the huts were even worse, with officers becoming bogged down in the mud, and many went into self-imposed hibernation, leaving their huts only to go to the wash-house and the *Abort*, and to attend to camp business. Peter Tomlinson:

Stayed in room most of the day owing to rain and mud outside. Feel filthy. I would give anything for a bath. We get a hot shower of sorts once a fortnight. Water on 2 minutes. Off for 3 and on for two again. 36 men under 12 half hearted trickles of hottish water. Ian [Macaskie] and Michael Lindley came round in morning. We had some soup together in No1 DH. I don't often eat mine in spite of my hunger. It's so repulsive. Mostly turnips floating about in liquid with a few potatoes a[nd] bits of stringy horse. It's hot — but that's about all. Supper ½ tin sardines, mashed potatoes. Bread (3 slices), margarine and Blutwurst. The latter looks something like a nasty railway accident. I found a tooth in mine last week. No stoppings!

The mud was worse still the next day, and it was impossible for anyone to walk even a short distance without getting covered in the stuff. But one Army officer, Captain J W M Mansel of the Queen's Royal Regiment, did pluck up the courage to pay a call on Douglas Bader, who was unable to leave his hut unless escorted by two men, usually Gardner and Lubbock. Meanwhile, Peter Tomlinson had tea

with Ian who had Richard Wood [Lieutenant R Wood, the Rifle Brigade] along to meet me. He seemed short of food so didn't eat much. Supper ½ tin herrings. Fried bread. 1 baked potato. 1 slice bread and Canadian cheese. The latter rather case hardened and reluctant to part with its silver paper covering. No letters. Despair of ever getting any.

The Spangenberg old lags were still anxious about personal parcels, as they had still received none. The Commandant was rumoured to have telephoned Spangenberg to find out what had happened. There were some 10,000 American and Canadian communal parcels at Warburg, about 4,000 of which had been listed in the stores ledger, and prisoners were hoping some would soon be issued, but under the present system of opening every tin, issues were slow in coming and food was going off. The Germans wanted to change over to giving out personal parcels, but the SBO insisted that communal food parcels should have priority.

During the night there was a hard frost, so that on the morning of Tuesday, 6 January prisoners were able to leave their barracks and go on *Appell* treading confidently for the first time in weeks. Peter Tomlinson had his morning brew with John Morley, a Lieutenant in the Buffs.

We chatted 'til soup time. Walked with Shutz [?] in afternoon. Sunny day after night of hard frost. Thank God — no mud. Exercise made me very hungry. Lost control and eat dinner and supper together. ½ tin meat loaf. Fried bread. Toast and jam. Damned hungry now 2200 hrs.

That night, to the delight of the Air Force contingent, British aircraft passed overhead — Hampdens on roving patrols over Northern Germany.

Prisoners looking through the southern fence the next morning saw the distant sky illuminated by fires. There had been more frost during the night, and the ground was rock-hard, and Tomlinson, who had "Slept on and off" awoke to find "Ice in the buckets again. Washed early to avoid crush. There are 16 of us to 2 basins so one has to be slippy. If only one could be alone for a bit. We have to do everything in a milling mass — even sleep."

Another unpleasant side-effect of the hard frost was that it froze up the drainpipes from the urinal in the latrines, so that urine flooded the floor and seeped out into the compound. The latrine area therefore became a place to be avoided. This was not difficult for Peter Tomlinson, who was

"Terribly constipated. I go about once a week. Crouched next to several embarrassed souls. It's like giving birth to a child on Piccadilly and almost as painful!"

At about 4pm a fog set in, and the goon-boxes and parcels hut in the distance were barely visible. Supper that evening for Peter Tomlinson was "½ tin stew, ½ tin peas." Overnight there was yet more frost, this time "Unbelievable...So bad that ½ doz. bottles of canteen lemonade (saccharine and H_2O) burst as they froze solid. They went off like bullets and woke everyone up. Slept in Mike Lindley's balaclava and scarf. Fully dressed. I was frozen."

On Thursday the 8th, the SBO received a letter from the OKW saying that if the undisciplined behaviour by junior officers in the camp was due to cramped conditions, then all their impedimenta should be removed to clear space in the huts. The SBO replied that both the OKW and the Protecting Power had already agreed that the camp was overcrowded, and that in any case the prisoners were entitled to their so-called "impedimenta" by the Geneva Convention.

A rumour was now circulating that the RAF contingent was to be moved to Saxony. "I hope not," wrote Tomlinson. "I have lots of army friends here and these journeys in cattle trucks are hell. Still no letters. It seems an age without news."

Despite the rumour of an impending move, Eric Foster called on "Nellie" Ellen and asked if he was still on the tunnelling list. Ellen assured him that he was. Foster asked if he could discuss his scheme further with "Hetty" Hyde, and Ellen said he would see what he could do.

On 9 January Tomlinson decided that it was

too cold to go out. Lay on my bunk and read Wilde's *De Profundis*. I know what he means when he says: "Behind joy and laughter there may be a temperament coarse, hard and callous. But behind sorrow there is always sorrow. Pain, unlike pleasure, wears no mask."

Despite the bitterly cold weather, the Germans announced a clothing parade for the ex-Lübeck prisoners — the opportunity for which Bader, Gardner, Lubbock and Captain Smith had been waiting since before Christmas. Collecting their escape kit from the committee, and wearing greatcoats over their civilian duds, they joined the parade at the gate and marched out of the compound towards the clothing store. Inside the store, under cover of a loud diversion planned by Captain P D Maud of the Somerset Light Infantry, Gardner picked the lock and the four slipped into the empty room. It was cold in the room, and outside, where Maud and his friends were faking the head-count, a thin snow carpeted the frosty ground. But darkness fell early, and at 8pm they heard a cacophony by the wire as Peter Tunstall created a diversion by rattling tins. The searchlights turned obligingly towards the noise, the signal for the four escapers to make their getaway. Gardner quietly opened the window. First out was Smith, followed by Lubbock, Bader and finally Gardner himself. In Indian file, they walked along the "High Street", Smith about fifteen yards in front of the other three, who were slightly bunched up. Smith had just reached the shadows when a German soldier ran out of one of the huts, apparently on his way to the latrines, and saw Bader, Gardner and Lubbock illuminated by the glare of the arc lamps. His face registered shock, and he started yelling *"Hilfe! Hilfe!"* ("Help! Help!") Jackboots crunched through the snow as guards zeroed in on them from all directions and in seconds the three were surrounded. But Smith had made good his escape.

The guards started jostling Bader and his two companions towards the guard-room and one of the NCOs, unaware that Bader had artificial legs, brought his rifle butt down, with bone-breaking force, on one of his feet to hurry him along. He gaped with amazement when the blow was received with equanimity. "We had difficulty in smothering our laughter in an otherwise depressing situation," Lubbock recalled later. The angry NCO banged harder and harder until one of his comrades explained why Bader felt no pain and told him to stop making a fool of himself. In the guard-room they were brought before Rademacher, who demanded to know how they had escaped. "We walked through the wire," said Bader. "Did you?" replied Rademacher. "Well, now you can try walking through the bars because you are going to the cells." He went away to make arrangements, but came back shortly afterwards red-faced and tight-lipped. The cells were already full — and there was a waiting list. They would have to go back to the compound and await their turn.

For the rest of the prisoners "kriegie" life had carried on as usual, Tomlinson receiving news from Ian that one of his three brothers, Paul, had proposed to his girlfriend Jean. "Shutz [?] came to tea. Nothing much to give him — but he said he wasn't hungry! John [Parker] went to Panto in the evening so I cooked supper ready for his return. We ate between us 1 tin sardines, fried potatoes, fried bread, porridge. Quite a blow out!"

Routine was disrupted that night when at 10.30, as a result of Bader & Co's escape attempt, the Germans conducted a head-count in every barracks. *Appell* the following morning was longer than usual, partly because it was conducted by a new officer unfamiliar with the ropes. Although he looked the personification of Teutonic efficiency, even down to his monocle, he forgot to carry pencil and paper. For the rest of the day the compound was crawling with Germans: the Commandant, limping and supporting himself with a stick; the *Lageroffizier*; another carrying what looked like a map case; and the monocled novice. "Tommy" Tomlinson, still mindful of feeling filthy, was not going to let these events deter him from "dhobying":

Washed my two handkerchiefs and only pair of pyjamas in morning — boiling some water on our tiny stove for the job. Ian and I visited Harold Hopper [Lieutenant H J A Hopper, Royal Armoured Corps] in the *Revier* [infirmary] after lunch. He has pneumonia and looks pretty bad. Poor devil! The noise in his room is as bad as in ours and he had 15 others in his "ward". I remember my fortnight there with the food poisoning. Pretty grim. Am reading Fenby's *Delius as I Knew Him*. A great book. How much the human mind and body can suffer — yet carry on. Or was Delius an exception? Bitter weather. I cannot sleep for the penetrating cold. Everything in the room is frozen solid when we wake up. No letters for an age. Oh well!

During the next two days, in which the weather turned colder, the heating was turned off in the No2 Dining Hall and the pipes froze up in the wash-houses, leaving the prisoners without water. Peter Tomlinson recalled Sunday, 11 January as the "Coldest day I have ever experienced. Really wicked. Stayed in my bunk all day with head below blankets." He interrupted his bed bashing towards the evening when he was "Asked out to tea by the Poles who had a magnificent repast waiting for me including Sauerkraut — which I can't stomach. But this treated Polish fashion was quite palatable as Sauerkraut goes. Took some time to go to sleep."

At last, on Monday, 12 January, he received a portrait postcard from some family friends, the Widderburns. "What joy!...gives me unspeakable joy and pleasure, particularly as it is a very good photograph of the whole family. Bless them. How nice to hear from them and learn I am not forgotten. Such kind good people."

Even more welcome was the bulk issue of Red Cross food that was made the following day: half a tin of *pâté de foie gras* ("of all things!"), one tin of bully-beef, half a tin of jam, one tin of "tunny" (tuna) fish and some Turkish cigarettes for each man. Tomlinson, along with some other prisoners, also enjoyed a hot shower that afternoon. "Life seems almost bearable again. Sweetened barley for supper. Very good."

On the 14th the Germans conducted a search of the No2 Dining Hall and warned prisoners that anyone leaving their huts in the meantime would be shot. Tomlinson stayed in his bunk and carried on reading *De Profundis*, which really impressed him. "Porridge for lunch. Have saved mine to eat tonight when I get really hungry." On evening *Appell* the *Lageroffizier* announced that in future all Battalions would be checked at the same time and that none would be dismissed until each Brigade total had been proved correct.

On Thursday, 15 January, at about 6.30am, a party of two hundred senior Army officers left for Spangenberg. It included Major-General Fortune, all Colonels and Lieutenant-Colonels (with the exception of Kennedy, who took over as SBO), and about a hundred and forty Majors. This was less than the 1,000 that both the Protecting Power and the OKW insisted should leave and therefore did little to ease the overcrowding. That morning only two of the taps were working in one of the wash-houses, still not much good for a camp now holding 3,500 officers and orderlies.

Later, on *Appell*, the prisoners had to stand on parade for thirty-five minutes in the biting cold owing to a dispute over the figure for the orderlies' Battalion, where the count had been chaotic, and lack of agreement over the number who had left for Spangenberg and the numbers out on working parties. After about twenty minutes the prisoners took to marching round in circles to keep warm. Those *krank im Zimmer* had to parade in one room in each hut, but Lieutenant-Colonel Kennedy, was told that in future there would be no such thing as automatic *krank im Zimmer*. Anyone who reported sick had to go to the camp infirmary and get a chit from the German MO. Things were worse at evening *Appell*, which lasted forty-five minutes. Afterwards Ian Macaskie, who had received a tobacco parcel, dropped in on Peter Tomlinson and gave him some De Rieke cigarettes. Tomlinson also drew half a Red Cross parcel in the evening. The half-parcel per man issue would continue over the next few days.

Appell next morning took half an hour. But kriegie morale received a boost from two sources. Firstly, the camp had running water again. Secondly, while they were on evening *Appell*, a lorry loaded with Canadian Red Cross packing cases arrived and the parade was told that another three were to follow. It would mean another half-parcel issue per head for the entire camp. Full-throated roars from the paraded prisoners.

On the down side, the British camp organisation was in chaos owing to the transfer of the "old and bold" to Spangenberg. These men had occupied leading positions in camp education, entertainment, sport and general administration, and although they had been replaced, the appointments had not been sufficiently promulgated. Consequently few prisoners knew who was responsible for running each department and were running around like headless chickens trying to track them down.

News also reached the compound that Captain Smith, who had made a clean getaway in the 9 January break, had been recaptured. Back in the compound, awaiting his turn in the cooler, he told Bader, Gardner and Lubbock that he had hidden aboard a cattle-truck and had been captured after five days of nearly freezing to death.

The next seven days were "Bitterly cold," recorded Tomlinson. "Spent most of my days on my bed trying to keep warm. Getting through a lot of books. Life seems very grim and hopeless and writing doesn't seem worthwhile."

On Saturday, 17 January the Germans announced that in future prisoners would have to leave their barracks for *Appell* fifteen minutes before they were due to parade and that *Appelle* were to last not less than twenty minutes. Tony Trumble decided on a change of address that day and moved in with another ex-Lübeck prisoner, "Flush" Kane. Two nights later there was another show in the camp theatre, a comedy called *The Black Eye* — once again to a professional and highly polished standard. The following day morale picked up again with an issue of mail and clothing. It was just as well that more clothing was handed out: the temperature that morning was -4°F (-20°C), with 36°F (2.22°C) of frost.

On 21 January "Hetty" Hyde wrote again to Kat:

BIG NEWS TODAY — I GOT MY TWO PARCELS YESTERDAY! THE TOBBACCO [sic] ONE WAS FROM THE B.A.T. WITH 1LB OF CAPSTAN IN IT, WHICH IS GRAND. THE OTHER WAS THE UNIFORM PARCEL THAT YOU SENT OFF IN AUGUST. THE TUNIC AND SLACKS WERE THERE...I SHALL LOOK AWFULLY SMART NOW! NO MAIL, EXCEPT XMAS CARDS FROM MY M.P. & DOT. I HAVE CHANGED MY QUARTERS SINCE I LAST WROTE. I NOW LIVE IN A SMALL ROOM (INHABITTED [sic] BY GEN. FORTUNE UNTIL HE LEFT LAST WEEK) WITH S/LD S S MURRAY, WHO IS THE OLDEST R.A.F. OFFICER KRIEGIE...VERY NICE CHAP...HE WAS PROMOTED S/LD ON THE SAME LIST AS I WAS, BUT MISSED HIS PROMOTION TO W/C BEING IN THE BAG. WE HAVE MADE A SMALL SKATING RINK HERE — I HAVEN'T RISKED MY NECK ON IT YET — 30° FROST YESTERDAY — SO IT FREEZES QUICKLY ENOUGH! COULD YOU SEND A BRACE OF PIPES IN MY NEXT CLOTHING PARCEL IN CASE THE OTHER IS A GONER?

Peter Tomlinson recommenced his diary jottings on Thursday, 22 January:

This last week has been incredibly cold. Temp. yesterday -36°. 2 letters from Mum bless her. Also 1 from Twink [David Tomlinson] and one from Aunty. Great fun. Have just heard that a clothing parcel for me has arrived in the camp. I can hardly sit still. I hope to draw it early next week. Went to supper with Shutz [?], Derek [Heaton-Nichols] and Peter [Harding] last night. Played bridge after. They gave me an excellent meal. Awfully pleased letters have started to come in again… ½ Canadian Red X parcel issued today. The days seem to pass fairly quickly — for which I am thankful. One becomes so introspective living this confined existence with no peace and solitude. Tempers fray all too easily and one lives selfishly only for letters and food parcels. One dreams of home and comforts continually but the great day when freedom, and all it stands for, will be mine seems immeasurably remote. A convict does at least know the length of his sentence.

Saturday the 24th was a day of excitement followed by disillusionment. A rumour had spread amongst the RAF that 10,000 parcels had arrived from Spangenberg and they decided to "bash" all their remaining food. It turned out that the consignment was only seven hundred personal parcels from Canada. When Captain John Mansel visited Bader, Gardner and Lubbock that afternoon for tea he found all three completely brassed off and that conversation with them was impossible. "God knows why," he wrote in his diary, "it was really most embarrassing." That night Al Matthews and Norman Thomas decided to gather in bets as to when the war would end, and trooped from hut to hut in search of wagers. With America now in the war, Mansel optimistically predicted September 1942! Al Matthews was in particularly good spirits, and in one room described the ice-hockey rackets in Canada.

On Sunday, 25 January Commander Beale gave a lecture in the theatre on the situation in the Mediterranean and Colin Dilly handed in a contribution to "The Quill" — a sheet of detailed plans for modellers of Elizabethan galleons. As the camp newspaper did the rounds, Dilly's plans would provide occupation for officers for months. Several of the Air Force contributed to "The Quill", among them Squadron Leaders John "Birdie" Barrett, Frank Campbell-Rogers, Don Gericke, Peter Mason and Frank Willan; and, from the junior officers, Harald Bjelke-Peterson, "Eski" Campbell, Edmund Cathels, Phil Cook, James Davies, Max Dunn, Edward Fairbank, John Green (an ex-Barth kriegie), Clive Hall, Derek Heaton-Nichols, R R Henderson, Wilf Hetherington, Eugeniusz Hubicki, Reg Jacoby, Theo Johnson, Fred Litchfield, Joe McCarthy, Al Matthews, Ian Potts, Fred Shorrock, Howard Taylor, Percy Thomas, Karel Trojacek, R A R White (RNZAF) and Gordon Wright. Among the contributors from the Fleet Air Arm was Nathaniel Hearle of the Royal Marines. Mainly they handed in drawings and paintings — the most prolific artist being Dilly — while on one occasion Matthews submitted a short piece on fishing in the Maritimes. Poor old Dilly came in for some ribbing over one of his paintings, of a strip between the warning-wire and the fence, which he had called "Herbaceous Border 1942 – VIB". Alf Mungovan recalls:

We kidded him a great deal about the colourful flowers, which we had not seen, until one day he invited us to join him by the wire. "Bend over and look at the scene from between your legs," he said. And sure enough, even to our untrained eyes the colours were indeed more intense than when viewed from the normal position.

On Tuesday, 27 January the temperature plummeted to -18°F (-27.8°C), followed by heavy snowfalls for the next three days. The water supply was frozen solid and the main pump burst, which would leave the camp without water for four days.

Eric Foster was finally able to have a discussion with "Nellie" Ellen about his proposed tunnel scheme. Ellen told him he would get his opportunity "as soon as possible". But Foster could not pin him down to a date. "I cannot commit myself at this stage," said Ellen. Feeling frustrated and impotent, Foster asked for an interview with the Senior British Officer, Lieutenant-Colonel Kennedy.

Over the past five months no new prisoners had been sent to Warburg, but several small parties arrived from Obermassfeld and various other hospitals, all of them having been wounded when they were captured in 1941. Their presence gave some substance to the rumour that the Germans were gathering all the sick and wounded in one camp in anticipation of resuming negotiations towards a POW exchange. Among them were: Acting Squadron Leader C G C Rawlins DFC, RAFVR; Flight Lieutenants F H Babcock RAFVR and R B Barr; and Pilot Officers J G N Braithwaite and W M MacKay RCAF.

At the beginning of the war Colin Guy Champion Rawlins had been a humble Volunteer Reserve Pilot Officer, but had been promoted to Flying Officer on 1 May 1940, Flight Lieutenant a year later and within less than a fortnight was a Flight Commander on his bomber squadron, No144, which when he was shot down was stationed at Hemswell. On 11/12 May 1941, eighty-one aircraft set out to bomb the harbour at Bremen. On the return leg, Rawlins's Hampden was bounced at about 0200 hours by *Oberleutnant* Helmut Woltersdorf of *II/NJG1*. Two of the crew were killed outright and the Hampden crashed at Hoogkarspel, six kilometres west-south-west of Enkhuizen. Rawlins's navigator, Pilot Officer R F J Featherstone RCAF, had been sent to Spangenberg; they were now reunited at Warburg and together would traipse through the same camps for the rest of the war.

Pilot Officer Braithwaite had also flown Hampdens from Hemswell, but with No61 Squadron. He had been shot down on 7/8 July 1941, on the same night as Peter Langmead, Eric Masters, Johnny Agrell and Donald Elliott. They had been sent to Frankfurt and Cologne in Halifaxes and Whitleys, but that night forty Hampdens from Nos 61 and 106 Squadrons were also put up with Mönchengladbach as their target. Two were lost. Braithwaite, who had taken off at 2300 hours, hit the Luftwaffe's night-fighter box defences across Belgium and Holland and was attacked by *Leutnant* Reinhold Knacke of *I/NJG1*. Knacke's air-gunners torched the aircraft and three of the crew burned to death. Braithwaite, his own face badly burnt, crashed the aircraft about twenty minutes after midnight at Meerssen, some six kilometres north-east of Maastricht. He spent almost six months in one hospital after another before fetching up at Warburg, and would be transferred to Stalag Luft III in May 1942.

Pilot Officer MacKay, from Calgary, Alberta, and Flight Lieutenant Robert Benjamin Barr had been involved in the RAF's major daylight attack on Brest harbour on Thursday, 24 July 1941 — the same elaborate and much-vaunted "Operation Sunrise" that saw Johnny Clayton enter the bag. MacKay was Wellington observer in No405 Squadron, Ronnie Morgan's old outfit. His pilot was the squadron's CO, Wing Commander P A Gilchrist DFC; and the rear-gunner, Flying Officer R G M Whigham, was not only the squadron's gunnery leader but also the son of a distinguished and highly decorated general. Gilchrist led his squadron off from Pocklington at 1130 hours and two of them were shot down by Me109s, along with eight other Wimpeys from Nos 12, 40, 75, 101, 103, 104 and 218 Squadrons. Flying Officer Whigham was killed when the Messerschmitts attacked. Gilchrist executed a crash-landing fifteen kilometres north-west of Brest. Along with his second pilot and the nose-gunner he evaded capture. MacKay and the wireless operator, Sergeant R H Westburg, were too badly injured to make a run for it and were captured.

Robert Barr had been on No144 Squadron, North Luffenham, with Anthony Hayward and "Pring" Pringle. His Hampden was shot down by Me109s and his observer and two air-gunners killed. He crash-landed not far from Landivisiau, twenty-one kilometres north-west of the target.

Four more prisoners arrived from Obermassfeld on Sunday, 1 February. They were Flight Lieutenant J L Nunn RAFVR; Flying Officer S H Dowse RAFVR, and Pilot Officers J D Beresford and J R Scott.

John Leslie Nunn had been shot down and badly wounded on 16/17 August 1941. He was a Manchester pilot on No97 Squadron, which five days previously had lost Jim Little and Mick Geoghegan to captivity and had since moved to Coninsgby. Nunn had taken off at 2250 hours to take part in the same raid on Düsseldorf as Hugh Keartland and the now deceased Pilot Officer Robinson. His aircraft was shot down by an Me110 from *I/NJG1* flown by *Hauptmann* Werner Streib. John Nunn gave the order to bale out, but one of the air-gunners, Sergeant H Currie, had been wounded and was unable to leave the aircraft. Nunn crash-landed the Manchester marginally inside the Belgian border. The two were taken to Aachen hospital, where Currie died from his wounds. The rear-gunner, Flight Sergeant P Williams, was also dead, having been killed after baling out. Nunn was subsequently moved to Dulag Luft, then to Hohemark clinic and then to Obermassfeld.

Pilot Officers Beresford and Scott were Spitfire pilots — the former from No54 Squadron, the latter from No610 (City of Chester) Squadron, both based at Hornchurch. They had been up on the same day that Wing Commander Joe Kayll, the Hornchurch Wing Leader and No54's CO, was shot down, that is, Wednesday, 25 June 1941. Indeed, young Beresford had his wings clipped on the same operation, "Circus No23", a raid on Longuenesse airfield near St-Omer. Following "Circus No23" there was an evening fighter sweep by the Biggin Hill, Hornchurch and Tangmere Wings in which four Spitfires were badly shot up by Me109s. One pilot was killed, two returned to base wounded, and Scott was shot down over France.

Sydney Hastings Dowse — a cheeky, fresh-faced twenty-two-year-old nicknamed "The Laughing Boy" — was a Londoner who had joined the RAFVR in July 1937. When the war started he was in No608 (North Riding) Squadron. An Auxiliary Air Force unit formed as a fighter squadron at Thornaby, in Yorkshire, in March 1930, No608 had been given a new role in 1939 as a General Reconnaissance unit within No16 Group. It flew Ansons, Blackburn Bothas, Blenheims and Hudsons. Dowse eventually transferred to No1 PRU, flying stripped-down Spitfires from Benson. On Friday, 15 August 1941 he was over Brest harbour photographing the German battleships *Scharnhorst* and *Gneisenau* when Me109s bounced him from up-sun. His Spitfire caught fire and he ditched not far from Brest. Despite a leg injury, he tried to swim ashore, where he hoped he could contact the Resistance. But as he neared the beach he saw a crowd of French women waving to him and heard them shouting welcomes to *l'aviateur anglais*. His hope of evading capture was stillborn; the activity on the beach drew the attention of everyone within earshot and Dowse was captured on making landfall.

After a period in the naval hospital at Brest he was transferred to the hospital at Stadtroda, from which he escaped on 1 December, only to be recaptured three days later at the Dutch border. He was thereupon transferred to the hospital at Obermassfeld attached to Stalag IXC, Bad Sulza. On 21 January 1942 he exchanged identities with a Canadian POW and mingled with a fatigue party. He then underwent another change of identity by acquiring a Belgian army uniform. While working in the German compound he ducked into the latrines, where he doffed his Belgian uniform under which he wore workman's attire. Thus disguised, he pretended to inspect a water-wheel near the wire fence and after a suitable interval walked nonchalantly through the gates. Although he had no forged papers, he did have some German money, so he walked to the local station and boarded the first of a succession of trains that would take him to Erfurt, Cologne and Werwitz. From there he continued on foot through deep snow towards the Belgian frontier. But the snow was two feet deep in places and by now Dowse was suffering from extreme exhaustion and snow blindness. For more than a day he wandered about in a complete daze, finally coming to his senses in a railway station as he was trying to buy a ticket to Brussels. He beat a hasty retreat and hid up in some nearby woods, setting out again after a few hours' rest. At last, towards dusk on Monday, 26 January 1942, he reached the Dutch frontier. Unfortunately he was spotted by the *Grenzpolizei* and fired upon. Unable to run because of frostbite, he was compelled to give himself up. After another spell in hospital, he was escorted to Warburg.

The day these men arrived at Oflag VIB a "latrinogramme" went round the camp that Warburg was to remain open for the duration of the war and that no more prisoners were to be transferred. It would be their "final resting place", and the POW complement would increase to 7,000. The following day Peter Tomlinson recorded:

Since last writing have grown quite used to snow and almost to the cold. The night before I drew my clothing parcel was fraught with excitement. I couldn't sleep. Comparable to Xmas Eve in one's childhood. At the parcel hatch at 10 sharp — praying hard for a lenient portion. 5 other officers in front of me. The waiting was hell. And then at last mine was put on the counter. A big one. Lovely. What a thrill. Visions of toothpaste, Rolls razor, towels, pyjamas, socks and shoes — above all shoes — flashed through my mind. The string was cut. The German censor had been alright with the others — so I wasn't worried. I'd give him some soap if necessary. The brown paper and cardboard was pulled aside and...oh God. My service overcoat (I have a Red X one) and my very best summer Anderson trousers. That's all. I nearly wept. But what is one more disappointment among so many.

On Wednesday the 4th, "Tommy" received a letter from his brother Paul. "Great rejoicing. This has taken four months to reach me. My rank wasn't clear so it went to Stalag VI[A]. Play much bridge, read, hope, worry, fret and pant for news from home. Such is one's life."

During the night of 5/6 February four blankets went missing from the camp de-lousing hut. They belonged to the Russians, had not been de-loused and were known to be infested with typhus. The hospital staff feared an outbreak of the disease. The blocked latrine drains had flooded again, and the hospital staff were likewise worried that, when the thaw came, the sports ground would be impregnated with filth, and that anyone who suffered open injuries would contract septicaemia.

Eric Foster, meanwhile, was still straining at the leash. He had already made the trap for his tunnel, in the temporary guise of an easy chair. Finally granted an interview with the SBO, he asked how high he was on the tunnelling list. The SBO said he could not reply until he had referred the matter to the Escape Committee. On Sunday, 8 February Foster, along with Nat Maranz and Warren Sandman, were called before Wing Commander Hyde. He told them that some Army officers had registered the tunnel scheme in October, and therefore had priority. It could be a court martial offence if they proceeded with their scheme without prior authority. Reluctantly, they resigned themselves to the situation and dissolved their syndicate.

On Monday, 9 February the Germans brought in labourers and carts and started cleaning up the camp, ready for an impending visit by the International Committee of the Red Cross. This turned out to be one representative, who arrived the next day, and was unimpressed by the German clean-up campaign. When he left, Rademacher's men conducted a search of the brick block, and were so painstaking that they ended up doing only a few rooms. Two days later they switched their activities to the bottom end of the camp.

The ex-Spangenberg kriegies were now receiving their personal parcels. These had apparently been at Spangenberg since 14 November. The Germans made no apology for this disgraceful state of affairs.

Suddenly, to his surprise, Eric Foster was given the green light by "Nellie" Ellen to start a tunnel. The fact that the Army officers had a lien on the potato store did not prevent him from digging a tunnel from his own barrack block. "How long will it be before you can start?" asked Ellen.

Foster paused, then said he could start almost immediately.

"But what about the trap?" asked Ellen. "Surely you know it'll take some time to prepare the trap!"

Foster explained that he had already made it, and showed him where it was. Ellen gave him a list of twenty-five officers who were on the escape roster, and from it Foster chose Christopher Cheshire, John Clelland, Oliver Hedley, Peter Pine and "Flip" Rance. The following day they installed their trap. After prising up several floorboards near the skirting board of Foster's room and making them into a solid section, they attached two angles carved out of wood. Then they fixed a frame under the floor so that when the section was being replaced it would easily slide back into position. To stop the section wobbling or being lifted up by the goons, they had cunningly built the frame with two slightly tapering sides and a sliding cross-brace. By sliding a knife between the section and the floorboards proper, they could move the cross-brace into place so that it slid into the two angles under the section. To lift the section, they simply ran the knife in the opposite direction.

Under the floor they carefully scraped up the surface layer of pine needles and dropped Foster's ready-made trap into the space. The trap consisted of a wooden tray filled with earth, and over this they spread the pine needles. Rance was appointed "Officer i/c Trap", a position of considerable responsibility, as he had to ensure that it was always carefully camouflaged and did not leave any tell-tale signs of wear and tear.

Sinking the vertical shaft began the next day, with two men taking turns being held upside down by their feet. The blood soon rushed to their heads and they could dig only for a short spell at a time. Finally they sunk a shaft seventeen feet deep and eighteen inches square, and at the bottom excavated a chamber seven feet long, six feet wide and six feet high to store clay pending dispersal. Within less than two weeks they were excavating the tunnel proper, working by the light of *Speisefett* lamps. For the next phase of the operation they intended to construct an underground railway, with a wooden trolley, so as to lighten the burden of transferring the clay from the face to the dispersal chamber. But at this point, two crises presented themselves: (i) lack of air, which caused the lamps to splutter out and the diggers to faint, and (ii) lack of timber with which to shore the tunnel and make the rails for their proposed trolley.

On Friday 13 February, the intense German security activity finally bore fruit, and the ferrets found a tunnel under No1 Dining Hall. The Commandant immediately put a ban on all entertainment in the makeshift theatre until further notice. Rademacher's men, in searching for the tunnel, had partially dismantled the building, and it struck Foster that this would be a good source for the supply of timber. That night, under cover of darkness and a team of stooges, Foster and his team crept out of their barracks and stole as much timber as they could, tying it into bundles with plaited string and stealthily dragging it back to their rooms. They now had their timber for shoring. For their railway tracks, they stripped wooden beadings from the hut walls. The trolley was made of bed-boards, with flanged wheels made from M&V tins. They made the rope, for pulling the trolley back and forth, by splicing together the string from Red Cross parcels. Sometimes they used the trolley to propel themselves along the tunnel at the end of a digging shift, thus avoiding the exhausting business of having to crawl its entire length. However, this caused too much wear and tear on the rope, the trolley and the railway lines, so they used this method as rarely as possible.

The problem of illuminating the tunnel would also have to be solved by theft. They decided to install electricity and "borrow" some flex from the camp's public address system. Equipped with makeshift cutters, they would have to shin up the telegraph poles at night to cut the wires down, and accordingly spent the nights of 12/13 and 13/14 February watching the movements of the guards patrolling the perimeter fence.

Yet more arrivals from Obermassfeld: Pilot Officers K H Anthony RCAF and W Beckingham; and Sub-Lieutenant (A) E K Margetts RNVR.

William Beckingham was Pilot Officer MacDonald's WOP/AG, and had been wounded in the daylight Blenheim raid on Rotterdam on 28 August 1941. Pilot Officer Anthony, another native of Toronto to swell the growing ranks of Canadians behind the wire, was from No403 Squadron, which was still under the command of Bren Morris when he was shot down on 19 August, the same day as Hurricane pilot "Jock" McKechnie. During the morning "Circus No81", consisting of six Blenheims, attacked Gosnay. The Luftwaffe reacted in force and five Spitfires were shot down. Three of the pilots were killed, one survived a ditching and was recovered by Air-Sea Rescue, and Anthony was captured.

Sub-Lieutenant Margetts was a Fleet Air Arm pilot whose squadron, No816, had been attached to Coastal Command at Detling for anti-shipping operations off the French and Dutch coasts. On Tuesday, 3 June 1941, while attacking enemy shipping, Margetts' Swordfish was shot down, his crew killed and Margetts himself badly wounded.

Undeterred by his abortive escape attempt by tunnel the previous October, Dennis Armitage had also embarked on another "dienst". This time he planned a considerably more ambitious tunnel. The space underneath the No1 Battalion huts, which the RAF and FAA occupied, was usually the final destination of most of the earth excavated from the little tunnels around the camp perimeter. Armitage discovered that there was still ample room for earth from his proposed tunnel, and decided that, rather than digging another hole from the perimeter area, he should start from his room in Barrack No6, which he shared with "Dim" Strong, "Buck" Casson and Doug Cooper. The tunnel would be driven in a northerly direction — opposite to that of Melville Kennedy's. It would be 300 feet long, and surface some 150 feet outside the camp, near the German quarters. The logic behind this was that the Germans would not suspect a tunnel to come up in that area. It would also take it beyond the range of the dog-handlers and searchlights. Three-hundred feet was an inordinate length to dig, but the disadvantages were largely outweighed by the fact that the dispersal of spoil would not be a problem. The dirt could be scattered underneath the same building, and there would be no kriegies staggering down the steps of the hut carrying loads of earth. Furthermore, when the ferrets saw the dirt piling up, they would blitz one of the huts nearest the perimeter, thinking that it must have come from there. It was a great inconvenience to have somebody digging from one's room, and Armitage sought approval from his Mess-mates, who assented, and two of them joined the team. Eventually there were ten men in the team, including "Basher" Beauclair and Douglas Cooper.

After cutting a trap-door in the floor, they dug a hole in the ground beneath and installed another trap, which they disguised with a little pile of dry earth. They then sunk a shaft some fifteen feet deep, and set off toward the wire. Everything went like clockwork. Like Eric Foster, Armitage decided to install an underground railway line, using strips of wood stolen from a hut that was being built in the compound. The trolley, too, was easy to make. The diggers filled it with earth and then dragged it along using a home-made rope. Lighting was a problem, because *Speisefett* lamps — as Foster had so often found — used up too much precious oxygen and tended to splutter out. Armitage and Beauclair, after some head-scratching and chin-rubbing, decided on the same solution as Foster: to install electric lighting using wire stolen from the loudspeakers. Beauclair and two others volunteered for the job.

Another issue of parcels was made on the 14th, but the carbide issue was late and most rooms had run out, so those without electricity were unable to read, write or carry on with their hobbies at night. Snow was falling every night, and on the twice-daily roll-calls the RAF had snowball fights, with Douglas Bader sitting on his stool while the snowballs whizzed past his ears.

That night the Foster gang rushed out of their barracks towards the wire, shinned up the loudspeaker poles, and using home-made wire-cutters secured several lengths of cable, other members of the team standing below rolling the cable into coils. Within ten minutes the wire was hidden in the tunnel, with the trap shut.

The next day, Sunday, 15 February, Wing Commander Hyde sent for Foster and told him that "Basher" Beauclair had also been poised to steal the cable, but had been beaten to it by Foster's team. He wanted to know if Foster would be prepared to share the wire with Beauclair. But Foster pointed out that there wasn't enough wire to go round, and Hyde accepted it. (As for Beauclair, he was a good sport and felt no resentment. He and Armitage pilfered what wire they could from around the camp, and eventually had a coil of about 600 feet.)

That day, Peter Tunstall and Dominic Bruce started a ten-day sentence in the cooler — punishment for their part in the escape attempt led by Peter Stevens. (By the end of his stint, Tunstall had clocked up no fewer than a hundred and five days of solitary.) Even in the cells they managed to put themselves in bad odour with the Germans, Bruce picking the locks and letting his fellow miscreants out of their cells to play cards, and Tunstall being found with a sketch of a gun-holster. The Germans were well and truly fed up with the pair of them, and decided to take them before a court martial.

Bader, Lubbock, Gardner and Smith were also undergoing their sentence in mid-February. They, too, had been "awarded" ten days each. On the seventh night, after the guard had locked up and gone, Gardner picked the lock of his cell door with a piece of wire and paid a visit on Bader who, lying on his bunk reading, was struck dumb. Bader joined him in the corridor and they unlocked Lubbock's cell. The trio then started exploring the cell block. They encountered no

Germans and discovered that only two doors lay between them and freedom. Bader wanted to make a break straight away, but the others advised against acting impetuously. Snow still lay on the ground, and they had no food, maps, compass or money. The Germans would not expect an escape from the cooler, and it would be a shame to spoil a good scheme with inadequate preparation. They decided to return to their cells. When the thaw came, they would earn a spell in solitary, have escape equipment smuggled in, and make their escape then. Three days later, when they returned to circulation, they registered the scheme with the Escape Committee, who set a date for May.

Oflag VIB was now all but cut off by snow from the world outside. A blizzard had blocked the road to Warburg with heavy drifts and in some places telegraph poles were completely covered. There was only a narrow path open to the railway station. While the kriegies were at last rejoicing in the plentiful supply of food, they resisted the impulse to "bash" it because no further supplies were likely until the snow had disappeared. More carbide for the goon-lamps had to be collected from the station, and as all the orderlies were on snow-clearing fatigues, Colonel Kennedy offered to get together an officers' fatigue party to do the job. The officers were, in any case, by now acting as their own orderlies, doing the washing up and fetching their own coal and rations. By Wednesday, 18 February the carbide issue was back to normal, with two days' ration being doled out that day and a further ration promised for three days' time. But clothing was still a vexing issue, as issues were still under German control. Their newspapers that day were full of Singapore falling, news that left the kriegies bewildered and embittered. Closer to home, typhus had broken out in the Russian compound. Two days later four dead Russians were taken into town for burial. On Sunday, 15 March, Bruce and Tunstall were sent to Colditz, which they reached the next day.

(3)

By early April the RAF were excavating at least four tunnels. "Bush" Kennedy's tunnel, which had been started from Barrack No7 in October, had been reopened in February, and despite flooding, falls and the discovery of the two dummy tunnels, was still lurching towards the wire. Squadron Leader Armitage's tunnel from Barrack No6, meanwhile, was making good progress. But the third, run by Eric Foster's syndicate, was encountering problems. The clay ceiling of the storage chamber was drying and falling out in big lumps. To shore it up they had to line the ceiling with bed-boards (stolen from a bunk belonging to one of their room-mates who was in the sick bay) and prop the boards up with the wooden posts that, until then, had lined the High Street. Lack of oxygen continued to worry them, and they set about designing some form of air pump. Their first effort — a fan attached to the motor of an electric razor and placed inside an air pipeline made of M&V tins set in the clay wall — was not at all satisfactory. Next they tried a kitbag, with the bottom removed, and flaps made of tin and the leather from boxing gloves. This seemed to work, pushing the foul air from the face of the tunnel back to the entrance.

As the tunnel neared the wire one of the digging shifts encountered a boulder that was too resistant to their improvised digging implements to break up and too big to roll along the tunnel to the chamber. Foster and Peter Pine, the Californian, decided to dig a pit in the floor, and dig around the rock so it would fall into the pit. They spent an entire shift picking the boulder free, until it fell into the pit with a thud that sent vibrations all the way up the tunnel. Those working in the chamber said it sounded like "a clap of thunder." It took another two shifts to fill the dome left by the rock and to shore the roof with timber.

They then discovered that the tunnel was veering to one side, and thus would not surface at the anticipated point of exit. Flight Lieutenant Lewis-Dale, who was a Bachelor of Science in Engineering and something of a mathematician, suggested they keep a lighted lamp hanging from the roof of the chamber. Diggers at the face could then keep a regular check to make sure the lamp was always in view as the tunnel forged ahead. To compensate for the stretch that was "off true", they excavated a second chamber, and Lewis-Dale made the necessary calculations for them to resume digging in the right direction. Thereafter they used the chamber as a staging post where

211

they could turn around on leaving the tunnel, rather than having to snake backwards the entire length.

Foster's tunnel was progressing smoothly, and nearing completion, when he was sent to the cooler for his last attempt to escape from Spangenberg. While he was undergoing his sentence one of Rademacher's "ferrets" discovered the electric wire leading to the tunnel entrance and a search was instigated. The Germans "blitzed" the barrack, but found nothing, a tribute to Rance's trap security. Not to be outdone, though, the Jerries dug a deep trench between the barrack block and the trip-wire, and finally broke through to the tunnel. Rademacher and his men filled it in using their usual insanitary method: with the ordure sucked from the *Abort* by the "honey-wagon". This was only one unpleasant by-product of tunnelling; another, recalls Clelland, was that "the only way of getting clean was a cold shower".

The fourth tunnel, also started in February, had its entrance in one of the orderlies' huts along the northern fence, and was being dug by a team of British, Canadians, Poles and Czechs twenty-five men strong. They planned to break well clear of the camp perimeter — a distance of about two hundred feet. The diggers, among them Joe Bryks, Maurice Butt, Wallace Cunningham, Sydney Dowse, "Danny" Król, David Lubbock and Karel Trojacek, kept the dimensions small — two feet wide and two feet six inches high — and hid the clay in the attic roof. Dirt and dust spilled between the cracks in the ceiling and onto beds, tables and utensils, making life unbearable for the hut's occupants. Although the clay was firm and the tunnel did not suffer as much from flooding as Kennedy's project, the diggers allowed themselves the luxury of shoring throughout, using boards taken from under the main floor of No2 Dining Hall. "The subsoil was clay and the winter rains ensured a real messy job," recalls Maurice Butt. "It was a cold, comfortless task lying in sodden long-johns." But the diggers drove on with grim determination, averaging a speed of about five feet a day. But as April approached, the hut ceiling started to sag ominously. "It became a race between the progress of the tunnel outwards and the ceiling sagging downwards," says Butt. The pregnant ceiling was a dead give-away and the Germans were bound to notice before long. It was also doubtful whether there would be enough roof-space for dispersal.

The Germans were also on the alert because of the number of escapes taking place. On the night of Friday, 10 April, three Army officers escaped, and the ferrets spent all the following morning searching the camp while the prisoners remained on *Appell*. Luckily, the tunnel withstood their scrutiny. Towards the middle of April, one of the diggers crawled to the face with a stick, which he prodded through the roof. Watchers in the compound saw it come up under the barbed-wire fence. They dug on a few yards more until Army surveyors assured them it was clear of the fence and indicated the point of exit.

Thirty-five men drew places on the tunnel. On the night of the break, Saturday, 18 April, the would-be escapers gathered in the hut in their various disguises. Wally Cunningham intended to travel with Douglas Bader, who was wearing a tunic roughly cut to resemble a civilian jacket. Lubbock told Bader he would never get through the tunnel because of the right-angle turn at the bottom of the shaft. It was very small. "Well, dammit," said Bader, "I'll take my legs off!" David Lubbock was enthusiastic, and offered to follow him down with his legs. Soon thirty-five men were lying head-to-toe along the tunnel.

The Czech flight lieutenant, Zdenek Prochazka, had the unenviable task of breaking through the last six feet of the tunnel to the surface. It took him four hours, and once he fainted through lack of air. At about 11pm stooges watching from the hut windows were appalled to see his head poke furtively out of the ground just outside the wire, in the glare of the searchlights, and almost in the middle of a path trodden by two sentries. The Army surveyors had blundered. Prochazka watched with open-mouthed horror as the sentries beat a path to each end of the wire, turned about, met in the middle, turned again, and proceeded once more along the wire. He bobbed down in alarm and a whispered conference ensued at the tunnel face. Then another prisoner poked his head out, saw the sentries' backs were turned, and nipped out. He ran into the darkness beyond the perimeter lights, followed by another. Two more followed, then a fifth. There, the exodus ended, because the two sentries met, and stayed there the rest of the night. The frustrated escapers started reversing up the tunnel and sneaking back to their own huts, where they hid their escape equipment and started tucking into their escape rations. The tunnel was discovered in the morning when one of the patrolling sentries nearly fell down the hole. While the Germans were digging it up, Bader stole a shovel from under their noses and they held a parade lasting ten hours while they searched the huts for it. But by then it was already hidden away in one of the other tunnels. Of the five men who had escaped, none was out longer than two weeks.

In the meantime, the less escape-minded prisoners were busy making themselves model gliders, much to the amusement of Colin Dilly, who on 5 April had written home:

BETTER WEATHER HAS BROUGHT ON A NASTY EPIDEMIC OF GLIDER-ITIS AMONG THE RAF. SOME VERY STRANGE AND COMIC PRODUCTIONS. CURIOUSLY THE WORST MADE SEEM TO DO THE BEST, WHILE A PERFECT BEAUTY, MARVELLOUSLY MADE (TAKING OVER A MONTH OF HARD WORK) DID SO BADLY IT'S NOW BEING RE-BUILT. IT HAD OVER THREE FOOT SPAN.

* * *

On the night of Monday, 27 April one of the most audacious escapes from Warburg was pulled off by two RAF and two SAAF officers. Eustace Newborn had noticed that the guard on the upper (western) double-gate went off duty at 7pm and that there was no sentry on the gates until the night patrol came on duty at 9pm. Thus for two hours the only watch was from the goon-boxes

Fig 15. Kriegie pastime at Warburg *(Wallace Cunningham)*

fifty yards away on either side. It was quite possible that during this time a number of escapers might be able to crawl underneath the gates without being seen.

In order to test this theory, Tony Ruffel spent a night in the barrack nearest the gate and after lights out started crawling towards it. The only cover was a shallow ditch about thirty feet away, which ran towards the gate at right-angles. Even then, anyone in the ditch was visible from the two goon-boxes. Nevertheless, Ruffel reached the first gate, loosened the wire on the bottom bar and measured the distance between it and the ground. He found that by bending the wire upwards and scooping a trench in the ground he could make room for a man to snake underneath. Wallace-Terry, Hugh Keartland and Gerry Williams decided to join him on the scheme. They arranged for a constant watch to be kept on guard movements, for two parties of diversionists to attract the attention of the tower guards on the appointed night, and for a system of signalling to warn them if they were in danger. Their escape equipment consisted of Army boots, a mixture of converted uniforms and civilian clothes, maps of Germany, Danzig and the Shaffhausen re-entrant, and shaving, washing and boot-cleaning kit. They had enough food to sustain them for twenty-four days — 15lb of Lubbock's Mixture each, with a little extra dried fruit and some Horlicks and Ovaltine tablets. Owing to the nature of their escape they were unable to carry greatcoats, blankets or groundsheets.

At 8.40pm on 27 April, Ruffel began to crawl towards the upper gate followed at three-minute intervals by the others. Over their converted uniforms they wore combinations dyed black. But it was not yet dark, and the moon was shining. As they crawled towards the ditch, pushing their rucksacks in front of them and getting covered in mud, some of the diversionists engaged the guards in conversation whilst others started a fight. All four men got underneath both gates and so well did the diversions work that the last man had time to bend the wire back into place and smooth over the ground they had disturbed. (As a result three Army officers were able to use this route two nights later.)

Outside the gate the four officers crawled to another ditch about six feet away. Two of them were still in full view of the patrolling guards as they arrived on duty, but as the guards almost invariably looked inwards towards the compound as they walked along the fence the two were not seen. By now it was almost dark and, despite the moon, they crawled past piles of timber and several sheds, reaching the cover of a partly built hut undetected. They had been crawling for an hour. Doffing their combinations, they shook hands all round and set off in pairs.

Ruffel and Wallace-Terry had planned to walk and jump goods trains to Danzig, where they had a "safe" address. Walking by night and resting by day they were free for a week before being recaptured in a railway marshalling yard searching for a train heading towards the Baltic ports. Peering at the destination labels, they were seen from the yard supervisor's hut and were suddenly surrounded by a posse of armed Germans.

Keartland and Williams headed for the Swiss frontier, kept going for seventeen days and covered two hundred and seventy-five miles before being caught. Williams spoke a little French and Keartland Afrikaans. They decided to pose as Belgian workers and hard-arse it to the frontier, jumping trains or using other forms of transport only as a last resort. If accosted by Germans they would claim to be going to whatever village was next on the map. However, it was their intention to walk at night and as far as possible avoid meeting anyone. At that time of year that meant spending seventeen out of every twenty-four hours either looking for or lying in hiding places.

On the first night they made good time, covering about twenty-five kilometres. During the day of Tuesday, 28 April they hid up on a hill above town. The cover was not good, but the day was fine and they managed to scrape most of the mud off themselves and their clothing.

On the second evening they continued on the road south, but at about 8.30pm a civilian on a bicycle overtook them, dismounted and began to ask questions. He was not quite satisfied with their "Belgian worker" story and he stayed with them, evidently intending to make further enquiries at the next village. After about ten minutes the two escapers branched off a small track to the left, leaving the civilian, and continued all night across country in a south-easterly direction. The next night they crossed the River Fulda using a small road-bridge and reached the *Autobahn* south of Kassel. They had travelled three or four miles down the *Autobahn* when Keartland began to complain about his feet. Although his Army boots were worn-in and well greased, they were bruising his Achilles tendon. They decided to stop and shelter in a Dutch barn full of hay. There they remained the whole day, cutting down their Army boots to relieve the pressure on the Achilles tendon. Several Germans entered the barn without seeing them.

Holding a whispered conference they arrived at the conclusion that the best way to travel was by walking along the *Autobahn* at night. Pedestrians and cyclists were forbidden and traffic was rare, mostly heavy transport lorries with one or two trailers attached. From then on they averaged twenty miles a day. Whenever they saw a vehicle the two escapers hid in a ditch or scrambled down an embankment and lay flat in the shadows until it passed. Once, when a cyclist approached without lights, he sheered off when he saw them. But they were soon suffering from physical and mental exhaustion, as on average they snatched only three or four hours' sleep a day. Even when the weather was fine, they spent the first four or five hours of their rest shivering violently, and it was often not until midday that they were warm enough to lie still. When they woke they found their legs and feet were terribly stiff, and the first few hours of each night's march were sheer agony. Most of the going was across flat country, and even at the smallest incline their breath came in short gasps and they could walk only at half their usual pace. Although reason told them that as time went on their rucksacks were becoming lighter, they seemed to weigh the same throughout the entire march.

Finding suitable cover for their day's rest was likewise no easy task. Young plantations with thick undergrowth afforded the best kind of cover, but most plantations in Germany were well tended by foresters who cleared away the undergrowth — most unfortunate from the escapers' point of view. Keartland and Williams often had to hide in ditches, covering themselves with dead grass, or holes in the ground covered with rubbish, or under piles of dead foliage. The concentrated food and the lack of water caused constipation, and this also made resting unpleasant. Trees and bushes scratched their hands and faces, and the wounds turned into festering sores, which took a long time to heal. After the first week each night's march was becoming so exhausting, and the prospect of finding good hiding places so discouraging, that they often felt like flopping down in the first hiding place that looked suitable.

They spent their eighth day of freedom — Tuesday, 5 May — in a wood about a mile from the *Autobahn*. At about 7pm, as they were about to start their evening meal of Lubbock's Mixture, a German NCO in his "walking out" uniform entered the wood with his girlfriend. They were looking for thick cover similar to that being enjoyed by the escapers. Inevitably, the NCO almost fell over them. He was immediately suspicious and, putting business before pleasure, started questioning them. Neither escaper had shaved since leaving Warburg, and he at first mistook them for Russians. When they said they were Belgian he let out a torrent of fluent French. Gerry Williams's schoolboy French could not compete. The game was up. The NCO promptly arrested them and, now thoroughly excited, proceeded to march them off. Fortunately, he carried no small arms, and the two simply ran off, leaving the NCO shouting in impotent rage with his girlfriend standing demurely beside him. The escapers found cover at the far end of the woods and stayed there until dark.

Fifteen nights after their escape they reached a fork outside Karlsruhe and took the branch leading to Stuttgart. By now they were so overcome with exhaustion that they forsook their resolution never to move except in darkness, and often succumbed to the temptation to take advantage of the last few hours before dawn to press on and cover a few extra miles instead of seeking somewhere to hide. Sometimes they carried on during the first few hours of daylight. Their last night on the run, 14/15 May, was one of the most depressing, with frequent thunderstorms and heavy showers soaking them to the marrow and ruining their maps. After passing through a small town on the way to Tuttlingen they took a wrong turning owing to the difficulty of finding signposts in the rain and darkness and a slight inaccuracy on their maps. Of the eighteen miles they walked that night, they had gone ten miles in the wrong direction before they discovered their error. After this they made an early stop in a forest two miles outside Wilberg. Morale was now a real problem. Usually when one escaper was at a low ebb the other was able to buoy him up. But physical weakness, increasing hunger, occasional thirst and the ever-present feeling of being a hunted animal, was a constant strain on the nerves. Once, Gerry

Williams, who carried cigarettes but had felt disinclined to smoke during the trip, lit up, only to throw half of it away in disgust.

The next day — Friday, 15 May — was the most miserable of all. Their bodies and clothes were soaked, and though the forest gave them security, the ground and trees were so wet that the only way they could stop shivering was by getting up and walking about. Neither of them had been warm or dry, or had had any sleep, for three days. Well aware that they were approaching the limit of their endurance, they decided that if they were ever to reach the frontier they should press on.

After washing and shaving they walked stealthily towards Wilberg. As they reached the outskirts of the town, they saw dozens of civilians. Not until it was too late did they realise that the presence of so many civilians, who had seen them, meant they would have to walk through the town in broad daylight — exactly the sort of thing they had tried to avoid during the past seventeen days. By now they were so dirty and dishevelled that they were bound to invite suspicion. Their clothes were soiled and worn, and Keartland had hardly any seat left to his trousers. Although none of the civilians spoke to them, almost everyone stared. They had reached the end of the town, and were about to rejoice upon the prospect of getting away with it after all, when a young policeman suddenly appeared and stopped them. Another came up behind them on a bicycle. Neither of the *Kripo* men swallowed their cover story. Moreover, they were armed, and the two escapers realised that resistance was out of the question and flight equally futile.

After averaging sixteen miles a night, Keartland and Williams had been recaptured within eighty miles of the Swiss frontier. To have foot-slogged such a distance at all was no mean achievement, especially considering the inadequacy of their maps and disguises. Their disappointment, bitter though it was, was thus tempered with pride. At the same time they were greatly relieved. At least now they would be warm and dry. One of them had lost eighteen pounds in weight and the other at least ten. Five days later, on Wednesday, 20 May, they were returned to Warburg. The "brown jobs" were very impressed with their performance, which they considered unprecedented and incredibly courageous.

Chapter Six

"Operation Olympia"

Oflag VIB, Warburg-Dössel, May–September 1942

During the absence of Keartland, Ruffel, Wallace-Terry and Williams from Oflag VIB, there had been yet more escapes. Not long after the four had made their break, Douglas Bader helped divert the sentries whilst three Army officers cut their way through the barbed-wire in broad daylight. The escapers were Major T Stallard of the Durham Light Infantry, Captain R K Page of the Royal Artillery and Lieutenant J A G McDonell of the Norfolks. Under cover of an elaborate system of signals and diversions they succeeding in cutting their way through, and had only to await the signal to get up and make for cover. Bader appeared on cue, crossing the rugby pitch with his usual swashbuckling gait and thereby attracting the attention of the goon in his box. At a signal, which he received without showing any sign of having done so, he started addressing the sentry. Pointing to his tin legs, he lifted one slightly as if to test it, then deliberately fell over. Two other RAF types were passing by and he shouted at them to come and help him. Fumbling with his straps, Bader took off the leg, waved it at the spellbound guard and shouted some well-rehearsed German phrases. But that was not the end of Bader's performance. Each time his friends picked him up, he slipped out of their grasp, falling to the ground and telling the sentry this was no way to treat a legless man. At last they managed to carry him off, the sentry watching all the time as they disappeared into the distance. In the meantime, the three Army officers had got clean away. Unfortunately, they were caught the following day.

Squadron Leader Armitage's tunnel had just reached the point where it was ready to break. However, the tunnellers had failed to reckon with the summer thunderstorms for which the Westphalian plains were notorious. A great pool of water about thirty feet wide and some twelve inches deep had started to form against the first hut that the tunnel had passed under. The clay subsoil was a sort of yellow-ochre, and the water seeped out coloured with clay — a dead give-way. Then it broke through into the tunnel, and Armitage took a team down to start baling out. Gradually the baled water began trickling out of the sides of his hut, and a yellow mud began forming around it. Rademacher's ferrets were on to it in a flash. One of them started walking through the block when the trap-door was still open. The men down below had no time to climb out, replace the trap and clear away the tell-tale signs of tunnelling. "Dim" Strong yelled at them to stay down and close the trap, and rushed out to obstruct the German, who pulled out his pistol.

Armitage was making his way towards the shaft when he suddenly saw two Germans climbing down the rope ladder and into the tunnel. There was little he could do but say: "Boo!" They jumped out of their skins and one of them fell into four or five feet of water in the well at the bottom. Armitage, himself chest-deep in water, helped him to his feet and then followed them both back up the rope ladder. When he popped his head out of the trap, under Doug Cooper's bed, there were sixteen Germans standing in the room, including Rademacher and the Commandant. Armitage had no clothes on — not even long-johns — as he used to strip off entirely when tunnelling. "I suppose I had better come up," he said. "I suppose you better had," replied Rademacher.

The Commandant was sitting in the only chair in the room, with all the other Germans spread out in a semicircle around him. He looked at Armitage, standing naked and filthy before him. "You are a fool," he said, at which point he flung out his arms and accidentally caught one of the goons standing beside him in the private parts. The whole situation seemed so ludicrous that Armitage suddenly burst out laughing. The Commandant must have assumed that Armitage was laughing at himself, and he laughed, too. When the Commandant laughed all the other goons had to laugh as well. So everybody stood there roaring with laughter for about thirty seconds. Then the Commandant decided it was getting out of hand and his face suddenly straightened. Everyone instantly stopped laughing. They then marched straight out of the room.

Unusually, no punishment was meted out on Armitage or any of the other men in the room except "Dim" Strong. Accused of advancing on the German "with clenched fist and flashing eyes", he was sentenced to ten days in the cooler, and his *Personalkarte I* was marked "especially obstinate and arrogant". Normally Armitage and the others, too, would have received at least a fortnight in the cooler, but they heard no more about it. The goons just filled in the shaft. After that, though, Armitage was through with tunnels. There had been a tremendous fall of earth during the rains and it had frightened him. He couldn't help thinking of the possibility that one of the diggers might be pinned down under a fall or drowned. Several of the very keen tunnellers at Warburg felt the same way, and from then onwards never dug again.

Meanwhile, Melville Kennedy's tunnel was proceeding apace. When the Germans had discovered the dummy tunnel, they had obligingly taken away the bags of clay stacked in the dispersal chamber and neglected to fill in the horizontal shaft. The tunnellers therefore used it to dump the clay from the second and third legs of the tunnel. As work progressed and the dummy tunnel filled up, they packed the clay round the brick skirting under the floor of the Army barracks. For the third leg, they allowed themselves the luxury of installing electric lighting, splicing together wire and fittings scrounged from every corner of the camp, and extended the railway line.

But again they found that the flooding made the walls and roof subside. Once, Kenneth Mackenzie was nearly buried alive by a ton of clay falling from the roof in an enormous lump. He pulled back in the nick of time. The fall left a huge, slanted dome in the roof, and to save time they decided to press on through the gap and shore up the roof. As the sledge was unable to negotiate the gradient, they turned this section of tunnel into a junction where they changed sledges. It also meant they had to place two more men in the tunnel to man the sledges, thus increasing the size of each shift. To safeguard against further mishaps, they started shoring up dangerous sections of the tunnel. For this the RAF kriegies sacrificed some of their bed-boards, replacing them with hammocks made from string saved up from Red Cross parcels.

The tunnel was by now curving up towards the surface, and had suffered so many falls that instead of being straight had developed at least four humps. Diggers were getting blinding headaches from lack of oxygen. The further they pushed ahead, the fouler the air became. To get round this, Mackenzie and a few others with an engineering bent devised an ingenious system to make air-holes which would also fox the "ferrets". Taking empty food tins of different sizes, they cut off the tops and bottoms to make hollow trowels. Then they made extending rods out of wood, joining them together with tubes made from yet more food tins, which had been cut in half, flattened out then rolled up to slip neatly round the end of each rod. Armed with this paraphernalia, they crawled along to the face and started boring an air-hole. One digger lay on his back and, starting with the biggest tin, twisted it into the roof so that the clay fell through it. Then he took the next size down and repeated the exercise, until he had a hole as long as his arm tapering towards the top. His partner then handed him a rod, which he fixed to another tin so as to cut away another section. As the air-hole progressed towards the surface, they extended the rods and used progressively smaller tins until at last they broke through into one of the gardens. The gardeners above camouflaged the hole with foliage and, when tunnelling ended for the day, covered it with a stone. As the tunnel forged ahead, they dug more air-holes at intervals.

At the beginning of May a rumour spread round the camp that some of the RAF were to be moved to their own camp, and before the week was out this was confirmed when the Germans announced that fifty Air Force and Fleet Air Arm officers were to be transferred to Stalag Luft III. Included on the list were Douglas Bader, George Baird, Joe Barker, Harry Bewlay, Don Blew, Braithwaite,

Brewster, Maurice Butt, John Clelland, Bob Coste, Charlie Crews, John Denny, Sydney Dowse, Ken Driver, Frank Dutton, Laurence Edwards, William Edwards, Ronald Ellen, Eric Foster, Peter Gardner, Alex Gould, Ray Hoppe, Frank Hugill, Hugh Keartland, "Bush" Kennedy, Tom Kipp, "Mike" Lewis, Lewis-Dale, "Liffey" McConnell, Sydney Murray, Peter Pine, Stan Reeves, Tony Ruffel, Arthur Steel, "Dim" Strong, James Taylor, Ken Toft, Dickie Troward, Tim Walenn, Richard Wallace-Terry, Mark Williams and some of the Fleet Air Arm officers, including Hugo Bracken and David Lubbock. Aircraftman 1st Class Larry Slattery was also listed: for the first time since being shot down in September 1939 he would be in a POW camp run by the Luftwaffe. Another odd case selected for the move was *Capitaine* Larmier, the Potez 63.11 observer who in July 1940 had been left behind at Spangenberg when his French compatriots had been transferred. Those who had been hard at work on tunnels for the past six months were seething, not least Melville Kennedy, who would be denied the chance of breaking from the warren-like tunnel he had engineered through one trial after another; "Liffey" McConnell, who had conceived the idea of the dummy traps, felt pretty much the same way.

On morning *Appell* on Saturday, 9 May they were advised that anyone who was unfit to walk the two miles to the railway station should report to the *Arzt* directly. The implication was that they would be provided with transport. Maurice Butt saw an opportunity to get one over the

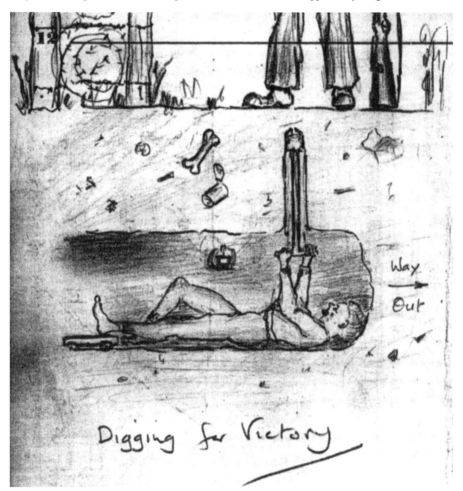

Fig 16. Drilling an air-hole in a tunnel at Warburg *(Wallace Cunningham)*

Germans. He had injured his left leg when he was shot down, and had already had trouble with it once during captivity. Although he knew that the Germans mainly had Bader in mind, he decided that Shanks's pony was not for him, either. After *Appell*, he dashed over to his room and vigorously applied a scrubbing brush to his left leg to simulate an abrasion, then paid a visit to the British MO, who in due time gave a list to the Germans. Before the *Arzt* appeared, Butt again applied the brush. The doctor looked at his leg, then at his medical card, and put him down for transport.

On Sunday, 10 May the fifty were paraded ready to leave the camp. For Bader, Butt and two others a pony and trap was laid on. As they passed the marchers on the way to the station they were greeted with derisive cat-calls. Arriving at the station first, the four were surprised and delighted to see they had been given a plush, first class carriage. On the wall above the seats the Germans had, by a peculiar oversight, left a diagrammatic map of the railway network, measuring two feet by one. Butt made a mental note to "win" it before the end of the journey.

When the rest arrived, they were ushered aboard, six to a compartment, with each guard in the corridor watching over two compartments. Then the Riot Act was read. Anyone attempting to escape or to approach the windows would be shot without warning. No one was to stand up in his compartment. Anyone wishing to use the toilet should make a request to the guard. The prisoners were bored. They had heard it all before.

After some boisterous banter they settled down and the train moved off. However, the journey to their new camp was to be a long one and after two days without washing and shaving, and with bottoms sore, they were feeling quite jaded. Before the last leg of the journey, the carriages were shunted into some sidings to await coupling to a new locomotive. "No sooner had a steam engine coupled up to the carriages," recalls Butt,

than Bader, noting our cheesed-off state, sprung up and said: "How about a cup of tea, chaps?" We looked up in amazement and some concern as he reached for his kitbag and dug a teapot out, followed by a packet of tea from a Red Cross parcel. Putting the kitbag back onto the luggage rack, he turned round and to our horror immediately opened the window wide, waving the teapot outside. The goons erupted into activity, shouting, in a high state of agitation, with rifles primed. An *Unteroffizier* appeared, followed by a *Feldwebel*, and after a while a *Hauptmann*. Revolvers were being waved around quite wildly and several rifles were pointed at the open window by the guards in the marshalling yard. Calmly, Bader explained that he wanted a brew of tea and wished someone to take the teapot to the engine driver in order to have the necessary boiling water added from the engine.

The officer did not want an immediate posting to the *Ostfront* just because his distinguished guest might cause a major incident, and, seeing that discretion was the better part of valour, gave the order, and the teapot was taken to the engine-room by a guard who was just as amazed as the rest of us. A cup of tea in the middle of Europe in the middle of the war. The Bader magic had worked again.

With our spirits rekindled, we set to work to prepare for the end of our journey. The boys in the next compartment distracted the guard with a long-winded dialogue about food, displaying items from Red Cross parcels and, to keep him really transfixed, sparing the occasional knob of chocolate — "You like that, yes?" etc. Thus the railway map, with its stiff cardboard backing, was taken from its frame on the wall of the carriage. It was sewn under the Scottish plaid lining of the leather horse-jacket I had confiscated from the enemy at Thorn. It required much skill and determination by David Lubbock to push a needle through the leather, hence he made only four penetrations, so that a single diagonal stitch about an inch long held the map from each of its top two corners. The idea was to walk through the search with it sandwiched behind the coat lining.

While the bulk of the prisoners walked the few hundred yards from Sagan station to the camp, Bader, Butt and other *Grands Blessés* were conveyed by lorry. Once in the *Vorlager*, they joined the main party for the usual search.

Bader, as usual, had the searchers in turmoil. "*Herr Hauptmann*, make sure you look inside my tin legs — they are full of contraband," he provoked. This froze the goons, and the officer in charge had already had his leg pulled and suffered loss of face from the teapot incident. He let Bader through with his tin legs stuffed with contraband.

Realising that hesitation was a loser, I threw myself at my searcher, suggesting that I stripped everything off. He was a little man, but with keen, watchful eyes. He seemed to sense that it would be ludicrous to doubt my innocence and let me by, after feeling with both hands between the leather jacket and my shirt, with us facing each other. Even the stiffness of the enclosed map on the back of his hand escaped his sensitivity. Then came the awkward walk away with the two white diagonal cotton strands shouting for attention. A pre-arranged diversion was in progress further along the line which focused attention away. Thus the confiscated black leather jacket got into yet another camp, this time carrying a bonus diagrammatic rail map.

(2)

Fearful of further purges, the RAF Escape Committee decided to break "Bush" Kennedy's tunnel ahead of schedule, even though it was only fifteen feet beyond the wire and would come up in a field of ripe corn. Almost a hundred men were down to go, among them Squadron Leader Sydney-Smith, Acting Squadron Leader Walter Williams, Paddy Denton, Hugh Falkus, Dennis Graham-Hogg, William Hunter, Hugh Lynch-Blosse, Kenneth Mackenzie, "Hank" Staniland, Ron Terry and Peter Valachos.

Eric Sydney-Smith went down first, followed by Peter Valachos. Unfortunately, the Germans had placed an outer patrol beyond the normal sentry beat, and the two thwarted escapees came crawling back to the hut to hold a hasty conference with the others. Some decided that snaking out under the sentries' noses was worth the risk. So Sydney-Smith went down again, followed by Hunter, Valachos, Terry and Staniland. As Sydney-Smith crawled out of the exit, by now almost blocked with crumbling earth, he snagged his braces, which snapped. Holding his trousers by the waist with one hand, he hauled himself out — directly in front of a waiting sentry, who waved his rifle in his face. Sydney-Smith didn't know whether to put up his hands or hold up his trousers, and for a while stood there, a comic figure, by turns putting up his hands, then quickly hitching up his trousers, until in the end he compromised by raising one hand and holding up his trousers with the other. Meanwhile, Bill Hunter was poking his nose out of the exit — only to find himself inches from the tip of a bayonet.

A riot squad ran into the camp, but in the chaos most escapers managed to reach their huts and disperse their escape equipment. For several days afterwards the Germans held long head-counts and conducted thorough searches of the huts and gardens. Luckily for the RAF, the third trap was in an Army barrack, so the Army copped most of the blame.

Those caught in the tunnel and at the mouth were sentenced to the usual punitive solitary confinement, but there was such a backlog that none of them would serve their time until they reached Oflag XXIB at Schubin in the autumn. Hunter decided that from now on, however, he would stick to a safer occupation, such as forgery.

The Germans flooded the tunnel, but it was not the last they were to hear of it. In their haste, they had left about fourteen feet of tunnel, between the trip-wire and the fence, to collapse and form a ditch. Kenneth Mackenzie and Dennis Graham-Hogg decided to drop into it and dig a blitz tunnel. Carrying a brown blanket apiece, they would crawl along the ditch to the outer fence and hide under the blankets until dark, then dig a shallow tunnel under the wire. They would be out of sight of the tower guards, effectively camouflaged by the fence-poles and the concertina wire that obscured their vision.

Organising a large band of circuit bashers, Mackenzie and Graham-Hogg positioned themselves in the middle, while two diversion parties distracted the tower guards. As the sentry patrolling the fence reached the farthest end of his beat, they dropped down into the tunnel, crawled to the end nearest the wire and hid under their blankets. Friendly shouts from passers-by

Goons in the Block.

kept them informed of German movements. After about thirty minutes, a stooge warned them that a sentry had stopped opposite them and was inspecting the tunnel remains. They tried to watch from beneath their blankets, but the sentry was screened from view by the wire coils. Somewhat perturbed, they had to face the possibility that he might still be there at dusk when the prisoners were locked in their huts. There would be nobody at hand to warn them of his presence or give them the "all clear". Eventually another stooge passed by, told them the sentry was still there — getting more and more agitated — and warned them to prepare to come back. Under cover of a mock fight started on the circuit, they crawled back into the compound and joined another band of evening strollers, inadvertently leaving behind one of the blankets. The guard, who knew by now that something was afoot, blew his whistle and the brawlers and strollers dispersed. Next morning, while bashing the circuit, Mackenzie and Graham-Hogg noticed the blanket was gone and that they had disturbed the ground while crawling into the ditch. This disturbance must have been what caught the sentry's eye. In any event, their frustration at their failure mingled with a certain relief; had they been caught on the wrong side of the trip-wire they might well have been shot without warning.

With the departure of Bader, Gardner and Lubbock, their plan to escape from the cells had to be aborted. But it was too good a scheme to waste, and the baton, as it were, was passed on to several other fractious prisoners who were due to serve their *Stubenarrest* time and keen to have a crack at escaping. Six were chosen, and they included the inveterate escaper "Pissy" Edwards, the Canadian Fleet Air Arm pilot Dickie Bartlett, the South African Don Gericke and the Danish Neil Svendsen. However, in the event one of the six had to stay behind, as Dickie Bartlett recalls:

Six of us had planned to go in twos but when I opened the cell door of my companion [Edwards], his feet were too swollen from flea bites [for him] to get his boots on, so I went on

222

**Fig 17 (*left*).
Barrack search by
German security
staff *(Wallace
Cunningham)***

**Fig 18 (*right*).
Workmen digging a
trench to unearth a
tunnel
*(P H Bear)***

my own. I hoped to get into Holland and tried getting on freight trains at night and hiding in the day. However, in [the] cells we had been living on a couple of slices of bread and some watery soup and after two days I decided I would try to keep going during the day. The first day when I was moving from one train to another, I accidentally walked into a small working party which was guarded by a soldier. He raised his rifle and had me covered within seconds. After a few days in the local cells, and I must admit, a bit of a worry when the word "Gestapo" was mentioned a few times, I was moved to Stalag Luft III.

***

The remnants of the RAF at Warburg had now received instructions from Hyde, via the Army Escape Committee, that no more escapes were to be attempted on the wire and that the northern part of the camp — the No4 Battalion area — was "off-limits" to clandestine activities. Although only a handful of the aircrew POWs knew it, the Army had planned to blow all the lights around the perimeter fence, along with the searchlights, and for numerous parties to climb the northern stretch of wire at several different places simultaneously with camp-made ladders. The scheme, which was codenamed "Operation Olympia" and would later be known as "The Warburg Wire-Job", was conceived by Major Tom Stallard, whom Bader had helped escape in April, and J R E ("Jock") Hamilton-Baillie, a twenty-three-year-old Lieutenant of Engineers who would shortly be promoted to Captain. The escape would take place on a dark, moonless night. As soon as pre-arranged diversions had begun to take effect the parties, each of about ten in number, were to storm the wire at certain selected points and, with the assistance of home-made ladders, go over the fence and run for it as fast as their legs could carry them.

The scheme had been proposed to the Escape Committee on 20 April, although it would not take place until the end of the summer and was intended to be the *grand finale* to the season's escaping activities. The Escape Committee had agreed that in the meantime no other "over the wire" scheme would be permitted, as this might prejudice the chances of the escape. Stallard and Hamilton-Baillie reckoned they could construct sixteen storming ladders, and that ten to twelve men might be able to escape over each ladder. The scheme could therefore be used by a large number of prisoners — anything from a hundred to one hundred and sixty.

It was a very ambitious project, and the Escape Committee was at first sceptical. Assuming that Stallard and his confederates could find enough wood to construct the ladders, they then had to manufacture them, hide them from the Germans, practise launching them and rehearse the actual scaling operation, all the time ensuring that the utmost secrecy be observed, for the greater the number of potential escapers and background workers involved, the greater the chances of a careless move or a slip of the tongue alerting the Germans.

Stallard suggested that the camp boundary lights be extinguished by throwing grappling-irons, attached to a long cord, over the electric light cables that ran round the camp just outside the fence. At a given signal the wires would be pulled down and, Stallard hoped, all the lights would go out at once, leaving the guards in complete darkness and considerable confusion while the ladders were placed against the fence.

The Escape Committee turned the scheme down. It was likely to cause casualties. But if Stallard could find a more certain method of extinguishing the lights, he would have the Committee's backing.

Stallard consulted an Army electrician, Major B D S ("Skelly") Ginn of the Royal Electrical and Mechanical Engineers, who had been captured at St-Valery-en-Caux on 12 June, 1940 . After two or three days of surveying the camp Ginn announced that he had discovered what he thought was a mains fuse-box in cobbler's workshop, which lay inside the camp. From this hut overhead cables ran directly to the guard-room outside the fence. He reckoned there was an even chance that these wires could be shorted out by pulling a spanner across the terminals using a length of string drawn through the window. The boundary lights — and possibly the searchlights as well — would then be put out of action. As the whole scheme depended on the lights being put out at a given moment, Stallard decided to test Ginn's theory by extinguishing them for a short time.

The shorting happened one night in May. Dusk was at about half-past ten, and that was when the camp lights were switched on in the main guard-room. The prisoners were supposed to be in bed by eleven o'clock, and by then the lights in their rooms had to be off. On this particular night the lights went out fifteen minutes early; the men were still undressing and making preparations to go to bed. As the extinguishing of the lights before the recognised time usually meant that the Germans had received an air-raid warning, the prisoners immediately gave a loud cheer. They followed their usual practice of going to the windows to see if there was any sign or sound of their own aircraft. There was none, but they noticed that in addition to the lights inside the camp those around the perimeter were out, too. They continued their preparations for bed in the darkness.

Stallard's test had worked perfectly, without leaving any traces to arouse suspicion. After this the Escape Committee gave him permission to prepare for the escape. Because speed over the wire was vital, Stallard & Co decided to construct only one ladder at first and to test it in a barrack block reserved for recreation. Situated near the middle of the camp to the south of the High Street, the recreation block was near the workshop, the gym, one of the washrooms and an *Abort*, but well away from the other buildings. It was used mainly as a music practice room.

The ladder was designed and constructed by Hamilton-Baillie, known to all as "H-B". It in fact consisted of two separate units: a ladder to mount the first fence, and a decking to bridge the gap between the two fences. The ladder itself was two feet wide and eleven feet long, with seven rungs. The top rung stuck out about eight inches each side of the two uprights. At the top, two chocks of wood projected downwards for about six inches; these were to act as claws, fastening on to the top strand of the overhanging wire apron. Stallard wondered whether the wire overhang would support the weight of the ladder once the mounting started, or whether it would simply collapse. But "H-B" was adamant that it would stand the weight, and that even if it did collapse the top of the ladder would simply tilt forwards and the claws would grasp the top strand of the fence proper. The decking was really nothing more than a duckboard eight feet long, with two runners sticking out three feet at either end. The runners projecting on the near, or camp, side acted as handles to assist the man launching the bridge. Nailed across the ends of the runners on the far side was a single stout spar (a hockey-stick handle proved eminently suitable). Having crawled along the decking on hands and knees, the would-be escaper grasped the spar firmly with both hands and dropped through the three-foot gap on to the ground outside the wire.

Stallard's teams were each to be built from a nucleus of four men — two of whom would be responsible for rushing the fence and setting up the ladder, while the third and fourth would make it secure. Prior to launching, the decking lay flat on top of the ladder. On approaching the wire, the two at the front (or top) of the ladder hoisted it up to arm's length and made sure that the chocks were engaged on the top strand of the overhang; they then stood at either side of the ladder to steady it. The two at the rear (or bottom) of the ladder first of all made sure that the feet of the ladder were firmly planted; number one then seized the bottom handles of the decking and mounted the ladder, pushing the decking in front of him, assisted from behind by number two and from the sides by the last two members of the team, numbers nine and ten (or eleven and twelve). The decking then slid into position, the front part falling on to the outer fence.

The amount of timber required to build the ladders was enormous. Each ladder would be eleven feet long, and the uprights each made of two planks nailed together (a single plank would not be strong enough). Each of the seven rungs would be about eighteen inches long. That meant at least fifty feet of timber per ladder. The bridge would be fourteen feet long, and here again the runners had to be made of two planks nailed together to give the necessary strength. The decking itself would need about twenty feet of wood. Thus each bridge would require between seventy and eighty feet. It amounted to a hundred and thirty feet of timber for each apparatus — and Stallard visualised building sixteen of them. Something approaching two thousand feet of timber had to come from somewhere; not an easy proposition when every yard of it had to be "won" and subsequently shielded from the enemy's grasp.

Then there was the question of the nails and rope: nearly a hundred nails and twelve feet of strong rope for each ladder. A decent length of strong rope simply did not exist in the camp — as tunnellers had found when seeking rope for their underground railway trolleys. They had to rely on pilfering short lengths of the string with which Red Cross parcels were tied up, splicing them together, and twisting or plaiting three or more into a rope.

The finished practice ladder was hidden in the recreation block. For the scaling experiment, two strong wires were stretched across the hut from wall to wall, six feet apart and ten feet high, to represent the double perimeter fence. There was just enough room under the roof for the first man climbing the ladder to push the extension up in front of him and tilt it over on to the second wire to form the bridge. The camp was never completely free of Germans, but with careful watching it was usually possible to practise the wire scaling two or three times before a warning was received. The ladder had then to be dismantled quickly, reassembled as shelves and covered with sheets of music, while one member of the team played a popular tune on the piano and the rest joined in the singing until the German passed the hut. The officer in charge of security and "stooging" for all nefarious goings-on was Captain Martin J Gilliat, of the King's Royal Rifle Corps, who ran an efficient team.

With his four-man launching teams in mind, Stallard approached Captain A S B Arkwright of the Royal Scots Fusiliers and Captain R J Fuller of the Royal Sussex Regiment; two officers from the Australian Expeditionary Force, Captain R R Baxter of 5th Infantry Battalion and Lieutenant J W K Champ of the 17th Infantry Battalion; another Australian, Captain D A Crawford of the 1st Anti-Tank Regiment; Wing Commander Joe Kayll and Squadron Leader Tony Trumble from the Air Force contingent; and, from the naval contingent, Lieutenant-Commander Norman Quill of the Fleet Air Arm. These men were potential team leaders. Stallard selected the bulk of each Army team either from officers he knew personally or based on recommendation, and Kayll and Quill did likewise. Some of the men were inveterate escapers, whilst others, although they had helped in various ways in other people's schemes, were never really in the forefront of activities, but had instead built up a reputation for reliability and alertness in assisting with even the most menial tasks involved in an escape bid.

By the middle of May, the teams had been chosen, most of them Army officers from the No2 Battalion barrack blocks, and Stallard invited each in turn to a secret meeting after 8.15 *Appell*. The meetings were held in a small room in the long brick building near the upper gate, which accommodated No5 Battalion.

Kayll's was a mixed team of Army, Navy and RAF. After swearing them to secrecy, Stallard boldly announced: "We are going to assault the wire. A considerable number of us are going over the fence at night — the exact number will be determined a little later on. We will use ladders to climb to the top of the wire, and platforms to straddle the distance between the two fences. The apparatus we will use is simple but effective; one has already been made, and it works."

After describing the scaling ladders, he went on: "We will operate from huts located close to the northern stretch of wire; the apparatus will be hidden there the evening of the day we go. Each assembly will be pushed out of the window with the platform resting on the ladder. Ten men will be designated to each apparatus."

He then demonstrated how to place the apparatus against the wire and how the first two men would scale the ladder, cross the decking, and drop to the ground.

"The remainder of the team will follow in rapid succession, and you will then run like bloody blazes!

"You are probably wondering about the searchlights, and the German patrols. Well, we have discovered a way around that, and have a positive way to fuse the lights — and I mean the entire camp lighting system!

"The method is secret and faultless," Stallard continued, "and we can put them off and on at will. You may recall that the lights all went out for about ten minutes a few nights ago." A low murmur buzzed round the room as the assembled officers recalled the incident. They were impressed. "That was us — the Germans thought it was an air-raid.

"Now, as for the patrols. We realise this is a rather difficult problem, but we are confident that it can be taken care of by creating a few simultaneous diversions. Full details have yet to be worked out. Your assault point will be on the wire behind No4 Battalion's huts, and about equidistant between the two closest towers — that is, about eighty yards from each sentry box. The timing will be such that both sentries are as far away as possible, but more about that later. At this stage of the planning, there may be other assault teams going over the wire elsewhere in the camp on the night, but we have yet to work out the practicalities involved."

There was a tense silence in the room. This was indeed a different proposation entirely from the usual tunnelling activities and "gate jobs". An audacious scheme, it required complete darkness, pukka equipment, sure-footed speed, and a tremendous element of surprise.

"I won't ask for any questions at this time," said Stallard, winding up the session. "I will ask, however, that you go over it yourself in your mind until our next meeting. Think about it carefully, as you might just happen to think of something we've overlooked. I will need to know by tomorrow afternoon whether you're in or out. If you'd rather not participate, then please let me know so that we can drum up a replacement quickly. There will be no stigma attached to any man who feels that he would rather pull out, as I won't deny it will be a pretty risky show. But if you do opt out, and it should become known that you have talked about the scheme, then you will be court-martialled!"

Shortly afterwards, the job of creating diversions was given to two of the Army officers, Albert Arkwright and Rupert Fuller; they spent many hours pacing round the camp with heads bent and brows knitted, trying to find a solution to the problem they had been set.

A few days after the meeting, Tom Stallard asked Kayll's tri-service team to gather for a rehearsal in the recreation block. Team No1, led by Baxter and Champ, and Team No2, led by Arkwright and Fuller, had already been given an initial try-out. The latter team had two Fleet Air Arm officers in addition to its complement of ten Army officers.

By the time Kayll and his men arrived, Martin Gilliat's stooging system had been set up to ensure they were not bothered by any snooping "ferrets". Stallard was already there, as well as Captain D H Walker of the Black Watch, who none of them knew. The hut was sparsely furnished

— just the battered old piano up against the far wall, a couple of racks along the wall containing sheet music, and two wooden beams about twelve feet apart which stretched from wall to wall at a height of about seven feet. Two strong wires had been strung between the beams, about eight feet apart, with more music sheets strung over them. All very innocent, but were the escapers in for a surprise!

Tom Stallard and David Walker crossed over to the music racks, and removed the sheet music. They then lifted the racks from the wall, and carried them, one on top of the other, into the middle of the room, where they swung one end upright and leaned it up against one of the taut wires. All of a sudden it struck Kayll and his men that the "rack" was actually one of the ladder assemblies, and the wires were meant to simulate the compound fences! It was ingenious in its simplicity and disguise. They watched in silence as Stallard grasped the handles of the platform, stepped swiftly up the ladder, assisted by Walker, and pushed it deftly across. The platform cleared the ceiling by a good foot or two, and dropped easily onto the further wire. Stallard crawled quickly across and, grasping the trapeze bar, dropped expertly to the floor. He was right — it worked!

The aim that day was to select the four-man launching team. Numbers One and Two would scramble over the apparatus first, with six others following quickly behind, and Numbers Three and Four going over last and effectively becoming Numbers Nine and Ten.

Before the session began, David Walker warned that the wire of the perimeter fences was a couple of feet higher than the wires in the room, and that the training apparatus was in fact shorter than the ones they would actually use on the night.

One by one Kayll's team had a go at it. They carried on for more than an hour, and managed three sorties per man. When their turn to go through the drill came around again they were designated Ladder Four. At this rehearsal Stallard pointed out that the camp electrical wires, which hung six feet above the top of the inner fence, were a potential hazard. If the decking hit those, the whole apparatus could topple over, so they had to be aware of this and make the necessary allowances in their training runs.

Before they packed up for the day Stallard told them: "A bit of news that may interest you — we have decided that only four ladders will be used on the night. We had at one time intended using anything up to sixteen teams with assemblies, but materials, training and diversions would have been too much of a problem. And so we are concentrating our efforts into your team and three others only, giving us a total of forty to get over the wire and away."

With regular rehearsals, each team reached the point where its members performed automatically. This increased their confidence. In time, Joe Kayll and Norman Quill emerged as Numbers One and Two in the tri-service team.

Towards the end of the month, once he was satisfied with the composition of his four teams, Stallard impressed upon them the importance of getting fit. "I want you to run at least a thousand yards a day," he said. "Walk at least three thousand, and play as much sport as you can without risking injury to yourself. You must realise that once you go over the wire you will have to run flat out for at least a thousand yards, and you won't be in shorts and shirts — you'll be fully dressed, and carrying a ten-pound pack, which is the maximum the Escape Committee will allow you to take with you over the wire."

(3)

Wednesday, 3 June, was the King's Birthday, and the Air Force kriegies surprised their Army and Navy compatriots by turning up for *Appell* in their best uniforms and forming up smartly — thus proving that they could be well turned-out and orderly if they wanted to. The only RN officer who wasn't caught unawares was Commander Beale, who had been briefed to expect a startling experience. But even he was thrown by the "buffed-up" RAF. He called out: "Parade!" and the pause that followed was like elastic pulled taut. On the command of "Attention!" there was a sound like a reverberating rifle shot as everyone clicked heels. The whole lot stood rigid at the 'shun and the total silence and discipline absolutely rattled the goons. Some of the Army battalions, having broken off, crossed the square to watch.

There was no way that the RAF were going to let their performance go unnoticed. The Germans, having done the count, twice saluted and "Gremlin George" dismissed the parade. The kriegies remained standing at attention. "One tiny little German guard behind the parade did not see George leave and remained on guard," Peter Harding remembers:

An Army band also celebrating marched towards us and made to pass through our ranks. The little guard — nicknamed "Napoleon" — tried to stop them, and finished up arresting the big drum and [the] drummer. As he marched his captive up the hill Gremlin George saw what was happening and laughed with us. Napoleon had to apologise and return the drum.

The RAF stayed on parade until, with a nod from "Hetty" Hyde, Commander Beale called the "Dismiss", at which they turned on their heels as one man. There was much gaiety and laughter as they fell out. "Took the piss out of them." "See the brown jobs watching?" "All good stuff." "Whacko!"

Afterwards they reverted to their usual slovenly behaviour — "to the mystification of the Germans," recalled Paddy Denton, "who couldn't comprehend the highly personal motives which existed in the Royal Air Force, perhaps more strongly, under duress, [and] with greater cohesion than with any other service."

On Monday, 22 June, Wing Commander Hyde wrote home:

SUMMER HAS ARRIVED AT LAST, THE LAST TWO DAYS HAVE BEEN QUITE GOOD. NO MAIL SINCE MY LAST LETTER, BUT RECEIVED ? lb State Express from Blokie Appleton (DROPPED INTO SCRIPT THEN, WITHOUT THINKING!). NO NEWS SO WILL CONTINUE MY NARRATIVE (LEFT OFF A COUPLE OF MONTHS AGO) — AT 1200 hrs WE HAVE LUNCH — A BOWL OF STEW, FLAVOURED WITH A "MARMITE" CUBE. AFTER WHICH ONE EXERCISES, READS, SLEEPS OR DOES ODD JOBS. WE GET A JUG OF HOT WATER AT 13.30 SO USUALLY WASH CLOTHING. EVERY MONTH OR SO WE GET ISSUED WITH CLEAN BED LINEN. TEA IS BREWED IN THE COOKHOUSE FROM RED CROSS TEA WHEN AVAILABLE, & BROUGHT ROUND BY ORDERLIES AT 16.00 Hrs. A COUPLE OF SLICES OF BREAD, MARG & JAM AS WELL. THE NEXT EVENT IS THE EVENING CHECK PARADE AT 18.15 HRS, WHICH USUALLY LASTS 15-30 MINUTES. ONE THEN GETS DOWN TO PREPARING THE MEAL OF THE DAY. A MEAT-ROLL, PORRIDGE OR TINNED HERRINGS FROM THE RED X PARCEL WITH A CUP OF TEA OR COCOA. WHEN ONE GETS AN AMERICAN OF GYPPIE PARCEL WE DO OURSELVES PROUD WITH COFFEE & A TWO OR THREE COURSE MEAL!

On Thursday, 25 June, Peter Valachos and Colin Dilly — of all people — were late on *Appell*. They were sent to the cells and released later in the day pending sentence. This would not be passed until 30 July, when each malefactor was awarded five days' *Stubenarrest*. However, the cells at Warburg were again overcrowded, and they would have to wait until January 1943 to carry out their sentence at Oflag XXIB, Schubin. On Monday, 29 June Tony Trumble was sent to the cooler to serve a ten-day sentence for helping an escapee. Whilst in the cooler he suffered another bout of dysentery.

The day after Trumble started his sentence another ten aircrew officers were transferred to Stalag Luft III, including Lou Barry, Willie Turner and some more Fleet Air Arm officers, among whom was Rupert Davies. This brough the number of prisoners so far moved to Sagan up to sixty.

Among those now left behind at Warburg were Mike Adams, Johnny Agrell, Dennis Armitage, Eddie Asselin, Roff Ayton, Bill Bakker, Robin Beauclair, "Skid" Bellairs, Harald Bjelke-Peterson, Tom Blacklock, Roger Boulding, Anthony Bridgman, Pete Brodie, Cyril Buckley, "Eski" Campbell, Frank Campbell-Rogers, Lionel Casson, Edward Chapman, Tom Churcher, Frank Clayton, Johnny Clayton, Douglas Cooper, "Crammy" Crampton, Wallace Cunningham, Paddy Denton, Colin Dilly, Les Dixon, Ken Doran, Kenneth Edwards, Donald Elliott, Robert ("Pissy")

Fig 19. Flying Officer Colin Dilly, drawn by Howard Taylor, Warburg 1942 *(Martin Dilly)*

HTAYLOR
42.

Edwards, Hugh Falkus, George Frame, Don Gericke, Trevor Griffith-Jones, Clive Hall, Peter Harding, Bill Hartop, Donald Hayes, Warren Hayward, Derek Heaton-Nichols, Oliver Hedley, Wilf Hetherington, Tony Hibell, "Jackie" Horner, Charles Howlett, Robin Hunter, William Hunter, Noel Hyde, Terance Hynes, Arthur Imrie, Reg Jacoby, Paul Jacquier, Theo Johnson, Michael and Terence Kane, Joe Kayll, Bill Keighley, Danny Król, Peter Langmead, Peter Leuw, James Leyden, Fred Litchfield, Hugh Lynch-Blosse, Logie MacDonald, Colin MacFie, Denis MacKarness, "Fiji" MacKay, Kenneth Mackenzie, Kenneth Mackey, Colin MacLachlan, Jim Margrie, Eric Masters, Albert Matthews, Joe McCarthy, "Jock" McKechnie, Allan McSweyn, Cecil Milne, Ronnie Morgan, Bren Morris, Alf Mungovan, "Spud" Murphy, Justin O'Byrne, Terrence Officer, "Barney" Oldfield, George Parker, John Parker, Jeff Peat, Tony Péronne, "Pring" Pringle, Harry Prowse, Norman Quill, Mark Redgrave, Derek Roberts, Ralph Roberts, Robin Ross-Taylor, Michael Roth, "Sammy" Sampson, Harry Sellers, "Betsy" Serjeant, Freddie Shorrock, Bill Skinner, Eric Trenchard Smith, Frank Smith, Hank Staniland, John Stephens, Peter Stevens, Eric Sydney-Smith, Bryan Tayler, Howard Taylor, Eric Templer, Percy Thomas, Frank Thompson, Peter Tomlinson, Tony Trumble, Charles Tudge, Paul Vaillant, Peter Valachos, Tom Walker, James Heber Ward, Peter Ward-Smith, Peter Whitby, Frank Willan, "Taffy" Williams and Gordon Wright.

The day the ten-man purge left, the Germans started another round of TAB inoculations. Two days later they ordered that until further notice prisoners would be allowed to write home only on letter-cards, not on letter-forms. This was a reprisal for the escape of Keartland, Ruffel, Wallace-Terry and Gerry Williams.

On Wednesday, 22 July, the SBO was informed that representatives of the Protecting Power would be visiting the camp the next day. The Swiss Commission duly turned up, and as they were doing their inspection, two YMCA officials arrived to ascertain the prisoners' needs in the way of books, clothes and sports equipment. A third commission then arrived, consisting of German engineers from the local *Wehrkreis*, who had come to inspect the drains and general sanitation.

Under the cover of all this confusion, five Army officers, with the help of the RAF, pulled off another "Swiss Commission" bluff similar to that previously carried out by the RAF at Spangenberg in 1941. Captain John Logan of the Argyll and Sutherland Highlanders was disguised as a *Hauptmann*, Captain A L Pope of the Royal Fusiliers as an *Oberleutnant*, and former Laufen old lag Lieutenant Terence Prittie as an *Unteroffizier*. They were to escort two members of the Swiss Commission, impersonated by Captain W Earle Edwards of the Royal West Kents and Lieutenant A P R Rolt of the Rifle Brigade, through the lower gate and out of the camp. They counted on the probability that so many civilian parties and German officers were inside the camp that the gate guards would not recognise them as impostors. The scheme had been gestating for months, with the Army faking their own "goon-skins" and the Fleet Air Arm providing the dress uniforms for conversion into civilian suits. At about 11am the five escapers donned their disguises, while the RAF's Duty Pilot system, on this occasion being directed by Martin Gilliat, kept an eye on goons coming in and out of the gate and sent runners to keep them posted of German movements. At twelve o'clock the escapers began to filter down to Barrack No7, mingling with sporting types on their way to the main wash-house. In Barrack No7 Frank Willan and Tony Bridgman had the rest of their kit laid out — home-made briefcases for the "Swiss Commission", Lubbock's Mixture, maps, compasses and forged papers. The RAF runners were not in on the details of the scheme, and their eyes nearly popped out of their heads when they entered the room to find two German officers and an NCO lying nonchalantly on their bunks! The escapers were joined by another Army officer, Major E A F Macpherson of the Argylls, posing as the SBO. He was to accompany them to the gate.

By one o'clock the "High Street" was crawling with officers on their way to and from lunch in No1 Dining Hall, and Gilliatt gave the escapers the green light. Willan thrust them out amongst a group of RAF officers, who were completely fooled by their appearance and whose remarks were typical — and comical: "That's a swine of a young Nazi lieutenant, isn't it?" "He damned well ought to be at the *Ostfront!*" "And a dirty little squirt of an under-officer, too!" From the escapers' point of view, these remarks were all very satisfactory. They reached the gate, had their papers inspected, and were let through without mishap. Outside the camp the three fake goons doffed their uniforms to reveal civilian workman garb underneath. Sad to say, none of the five escapers made the home run. The longer they were out, the shabbier their appearance became, and this proved their undoing.

At the end of July, Allan McSweyn also escaped through the gate. Having taken part in two tunnel projects that had been discovered, he decided to hide in the bread cart. Converting and dyeing an RAF NCO's uniform into something resembling a suit, he settled into the cart and allowed the orderlies to wheel him out of the gate. He was away for two days. Crossing an enclosed field, he was spotted by two alert goons and returned to the camp for the customary fourteen days' solitary.

Although the RAF tunnellers had pretty well shot their bolt by August, several Army tunnels were being dug. Most were discovered by the highly active "ferrets" before they could be broken. If nothing else, the Germans picked up more knowledge of escape tactics, which made subsequent bids harder. Rademacher's men would suddenly assault a particular hut, strip each room bare, and go over each inch minutely, rapping on walls and floors, alert for the hollow sounds that would give away the tunnel or the hide they knew must exist. In August alone the Germans found five tunnels. As a result there was a general tightening-up of security, and German preventive measures inside the camp increased alarmingly, seriously limiting practice sessions for "Operation Olympia".

One afternoon David Walker told Kayll's team that from the signal to go they were taking at least eighty seconds per man to sortie. He wanted the time down to sixty seconds.

"When you go over that fence," he said, "things will happen very quickly. We are confident that the diversions will be effective to a degree, but it is essential that you are all well clear before any goons arrive on the scene." A week later their time was down to sixty-three seconds. Walker told them that Ladder Three (led by Captain David Crawford) was now below the one-minute mark, and this urged them on even more.

Walker now introduced another man — a Number Eleven — into Kayll's team. He was to be the "anchor man", and it would be his task to climb the ladder on the heels of Number Ten, tightly gripping the handles of the platform to prevent it from tilting while the last man went across. He would then return to his quarters.

With the help of the Escape Committee the potential escapers had been planning their routes. Master maps of all areas were smuggled into the camp in games parcels addressed to Army officers (but only two RAF officers received any). They were printed on very fine tissue paper and were exact in every detail. The camp's backroom boys had cleverly constructed a printing press. Using heavily strained jelly crystals from Red Cross parcels they made the base. Once this jelly base was set hard, they were able to etch the map details onto it in very fine relief, and with ink made from indelible pencils they could run off as many copies as they wanted. One of the RAF map-makers, Johnny Clayton, would use this method at Schubin and Sagan, and by the end of the war produced 4,900 maps. The escapers were also given handmade compasses with a magnetised needle set on a cork swivel. A small speck of luminous paint from a disused watch on the end of the needle would indicate north by night.

All this time, "Thomas Cooks", the forgery department run by Captain John Mansel, was working unremittingly at producing the wide variety of documents to be carried by the escapers. Most of the latter, once outside the camp, hoped to be able to pass themselves off as foreign workers. There were several millions of these unfortunates in Germany, brought in to work for the German war effort from all the countries overrun by the Nazis, and every one of them, man and woman, was obliged to carry a fistful of identity cards and permits according to nationality and occupation. These included an *Ausweis* (permission to travel within the Reich) and an *Arbeitskarte* (a worker's identity card), along with an *Urlaubsschein* (leave pass) and such items as ration books and military service exemptions. Identity cards were changed fairly frequently. It was essential that a forged pass should be up to date if the bearer hoped to bluff his way out of Germany. The collection and collation of the necessary information, and the acquisition of the various genuine passes, letters of introduction and maps, was in the hands of the Intelligence teams, who supplied the information upon which the forgers based their work.

The originals were typewritten, but as long as hand-produced forged permits were well drafted and properly stamped, they would almost certainly pass. There were also typed letters of recommendation which both German and foreign workers carried, explaining in more detail their reason for travelling. Imitating German typescript with a paintbrush was extraordinarily laborious work, as every letter had to be both vertically and horizontally aligned. German letterheads were often in raised type and in Gothic script. Producing these became a great art; indeed, so accomplished were the forgeries that the Germans were convinced they were being produced on a printing press, and on at least one occasion made a determined effort to search the camp for it.

Paper was fairly easy to obtain. Typing paper, artists' watercolour paper, the fly-leaves from books, and toilet paper — all could be filched or borrowed without arousing much suspicion. But German pen-nibs were unsatisfactory owing to poor quality, and a lot of work was done with a fine watercolour brush. Mansel used diluted ivory black Indian ink, building up each stroke to achieve a consistent overall colour. This avoided damaging the surface of the paper and looked more like genuine printing. The forged document was completed with signature and even, where necessary, embossing. A document with Roman lettering might take up to sixty hours to complete; a Service travel permit in Gothic lettering could be done in far less time.

Mansel's forgery team included any escape-minded officer with artistic leanings. One of the leading forgers from the RAF contingent, Gilbert Walenn, had been purged to Sagan. But Mansel still had Colin Dilly, Harald Bjelke-Peterson, Bill Hunter, Peter Mason and Howard Taylor. From the Army he had Lieutenant R H H Eastman of the 3rd Royal Tank Regiment, who had taken part in the defence of Calais in May 1940. He had been a handicraft teacher before the war, and was an expert in lettering (he had been coached by Daisy Alcock, who later produced the *Commemorative Book* in Westminster Abbey for those who fell in the war). His career as a POW forger had begun the previous autumn, when he saw a German guard drop his pass in the camp. Eastman helpfully picked it up for him, taking a good look at it as he did so. He then made two imitations, one of which Peter Stevens had used when trying to lead his fatigue party out of the camp in December. Eastman pretended that his hobby was heraldry, using it as a pretext to obtain the materials necessary to make authentic-looking German papers. Stevens often helped with the German wording.

"The Germans used to come and peer over my shoulder at my work," Eastman recalled, "but they never looked underneath, and therefore always missed the forgeries."

When the Germans were satisfied that his work was not subversive, they stamped it with an official pass, which he was then able to imitate, even to the small imperfections on the outline of the stamp.

The forgers did a lot of their work in the canteen — under the guise of "study" — getting up very early to get the best chance of peace and quiet. The contents of the canteen, set out for easy access on shelves — including pens, inkpots and writing paper — provided the necessary camouflage for the forgers' work, while the various bulk stores provided hiding places easy of access in emergency. Lookouts were posted at all relevant times to protect the forgers from being surprised on the job.

Following instructions, the would-be escapers had all been hoarding nails. They were going to need a large quantity of them when the time came to make the ladders. They pulled them out of doors and walls, found them on the ground and pinched them from unsuspecting civilian German carpenters. It was quite surprising how the quantity built up. The platforms for the ladders would come from the ceilings of the huts.

At midnight on Monday, 17 August, the Germans found yet another tunnel. A Riot Squad marched into the camp and turfed everybody out of their beds for a head-count, interrupting the work of other tunnellers digging by night.

"The weather here is quite hot now," wrote Wing Commander Hyde to his wife on Wednesday, 19 August:

THE CANTEEN HERE GOT HOLD OF AN OLD VIOLIN REPUTED TO BE WORTH RM 4,000, SO THEY RAFFLED IT & SPUD MURPHY HAS WON IT! HE DOESN'T PLAY IT & DOESN'T KNOW WHAT TO DO WITH IT! SOMEONE HAS OFFERED HIM £50 FOR IT, BUT, IF HE CAN GET IT HOME & IT IS GENUINE, IT SHOULD BE WORTH ABOUT £200.

A POW camp was a great place for rumours, and these stories usually concerned the progress of the war, but now a new crop of rumours spread through the camp like wildfire. They were most disturbing from the escapers' point of view, as they said that the camp was to be split up. On 20 August confirmation came when all Army officers of the rank of Major and above or over thirty-five years of age were given a week's notice that they were to be moved to Oflag IXA/Z at Rotenburg. On Wednesday, 26 August, the RAF and FAA contingents were told they, too, would be moving to their own camp. This move did not take place, but the transfer of the army officers did, and they left Warburg on 27 August. But here was one noticeable absentee. Major Tom Stallard had gone into hiding.

The transfer to Rotenburg had culled five of the thirty-five Army officers who had been trained for "Operation Olympia". In order to keep the four teams up to quota another five Air Force officers were recruited to fill the gaps, including Allan McSweyn, who had recently been released from the cooler, Don Gericke and Clive Hall. The Army officers who had been trained on Ladder Four were dispersed amongst the other three teams, and the new RAF recruits joined Kayll, Quill and Trumble. Ladder Four now consisted entirely of RAF and Fleet Air Arm officers. McSweyn, Gericke, Hall and the other two newcomers to the scheme were given some hurried training and instructed to finalise their travelling plans. The break would take place any night now. Stallard wanted cloud, wind and possibly rain, but lately the moon had been full and the weather clear and fine. The prospective escapers were getting edgy. Every day they pounded the dust of the compound and the perimeter road, building up strength and gazing impatiently at the mockingly clear skies.

Lieutenant-Colonel Kennedy, the SBO, demanded an audience with the Commandant, now *Oberstleutnant* Brinkord, who had replaced Gall in April or May. Kennedy was promised at least forty-eight hours' notice of any move. That was some reassurance, but the escapers became increasingly restless with each passing day.

On Friday, 28 August Brinkord informed Lieutenant-Colonel Kennedy that the entire camp would be evacuated on 1 September. However, later that day the move was again postponed. The situation was becoming fraught, to say the least, and on 29 August the "Operation Olympia" teams were summoned one by one to a meeting in David Walker's room.

"From now on, you are on twelve hours' notice," said Tom Stallard. "The assault area will be between Barrack Nos 20 and 21. There is quite a large back-up team, which has been specially selected to lay on the diversions, and I can assure you that there is going to be considerable noise and confusion going on while our escape is in progress. Grapples with empty tin cans on them will be tossed into the coiled wire and jangled with a rope. People in nearby huts will create as much din as possible. They will bang drums, blow trumpets and generally kick up a fuss. We will time our departure so that the patrolling goons are as far away from the assault area as possible, and we are quite convinced that the Germans will panic — they won't know what the hell is going on!"

Ladders One and Two would be assembled in Barrack No27, which was now empty. The other two teams would assemble their apparatus in Barrack No25.

"When we go over, we will fan out," Stallard continued. "Later, David Walker will show you the direction each of you is to take. Now — one other very important thing. We know that there is a standing patrol of Germans in the hayfield beyond, but they change their position every night. Should you run into the patrol, you must surrender immediately and keep them there! Somehow you must hold them for at least three minutes. If you're caught, you're caught — you don't make any further attempt to get away. Understood?"

The assembled men agreed, somewhat reluctantly.

Indicating Captain R A Johnstone of the Royal Engineers, he went: "Now, in conclusion, Captain Johnstone will be in charge of the whole operation from the compound. His word will be law. He will give the order to go from the compound and if, in his judgement, it is necessary he will give the order to stop. As from now, no more rehearsals will take place. Word will be passed to you when it is on!"

The next day, Sunday, 30 August, Lieutanant-Colonel Kennedy received his forty-eight hours' notice that the camp was to be evacuated. Although the conditions were by no means ideal for their purpose, it was decided to sortie that evening. But at lunchtime a bombshell dropped. A young English Lieutenant, John Dupree of the Seaforth Highlanders, had been accidentally electrocuted while working in a tunnel from Barrack No13, which had its entrance in a coal cellar off the hut kitchen. The officer in charge of the day shift, Lieutenant D A Cruickshank of the Royal West Kents, was operating the air pump at the bottom of the shaft supplying air to the naked Dupree, who had wriggled his way up to the working face of the tunnel with a small sand dispersal trolley, and his assistant, Captain Michael Borwick of the Scots Greys. Dupree had been working lying in water, at the face of the extremely narrow shaft, which was lit by a small bulb hanging from some piecemeal wiring running along the roof. The wire was not as well insulated as the workers would have liked, but insulating materials were hard to come by. A short time later Cruickshank heard Borwick yelling down the tunnel to switch off the electric current, which he did immediately. A few moments later an ashen Borwick came flying backwards out of the tunnel.

"Dear God, help him!" he cried. "There's been an accident!"

Cruickshank dived into the mouth of the dark hole and scrambled frantically along the pitch-black tunnel, eventually encountering Dupree's inert body.

Dupree had been hauling a dispersal trolley carrying a new length of air pipe. The projecting end of the pipe had caught a coil into which spare electric cable was wound to allow for the light moving forwards. The wire had been pulled down and become entangled with the trolley rollers. Obviously, Dupree had come back from the face to try to untangle it. A join in the wire had broken and a live end had fallen across his bare back, electrocuting him. Cruickshank tried desperately to pull Dupree back along the shaft, but the dead weight of the man, plus the cramped confines of the tunnel, made it an impossible task.

There was only one thing to do — sacrifice the tunnel in the hope that Dupree might be saved. Cruickshank scrambled backwards out of the tunnel, and found Borwick and the others in the day team waiting anxiously outside the mouth of the shaft in the coal cellar. A few seconds later they were all pounding on the locked cellar door, and a surprised orderly let them out. They quickly alerted a German sentry, and then someone rushed over to inform the Escape Committee. They had to get Dupree out in a hurry, and the only way they thought possible, having heard of Cruickshank's difficulty, was by digging from above the shallow tunnel in the compound.

Captain Frank Weldon, of the Royal Artillery, rushed to the scene, and while "Jock" Hamilton-Baillie and some others frantically dug from above, he ran into the coal cellar with a length of rope, squirmed desperately up the shaft and tied the rope around Dupree's cold legs. Once back in the pump chamber he and Captain "Johnny" Johnstone hauled on the rope, and after an incredibly superhuman effort they managed to drag Dupree's body back along the tunnel. The heavy body was hauled upright and pulled up and out by the others in the cellar, Germans included, and then quickly carried into the kitchen. Frank Weldon collapsed with his exertions.

Bill Bakker was one of the few officer aircrew who witnessed part of the tragedy:

I have seen the mishaps with the Army tunnel with RAF involvement. I was watching from our block, as a stooge. Suddenly an escapee, a man in a digger's outfit — underwear, and covered in mud — came running across shouting for help, as his mate had been electrocuted, underground. A sight I will never forget!

Several MOs, both German and British, worked hard at reviving Dupree, but to no avail. They eventually gave up and declared Dupree beyond help.

Once news of Dupree's death had swept through the camp, Lieutenant-Colonel Kennedy found himself with a difficult and delicate decision to make. Should he allow "Operation Olympia" to go ahead in light of the day's tragedy? He hurriedly called a conference, and the members of the Escape Committee each stated their own thoughts on the subject. Some insisted that the escape be postponed, while others indicated that the teams of men had been working for many weeks, and that as the camp was being evacuated shortly they should be permitted to make good their escape. Finally, Kennedy announced his decision.

"You go, Tom!" he told Stallard. "You go because I know that is what young Dupree would have wanted you to do!"

That afternoon Joe Kayll, Tony Trumble and Norman Quill, from Number Four Ladder, and Douglas Crawford, in charge of Number Three Ladder, crossed to Barrack No25, where they met some Army sappers and climbed into the loft through a well-concealed trap-door. With purloined hammers and saws they got to work constructing the four sets of ladders. The construction team worked fast, and in two hours had two perfect sets of apparatus. They dyed them purple with indelible lead dye so that they would not stand out in the dark. Two identical sets of ladders were being made for the other two teams in the loft of Barrack No27.

After *Appell* the RAF escapers informed their closest friends they were going out that night. They told them out in the open, one or two at a time, but could not tell them just how it would be accomplished. At 8pm the escapers were dressed and ready to go. At 8.45, in the gathering gloom, teams Three and Four made their separate ways to Barrack No25. Swiftly they took their storming apparatus from the ceiling and, covered by an alert team of stooges, carried them the short distance to their assembly area in Barrack No21, where they greased the wooden runners with *Speisefett*. Zero hour was 9.30pm.

The compound "controllers" were outside, ostensibly walking around before turning in for "lights-out" at 11 o'clock. The Germans allowed such walks up until this hour, so the officers did not appear suspicious as they strolled casually around the area, chatting and smoking.

Back in Barrack Nos 20 and 21, the escapers blackened their faces with soot from the stoves and pulled balaclava helmets over their heads. They ended up a sinister-looking lot. Like actors waiting for a play to begin, they wandered back and forth, making last-minute adjustments to their clothing and their packs. There was some desultory conversation, but generally they kept quiet, each man absorbed in his own thoughts.

At 9.25 Kayll, McSweyn and two other members of Ladder Four took up their positions by the apparatus. The other six, and No11, the "anchor man", stood behind them. The tension in the room was palpable. Suddenly, at 9.30, the camp was plunged into darkness, and they jumped out of their skins. But they weren't being given the signal to go. What was wrong?

Captain Johnstone was waiting for the sentries to reach the far end of their respective beats. Finally he gave the signal from the compound, and the controller bellowed: "Go!" This was it! Forty black-faced escapees instantaneously sprang into action. Kayll and McSweyn leapt out of their window, while two other members of the team pushed their apparatus out behind them. They grabbed the front end and pulled it out. Quill and an RAF escaper grabbed the other end on their way out, and the four of them raced towards their spot at the wire. The trip-wire had been whitewashed earlier to ensure they wouldn't run into it. Once across the warning wire, Kayll and McSweyn pushed their end up high, and Numbers Three and Four rammed their end into the ground beside the inner fence.

All around the camp bedlam had broken loose, as the diversions created complete pandemonium among the guards. They had no idea what was going on in the darkness and they didn't know which way to turn, although most of their attention was attracted to the noise of men shaking the barbed-wire fence a long way from where the escape was actually taking place. The two sentries in the closest towers were busy shouting down at two groups of men who had thrown up dummy ladders, and who were now scurrying back to their quarters, having ordered the guards, in German, not to take their eyes off the ladders.

Kayll leapt onto his ladder with the bottom end of the platform firmly grasped in his hands, whilst Nos 2, 3 and 4 held him steady. He climbed a couple of steps, and with all the strength he could muster slid the heavy platform upwards and across the two fences. As it fell into place he was up and over in a flash. The platform effectively straddled the wire, and he swung deftly through the hole at the far end, using the hockey-stick "trapeze bar", hit the ground and took off in a crouching run. Behind him the diversions were in full swing, and the wire twanged loudly as it shifted back and forth through the holes in the posts. The familiar, high-pitched and hysterical shouts of the Germans indicated their complete confusion.

McSweyn was all of three feet behind Kayll. As he was following him up the ladder he heard behind him a loud obscenity in a familiar Australian accent. Clive Hall was having trouble at the foot of the ladder. But McSweyn did not hesitate for a second as he repeated Kayll's smooth actions. He began sprinting after Kayll, and was about twenty yards clear when he heard a rifle-shot split the night air. He ran fast, crouching low, and charged through a field of turnips. Behind him, the machine-guns in the towers rattled as the excited sentries fired wildly at the ant-like army racing pell-mell from the camp. He sped on into a field of hay, bullets occasionally whining overhead, then slowed down a little.

Then, suddenly out of the darkness: "*Halt! Halt!* Or we fire!"

Ten hysterical Germans sprang from behind a stack of hay. McSweyn had run smack into the middle of the standing patrol. In seconds he was surrounded. The sentries were over-wrought with excitement, jabbing rifles and pistols into his back. Choked up with exertion and frustration, he

Fig 20. Operation Olympia. An impression by Phillip Bear as described by Michael Roth
(P H Bear)

stood gasping, and a few moments later noticed that two of the Army escapers had also been caught. They were Jack Champ and Rex Baxter, although he didn't know their names. Soon another recaptured escapee was thrust breathlessly in their midst.

The German *Unteroffizier* was furious, and obviously confused by the rapid events of the past few minutes. This was no time for heroics, as the guards were jumpy, but the recaptured escapers knew they now had a job to do — keep the guards with them so as to give the others a better chance. The requisite three minutes stretched before them like an eternity.

"How many have escaped?" screamed the *Unteroffizier*. "How many away?"

They stalled, and he barked: "Answer me, or you will be shot. Right now!"

"Four men!" said Baxter. "Four men, that's all. You have us all!"

"How did you get out?" yelled the *Unteroffizier*, his face inches from Baxter's. "How did you get past the wire?"

"We jumped over it," replied Baxter, with complete composure. "It was easy!"

"You lie!" spat the German. "You lie, you lie! It is impossible!"

They stood mute as he ranted on, but they had the grim satisfaction of knowing that the precious three minutes had now slipped by. Despite the constant scampering of feet as the other escapers disappeared into the darkness of the night, the patrol was still standing with their four captives instead of giving chase. These four had been unlucky, but it was immediately clear that, in essence, the scheme had worked.

Shortly afterwards, prodded violently with rifles, they were unceremoniously marched to the guard-house. Then two others joined them; so far, six in all had been caught. They were made to strip stark naked, and then lined up in the corridor, well away from the wall and about three feet apart. Talking was *streng verboten*. Six wary guards with rifles and fixed bayonets stood facing them from the other wall; they looked excited and jittery, so the six prisoners stood still. The lights were still out, and two hurricane lamps flickered eerily on the far wall.

After a while *Hauptmann* Mahlaw, the much-hated "Bulk Issue", strode in. Paunchy and pompous in his massive greatcoat with flamboyant velvet collars, he was red in the face with ill-concealed fury as, by the dim light of the lanterns, he walked slowly along the pathetic line-up. Silently he shook his gloved fist in each of their faces. He turned at the door, looked back and snarled at them.

"Verdammte englische Schweinhunde!"

They remained standing in the passageway for about two hours. They were cold, weary and thirsty, but also quite elated. Guards rushed in and out in a panic. Officers and NCOs shouted orders, and the six heard the screech of tyres as motor vehicles careered off into the night.

Around midnight things settled down a little. A guard strutted down the corridor, barked an order, and Baxter and Champ were escorted, still naked, for interrogation. Then it was McSweyn's turn. In the small dimly lit interrogation room he saw the contents of his pack laid out on a small table, behind which sat Rademacher, his face swollen and red with rage and his knuckles white. McSweyn's ration of Lubbock's Mixture, his precious hoard of chocolate, and his maps and compass, all lay in orderly fashion in front of Rademacher's trembling fists. He looked up at McSweyn as if he could throttle him, took in his discomfort and nakedness, and sat back.

"You have been brought here for interrogation," he said. "I am sure that you will co-operate, just as I am sure that you know the consequences of your stupid escape attempt. You have read the notices from the *Oberkommando der Wehrmacht*, warning you of what might happen. You have nothing to lose by answering a few questions."

He paused for effect, and hinting that the Gestapo might intervene, added: "It may even save your life!"

Picking up one of Johnny Clayton's maps, he went on: "We have already examined your escape equipment, and we know how you got out." He looked McSweyn in the face "Where did you get the ladders, and how many of you were there? Where did you get the maps? How did you plan to get out of Germany? Answer me — NOW!"

McSweyn calmly gave him his name, rank and service number.

Rademacher glared at him. "You are being very foolish!" he said. "Why not be sensible and answer my questions? We will find the answers eventually, so why not tell us now? Come along; you will explain the whole plan, and things may go a little easier for you when punishments are given to the participants! I am sure you are aware what these punishments may be. It is a very serious charge you will face. Your answer, please!"

McSweyn repeated the formula.

Rademacher exploded, yelling and screaming in unintelligible German. It was a frightening sight. He jumped up from his chair and slammed his fists repeatedly onto the table, making everything fly into the air. McSweyn stood still, blinking. He was frightened lest Rademacher pull out his revolver and start shooting. He could sense the guards behind him go stiff with fear.

"Raus!" screamed the furious Rademacher. *"Raus!"*

McSweyn needed no further encouragement. Turning to flee the room, he was grabbed by the arms and escorted back to the sanctuary of the corridor. One by one his companions were taken away to undergo similar treatment, but Rademacher learnt nothing from them, either.

As the long night dragged on, McSweyn was overcome by tiredness, but the guards relaxed a little and one by one the six men were allowed to go to the toilet.

At about 6am the lights came back on — courtesy of the British! Just after seven o'clock the unpredictable Germans gave them back their underclothing, shirts, socks and boots, and they were permitted to dress. Half an hour later they were escorted to the main camp gate and they were free to return to their quarters. They couldn't believe their good fortune as they walked quickly along the "High Street", talking animatedly about the events of the night — the first chance they had had to do so — and eager to find out from some of the others how the rest had fared. They were curious as to how many had escaped.

Two of the teams had been completely successful — Ladders One and Two had between them cleared twenty men over the wire. On Number Three Team, Doug Crawford, Captain A J Hands of the King's Own Royal Rifle Regiment, and four others managed to scramble over before the order to return was given by Captain Johnstone. Ladder Four, the hastily reconstituted RAF and FAA team, managed to get only two of their number away, McSweyn and Kayll; the latter was still on the loose. Twenty-eight men out of a possible forty had got over the wire. Six of them had been retaken, so it now appeared they had twenty-two "gone aways"— not a bad effort. The only casualty was an Army officer who had sustained a slight bullet wound to the heel.

Michael Roth had observed the escape from a position of safety in one of the barracks. "It was a very fine effort…It is a miracle no one was killed...The Germans were convinced that the special ladders had been dropped from the air. I am surprised the escape was not made into a film."

The next morning the escape apparatus were still straddling the wire, a symbol of their triumph, and an official photographer was busy snapping away with his Leica. Alas! for posterity, he was not from the OKW, but was merely a civilian photographer from Warburg under contract to the Wehrmacht. At the end of the war he destroyed his entire archive, and only six photographs taken at Oflag VIB have survived.

Joe Kayll was out one week. He had spent so much time helping prepare others for the escape that he had not given much thought about what to do once outside the wire, and although he had warm clothes he had no papers. He decided to hard-arse it to Switzerland, walking down the *Autobahn* at night and hiding by day. There wasn't much traffic at night, and whenever he did see headlights he lay by the roadside until the vehicle was comfortably past, and then carried on walking. As soon as it started to get light he found a wood and stayed there for the day. On his fifth morning of freedom he was building a little nest for himself in the middle of a wood when a gamekeeper, the bane of many an escaping prisoner of war, appeared with his dog and baled him up with his shotgun.

Two days after the escape, on Tuesday, 1 September, all the remaining Army officers in the camp began entraining for the new camp, Oflag VIIB, at Eichstätt in Northern Bavaria. It was here that they learnt several months later that the first three over the wire — Rupert Fuller and Albert Arkwright, along with Henry Coombe-Tennant of the Welsh Guards — had made it back to England. Walking to Holland, they had contacted the Dutch Underground. After staying in a sympathetic farmer's barn for nine days, they had eventually been passed along the famous "Comet" line through Belgium, France and Spain and finally home to England.

On Friday, 4 September the remnants of the RAF and FAA contingent were sent to Oflag XXIB, at Schubin, near Bromberg in Poland — and fewer than sixty kilometres (about thirty-seven miles) from Thorn, the scene of the *Strafe* in 1941. The day began with the prisoners being woken up and searched at 4am. The whole business took almost five hours, but by 9.30 am they were sitting in second class railway carriages at Dössel station. They arrived at Schubin at 5am on 5 September. A week later, Joe Kayll was escorted in to the camp and "awarded" forty days in the cells.

Hugo Bracken summed up the experience of Warburg as follows:

(i) Being shot down and taken prisoner is a fairly traumatic experience from which it takes some time to recover. Most of the aviators at VIB had been prisoners for some time and had recovered.

(ii) The Germans did not make such a deliberate attempt to humiliate us [as they had done at Oflag XC]. The morale in the camp was better and the general attitude was one of "standing up" to the Germans, which was lacking at Lübeck.

(iii) We got Red Cross parcels, which we did not get at Lübeck, and more regular mail.

(iv) Probably the most important was that we got regular BBC news, which we did not get at Lübeck, and the news was better. In the summer and early autumn of 1941 the Germans were winning victory after victory on the Eastern Front, and there was quite a possibility that, if this continued, Russia would be knocked out of the war. If this happened, Britain would be fighting on alone with very little prospect of avoiding a humiliating peace. Things were also going badly in North Africa. By the winter it became clearer and clearer that the Germans had failed to knock Russia out of the war. Furthermore, in December America came into the war, which transformed the situation.

There was no telling what Sagan and Schubin held in store, although David Lubbock would later sum up his experiences of various POW camps in four pithy lines:

Dulag Luft was a mockery... "For you the war is over." Oh yeah? Lübeck was sadistic. Warburg, with all the army officers, was for us almost a relaxing interlude. Schubin was the easiest camp from which to escape and reach Sweden. Sagan was the most efficiently run and the prisoners most closely guarded.

Notwithstanding the many fillips to kriegie morale at Warburg, in three years of war not one aircrew prisoner from Spangenberg, Thorn, Lübeck and Warburg had made a home run — or come anywhere near it. As far as the Warburg prisoners knew, Roger Bushell and Jaroslav Zafouk were still at large (they had, in fact, been recaptured after months of hiding out in Prague), but so far the honours had gone to the Third Reich. Nevertheless, Warburg had been a training ground for newly captured RAF and FAA prisoners, who had learned how to shore tunnels, how to construct trolleys and underground railway lines from filched materials, how to scale the wire, and the clandestine arts of forgery, map-making and escape security. They would put their knowledge and experience to the test in Schubin and Sagan. As for Commander George Beale, in view of the cat that he was not in the Royal Navy's aviation branch (although he had been in charge of RAF and FAA parades at Warburg and would be so again at Schubin), he would eventually be transferred to Marlag und Milag Nord, the *Kriegsmarine* camp for Royal and Merchant Navy prisoners at Westertimke. There, he would lead the camp's Escape Committee.

The three Czechs who had been captured in September 1940 — Vaclav Kilian, Zdenek Prochazka and Karel Trojacek — were separated by the time Warburg closed. Prochazka alone was sent direct to Stalag Luft III. Kilian had already been moved to Oflag VIC at Osnabrück, which had opened in July 1941, and would turn up at Sagan much later. Shortly afterwards, Trojacek was transferred to a French camp, Oflag VIA at Soest. He was then moved to Oflag IXA/Z, Rotenburg, and thence to Oflag IXA/H, where he remained from 14 September 1942 until 14 March 1943, when at last he was escorted to Stalag Luft III. On 2 September 1944 Trojacek was moved again, to Stalag Luft I, along with Kilian, and on 22 September Prochazka was sent to Colditz. Throughout this time all three were periodically interrogated and intimidated by the Berlin Gestapo, until on 6 January 1945 Trojacek was also removed from Stalag Luft III and sent to Colditz, arriving on the 9th. There, Prochazka and Trojacek awaited liberation by the US Army.

Appendices

Services:
AuxAF Auxiliary Air Force
FFAF Free French Air Force
RAAF Royal Australian Air Force
RAFO Reserve of Air Force Officers
RAFVR Royal Air Force Volunteer Reserve
RCAF Royal Canadian Air Force
RM Royal Marines
RN Royal Navy
RNNAS Royal Netherlands Naval Air Service
RNR Royal Navy Reserve
RNVR Royal Navy Volunteer Reserve
RNZAF Royal New Zealand Air Force
SAAF South African Air Force

Ranks:
Air Forces:
AC1 Aircraftman 1st Class
P/O Pilot Officer
F/O Flying Officer
F/L Flight Lieutenant
S/L Squadron Leader
W/C Wing Commander
G/C Group Captain

Other services:
L/A Leading Airman (RN)
Mid Midshipman (RN)
N/A Naval Airman (RN)
Ty S/Lt Temporary Sub-Lieutenant (RN)
Ty Lt Temporary Lieutenant (RN)
2/Lt Lieutenant (SAAF)
S/Lt Sub-Lieutenant (RN)
Sy Lt Supply Lieutenant (RN)
Lt Lieutenant (FFAF, RN, SAAF, Army)
Lt Cdr Lieutenant Commander (RN)
Cdr Commander (RN)
Capt (RM, RN, SAAF)

Note: The prefix "A" before a rank indicates acting rank

Decorations:
AFC Air Force Cross
DFC Distinguished Flying Cross
DFM Distinguished Flying Medal
DSC Distinguished Service Cross (RN)
DSO Distinguished Service Order
MC Military Cross
* Bar to decoration

Prisoner of War Camps:

D185	Dulag 185, Salonika, Greece
DL	Dulag Luft, Oberursel
F15	Fort XV, Thorn
O2A	Oflag IIA, Prenzlau
O4C	Oflag IVC, Colditz
O5B	Oflag VB, Biberach
O6A	Oflag VIA, Soest
O6B	Oflag VIB, Warburg
O6C	Oflag VIC, Osnabrück
O7B	Oflag VIIB, Eichstätt
O7C	Oflag VIIC, Laufen
O9A/H	Oflag IXA/H, Spangenberg
O9A/Z	Oflag IXA, Rothenburg
O10A	Oflag XA, Itzehoe
O10C	Oflag XC, Lübeck
O21B	Oflag XXIB, Schubin
S9C	Stalag IXC, Bad Sulza (Mulhausen)
S12A	Stalag XIIA, Limburg an der Lahn
SL1	Stalag Luft I, Barth
SL3	Stalag Luft III, Sagan

Appendix I

The Prisoner-of-War Code of the Geneva Convention, 1929

Weimar Germany was one of the first of the thirty-eight powers represented in Geneva on 27 July 1929 to sign the Prisoner-of-War Code and the Red Cross Convention. These had their origins in the first, semi-official, Geneva Convention called in 1863, which was followed a year later by the first international laws of war regarding the treatment of the sick and wounded. Known collectively as the Red Cross Convention, they were ratified by forty-one states and revised in 1906. On 18 October 1907, the Red Cross Convention was extended by the Hague Convention, which for the first time in history laid down the rights and obligations of prisoners of war. But the Great War proved both Conventions inadequate and they had to be revised yet again. The 1929 Prisoner-of-War Code contained no less than ninety-seven specific articles, the most pertinent of which can best be summarized as follows:

ARTICLE 2. A prisoner of war shall be under the control of the hostile power, not of the individuals or units that have captured him.

ARTICLES 2 & 3. POWs are to be protected by the detaining power from violence, insults and public curiosity, and must not be subject to reprisals for military actions. They shall be segregated according to rank — officers in one compound, NCOs and "other ranks" (ie, those below the rank of full corporal) in another.

ARTICLE 5. A POW under interrogation is obliged to give only his name, rank and service number, and must not be forced to give information on his armed forces or his country. He must not be threatened, insulted, or exposed to unpleasantness or disadvantages should he refuse to reply.

ARTICLE 6. All his personal effects are to be held initially by the detaining power and, along with identification documents, must eventually be handed back. Identity discs, badges of rank and decorations are not be taken from him. Only arms and military equipment can be confiscated.

ARTICLE 7. Newly captured prisoners must be removed from the fighting zone as soon as possible but, "Evacuation of prisoners on foot may normally be effected only by stages of 20 kilometres (12 miles) a day, unless the necessity of reaching water and food depots requires longer stages".

ARTICLES 8 & 10. Immediately after capture or, at most, within one week of arriving at a permanent camp, a POW is entitled to write directly to his family and to POW and relief agencies, stating that he is a prisoner and indicating whether or not he has been wounded; thereafter he is entitled to send at least two letters and four cards per month. Parcels addressed to him can contain food, tobacco, clothing, medical supplies and articles of a religious, educational and recreational nature.

ARTICLE 9. Prisoners are to be given complete religious freedom, including a chaplain and provision for religious services. Captives qualified as doctors, dentists, chaplains, etc, if required to act as such, shall not then be considered prisoners of war but "protected personnel", and shall be entitled to visit prisoners working outside the camp.

ARTICLE 11. The food provided by the detaining power shall be of the same quantity and quality as that given to its own base troops (in Germany, members of the *Ersatzheer*, or Army Reserve, which guarded POWs) and means shall be provided for cooking these and any additional rations that prisoners procure. Tampering with their food as a disciplinary measure is forbidden.

ARTICLES 12-21. Prisoners are to be grouped according to nationality, language and customs, and are not to be separated, without their consent, from other prisoners from their own branch of the armed forces. POW camps must be comparable to accommodation for the detaining power's own depot troops; located in healthy areas away from the battle zone; and have sufficient running water, sanitary facilities, heating, fresh-air exercise space and bomb shelters, and a canteen stocking everyday articles such as soap, toothbrushes, combs and hair oil at prices not above those prevailing locally. The clothing provided shall include decent underwear and footwear.

The next twenty-five articles deal with discipline and organisation. They lay it down that POWs are at all times subject to the laws of the detaining power's armed forces. Thus, all "other ranks" are required to salute all officers of the detaining power, while officers are required to salute equals and superiors in rank. The camp commandant can put them under arrest for disobedience, disorderly behaviour or violation of camp orders. But they are only to be "reasonably restrained", and not strictly confined unless absolutely necessary. POWs are also entitled to legal counsel before signing any legal documents and to a trial for serious breaches of camp discipline. Trial is to be by military court, unless the laws of the detaining power expressly give jurisdiction to the civil authority. But no prisoner can be punished by both military and civil court for the same act.

Prisoners are allowed to select a representative to confer with the camp commandant and his staff and to take charge of the distribution of Red Cross supplies. This individual will listen to the grievances of his men and discuss them in private with representatives of the protecting power, who are to ensure that the Geneva Convention is upheld by the detaining power. If the protecting power concludes that the grievances are legitimate, they are to be passed on to the camp commandant. Protecting power representatives, as well as representatives of the International Committee of the Red Cross and members of approved relief agencies, such as the Young Men's Christian Association, have the right to visit camps and report on their conditions.

ARTICLES 50-54 of the Code recognise the duty of a prisoner to escape, and forbid harassment or reprisals in the event of recapture, such as corporal punishment, confinement in cells not illuminated by daylight, any form of cruelty, the stripping of rank, and collective punishment for an individual act. A recaptured escapee shall be subject only to disciplinary punishment — no more than thirty days' solitary confinement. The same applies to those who have aided and abetted him, unless they have committed acts of violence or murder. (Under Article 48, however, the detaining power is permitted to create "special camps" as repositories for difficult captives.)

ARTICLE 67. Medical inspections are to be carried out once a month and prisoners given access to an infirmary on the camp site. Seriously ill POWs must be admitted to civilian or military hospitals for treatment at the expense of the detaining power.

ARTICLE 68. Inspection commissions consisting of a doctor each from the detaining power, the protecting power and the enemy power shall be permitted to examine and interview critically ill prisoners who have been put forward for repatriation or exchange. Those who pass are to be sent to a neutral port for their return home.

ARTICLE 84. A complete copy of the POW Code shall be posted "in places where it may be consulted by all prisoners" and in their natives language(s).

APPENDIX II

The POW Organisation of The War Office and the Red Cross

While Nazi Germany had been shaping its policy towards future prisoners of war from as early as 1938, Britain did not confront the possibility that large numbers of its servicemen might end up behind barbed-wire until it was forced to do so. Only after the outbreak of hostilities did the Foreign Office set up a POW Department, which would be led throughout the war by Sir Harold Satow, and only when the German offensive against the Low Countries and France was well under way in May 1940 did the War Office set up a Prisoner of War Directorate.

Both departments, along with the Army Council, displayed a stiff-necked attitude, a distinct lack of urgency and a surfeit of confusion in dealing with prisoner of war affairs. When, in September 1939, the Foreign Office received two POW letters — one from a bomber pilot, Squadron Leader S S Murray, and the other from his second pilot, Pilot Officer A B Thompson — via Goering and his diplomatic contacts in Sweden, the civil servants complained because they had not gone through authorised Red Cross channels. Seven months later, in April 1940, the Army Council informed the Joint War Organisation of the British Red Cross and Order of St John of Jerusalem that it expected only 2,000 officers and men to be captured in the immediate future. On 15 June, when the British Expeditionary Force was evacuating through Dunkirk, the number of prisoners registered was only 1,345 — well within the Army Council's optimistic forecast. But thousands of personnel had been left behind in France, and slowly but surely the number of prisoners being registered increased. By the end of June it stood at 2,111, and by the end of July at 4,000. Even at that late stage the Army Council was unable to give the Red Cross any indication of what it thought the final figure would be. Not until November did the Council disclose the full figure of 44,000.

The Prisoner of War Directorate had representatives from all three Services and eventually spawned a number of sub-committees. They listed British POWs in enemy hands, including each man's name, rank and service number, and the designation and location of the camp in which he was held; attended to the welfare of prisoners; dealt with prisoners' pay and allowances; maintained contact with their next-of-kin and relatives; supplied their military clothing, which it sent through the Red Cross; negotiated repatriation schemes; and regulated the voluntary organisations which helped POWs. These included the International Committee of the Red Cross (ICRC), the Joint War Organisation, the Young Men's Christian Association, the Relatives' Association and the International Student Body. The POW Directorate also took on responsibility for the welfare of Czechoslovakian, Polish, French, Belgian, Dutch, Norwegian and Greek POWs who had been captured while serving in His Majesty's Forces and whose governments were in exile in Britain. It also established an Imperial Prisoner of War Committee, which attended to the needs of Dominion POWs in German and Italian hands; on this sat representatives of the armed forces of Canada, Australia, New Zealand and South Africa.

Whenever it received a new list of prisoners from Germany's *Wehrmachtsauskunftsstelle für Kriegsverluste und Kriegsgefangene* (Armed Forces Information Office for Casualties and POWs), the Information Bureau in London notified the War Office's POW Directorate, and the POW Department of the Foreign Office, and also sent lists to the Joint War Organisation. The latter also established a special section called the "Wounded, Missing, and Relatives Department" to deal with the problems of missing men who could not be traced. It worked in close collaboration with the Admiralty, the War Office and the Air Ministry, each of whom sent it lists of all men missing in action. With the help of the ICRC it followed up the smallest clues in order to trace missing men.

Another means by which the POW Directorate received information about prisoners of war was by German radio. During the first year of the war, Josef Goebbels, the German propaganda minister, and his "editor and speaker" for foreign broadcasts at the *Reichsrundfunk* at Berlin-Charlottenburg, William Joyce ("Lord Haw-Haw"), had a British audience two-thirds the size of the BBC's. To keep the British public tuned in, Joyce regularly broadcast prisoners' names from the *Rundfunkhaus* in Masurenallee, or from satellite stations such as the *Bremensender* and *Hamburgsender*. Squadron Leader Murray, Flight Lieutenant R H Edwards and Pilot Officers H E L Falkus and A B Thompson all had their capture announced over German radio. Occasionally POWs were brought before the microphone to relate details of their capture. Lord Haw-Haw's news was passed on even when it was not heard by immediate relatives. Both the War Office and the Joint War Organisation regarded these unofficial reports with scepticism, taking the view that they could not be checked and that, moreover, British citizens who had been informed that their husband, son or brother was a POW might be devastated when reliable details confirmed that he had in fact been killed. This scepticism seems to have been ill-founded, however, as, apart from occasionally misspelling the names of those captured, the Germans seldom communicated unreliable information on this subject except towards the end of the war when the Reich was crumbling from within as well as without. (In fact, of all the Allied nations involved in the Western theatre, it was the British who first gave up keeping accurate POW records, sometimes being three camps behind in prisoner transfers. Even as late as 1945, Ernie Mullins and Alf Mungovan were listed as still being in Oflag VIB.)

In any event, the War Office forbade prisoners of all ranks from using German radio to transmit messages home under any circumstances, but a few prisoners were naturally tempted to use this means of letting their families know that they were safe. This undoubtedly owed something to the fact that very few prisoners — even the most senior officers and NCOs — were informed about Britain's POW arrangements. The same applied to their relatives. It was not until 1943 that the War Office issued *A Handbook for the Information of Relatives and Friends of Prisoners of War*, and the government only handled questions about POWs in the House of Commons through a junior Minister. "I am astonished," says Hugo Bracken today, "how very few questions were asked in Parliament about POWs between 1940 and 1944. I have only been able to find two in 1940, four in 1941, one in 1942 and two in 1943." Thus it was easy for both prisoners and their families back home to believe that they were being conveniently ignored.

British officialdom's attitude towards POWs is again illustrated by the reluctance with which it agreed to establish a sea-route for sending them parcels of food, clothing and other essentials. On 2 September 1939 the British Red Cross Society and the Order of St John of Jerusalem had merged — as they had done in the Great War — into the Joint War Organisation, under the chairmanship of Sir Arthur Stanley, to bring relief to sick and wounded British servicemen and to ameliorate the lot of British prisoners of war. The Emergency Committee that had convened to ratify this agreement had already devised the machinery to meet these requirements. This consisted of an Executive Committee, chaired by Lord Cromer, with Major-General Sir John Kennedy, a distinguished soldier, as vice-chairman; and fifteen departments, one of the most important of which was the Prisoners of War Department, with Lord Clarendon in charge, and Field Marshal the Lord Chetwode among the distinguished members of its committee. (In June 1940 Lord Chetwode became vice-chairman of the Executive Committee. In September 1941 Lord Clarendon was succeeded by Major-General Sir Richard Howard-Vyse.)

The main task of the Prisoners of War Department was to supplement official ration scales by providing food, equipment and services that would bring the standard of prisoners' comfort up to the level the public would themselves expect. But this was by no means easy — for in effect it found itself supplying much that should have been normal issue, owing to the fact that the Germans consistently underfed their prisoners. A booklet entitled *Prisoner of War*, published by the British Red Cross more than a year after its first major inspection of the camps in February 1941, pointed out that, in contravention of the POW Code, the food issued to prisoners sometimes fell below the standard of that issued to German garrison troops and that "if it were not supplemented from outside, British prisoners would be in a poor way".

The War Office handbook went further: "...the German Government have committed serious breaches of the Convention. Of these, the most grievous is their failure to provide men with adequate food and clothing." More specifically, the Germans had estimated the cost of keeping a prisoner of war at 1.20 *Reichsmark* a day, the sterling equivalent of eleven shillings (11/-) a week. But they fed non-working prisoners — mainly officers and Senior NCOs — on one shilling and two pence a week (1/2d), that is, less than the provision for a non-working civilian. Even with Red Cross parcels British prisoners were receiving less than half the calories that German prisoners were consuming in Britain and Canada. They were, in effect, being systematically starved. British other ranks engaged in heavy labour in coal mines received only slightly better rations and those working on farms were given "extras" by the farmers, who had a vested interest in ensuring they could work at their best.

Thus Red Cross food parcels became more a necessity than merely a luxury, and accordingly POWs turned to the Red Cross for their bare means of subsistence. Lord Cromer ruled that the British Red Cross should always keep a large reserve of food parcels "in the pipe" to meet this contingency, and Mr (later Sir) Montague Eddy, in charge of transporting parcels, did his utmost to maintain the flow.

Up to the fall of the Low Countries and France, prisoners of war in Germany received Red Cross food parcels either by postal service from Britain or by road and rail from Belgium via Holland. But the 1940 campaign closed the latter route. It was not until December, by which time some members of the RAF had been prisoners for more than a year, that the British Admiralty opened a loophole in the blockade of Occupied Europe to allow ships chartered by the Red Cross to ferry vital foodstuffs, clothing and medical supplies between Lisbon and Marseilles so they could be sent on to Geneva. The first vessel, the *Julita*, sailed before Christmas 1940, and thus began a regular service controlled at all times by the Red Cross. Even then, the British Red Cross was subject to severe criticism by Members of Parliament, and letter-writers to *The Times*, who doubted the value and efficiency of its parcels service.

As the war progressed and the number of POWs increased, this enterprise was vastly expanded until there were ten standard types of food parcel, each containing slightly different foodstuffs but of similar calorific and nutritional value. Each contained ten shillings' worth of food, bought at cheap rates, not subject to the usual duties and tax, and worth at least eighteen shillings by 1944. The main ingredients were meat, fish, tea, cocoa, margarine (with added vitamins), pudding mixture, cheese-, egg-, and milk-powders, chocolate, jam and biscuits. Cigarettes went in separate parcels.

The Red Cross also sent standard medical parcels, books, musical instruments, play-scripts, stage make-up and sports equipment, much of it supplied by the YMCA. Standard medical parcels — containing disinfectants, soap, bandages, gauze, lint, drugs and aspirins — were sent from London to Geneva every week, while the Invalid Comforts Section supplied special parcels for the sick. One was a "milk parcel" and the other an "invalid parcel". A typical milk parcel contained one tin each of Benger's food, Allenbury's, Horlicks, creamed rice, lemon-curd, custard, tomatoes and arrowroot; two tins each of Nestlé's milk, Ovaltine, cheese, dried eggs and Yeatex, plus tomato sauce, barley sugar and chocolate. Hundreds of these were packed a week into small tins. The invalid parcels contained more solid food — minced beef or sliced meat, tinned fruit, tinned salmon, meat and vegetable extracts, cod-liver oil and malt, glucose and honey. At Geneva there was usually a balance of 40,000 milk parcels and another 40,000 special food parcels. This was calculated on the assumption that five percent of POWs at any one time would need medical attention. From Geneva they were sent to senior medical officers at prison camps and POW hospitals to use as required. In addition to these there was an "occupational parcel", which contained patterns and material for making such things as slippers, waistcoats, belts, patchwork quilts, wall-pockets and tapestries.

"Utility" parcels of books could also be sent by certain specified booksellers, and cigarettes, pipes and tobacco by selected tobacconists. A prisoner's next-of-kin could send clothes three times a year.

While utility parcels were addressed directly to individual prison camps, all other parcels had to go by what the authorities called the "Parcels Roundabout". At the beginning of the war parcels were packed at St James's Palace, London, which sent out a mere twenty-six parcels a week. But after Dunkirk, when the number of POWs increased, the packing centre was moved to North Row, just off Park Lane, with another for next-of-kin parcels at Finsbury Circus. Many voluntary packing centres opened throughout England, the figure eventually reaching seventeen, plus another six in Scotland, including a centre for next-of-kin parcels in Glasgow. Parcels packed in Scotland were popular with prisoners because they contained oatmeal.

If a POW's wife wanted to send a next-of-kin clothing parcel it had to go first to Finsbury Circus, London, or to the packing centre in Glasgow, along with a list of contents. It was then unpacked, examined and repacked. At the Finsbury Circus centre a hundred girls — about eighty of them volunteers — worked at long trestle tables in a large room, and as soon as the postman delivered the parcel one of the girls unpacked it, spread its contents out on the table and examined them. First, she checked the "coupon goods". Next-of-kin were allowed special coupons with which to buy clothes for prisoners, and any unused coupons had to be returned when the parcel was delivered to the packing centre. However, some next-of-kin had been known to use the coupons for themselves. To make sure the items of clothing tallied with the number of coupons used, the girls subjected each parcel to careful scrutiny. Whenever there was a discrepancy, the parcel was delayed until it was accounted for and, if possible, rectified.

The next check was for contraband. No money, stamps, stationery or playing cards could be sent privately (playing cards could be sent only in Red Cross games parcels). Nothing in tubes was allowed, as these could contain messages, and neither were food (except chocolate), medical comforts or cigarettes. Pictures and photographs had to go in separate letters. Dozens of parcels a week arrived at the centre containing pots of jam, home-made cakes or sweets. The girls had to take them all out and mark them "return to sender". They also had to search diligently for hidden messages — a favourite hobby with relatives, who would write endearments on thin paper and stuff them in the toes of slippers and the ends of glove-fingers. Some wives embroidered coded messages as patterns on clothes. These messages were normally innocent, but if the German censors discovered them they would naturally assume otherwise and delay issuing the parcel.

Once the girl had checked the contents, and made sure they tallied with the list inside the parcel, she had to repack them, firstly in corrugated cardboard, then in extra-strong, waterproof brown paper, which she tied up with string. (On average, the British Red Cross got through two hundred miles of string per week.) The parcel was now ready to start its journey. Until it reached Lisbon it was under the control of the General Post Office, who might receive it that same evening. However, the GPO sometimes had to hang on to it for as long as three weeks while the Ministry of War Transport awaited room on a convoy.

Vessels chartered by the ICRC sailed from Britain, the Dominions, the USA and South America to Lisbon and Genoa, where parcels from all these countries converged before being sent by sea to Marseilles and by rail to Geneva. (Experience had shown that trying to take the parcels overland through Spain was a hopeless proposition. Spain was unable to look after its own affairs, let alone help the Allies.) At Lisbon a stock of five or six weeks' food was always held over so that no ship was left idle upon its return from Marseilles. Another five million were also stockpiled at Geneva, where the Red Cross rented huge warehouse and piled parcels from the floor to the ceiling rafters, in case of delays abroad. Later in the war a northern sea route to Göteborg, Sweden, was established and from there stores were ferried across the Baltic to Lübeck and other ports in north Germany. From Britain there might be as many as 100,000 food parcels a week, plus five million cigarettes, as well as next-of-kin parcels. Another 100,000 food parcels a week came from Canada. Bulk food came from Argentina. Books were sent out by the Joint War Organisation at the rate of about a thousand a week, until by 1943 some 25,000 volumes stood on the shelves at the reserve library in Geneva.

A ship's cargo was usually made up of severnty-five per cent food parcels and the rest next-of-kin and other personal parcels. The latter were always given priority. When they reached Lisbon, they would go into the first available ship, and only when they were stowed away in the holds was the space left over filled with standard food parcels to add to the floating stock at Geneva. There, hundreds of people were employed in the enormous task of classifying and sorting out the parcels. The food parcels were drawn from the stockpiles at a rate of one per man per week. Early in the war the parcels were addressed to individuals. But details of a new prisoner might not reach home for weeks or even months, in which case he would have to survive on the poor German diet and the charity of his fellow-prisoners until his own parcels arrived. If a man moved camp he might never get the parcel meant for him. (To give the Germans credit, they set up a "lost parcels" centre at Stalag XIIA, and regularly published lists of unclaimed parcels in their POW propaganda rag, *The Camp*.) Later the system was changed and the parcels sent in bulk to the camps, where they were shared out. Clothing and next-of-kin parcels were sorted out in Geneva first by country, then by camp. The ICRC then had to arrange with the German authorities for sufficient box-wagons to transport the parcels from the Swiss border to the camps.

Eventually the ICRC had eight ships in regular service. They ranged in size from the 1,000-ton *Padua* to the 5,000-ton *Malange*, which could carry 360,000 Red Cross food parcels on a single voyage. As many as possible were used at a time, but this was subject to the availability of crews, who had to be neutral — mainly Swedes, Portuguese and Spaniards. Each timetable and route had to be agreed between the enemy power and the detaining power, which then granted the vessel safe conduct. The Red Cross had to give the warring powers six days' notice before the ships could leave Lisbon, and make sure each ship was properly painted with large red crosses and installed with special lighting to illuminate the signs at night. Every ship's captain knew that any deviation from the agreed course could be fatal. Each ship took about a month to make the round trip from Lisbon to Marseilles and back again. Unloading at Marseilles was never easy because there was no British supervision for foreign labour. Even when the supplies were unloaded their onward transmission could only be guaranteed after lengthy arguments between Red Cross delegates and the German authorities had secured the use of Germany's precious rolling stock. There might be anything up to five weeks' delay before the parcels moved again. The rail journey to Geneva could take as long as three weeks. A next-of-kin parcel might take as long as four or five months to make the whole journey from Finsbury Circus to its final destination.

Anything that was required urgently — such as special drugs, trusses, spectacles and false teeth — was sent by air, usually by the Invalids Comfort Section of the Red Cross Prisoners of War Department. A request would be sent from Germany by cable and the item packed in London, if possible, on the same day. There was always a censor at the packing centre, so time was saved there from the outset. Once packed, the item was immediately sent by "Clipper" to Lisbon, where it was collected by a post-office official who took it across to the office of the German airline. The supply of artificial limbs was, however, more complex. Amputees were examined by an International Orthopaedic Commission, which had permission to investigate every single maimed British prisoner in Germany. Those who needed artificial limbs were sent to *Lazarett* IXC, the POW hospital at Obermassfeld.

Formerly a large agricultural school, this was a crude, ill-equipped building, which, by 1943, would house about a thousand, mainly British, Army POWs and about fifty RAF. Under the supervision of a German doctor — a jack-booted Army *Oberst* — and his orderlies and guards, it was run by British MOs: a former orthopaedic surgeon, Major W E Tucker; and Major W R Henderson RAMC, a neurologist. They had a staff of about sixty officers and men of the RAMC. Nearly all had volunteered to stay behind and care for the wounded after the fall of Dunkirk. Despite the poor accommodation and inadequate equipment and medical supplies, they worked unstintingly for five years, overcoming German restrictions and carrying out major surgery on many thousands of undernourished prisoners. Dressings were sterilised daily by two Welsh Guardsmen using the boiler of a 19th-century road steam engine in an adjacent yard. Tucker, who had been an England Rugby forward and a Cambridge Blue, and was well into his forties, pioneered the practice of moving muscles while still in plaster casts, and insisted that patients exercise daily. Artificial limbs were made by a team of Swiss experts in Geneva, who travelled to Obermassfeld to fit them.

Unfortunately, the fact that the Red Cross sent food, medical and comfort parcels did not mean they always arrived at their destination nor that, if they did arrive, they were still intact. "The statement that parcels were released from stock at the rate of one per week," says Hugo Bracken,

gives the impression that the prisoners received parcels at that rate in the camps. That is absolute nonsense. I got part of a parcel in Dulag Luft [in August 1941] and then nothing while I was at Oflag XC, Lübeck, until I reached Oflag VIB, Warburg, at the end of October. After Stalag Luft III was evacuated at the end of January 1945 until we reached the United Kingdom in June I never saw a Red Cross parcel. In between those dates the issue of Red Cross parcels never exceeded one per room per week, or between one-eighth or one-twelfth of a parcel per man per week. I have checked this with a number of POWs, who are in general agreement with this. Had we received one parcel each per week we would all have needed a long course with Weight Watchers when we got home. Also I can recall only seeing one or two British Red Cross parcels; virtually all were either Canadian or American in Stalag Luft III.

There were from time to time rumours that the Germans had pinched some of them. These were investigated and proved to be unfounded. On the other hand, to our shame, it is a fact that Red Cross parcels were subject to a certain amount of pilfering by dockers in this country and elsewhere.

In April 1942 there was again a serious shortage of food parcels. Packing had been cut down in Britain, and one of the ships chartered in Geneva had an accident and was out of commission for three months. The ICRC drew on its reserves in Geneva, until eventually they ran out. Eventually, normal service was resumed, and from then on POWs received Red Cross parcels at the rate recalled by Hugo Bracken.

Despite these shortcomings, the activities of the ICRC, the British, American and Canadian Red Cross, and the various POW relief agencies can be looked upon as one of the great success stories of the war. The death rate among British POWs in Germany and Italy was only 5.5 per cent for the Army, 2 per cent for the Royal Navy and 1.5 per cent for the RAF — and that includes those killed trying to escape. Thus, there is hardly an ex-POW who has not at some time or another expressed undying gratitude for the help the relief agencies provided. The cost of administering such relief was also low. It cost the British Red Cross only eleven pence in the pound, to collect funds, plus two-pence-halfpenny in the pound for expenses in its headquarters. Without this expenditure, the Red Cross believes, British and Dominion POWs on the Continent would have died in their hundreds. However, Captain Bracken, once again, argues that

such a catastrophe would never have been allowed to happen. Either the Germans would have been forced to increase the rations or the Allied governments would have been forced to provide the food —

indeed, it can be argued that they should have done so anyway, rather than relying on private charity. In all probability there would have been reprisals against German POWs, and it should be remembered that after the German defeat in Tunisia the Allies were in an advantageous position, holding far more German prisoners than the Germans held British and Americans. It would, however, be true to say that we would have arrived back home in far worse shape than we did.

Until they received their first Red Cross parcels, prisoners taken in 1940 relied upon the charity of civilians they had encountered as they marched in POW columns through France, Belgium and Holland — and relatives and unknown benefactors on the Continent — who sent personal parcels to many prisoners who in turn shared the contents with their less fortunate fellows.

APPENDIX III
The POW Pay Scandal

The Whitehall Departments responsible for POW financial affairs did not have the same charitable outlook as the Red Cross. It was the job of these Departments to ensure that only properly authorised expenditure was made by and on behalf of POWs and that the regulations that governed the economic blockade of Germany were enforced. But they were also responsible for ensuring that POWs continued to be paid; that their captors gave them sufficient advances on the pay accumulating back home; that the goods they bought in POW camp canteens gave value for money; that their next-of-kin were given a sufficient allowance throughout the war; and that, finally, the detaining powers should be reimbursed after the war, while returning prisoners received the back-pay that had accumulated and were reimbursed for unreasonable expenses incurred whilst in captivity. It goes without saying that it was also incumbent upon these offices to keep prisoners of war informed of their financial affairs and any other measures taken on their behalf, even if only to maintain their morale.

Pay procedure was provided for in the POW Code of the Geneva Convention and governed by private arrangements between belligerent powers. According to Article 23 of the Convention, officer prisoners should receive from the detaining power the same pay as that given to its own officers of equivalent rank who were also POWs, on condition, however, that it did not exceed that to which they were entitled from the armed forces of the country which they had served. This pay was to be granted in full, once a month if possible, and without being liable to any deductions for expenses incumbent on the detaining power, even when they were in favour of the prisoners. The Article went on to state that the rate of exchange applicable to this payment should be fixed by an agreement between the belligerents. In the absence of any such agreement, the rate adopted should be that in force at the time of the outbreak of hostilities. All payments made to prisoners had to be reimbursed at the end of hostilities by the power in which they had served. It was generally agreed that the advances in pay made by the Germans would be in the form of *Lagergeld*, or camp currency.

The conditions and pay of NCOs and other ranks were governed by Articles 30 to 34 of the Convention. Officers could not be forced to work, and neither could NCOs be forced to work outside the camps, although they could volunteer. Other Ranks could be forced to work provided this did not involve direct war-work — for instance, making munitions. Article 34 laid it down that prisoners should not be paid wages for work connected with the administration, management and maintenance of the camps. However, prisoners used for other work were entitled to wages, to be fixed by agreement between the belligerents.

Article 24 of the Convention laid it down that the belligerent powers should agree to the maximum amount of ready money that POWs of various ranks should be allowed to keep in their possession. Any surplus taken from or withheld from a prisoner was to be entered into his account, the same as any deposit made by him, and was not to be converted into another currency without his consent. Pay to the credit of their accounts should be given to POWs at the end of their captivity. During their imprisonment, facilities were to be granted them for the transfer of these amounts, in whole or in part, to banks or private persons in their country of origin.

So much for the terms of the POW Code. What actually happened was markedly different. While the Germans often breached the pay provisions of the Convention, the British authorities, by and large, acted in violation of their spirit. With the exception of the Air Ministry, the support of the Service Ministries for measures to mitigate the circumstances of prisoners of war was, to say the least, lukewarm. As a result of this, and Treasury-inspired opposition, the Service machinery worked very slowly and much to the disadvantage of prisoners.

In working out its pay policy, Whitehall gave consideration very early in the war to two requirements. Firstly, there was the probability that the enemy would have to be reimbursed for any issues of camp-pay to officers. If deductions were not made at home from the pay of officer POWs then the money to reimburse the enemy would have to be met from the Public Purse. Secondly, the government calculated all pay and allowances from the point of view of conserving as much money as possible in each prisoner's account in this country, ready for when he was repatriated. In effect, once the detaining powers had been reimbursed, the returning prisoners should receive a refund comprising camp money exchanged on arrival home, any sums credited to their accounts up to that time, and credits adjusted on the basis of any information brought back from Germany. Contributions and levies to communal funds and money spent in POW camps would not be refunded.

In anticipation, the Ministry of Defence docked a third of all officers' pay at source. In all, £1.7 million was deducted from the pay of officers in German camps throughout the war. The deductions from the pay of RAF officers and of the Dominion and Allied Air Forces serving with the RAF were held in a suspense account by the Air Ministry and eventually amounted to £646,365. However, the War Office proceeded in a dilatory manner and the steps it took to inform members of the armed forces about their financial affairs should they become prisoners were inadequate.

Hostilities commenced within hours of Britain declaring war against Germany, and a number of aircrew were taken prisoner within the next few days. Whilst sea and air warfare continued, land forces did not clash until the German invasion of Norway in April 1940. By then more than fifty British and Dominion aircrew had been captured. The fighting in Norway went on until after the German invasion of France and the Low Countries on 10 May 1940. All Service departments had by this time realized that the so-called "Phoney War" had ended. In the event of major battles prisoners might be taken in large numbers. Yet no agreement was reached with Germany about either the rates of pay to be issued to officers or the exchange rates to be used. Clearly, action was necessary.

Accordingly, on 16 May 1940, the War Office issued a Special Army Order, No71/1940, which laid it down that from the day after capture pay would be adjusted according to the camp-pay issued by the detaining power and that deductions would be made at rates notified from time to time by the Army Council. Marriage allowance would continue, but no other allowances were admissible beyond the day preceding capture. This order was followed by an Army Council Order, which specified the deductions that would be made from the pay of officers. The deductions announced were significantly larger than those that were subsequently agreed with the Germans, although officers' accounts were eventually adjusted and the difference refunded. It is unlikely, however, that many Army officers saw either order, as the war in the West had been going on for six days before the first was promulgated.

On 10 June 1940 Italy declared war on Britain and France. This added to the problems relating to officer POWs' pay since different deductions based on a different exchange rate would apply between those who were captured by the Germans and those captured by the Italians. Despite the greater risks of aircrew being taken prisoner, the Air Ministry issued no order until 11 July 1940. It was the only one issued by the Air Ministry throughout the entire war. AMO 463 was shorter than the Special Army Order since it dealt only with the pay of officers; otherwise it differed significantly in only one respect, in that it specified the deductions to be made: £6 a month from the pay of pilot officers and flying officers, and £8 a month from that of flight lieutenants and above. Again, these were provisional rates and were amended later on, with officers' accounts being adjusted. However, it is estimated that some 135 RAF officers were shot down and captured before this AMO was promulgated. No follow-up was ever issued giving the actual rates used and no information was given at briefings or Escape and Evasion lectures prior to operations. The same applied to arrangements for the transfer home of savings — or credits — against camp pay.

Finally, the Admiralty issued Admiralty Fleet Order (AFO) 2881/40 on 1 August 1940. Again, this was shorter than the Army Order and specified the deductions to be made which, rank for rank, were the same as those in the AMO. These, too, were subsequently amended.

Negotiations with both the Germans and the Italians started before the end of 1940. Britain and Germany reached an agreement in January 1941 that each side would provide food and accommodation for officer prisoners without charge, and on the relative ranks between the armed forces of each side. But a long wrangle ensued about exchange rates. It was difficult to apply Article 23 of the POW Code because in 1939 the Germans operated a system of multiple exchange rates which varied according to what use the foreign currency was to be put. The rate of exchange to be used was vital because it would determine the amount each side would have to reimburse the other once the war was over. Britain favoured the rate of

22 *Reichsmark* to the pound sterling, while the Germans suggested RM10 to the pound. However, Britain was in a weak bargaining position, as the Germans by then held more than 1,500 British and Commonwealth officers prisoner while Britain held less than five hundred of theirs, and the scale of pay for German officers was lower than that for the British. Finally, in February 1941 — seventeen months after the war had started — the two sides agreed a rate of RM15. This defeated Britain's plans, which were, firstly, to secure the highest rate possible, so as to reduce the amount payable to enemy prisoners at the expense of the British tax-payer, and, secondly, to preserve the largest amount of pay due to British prisoners upon their repatriation.

British officer prisoners in Germany received news of this on 18 February 1941, when a letter reached the Army camp, Oflag IXA/H, Spangenberg, from the American Embassy. The letter, addressed to Army officers, specified that they were being paid RM15 to the pound sterling, and that deductions from their pay might be made after the war for clothes received in Red Cross parcels. However, Spangenberg was the only camp that received such information, and in any case the letter made no mention of savings. A similar announcement by the Admiralty is on record in the form on AFO 3023/41, issued on 17 July 1941. There is no evidence of an Air Ministry Order being promulgated in the RAF camp at Barth nor in Spangenberg, where the RAF were in a minority; if there was an AMO, then it was given a low priority. On 17 May 1941, these same Army prisoners, by now in Fort XV, Thorn, received news that all their credit and cash in hand at the end of the war would be exchanged. Again, there is no record of any such information being promulgated in the RAF camp at Barth.

As it was, the rates of pay issued each month to officer POWs in Germany, along with deductions made at home, were calculated as follows:

RN	ARMY	RAF	CAMP-PAY (GERMANY)	DEDUCTIONS IN U.K.
Captain	Colonel	Grp Capt	RM 150	£10 0s 0d
Commander	Lt Col	Wing Cdr	RM 120	£8 0s 0d
Lt Cdr	Major	Sqn Ldr	RM 108	£7 4s 0d
Lieut	Captain	Flight Lt	RM 96	£6 8s 0d
Sub Lieut	Lieut	Flg Officer	RM 81	£5 8s 0d
A/Sub Lnt	2nd Lnt	Pilot Officer	RM 72	£4 19s 0d

By 1942, a flight lieutenant in the RAF was being paid £36 5s 0d a month. After Income Tax and National Insurance contributions he was left with a net pay of £26 9s 0d. Even if the Germans issued the equivalent of £6 4s 0d in camp currency, it would amount to only 24 per cent of his net pay. Royal Navy lieutenants were at an even greater disadvantage. They were paid £27 4s 0d a month, and after Income Tax and NI contributions were left with £20 9s 0d. An RN lieutenant issued with the same amount of camp currency would therefore have 31 per cent of his net pay deducted. An Army lieutenant, in 1942, would be losing as much as 34 per cent.

No information explaining the rates in such detail was circulated either to aircrew POW camps or at home. This was despite the formation, in late 1940, under the Prisoner of War Directorate, of the Inter-Departmental Prisoner of War Co-ordinating Committee (Finance). Chaired by the Foreign Office, it had representatives from the Treasury, all three branches of the armed forces and officials from the Dominion governments. The ICCF, as it became known, administered the pay and allowances of Allied and Dominion POWs in the European theatre, as well as those of the Allied governments in exile, and took on responsibility for financial dealings with the Germans, the Italians, the Protecting Power and the ICRC. It would recover costs at a later date, but meanwhile Dominion officers had deductions made from their pay at the same rate as British officers of equivalent rank, as did the French, Belgians, Poles and Czechs captured while serving with the British armed forces. The ICCF later became Sub-Committee B of the Imperial Prisoner of War Committee.

The failure of this committee to issue accurate and up-to-date information regarding pay and deductions was not for want of opportunity. In 1941 a pamphlet entitled "The Duties of a Prisoner of War" was issued to all members of the armed forces. Yet it made no mention of camp-pay or credits. Aircrew also received Escape and Evasion briefings prior to flying on operations, and although these covered the rights and obligations of POWs, the matter of pay was again neglected.

At the end of 1941 the Air Ministry representative on Sub-Committee B voiced his concern about the paucity of information about pay so far sent to camps in Germany. He strongly urged that more information be sent. The chairman put up some resistance, but ultimately work began on a suitable document, which became known as the "Camp Leaders' Guide". Apart from information of a general nature, such as procedures for divorce and financial arrangements for prisoners' families, this Guide would contain, for the first time, an undertaking that the British government would refund credits at the agreed rates of exchange after the war and would point out that camp currency would be subject to income tax. However, administrative delays would prevent it from being ready before August 1944, by which time it was too late to reach many of the camps. In lieu of this, letters were sent by each Service ministry to the senior officers in each camp giving details of deductions in pay and credit arrangements — but not until autumn 1943, four years after the war had started. In the meantime, copies of the Geneva Convention, with its relevant clauses on pay, were seldom given to Senior British Officers in camps in Germany or even posted for prisoners to see; not that this would have helped, for the Convention did not mention deductions from pay. British POWs had no idea that the exchange rates agreed between the two sides left them much worse off than German and Italian prisoners.

It is quite clear from the foregoing that Whitehall's pay policy was poorly promulgated. However, even if the opposite had been the case, the policy would not have worked. For it was based on a patchy knowledge of conditions in POW camps and was therefore completely unrealistic.

During the summer of 1940, in Oflag VIIC, Laufen, camp-pay was issued every ten days instead of every seven and even then officers received only half of that to which they were entitled, *and* at an unfavourable rate of exchange. In most camps, token money was issued monthly, except during the first and last few months of war, when conditions in Germany were chaotic. Royal Navy and Royal Marine officers were paid one rank lower than the RAF by the Germans owing to a dispute about relative ranks. The pay was in the form of *"Wehrsold"*, which looked like large bus tickets and were in denominations ranging from 10 *Lagermark* to 10 *Pfennige*. The possession of genuine currency was a punishable offence, and such money was confiscated without being credited to the culprit's account. But there in any case was very little that prisoners in Germany could buy. Protecting Power and Red Cross reports of conditions in POW camps in Germany revealed the following about camp canteens:

1941:

May	Oflag IXA/H, Spangenberg	Not bad
	Oflag IVC, Colditz	Not bad
July	Oflag IXA/H	Very badly stocked
	Stalag Luft I, Barth	Not bad
October	Oflag VIB, Warburg	No canteen
	Oflag IXA/H	Very badly stocked
December	Oflag VIB	Not good
(two visits)	Oflag VIB	Extremely poor

1942:

February	Oflag VIB	Very small supply to canteen
April	Oflag VIB	Not well provided

Permission to transfer money to other camps refused

To make matters worse, the Germans levied a ten per cent tax on purchases from camp canteens, and inflation in Germany was increasing at a faster rate than in Britain, thus eroding further the value of camp money. Britain tried to get the issues halved for prisoners of both sides, but the Germans refused, as the camp canteens in Britain and Canada were well stocked and German prisoners could use their camp-pay effectively. The Germans did, however, indicate that they had no objection to the British proposal being adopted unilaterally. This the British government was unwilling to accept; it withdrew the proposal — without explanation, then or since.

Even assuming that camp money was issued regularly and in full, it would have been difficult, if not impossible, for POWs to hang on to it for exchange upon repatriation. For the sad fact is that all prisoners changed camps at least once during their period of internment, while hundreds changed camps between three and nine times. Within two weeks of the letter from the American Embassy reaching Spangenberg in

February 1941, for instance, the camp was cleared out and all the prisoners sent to the *Straflager* at Thorn. In the year that followed all were moved at least three times and some as many as four.

These moves often took place without sufficient warning or adequate transport, and often ended at squalid and disorganised camps. Prisoners on these "purges", as they were called, were lucky even to get proper rations, let alone space in which to store heaps of dirty *Lagergeld*. Escapers were even less fortunate. There was no guarantee that a man who had escaped would be returned to the same camp upon recapture, and he certainly could not expect his old pals to look after his *Lagergeld* while he spent the rest of the war in another camp. (Besides, there was a much more urgent use for *Lagergeld*, associated with the lack of toilet-paper.) Escapers also had money docked from their camp accounts as fines. On one occasion, when a tunnel was discovered at Stalag Luft I, Barth, the Germans imposed a fine of 4,500 *Reichsmark*.

Towards the end of 1941 Germany proposed that lists of credits be sent to the British authorities from the camps — but two years of negotiations were to elapse before this scheme started to operate. Even then, not all prisoners would have their accounts credited, either because the Germans lost accounts when they transferred prisoners from one camp to another, or because the information from camps did not reach home, or because the authorities took no action on the information received. In the meantime, during periods in which supplies of Red Cross parcels were held up, Air Force prisoners in Stalag Luft I, existing on a meagre German diet, had perforce to spend camp-pay on food that should have been issued by the enemy. They were to confront another problem later, in Stalag Luft III, when the Germans decided that administering camp-pay was too much bother and the issues of *Wehrsold* to individual prisoners ceased.

The behaviour of the British Government contrasts markedly with that of other Allied administrations, who either made no deductions in pay, got the issues of camp currency reduced, or undertook to refund nearly all the deductions made. Dominion officers were already better paid than those in the RAF, and neither the Australians nor the New Zealanders paid income tax while serving overseas. Nevertheless, their governments decided to adopt a more charitable stance towards the question of deductions and refunds in the light of privation, hardship and degradation that POWs suffered and in view of the very low, and at times non-existent, value of the currencies in which advances in pay were made. The British government possessed the same knowledge, but preferred to be penny-pinching.

Thus, while British officers POWs were being underfed by their German captors and using camp-pay to supplement their paltry rations, back home the authorities who were supposed to be looking after their interests were docking one-third of their pay. After the war, the Ministry of Defence and the Treasury would go into mental contortions to wriggle out of paying them back, even going so far as to suggest that ex-POWs were already as well off, if not better off, than those who had not been captured because they had been unable to spend their pay! To add insult to the injury, they claimed that refunds to former officer POWs "would be unfair to those who continued to fight". As this book has shown, the RAF continued to fight for their country even when behind barbed-wire.

APPENDIX IV

RAF and Dominion Air Force and FAA POWs in Laufen, Biberach, Lübeck and Warburg, June 1940–September 1942

Rank and name	POW No	Date Captured	POW Camps
Officers:			
A			
P/O M T H Adams	3751	01/02 09 41	O10C O6B O21B
P/O J D Agrell	1636	07/08 07 41	O7C O10C O6B O21B
P/O M F Andrews	1375	27 06 41	O9A/H O6B O21B
P/O K H Anthony RCAF	39323	19 08 41	S9C O6B SL3
A/S/L D L Armitage	3800	21 09 41	O10C O6B SL3 O21B
P/O J E T Asselin RCAF	3753	04 09 41	O10C O6B O21B
Lt (A) A O Atkins RN	1262	22 09 40	O9A/H O6B O21B
P/O R S Ayton DFM	1346	10/11 05 41	O9A/H O6B O21B
B			
P/O D G Baber	3765	05/06 08 41	O10C O6B O21B
A/W/C D R S Bader DSO* DFC*	3797	09 08 41	O10C O6B SL3
P/O G M Baird	61	20 10 40	SL1 O9A/H F15 O9A/H O6B SL3
F/L W Bakker (Dutch)	3789	30 08 41	O10C O6B O21B
P/O J Barker	1370	18/19 07 40	O9A/H O6B SL3
F/L R B Barr	18391	24 07 41	S9C O6B O21B
S/L J H Barrett	3794	15/16 09 41	O10C O6B O21B
P/O L B Barry RAFVR	3642	12 02 41	O10C O6B SL3
Sub-Lt (A) R E Bartlett RN	92	13 06 40 (31 08 40)	SL1 O9A/H F15 O9A/H O6B SL3
P/O G H Batchelor	—	09 07 41	S9C O10C Died 15 04 42
F/O T A Bax	1352	09 06 41	O9A/H O6B O21B
P/O A J Beales	3813	18 09 41	O10C O6B SL3
F/L H T Beare RCAF	3781	10/11 09 41	O10C O6B O21B
P/O R F Beauclair	154	26/27 07 40	SL1 O10C O6B O21B
P/O W Beckingham	39322	28 08 41	S9C O6B SL3
Sub-Lt (A) L E R Bellairs RN	3719	30 07 41 (09 08 41)	O10C O6B O21B
P/O H J Bell-Walker	9664	12 08 41	S9C O6B O21B

P/O J D Beresford	39161	25 06 41	O10C O6B O21B
P/O J W Best	272	05 05 41	D185 O5B DL SL1
F/L D R S Bevan-John	3324	06 06 41	D185 O10C DL O10C O21B
P/O H R Bewlay	—	07 11 39	O9A/H F15 O9A/H O6B SL3
P/O R M M Biden RAFVR	239	13 08 40	SL1 O9A/H F15 O9A/H O6B O21B
P/O H R Bjelke-Peterson	1263	28/29 09 40	O9A/H O6B O21B
Sub-Lt (A) T E Blacklock RNVR	3673	30 07 41	O10C O6B O21B
F/O D Blew	594	11 05 40	O9A/H SL1 O9A/H F15 O9A/H O6B SL3
F/O J H L Blount	3682	09 04 41	O10C O6B O21B
Sy Lt H F Bond RN	3668	30 07 41	O10C O6B SL3
F/O R J E Boulding	135317	06 41	O9A/H O6B O21B
F/L J C Bowman RAFVR	1241	21 07 40	O9A/H O6B SL3
Lt H H Bracken RN	3664	30 07 41	O10C O6B SL3
P/O J G N Braithwaite	9973	07/08 07 41	S9C O6B SL3
F/O P E Bressey RAFO	1124	40	O9A/H SL1 O9A/H F15 O9A/H O6B O21B
P/O A J Brewster	1354	19/20 06 41	O9A/H O6B SL3
S/L A O Bridgman DFC	1264	23/24 09 40	O9A/H F15 O9A/H O6B O21B
P/O P S E Briggs RAFVR	1355	16 06 41	O9A/H O6B O21B
P/O P G Brodie	1242	19/20 08 40	O9A/H F15 O9A/H O6B O21B
F/O D Bruce	1356	09 06 41	O9A/H O6B O4C (16 03 42)
F/L J Bryks (Ricks) (Czech)	1363	17 06 41	O9A/H O6B O21B
F/O C Y Buckley	114	09 06 40	SL1 O10C O6B O21B
A/S/L H Budden DFC	3709	12/13 08 41	O10C O6B SL3
P/O H F Burns	1285	26 10 40	O9A/H F15 O9A/H O6B O21B
F/O R M Burns	595	10 05 40	O9A/H SL1 O9A/H F15 O9A/H O6B SL3
Sub-Lt (A) R A Burroughs RNVR	3718	04 08 41	O10C O6B SL3
P/O J C W Bushell RAFVR	156	26/27 07 40	SL1 O10C O6B O21B
S/L R J Bushell, AuxAF	621	23 05 40	DL SL1 O10C
F/O A R Butcher	22728	22 05 41	O10C O6B O21B
P/O M G Butt RAFVR	241	27/28 08 40	SL1 O9A/H F15 O9A/H O6BSL3

C

P/O B D Campbell RCAF	1637	02/03 07 41	O7C O10C O6B O21B
A/S/L F L Campbell-Rogers	3655	23 07 41	O10C O6B O21B
F/L J A Cant	3711	16/17 08 41	O10C O6B SL3
P/O S Carter RAFVR	1386	30 06/01 07 41	O9A/H O6B SL3
F/O L H Casson DFC AuxAF	3725	09 08 41	O10C O6B O21B
F/O E C Cathels	3746	27 08 41	O10C O6B O21B
P/O W Cebrazynski (Pole)	1366	18/19 06 41	O9A/H O6B O21B
P/O O Cerny (Czech)	3663	16/17 07 41	O10C O6B O21B
P/O W C Chadwick	3731	12 08 41	O10C O6B O21B
F/O E F Chapman RAFVR	1342	08 05 41	O9A/H O6B O21B
P/O W W Chciuk (Pole)	3742	24 07 41	O10C O6B O21B
F/L C C Cheshire	3712	12/13 08 41	O10C O6B SL3
F/O T F C Churcher	3442	26 05 41	D185 O10C DL O10C O6B O21B
P/O F T Clayton	3679	06/07 08 41	O10C O6B O21B
F/O J F Clayton DFM	3683	24 07 41	O10C O6B O21B
P/O E J Clelland	358	28/29 11 40	SL1 O9A/H F15 O9A/H O6B SL3
Lt I M Coetzee SAAF	3677	13 06 41	O10C O6B O21B
P/O G W Cole	3739	14/15 08 41	O10C O6B SL3
A/S/L L E Collings RAAF	3710	25 07 41	O10C O6B SL3
P/O P W Cook	1243	19/20 08 40	O9A/H F15 O9A/H O6B O21B
S/L H D H Cooper DFC	3795	01 07 41	O10C O6B O21B

P/O R M Coste	2029	09 39	O9A/H F15 O9A/H O6B SL3
Lt P Courcot FFAF	22731	26 05 41	O10C O6B O21B
P/O D Cowley	—	27 06 41	O10C O6B O21B
F/O R T R Cowper	3791	13 09 41	O10C O6B SL3
P/O J G Crampton	1632	14/15 07 41	O7C O10C O6B O21B
F/O C A R Crews DFC	328	11 05 40	
			O9A/H SL1 O9A/H F15 O9A/H O6B SL3
F/O A P Culverwell AFC RAFVR	3670	02 08 41	O10C O6B O21B
F/O W Cunningham DFC	3744	28 08 41	O10C O6B O21B

D

P/O C Daszuta (Pole)	3799	17 09 41	O10C O6B SL3
P/O J I Davies RCAF	3790	15/16 09 41	O10C O6B O21B
Sub-Lt (A) R L G Davies RN	1244	22 08 40	O9A/H F15 O9A/H O6B SL3
P/O A H Deacon	465	28 05 40	O7C DL SL1
S/L C H Deakin (S Rhodesian)	3316	06 06 41	D185 O10C DL O10C O6B O21B
P/O J R Denny	361	28/29 11 40	SL1 O10C O6B SL3
P/O I P B Denton	3654	25/26 07 41	O5B DL O10C O6B O21B
P/O R V Derbyshire	327	14/15 11 40	SL1 O9A/H F15 O9A/H O6B SL3
Sub-Lt (A) H Deterding RNVR	1266	22 09 40	O9A/H F15 O9A/H O6B O21B
F/O C N Dilly	3450	06 06 41	D185 O10C DL O10C O6B O21B
P/O P L Dixon RAAF	3657	14/15 07 41	O10C O6B O21B
P/O G T Dodgshun	508	21/22 05 40	
			O9A/H SLI O9A/H F15 O9A/H O6B SL3
S/L K C Doran DFC*	501	30 04 40	O9A/H SL1 O10C O6B O21B
P/O R O H Downe	3782	13 09 41	O10C O6B SL3
F/O S H Dowse RAFVR	39320	15 08 41 (20 08 41)	S9C O6B SL3
F/L G G F Draper	3669	07 08 41	O10C O6B SL3
Capt K W Driver DFC SAAF	1371	14 06 41	O9A/H O6B O21B
F/L L S Dunley RNZAF	1348	10/11 04 41	O9A/H O6B O21B
P/O N M Dunn RAAF	1357	16 06 41	O9A/H O6B O21B
F/L R McD Durham	3722	12/13 08 41	O10C O6B SL3
F/L F G Dutton	364	21/22 04 40	SL1 O9A/H F15 O9A/H O6B SL3
P/O F P N Dyer	3303	06 06 41	D185 O10C DL O10C O6B SL3

E

Lt (A) A T Easton RN	—	25 07 41	O10C O6B SL3
P/O R Edge	291	18 04 41	D185 O5B DL SL1
P/O K C Edwards, AuxAF	3645	16/17 07 41	O5B DL O10C O6B O21B
P/O L H Edwards	6	06 09 39	O9A/H F15 O9A/H O6B SL3
F/L R H Edwards	161	28/29 07 40	SL1 O9A/H F15 O9A/H O6B O21B
F/O W H Edwards DFC	326	12 05 40	
			O9A/H SL1 O9A/H F15 O9A/H O6B SL3
F/L R A G Ellen	162	13 08 40	SL1 O9A/H F15 O9A/H SL3
P/O D A Elliott RCAF	1620	07/08 07 41	O7C O10C O6B O21B
P/O G A Eperon	2870	24 07 41	O10C O6B O21B

F

F/O E T Fairbank	1373	23 06 41	O9A/H O6B SL3
P/O H E L Falkus	2256	01 06 40	S12A O2A SL1 O10C O6B O21B
P/O R F J Featherstone RCAF	1345	11/12 05 41	O9A/H O6B O21B
S/L S S Fielden	3788	07/08 09 41	O10C O6B SL3
Lt C H Filmer DSC RN	457	13 06 40	SL1 O10C O6B O21B
F/L M J Fisher RAFVR	1245	16/17 08 40	O9A/H F15 O9A/H O6B SL3
P/O J E A Foster RAFVR	1268	14/15 06 40	O9A/H F15 O9A/H O6B SL3
P/O W M W Fowler	138430	06/01 07 41	O9A/H O6B O21B
P/O G M Frame RAFVR	1380	27/28 06 41	O9A/H O6B O21B

256

F/O J H Frampton	1337	16/17 01 41	O9A/H O6B O21B
F/L C H Fry	3339	16 05 41	D185 O10C DL O10C O6B O21B
F/L G M Fuller	3659	25/26 07 41	O10C O6B SL3

G

A/F/L P M Gardner DFC	3801	11 07 41	O10C O6B SL3
F/L R Garside	3425	06 06 41	D185 O10C DL O10C O6B O21B
F/O M G Geoghegan	3720	12/13 08 41	O10C O6B SL3
S/L D B Gericke	1341	12 04 41	O9A/H O6B O21B
P/O J R Gibbon	3732	12/13 08 41	O10C O6B SL3
P/O T R Gilderthorpe	997931	08/01 09 41	S9C O6B O21B
P/O J T Glover	510	19/20 05 40	O9A/H F15 O9A/H O6B O21B
P/O L J E Goldfinch	301	28 04 41	D185 O5B DL SL1
F/L A D Gosman	3713	12/13 08 41	O10C O6B O21B
P/O A H Gould	1269	20/21 07 40	DL O9A/H F15 O9A/H O6B SL3
P/O S A Graham RCAF	3807	—	O10C O6B O21B
F/O D Graham-Hogg	3656	18 07 41	O10C O6B O21B
P/O J H Green	465	10/11 02 41	SL1 O10C O6B SL3
F/O P O V Green	3783	07 07 41	D185 O10C O6B O21B
P/O C A S Greenhill DFC	3721	—	O10C O6B SL3
Lt (A) P J Greenslade	3676	30 07 41	O10C O6B O21B
F/L T Griffith-Jones	3762	09 07 41	O10C O6B O21B
P/O J Grocott RAFVR	—	29 08 41	O10C O6B O21B

H

P/O T H Hadley RAFVR	245	10/11 09 40	SL1 O9A/H F15 O9A/H O6B O21B
F/L C M Hall RAAF	389	07/08 09 41	O10C O6B O21B
P/O N D Hallifax	1306	15 05 40	S9C O9A/H O6B S9C
P/O A J C Hamilton	1376	06 06 41	O9A/H O6B SL3
Lt (A) M A J J Hanrahan RN	1270	22 09 40	O9A/H F15 O9A/H O6B SL3
F/O P Harding	3748	27 08 41	O10C O6B O21B
P/O T Harrison	—	23 06 41	S9C O6B SL3
P/O W C Hartop	1349	01 04 41	O9A/H O6B O21B
P/O D K Hayes	1271	29/30 09 40	O9A/H F15 O9A/H O6B O21B
P/O A E Hayward	3752	25/26 08 41	O10C O6B O21B
F/O B W Hayward	204	23/24 04 40	O9A/H F15 O9A/H O6B O21B
Lt N M Hearle RM	1246	22 08 40	O9A/H F15 O9A/H O6B SL3
Sub-Lt (A) H N C Hearn RN	1272	23 09 40	O9A/H F15 O9A/H O6B SL3
P/O H Heaton	3764	12/13 03 41	O10C O6B SL3
F/L D G Heaton-Nichols	22	30 09 39	O9A/H F15 O9A/H O6B O21B
F/L J O Hedley	3772	—	O10C O6B O21B
P/O R R Henderson RCAF	3728	18/19 08 41	O10C O6B O21B
P/O W Hetherington	1383	29/30 06 41	O9A/H O6B O21B
P/O E Hewson	3724	23 06 41	O10C O6B O21B
P/O A J Hibell	3775	15/16 09 41	O10C O6B O21B
P/O G H Hill	3734	12 08 41	O10C O6B SL3
F/O D S Hoare	580	25 05 40	
			O9A/H SL1 O9A/H F15 O9A/H O6B SL3
P/O L P R Hockey RAFVR	410	21/22 05 40	O7C DL SL1
P/O K N Holland	1358	16/17 06 41	O9A/H O6B O21B
P/O W H Holland	1377	27 06 41	O9A/H O6B SL3
P/O J R Hoppe RAFVR	371	04/05 12 40	SL1 O9A/H F15 O9A/H O6B SL3
P/O F G Horner	3761	08 07 41	O10C O6B O21B
Sub-Lt (A) C V Howard RN	3674	30 07 41	O10C O6B SL3
F/L C R C Howlett	3298	06 06 41	D185 O10C DL O10C O6B O21B
F/L E Hubicki (Pole)	1390	29/30 06 41	O9A/H O6B SL3
P/O F Hugill	1127	14 06 40	O9A/H F15 O9A/H O6B SL3

P/O R C A Hunter RCAF	1633	15/16 07 41	O7C O10C O6B O21B
P/O W J Hunter RAFVR	3648	25 07 41	O5B DL O10C O6B O21B
F/O T Hutton	5005	06 06 41	D185 O10C O6B SL3
W/C N C Hyde	628	08/09 04 41	SL1 O10C O6B O21B
P/O T G Hynes	248	29/30 08 40	SL1 O10C O6B O21B

I

Lt J C Iliffe RN	1273	13 09 40	O9A/H F15 O9A/H O6B SL3
P/O A M Imrie (S Rhodesian)	503	14 05 40	
			O9A/H SL1 O9A/H F15 O9A/H O6B O21B
P/O J G Ireton	3649	24 07 41	O5B DL O10C O6B SL3

J

A/F/O W F Jackman RAFVR	1389	01 07 41	O9A/H O6B O21B
F/O R H Jacoby	581	23 05 40	
			O9A/H SL1 O9A/H F15 O9A/H O6B O21B
F/L P J F Jacquier FFAF	36	24 05 41	O6B O21B
P/O K Jaklewicz (Pole)	1367	18/19 06 41	O9A/H O6B SL3
P/O J Janicki (Pole)	3814	18/19 07 41	O10C O6B SL3
P/O T F S Johnson	1247	19/20 08 40	O9A/H F15 O9A/H O6B O21B
P/O F M V Johnstone	3758	28 08 41	O10C O6B SL3
P/O K Jones	124	20/21 07 40	SL1 O10C O6B O21B

K

S/L M M Kane MBE	3708	18/19 08 41	O10C O6B O21B
P/O T M Kane	63	23 09 40	SL1 O9A/H F15 O9A/H O6B O21B
P/O I A Kayes	3684	05/06 08 41	O10C O6B SL3
W/C J R Kayll DSO DFC AuxAF	1374	25 06 41	O9A/H O6B O21B
P/O H G Keartland SAAF	—	16/17 08 41	O10C O6B SL3
S/L F J B Keast RAFO	468	17/18 02 41	SL1 O10C O21B
Sub-Lt (A) A P Keep RN	3671	30 07 41	O10C O6B SL3
F/L F W S Keighley	1275	29 07 40	O9A/H F15 O9A/H O6B O21B
P/O D E Kennedy RAFVR	3756	16 06 41	O10C O6B SL3
F/O M N McF Kennedy	164	31 07 40	SL1 O10C O6B SL3
P/O J McB Kerr RNZAF	1359	19/20 06 41	O9A/H O6B SL3
F/L V Kilian (Czech)	3771	23/24 09 40	DL O7B O10C O6B O6C SL3
F/L T R Kipp RCAF	3667	02/03 08 41	O10C O6B SL3
P/O I C Kirk	1276	02/03 09 40	O9A/H F15 O9A/H O6B SL3
P/O J F Knight RNZAF	3808	—	O10C O6B SL3
P/O M Kozinski (Pole)	1628	10/11 07 41	O7C O10C O6B O21B
F/L L Kozlowski (Pole)	1391	29/30 06 41	O9A/H O6B O21B
F/L S Z Król (Pole)	1392	02 07 41	O9A/H O6B O21B
P/O W Krupowicz (Pole)	1393	03/04 07 41	O9A/H O6B O21B

L

F/O H W Lamond	45	28 04 41	D185 O5B DL SL1
F/O P Langmead	1631	07/08 07 41	O7C O10C O6B O21B
Cpte Larmier, *Armée de l'Air*	—	10 05 40	O9A/H F15 O9A/H O6B O21B
F/O D F Laslett	511	21/22 05 40	
			O9A/H SL1 O9A/H F15 O9A/H O6B SL3
P/O J B Leetham	3784	06/07 09 41	O10C O6B O21B
F/O W N Lepine	1129	18 05 40	
			O9A/H SL1 O9A/H F15 O9A/H O6B SL3
P/O P A Leuw	3652	19/20 07 41	O10C O6B O21B
F/L W J Lewis DFC	3785	07/08 09 41	O10C O6B SL3
F/L E H Lewis-Dale	3340	20 05 41	D185 O10C DL O10C O6B SL3

F/L J N Leyden	1125	26 05 40	
			O9A/H SL1 O9A/H F15 O9A/H O6B O21B
F/L F L Litchfield	3716	05/06 08 41	O10C O6B O21B
F/O J A Little	3717	12/13 08 41	O10C O6B SL3
S/L S G Long RAFO	3707	17 06 41	O10C O6B SL3
P/O G F Lowes	3815	23 07 41	O10C O6B SL3
Sub-Lt (A) D M Lubbock RNVR	3804	30 07 41	O10C O6B SL3
S/L E H Lynch-Blosse	472	12/13 03 41	SL1 O10C O6B O21B

M

P/O W L MacDonald	3745	28 08 41	O10C O6B O21B
F/L C H MacFie DFC, AuxAF	1629	05 07 41	O7C O10C O6B O21B
P/O D F M Mackarness	102	06/07 07 40	SL1 O10C O6B O21B
P/O A W MacKay	3662	19/20 07 41	O10C O6B O21B
P/O W M MacKay RCAF	—	24 07 41	S9C O6B SL3
F/O K W Mackenzie DFC AFC	3802	29 09 41	O10C O6B O21B
P/O W K Mackey RCAF	3780	07/08 09 41	O10C O6B O21B
F/O A C MacLachlan	40	01 10 39	O9A/H F15 O9A/H O6B O21B
F/L R I C Macpherson	582	16 05 40	
			O9A/H SL1 O9A/H F15 O9A/H O6B SL3
P/O S Maciejewski (Pole)	3660	17 07 41	O5B O10C O6B SL3
P/O N Maranz	1372	21 06 41	O9A/H O6B SL3
F/O M Marcola (Pole)	3704	09/10 07 41	O10C O6B SL3
Sub-Lt (A) E K Margetts RNVR	39325	03 06 41	S9C O6B SL3
P/O J D Margrie	1381	27/28 06 41	O9A/H O6B O21B
Lt (A) D T R Martin RN	1128	13 06 40	
			O9A/H SL1 O9A/H F15 O9A/H O6B O21B
P/O E C Maskell	3738	17/18 08 41	O9A/H O6B SL3
A/S/L P Mason	3321	06 06 41	D185 O10 DL O10C O6B O21B
F/L E A Masters	1630	07/08 07 41	O7C O10C O6B O21B
P/O A W Matthews	1261	10 05 40	O9A/H F15 O9A/H O6B O21B
F/O R D May	3433	26 05 41	D185 O10C DL O10C O6B SL3
P/O J W McCarthy RCAF	3763	07/08 09 41	O10C O6B O21B
F/L R J McConnell	410	10/11 02 41	SL1 O10C O6B SL3
P/O J P McKechnie	3729	19 08 41	O10C O6B O21B
P/O R C D McKenzie	1248	08 06 40	O9A/H F15 O9A/H O6B SL3
F/O N W McLeod	3650	24 07 41	O10C O6B SL3
P/O J F McPhie	16247	13 06 40	SL1 O10C O6B SL3
P/O A F McSweyn RAAF	—	29/30 06 41	O9A/H O6B O21B
F/L B Mickiewicz (Pole)	3747	29 08 41	O10C O6B SL3
P/O L Miller DFC	24	19/20 05 40	O9A/H F15 O9A/H O6B O21B
Sub-Lt (A) R S Miller RNVR	3672	30 07 41	O10C O6B SL3
S/L A F H Mills RCAF	3706	12 08 41	O10C O6B SL3
F/O C D Milne	412	40	SL1 O10C O6B O21B
F/O J C Milner	393/419	19 05 40	SL1 O9A/H F15 O9A/H O6B SL3
F/O R G M Morgan	3653	14/15 07 41	O10C O6B O21B
S/L B G Morris	3705	21 08 41	O10C O6B O21B
P/O E R Mullins	504	14 05 40	O9A/H SL1 O10C O6B SL3
P/O A W Mungovan	324	11 05 40	
			O9A/H SL1 O9A/H F15 O9A/H O6B O21B
F/O M I Murdoch	330	15 05 40	O9A/H SL1 O10C O6B O21B
F/O K H P Murphy	207	29/30 04 40	
			O9A/H SL1 O9A/H F15 O9A/H O6B O21B
P/O H M Murray	1130	11 05 40	
			O9A/H SL1 O9A/H F15 O9A/H O6B SL3
S/L S S Murray	60	08/09 09 39	O10A O9A F15 O9A O6B SL3
P/O W E Myhill	8348	22 05 41	O10C O6B SL3

N

Name	No.	Date	Codes
Lt A D Neely RN	420	28 05 40	O7C DL SL1
Lt E C Newborn SAAF	1360	14 06 41	O9A/H O6B O21B
P/O B T J Newland (S Rhodesian)	1617	13 08 40	O9A/H F15 O9A/H O6B O21B
F/O W M Nixon	1249	16/17 08 40	O9A/H F15 O9A/H O6B SL3
F/L J L Nunn	39318	16/17 08 41	S9C O6B SL3

O

Name	No.	Date	Codes
P/O D G O'Brien	597	10 05 40	O9A/H SL1 O9A/H F15 O9A/H O6B O21B
P/O J H O'Byrne RAAF	3735	09 08 41	O10C O6B O21B
P/O T L W Officer RAAF	1378	17 06 41	O9A/H O6B O21B
P/O W R Oldfield	3760	29/30 04 41	O10C O6B O21B
Sub-Lt (A) J S Olsen RN	3664	30 07 41	O10C O6B SL3
P/O D B Organ	3766	31 08/01 09 41	O10C O6B O21B

P

Name	No.	Date	Codes
F/O J Palka (Pole)	1627	03/04 07 41	O7C O10C O6B O21B
F/O S H Palmer RAFVR	475	12/13 03 41	SL1 O10C O6B O21B
P/O G Parker	1250	14/15 08 40	O9A/H F15 O9A/H O6B O21B
F/O J A G Parker (S Rhodesian)	3803	—	O10C O6B O21B
Pro Ty Sub-Lt (A) W Parsons RNVR	3678	30 07 41	O10C O6B O21B
P/O D Paterson	1351	—	O9A/H O6B SL3
F/L W J Peat RCAF	3779	07/08 09 41	O10C O6B O21B
F/L S G L Pepys	583	23 05 40	O9A/H SL1 O9A/H F15 O9A/H O6B SL3
P/O J W P Perkins	1251	5/6 07 40	O9A/H F15 O9A/H O6B SL3
A/F/L A M D Péronne FFAF	382	15 06 41	O6B O21B
P/O H W Pickstone	3767	21 08 41	O10C O6B SL3 O21B
S/L S Pietraszkiewicz (Pole)	3810	21 09 41	O10C O6B O21B
P/O P R I Pine RCAF (American)	1624	08 07 41	O7C O10C O6B SL3
A/S/L T W Piper	3647	19 07 41	O5B O10C O6B O21B
P/O I G G Potts	1122	01 06 40	O9A/H SL1 O9A/H F15 O9A/H O6B SL3
P/O R G Poulter	1382	27/28 06 41	O10C O6B SL3
Sub-Lt (A) D A Poynter RN	1278	22 09 40	O9A/H F15 O9A/H O6B SL3
P/O I G St C Pringle	3755	25/26 08 41	O10C O6B O21B
F/L Z Prochazka	3770	23/24 09 40	DL O10C O6B SL3
F/O H A R Prowse	1626	04 07 41	O7C O10C O6B O21B
F/O R E W Pumphrey, AuxAF	598	20 05 40	O9A/H SL1 O10C O6B O21B

Q

Name	No.	Date	Codes
Lt Cdr N R Quill RN	1279	09 10 40	O9A/H O6B O21B
P/O J P Quirke	167	30 06 40	SL1 O10C O6B O21B

R

Name	No.	Date	Codes
P/O E A Rance RAFVR	3727	11 08 41	O10C O6B SL3
A/S/L C G C Rawlins DFC, RAFVR	6424	11/12 05 41	S9C O6B SL3
S/L M E Redgrave	1362	11/12 06 41	O10C O6B SL3 O21B
P/O S Reeves	1405	30 05 41	O9A O6B SL3
P/O C D Roberts	3737	18/19 08 41	O10C O6B O21B
P/O R Roberts	1252	15 08 40	O9A/H F15 O9A/H O6B O21B
P/O H B Robertshaw	3741	18/19 08 41	O10C O6B SL3
P/O T M Robinson	—	16/17 08 41	O10C Killed 10 10 41

Name	No.	Date	Codes
P/O C I Rolfe	1397	02/03 08 41	O9A/H O6B SL3
Lt (A) R Ross-Taylor RNVR	3714	30 07 41	O10C O6B O21B
F/O M H Roth	333	10 05 40	O9A/H SL1 O10C O6B O21B
Lt A S Ruffel SAAF	3792	25 05 41	O10C O6B SL3
F/L A A Rumsey RAFO	1286	26 10 40	O9A/H F15 O9A/H O6B SL3

S

Name	No.	Date	Codes
F/L D N Sampson	3733	14/15 08 41	O10C O6B O21B
P/O W J Sandman RNZAF	1379	27 06 41	O9A/H O6B SL3
S/L S Scibior (Pole)	3811	05/06 08 41	O10C O6B O21B
P/O J L Scott	272	25/26 07 40	SL1 O10C O6B O21B
P/O J R Scott	39319	25 06 41	S9C O6B SL3
F/O S T Sedzik (Pole)	1368	11/12 06 41	O9A/H O6B O21B
P/O H J Sellers	1622	15/16 05 41	O7C O10C O6B O21B
Lt H K Serjeant RN	3715	30 07 41	O10C O6B O21B
F/L P J S Shaughnessy DFC	3643	12/13 06 41	O5B O10C O6B O21B
A/F/L M C G Sherwood	3646	25/26 07 41	O5B O10C O6B SL3
P/O F W Shorrock RCAF	3740	18/19 08 41	O10C O6B O21B
P/O R Shuttleworth	3816	29/30 09 41	O10C O6B SL3
P/O J E Simmonds	1634	06/07 07 41	O7C O10C O6B O21B
F/O H Skalski (Pole)	3749	27 08 41	O10C O6B O21B
P/O H A T Skehill	1253	16/17 08 40	O9A/H F15 O9A/H O6B SL3
P/O W M Skinner DFM	1623	06 07 41	O7C O10C O6B O21B
AC1 L J Slattery	84	03/05 09 39	O9A/H F15 O9A/H O6B SL3
F/L J R T Smalley DFC	1280	08 10 40	O9A/H F15 O9A/H O6B O21B
P/O J B Smiley	947	23 05 40	O7C DL SL1
S/L E T Smith	1364	17 06 41	O9A/H O6B O21B
S/L F G L Smith DFC	1287	26 10 40	O9A/H F15 O9A/H O6B O21B
P/O W J S Smith	3796	17/18 09 41	O10C O6B O21B
P/O W A Sojka (Pole)	1369	11/12 06 41	O9A/H O6B O21B
F/O W A Staniland	3736	12 08 41	O10C O6B O21B
P/O A J J Steel	1281	30 09/01 10 40	O9A/H F15 O9A/H O6B SL3
F/L J W Stephens DFC*	519	23 06 40	O9A/H SL1 O10C O6B O21B
F/L P Stevens	3786	07/08 09 41	O10C O6B O21B
A/S/L D M Strong	3793	10/11 09 41	O10C O6B SL3
P/O A W Sulston	3723	15/16 05 41	O10C O6B SL3
F/L N H Svendson DFC (Dane)	1387	30 06/01 07 41	O9A/H O6B O21B
A/S/L E Sydney-Smith	3651	16 07 41	O10C O6B O21B
F/L T E Syms	1288	13 08 40	O9A/H F15 O9A/H O6B O21B

T

Name	No.	Date	Codes
F/L T H B Tayler	3666	25/26 07 41	O10C O6B O21B
Lt A Taylor RN	1254	22/23 08 40	O9A/H O6B SL3
P/O H H Taylor	584	19 05 40	O9A/H SL1 O9A/H F15 O9A/H O6B SL3
F/O J M Taylor	256	04/05 09 40	SL1 O9A/H F15 O9A/H O6B SL3
F/O E R Templer	3754	24/25 08 41	O10C O6B O21B
F/L R F Terry RAAF	2685	02/03 08 41	O10C O6B SL3
F/O N M Thomas	1401	12 05 40	O9A/H SL1 O9A/H O6B O21B
P/O P A W Thomas	352	14/15 11 40	SL1 O9A/H F15 O9A/H O6B O21B
P/O A B Thompson	59	08/09 09 39	O10A O9A/H F15 O9A/H O6B O21B
F/L F Thompson RAAF	3675	25/26 07 41	O10C O6B O21B
P/O F K Thornton	3680	—	O10C O6B O21B
F/O J Tilsley	38	16 10 39	O9A/H F15 O9A/H O6B O21B
P/O J A Timmis	5001	19 08 41	S9C O6B SL3
P/O K S Toft	126	17 05 40	SL1 O9A/H F15 O9A/H O6B SL3
F/L P Tomlinson RAFO	3805	09 08 41	O10C O6B O21B

P/O W B Towler	3812	19/20 09 41	O10C O6B SL3
F/L K Trojacek (Czech)	3769	23/24 09 40	DL O10C O6B O6A O9A/Z, O9/A/H SL3
F/L R E Troward	340	16 11 40	SL1 O9A/H F15 O9A/H O6B SL3
S/L A J Trumble	3211	06 06 41	D185 O10C DL O10C O6B O21B
S/L H J C Tudge	1621	10 07 41	O7C O6B O21B
F/O P D Tunstall	258	26/27 08 40	
			SL1 O9A/H F15 O9A/H O6B O4C (16 03 42)
Sub-Lt (A) G L Turner RNVR	3681	30 07 41	O10C O6B SL3
S/L W H N Turner DFC	332	18/19 05 40	O9A/H SL1 O10C O6B SL3

V

F/L P F R Vaillant	1283	27/28 08 40	O9A/H F15 O9A/H O6B O21B
F/O P J Valachos DFC	3429	06 06 41	D185 O10C DL O10C O6B O21B
P/O P P Villa	1365	16 06 41	O9A/H O6B SL3

W

F/L G W Walenn	3776	10/11 09 41	O10C O6B SL3
F/O G E Walker	1120	20/21 06 40	O9A/H F15 O9A/H O6B O21B
P/O R A Walker	1388	02/03 07 41	O9A/H O6B SL3
F/O T L Walker RAAF	3774	10/11 09 41	O10C O6B O21B
F/L R P Wallace-Terry	—	07/08 09 41	O10C O6B SL3
P/O J H Ward	1635	14 06 41	O7C O10C O6B O21B
P/O P Ward-Smith	1619	10 07 41	O7C O10C O6B O21B
S/L R N Wardell	1618	13 08 40	O9A/H O6B O21B
P/O R D Wawn	1255	25/26 08 40	O9A/H F15 O9A/H O6B O21B
F/L M C Wells	331	10 05 40	
			O9A/H SL1 O9A/H F15 O9A/H O6B SL3
P/O J Whilton	513	21/22 05 40	O9A/H F15 O9A/F O6B SL3
F/O P G Whitby	1256	16/17 08 40	O9A/H F15 O9A/H O6B O21B
P/O R A White	3798	16 07 41	O10C O6B SL3
P/O R A R White RZNAF	1350	21 05 41	O10C O6B O21B
P/O R T C O White	3778	11/12 09 41	O10C O6B O21B
P/O F R Wilbraham	3777	07/08 09 41	O10C O6B O21B
A/S/L F A Willan DFC	260	08/09 09 40	SL1 O10C O6B O21B
F/O G S Williams	3787	10/11 09 41	O10C O6B O21B
P/O M G Williams	3726	18 08 41	O10C O6B SL3
A/S/L W R Williams	3644	24 07 41	O5B DL O10C O6B O21B
F/O H C Winter-Taylor	3773	29 08 41	O10C O6B O21B
P/O I K Woodroffe	1343	09/10 05 41	O9A/H O6B O21B
F/L G O M Wright	599	14 05 40	
			O9A/H SL1 O9A/H F15 O9A/H O6B O21B

Z

F/O J Zafouk (Czech)	3661	16/17 07 41	O10C O4C

APPENDIX V

RAF and Dominion Air Force and FAA POW Escape and Clandestine Activities in Laufen, Lübeck and Warburg, June 1940–September 1942

P/O J D Agrell	Tunnels O6B
P/O M F Andrews	Tunnels O6B
A/S/L D L Armitage	Tunnels O6B
P/O J E T Asselin RCAF	Tunnels O6B
A/W/C D R S Bader DSO* DFC*	Hospital window, St-Omer. Tunnel (discovered) DL.Gate, tunnels, diversions O6B
F/L W Bakker (Dutch)	Forgery, tunnels O6B
P/O J Barker	Tunnels O6B
S/L J H Barrett	Tunnels, forgery O6B
F/O L B Barry	Tunnels, news-reading O6B
Sub-Lt (A) R E Bartlett RN	Tunnels, walk-outs O6B
P/O R F Beauclair	Train. Tunnels O6B
P/O H R Bewlay	Tunnels, Escape Committee O6B
P/O H R Bjelke-Peterson	Forgery O6B
F/O D Blew	Tunnels O6B
F/L J C Bowman	Tunnels O6B
Lt H H Bracken RN	Letter-codes, tunnels O10C & O6B
S/L A O Bridgman DFC	Bribery, tunnels, forgery O6B
P/O P G Brodie	Tunnels O6B
F/O D Bruce	Tunnels, walk-outs O6B
F/L J Bryks (Ricks) (Czech)	Tunnels O6B
F/O C Y Buckley	Tunnel O10C. Tunnels O6B
A/S/L H Budden DFC	Tunnels O6B
P/O H F Burns	Tunnels O6B
F/O R M Burns	Tunnels O6B
P/O J C W Bushell	Tunnel O10C. Tunnels O6B
S/L R J Bushell AuxAF	Tunnel O10C. Train

P/O M G Butt	Tunnels O6B
P/O B D Campbell RCAF	Forgery O6B
F/L F L Campbell-Rogers	Tunnels O6B
F/L L H Casson DFC	Tunnels O6B
F/O E C Cathels	Forgery O6B
P/O W Cebrazynski (Pole)	Tunnels O6B
P/O O Cerny (Czech)	Tunnels O6B
P/O W W Chciuk (Pole)	Tunnels O6B
F/L C C Cheshire	Tunnels O6B
F/O J F Clayton DFM	Maps O6B
P/O E J Clelland	Tunnels O6B
Lt I M Coetzee SAAF	Tunnels O6B
P/O P W Cook	Tunnels, forgery O6B
S/L H D H Cooper DFC	Tunnels, construction O6B
P/O D Cowley	Tunnels O6B
P/O J G Crampton	Tunnels O6B
F/O C A R Crews DFC	Tunnels O6B
F/O W Cunningham DFC	Tunnels O6B
P/O C Daszuta (Pole)	Tunnels O6B
P/O J I Davies RCAF	Forgery O6B
P/O J R Denny	Train. Tunnels O6B
P/O I P B Denton	Tunnels O6B
Sub-Lt (A) H Deterding RNVR	Tunnels O6B
F/O C N Dilly	Forgery O6B
P/O P L Dixon RAAF	Tunnels O6B
P/O G T Dodgshun	Tunnels O6B
S/L K C Doran DFC*	Tunnels O10C O6B
F/O S H Dowse	Hospital gate S9C. Tunnels O6B
Capt K W Driver DFC SAAF	Tunnels O6B
P/O N M Dunn RAAF	Forgery O6B
F/O L H Edwards	Tunnels O6B
F/L R H Edwards	Tunnels, wire O6B
F/O W H Edwards DFC	Tunnels O6B
F/L R A G Ellen	Train. Tunnels, Escape Officer O6B
P/O D A Elliott RCAF	Tunnels O6B
P/O G A Eperon	Tunnels O6B
F/O E T Fairbank	Forgery O6B
P/O H E L Falkus	Tunnels, maps, compasses, clothing O6B
P/O R F J Featherstone RCAF	Tunnels O6B
S/L S S Fielden	Tunnels O6B
Lt C H Filmer DSC RN	Tunnel O10C. Train (abortive). Tunnels, wire, gate O6B
P/O J E A Foster RAFVR	Tunnels, letter-codes, loaded parcels O6B
F/L P M Gardner DFC	Tunnel (discovered) DL. Tunnels, gate O6B
S/L D B Gericke	Tunnels, gate, wire, forgery O6B
P/O A H Gould	Tunnels O6B
S/L D Graham-Hogg	Tunnels O6B
P/O J H Green	Forgery O6B
F/O P O V Green	Wire DL. Tunnels, wire O6B
F/L T Griffith-Jones	Tunnels O6B
P/O T H Hadley	Tunnels O6B
F/L C M Hall RAAF	Train. Tunnels, wire, forgery O6B
F/O B W Hayward	Tunnels O6B
P/O H Heaton	Tunnels O6B
F/L D G Heaton-Nichols	Forgery O6B
F/L J O Hedley	Tunnels O6B
P/O R R Henderson RCAF	Forgery O6B
P/O W Hetherington	Tunnels, forgery O6B

F/O D S Hoare	Tunnels O6B
P/O J R Hoppe	Tunnels O6B
F/L E Hubicki (Pole)	Tunnels, forgery O6B
P/O F Hugill	Tunnels O6B
P/O W J Hunter	Tunnels, forgery O6B
P/O T G Hynes	Tunnel O10C. Tunnels O6B
P/O A M Imrie (S Rhodesian)	Tunnels O6B
F/O R H Jacoby	Forgery O6B
F/L P J F Jacquier FFAF	Tunnels O6B
P/O K Jaklewicz (Pole)	Tunnels O6B
P/O J Janicki (Pole)	Tunnels O6B
P/O T F S Johnson	Tunnels, forgery O6B
S/L M M Kane	Wire O10C. Tunnels O6B
P/O T M Kane	Tunnel O10C. Tunnels O6B
W/C J R Kayll DSO, DFC, AuxAF	Tunnels, wire O6B
P/O H G Keartland SAAF	Train. Tunnels, wire O6B
F/L F W S Keighley	Tunnels O6B
F/O M N McF Kennedy	Tunnel O10C. Tunnels, gate O6B
F/L V Kilian (Czech)	Tunnels, clothing O6B
F/L T R Kipp RCAF	Tunnel O10C. Tunnels O6B
P/O M Kozinski (Pole)	Tunnels O6B
F/L L Kozlowski (Pole)	Tunnels O6B
F/L S Z Król (Pole)	Tunnels O6B
P/O W Krupowicz (Pole)	Tunnels O6B
F/O P Langmead	Tunnels O6B
F/O D F Laslett	Tunnels, gate, wire O6B
F/O W N Lepine	Tunnels, gate, wire O6B
P/O P A Leuw	Tunnels O6B
F/L W J Lewis	Train. Tunnels, maps O6B
F/L E H Lewis-Dale	Tunnels, surveying, compasses, construction O6B
F/L J N Leyden	Tunnels O6B
F/L F L Litchfield	Forgery O6B
Sub-Lt (A) D M Lubbock RNVR	Tunnel (discovered) DL. Gate O6B
S/L E H Lynch-Blosse	Tunnel O10C. Tunnels, maps, compasses, clothing O6B
F/O C H MacFie DFC	Tunnels O6B
P/O D F M Mackarness	Tunnel O10C. Tunnels, wire O6B
P/O A W MacKay	Tunnels O6B
F/O A C MacLachlan	Tunnels O6B
P/O J W McCarthy RCAF	Tunnels, forgery O6B
F/L R J McConnell	Tunnels, construction O6B
P/O J P McKechnie RAAF	Tunnels, construction O6B
P/O R C D McKenzie	Tunnels O6B
P/O A F McSweyn	Tunnels, gate, wire O6B
P/O S Maciejewski (Pole)	Tunnels O6B
F/O K W Mackenzie DFC AFC	Tunnels, construction O6B
F/L R I C Macpherson	Tunnels O6B
P/O N Maranz	Tunnels O6B
F/O M Marcola (Pole)	Tunnels O6B
Lt (A) D T R Martin RN	Tunnels O6B
A/S/L P Mason	Forgery O6B
F/L E A Masters	Tunnels O6B
P/O A W Matthews	Train. Tunnels, forgery O6B
F/L B Mickiewicz (Pole)	Tunnels, construction O6B
P/O L Miller DFC	Tunnels O6B
F/O C D Milne	Tunnel O10C. Tunnels, wire O6B
F/O J C Milner	Tunnels, gate O6B
S/L B G Morris	Wire O10C. Tunnels, wire O6B

P/O A W Mungovan	Tunnels O6B
F/O K H P Murphy	Tunnels O6B
P/O H M Murray	Tunnels, wire O6B
Lt E C Newborn SAAF	Tunnels, wire O6B
P/O B T J Newland (S Rhodesian)	Tunnels O6B
P/O D G O'Brien	Tunnels O6B
P/O T L W Officer RAAF	Tunnels O6B
P/O W R Oldfield	Tunnels O6B
F/O J Palka (Pole)	Tunnels O6B
F/O S H Palmer RAFVR	Tunnel O10C. Tunnels, gate, clothing, maps, compasses O6B
P/O G Parker	Tunnels O6B
F/O J A G Parker (S Rhodesian)	Tunnels, wire O6B
F/L S G L Pepys	Forgery O6B
A/F/L A M D Péronne FFAF	Tunnels O6B
P/O H W Pickstone	Forgery O6B
S/L S Pietraszkiewicz (Pole)	Tunnels O6B
P/O P R I Pine RCAF (American)	Tunnels O6B
S/L T W Piper	Tunnels, security O6B
P/O I G G Potts	Tunnels, wire, forgery O6B
Sub-Lt (A) D A Poynter RN	Tunnels O6B
F/L Z Prochazka	Tunnels O6B
F/O H A R Prowse	Tunnels O6B
Lt Cdr N R Quill RN	Wire O6B
P/O E A Rance	Tunnels O6B
P/O T M Robinson	Train (killed)
Lt (A) R Ross-Taylor RNVR	Tunnels O6B
Lt A S Ruffel SAAF	Wire DL. Train. Tunnels, wire O6B
P/O W J Sandman RNZAF	Tunnels, wire O6B
S/L S Scibior (Pole)	Tunnels O6B
F/O S T Sedzik (Pole)	Tunnels O6B
P/O H J Sellers	Tunnels O6B
Lt H K Serjeant RN	Tunnels O6B
F/L P J S Shaughnessy DFC	Tunnels O6B
P/O F W Shorrock RCAF	Forgery O6B
P/O R Shuttleworth	Tunnels O6B
P/O J E Simmonds	Tunnels O6B
F/O H Skalski (Pole)	Tunnels O6B
P/O H A T Skehill	Tunnels O6B
P/O W M Skinner DFM	Tunnels O6B
F/L J R T Smalley DFC	Tunnels, maps, forgery O6B
P/O W A Sojka (Pole)	Tunnels O6B
F/O W A Staniland	Tunnels O6B
F/L J W Stephens DFC*	Tunnels, wire O6B
F/L P Stevens	Tunnels, gate, bribery, forgery O6B
S/L D M Strong	Tunnels O6B
P/O A W Sulston	Tunnels O6B
F/L N H Svendsen DFC (Dane)	Tunnels, gate, wire O6B
S/L E Sydney-Smith	Tunnels, news-reading O6B
F/L T E Syms	Tunnels O6B
F/L T H B Tayler	Tunnels O6B
P/O H H Taylor	Tunnels, wire, forgery O6B
F/L R F Terry RAAF	Tunnels O6B
P/O P A W Thomas	Tunnels, forgery O6B
P/O A B Thompson	Tunnels O6B
F/O J Tilsley	Tunnels O6B
P/O K S Toft	Tunnels O6B
F/L P Tomlinson	Tunnel (discovered) DL. Tunnels O6B

F/L K Trojacek (Czech)	Tunnels, forgery O6B
F/L R E Troward	Tunnels, gate, wire O6B
S/L A J Trumble	Wire, diversions O6B
F/O P D Tunstall	Tunnels, gate, wire O6B
S/L W H N Turner DFC	Letter-codes, loaded parcels O6B
F/L P F R Vaillant	Tunnels O6B
F/O P J Valachos DFC	Tunnels O6B
F/L G W Walenn	Forgery O6B
F/L R P Wallace-Terry	Train. Tunnels, gate, wire O6B
P/O J H Ward	Tunnels O6B
P/O P Ward-Smith	Tunnels O6B
S/L R N Wardell	Tunnels, gate O6B
P/O R D Wawn	Tunnels O6B
F/L M C Wells	Tunnels O6B
F/O P G Whitby	Tunnels O6B
P/O R A R White RZNAF	Forgery O6B
P/O F R Wilbraham	Train. Tunnels O6B
A/S/L F A Willan DFC	Tunnels, forgery, disguise, security O6B
F/O G S Williams	Tunnels, gate, wire O6B
A/S/L W R Williams	Tunnels, escape intelligence O6B
F/O H C Winter-Taylor	Tunnels O6B
F/L G O M Wright	Tunnels, construction, forgery O6B
P/O J Zafouk (Czech)	Train

Appendix VI

Chronology of Escape Attempts, June 1940– September 1942

Date and Location	Participants	Method	Result
1940			
June-September			
Oflag VIIC, Laufen	Lt A D Neely RN	Tunnel	Transferred
1941			
17 August			
St-Omer Hospital	A/W/C D R S Bader	From window by rope of knotted bed-sheets	Recaptured
August-September			
Dulag Luft	A/W/C D R S Bader A/F/L P M Gardner DFC F/L P Tomlinson Sub-Lt (A) D M Lubbock RNVR	Tunnel	Discovered
Dulag Luft (Hohemark Clinic)	F/O P O V Green Lt A S Ruffel SAAF	Wire	Recaptured
20/21 September			
En route from Dulag Luft to Oflag XC	F/L R T Wallace-Terry F/L C M Hall, RAAF	Escaped from moving train	Recaptured
September-October			
Oflag XC	S/L R J Bushell, AuxAF S/L K C Doran DFC* S/L E H Lynch-Blosse F/L T R Kipp RCAF F/O M N McF Kennedy F/O S H Palmer P/O R F Beauclair Lt C H Filmer DSC, RN Lt H H Bracken, RN	Tunnel	Abandoned when camp evacuated
8 October			
Oflag XC	F/L T R Kipp RCAF	Hid in tunnel when camp evacuated and cut through wire	Recaptured
8 October			
Oflag XC	S/L M M Kane S/L B G Morris	Hid in camp when prisoners transferred	Recaptured

Date and Location	Participants	Method	Result
8/9 October *En route* from Oflag XC to Oflag VIB	S/L R J Bushell AuxAF P/O J Zafouk	From cattle-truck outside Hannover	Reached Prague, but recaptured in 1942
As above	P/O T M Robinson	As above	Fell under train wheels and was killed
As above As above	Lt C H Filmer DSC, RN P/O H G Keartland SAAF	As above Escaped from moving train	Aborted Recaptured almost immediately
As above	F/L W J Lewis P/O R F Beauclair P/O J R Denny P/O P Stevens	As above	Recaptured
28 October Oflag VIB	F/L J Bryks F/L S Król F/L L Kozlowski P/O J E T Asselin RCAF P/O R F Beauclair P/O O Cerny	Tunnel	Recaptured
1 December Oflag VIB	F/O D Bruce AFC F/O S H Palmer F/O P D Tunstall P/O P Stevens	Disguised as Germans tried to lead party of "orderlies" out of upper gate	Aborted owing to defect on gate passes
Oflag VIB	*13 December* As above (second attempt) (Also involved were F/O M N McF Kennedy and Lt C H Filmer DSC, RN)	As above	Discovered
1942 *9 January* Oflag VIB	A/W/C D R S Bader A/F/L P M Gardner DFC Sub-Lt (A) D M Lubbock RNVR Capt. C J A Smith, Gen. List	Escaped from Clothing Store	Bader, Gardner and Lubbock discovered; Smith escaped and recaptured
18/19 April Oflag VIB	Five RAF officers	Tunnel	Recaptured

Date and Location	Participants	Method	Result
27/28 April Oflag VIB	F/L R P Wallace-Terry F/O S G Williams Lt A S Ruffel SAAF P/O H G Keartland SAAF	Under wire near upper gate	Recaptured
May Oflag VIB	S/L E Sydney-Smith	Tunnel	Caught at tunnel exit
Oflag VIB	F/O K W McKenzie DFC AFC F/O D Graham-Hogg	"Blitz" tunnel from dig left by filling in tunnel above	Aborted
Oflag VIB	S/L D B Gericke F/L N H Svendsen DFC Sub-Lt (A) R E Bartlett RN F/L R H Edwards (aborted) Plus two other RAF officers	Escaped from solitary Confinement cells	Recaptured
July Oflag VIB	P/O A F McSweyn RAAF	Through gate in bread cart	Recaptured
30/31 August Oflag VIB	W/C J R Kayll DSO DFC P/O A F McSweyn RAAF	Over wire with scaling ladders ("Operation Olympia")	Recaptured
27/28 April Oflag VIB	F/L R P Wallace-Terry F/O G S Williams Lt A S Ruffel SAAF P/O H G Keartland SAAF	Under wire near upper gate	Recaptured
May Oflag VIB	S/L E Sydney-Smith	Tunnel	Caught at exit
Oflag VIB	F/O K W Mackenzie DFC AFC A/S/L D Graham-Hogg	"Blitz" tunnel from ditch left by filling in tunnel above	Aborted
Oflag VIB	S/L D B Gericke F/L N H Svendson DFC Sub-Lt (A) R E Bartlett RN F/L R H Edwards (aborted) Plus two other RAF officers	Escaped from solitary confinement cells	Recaptured
July Oflag VIB	P/O A F McSweyn RAAF	Through gate in bread-cart	Recaptured
30/31 August Oflag VIB	W/C J R Kayll DSO DFC P/O A F McSweyn RAAF	Over wire with scaling ladders	Recaptured

APPENDIX VII
Selected
Biographical
Sketches

ANDREWS, Mervyn Frank ("Andy") Born 1919. No19 Squadron, Duxford (Spitfires). **Post-war:** Demobilised 1945 as Flight Lieutenant. Admitted to the ICAEW in 1950 and remained in full-time practice as a chartered accountant specialising in expert witness work. Died in Bristol Royal Infirmary on 24 May 2003, aged 84, leaving a wife, Sandra, several children and an extended family.

BADER, Douglas Robert Steuart Born St John's Wood, London, 21 02 1910. Infancy in India, then UK. Educated at Temple Grove Prep School, Eastbourne; St Edward's School, Oxford (scholarship). Entered RAF College, Cranwell (prize cadetship), in September 1928. Commissioned 26 07 1930. Posted No23 Sq, Kenley. Represented squadron in pairs aerobatic competition, Hendon Air Display, 1931. Lost legs after crashing in unofficial aerobatics display at Woodley aerodrome, Berkshire, 14 12 1931. Artificial limbs, then ground job. F/O 06 06 1932. Retired (1st) 30 04 1933. Aviation Department of Asiatic Petroleum Company (later Shell). Married (1st) Thelma Edwards, 1933. Returned to RAF 1939. (CFS Upavon for flying test, 18 10 1939. Re-employed as a regular officer, 26 11 1939.) Refresher course also at Upavon. Joined No19 Sq, Duxford (Spitfires), 07 02 1940, as F/O. Promoted F/L on 12 03 1940 and posted to No222 Sq, Duxford (Spitfires), as Flight Commander. Promoted Acting S/L, CO No242 Sq, Coltishall (Hurricanes). Acting W/C Flying, Tangmere Wing, No12 Group, Duxford, on 19 03 1941. 20 e/a destroyed, 2 shared and 1 probable. Awarded DSO, 01 10 1940; DFC, 07 01 1941; Bar to DSO, 15 07 1941; Bar to DFC, 09 09 1941. 2 Mentions in Dispatches. **Post-war:** CO, Fighter Leaders School, Tangmere, June 1945; then CO Essex Sector, No11 Grp, North Weald. Confirmed W/C 01 07 1945. Organized Battle of Britain flypast, 15 09 1945. Retired (2nd) on 21 07 1946, retaining rank of G/C. Rejoined Shell. Made *Chevalier, Légion d'Honneur*; awarded *Croix de Guerre avec Palm*, and 3rd Mention in Dispatches, 1947. Managing Director, Shell aircraft fleet, 1952; retired 1969. CBE for services to disabled, 1956. Director, Trafalgar Offshore Ltd. Member, Civil Aviation Authority, 1972-78. Thelma died 1971. Re-married Mrs Joan Eileen Murray, 1973. Made KBE, June 1976. Died 5 September 1982 of a heart attack.

BAKKER, William ("Dutch") Born Den Helder, Holland, 26 11 1911. Educated at High School. Royal Military Academy (KMA), 1930-33, then one year as 2nd Lieutenant in Infantry Regt. Flying training, 1935-36. Fighter pilot, 1936-37. Flying instructor, 1937-40. Escaped to England (arriving at Milford Haven) via Belgium and France (Cherbourg) when Germans invaded Holland, May 1940. Joined RAF. No1 (Coastal Command) OTU, Silloth, as instructor on Bothas (also test flights in Hurricanes). Dutch Royal Navy flying unit, Porthcawl, Wales, end 1940. Unit moved to Leuchars, early 1941, and became No320 Sq, Coastal Command (Lockheed Hudsons). **Post-war:** Lived in Heerde, Holland, until his death in late 1990s.

BARRY, Louis Brull ("Lou") Born in 1909 and grew up in Hungary, where his father, noted rower W A Barry, taught him to scull and to ride on the estate on which he was employed. Between the wars he was a professional sculler on the Thames, winning the Doggetts Coat and Badge in 1927, and gaining the championship of England in 1936. Also worked as a professional rowing coach, first in Ireland and then in Italy, where in 1936 he coached the Italian Olympic team. When war broke out he joined the RAF, qualified as a navigator and air-gunner and joined No217 Squadron, St Eval, Coastal Command. **Post-war:** Awarded the MBE. Worked in Austria in Air Intelligence, where he remained until his retirement in 1965 as a Squadron Leader. He also continued to coach rowing — he became involved in the Tideway Scullers' School — and he took the British crews to the Olympics in Tokyo in 1964, and to Montreal in 1976. At the time there was no official British National squad, nor was there any position of head coach, but Barry was generally acknowledged to be the expert. When he died, on 8 April 1991, he was the last surviving professional sculling champion of England. He was 82.

BEWLAY, Harry Ryland ("Bugger"/"Pop") Born King's Norton, Birmingham, 13 11 1911. Educated at Hallfield Prep School, Edgbaston, and Wrekin College, Wellington. Joined King's Royal Rifle Corps at Whittington Barracks, then joined RAF 1936 on Short Service Commission. Trained at Perth (Tiger Moths) and Netheravon (Hawker Hinds). Posted to No18 Sq (Fairey Battles) at Upper Heyford, then to No57 Sq, also at Upper Heyford (Blenheim Mk1s). **Post-war:** Demobbed 1945. Joined Inland Revenue in Weston-super-Mare, Somerset, then moved to Australia where second child was born. Returned to UK after 18 months and worked as salesman for Orchard Tyres, retiring at age 62.

BLACKLOCK, Tom E Interrupted Naval Architecture studies at Liverpool University to volunteer for Fleet Air Arm, 1939. Joined HMS *Victorious* 1941. **Post-war:** Demobbed February 1946. Returned to Liverpool University, graduating in 1949. Worked at Vickers, Barrow, until retirement in 1982, with a three-year break as Warehouse Superintendent for a shipping firm. Retired to Cumbria.

BOULDING, Roger John Eric Born 19 11 1919. Joined RAF on Short Service Commission in June 1938. No6 E&RFTS, Sywell, Northants (Tiger Moths), 29 08 1938; No8 FTS, Montrose, November 1938; No11 FTS, Shawbury; Armament Training Camp, Penrhos, June 1939. Joined No. 52 Sq, Upwood, July 1939, flying Fairey Battles and Avro Ansons. Commissioned P/O, 29 08 1939. No98 Sq, Hucknall, October 1939. No142 Sq, France (Battles), November 1939-May 1940. Escaped from France in an abandoned Tiger Moth, arriving at RAF Hawkinge. Volunteered for Fighter Command and posted to No74 (Tiger) Sq, Kirton-in-Lindsey (Spitfires), 22 8 1940. 1 e/a destroyed, 1 shared, 1 damaged. Promoted to F/O, 03 09 1940. Time-promotion as POW: F/L 03 09 1941 and S/L 01 07 1944. **Post-war:** Permanent Commission, 1945. Refresher training at No6 (P) AFU, 25 09 1945, and No10 OTU, Abingdon, 12 02 1945; converted to Lancasters at No1553 HCU, North Luffenham. CO, No35 Sq (Lancasters), Stradishall, 30 01 1947. HQ Bomber Command, 22 10 1948. No203 AFT, Driffield, May 1950, then two months at Central Fighter Establishment, West Raynham. CO, No249 Sq, Devesoir, Egypt (Vampires), 24 10 1950-02 05 1953. Promoted to W/C, 01 01 1954. Retired from RAF 29 11 1966. Ran hotels and restaurants with wife until retirement in 1987. Died 9 August 1993.

BRACKEN, Hugo ("Bungie") Joined Royal Navy as cadet, January 1926. RN College, Dartmouth. Cadet and Midshipman on two different battleships in Mediterranean Fleet, 1929-32. Sub-Lt 1932, courses at Greenwich and Portsmouth. Fishery protection ship, HMS *Hairbell* (the last coal-burning ship in the Navy), 1933. Volunteered for Air Branch 1934. Six months' pilot training at No1 FTS, Leuchars (Avro 504N, Fairey IIIF, Fairey Seal). Dual commission as Sub-Lt, RN, and F/O, RAF. Torpedo-bomber training, Gosport (Blackburn Baffin). Deck-landing training. Then to HMS *Furious* to squadron equipped with Baffins. HMS *Courageous* and Lee-on-Solent (Blackburn Sharks). Armament training. Re-equipped with Fairey Swordfish owing to design fault in Sharks. On first observer training course, 1938. Conversion course to Walruses. Destined for HMS *Glasgow* 1939 (two Walruses) but ship not ready, so transferred HMS *Suffolk*. At start of war, on the northern patrol, between Orkneys, Shetlands and Iceland. *Suffolk* rammed by merchantman. Walruses transferred to Hatston for anti-submarine patrols. Back to *Suffolk* for Norwegian campaign. *Suffolk* damaged by German dive-bombers and Walruses returned to Hatston for further anti-submarine patrols. As Lt, CO No701 Sq (six Walruses) formed 08 05 40 to make shore-based patrols from Harstad, Norway. Went to Norway on HMS *Glorious*, also equipped with No46 Sq (Hurricanes). Arrived Harstad 18 08 440. Returned to Scapa Flow on HMS *Ark Royal*, landing on 08 06 40, flying patrols on the way. HMS *Argus* to Iceland, establishing three bases for reccos and patrols. Squadron disbanded, October 40. Senior observer newly formed No827 (torpedo-bomber) Sq working up at Crail. Anti-submarine patrols from Stornaway. Ministry of Aircraft Production, London, i/c cockpit design for RAF and FAA single-seater a/c, 1941. Senior Observer, No827 Sq (Fairey Albacores), HMS *Victorious*, June 1941. **Post-war:** Captain of fishery protection patrol. Conducted first "Cod War" against Iceland. Made CBE.

BUSHELL, Roger Joyce Born Springs, Transvaal, 30 08 1910. Educated at Wellington College; Brasenose College, Oxford (Law); University of Grenoble. Pre-war practising barrister and olympic skier. Joined Auxiliary Air Force, No601 (County of London) Sq, "The Millionaires". Went solo 06 08 1932 and obtained "A" licence three days later. Flew Westland Wapiti I, Hawker Hart I, Gloster Gauntlet II and Blenheim If. Performed in Empire Air Display, May 1838. CO, No92 Sq (Blenheim MkIF, Spitfire MkII),

October 1939. First South African and AuxAF officer to command a squadron. S/L confirmed, 01 01 40. Shot after mass escape from Stalag Luft III, 29 03 1944. Cremated at Saarbrücken.

BUTT, Maurice Born Chislehurst, Kent, 31 08 1919. Educated at Nantwich & Acton Grammar School. Apprentice to Armstrong Whitworth Aircraft, Coventry, 1936-39, workshop and wind-tunnel. Tested Avro Manchester fuselage and wing models, autumn 1938. RAFVR, Sergeant Pilot, 1938. Flying training at Ansty. Called up for full-time service, 1939. Training at Hullavington and Ternhill, 1939/40. Assessed exceptional as pilot, February 1940. Commissioned P/O June 1940; posted to Harwell. Joined No149 (East India) Sq, Mildenhall (Wellingtons, No3 Group, Bomber Command), August 1940, as second pilot. **Post-war:** Structural engineer with steelwork contractors in Banbury and London. Senior lecturer in Structural Engineering, 1967-79. Retired to Norfolk. Has sat on Coventry Council since 1989.

CASSON, Lionel Harwood ("Buck") Born Sheffield 1915. Joined No616 Sq, AuxAF, Doncaster, 06 04 1939. Called to full-time service, August 1939. No2 FTS, Brize Norton, 01 10 1939. Rejoined No616 Sq (Gloster Gauntlets and Fairey Battles) at Leconfield, 06 04 1940. No6 OTU, Sutton Bridge, 28 04 1940. No501 Sq, Arras, France, 14 05 1940. Evacuating France, the train was bombed and he made his way to Cherbourg and by ship to Southampton. Joined No79 Sq, Biggin Hill (Hurricanes), 17 05 1940. Re-joined No616 Sq, Leconfield, 07 07 1940. Re-equipped with Spitfires. One "kill" and two shared as fighter pilot. Promoted F/O 03 12 40. Awarded DFC, 16 09 1941. Time-promotion to F/L, 03 12 41, whilst POW. **Post-war:** Demobilised 12 11 1945. Rejoined Royal Auxiliary Air Force 03 05 1947. F/O No616 Sq, Finningley. Appointed CO, 02 10 1950. Awarded AFC, 01 06 1953. Released November 1954 as S/L.

CHAPMAN, Edward ("Tug-Boat Ted") Born 01 05 1906. Merchant Navy cadet, HMS *Worcester*, Greenhithe, 1921-23. Then wine trade. Married 03 03 1936, one son (Anthony, born 1945). On outbreak of war volunteered for Navy, but Navy was full; tried Army, but minimum length of service was seven years; then went direct to Admiralty and was accepted by Navy, also by RAF, Royal Marines and Westminster Dragoons. RAF accepted first, in February 1940, so he joined RAF Marine Craft Section (High Speed Launches). Posted to Calshot, then Grimsby, October 1940-Feb 1941; then Dover. MCS became Air-Sea Rescue Service. S/Ldr posting, Gibraltar, March 1941, but captured before embarkation. **Post-war:** Stayed in RAF. Retired September 1966 as S/L. Supervised German market for sherry for more than twenty-five years. Pioneered plonk, 1966, creating nineteen different brands. Bought a bonded store near Sally Line at Ramsgate, working as Marketing Director. Retired in 1984 when sponsor died and his son took over. Fellow, Institute of Directors. Lived in Hove, East Sussex, until his death in late 1990s.

CLELLAND, Ernest John Born 12 12 1920, Southall. Educated at Kimbolton School. Joined RAFVR 04 07 39. Mobilised 02 09 39. **Post-war:** Granted Permanent Commission. Retired in 1948 on medical grounds as S/L. From January 1957, lecturer in English Language & Literature in the interpreters' department at Louvain University, Belgium. Lives in Brussels.

COOPER, Herbert Douglas Haig Born Northern Ireland. Entered RAF on Short Service Commission, December 1936. No110 (Hyderebad) Sq, Wattisham (Blenheim MkIV, No2 Group, Bomber Command). Completed tour. Awarded DFC. Then No21 Sq, Watton (Blenheims, No2 Group). Captured towards end of tour. **Post-war:** Released from RAF 1946 as S/L. Took over family business of running local cinema, Strabane, Co. Tyrone. Magistrate, Juvenile Courts; member of Board of Visitors at nearby prison. Active in RAF Association. Lives in Strabane.

CUNNINGHAM, Wallace ("Jock") Born Glasgow, 04 12 1916. Educated Oatland School, then Govan House School and Strathclyde University. Trained as Mechanical Engineer with Watson-Laidlaw, manufacturers of sugar machinery, then worked as engineer in Glasgow and Kent. Joined RAFVR at Prestwick, August 1938, and trained at Rochester (Tiger Moths, Hawkers Hart and Hind, Avro Tutors). Called up September 1939 as Sergeant. No11 Intermediate FTS, Shawbury, Shropshire (Harts and Audaxes). No5 OTU Aston Down, Gloucestershire, May 1940 (Miles Masters, Harvards, Spitfires). Commissioned P/O 08 06 40. No19 Sq, Duxford, (No12 Group, Fighter Command, Spitfires), June 1940. Awarded DFC 08 10 40. Promoted F/O 01 06 41. Four e/a destroyed, plus two shared. Time-promotion to F/L, 01 06 42, whilst POW. **Post-war:** Released from RAF 1946. Rejoined previous employers in Kent. Returned to Glasgow 1960 as a Chief Engineer. Became Sales and Engineering Director. Then in chemical, food and textile industries. Travelled widely in USA, Far East, Russia and Communist Bloc. After retirement retained as design consultant. Lives in Muirend, Glasgow.

DAVIS, Rupert ("Pud") Born 1916. Trained for Merchant Navy on HMS *Worcester*, Greenhithe. Transferred to RN, then FAA. Midshipman on carrier HMS *Glorious*. **Post-war:** actor in theatre, radio, film and TV. Played Georges Simenon's fictional detective, Maigret, in fifty-two episodes for BBC TV, 1960-64, and named TV actor of the year 1963. Had to struggle to shake of his Maigret image and despite a few later film appearances died of cancer, penniless, in 1976.

DENTON, I P B ("Paddy") Born North Wales, 1920. Educated at Shrewsbury. Apprenticeship with Ruston & Hously, manufacturers of marine and diesel engines, Lincoln, September 1938-September 1939. Army Reserve. Transferred to RAF, 1940. Trained at: Babbacombe, near Torquay; Cambridge; Perth (Tiger Moths); Moosejaw, Saskatchewan (Airspeed Oxfords and Harvards); Abingdon OCTU (Whitleys); and Stanton Harcourt. Joined No102 Sq, Topcliffe, Yorkshire (Whitleys, No4 Group, Bomber Command). **Post-war:** Joined his family firm of construction engineers. Travelled widely in UK, on the Continent and in India. Retired 1979, to Little Budworth, Cheshire, owing to ill-health. Involved in design, construction and creation of Oulton Park Motor Racing Circuit. Author and poet. Died 6 September 1991 of a stroke.

DILLY, Colin Noel Born Lowestoft, 10 December 1899. Educated at Lowestoft Grammar School and Goldsmith's College. Joined RNAS as a pilot in 1917, flying RE8 and DH9A. Commercial artist, 1918-1939. Commissioned RAFVR, 18 10 1939. Codes and cyphers officer, Egypt, Greece and Crete. **Post-war**: resumed career as commercial artist. Central Office of Information as illustrator until retirement in 1965. Wife died 1985. Dilly died 20 May 1987. One son, Martin.

DUNN, Norman Maxwell Born Sydney, Australia, 1916. Went into accountancy, then joined RAAF and was the first officer commissioned under the Empire Air Training Scheme. **Post-war:** Chairman of the Council of the Australian Telecommunications Development Association. Lives in St Ives, NSW.

EDWARDS, Kenneth Charles Born St Mary's Cray, Kent, 15 November 1910. Engineer and draughtsman. Joined No600 (City of London) Sq, Auxiliary Air Force, Hendon, in 1936; began training as air-gunner in April 1936. Promoted Sergeant 1939. Called up for full-time service to No600 Sq on 24 08 1939; squadron posted to Manston, October 1939. Commissioned P/O 08 08 1940. Squadron rested at Catterick, October 1940. Edwards posted as AG to Bomber Command, No150 Sq, Newton (Wellingtons, No1 Group), January 1941. Completed 14 ops. Promoted to F/O 08 08 1941. Time-promotion to F/L 08 08 1942 whilst still a POW. **Post-war:** Released from RAF August 1945, as F/L. Middle management and Civil Service (MOD). Lives in Sevenoaks, Kent.

FALKUS, Hugh Edward Lance Born in Cheam, SW London, on 15 May 1917. Educated at East Anglian School, Culford. Joined RAF on Short Service Commission in 1937. Married (1st) in 1939 (two sets of twins; marriage dissolved 1947). P/O in No222 Sq, Duxford, 1940. **Post-war:** Freelance broadcaster, BBC, and making documentary and wildlife films. Married (2nd) January 1952, but wife drowned 12 05 1952; (3rd) 1952 (dissolved 1958); (4th) 1958. Wrote sitcoms for TV, broadcast for *Children's Hour*, wrote more than thirty scripts for *The Undersea World of Jacques Cousteau*, then independent director of (and occasional actor in) prize-winning nature films and author of, among others, *Sea Trout Fishing* (1962), *Freshwater Fishing* (1975) and *Salmon Fishing* (1984). Partial autobiography, *The Stolen Years* (1968). Died April 1996.

GARDNER, Peter Melvill Born in Grimsby, 01 July 1918. Joined RAF on Short Service Commission in November 1937. No5 FTS, Sealand, 05 03 1938. Posted to No32 Sq, Biggin Hill, on 17 09 1938, as Acting P/O. Confirmed as P/O 29 11 1938. Attached to No3 Sq, France, May 1940. Returned to No32 Sq, June 1940. 8 e/a destroyed, 1 shared. Promoted to F/O 29 08 1940. Awarded DFC, 30 08 1940. Posted to No45 Sq, Hornchurch, as Flight Commander, June 1941. Time-promotion to F/L 29 08 1941 and S/L 01 07 1943 whilst a POW. **Post-war:** Stayed in RAF. Retired from service on 31 07 1948 as S/L. Died 23 May 1984.

GOULD, Alexander Herbert Born New Zealand, but family moved to USA 1918; then to UK; then finally to Australia, 1922. Educated North and Central Queensland, New South Wales Agricultural College, Hawkesbury Agicultural School, and Sydney University. Infantry militia, 1936-37. Joined RAAF, 1937. Stations, RAF 1938-40: Netheravon, Rissington, Manston and Hemswell. Commissioned P/O 07 03 39. **Post-war:** Returned to Australia and settled in Bundanoon, NSW, where he was active in the RAAF Ex-POW Association. Published *Tales from the Sagan Woods*, 1994.

GRIFFITH-JONES Trevor Born 03 September 1913. Joined RAF 03 September 1940. Married 10 05 1941. **Post-war:** died of severe heart disease 11 March 1968.

HARDING, Peter Born Forest Hill, London, 11 May 1919. Educated at Dulwich College, 1931-37. Was OTC Platoon Sergeant, receiving colours in shooting eight. Studied metallurgy at the Royal School of Mines, Kensington, 1937-39. Summer vacation 1938 as 8th engineer on 11,000-ton freighter SS *Africa Star* sailing ten-week round trip to Rio de Janeiro, Santos and Buenos Aires carrying meat, bananas and oranges; in charge of engine-room on return voyage. Joined London University Air Sq, 1939, trained on Avro Tutors at Northolt with RAF instructors, and on Hawker Hinds and Harts at summer camps. Commissioned P/O in RAFVR, June 1939. Prohibited from joining up Sept 1939 because "in reserved occupation". Students evacuated to Swansea University in 1939 to complete studies. Studies neglected (drink, driving, rugger) and failed exams. (Summer vacation job making Ack-Ack and 18-inch guns at Beadmore's, Glasgow.) Asked to be called up, informed still "reserved", but binned letter and joined RAF anyway. Hatfield ITW for short refresher (Tigers), then Cranwell (Ansons) and Montrose (Masters). Army Co-operation course at Old Sarum (Lysanders). Posted to No225 Sq, Tilshead. Volunteered for PRU on Spitfires. Converted to Spitfires by Geoffrey Tuttle on dual-controlled Battle. Posted to No1 PRU, Benson, Oxon. Then No3 PRU, Oakington, as F/O. **Post-war:** Demobbed VJ-Day + 1 unfit for flying with chronic bronchitis. Returned Royal School of Mines October 1945 to repeat third and final year. Received 2nd Class Honours in metallurgy, 1947. Joined H J Enthoven & Sons, Lead Smelters and Refiners, late 1947; rose to Works Manager, then Technical Director. Taken over by Billiton of The Hague and then by Royal Dutch Shell. Responsible for technical co-ordination of works at home and abroad and for pollution control. Retired in 1980 and did eight years' consultancy work. Married in 1952 (three sons). Lives in Chislehurst, Kent.

HYDE, Noel Challis ("Hetty") Joined RAF in September 1929. No208 Sq, Egypt, 1932-36. Promoted to S/L on 01 08 38. Took part in gunnery trials for Spitfire and Hurricane. Flight Commander, No44 Sq, Waddington (Hampdens, No5 Group, Bomber Command), October 1940. CO, No207 Sq, Waddington (Manchesters, No5 Group), November 1940-April 1941. **Post-war:** RAF Staff College, Bulstrode, May 1945-November 1947. HQ Combined Airlift Task Force, Berlin, November 1948. Station Commander, RAF Binbrook, April 1952-August 1953. Commandant, CFS Upavon, April 1956-December 1958. C-in-C, Royal Malayan Air Force, November 1957-November 1961. Retired from the RAF as an Air Commodore in 1962. Ten years working for charitable organisations. Active in RAF EX-POW Association and CFS Association, 1959-86. Died, September 1987.

JOHNSON, Theo Faire Storrer Born Wellington, New Zealand, 12 May 1919 then moved with family to Hamilton. Joined State Insurance Department of NZ Public Service. Joined RNZAF in 1938. Initial Training at No1 FTS Wigram. Sailed for UK, March 1940. P/O, No51 Sq, Linton-on-Ouse (Whitleys, No4 Group, Bomber Command); flew two ops. **Post-war:** Released from RAF, 1945. Studied Town & Country Planning in UK at Manchester University, 1945-48. Married Vivien Steuart Symonds, 07 01 1947 (one son). Returned to NZ Public Service. Final post was Director of Town & Country Planning Division, Ministry of Works. Died 6 March 1972 of stomach cancer.

KAYLL, Joseph Robert Born Sunderland 12 April 1914. Educated at Aysgarth School, near Bedale, Yorkshire, and Stowe. Started work at age sixteen as mill-boy in family firm of Joseph Thompson & Co. Sawmills, Sunderland. Gained "A" Licence in 1935 and joined the Auxiliary Air Force, No607 (County of Durham) Sq, Usworth. Trained on Avro 504N, Wapiti and Hawker Harts and Demons. Squadron finally equipped with Gladiator MkI and MkII. Promoted to F/L 1937. Appointed "A" Flight Commander 1939. Called to full-time service with No607 Squadron (No13 Group, Fighter Command), 24 08 1939. Moved to Merville, near Vitry-en-Artois, France, as part of AASF, on 15 11 1939. Shared airfield with No615 Sq (also Gladiators). Appointed CO of No615 Sq (No61 Fighter Wing), March 1940. Squadron moved to Le Touquet to convert to Hurricanes, 20 50 1940; returned to Merville, 11 05 1940. Ops in Northern France from 16 05 1940. Returned to Kenley 20 05 1940. Awarded DSO and DFC on 31 05 40. Squadron "rested" at Prestwick, 31 08 1940; stationed at Northolt, 10 10 1940. Battle of Britain "ace". As fighter pilot, 12 kills, plus 1 shared and two probables. HQ Fighter Command, Bently Priory, 30 12 1940, as S/L Tactics. Appointed W/C Flying, Hornchurch, 02 06 1941. **Post-war:** Mention in Dispatches, 28 12 45. Demobilised in 1946 as W/C. Made OBE, 26 06 46. Asked to re-form No607 Sq at RAF Ouston, Northumberland, with Spitfires. Relinquished command 1949. Returned to Thompson's Sawmills. Lived in Sunderland until his death on 3 March 2000.

LEWIS, Wilfred John ("Mike") Born Port Hope, Ontario, Canada, 24 March 1918. Educated at Port Hope High School. Mechanical engineer, Mathew's Conveyer Company, 1936-38. To UK for Short Service Commission in the RAF. FTS, Sealand, Chester, 1938. Air Navigation School, Manston. Joined No44 (Rhodesia) Sq, Waddington (Hampdens, No5 Group, Bomber Command), August 1939. Completed tour. Awarded DFC. Then posted to No207 Sq, Waddington (Manchesters, No5 Group), as F/O. Completed tour.

LUBBOCK, David Miles Born 1911. Nutrition research, Rowett Institute, Aberdeen, 1932-39. married, 1939. Joined Fleet Air Arm, September 1939. Training, Lee-on-Solent, Ford and HMS *Conder*, Arbroath. Posted No828 Sq, Torpedo Spotter Reconnaissance (Fairey Albacores), training at Machrihanish, Mull of Kintyre. Then squadron moved to Hatston, Orkneys, for anti-submarine patrols; finally sailed with HMS *Victorious*, July 1941. **Post-war:** Mention in Dispatches 19 03 46 for services as POW. Returned to Rowett Institute, then asked by United Nations to help establish Food and Agriculture Organisation. After five years returned Scotland to farm. For next twenty years from time to time helped FAO member nations to help improve the feeding and nutrition of their peoples. Lived in Brechin, Scotland, until his death in 1993.

MacFIE, Colin Hamilton Born Cheltenham, Gloucester, 12 June 1920. Joined No611 Sq, Auxiliary Air Force, 12 03 1939. Called to full-time service as P/O with No611 Sq on 26 08 1939. Appointed Flight Commander, No616 Sq, Coltishall, 07 09 1940. Promoted to F/O on 06 04 1941. Credited with 2 "kills" and 3 e/a damaged. Awarded DFC on 08 08 1941. Time-promotion to S/L on 01 07 1944 whilst POW. **Post-war:** Permanent Commission in RAF. CO, No1 Sq, October 1946-July 1947. CO, No3 Sq, July 1947-November 1949. Retired from RAF on 18 10 1963 as S/L. Died in 1982.

MACKENZIE, Kenneth William Born Belfast, 08 June 1916. Educated at Methodist College, Belfast. Engineering apprenticeship, Harland and Wolff. Studied for engineering degree at Queen's University, Belfast. Learned to fly 1935 at the North of Ireland Aero Club, Newtownards. Joined RAFVR in 1939. No23 E&RFTS, Sydenham. Called up 03 09 1939. Training began at No3 ITW, Hastings, 28 12 1939. Then No5 FTS, Hanworth, 25 02 1940, and No4 FTS, South Cerney, 25 05 1940. Commissioned P/O on 28 08 1940. No6 OTU, Sutton Bridge, 30 08 1940, for Hurricane conversion. Joined No43 Sq, Usworth, on 21 09 1940. Posted to No501 Sq, Kenley, 29 09 1940. As fighter pilot, 10 "kills", three shared and one damaged. Awarded DFC on 25 10 1940. Posted to No247 Sq, Predannack, 19 06 1941, as Flight Commander. Promoted to F/O on 24 08 1941. Time-promotion to F/L whilst POW on 24 08 1942. Repatriated from Stalag Luft III, October 1944. Posted to No53 OTU, Kirton-in-Lindsey, on 09 12 1944, as instructor. Then to No61 OTU, Keevil, as Flight Commander, on 17 06 1947. **Post-war:** Stayed in RAF. Promoted to S/L on 01 08 1947. Awarded AFC on 01 01 1953. Promoted W/C on 01 01 1954. Retired from the RAF on 01 07 1967 at own request to become deputy Commander of the Zambian Air Force. Subsequently became Managing Director of Air Kenya Limited, and finally an aviation consultant in Nairobi. At various times was Hon Secretary of the Battle of Britain Fighter Pilots' Association, Chairman of the RAF Motor Sports Association, and Chairman of the RAF Officers' Association, East Africa. War memoirs, *Hurricane Combat*, published in 1987. Married (twice), with one daughter and two step-sons. Retired to Cyprus.

McCONNELL, Robert James ("Liffey") Born 19 May 1913 in Carrigans, Omagh, Co. Tyrone, son of a farmer. After education at Dunmullan Public Elementary School and Omagh Academy, started training as an accountant but left to join RAF on a Short Service Commission in1935. Trained at Coventry and Uxbridge on the Avro Cadet, and gained his pilot's licence (No11234) on 22 12 1936. After advanced flying training on Hawker Harts at Digby, Yorkshire, posted to No21 Sq, then No82 Sq, Watton. Flew some of the earliest bombing raids over Holland. Was shot down in May 1940 and evaded, and after hospitalisation went on a refresher course at No11 FTS, Shawbury. Was shot down again in 1941 and captured. **Post-war:** Released from RAF as F/L and returned to farming. For twenty-three years monitored the weather for Aldergrove meteorological station. Died 8 July 1992.

McSWEYN, Allan Frank Born Rockdale, near Sydney, in 1919. Enlisted in RAAF in September 1939 and joined No1 Course of the Empire Air Training School. Trained at Somers, Victoria, and Narromine, NSW. Shipped to Canada in 1940 to train at Uplands, Ottawa, on Yales and Harvards. December 1940 arrived in UK and sent from Uxbridge to Lossiemouth for bomber training. Posted to No115 Sq, Marham (Wellington IC). Made "home run" in 1943. After refresher course at Cranwell posted to No105 Transport OTU at Bramcote, training "operationally expired" pilots for transport and civil aviation duties. Married in Winchester on 06 03 1944. Received MC for his escape and AFC for post-escape flying work on

10 07 1945. Left RAAF as a F/L. **Post-war:** Returned to Australia. Joined Trans Australian Airlines and became their Queensland manager. After ten years with TAA he left to set up his own business, which he ran for years. After a period as general manager of an engineering business he retired to the Gold Coast.

MUNGOVAN, Alfred W ("Alf") Junior clerk, Mark Brown's Wharf near Tower Bridge, London. Joined RAF on a Short Service Commission in October 1938. Trained at No11 FTS, Shawbury, 1939. Commissioned P/O on 03 09 39 and posted to No88 Sq. and went to France with AASF (Fairey Battles). **Post-war:** Signed on for another four-year Short Service Commission. Transferred to Administrative Branch. Served two years in India, mostly as Station Administrative Officer. Returned to UK in February 1948, then to Ballykelly, Northern Ireland. Married 1948. Transferred to HQ, No19 Group, Mount Batten, in October 1948 as Senior Personnel Staff Officer. Retired from RAF in May 1950, retaining rank of S/L. Then for seven years a sales rep for a Midlands chocolate manufacturer covering the Home Counties. Bought confectionery shop in Stanmore, 1956. Emigrated to Australia, March 1966. Settled in Modbury, South Australia, and spent six years as an arts and crafts rep. With colleague founded Premier Arts Supplies PLC, 1973, which has become the largest business of its kind in South Australia. Semi-retired as from 1980, but still retained an interest in the business as a director.

PIETRASZKIEWICZ, Stanislaw Andrzej Born in Minsk Litewski, Poland, on 20 04 1906. Entered the second class of the Aviation Cadet School and in 1939 became an instructor. Fled Poland after the German invasion and joined the *Armée de l'Air*, in which he was a flight commander. After fall of France joined RAF and became the first CO of No307 (Night Fighter) Squadron. At his own request was transferred to day fighters and posted to No616 Squadron. Then became the first CO of No315 squadron. Credited with three enemy a/c destroyed, plus one damaged and one "probable". **Post-war:** Settled in South Africa.

POYNTER, Douglas Arthur Born 1921. Entered Royal Navy 1948 and trained as an Observer (Air). Served on HMS *Glorious* and HMS *Furious*. **Post-war:** MBE 19 03 46 for services as POW. From 1945 to 1955 various appointments at sea, on-shore and on courses as Lieutenant and subsequently Lieutenant-Commander. Promoted Commander, 1955, and Captain, 1962 and was Executive Officer on HMS *Terror* and Signals Officer in Far East. Deputy Director of Naval Signals, 1963. Senior Officers' War Course, 1965. Defence, Naval, Military and Air Attaché in Santiago, Lima and Quito, 1966-67. Appointed Commander of the Royal Victorian Order, 1968. Director of Naval Signals, 1969. Appointed *Aide-de-Camp* of HM the Queen, 1971. Retired from RN, 1972. Naval Regional Officer, London Area, 1972-80. Elected to Waverley Borough Council, 1983, and up to 1992 was Chairman, then Vice-Chairman, of the Finance Committee. From 1992 onwards, committee member of his local Conservative Association and Residents' Association. Lives in Farnham, Surrey.

PROWSE, Harry Arthur Robin Joined RAF on Short Service Commission, May 1939. Training: No8 E&RFTS, Woodley, 30 05 1939; No13 FTS, Drem, 11 08 1939; No15 FTS, Lossiemouth. Posted to No9 Bombing & Gunnery School, Penrhos, as staff pilot, on 06 01 1940 and commissioned P/O. Then to No4 Ferry Pilots' Pool, 16 05 1940, followed by posting to No7 OTU, Hawarden, on 05 09 1940, converting to Spitfires. Joined No226 Sq, Wittering, on 16 09 1940. Transferred to No603 Sq, Hornchurch, 20 10 1940. 3 e/a destroyed. Promoted to F/O on 01 06 1941. Time-promotion whilst POW to F/L on 01 06 1942. **Post-war:** Flying refresher course at No5 (P) AFU, Atcham (Harvards), 16 10 1945-03 01 1946. Released from RAF but returned for one year. Went to No61 OTU, Keevil, for refresher course on Spitfires on 18 06 1946. Instructor at Keevil, 18 07 1946. Released from the RAF on 06 06 1947. Sailed for Brazil with wife in September 1947 and managed a 17,000-acre estate until he retired in December 1983.

ROBERTS, Ralph Joined No616 Sq, Auxiliary Air Force, at Doncaster in March 1939. Called to full-time service as Acting P/O on 24 08 1939 and awarded wings in September. P/O confirmed 04 09 1939. Converted to Hurricanes at Fighter Pool, St Athan. Then to Ferry Pilots' Pool, Fenton. Posted to No615 Sq, Vitry-en-Artois (Gladiators, Hurricanes), on 01 01 1940. Squadron operated from Manston during Dunkirk evacuation and from Kenley during the Battle of Britain. Posted to No64 Sq, Kenley, in August 1940. 1 e/a destroyed. Time-promotion whilst POW: F/O 04 09 1940; F/L 04 09 1941. **Post-war:** Released from RAF on 09 03 1946 as F/L. Died 1994.

ROTH, Michael Herriott ("Maggie") Born 1919. Joined the RAF on a Short Service Commission in 1936. Promoted to F/O 18 04 39. **Post-war:** Professional magician in Canada until retirement. Wrote a memoir of his POW experiences called "The Unhurried Years", which was accepted by an agent of William

Collins & Sons in Canada but later turned down in favour of Eric Sydney-Smith's biography of "Wings" Day. Lived in Toronto until moving in to a retirement home in the mid-1990s.

RUFFEL, Anthony Stanford Born in Bloemfontain, South Africa, 30 December 1915. Educated at Grey College, Bloemfontain. Employed by Cooper, MacDougall & Robinson, manufacturers of animal health products. Joined SAAF at Pretoria ITW in 1940. Passed out as Lt pilot at AFS Vereeniging. Posted to No1 Sq SAAF at Fuka (Hurricanes, No204 Group, Western Desert AF), May 1941. **Post-war:** Married his fiancée, a former WREN, in Cornwall in July 1945 (three children). Returned to South Africa and demobbed in October 1945; went back to pre-war employers. Started own business, also animal health products, in 1947, and ran it until he sold it in 1970 and retired to Riviona, RSA.

SKINNER, Wilfred Malcolm ("Bill") Born in Gloucester, the son of an ex-RFC pilot. Educated at Merchant Taylors' School and in April 1937 while working for the Midland Bank joined RAFVR. Clocked up sufficient flying hours and reached required standard to undergo full-time training in regular RAF at No5 E&RFTS, Hanworth. Posted to No74 Sq, Hornchurch, on 10 06 1939 as a Sergeant Pilot. 6 e/a destroyed, 3 shared, 1 damaged during Dunkirk and Battle of Britain. Awarded DFM on 24 12 40. Then to No59 OTU as Instructor, March 1941. Commissioned P/O on 17 05 1941. Rejoined No74 ("Tiger") Sq at Rochford on 10 06 1941. Time-promotion as POW: F/O 17 05 1942; F/L 17 05 1943. **Post-war:** Released from the RAF in 1946 as F/L. Rejoined Volunteer Reserve as F/O on 12 10 1947.

STEVENS, Peter ("Steve") Born London, 13 April 1917. Student, London School of Economics. Left LSE and joined RAFVR on 03 09 1939 as Aircraftman 2nd Class at No1 Depot, Uxbridge. Then to Finningley on 11 11 1939. Under training as pilot, No5 ITW, 05 12 1939-20 01 1940. No33 Maintenance Unit, 21 05 1940. No50 Group Pool, 09 06 1940. No51 Group Pool, 29 07 1940. No11 Service FTS, 01 08 1940. Sergeant Pilot, 31 10 1940. Commissioned P/O on 02 11 1940; sent to No2 School of Air Navigation. Then No16 OTU, 04 01 1941. Posted to No144 Sq, Hemswell (Hampdens, No5 Group, Bomber Command), on 07 04 1941. Flew 25 ops. Promoted to F/O (war substantive) on 02 11 1941. F/L (war substantive), 02 11 1942. **Post-war:** Stayed with RAF. Interpreter, Control Commission, British Forces of Occupation, Germany, 06 07 1945. Interpreter, Air Division, CC BFO, Germany, 13 08 1945, as Acting S/L. Awarded MC on 17 05 1946 for services as a POW. Appointed Personal Assistant to Air-Vice Marshal Davidson, Deputy Chief of Air Defence, HQ Air Division, BFO in Germany, 01 07 1946. Administrative officer GDR, CC, BFO, Germany 11 09 1946. Resigned commission 14 09 1946 and took Intelligence posting in Air Branch as Acting S/L 16 12 1946. Released 01 03 1947 (last day of service 29 06 1947). Emmigrated to Canada in April 1952. Personnel Manager of Bristol Aeroplane Company, May 1952-October 1958. Joined RCAF VR on 26 09 1952. Married 1953 (two sons). Director, Labour Relations for Canadian Construction Association, Ottawa, November 1958-October1966. Executive, National Concrete Producers' Association, Toronto, October 1966-June 1968. Executive V-P, Housing and Urban Development Association of Canada, Toronto, July 1968-July 1979. Died on 15 July 1979 from coronary caused by chemotherapy for cancer.

STRONG, David Malcolm ("Dim") Born 30 September 1913. Educated at Cardiff High School. Joined the RAF in 1936. Bomber Command, 1937-41, Flight Commander (S/L) in No104 Sq (Wellington MkII), Driffield. Awarded AFC in 1941. **Post-war:** Officer Commanding RAF Jurby and RAF Driffield, 1946-48. Staff College, 1949. Staff Officer, Rhodesian Air Training Group, 1949-51. Directing Staff, Staff College, 1952-55. Air Warfare College, 1956. OC, RAF Coningsby, 1957-57. Director of Personnel, Air Ministry, 1959-61. Senior Air Staff Officer, RAF Germany, 1962-63. Made CB in 1964. OC, RAF Halton, 1964-66. Retired from the RAF in 1966 as an Air Commodore. Married 19 03 1941 (two sons, one daughter). Retired to Wendover, Buckinghamshire, and was active in the RAF Ex-POW Association's Officers' Dining Club.

THOMAS, Percy Ainsworth Ward Born 1913. Educated at Wellingborough. Trainee executive, London Transport. Joined RAF on Short Service Commission and trained at Derby and Kinloss. **Post-war:** Pro-am golfer and author (as Pat Ward-Thomas): *Masters of Golf, The Long Green Fairway, World Atlas of Golf* (co-author), *Royal and Ancient, Shell Golfers Atlas*. Partial memoir, *Not Only Golf* (Hodder & Stoughton).

THOMPSON, Alfred Burke ("Tommy") Born Penetanguishene, Canada, 8 August 1915. Joined the RAF in 1937. **Post-war:** Osgoode Hall Law School, Toronto, 1945-48. Married Nora Jackson, 1946 (eight children, eight grandchildren). Lawyer, Penetanguishene, 1948-1967. Mayor of Penetanguishene 1957/8. Assistant Crown Attorney, Simcoe County, 1966-80. Retired in 1980. Died 9 August 1985.

TOMLINSON, Peter ("Tommy") Born in London, 19 April 1916 and educated at Tonbridge in Kent. Commissioned in the Reserve of Air Force Officers in 1935. Called up 1939 and after training posted to No7 Sq, Bomber Command. Was pilot and Personal Assistant to AVM A T Harris, AOC No5 Group, Grantham, from Sept 1939 to February 1941. Transferred to ops, going to No3 PRU, Oakington, Cambridgeshire, and then to No1 PRU, Benson, when No3 disbanded. **Post-war:** Returned to Harris as PA and went with him to South Africa to create South African Marine Corporation, which grew into giant shipping company. Lived in Sea Point, RSA, from 1954. Now deceased.

TRUMBLE, Anthony John Born Whipps Cross, Essex, 15 December 1915. In India, 1920-29. Education: no formal tutor before age nine, then Wanstead High School (a co-educational fee-paying school). Joined RAF on a Short Service Commission on 15 March 1935. Training at No5 FTS, Sealand, 30 03 1935. Then at ATS (Hawker Furies). Distinguished pass with enhanced seniority; promoted F/O two months early. Posted to No56 Sq, North Weald (Bristol Bulldogs, then Gloster Gauntlets), on 28 02 1936. Attached to RAF Calshot, 22 06 1936, for floatplane conversion, then sent to No1 FTS, Leuchars, for FAA conversion, and Gosport for deck landing training. Joined No801 (Fleet Fighter) Sq, Southampton and HMS *Furious*, 25 09 1936. Posted on 06 05 37 to No800 (Fleet Fighter) Sq (Nimrods), based on HMS *Courageous*; and on 21 11 1938 to No803 (Fleet Fighter) Sq (Skuas) as commander "B" Flight on HMS *Ark Royal*. Followed by Staff duties HQ No23 Group, Flying Training Command, Grantham, 31 03 1939. Married 24 06 1939 (one daughter, two sons). Air Intelligence duties (debriefing crews returning from ops) RAF Component to BEF, Arras, France, 26 08 1939. Promoted to F/L on 15 09 1939. Appointed Commander "B" Flight on No264 Sq, Duxford (Defiants), June 1940, carrying out night-flying operations from Fowlmere and then coastal strikes from Martlesham Heath. Left No264 Sq, early July, and joined No418 Flight (Hurricanes) on HMS *Argus* at Greenock, 18 07 1940, destined for Malta. Sailed 23 July; flew Hurricanes off to Luqa, Malta on 02 08 1940. No418 Flight re-designated as No261 Sq on 16 08 1940. Promoted to Acting S/L on 10 12 1940 and took over the squadron. Staff duties at "Z" Wing (Fighter Plans), HQ Middle East 25 02 1941. Station Commander RAF Heraklion, Crete April 1941. Time-promotion while POW to Acting W/C on 01 03 1942. **Post-war:** Permanent Commission (backdated to 15 05 35). Air Ministry attachment, debriefing RAF ex-POWs in deptartment DPS. POW (INF), 23 05 1945-07 07 1945. (Made OBE for this work on 28 12 1945). Refresher flying course, No7 FIS, Upavon; course at School of Air Transport, Netheravon. CO Metropolitan Communications Sq, Hendon, 10 08 1945 (114 aircraft of fourteen different types). Promotion to W/ C confirmed on 01 07 1947. Department SASO, No46 Group. Staff College course, Andover, 1948. Stayed on as Instructor, 1949-52. Senior Admin/Station CO, CFS Little Rissington, 1952/3. Air Ministry, Maritime Air Operations, 1953-55 (planned air cover for Fuchs' trip to the Antarctic). Promoted to Group Captain 01 01 1956. CO, No7 School of Recruit Training, Shropshire, 1956-58. Senior RAF Personnel Officer, Far Eastern Air Force, Singapore, 1958-60. Senior Coastal Command appointment, 1960-63. Then to MOD, as Chairman, Overseas Establishment Committee, up to November 1965. Retired from the RAF on 03 05 1966. Made officer of the Order of Leopold II of Belgium for services to Belgian Air Force. Retired to Devon. Died 21 April 2004 aged 88.

VALACHOS, Peter Born Brantford, Ontario, Canada, 1 October 1915, son of a Colborne Street candy store owner. Joined RAF on a Short Service Commission on 28 09 1938. Posted to No99 (Madras Presidency) Sq, Newmarket (Wellingtons, No3 Group, Bomber Command), as pilot. Flew 30 ops. Mention in Dispatches and recommendation for the DFC, 1940. Posted to No148 Sq, Malta. Flew another ten ops. Then to HQ, Cairo. Promoted to F/L in May 1941, appointed officer i/c ground defences, RAF Heraklion, Crete. **Post-war:** Invested with the DFC in 1945 by King George VI at Buckingham Palace. Transferred to RCAF. Stayed eight months, then served in artillery with the Canadian militia. Worked for Ontario Ministry of Industry and Tourism for twenty years. After retirement, continued as tourism consultant and assisted Canadian Executive Service Overseas in finding experts to send to developing countries. More than 90 hours as private pilot. Amateur theatre, Canada. Retired to Brantford, Ontario.

WARD, James Heber Born Sheffield, Yorkshire, 2 June 1918. Worked in Hull sales office of large silversmiths company. Joined RAFVR and flew each weekend at Brough. Commissioned P/O and posted to No73 (Hurricane) Sq (No204 Group, Western Desert Air Force), based at Mersah Matruh, Egypt. **Post-war:** Demobbed as F/L.

APPENDIX VIII

Amendments
and Additions to
Wire and Walls

page 10: "*Stadt Acrchive*" should read "*Stadtarchiv*"

page 19: "Sir Cedric Gibbon" should read "Sir Edward Gibbon"

page 33: "*Reichsmarks*" should read "*Reichsmark*"

page 33 (cont): "Oflag VIB, Warburg" should read "Fort XV, Thorn"

page 35: "March 1941" should read "February 1941"

page 46: "*Ostenfliegergruppe*" should read "*Küstenfliegergruppe*"

page 50: "had been" should be "has been"

page 54: for "left" (line 2) read "right"; for "right" (line 5) read "left"

page 56: for "bother" (line 5) read "brother"

page 56 (cont): for "Ludwig the Peaceable" read "Ludwig the Peaceful"

page 64: "Saturday, 28 September" should read "Thursday, 28 September"

page 64 (cont): "Saturday, 12 October" should read "Saturday, 21 October"

page 66: "*Marineflakabteilung 246*" should read "*Marineflakabteilung 264*"

page 71: for "became" (line 16) read "become"

page 81: "58 degrees of frost" should read "14.45C (58°F) of frost"

page 82: for "April 1940" substitute "May 1940"

page 85: "first RAF operation" (line 45) should read "first RAF offensive operation"

page 103: "Hampden" (line 17) should read "Whitley MkV"

page 118: "Sergeant Larry Slattery" should read "Aircraftman 1st Class Larry Slattery" (although he was later promoted to Sergeant along with all RAF other ranks)

page 119: The entry for George Skelton should be amplified as follows: "Skelton was eventually sent from Hohemark to Stalag Luft I, then to Obermassfeld, from which, despite his wounds, he attempted to escape. This earned him a place in Colditz, which closed it gates behind him on 12 May 1941. Two years were to elapse before he could use his arm; in 1943 he would be repatriated."

page 119: "less than two months" should read "for only three months"

page 119 (cont): "at the end of August 1940" should read "the first week of October1940"

page 122: "August purge" should read "October purge"

page 126: for "bombs" (line 15) read "mines"

page128: "Pilot Officer R M Biden" (line 27) should read "Pilot Officer R M M Biden RAFVR"

page128 (cont): the word "port" (line 29) should be followed by "engine"

page 129: after "...Oberursel." (line 30) add new sentence: "Pilot Officer Robert Murphy Mervyn Biden was initially sent from Dulag Luft to Stalag Luft I and would turn up at Spangenberg in February 1941"

page 133: for "*IV/JG27*" (last line) read "*IV/JG77*"

page 134: "Reserve of Air Force Operators" (line 3) should read "Reserve of Air Force Officers"

page 136: delete "P L Dakeyne" (line 37)

page 136 (cont): add "R M M Biden RAFVR" (line 39)

page 140: "fourteen or sixteen to a room" (line 3) should read "fourteen, sixteen, eighteen or twenty-two to a room"

page 143: "moved" (line 26) should read "moving"

page 153: amend "and two Army officers, one of whom was Lieutenant Peter Methuen of the Queen's Royal Regiment." (lines 41 and 42) to "and two Army officers, Captain Henry E Duff of the Royal West Kents and Lieutenant Peter Methuen of the Queen's Royal Regiment."

page 158: Flight Lieutenant Skelton (line 9) was then at Oflag IVC, Colditz, for attempting to escape from *Lazarett* IXC.

page 158 (cont): According to the Red Cross, Pilot Officer P J Coleson (line 10) had a fractured skull and a broken ankle and had lost an eye, but was responding well to German medical treatment, his face giving "no indication of the seriousness of his injuries". His POW number was 30918.

page 162: "as 12.00 GMT" (line 7) should read "at 12.00 GMT"

page 163: "take over HSL" (line 45) should read "take over HSL 143"

page 167: for "Friday" (line 16) read "Thursday"

page 169: "forward" (line 10) should be followed by "base"

page 171: "sever icing" (line 5) should read "severe icing"

page 173: After "During the afternoon" (line 3) add "of Tuesday, 17 June,"

page 174: "with the exception of the WOP/AGs" (lines 32/33) should read "with the exception of the wireless-operator"

page 174 (cont): "All baled out safely" (lines 38/39) should read "All those still alive baled out safely"

page 174 (cont): "*II/NGJ1*" (line 44) should read "*II/NJG1*"

page 176: The entry for Król should conclude: "He had already flown on ten sweeps when on the afternoon on 2 July No74 Squadron was ordered up to roam the skies over France while twelve Blenheims were being escorted on "Circus No29" to Lille. Four RAF fighter pilots, including Król, were shot down by Me109s."

page 180: "for rates" (line 19) read "rats"

page 181: for "Monday, 28 August" read "Thursday, 28 August"

page 184: "The police" (line 5) should read "One of the policemen"

page 184 (cont): "Tuesday, 29 August" should read "Friday, 29 August"

page 190: George Skelton (paragraph one) had in fact been returned to Colditz, where he remained until 18 August 1942

page 190 (cont): "St Valéry-sur-Somme" (paragraph one) should read "St-Valery-en-Caux"

page 196: After "survival gear he needed" (line 24) insert "and began paddling."

page 196 (cont): for "rowing" (line 26) read "paddling"

page 199: "all but one of the rest were killed" (line 4) should read "all but one of the other pilots shot down were killed"

page 203: Squadron Leader Davie's full name was Norman Scott Ferguson Davie.

page 207: "swollen too much" (line 18) should read "swollen so much"

page 207 (cont): the aerodrome at Morlaix was the base of *I/JG2*

page 209: "Eventually came" (line 30) should read "Eventually there came"

page 211: "No73 Squadron, formed in May at Sidi Haneish" should read "No73 Squadron, a fighter unit originally formed during the Great War and which since April 1941 had been based at Sidi Haneish"

page 213: Dr Laust was in fact Major L W Lauste of the RAMC (POW number 3682). He was later transferred to the POW infirmary at Stalag VIIIB

page 214: the "branch line" (line 214) was the *Kanonenbahn* referred to in Chapter One.

page 214 (cont): for "February 1941" read "February 1942"

page 226: "October 1941" should read "September 1941"

page 228: delete "to told" (line 16)

page 228 (cont): "The prisoners found their tunics, greatcoats and hats in a large heap in the courtyard. All unit badges and buttons, badges of rank and medal ribbons had been cut off and taken away." (lines 32/32) This was in contravention of Article 6 of the POW Code of the Geneva Convention.

page 232: Add:
P/O R M M Biden RAFVR   239   13 08 40   SL1 O9A/H F15 O9A/H O6B

page 232 (cont): The date of P/O H F Burns' capture should read 26 10 40

page 233: "F/L R M Coste" should read "P/O R M Coste". His POW number was in fact 20.

page 233 (cont): P/O W M W Fowler's camps should read "O9A/H O6B"

page 234: F/O G E Grey-Smith's camps should read "O9A/H SL1 O9A/H SL1". When Stalag Luft I was closed down he went to Stalag Luft III, and in 1943 was finally repatriated.

page 234 (cont:) P/O N D Hallifax's POW number should be 1396.

page 235: Delete "P/O E C Maskell" and all subsequent references on that line.

page 236: P/O C I Rolfe's camps should read "O9A/H O6B"

page 236 (cont): F/L G Skelton's camps should read "O9A/H DL S9C O4C O9A/H O4C SL3"

page 236 (cont): The details for S/L F G L Smith DFC should read "26 10 41" and "O9A/H F15 O9A/H O6B". The POW number given is correct.

Sources and Bibliography

Interviews:
H H Bracken, E F Chapman, H D H Cooper, Martin Dilly (C N Dilly), H E L Falkus, P Harding,
W J Lewis, P B ("Laddie") Lucas (D R S Bader), A S Ruffel, Marc H Stevens (Peter Stevens),
D M Strong, Peter Tomlinson, A J Trumble, P J Valachos

Correspondence:
W Bakker, R E Bartlett, H R Bewlay, T Blacklock, D Blew, R J E Boulding, H H Bracken, D Bruce,
Mrs M A Butler (R J E Boulding), M G Butt, E F Chapman, E J Clelland, H D H Cooper, Nora Crete
(A B Thompson), W Cunningham, I P P Denton, Martin Dilly (C N Dilly), N M Dunn, K C Edwards,
H E L Falkus, A H Gould, P Harding, H Hearn, J Heber Ward, Mrs Vivien Johnson (T F S Johnson),
J R Kayll, W J Lewis, D M Lubbock, P B ("Laddie") Lucas (D R S Bader), E H Lynch-Blosse,
Mrs K M H McConnell (R J McConnell), A W Mungovan, D Poynter, Jane Preese (N C Hyde),
Mrs Celia Rambaut (I P P Denton), M H Roth, Norman Ruddock (J R McConnell), A S Ruffel,
W A Staniland, Marc H Stevens (Peter Stevens), D M Strong, Peter Tomlinson, R E Troward,
A J Trumble, P J Valachos, R B Ward, Mrs P White (T Griffith-Jones)

Wartime Logs, letters and diaries:
W Bakker, W Cunningham, N C Hyde, A J Trumble, P Tomlinson

Unpublished manuscripts:
DENTON, I P B: "Untitled Memoir, Vol.1940-45"
KING, Gunner Cyril: "Left Behind"
ROTH, M H: "The Unhurried Years"
VON LINDEINER-WILDAU, *Oberst Freiherr* Freidrich-Wilhelm: "Memoirs"

Audio-tapes:
H H Bracken, W Cunningham

Official Documents:
Air 20/2336 Alphabetical lists of RAF, RAAF, RCAF, RNZAF and SAAF POWs in Germany
MI9/S/PG(G)/1629: Account of escape of P/O A F McSweyn RAAF
WO 165/39: MI9 War Diary
WO 208/3242: Historical Record of MI9

Archives and Museums:

Bundesarchiv, Freiburg im Breisgau; Imperial War Museum, Lambeth; Fleet Air Arm Museum, Ilchester;
Public Record Office, Kew; *Stadtarchiv* Warburg

Secondary Sources:

ARKRIGHT, Maj A S B, MC, *Return Journey* (Seeley, Service & Co Ltd, 1948)
ASHWORTH, Chris: *RAF Coastal Command, 1936-1969* (Patrick Stephens Ltd, 1992)
BARBER, Noel: *Prisoner of War* (Harrap & Co, 1944)

BECKWITH, E G C (Ed.): *The Mansel Diaries* (Privately Printed, 1977)

BICKERS, Richard Townshend: *The Desert Air War, 1939-45* (Leo Cooper, 1991)

BOITEN, Theo: *Blenheim Strike* (Air Research Publications, 1995)

BOITEN, Theo: *Bristol Blenheim* (The Crowood Press Ltd, 1998)

BRICKHILL, Paul: *Reach for the Sky* (William Collins & Sons, 1954)

BRICKHILL, Paul, and NORTON, Conrad: *Escape to Danger* (Faber & Faber, 1946)

CHAMP, Jack, and BURGESS, Colin: *The Diggers of Colditz* (Orbis Publishing Limited, 1985)

CHESHIRE, Leonard: *Bomber Pilot* (Hutchinson, 1943)

CHORLEY, W R: *RAF Bomber Command Losses of the Second World War:*
  Vol. 1: 1939-40 (Midland Publishing, 1992)
  Vol. 2: 1941 (Midland Publishing, 1993)

COSSEY, Bob: *Tigers: The Story of No. 74 Squadron RAF* (Arms & Armour Press, 1992)

CRAWLEY, Aidan: *Escape from Germany* (HMSO, 1985)

CRAWLEY, Aidan: *Leap Before You Look* (Collins, 1988)

CULL, Brian, and MINTERNE, Don: *Hurricanes Over Tobruk* (Grub Street, 1999)

DELARUE, Jacques: *The Gestapo: A History of Horror* (Paragon House, 1987)

DONNELLY, G L "Larry": *The Whitley Boys* (Air Research Publications, 1991)

DUNCAN, Michael: *Underground from Posen* (William Kimber & Co Ltd, 1954)

FOOT, M R D, and LANGLEY, J M: *MI9 — Escape and Evasion, 1939-1945* (The Bodley Head, 1979)

FORD-JONES, MARTYN R: *Bomber Squadron: The Men who Flew with XV* (William Kimber, 1987)

FORMAN, John: *Fighter Command War Diaries, Vol. 2: September 1940 to December 1941* (Air Research Publications, 1998)

FOSTER, Eric: *Life Hangs by a Silken Thread* (Astia Publishing, 1992)

GRETZYNGIER, *Robert: Poles in the Defence of Britain* (Grub Street, 2001)

JACKSON, Robert: *Before the Storm: The Story of Bomber Command 1939-42* (Arthur Barker, 1972)

LUCAS, Laddie: *Flying Colours: The Epic Story of Douglas Bader* (Hutchinson & Co, 1981)

LYNCH-BLOSSE, Hugh: *Wings — and Other Things* (Square One Publications, 1990)

MACKENZIE, K W: *Hurricane Combat* (William Kimber, 1987)

McNEILL, Ross: *Royal Air Force Coastal Command Losses of the Second World War, Volume 1, 1939-1941* (Midland Publishing, 2003)

MIDDLEBROOK, Martin, and EVERITT, Chris: *The Bomber Command War Diaries* (Midland Publishing Ltd, 1996)

MOYLE, Harry: *The Hampden File* (Air Britain, 1989)

NEAVE, Airey: *Saturday at MI9* (Hodder & Stoughton Ltd, 1969)

PAINE, Lauran: *German Military Intelligence in World War II: The Abwehr* (Military Heritage Press, 1984)

PAPE, Richard: *Boldness Be My Friend* (Elek Books Ltd, 1953; rev. edn. Granada Publishing Ltd, 1984)

PAPE, Richard: *Sequel to Boldness* (Odhams Press Ltd, 1959)

PRITTIE, T C F and EDWARDS, W Earle: *South to Freedom* (Hutchinson & Co, 1946)

QUARRIE, Don: *Oflag* (The Pentland Press Ltd, 1995)

REID, Major P R, MBE MC: *The Colditz Story* (Hodder & Stoughton, 1952)

REID, Major P R, MBE MC: *Colditz: The Full Story* (Macmillan, 1984)

SAUNDERS, Hilary St George: *The Red Cross and The White* (Hollis & Carter, 1949)

SHORES, Christopher: *Dust Clouds in the Middle East* (Grub Street, 1996)

SHORES, Christopher, et al: *Air War For Yugoslavia, Greece and Crete, 1940-41* (Grub Street, 1987)

THROWER, Derek: *The Lonely Path to Freedom* (Robert Hale, 1980)

WRAGG, David: *The Fleet Air Arm Handbook* (Sutton Publishing, 2001)

WYNN, Kenneth G: *Men of the Battle of Britain* (CCB Associates, 1999)

Newspapers and Periodicals: *The Camp, The Kriegie, The Times, The Daily Telegraph, The Daily Mail*

Index

284

287

162, 164, 172, 201, 214, 243, 246, 250-53
Gestapo, 22, 25-26, 30, 60, 109-11, 127, 143, 148, 223, 237
Ghent, Belgium, 90
Ghost Train, The (play), 69
Gibbon, P/O J R, 97, 99
Gibraltar, 26, 101
Gibson, Sgt W R, 64-68
Gieves' (London tailors), 174
Gifford, P/O M H, RCAF, 107
"Giglis", *see:* Escape equipment
Gilchrist, W/C P A, DFC, 206
Gilderthorpe, P/O T R, 175, 186-87
Gilliat, Capt M J, King's Royal Rifle Corps, 225-26, 230
Gillies, F/O J A, AuxAF, 28
Gildner, *Oberfeldwebel* Paul, 80
Ginn, Maj B D S ("Skelly"), REME, 224
Githeon, Greece, 56
Gladstone, W E, 153
Glagow, Scotland, 245
Gloucestershire Regiment, 46, 170
Glover, P/O J T, 161
Gneisenau, 61, 207
Godwin, F/S C A, 87
Goebbels, Josef, 42, 243
Goering, *Reichsmarschall* Hermann, 21, 23, 25, 49, 124, 135, 243
Gold Coast (Africa), 196
Golders Green, 118
Goldfinch, P/O L J E, 54, 56-60, 69, 75
"Goon-baiting", 170, 180-182
Gosman, F/L A D, 97, 99, 102, 107, 114, 154
Gosnay, France, 98, 129, 145-46, 187, 209
Göteborg, Sweden, 246
Gould, P/O A H, 161, 175, 179, 194, 197, 219
Goumin, *Commandant* Georges, FFAF, 128
Government, HM, 244, 250, 252-53
Government, Swiss, 191
Gowland, Sgt J C, 118
Graham, P/O S A ("Blackie"), RCAF, 144, 175
Graham-Hogg, F/O D, 75, 80, 177, 185, 221-22
Grantham, Lincolnshire, 143
Gravelines, France, 80, 100, 104
Great Britain, 20, 26, 32, 33, 37, 44-46, 91 *passim*, 55-56, 65, 68, 71, 76, 101, 111-12, 118-19, 135, 148, 160, 174, 183, 186, 238-39, 243-44, 246-47, 250-52
Great Central Hotel, Marylebone, 24 (*See also:* London Transit Camp)
Great War, 21, 23, 25, 27, 29, 34, 37, 41, 46, 71-72, 74-75, 122, 143, 170, 182, 244
Greater Germany, *see:* Germany
Greece, 54-55, 57-58, 71-72, 74-75, 128-129, 165; German invasion of, 55-56, 71; Italian invasion of, 56
Green, P/O J H, 84, 205
Green, F/O P O V ("Ollie"), 53, 115, 121-23, 127, 149
Greenhill, P/O C A S, DFC, 87
Greenslade, Lt (A) P J, RNVR, 87, 92, 94, 150

"Gremlin George", *see:* Kraus, *Hauptmann*
Grense Jacobselv, Finland, 94
Grenzpolizei, 22, 207
Grey-Smith, F/O G E, 186
Griffin, L/A H C G, 92
Griffith-Jones, F/L T, 107, 114, 149, 229
Grimsby, Yorkshire, 141
Grocott, F/O J, RAFVR, 121, 144, 149
Gross Glockner, Germany, 42
Guidi, Greece, 75
Guymer, Sgt H N, RNZAF, 88
Gwyn-Williams, Sgt, 52

H
Haamstede, Holland, 89
Hadley, P/O T H, RAFVR, 161
Haelen, Holland, 103
Hague Convention, 22
Haig, Field Marshal Douglas, 115
Haines, Sgt G, 90
Hainaut, Belgium, 32
Hall, Sgt C, 116
Hall, F/L C M, RAAF, 124, 127, 205, 229, 233, 235
Hall, P/O W I, 132-34, 136-37, 139
Haller, Lt G A, SAAF, 123
Hallifax, P/O N D, 190
Hamburg, Germany, 61, 80, 88, 108, 118, 143, 145, 153, 157-59;
Hamburgsender, 244
Hamilton, P/O A J C, 74, 161
Hamilton, Ontario, 112
Hamilton-Baillie, Lt (later Capt), J R E ("Jock"), Royal Engineers, 223-25, 234
Hamm, Germany, 165
Hammersmith, London, 143
Hammond, Sgt A ("Wally"), 108
Handbook for the Information of Relatives and Friends of Prisoners of War, A (1943), 244
Hands, Capt A J, King's Own Royal Rifle Regt, 238
Hanrahan, Lt (A) M A J J, RN, 162
Hanover, 50, 64, 76, 81, 87-88, 102, 158, 165
Hardelot, France, 104
Harding, F/O P, RAFVR, 107, 112-14, 149, 187, 193, 205, 228-29
Harger, *Hauptmann* (Oflag VIB), 170, 180-82
Harnett, Sgt R V, 64
Harper, Sgt R, 125-126
Harris, Air Marshal A T, CB, OBE, AFC, 70, 143, 160, 195
Harris, Mrs J, 143, 195
Harrison, P/O T, 132-34
Harrow, Middlesex, 26
Hart Sgt W, 103
Hartop, P/O W C, 161, 229
Hasselt, Belgium, 103
Hawkes, Sgt A W, 102
Hayes, P/O D K, 161, 229
Hayward, P/O A E, 107, 111, 206
Hayward, F/O B W, 161, 229
Hazebrouck, France, 112, 187
Heard, Sgt A H, 145
Heard, Capt the Rev R G, Royal Army Chaplain's Department, 42
Hearle, Lt N M, RM, 162, 205
Hearn, Sub-Lt (A) H N C, RN, 162

Heaton, P/O H, 107-9, 114, 177
Heaton-Nichols, P/O D G, 161, 179, 188, 205, 229
Hedley, F/L J O, 115, 149, 177, 208, 229
Heer, das, see: Army, German
Heeren, Gs H F, RNNAS, 119-20
Helsinki, Finland, 93-94
Helvitia Hotel, Heraklion, 74
Hemer bei Iserlohn, *see:* **Prisoner of War camps**
"Helpers", 26 (*See also:* Escape Lines; Evasion)
Henderson, P/O R R, RCAF, 102-3, 205
Henderson, Maj W R, RAMC
Hengelo, Holland, 126
HMS *Furious*, 92
HMS *Glorious*, 33
HMS *Victorious*, 92-93, 101
Heraklion, Crete, 74 (*See also:* **Stations**)
Herman, *Felbwebel* (at Laufen), 45
Hetherington, P/O W, 161, 205, 229
Hewson, P/O E, 87, 90-91
Heydrich, *SS-General* Reinhard, 22
Hibell, P/O A J, 115, 118, 149, 175, 229
Hièque, *Madame*, 138-139
Hièque, *Monsieur* J, 134-35, 138-39
Highgate, North London, 26 (*See also:* Caen Wood Towers; IS9)
Hill, P/O G H, 97-98, 187
Hill, Sgt J E, 101
Hitler, Adolf, 20, 22, 25, 149
Hitlerjugend, 60, 161, 191
Hoare, F/O D S, 161
Hockey, P/O (A/F/L) L P R, 31-32, 34, 35, 42, 49, 144
Høckner, Oberleutnant Walter, 74
Hoffman, *Kapitän zur See*, Kurt, 62
Hohemark Clinic, see: **Prisoner of War hospitals**
Hohensalzburg, *Schloss*, 42
Holden, A/S/L K, 129-30
Holiday, Sgt G D, 82
Holland, 24, 26, 33, 47, 50, 64, 76-81, 89-91, 98, 102-4 *passim*, 167, 107, 111, 113, 116, 119-20, 125-26, 143, 145, 152, 192, 196, 206-7, 209, 223, 238, 245, 248; German invasion of, 20
Holland, Major J F C, DFC, 24
Holland P/O K N, 161
Holland P/O W H, 161
Holmark, Germany, 139
Holstum, Germany, 145
Hoogkarspel, Holland, 206
Hooker, C W R, 28
Hooley, Sgt R D, 126
Hoppe, P/O J R ("Hoppy"), RAFVR, 161-62, 194, 197, 219
Hopper, Lt H J A, Royal Armoured Corps, 203
Hordern, P/O S S, 146
Horner, P/O F G, 107, 112, 229
"Horst Wessel Lied", 175
Howard, Sub-Lt (A) C V, RN, 87, 92, 94
Howard-Vyse, Maj-Gen Sir Richard, 244
Howe, Capt R H ("Dick"), MC, Royal Tank Regiment, 49
Howell, W/C Edward, 127-29, 171-72
Howlett, F/L C R C, 70, 72, 74, 80, 229
Hubicki, F/L E, 161, 205
Hughff, Sgt J E, 76
Hugill, P/O F, 161, 219

288

294